The Mesolithic in Britain

The Mesolithic in Britain proposes a new division of the Mesolithic period into four parts, each with its own distinct character.

The Mesolithic has previously been seen as timeless, where little changed over thousands of years. This new synthesis draws on advances in scientific dating to understand the Mesolithic inhabitation of Britain as a historical process. The period was, in fact, a time of profound change: houses, monuments, middens, long-term use of sites and regions, manipulation of the environment and the symbolic deposition of human and animal remains all emerged as significant practices in Britain for the first time. The book describes the lives of the first pioneers in the Early Mesolithic; the emergence of new modes of inhabitation in the Middle Mesolithic; the regionally diverse settlement of the Late Mesolithic; and the radical changes of the final millennium of the period. The first synthesis of Mesolithic Britain since 1932, it takes both a chronological and a regional approach.

This book will serve as an essential text for anyone studying the period: undergraduate and graduate students, specialists in the field and community archaeology groups.

Chantal Conneller is a Senior Lecturer in early prehistory at Newcastle University. She is author of *An Archaeology of Materials* (2012) and *Star Carr: A Persistent Place in a Changing World* (2018).

Routledge Archaeology of Northern Europe

The British Palaeolithic
Human Societies at the Edge of the Pleistocene World
Paul Pettitt and Mark White

The Neolithic of Britain and Ireland
Vicki Cummings

Iron Age Lives
The Archaeology of Britain and Ireland 800 BC – AD 400
Ian Armit

The Mesolithic in Britain
Landscape and Society in Times of Change
Chantal Conneller

Formative Britain
The Archaeology of Britain AD 400 – 1100
Martin Carver

For more information about this series, please visit: https://www.routledge.com/Routledge-Archaeology-of-Northern-Europe/book-series/ARCHNEUR

The Mesolithic in Britain

Landscape and Society in Times of Change

Chantal Conneller

LONDON AND NEW YORK

First published 2022
by Routledge
4 Park Square, Milton Park, Abingdon, Oxon OX14 4RN

and by Routledge
605 Third Avenue, New York, NY 10158

Routledge is an imprint of the Taylor & Francis Group, an informa business

British Library Cataloguing-in-Publication Data
A catalogue record for this book is available from the British Library

Library of Congress Cataloging-in-Publication Data
A catalog record has been requested for this book

ISBN: 978-1-138-79042-1 (hbk)
ISBN: 978-1-138-79043-8 (pbk)
ISBN: 978-1-003-22810-3 (ebk)

DOI: 10.4324/9781003228103

Typeset in Times New Roman
by MPS Limited, Dehradun

Contents

Figures

Tables

Acknowledgements

First, I would like to thank the British Academy, whose award of a mid-career fellowship permitted me to finish this book within the terms of my natural lifespan. Thanks also to the intrepid readers who commented on the entire draft: Andrew David, Graeme Warren and Caroline Wickham-Jones. Ben Elliott, Aimee Little and Tom Yarrow provided useful input on specific chapters and issues. The project has hugely benefited over its various iterations from the input of Tom Higham, Alex Bayliss and Seren Griffiths on the dating side. I would also like to thank Fraser Sturt for generously generating new sea-level maps for this book; to Charlie Rowley for her rigorous work on the maps in chapters 2–4, and to Salvatore Basile for chapters 5–6 maps.

A book that covers so much material can only be completed through the generous efforts of a huge number of people, who have provided images, answered queries and introduced me to their sites. I would like to thank: Cathy Barnett, Nick Barton, Alex Bayliss, Martin Bell, Martin Blundell, Fraser Brown, Alison Burns, Sophy Charlton, Mike Church, Andrew David, Mike Donnelly, Ben Elliott, Mike Farley, Nyree Finlay, Eric Grant and colleagues, Seren Griffths, Susanna Harris, Gill Hey, Brian Howcroft, Clive Hudson, David Jacques, Kay Kays, Jodie Lewis, Tom Lord, Nicky Milner, Steve Mithen, Garry Momber, Graham Mullan, Nick Overton, Susann Palmer, Steph Piper, Stephen Poole, Matt Pope, Paul Preston, Gary Robinson, Peter Rowley-Conwy, Rick Schulting, George Smith, Penny Spikins, Barry Taylor, John Thorp, Clive Waddington, Elizabeth Walker, Graeme Warren, Caroline Wickham Jones, Karen Wicks, Linda Wilson. A special thanks goes to Roy Froom for his generous tour of the Kennet Valley sites, to John Davies for his introduction to the Mesolithic of Northumberland and to the late Pat Stonehouse for his appreciation of the Pennine Mesolithic landscape. I have learnt a huge amount about the British Mesolithic from PhD students I have worked with and would like to thank Hannah Cobb, Amy Gray Jones, Jim Leary, Nick Overton, Ray Nilson, Ellen McInnes, Lawrence Billington, Alison Burns, Julie Birchenall and Tom Lawrence for their insights. This book has also benefitted from discussions over many years with Ed Blinkhorn, Ben Elliott, Roger Jacobi, Aimee Little, Stephen Poole, Graeme Warren and Tom Yarrow. All errors are of course my own.

A lot of this book is based on work on lithic collections and museum archives. In times when local museums are under threat from reduced funding, I must emphasise how vital these visits have been. I would like to thank the following people who have generously facilitated access to their collections: Jill Greenaway (Reading Museum), Brett Thorn (Buckinghamshire County Museum), Andrew Parkin (Great North Museum), Ross Turle and David Allen (Hampshire Museums), Lisa Brown

(Wiltshire Museum), Ann Vernau (Three Rivers Museum Trust), Richard Sabin (Natural History Museum) and Nick Ashton, Jill Cook Claire Harris and Claire Lucas (British Museum).

Thanks also to Kangan Gupta and all the other members of the Routledge editorial team, whose patience I have tested over the years.

And finally to Aimée Little, Lesley McFadyen and Beccy Scott, and to Roger Jacobi, who set me on to this task.

Basemap data acknowledgements:
The maps produced for this volume contain public sector information (OS Strategi 2016.01 and OpenRivers 2018) licensed under the Open Government Licence v3.0 and open data (Pope 2017 UK Shaded Relief Tiff) licensed under the Open Data Commons Public Domain Dedication and License (PDDL) v1.0.

Note on radiocarbon dating:
All radiocarbon dates have been calibrated using IntCal13 (Reimer et al. 2013) and OxCal version 4.3 (Bronk Ramsey 2009). Date ranges are given at 95% probability unless noted otherwise.

1 Hunting and gathering time

Chronological frameworks and key themes

The Mesolithic was a time of profound change: Houses, monuments, middens, long-term use of sites and regions, manipulation of the environment and the symbolic deposition of human and animal remains all emerged as significant practises in Britain for the first time. These developments occurred during a period when environmental change was, at times, rapid and transformed the appearance of a place over the course of its inhabitation. However, this is not the traditional picture of the Mesolithic. Instead, the period has been represented as homogenous: Hunter-gatherers focused on routine economic practises in an endlessly repeating seasonal round. Perhaps at best the Mesolithic is seen as shifting from a way of life based on hunting large terrestrial mammals in the Early Mesolithic (as at Star Carr) to marine adaptations in the Late Mesolithic (on Oronsay); here 'the specific is abstracted to the general' (Elliott and Griffiths 2018, 349) due to a perceived lack of evidence and reliance on the few sites with faunal remains. Poor chronological resolution has serious consequences for the period, perpetuating characterisations of the Mesolithic as timeless and unchanging. The poverty of our chronologies appears even more acute as recent ground-breaking advances have produced refined chronologies for adjacent periods (Bayliss et al. 2007; Jacobi and Higham 2011).

This book aims to shed new light on the temporality of the Mesolithic occupation of Britain: Tracing the ebb and flow of inhabitation, the structure of settlement practises and the appearance of new and distinctive ways of life during the period. Above all, we need to see the Mesolithic as a historical process in which new ways of life emerge that both build on and reinterpret past practises. I present here a new chronological scheme for the period, where the Mesolithic is divided into four parts. This new chronology for the Mesolithic is based on a modest radiocarbon dating programme, audit of existing estimates and archive research. This has permitted refinement of existing typochronological schemes that have been used to develop new understandings of the timing and duration of settlement forms and features across Britain between 9500 and 4000 cal BC. The Mesolithic saw the first long-term, uninterrupted occupation of Britain for tens, perhaps hundreds, of thousands, of years: The Mesolithic was the origin of qualitatively new forms of human relationship with place, as landscapes acquired long-term histories for the first time, and particular locations took on meaning through new social and ritual practises of construction and deposition.

The remainder of this introductory chapter will be concerned with time, or more properly, with periodisation. How have archaeologists and quaternary scientists, from those first to recognise the Mesolithic, created order from the particular detritus of the period: The lonely scatters of charcoal and stone tools on bleak moorlands, the pollen

DOI: 10.4324/9781003228103-1

records of the peats, the lithic scatters of river valleys and sandy heathland and the rarer finds of animal bones and large structures?

Typological chronologies

The concept of the Mesolithic – as a hiatus between the Palaeolithic and Neolithic – was first mooted in the late 19th century and became linked with microlithic industries following the work of Piette at Mas d'Azil in 1895 (despite the fact that these industries eventually proved to be neither Mesolithic nor truly microlithic). The Mesolithic only really gained common currency in Britain in the 1920s and 1930s, when further fieldwork had been undertaken and the first writers of syntheses were able to take account of richer continental comparators (Burkitt 1926; Childe 1925; Clark 1932). Since then, a number of typological differences have been noted in the form of stone tools, more specifically microliths (see Box 1.3 for definitions and a discussion of the significance of these tools). Microliths have been the focus of these endeavours because they are found on most sites and, in contrast to other tool types, display considerable variation. This has been interpreted in different ways: Some variation, from work of the earliest researchers onwards, has been seen to have a temporal basis, but at other times different styles have been seen as contemporary, the product of different regional signatures, or more explicitly different groups of people with different styles of armature. There has even been a resurgence in explanations that equate microliths with people in recent years, returning full circle to the interpretations that established the Mesolithic in the 1930s.

The first to notice variation within the British material was the pioneer of Mesolithic studies, Francis Buckley (Box 1.1). In the course of his extensive fieldwork in the Central Pennines (Buckley 1921, 1924) he noted two distinct types of microlithic industry, which were found at different stratigraphic levels and thus considered to have a temporal basis. Buckley christened these broad blade and narrow blade (Figure 1.2), based on the width of the microliths recovered (Switsur and Jacobi 1979). Subsequent work suggests the former have a width of greater than 7 mm, while the latter are 5 mm wide or less (Pitts and Jacobi 1979). While it is clear Buckley's definition refers to microliths, Preston (2012) argues he implicitly included laminar debitage in his assessment of his material. Initially the 'narrow blade' industries were thought to be earlier on the basis of their supposed greater depths at Warcock Hill (Petch 1924; Woodhead 1929). Clark (see Box 1.2 noted their correct position, though labelling the microlith forms 'non-geometric' and 'geometric', respectively. He drew parallels between these types and those in particular continental industries: Non-geometric types were found in the Southern Scandinavian Maglemosian, while geometric types were similar to the French Sauveterrian (Clark 1932). This division between these microlith types was confirmed through cluster analysis of microlith types from a wide range of assemblages across England and Wales by Jacobi (1979). Jacobi, working with Roy Switsur, linked these clusters to radiocarbon dated samples (see below), confirming their hypothesised temporal patterning (Switsur and Jacobi 1979).

The terms 'Early Mesolithic/Maglemosian/non-geometric/broad blade' and 'Late Mesolithic/Sauveterrian/geometric/narrow blade' were used interchangeably for a few decades. Maglemosian and Sauvetarrian dropped out of use earliest as Mesolithic archaeologists in Britain became less interested in culture-historical frameworks and work by continental archaeologists redefined the Maglemosian and Sauveterrian in

Box 1.1 Francis Buckley (1881–1948), pioneer of Mesolithic research

Francis Buckley (Figure 1.1) came from a wealthy Yorkshire family and, before the First World War, practised as a barrister. His experiences in the war shaped Buckley as an archaeologist (Griffiths and Saunders 2020), for in France he encountered stone tools. He took to scouring the spoil heaps from the excavated trenches for Prehistoric remains, a task that left him dangerously exposed. In the war, he served as an 'Observer', working with maps and monitoring enemy movements to direct shelling. The skills he developed in producing military landscape sketches and trench plans formed the basis for his archaeological recording after the war, while his life in the trenches led him to become a skilled observer of the relationship between stone tools and sedimentary contexts.

Figure 1.1 Francis Buckley (copyright Gallery Oldham)

Damaged by his experiences, Buckley did not work in the law following his return from France. Instead, he wrote – wartime memoirs and archaeological notes – and henceafter avoiding enclosed spaces (ibid), he took to walking the moors above his home near Saddleworth, collecting material from erosion scars and excavating small trenches. Particularly in the years following the war, he worked intensively, digging in snow on Christmas day in the 1920s and amassing a huge collection of lithic material. His notebooks record discovery of around 8000 pieces of flint just from March Hill between 1920 and 1923 (Griffiths and Saunders 2020). Between 1920 and 1924, over 6000 pieces from March Hill were deposited at the Tolson Museum, Huddersfield (Petch 1924), with many more distributed to museums across the country. Buckley also accumulated key collections from the Northumbrian coast, where his wife Bebba's family lived.

In his studies of lithic material, Buckley recognised key typological features that differentiated both early and late industries and divisions within the Early Mesolithic. Buckley was unusual in not just collecting flint but in recording spatial patterns, hearths and other site furniture and collecting charcoal and other charred material (Spikins 1999, 2002). These were subsequently used in the first systematic Mesolithic dating programme (Switsur and Jacobi 1975).

Details of his work are entered in his notebooks, lodged in the Tolson Museum, Huddersfield, and summarised in two publications – *A Microlithic Industry, Marsden, Yorkshire* (Buckley 1921) and *A Microlithic Industry of the Pennine Chain* (Buckley 1924). Buckley loaned his notebooks to Clark when the latter was working on his synthesis of the British Mesolithic (Clark 1932). Buckley's work appears a strong influence on both illustrations and text, though one that is perhaps not fully acknowledged.

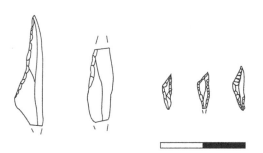

Figure 1.2 'Broad blade' microliths (left) and 'narrow blade' microliths (right)

the more chronologically and geographically restricted terms currently used. Clark's non-geometric and geometric division is still employed, but hampered by the fact it is not a very accurate description of early and late microliths. While early assemblages are dominated by obliquely blunted points, there are also a range of geometric forms: Broad isosceles and scalene triangles, trapezes and rhomboids. Similarly, while the range of geometric forms increases in Late Mesolithic assemblages, non-geometric forms are still present.

The terms 'broad blade' and 'narrow blade' have become increasingly common and have migrated at some point from terms to describe microliths to be used to describe early and late technological systems. As relatively untested terms to describe technological systems lasting millennia, these three phases into zones as they are clearly inadequate. Technological schema in Mesolithic Britain are extremely variable and raw material-dependent. The terms 'broad blade' and 'narrow blade' have become particularly popular in areas of Britain where there is a shift in raw material use between Early and Late Mesolithic, with use of local, smaller, often poor quality stone in the latter, in particular in Scotland and Northern England. In this context, the term is often simply used to reference the fact the material is quite small, rather than reflecting any detailed comparative metrics. In some of these regions, bipolar reduction on an anvil is a key technique to deal with extremely small beach pebbles. Here, bladelets are mostly lacking; yet, the term is still used. In the chalklands of Britain, it is unclear whether there is a narrowing of laminar products between Early and Late Mesolithic. A systematic study by Pitts and Jacobi (1979) of 21 assemblages from Southeast England suggested this was not the case and that the term 'broad and narrow blade' should be abandoned apart from in reference to microliths. However, Pitts and Jacobi measured all debitage and used length:breadth ratios to report their results, so results may differ from schemes that only focus on laminar products. Varied raw material-dependent technological strategies are also present in Southeast England. At Broxbourne 105 on the river Lea in Hertfordshire, large gravel flint was simply smashed into angular chunks, for example. No laminar production is in evidence. While in some regions, and at certain times, we can see an Early Mesolithic focused on blade and bladelet production and a Late Mesolithic where some neat bladelets are often present, the terms 'narrow' and 'broad blade' are not useful as a widespread means to periodise the Mesolithic. It may be found helpful in some regions, but the detailed metrical and technological studies remain to be undertaken.

We are left then with a metrical definition based on microliths, which does seem useful, and the terms 'Early' and 'Late Mesolithic'. These latter have been dealt a blow by modelling of radiocarbon dates for sites with 'broad' and 'narrow' microlith forms (see section below on radiometric dating), which has suggested a time-transgressive shift between 'early' and 'late' types of significant duration (Waddington et al. 2007). This study has been complicated by the role of particular microlith assemblages, known as 'Horsham' (see below), treated as Early Mesolithic by Bayliss and Waddington and in similar studies (Reynier 2005), but grouped with late types in the Pitts and Jacobi (1979) study. The ambiguous status of these forms leads us to a closer look at the variability within Early and Late Mesolithic microlith assemblages and whether an understanding of these can improve our typochronologies.

Understanding variability: The Early Mesolithic

Variability within assemges subsequentln as Early Mesolithic was recognised nearly a century ago. Francis Buckley (see Box 1.1) separated two sites he dug on Warcock Hill in the Central Pennines according to the types of broad microliths he found there (Buckley 1924) (Figure 1.3). A little later, Grahame Clark (1934) suggested that the idiosyncratic hollow-based microliths (Figure 1.4) found in the Horsham area might be indicative of a 'homogenous culture'.

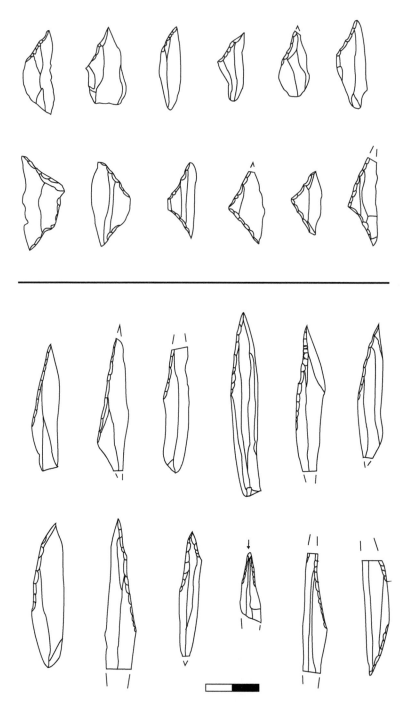

Figure 1.3 Early Mesolithic microlith forms: Star Carr types from Star Carr (rows 1 and 2), Deepcar types from Lackford Heath (rows 3 and 4)

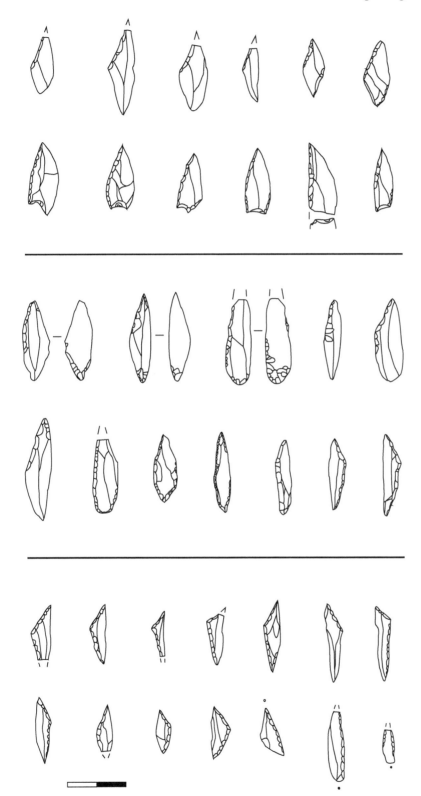

(caption on next page)

Figure 1.4 Middle Mesolithic microlith forms: Horsham types from Longmoor (rows 1–2), Honey Hill types from Asfordby (redrawn after Cooper and Jarvis 2017) (rows 3–4), Variably Lateralised Scalenes from Howick (rows 5–6)

Radley and Mellars (1964), in a discussion of the typological affinities of the assemblages from the site of Deepcar, South Yorkshire, built on Buckely's work to suggest two Early Mesolithic assemblage types could be discerned in the Central Pennines (Figure 1.3). The assemblage from Deepcar was characterised by the presence of slender obliquely blunted points (including a proportion with retouch on the leading edge) and points with one edge blunted (see Box 1.3). The vast majority (c.95%) of the assemblage was manufactured on opaque white flint. Mellars compared the Deepcar assemblages with those from Lominot sites 2 and 3, Windy Hill 3, Warcock Hill North and Warcock Hill South, all situated in the Central Pennines. All but the latter were similar in microlith form and the raw material utilised. Warcock Hill South, however, was characterised by the presence of broad obliquely blunted points, isosceles triangles and trapezes and by the use of a range of clear brown, speckled grey and red flint and was thus similar to the assemblage recovered by Grahame Clark from Star Carr (see Box 1.2). Mellars also linked these types with similar assemblages found in both Southeast and Southwest England. Subsequent work by Roger Jacobi (1978a) showed that the distinction made mainly between Pennine assemblages could be extended throughout Northern England. Assemblages from the sites of Pointed Stone 2 and 3 on the North York Moors displayed similar microlith morphology and use of raw materials to Star Carr and Warcock Hill South, while others were similar to Deepcar (Jacobi 1976, 1978a). Subsequent work (Reynier 1997, 2005) has suggested that similar typological distinctions could be extended throughout the rest of England and Wales, though without the different raw materials characteristic of Northern England.

Box 1.2   Grahame Clark

Grahame Clark was born in 1907, the son of a stockbroker who survived active service in the First World War, but died of influenza on his journey home (Coles 1997). From childhood, Clark was interested in archaeology, collecting flints from the landscape around his home on the South Downs. He published accounts of his findings in his school magazine before graduating to artefacts studies for regional archaeology journals. In 1926, he arrived at Cambridge University. This was a time when archaeology was first being established as an academic discipline; the first university posts in Prehistoric archaeology were established and the first degree programmes institutionalised. Gordon Childe was appointed at Edinburgh University in 1927; Miles Burkitt first taught Prehistoric archaeology at Cambridge in 1915 (Smith 1994). To teach archaeology, archaeological finds needed to be organised, rationalised and most of all synthesised. To this end, Gordon Childe, Miles Burkitt and Dorothy Garrod all began assessment of the Mesolithic in the mid-1920s, but it was Clark who brought this process to fruition in the 1930s.

At Cambridge, Clark was taught by Miles Burkitt; following his graduation, Clark embarked on the first PhD project on a Prehistoric theme. Despite describing Mesolithic cultures as 'numerous and somewhat monotonous' (1926, 250), Burkitt suggested Mesolithic Britain to Clark as a thesis topic (Clark 1974). Clark's doctoral thesis (published in 1932 as *The Mesolithic Age in Britain*) was the first major synthesis of the period. It consists, apart from a short introductory chapter, of a systematic inventory of Mesolithic finds from Britain in relation to continental classificatory schemes. This is Clark in his initial typological mode, which he represented in his future work as limited and outmoded. However, at the time this initial organisation of Mesolithic data was vital; furthermore, in this book Clark was keen to promote a pan-European perspective on archaeology, which he saw as an important corollary to the more local focus of archaeology at the time.

Clark became a hugely influential figure, both in Mesolithic studies and in the discipline more broadly, whose career spanned a time of huge changes in archaeology. When Clark first became interested in the subject, archaeology was still the preserve of the gentlemen of learned societies. These people were landowners and professional men, but there were few salaried archaeologists among them. By the time Clark retired in 1974, archaeology was firmly established as a profession. Clark was influential in these changes. In the 1930s, Clark and his friends Stuart Piggott and Charles Phillips saw themselves as 'Young Turks' (Piggott 1994, cited in Smith 1999), who were transforming a myopic, artefact-focused archaeology. They chafed against what they saw as the parochialism of certain of the old guard of gentlemen amateurs. An instructive example of the work of the 'Young Turks' can be seen in the renaming of the Prehistoric Society of East Anglia to more accurately reflect its national – and indeed international – scope. Still echoing legends have Clark's supporters heroically racing across the fens in a MG sportscar borrowed from marmalade baron Alexander Keiler, to cast their votes in favour of a name change to The Prehistoric Society. This legend (as indeed many surrounding Clark) has unfortunately been exaggerated (Smith 1999); the decision was in fact made through a postal vote, balloting the entire membership, and Clark's work as editor of the Society's *Proceedings* from 1933 was probably more crucial in shifting towards an international focus.

Clark published several pieces tracing his intellectual biography (Clark 1972, 1974). We can perhaps think of these pieces, though usually factually correct, as an attempt to create a narrative from something that was perhaps rather more piecemeal. Clark viewed himself as passing through three stages: Typological, stratigraphic and functional. He represents the shifts between stages as clean breaks (often with a Eureka! moment involved), where a new (and superior) type of archaeology supplanted an older (and flawed, or even worse, uninteresting) approach. In his history, Clark plays up certain intellectual influences and neglects others (for example, both the influence of Gordon Child and Francis Buckley on his early work).

In the mid-1930s, Clark suggests that his research objectives had begun to take a new direction – a desire to situate artefacts in their environmental context. He states that this shift was stimulated by two major factors: First, his growing awareness of the pioneering work on environmental reconstruction in Scandinavia following his first visit in 1929 (Clark 1936, ix); second, by his acquaintance with the Godwins (who pioneered the Swedish technique of pollen analysis in this country) and the involvement of Clark, the Godwins and Charles Phillips in the Fenland Research Committee. Clark was initially drawn to environmental research as a means of providing a chronology for Mesolithic sites such as Peacock's Farm, Shippea Hill (see Box 4.4), but he became increasingly interested in the way that material culture and the environment interacted. This new viewpoint was crystallised in *The Mesolithic Settlement of Northern Europe* (Clark 1936). This book contains a mixture of typological analysis and a 'real, if unsophisticated, appreciation of the significance of the physical environment' (Clark 1974, 37–8). Clark's description of the way of life of 'Maglemose Folk' (living during the summer by rivers, lakes and fens; fishing, fowling, hunting with their dogs and eating hazelnuts), went some way towards fulfilling his wish that archaeology should be 'the study of how men lived in the past' (Clark 1939).

His views were developed in the subsequent publication *Archaeology and Society* (1939). Here, he followed the anthropologists Malinowski and Radcliffe-Brown, whose work he had encountered as a student, and viewed society as a functioning system whose goal was self-perpetuation. The environment was viewed as a constraining factor, influencing all aspects of the system, but in particular (according to Clark) the technology and economy of a society. He also emphasised these two components as potentially the most knowable to archaeologists, as well as being the most immediate to the perpetuation of life. Because all components were closely interdependent, to know of environmental conditions and also of the economy was thus to know something of how society functioned. So, Clark sought new kinds of data – data that transformed artefacts from cultural markers to economic indicators and that transformed ecofacts from chronological markers to evidence for the environmental context upon which the system was based.

This sort of work needed a site with good organic preservation. One of Clark's aims in establishing the Fenland Research Committee was undoubtedly to find such a site; however, Peacock's Farm did not fit the bill because it lacked preserved organics. The excavation of Farnham in Surrey in 1937–1938 in a joint publication with W.F. Rankine (the leading Mesolithic fieldworker in Southern England), was another attempt to find such a site (see chapter 4). This excavation failed to yield either ecological information or structures; Clark was sorely disappointed (Fagan 2018). The search was interrupted by the war; however, an opportunity to realise his aims finally presented itself when John Moore, an amateur archaeologist active in East Yorkshire, brought to his attention a site of suspected 'Maglemose type', with good organic preservation.

This was Star Carr (see chapter 2). The excavations were completed in 1951, the year before Clark was awarded Cambridge's Disney professorship; this is Clark's work at its apex. Here, a combination of new ideas about how to interpret archaeological remains, an unusually well-preserved site, the role of the site in Clark's subsequent teaching and a timely and innovative publication combined to produce a hugely influential account of the site. The publication was in Clark's name alone: John Moore, who had undertaken the initial excavation, was side-lined in a way Bill Rankine had not been ten years earlier. While the archaeology of the site is discussed in detail in chapter 2, several features of the excavation can be highlighted as a result of their future influence. Particularly important were Clark's considerations of seasonality and subsistence. Although seasonality had been considered during the earliest

Scandinavian excavations, it began to preoccupy Clark when he became familiar with the work of the anthropologist D. Thomson, who observed that the Wik Monkan of Arnhem Land used a different array of equipment at different times of the year (Thomson 1939). This variability in material culture would have been distinguished by archaeologists of the time as the products of different groups. Thus, Clark had a desire to view artefacts in functional terms, rather than as cultural markers. His calculations of the actual amount of meat represented by the faunal remains, relating it to a group's calorific requirements, subsequently were taken up by the palaeoeconomy school (e.g. Vita-Finzi and Higgs 1970). Although the site of Star Carr has subsequently undergone many revisions and reinterpretations (see chapter 2), Clark's investigations remain an impressive picture of the way of life of a group of Mesolithic hunter-gatherers, and as an example of what can be achieved by asking new questions and examining new classes of data, seemed to call into question the value of earlier excavations (Trigger 1989, 268).

Two decades later, Clark returned to the Star Carr data in order to expand his interpretation of the site to incorporate a consideration of the group's annual territory (Clark 1972). He had become strongly influenced by Tansley's concept of an ecosystem, which he was the first to apply to archaeology in *Prehistoric Europe: The Economic Basis* (1952). He used Vita-Finzi and Higgs' (1970) site catchment model, listing the available resources during the supposed winter stay and relating the number of red deer in this territory to the calorific requirements of a human group. Clark attempted to reconstruct the whole settlement system by suggesting, on the basis of the migration patterns of red deer, that human groups had a similar upland/summer, lowland/winter pattern as their prey and that the people who wintered at Star Carr spent their summers hunting deer on the North York Moors.

Clark's legacy to Mesolithic research centres on Star Carr. It is a site that has come to dominate Mesolithic studies, partly as a result of preservation, partly as a result of its innovative publication. It served as the cornerstone to Clark's economic approach to the Mesolithic that dominated the period for many decades. Clark's position as Disney professor in one of the few institutions in those early years that taught archaeology reinforced its significance: Clark taught his students about Star Carr; many became lecturers and taught their students. Cambridge prehistory, within which Star Carr played a central part, spread across the globe (Clark 1989). The Star Carr publication also marks a shift in the role lithic material played in Clark's work, from central in the 1930s, to one subsidiary, to faunal remains. This attitude was echoed by Clark's students, and as a result, lithics, the main class of evidence for Mesolithic studies, was neglected until Jacobi's work in the 1970s. Finally, the Star Carr publication was in Clark's name alone; John Moore, the discoverer of the site, was side-lined in a way that Bill Rankine had not been in the Farnham report a decade previously. Clark's professionalisation of the discipline had the effect of marginalising the skilled amateur archaeologists who had established the Mesolithic as a period of prehistory and who have contributed so substantially to Mesolithic studies subsequently.

Honey Hill-type assemblages were the latest of the Early Mesolithic types to be fully distinguished. Jacobi (1978b), in his survey of the Mesolithic of England and Wales, noted that some assemblages in the midlands and East Anglia were characterised by microliths with inversely retouched bases, which ranged from pointed- to rounded-base forms (Figure 1.4). The assemblage type was named by Saville (1981a,b) on the basis of his analysis of the site of Honey Hill, Elkington, Northamptonshire. Saville also noted the distinctiveness of the inversely retouched bases and produced a distribution map for sites in the English midlands.

More recently, Reynier (1997, 1998, 2005) has refined understandings of the different assemblage types. In addition to analysis of microlith form and other tool types (see Box 1.3), this work included an analysis of technological schema associated with the various types, though the utility of this is limited by the small number of assemblages analysed and its narrow geographical focus. Reynier also suggested a chronological dimension to these different types. Working with un-calibrated radiocarbon dates, he argued that Star Carr assemblages appear in Britain first, at around 9700 radiocarbon years BP (c.9200 cal BC), with Deepcar assemblages occurring after, around 9400 BP (c.8700 cal BC), and Horsham assemblages – characterised by the presence of hollow-based Horsham points – from c.9000 BP (c.8250 cal BC). However, the dating evidence suggested that the different assemblage types did not displace the preceding facies, so that after 9000 BP all three appear to have been contemporary (c.8250 cal BC). Honey Hill types were not included in this discussion because they were at that point in time undated. However, since some Honey Hill types were present in some Horsham assemblages (e.g. Beedings Wood), Reynier suggested that Honey Hill assemblages belonged to a similar time-frame to Horsham types. A set of dates for Honey Hill assemblages was finally provided through excavations of Asfordby, Leicestershire (Cooper and Jarvis 2017), where radiocarbon measurements centred on 8000 cal BC, suggesting that Honey Hill and Horsham-type sites were broadly contemporary.

Box 1.3   Reynier's definitions of Star Carr, Deepcar, Horsham and Honey Hill assemblage types

Star Carr-type assemblages

Star Carr assemblages are characterised by broad obliquely truncated points and large isosceles triangles and trapezes (Figure 1.3). Microliths are slightly more likely to be lateralised to the left (60%) (Reynier 2005). Other tools include scrapers, well-made burins, truncations, awls (including the distinctive bilaterally retouched meche de foret) and axes. Microdenticulated pieces are rare.

Deepcar-type assemblages

Deepcar assemblages are dominated by narrower, elongated obliquely truncated points, sometimes with retouch on the leading edge, which grade into partially and fully backed forms (Figure 1.3). Trapezes and triangles are still present, but in reduced numbers. Rhomboids also occur, as do curve-backed pieces in some assemblages (e.g. Oakhanger V/VII). Lateralisaton tends more to the left (>70%) (Reynier 2005). Scrapers are the most common tool form after microliths. Some burins are found, but these are poorly made. Truncations, awls, microdenticu-lates and axes are also present in varying numbers. Rods, a type unknown from Star Carr assemblages, are also occasionally recovered. Jacobi suggest that these were used as strike-a-lights and are the functional equivalent of the heavily abraded cores found in Star Carr-type assemblages (Jacobi et al. 1978, 214).

Horsham-type assemblages

Horsham assemblages are characterised by hollow-based points and other basally modified forms (Figure 1.4). Obliquely truncated points still dominate though, and these are strongly lateralised to the left (>95%) (Reynier 2005). Obliquely truncated point are short and broad, more similar to Star Carr than Deepcarr examples. Rhomboids are more common than in Deepcarr assem-blages, and triangles persist, but trapezes are absent. Beyond microliths, scrapers and truncations are common, while axes, burins and microdenticulates are present but rare. Chamfered pieces are a notable aspect of these assemblages.

Honey Hill assemblages

The distinctive feature of Honey Hill assemblages is the presence of inversely retouched basally modified pieces (5–20%) (Figure 1.4). Obliquely truncated and partially backed points are present in varying numbers (20–60%), often with retouch on the leading edge. These are small in comparison to the obliquely truncated point in Star Carr-type and Deepcar-type assemblages. Also found within these assemblages are curve-backed pieces, lanceolates, isosceles triangles and rhomboids. Some small scalene triangles are present, and there has been debate as to whether these are intrusive, or herald a shift towards later Mesolithic microlith types. Lateralisation of obliquely blunted points is strongly to the left (>90%) (Reynier 2005). As with Horsham-type assemblages, scrapers are common, but burins are rare. Axes are present in some assemblages.

Understanding variability: The Late Mesolithic

There has been rather less work on variation in the Late Mesolithic. Much of this was undertaken by Roger Jacobi in the 1970s. He used cluster analysis to group 151 mi-crolith assemblages across England and Wales and to suggest a number of groupings that had either a regional or chronological basis. Four Late Mesolithic clusters were identified in his early work (Swsur and Jacobi 1979). Cluster D, the largest, consisted of assemblages dominated by narrow scalene triangles (Figure 1.5). This grouping was mainly, though not exclusively, found in Northern England and included both low-land and upland locations. Cluster E, dominated by narrow, straight-backed bladelets known as rods, was more restricted in its location (Figure 1.5). These assemblages are found in the upland areas of the Pennines and the North York Moors and were

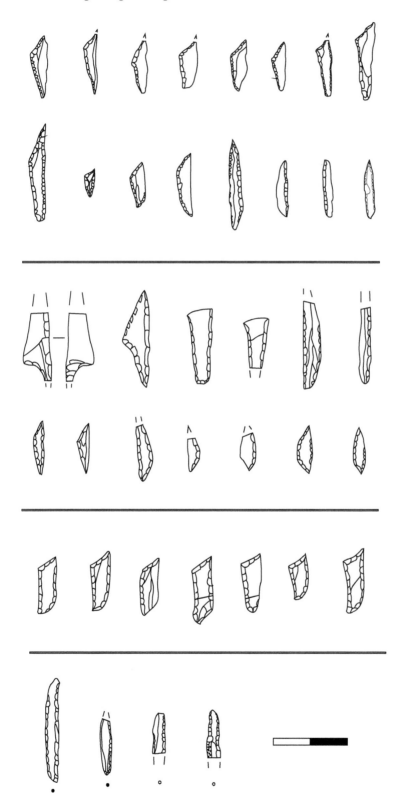

(caption on next page)

Figure 1.5 Late Mesolithic left lateralised triangles and backed bladelets from March Hill Carr (rows 1–2). Final Mesolithic microliths: A micro-tranchet assemblage from Stratford's Yard (rows 3–4); a rod microlith assemblage from March Hill Top (row 5); four-sided pieces from Readycon Dene (row 6)

suggested on the basis of two radiocarbon dates to belong to the very end of the Mesolithic. Cluster C was small, consisting of only three sites, and consisted of assemblages dominated by four-sided types (Figure 1.5). The only dated site in this cluster suggested it too belonged to the end of the Mesolithic. The final cluster (B) encompassed assemblages across England and Wales. It is distinguished from the others by the inclusion of early microlith types along with narrow microliths. This cluster seems a product of three different factors: 1. chronological mixing, as at Farnham pit 2 and Selmeston pit 1; 2. the inclusion of Honey Hill assemblages (see above); and 3. Discrete assemblages belonging to the start of the Late Mesolithic, which do seem to have more obliquely blunted points than others (e.g. Prestatyn). In his later regional syntheses, Jacobi drew on his cluster analysis to suggest particular regional groupings, such as a crescent- and lanceolate-dominated southwest group (Jacobi 1979). This group he later recognised extended across Southern Britain (Jacobi and Tebbutt 1981).

As part of his research on the Mesolithic in the 1970s, Jacobi examined all Mesolithic collections then known from England and Wales (Jacobi 1975). In addition to his cluster analysis, he produced a microlith-type list (Figure 1.6), which has been used in this book as the basis for the categorisation of different microlith forms. Since Jacobi's studies of the late 1970s and early 1980s, there has been relatively little typochronological work focused on the majority of the Late Mesolithic. Ellaby (1987) has suggested the start of the Late Mesolithic in Southeast England may be characterised by assemblages dominated by backed bladelets, and the dating of a composite tool from Seamer K, North Yorkshire has raised the possibility that there may have been a similar phase in Northern England. Barton and Roberts (2004) have concurred with an earlier suggestion by Jacobi that microscalenes and other more elaborate forms such as microtranchets, four-sided pieces and microcrescents post-date 6000 BC in England.

Most work has focused on the rod microlith assemblages, Jacobi's cluster E, which he saw as belonging to the very end of the Late Mesolithic. Fieldwork by Penny Spikins (2000) in the Central Pennines and by Richard Chatterton (2005) in the Northern Pennines confirmed Jacobi's thesis that these dated to the very end of the Mesolithic. Griffiths (2014), in a review of Late Mesolithic and Early Neolithic radiocarbon dates, noted some late dates for groups of straight-backed bladelets in Southern England and Wales, particularly at Lydstep Haven and the Fir Tree Field Shaft, both of which also date to the last centuries of the Mesolithic period. Whether these are part of the same phenomena as the 'rod' sites of the Pennines and North York Moors is more difficult to determine: The Pennine rod sites are also distinguished by a shift in raw material use, making their difference from earlier assemblages clearer. The issue is also hampered by a lack of clear definition for backed bladelets and rods (see discussion in chapter 6). Rod microliths in the Pennines tend to have steeply retouched single or double backing (the latter sometimes more akin to Jacobi's needle point). The microliths from Lydstep and Fir Tree Field do not fall into the latter definition, and both assemblages are probably more accurately described as backed bladelets. More work needs to be done to understand if there is a rod microlith phase beyond the Pennine chain.

But what about Scotland?

It may not have escaped the reader's notice that these typological schemes have almost entirely been enacted on material from England and Wales. In Scotland, there has been a healthy scepticism about whether even a chronologically distinct broad microlith and narrow microlithic division can be made. This is partly

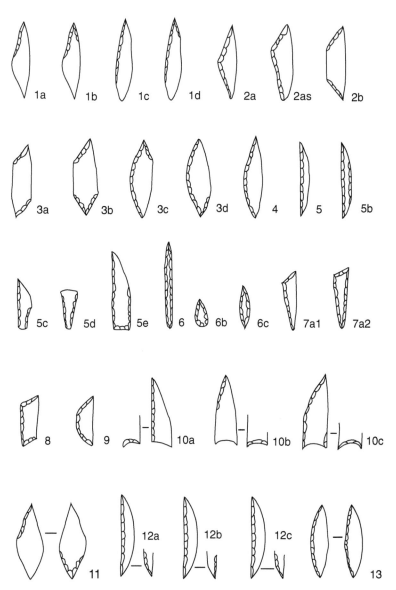

(caption on next page)

Figure 1.6 Jacobi's microlith types (redrawn from Jacobi 1978b) with additions. 1a. Obliquely blunted point. 1b. Obliquely blunted point with retouch on the leading edge. 1c. Partially backed point. 1d. Partially backed point with retouch on the leading edge (1c and 1d are the author's additions to Jacobi's types and are useful for distinguishing Deepcar assemblages). 2a Isosceles triangle. 2b. Large scalene triangle. 2c. Trapeze. 3a. Rhomboid/3b–d. Various forms of lanceolate. 4. Curve-backed piece. 5. Backed bladelet. 5b. Double-backed bladelet. 5c. Asymmetric micro-tranchet. 5d. Symmetric micro-tranchet. 5e. Piece with square base. 6. Needle-point. 6b. Pear. 6c. Sauveterre point (known as Fine Point in Scotland). 7a. Scalene triangle (two sides retouched). 7b. Scalene triangle (three sides retouched). 8. Four-sided piece. 9. Crescent. 10a and 10c. Different forms of Horsham point; the basal retouch can be inverse or dorsal. 10b. Tardenois point (this can also have a straight basal truncation). 11. Honey Hill point. 12a–c. Various forms of backed bladelet with inverse retouch. 13. Curved-backed with inverse retouch

due to the unfortunate habit of broad microliths turning up in later assemblages; these tend, however, to be ploughzone sites found along favoured places, particularly along rivers. Early-type microliths have also been associated with Late Mesolithic dates, particularly at Morton A, where an almost exclusively early-seeming assemblage is broadly associated with mainly seventh and sixth millennium dates, and at Lussa Wood I on Jura where eighth and seventh millennium dates have been obtained (though here the use of bulked charcoal on a site of mixed date is a more readily identifiable explanation). In more recent years, as some discrete early assemblages have been located, archaeologists working in Scotland appear more ready to accept that a chronologically distinct Early Mesolithic with features similar to those found in England and Wales (and Northwest Europe more broadly) does exist in the region.

In a region dominated by narrow microlith assemblages, there has been more work on the dimensions of variability. Work by Nyree Finlay in the context of the Southern Hebrides Mesolithic project (SHMP) found little chronological basis for microlith variability in the assemblages examined (Finlay et al. 2000); Mithen suggested variability amongst these sites might instead have a functional component, the higher proportion of backed bladelets at Staosnaig perhaps being related to use of this site for plant processing (Mithen 2000). If there is chronologically based typological variation amongst Scottish Late Mesolithic assemblages, the SHMP sites, consisting of huge assemblages from sites without stratigraphic separation and with relatively few radiocarbon dates are not the places to find this. However, it is clear from Finlay's analysis that there is considerable overlap between forms in this region: Scalene triangles grade into crescents, which grade into fine points and backed bladelets. This appears the case in more than one region of Britain, where there is use of very small packages of raw material and a trend to hyper-microlithisation.

Environmental frameworks

Mesolithic archaeologists have also drawn on the chronological schemes developed to understand Early and Mid-Holocene vegetation history, though this has been more a feature of research on the continent. In 1940, Harry Godwin, a pioneer of pollen analysis, proposed a three-fold division of the Holocene vegetational history of Britain. Though this division was based primarily on his work on the deep peat sequences of the East Anglian fens, it was detectable, he suggested, across England and Wales. These changes were attributed to climate: A period of increasing warmth, followed by maximum warmth and then a climatic downturn, but one of decreased severity compared to the first. These were seen to affect the major tree species in different ways, with an early radiation of the more tolerant birch, followed initially by pine and then more warmth-loving hazel, oak and elm and finally alder. In the third phase, these trees diminished, and birch again increased with beech and hornbeam. Godwin further subdivided these three phases into zones as follows:

Zone IV
Birch-pine zone. During this period, birch was dominant with pine, the only other important tree. Willow was also present.

Zone V
Pine zone. Here birch was replaced by pine, with hazel beginning to expand rapidly and the appearance of other thermophilous trees. This zone was subsequently redefined to correspond with the rise in hazel (Godwin 1956).

Zone VI
Pine-hazel zone. This was divided into three:

VIa Pine and hazel dominant, elm expands rapidly, oak less important.
VIb Pine and hazel dominant, oak pollen equals or exceeds elm.
VIc Reduction of hazel, expansion of lime and alder.

Zone VII
Alder-oak-elm-lime zone. Pine is replaced by alder, lime expands considerably. Divided into VIIa and VIIb on the basis of the sudden decline of elm.

Godwin saw his divisions as applicable across Britain, though he acknowledged the presence of regional climatic-vegetational zones, where climatic changes led to 'equivalent but not identical' outcomes (Godwin 1940a, 388). The synchroneity of these changes are assumed. While acknowledging the influence of local factors, such as soil types, on vegetation, these factors are generally downplayed in an attempt to establish a sequence.

Godwin correlated his zones V and VI with the Mesolithic. Zone VI was equated with the Boreal climate phase in the Blytt-Sernander system (Figure 1.7). This was a system of climate sub-division for the Holocene, developed by the botanists Blytt and Sernander on the basis of peat bog and lake stratigraphy in Southern Scandinavia. These subsequently became related to pollen sequences and zones, and their use was extended across Northern Europe (Table 1.1).

The equation of Godwin's pollen zones with continental pollen zones and Blytt-Sernander phases facilitated their increasing use by archaeologists as chronostrati-graphic units. In Britain, this was initiated by Godwin (1940a), who attempted to correlate archaeological periods with his zones, pointing out, for example, that the site at Broxbourne was sealed below a zone VI peat, while his work at Star Carr extended the Mesolithic back into zone IV and facilitated a comparison with sites in Southern Scandinavia. Here, he stated, 'there is good reason to regard

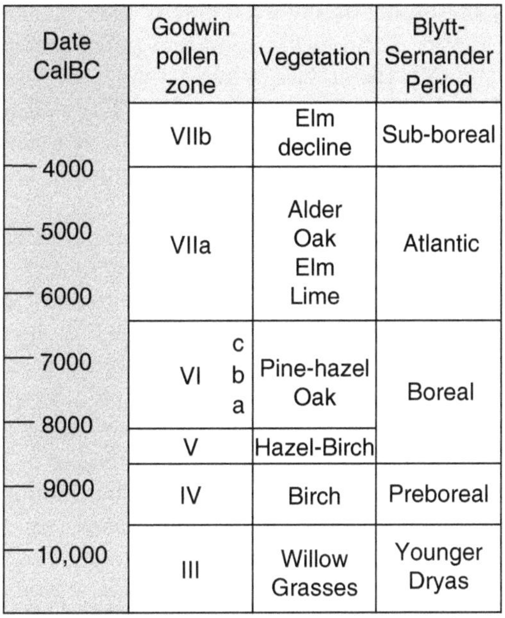

Date CalBC	Godwin pollen zone		Vegetation	Blytt-Sernander Period
	VIIb		Elm decline	Sub-boreal
— 4000				
— 5000	VIIa		Alder Oak Elm Lime	Atlantic
— 6000				
— 7000	VI	c b a	Pine-hazel Oak	Boreal
— 8000	V		Hazel-Birch	
— 9000	IV		Birch	Preboreal
—10,000	III		Willow Grasses	Younger Dryas

Figure 1.7 Correlation of Godwin's pollen zones with Blytt-Sernander zones

Table 1.1 Blytt-Sernander zones

Blytt-Sernander zone	*Climate*
Preboreal	Sub-artic
Boreal	Warm and dry
Atlantic	Warm and wet. Oceanic
Sub-boreal	Warm and dry. Continental
Sub-atlantic	Cold and wet. Oceanic

these zones [IV and V] in Denmark and Britain as synchronous' (Godwin 1954, 68). This suggested a potential for pollen-stratigraphy to permit British Mesolithic archaeologists to tap into better dated chronological sequences. Subsequent work on Mesolithic sites took care to match sequences to Godwin's pollen zones: Churchill's work at Thatcham suggested the evidence could be mapped to zone V/VI or boreal (Churchill 1962). By the 1950s, the Blytt-Sernander zones were fully combined with Godwin's zones and tied to archaeological periods in a convenient chronological system for the Holocene (Godwin 1956).

Pollen-stratigraphic dating was seen to hold considerable potential before the widespread use of radiocarbon dating. This was also a time when pollen analysis of mineral soils was being pioneered by Dimbleby (1957, 1985). If pollen assemblages from buried soils provided an accurate representation of a phase of ancient vegetation, these could be correlated with the archaeological remains preserved within these soils, and offered much greater dating potential in comparison to the rarer juxtaposition of Mesolithic sites and contemporaneous peat bogs, which had been the traditional focus of pollen analysis. Dimbleby contributed environmental and pollen stratigraphic evidence to the interpretation of many Mesolithic sites (e.g. Dimbleby 1959; Keef et al. 1965; Rankine and Rankine 1960). However, it is now apparent that pollen can move through these soils from above, and the soils themselves, while active, incorporate a time-averaged pollen assemblage, affected by issues of preservation. The pollen assemblage from Longmoor (a site in a sandy podzolised sediment) suggested an Atlantic date for the Mesolithic site, whereas the radiocarbon dates indicate the occupation was at least a millennium earlier (Reynier 2005).

From the 1970s onwards, as more radiocarbon dated pollen profiles became available, the extent to which Godwin's zones were diachronous and affected by local factors, such as soil type, fluvial regimes and woodland disturbance, became clear (Smith and Pilcher 1973), leading Birks (1982, 101) to recommend they should be abandoned as chronostratigraphic markers. Birks' (1989) own work demonstrated the time-transgressive nature of vegetational changes. His isochronic maps used radiocarbon dates to plot the spread of various tree types. Oak, for example, took 1500 radiocarbon years to spread from Southwest England to Southern Scotland. Bennet (1989) recommended the use of local pollen assemblage zones that then might be correlated, using radiocarbon dating, to produce regional pollen sequences. His work indicated that regional pollen sequences across Britain were not simply asynchronous, but also not comparable in composition. The Blytt-Sernander zones, which by this time were functioning more as vegetational chrono-stratigraphic zones than climatic markers, were also seen as subject to the same issues (Godwin 1975). Their use lingers as a convenient, if imprecise, chronological shorthand, but they have been largely superseded by radiocarbon dating.

Radiometric chronologies for the Mesolithic

Despite one of the first radiocarbon dates for a British site being obtained from Star Carr, just a couple of years after the technique was first used, relatively little systematic work was done in the subsequent two decades. Instead, occasional dates were obtained for key sites, though more was made of environmental sequences associated with Mesolithic sites as a dating method, for example, at Thatcham. In the 1970s, Roger Jacobi, in collaboration with Roy Switsur, collected samples from amongst the charcoal and charred hazelnut preserved in museum collections, from his collaborations with local archaeologists and from his own excavations. These measurements, combined with those few pre-existing estimates, resulted in a record of 43 radiocarbon dates for Mesolithic sites by 1979. These measurements suffered from the problems of their day. These included large standard deviations and no means to calibrate results. Charcoal measurements were often made on unidentified wood, and often bulked from more than one feature. Dates on bone were similarly bulked and did not always include samples with evidence for human modification. In future years, Jacobi (1994) found many of these unsatisfactory.

In the following decades, while Mesolithic studies in England languished, Wales saw a new dating programme through the work of Andrew David, while Mesolithic fieldwork in Scotland took off. Much of the work in Scotland was accompanied by high-quality dating programmes with rigorous targeting of short-lived samples from sealed archaeological features, and the fieldwork of Caroline Wickham-Jones should be noted as leading the way in this respect. This began to result in a much better understanding of the chronology of the Mesolithic in Scotland, in particular the timing of movement into the far north and the islands.

Improved dating in England happened incrementally, mostly as part of new developer-funded work (e.g. Ellis et al. 2003), along with a small number of research projects (e.g. Spikins 2002). Particularly important amongst these for understanding the temporality of Mesolithic occupation was the work by Petra Dark at Star Carr (Mellars and Dark 1998). She dated charcoal samples found at different levels of an environmental sequence. By studying the distribution of dates in relation to the stratigraphic level she was able to 'wiggle match' these to the radiocarbon calibration curve. By using these dates to estimate the rate of peat formation, she was able to suggest human occupation (indicated by the charcoal proxy) for a period of 80 years, then a gap of 100 years, within which only very occasional visits occurred, followed by a second phase of 150 years, during which visits to the site were less frequent than during phase 1.

Despite these advances, it was telling that when Reynier published his typo-chronological review of the Early Mesolithic in England and Wales, a review that included auditing all known dates, only 27 were considered sufficiently robust for inclusion in the analysis. In this attempt to understand the chronology of Early Mesolithic assemblage types, Reynier was hampered by lack of calibration and the presence of radiocarbon plateau at 9600BP and 9000BP, permitting only an imprecise understanding of the possible longevity of the various types (see above).

In subsequent years, the use of Bayesian modelling has begun to provide un-precedented understandings of the occupation of certain Mesolithic sites. The combination of numerous radiocarbon measurements with statistical modelling based on stratigraphy has offered new insights into the dating and duration of occupation of key sites. First of these was the Mesolithic structure at Howick (Waddington et al. 2007). Modelling of the phases suggested a duration of occupation for this feature of between 100 and 300 years (see chapter 4). The work at Howick was accompanied by a study of the dating of the transition from Early to Late Mesolithic, which suggested the process was time-transgressive. This work did not distinguish between different types of assemblage, and by including Horsham sites with the Early Mesolithic group, its significance was difficult to gauge, beyond showing Late Horsham sites in the south were contemporary with assemblages containing narrow scalene triangles in the north. The dates for the earliest sites with narrow scalenes were suggested to show an east-west spread; this was hypothesised to reflect the presence of marine-adapted groups pushed westwards from an ever-shrinking Doggerland.

An extensive Bayesian model was also made for Star Carr following the recent excavations (Bayliss et al. 2018). This primarily drew on the deep stratigraphy of the wetland area, the more intensively occupied dryland area being more difficult to tie in to this sequence. The modelling indicated routine occupation of the site for a period of more than 800 years. During this time, the focus of activities changed, but key themes and modes of engaging with the landscape remained (see chapter 2).

As part of this work, the different types of Early Mesolithic industries were modelled, along with the emergence of assemblages dominated by narrow scalenes (Conneller et al. 2016a). Due to the paucity of dates for basally modified assemblages, these were lumped together in a single group, which is less than ideal. The model indicated the following results (Figure 1.8):

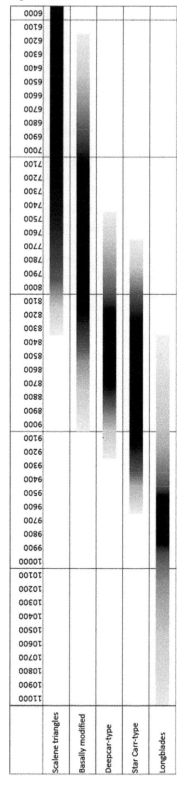

Figure 1.8 2016 model of Early Mesolithic assemblage types (Conneller et al. 2016a)

1. Star Carr-type assemblages first appeared in *9805–9265 cal BC (95% probability; start Star Carr-types)*, probably in *9495–9290 cal BC (68% probability)*. Star Carr-type assemblages disappeared in *8230–7520 cal BC (95% probability; end Star Carr-type)*, probably in *8165–7835 cal BC (67% probability)* or *7830–7815 cal BC (1% probability)*.
2. Deepcar-type assemblages first appeared in *9460–8705 cal BC (95% probability; start Deepcar-type)*, probably in *9090–8775 cal BC (68% probability)*. Deepcar-type assemblages disappeared in *8200–7240 cal BC (95% probability; end Deepcar-type);* probably in *8075–7620 cal BC (68% probability)*.
3. Basally modified microlith-type assemblages first appeared in *9280–8305 cal BC (95% probability; start basally modified)*, probably in *8690–8335 cal BC (68% probability)*. Basally modified microlith-type assemblages disappeared in *7030–5845 cal BC (95% probability; end basally modified type;* Figure 1.6), probably in *6960–6460 cal BC (68% probability)*.
4. Small scalene triangles first appeared in *8315–7765 cal BC (95% probability; start scalene triangles)*, probably in *8045–7795 cal BC (68% probability)*.

In essence, though providing more precise calendar dates, this study replicates the findings of Reynier, suggesting successive appearance of Star Carr, Deepcar and basally modified types, followed by co-existence of these forms. There are some hints, though, that there may be different sequences in different parts of Britain. At Star Carr, for example, a few Deepcar-like microliths appear in the upper parts of the peat sequence, while recent dates for Deepcar sites in the north suggest an appearance from around 8500 cal BC, a time when occupation at Star Carr was probably ending. In Southern England, Star Carr sites are extremely rare, and the significance we can attach to the single dated site at Broxbourne 104 is unclear. In Wales, there are very late dates for Star Carr-type sites and some typological differences; we should probably question whether these should be grouped with the sites from Northern England.

The 2016 study was focused on Star Carr, Deepcar and Horsham assemblages based on extensive work, including archive visits. British Academy funding in 2018–2019 permitted more comprehensive work on the Late Mesolithic, including further collation of radiocarbon measurements, some archive work on key later Mesolithic assemblages and some targeted radiocarbon dating. Late Mesolithic dates were linked, where possible, to particular microlith types. Modelling of these results, targeting in particular major shifts in scalene triangle forms and novel late microlith types, was undertaken by Seren Griffiths (Conneller and Griffiths in press). This provides part of the basis for the new periodisation of the Mesolithic presented here. In some ways, the aim of this typochronological work is a bit different from previous attempts. While assemblage types have been modelled, the primary aim has been to produce a new periodisation for the Mesolithic that can be used to emphasise how life changed between 9300 and 3900 cal BC.

Towards a new synthesis

To understand the Mesolithic, it is essential to move beyond the current early/late division and focus on the Mesolithic as regional varied, temporal and historical processes. There is, as elucidated by Elliott and Griffiths (2018), currently a difficulty in connecting the scales at which Mesolithic studies operate: The broad-scale often homogenised period divisions, in which the focus remains on the dynamism of the transition rather than ongoing temporal change, and the short-term site histories and events measured by radiocarbon dating. Their solution is to use well-dated sites and artefacts to move between scales, and this is something that is attempted in this book. However, there are many regions where, due to either preservational issues or Mesolithic lifestyles that do not generate convenient sealed contexts for radiocarbon datable samples, radiometric dating will rarely be feasible. As a result, we need to improve typochronological dating, simply as a temporal anchor for the vast majority of Mesolithic evidence.

While typochronological work leads to periodisation and thus potentially to the homogenisation critiqued by Elliott and Griffiths, this has been a feature of some approaches more than others. Jacobi, for example, though often focused on typochronology, was influenced by David Clarke's approach to typology (Reynier 2005) and thus highlighted processes of change and variation rather than segmented, homogenous periods. I would argue that typochronology can be the basis of creating a more heterogenous Mesolithic, in that it permits a discussion of undated sites in their proper order and context and thus means we do not have to rely on the few key sites that have organic preservation. Lucas (2019) makes the point that while change happens all the time, periodisation is a means of identifying relevant change; relevance is defined on the basis of the synchronicity of changes in a number of different features. Lucas works in historic periods, and whether synchronicity can ever be determined in early prehistory is a moot point. In this book, typochronology has been used to break down the Mesolithic into useful segments for analysis, some of which do seem to be related to a broader suit of new settlement feature, and thus might be seen as examples of 'relevant' change. All though show change throughout.

The Mesolithic is divided in this book as follows:

Early Mesolithic. 94th/93rd century to 82nd/80th century. This encompasses assemblages with Star Carr, Deepcar, Nab Head and Cramond types of microlith (Figure 1.3). Star Carr and Deepcar are previously defined types. Nab Head types are a Southern Welsh Early Mesolithic form, previously seen as a Star Carr type, but distinguished from these by the presence of broad scalenes rather than broad isosceles triangles. Cramond type is currently unique to Cramond, but presumably representative of groups in now submerged areas of Doggerland. Previously it has been suggested to fall into the Middle Mesolithic as it has a basally modified microlith and forms – obliquely blunted points, curve-backed pieces and isosceles triangles – common to Middle Mesolithic sites in Britain and on the continent, though in unique combinations. Others have argued it is Late Mesolithic, though this does not seem to be the case on the basis of microlith types illustrated (Saville 2008; Figure 1.4). As Ritchie (2010, 23) states of Cramond, in the only typological review of the Scottish Mesolithic: 'this assemblage clearly includes forms that are typical of broad blade assemblages'. A recent review by Ballin and Ellis (2019) sees it as 'hybrid'. In recognition of its early date, it is included in Early Mesolithic types.

Middle Mesolithic. 82nd century to 70th century. This includes three main types, the Horsham and Honey Hill assemblages described above and assemblages with variably lateralised scalenes (VLS), as well as assemblages including basally modified forms that do not easily fit into the tighter type definitions (Figure 1.4). VLS assemblages are found in Scotland, Northern England and North Wales and are characterised by the presence of narrow scalene triangles. While these tend to have more left lateralised scalenes (if the microlith is orientated with the short side up-permost, this is the retouched side, as shown in Figure 1.4), a considerable minority of right lateralised examples are present (proportions are usually along the lines of two left lateralised triangles to one right). These scalenes are accompanied by small narrow obliquely blunted points, part-backed pieces, and sometimes backed blade-lets and crescents. VLS assemblages shift to assemblages associated with pre-dominantly left lateralised scalenes at around 7200 cal BC (Conneller and Griffiths in press). Middle Mesolithic basally modified forms seem to linger slightly later to c.7000 cal BC.

Late Mesolithic. 72nd century to 52nd century. Composition of microlith assem-blages in this period is more varied, based on fluctuating proportions of mainly left lateralised scalenes, narrow-backed bladelets and crescents (Figure 1.5). At times, triangles are hyper-microlithised, and there is a tendency to more examples with three sides retouched than amongst VLS assemblages. Some of the variation between forms may have a chronological and regional component. Ellaby (1987), for example, sug-gests that assemblages dominated by narrow-backed bladelets represent the earliest post-Horsham evidence in Southeast England, and there is a similar date for a com-posite tool with backed bladelets inserts from Seamer K in North Yorkshire (David 1998). However, it is clear that for large parts of the Mesolithic, this variation between types does not have a chronological dimension, particularly in Scotland, where there has been the suggestion that there is a functional element to variation in microlith types (Mithen 2000; Wickham-Jones and Dalland 1998). In many areas, particularly but not exclusively where raw material is in small, poor-quality packages, there is considerable continuity between types, particularly between scalenes and crescents (Finlay 2000).

Final Mesolithic. 52nd to 39th century. In parts of Britain, though not others, new microlith types appear in the final millennium of the Mesolithic (Figure 1.5). Symmetric and asymmetric micro-tranchets are found from Sussex to Cumbria. Asymmetric micro-tranchets (often with inverse retouch, Bexhill points) are well dated (at Bexhill; Champness et al. 2019), symmetrical microtranchets rather less so. A single early fifth radiocarbon date from Stratford's Yard, Chesham (Stainton 1989), could suggest a broadly similar currency to Bexhill; however, this measure-ment is on bulked bone from a repeatedly occupied site. Recent work by Spencer Carter (2014) suggests that microtranchets in the north also belong to the fifth millennium. Jacobi (1979) suggested that four-sided microliths were also relatively late in the sequence. A single radiocarbon date of 4350–3785 cal BC (4250–3960 cal BC at 67.7% confidence) (5260 ± 130; BM-449) from Wawcott I suggests a very late date for this type. The Wawcott sites seem in general to be favoured places of re-peated activity (Froom 2012), though amongst these Wawcott I appears a reason-ably discrete assemblage. Griffiths (2014) has demonstrated that rod sites in the Pennines date to the last centuries of the Mesolithic. These sites are distinguished by their size, location and raw material use. Griffiths has noted similar late dates for composite tools with backed bladelet inserts in Southern England and South Wales , though it is not known whether these are accompanied by similar changes in lifestyle to those on the Pennines or simply fortuitous survivals of types that spanned the entire Late Mesolithic. In Scotland, there is currently no evidence for changes in microlith forms in the fifth millennium, and any periodisation here needs to be on the basis of radiocarbon dates.

Box 1.4   What is a microlith?

Much of the chronology assembled in this book is based on the form of microliths. But what is a microlith? Microliths are small retouched tools, traditionally equated with the points and barbs of arrows, but now seen to have a much broader function as flexible components in composite tools. They range in size from up a few centimetres in length in Early Mesolithic Deepcar industries to a few millimetres in length on some Late Mesolithic sites, with hyper-microlithisation associated with the last millennia of the Mesolithic (Barton and Roberts 2004; Jacobi 1979). The strict technological definition of a microlith is based on their production through use of the microburin technique (Figure 1.9). In this method, a blade blank is selected, a notch is created and it is used to snap the blade. This produces two pieces. The first, the waste product, is known as the microburin, so-called as it was initially considered to represent a very small engraving tool. The second piece is the microlith, which then underwent further retouch to remove the snap facet and to form the desired shape. The ratio of microliths to microburins on a site has been used to understand the respective balance between production or gearing up and discard (Mellars 1976a; Myers 1986). More recent work, however, indicates that the microburin technique was not always used, particularly in the Late Mesolithic. Experimental production also shows that even when this technique is employed, in around 20% of cases no visible microburin was produced (Finlay 2003).

Early accounts stressed the use of microliths as arrow armatures, and the Mesolithic came to be seen as 'the age of red deer or of bowmen' (Rozoy 1984). Some accounts equated sites dominated by microliths with male-only hunting parties (Mellars 1976a). If this were the case, it seems that no women ventured north of the Trent between 8500 and 4000 cal BC. From the 1980s onwards, microwear began to be used in assemblage analysis, and a wider variety of uses for microliths was suggested (e.g. Finlayson 1990; Healy et al. 1992), reinforcing the work of David Clarke (1976), who highlighted the varied role of microliths in ethnographic contexts. Much of this early work is characterised by use of different methods of cleaning and analysis and incomplete reporting, making its comparability and significance difficult to assess (Evans 2009). More recent research shows that, in general, where use traces are present, these are associated with a projectile function (see Table 1.2), though the

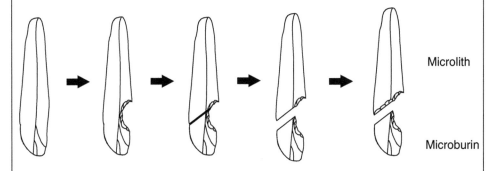

Microlith

Microburin

Figure 1.9 The microburin technique of microlith production

Table 1.2 Results of functional analyses of microliths

Site	Period	Total	Projectile	Projectile?	Cutting hide	Cutting meat	Cutting meat/hide	Piercing hide	Bone/wood	Plant	Piercing soft material	Reference
Star Carr	EM	16	6	2			4	2	1	1	1	Conneller et al. (2018a)
East Barns	MM	17	11	4	1			1				Evans (2009)
Asfordby	MM	27	16		1	7			2	1		Evans (2017)
North Park Farm	Mixed	24	13		2	2	6	1				Evans (2009)
Runnymede	Mixed	13	7	5		1					1	Evans (2009)
Malham Tarn A	LM	14	13					1			1	Evans (2009)
Goldcliff A and J	LM	2	1				1					Bell (2007)

problems associated with the identification of projectiles should be noted (Rots and Plisson 2014). The vast majority of microliths in analysed assemblages register no wear-traces at all, and experimental work demonstrates that only around one third of tools used as projectiles will show traces of use (Dockall 1997). That said, microliths are by no means uniquely projectile points, with notable secondary uses as knives in processing animal carcasses, in plant-based crafts such as basketry and as piercers. This is the case throughout the Mesolithic. Though we have no way of knowing who regularly undertook these various activities, as Finlay (2000) notes, this evidence prevents microliths being used as a signifier of male action or the simple equation of microlith-dominated sites with male hunting parties (Mellars 1976a).

There is certainly more work to be done in unpicking these patterns, as microliths have varied forms, and some lend themselves more readily to a variety of tasks than others. Evans (2009) suggests that at some sites longer backed bladelets, particularly those lacking retouch on the leading edge, are more likely to have been used as knives. A much more extensive microwear study of 467 Preboreal and Boreal Mesolithic microliths from Verrebroek, Belgium, found a strong association of microliths with projectile function, though a handful had been used in plant working (Crombé et al. 2001). This study explored means for identifying barbs as well as tips and thus was able to offer some insights into hafting arrangements. Crombé et al. (2001) note the earlier Mesolithic assemblages are characterised by either use of partially backed points, obliquely blunted points, triangles or crescents. The former only seem to have been used as arrow tips, whereas the three other types could be used as tips or barbs, though triangles and crescents tended to be the latter. Boreal Mesolithic assemblages are characterised by the appearance of microliths with basal modification; these seem always to have served as arrow tips, while scalenes were used as barbs.

To understand hafting arrangements in British contexts, we must turn to the isolated clusters of microliths found mainly in upland regions of England and Wales. While there is only one of these clusters where a haft is potentially preserved (David 1998), many are likely to represent lost arrows, though there is some ambiguity to this pattern that will be discussed further below. Myers (1989) has suggested the shift between traditional Early and Late Mesolithic was associated with a change in projectile form, from arrows with a tip and one or two barbs, to tools with a much greater number of barbs. The fact that Early Mesolithic arrows incorporated fewer components makes them more difficult to spot, and as a result the Lilla Loshult arrow from Sweden has been taken as model of Early Mesolithic types, though this dates around 8000 cal BC, effectively the time of the Early/Middle Mesolithic transition in Britain. The Loshult arrow measures 102 cm and has an isosceles triangle as a tip and an obliquely blunted point as a barb (Larsson et al. 2016). The few potential Early Mesolithic groupings suggest a similar arrangement. A cluster of three obliquely blunted points was found in the wetland at Star Carr (Figure 1.10). Micro-wear suggests that one was used as a tip, while the others may have been barbs. In the absence of a haft, it is impossible to determine whether this is a complete projectile or just a fragment, a caveat that also applies to the remainder of this discussion. However, the only other recorded group of early microliths, from the site of Warm Withens in the Central Pennines, also

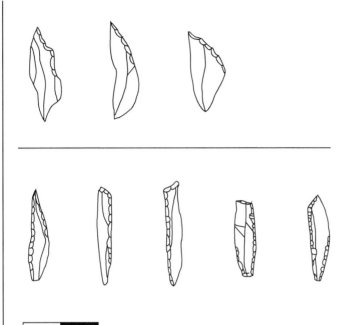

Figure 1.10 Microliths from possible composite tools from Star Carr: Early Mesolithic
(above); Middle Mesolithic (below)

consists of three components (Myers 1987). At Star Carr, three Deepcar-type
obliquely blunted points were found in the upper levels of the peat. All had
been used as barbs (Conneller et al. 2018a,). None had retouch on the leading
edge, which Evans' (2009) study suggests is a feature related to projectile use.
We might thus envisage a scenario where Deepcar arrows were barbed with
obliquely blunted points and tipped with examples with retouch on the leading
edge. Cooper and Jarvis (2017) have suggested improvements in projectile
technology towards the end of the Early Mesolithic with the use of leading-
edge retouch, as well as the appearance of crescents and lanceolates on Late
Deepcar sites.

Middle Mesolithic Britain can be divided into two provinces with different
sets of projectile technology. In large areas of Southern Britain, basally
modified forms proliferated. Research at the site of Asfordby indicates that
many of the more elaborate forms, Honey Hill points, lanceolates and
Sauveterrian points were used as arrow tips. These appear part of a broader
European trend towards innovation in flint-tipped arrow technology, with
improvements in the hafting technologies, as bone and antler points fell out of
use (Crombé et al. 2001).

In the Middle Mesolithic of Northern Britain, a process of miniturisation of
microliths commences. A second cluster of microliths found at Star Carr from
much higher in the peat consists of four scalenes and a partially backed piece
with retouch on the leading edge (Figure 1.10). The latter is likely to have been
the tip, though no wear traces were found. The triangles are variably lateralised

examples, suggesting this arrow dates to between 8200 and 7200 cal BC. The triangles form two symmetrically opposed pairs; each pair having slightly different morphology. A potentially contemporary cluster of elegant narrow elongated scalenes with variable lateralisation and numbering between six and nine was recovered from Waun Fignen Felen 9 (Figure 16 in Barton et al. 1995). Finally, of potential Middle Mesolithic composites is an example consisting of five left lateralised scalenes and four right lateralised scalenes from Urra Moor on the North York Moors. Though we cannot be certain these are complete tools, these Middle Mesolithic examples suggest the shift to an increased number of barbs occurs at this time. Myers (1989) has suggested that this shift made arrows more reliable, in that damage to a single barb was less likely to compromise functionality, which would have been important when increasingly dense woodland made hunting more difficult and time scheduling for repair less predictable.

Probably dating slightly later and to the start of the Late Mesolithic is the potentially hafted composite tool from Seamer K (Figure 1.11). This collection of microliths was seemingly in alignment with a very decayed piece of wood, but no microwear traces were present to confirm its function (David 1998). Though some microliths are snapped, this group consists of 16 backed bladelets, most with retouch on the leading edge. A radiocarbon date of 7540–6670 cal BC was obtained on the wood associated with the microliths. This is the only dated Late Mesolithic composite. To understand more about Late Mesolithic hafting arrangements, we can turn to the evidence provided from a series of isolated groupings of microliths found mainly on the Pennines and North York Moors (see Table 1.3). These have generally been considered to represent lost arrows (Jacobi 1975), though Myers has suggested some may be caches (Myers 1989). Formal deposition of tools associated with special activities is also a possibility. Most of these are undated and cannot be differentiated between Late and Final Mesolithic, apart from three which belong to the Final Mesolithic. Late fifth millennium dates have been obtained for the groupings of backed bladelets recovered from Lydstep and Fir Tree Field, while a group consisting of an asymmetric microtranchet (probably serving as the arrow tip), five scalenes and a fragment from Urra Moor on the

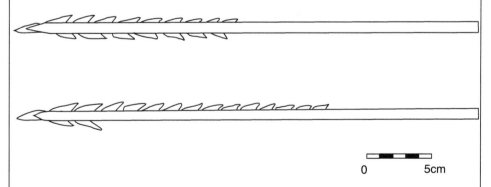

0   5cm

Figure 1.11 Potential hafting arrangements for the Seamer K microlith cluster (redrawn after David 1998)

Table 1.3 Finds of isolated microlith clusters

Site	Scalenes (left lateralised)	Scalenes (right lateralised)	Micro-isosceles	Backed bladelets	Four-sided	Broken/ uncertain	Other	Reference
White Hassocks	43					1		Myers (1987); Jacobi archive
Waun Fignen Felen 1	12							Barton et al. (1993)
East Bilsdale Moor	9					2		Myers (1987); Jacobi archive
Money Howe	9					0		Myers (1987); Jacobi archive
Blubberhouses Moor	9					2		Myers (1987); Jacobi archive
Store Moor	8							Myers (1987); Jacobi archive
Risby Warren V	8?	1						Myers (1987); Jacobi archive
Urra Moor	7					5		Myers (1987); Jacobi archive
Store Moor	7					1		Jacobi archive
Calderbrook Moor	7						1	Myers (1987); Jacobi archive
Waun Fignen Felen 9	>6							Barton et al. (1993)
White Gill	6					1		Myers (1987); Jacobi archive
Blubberhouses Moor	6					0		Myers (1987); Jacobi archive
Urra Moor	5						1	Myers (1987); Jacobi archive
Urra Moor	5	4				1		Myers (1987); Jacobi archive
South side Cupwith Hill	4							Myers (1987); Jacobi archive
Star Carr	4						1	Conneller et al. (2018a)
White Hill Summit G	3					1		Myers (1987); Jacobi archive
Top of Windy Hill	2					1		Myers (1987); Jacobi archive
NW of Windy Hill			4					Myers (1987); Jacobi archive
Manshead Hill			6			1		Myers (1987); Jacobi archive
Windy Hill 5				68				Poole (pers comm.)
Urra Moor				22				Myers (1987); Jacobi archive
Tag Heys				17				Myers (1987); Jacobi archive
Seamer K				16				David (1998)
Holiday Hill				14				Myers (1987); Jacobi archive
Cockayne I				13				Myers (1987); Jacobi archive
Seamer K				13		1		David (1998)
Arnsgill Ridge				11			3	Myers (1987); Jacobi archive

(*Continued*)

Table 1.3 (Continued)

Site	Scalenes (left lateralised)	Scalenes (right lateralised)	Micro-isosceles	Backed bladelets	Four-sided	Broken/uncertain	Other	Reference
Cow Ridge				7				Myers (1987); Jacobi archive
Fir Tree Field Shaft				7				Griffiths (2014)
Sil Howe Bog				6				Myers (1987)
SW of March Hill				3	1			Myers (1987)
Lydstep Haven				2				Jacobi (1980a,)
Urra Moor					25			Myers (1987); Jacobi archive
Readycon Dene	1				21	13		Myers (1987); Jacobi archive
Dry Clough					14			Myers (1987); Jacobi archive
Rosedale					12	4		Myers (1987); Jacobi archive
March Hill					9			Myers (1987)
Culvert Clough					7			Poole (pers comm.)
Near Windy Hill					7	10		Myers (1987); Jacobi archive
Warcock Hill North					7	6		Myers (1987); Jacobi archive
Windy Hill 3					5			Myers (1987); Jacobi archive
March Hill					3			Myers (1987)
Badger Slacks					2			Myers (1987); Jacobi archive
Boxing Hole					2			Myers (1987); Jacobi archive
Oxy Grains Bridge					2	1		Myers (1987)

North York Moors is likely to belong to the fifth millennium on a typological basis. The dating of the remainder of the groups is less certain, though the rather limited evidence available suggests that four-sided microliths may also fall into the Final Mesolithic, as may the Pennine backed bladelet groupings at Windy Hill 5 and Tug Heys.

A feature of these Late/Final Mesolithic groupings is the homogeneity of the microlith forms in each cluster; it is seemingly rare for these composites to have different forms for tips and barbs unless microtranchets were involved. This is interesting considering the co-existence of scalenes and backed bladelets throughout much of the Mesolithic; they seem never to have been incorporated into the same tool. There have been suggestions that these different forms may have had different functions (Finlayson and Mithen 1997; Wickham-Jones and Dalland 1998). These Late and Final Mesolithic groupings are also characterised by use of the same raw material type for all pieces in the group, at times all microliths seemingly produced from the same flint or chert nodule. This appears particularly true for groups of triangles: Of 13 examples where material is noted in the Jacobi archive (British Museum) only two appear to incorporate flint from more than one nodule. Of the latter, one example from Money Howe consists of two identical scalenes in yellow flint without retouch on the leading edge and seven scalenes on grey flint with retouch on the leading edge. These patterns perhaps tell us something about the rhythm of microlith manufacture and the individuals involved. All the microlithic components seem to have been made at the same time by the same person, and they seem rarely to have been repaired. The Money Howe composite is a rare case when the products of more than one individual's knapping were probably incorporated into a single tool. This example may also suggest some level of aesthetics was involved, in that two microliths in a contrasting colour seem to have been paired. The skill involved in producing identical-shaped pairs can also be seen in Figure 1.10. Though these usually seem to have depended on the labour of one individual knapper, composite tools are more than just their lithic components and incorporated the work involved in the management of woodland for hafts, the sourcing of birch bark and the pyrotechnic skills involved in birch tar production. As Finlay (2003) has discussed, the complete tools are likely to be the product of multiple authorship and as such may have served as metaphors for models of social relations amongst Mesolithic groups.

Amongst these isolated microlith clusters are groupings that seem to represent more than lost arrows, forming complex composite tools, markers or caches. The most notable example is the set of microliths found by Francis Buckley at Readycon Dene, near White Hill in the Central Pennines (Figure 1.12). Here 35 four-sided microliths were found in a linear arrangement, spaced at 2.5–3 cm intervals to a length of nearly 2 m (Petch 1924). A similar arrangement at Urra Moor consisted of 25 four-sided microliths spaced at gaps of 5–7 cm over a length of 125–190 cm (Jacobi archive). While these could represent complex tools such as spears or saws (and like the arrows both groupings incorporate microliths of the same colour flint), objects this size are less easily lost than arrows. Another possibility is landscape markers; forming parts of decorated posts.

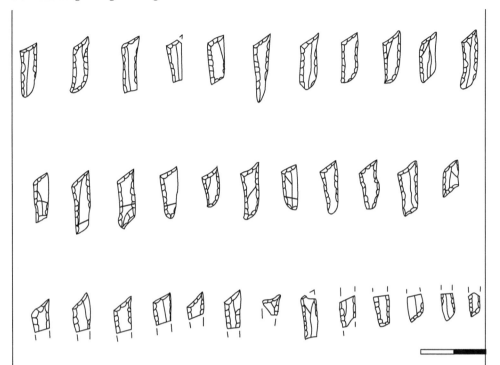

Figure 1.12 Group of rhomboids found by Francis Buckley at Readycon Dene (redrawn from the Jacobi archive)

Other groupings seem to represent caches: 92 microliths from an assemblage of 102 were recovered by Pat Stonehouse at Pule Bents in the Central Pennines (Stonehouse 1997). Most are backed bladelets, but seven scalenes were also recovered. Though most of the backed bladelets were manufactured from a brown flint, a variety of cherts were also used, and the triangles tended to be made from chert. Stonehouse also notes considerable variation in the morphology of the backed bladelets. These factors suggest this microlithic assemblage is the product of different processes to the lost composites. The distribution pattern of a main cluster and tail suggests that the microliths may have been originally deposited together, with some subsequently moved downslope through colluviation. Clusters of microliths that might represent caches have also been recovered at Warcock Hill IV (around 90 in a space of 4 square feet) (Stonehouse 1997) or at Beely Moor in Derbyshire (80 examples) (Hart 1981, 32); in both cases, these were associated with occupation debris.

The isolated groupings of lost arrows are the building blocks of the microlithic assemblages found on Mesolithic sites. What started as composites, usually made from the same materials and incorporating the same forms, were broken, at times repaired or repurposed; individual components or the entire tool were lost or discarded on settlement sites; over time the fragments of these individual styles became the palimpsests of different forms we know today. Small, short-term sites often have very homogenous microlith assemblages; larger, denser sites tend to have high diversity; microlith diversity is thus a measure of time. Small sites with diverse microlith assemblages seem to occur in specific environments: The Goldcliff sites, for example, have diverse but small microlith assemblages (see chapters 5 and 6), no doubt reflecting numerous ephemeral occupations over a long period of time while the intertidal zone was exploited.

And finally, did microlith form, something of an obsession to analysts, matter to Mesolithic people? At times it probably did, particularly perhaps when new forms relating to changes in projectile technology emerged in the Middle Mesolithic and the Final Mesolithic; these new techniques spread widely and seem to have been valued. At other times, forms seem less important, with types, particularly small triangles and crescents, grading into each other and persisting unchanged for long periods of time. Finlay (2003) makes the point that in the composite tool, most of the microlith form is hidden; the same is the case during production due to their small size. If these carried messages about individual or group identity, they could not be easily read. Despite this, particular structures of production, for example, relating to lateralisation were followed for long periods, and minute variations in size and form may have been individual production signatures.

Conclusions: Mesolithic histories

In this introductory chapter, a typochronological scheme has been used to propose a new periodisation of the Mesolithic in Britain. The scheme is based on changing microlith forms, by simple virtue of the fact that stone tools, in contrast to other artefacts, are relatively indestructible, and microliths, more than other tool types, vary across the period. However, as Lucas (2019) points out, different objects show different rhythms of change; if another material were available, different patterns might be discerned, and indeed, some practises, such as burial, seem to persist across boundaries produced by changing microlith forms (Conneller 2006).

Many of the divisions enacted by this scheme can best be seen as a heuristic for dividing and comparing our data, though at times changes in microlith form seem to be accompanied by other 'relevant' changes: Shifts in settlement forms and features, changing patterns of resource exploitation and environmental changes, though the exact temporal relationship of these, and indeed any causality, is difficult, if not impossible, to discern. The remainder of the book will focus on these changes, creating a new temporal narrative, as people moved into Britain, settled into different areas and created new landscape histories of occupation. Britain has seen many people come and go over the millennia. What has united them is their knowledge of and inhabitation of these landscapes. While many places have changed significantly in the last 11,000 years – Doggerland has been inundated, while the lakes of glacial meltwater, the sandy hazel groves and the tufa springs are now gone – perhaps something in the structure of these Mesolithic landscapes remains recognisable to those of us who now inhabit them.

2 Pioneers in the north

Preboreal and Early Boreal settlement, 9500–8200 BC

Pioneers in a new land

Some time during the 94th century BC, the first Mesolithic groups arrived in Britain. They moved into a landscape that was probably empty of people, deserted by the last Upper Palaeolithic groups during an Early Holocene cold snap (the Preboreal Oscillation). These dark-skinned people moved into a landscape very different from today. With relative sea-levels much lower, Britain was an upland peninsula, on the northwest margin of the European landmass. To the east lay Doggerland, a low-lying landscape of rivers, lakes and wetlands; to the south a huge embayment and the estuary of the great Channel River, into which most rivers of Northern Europe drained (Figure 2.2).

In Britain, stands of birch and pine were starting to grow in lowland areas, across a landscape that a few generations earlier had been open, scrubby grassland (Figure 2.3). The herds of reindeer and horse exploited by Upper Palaeolithic groups had moved north, and the landscape became populated by animals more tolerant of woodland: Bears, wolves, lynx, elk, red deer, roe deer, wild cattle (aurochs) and wild pig. Squirrels and pine marten inhabited the canopy.

In the lowland areas that the first pioneers favoured, this was a landscape of water. In the north, large lakes, created by glacial meltwater and fringed with reeds and rushes, attracted flocks of migratory birds. Pike and perch swam in their depths. Large rivers with huge floodplains meandered through the valleys. As the course of these rivers shifted in this unstable landscape, cut-off meanders became ponds and small lakes. Beavers blocked watercourses and flooded whole valleys.

The Channel River/embayment seems to have been a longstanding barrier to human movement from the south (Pettitt and White 2012), and the first Mesolithic groups, as with Palaeolithic pioneers, entered Britain from the east. These were groups who had exploited the coasts, lakes and rivers of Doggerland for generations. Rockman (2003) has described how hunter-gatherer groups colonising new landscapes seek out familiar environments. Mesolithic people followed this pattern, settling on the edge of the familiar lowland lakes and rivers they had known in Doggerland; all of the earliest Mesolithic evidence comes from these settings.

In the south, people moved into Britain along the river systems, camping on gravel islands and terraces rising above the floodplains. The lifeways of the first groups in Southern England will be discussed in the following chapter. In the north, Mesolithic

DOI: 10.4324/9781003228103-2

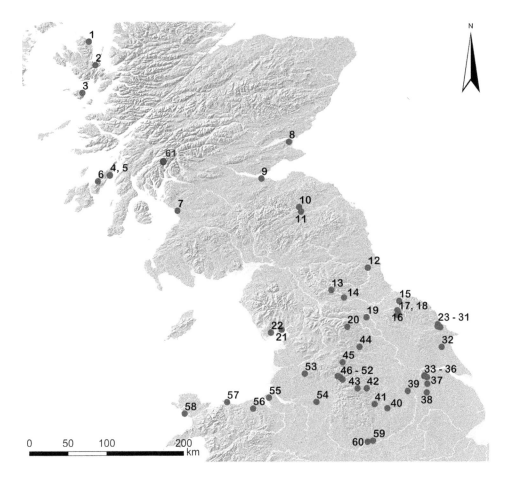

Figure 2.1 Location of the sites discussed in the text (1. An Corran, 2. Clachan Harbour, 3. Kinloch, 4. Lussa Wood 1, 5. Lussa Bay, 6. Glenbatrick Water Hole, 7. Shewalton Moor, 8. Morton A, 9. Cramond, 10. Craigsford Mains, 11. Dryborough Mains, 12. Sheddon's Hill, 13. Staple Crag, 14. Towler Hill, 15. Highcliff Nab, 16. Urra Moor, 17. Pointed Stone 2 and 3, 18. Money Howe I, 19. Little Holtby, 20. South Haw, 21. Kent's Bank Cavern, 22. Bart's Shelter, 23. Seamer L, 24. Seamer K, 25. Seamer C, 26. No Name Hill, 27. Flixton I, 28. Star Carr, 29. VPD, 30. Flixton School, 31. Barry's Island, 32. Brigham Hill, 33. Bagmoor, 34. Roxby Sands, 35. Sheffield's Hill, 36. Risby Warren, 37. Manton Warren I, V and Manton Pond, 38. Willoughton A, 39. Misterton Carr I, 40. Whaley Rockshelter, 41. Unstone I, 42. Deepcar, 43. Mickleden 1–4, 44. Pike Low 1, 45. Nab Water, 46. Lominot 2, 3 and C, 47. Pule Hill Base, 48. Warcock Hill North, 49. Warcock Hill South/Turnpike, 50. Waystone Edge 1, 51. White Hassocks 1 and 2, 52. Windy Hill 3, 53. Rushy Brow, 54. Tatton Mere, 55. Greasby, 56. Ffynnon Beuno, 57. Ogof Pant-y-Wennol, 58. Aberffraw/Trwyn Ddu, 59. Swarkestone Lowes, 60. Potlock)

groups may have migrated along the coast of Doggerland and the now submerged coast of the British Isles, at times moving inland to occupy lakeland landscapes such as existed in the Vale of Pickering and in Holderness. The sites in the Vale of Pickering show strong coastal connections, and the presence of similar, but undated, microlith

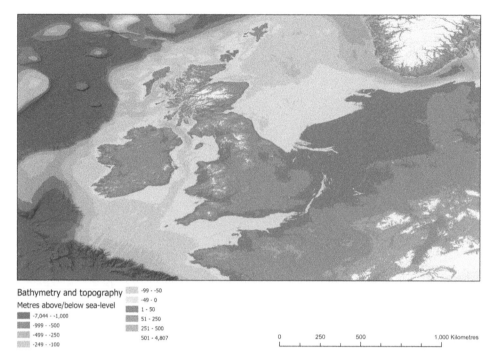

Bathymetry and topography
Metres above/below sea-level

■ -7,044 - -1,000
░ -999 - -500
░ -499 - -250
░ -249 - -100

░ -99 - -50
░ -49 - 0
■ 1 - 50
■ 51 - 250
░ 251 - 500
  501 - 4,807

0   250   500   1,000 Kilometres

Figure 2.2 Palaeogeographic model of Britain at 9000 cal BC (Image Fraser Sturt. Bathymetry provided by EMODnet Bathymetry Consortium (2020): EMODnet Digital Bathymetry (DTM). https://doi.org/10.12770/bb6a87dd-e579-4036-abe1-e649cea9881a, Topography produced using Copernicus data and information funded by the European Union (EU-DEM))

types in the basal layers of the site of An Corran, on Skye (Saville et al. 2012), amongst later occupation at Kinloch on Rùm (Wickham-Jones 1990) and by lithics from a pre-7600 cal BC layer at Clachan Harbour on Raasay (Ballin et al. 2015), suggest rapid coastal colonisation by hunter-gatherer groups.

Most of the Early Holocene coastline of Britain is now submerged, and coastal sites of this date are lost. In some parts of Scotland, the situation is different, and the complex interplay of sea-level rise and isostatic rebound of land once depressed by huge ice sheets means that on the north coast of Skye relative sea-level at around 9000 BC was similar to today. An Corran would have been, as today, a coastal site and may represent a rare trace of groups moving mainly along the coast. In Norway, isostatic uplift has left sites along the Early Mesolithic coastline stranded in the mountains, at up to 300 m above present sea-level. Evidence from these sites indicates that small marine-focused groups moved extremely rapidly along the coast, from Western Sweden to the northernmost part of Norway in 200–300 years (Bjerck 2009). A similar coastal focus amongst the earliest groups in the north may explain the presence of these early microlith types on Skye.

While pioneers may have sought out familiar *sorts* of landscapes, such as lakes and rivers, the evidence indicates that these quickly moved beyond simply representing generic types of location, and became important places in their own right. This can

Figure 2.3 Birch woodland at Hatchmere, Cheshire, analogous to that encountered by Early
Mesolithic groups (copyright Barry Taylor)

most clearly be seen at Star Carr, where the actions undertaken during a small-scale
pioneer occupation made the site into a significant place, encouraging future visits and
guiding subsequent activities at the site. This is just part of a broader pattern where
this once-empty landscape was quickly imbued with significance. Jacobi (1981) long
ago pointed out the tendency for Early Mesolithic sites to cluster in a restricted area,
no doubt the product of people returning repeatedly to areas that had quickly gained
significant histories.

The Early Mesolithic evidence from Briain can be grouped into two: The evidence
from the north, of groups focused on coasts, lakes and surrounding uplands, and that
of the south, focused on river valleys. Parts of the midlands do not seem to have been
occupied in the earliest part of the Mesolithic (Cooper and Jarvis 2017). The various
Early Mesolithic groups that inhabited these two areas had different histories, moved
into Britain from different areas, and pursued different ways of life on the southern
and northeastern margins of the British peninsula, respectively. These two groupings
will be discussed in the following two chapters. In the first of these, we will follow the
pioneers in the north.

9300 BC: Colonisation of the north

Current evidence indicates that people who made Star Carr-type assemblages (see
chapter 1) were probably the earliest Mesolithic groups to arrive in Britain, with the
initial colonisation dating to between 9400 and 9300 cal BC (Conneller et al. 2016a).

The earliest Mesolithic sites in Northern England come from the Vale of Pickering (see below), though it is probable that this is simply a function of the extensive fieldwork that has been undertaken in this area. The evidence from the Vale of Pickering suggests that people were moving into a landscape where woodland was developing in lowland areas. Initially, this probably consisted of small stands of birch trees in a landscape that was still relatively open, though birch woodland developed in the following centuries (Blockley et al. 2018). Upland areas of Britain and the far north would have remained open grasslands at this time. There is some slight evidence to suggest that elk may have been an important prey species for the earliest colonisers, as it appears to have been in Southern Scandianvia (Jessen et al. 2015); however, there appears to have been a diverse range of animals populating the open woodlands of the late tenth millennium BC, with red deer, elk, aurochs and wild pig all found in contexts predating 9000 BC (Conneller and Higham 2015; Milner et al. 2018).

Following the rapid warming at c.9700 cal BC that marks the end of the Pleistocene, the Early Holocene has traditionally been considered as characterised by a warm, generally stable climate, albeit one with a more continental climate while Britain was attached to the European landmass. However, evidence from Greenland Ice Cores indicates centennial-scale climatic oscillations throughout the Holocene (Mayewski et al. 2004), including a number of more pronounced downturns. While the most serious of these, the 8.2 event, is discussed in chapter 5, the first millennium of the Holocene saw two notable short-lived climatic downturns. The first of these, the Preboreal Oscillation at around 9400 cal BC, probably predated the appearance of Mesolithic groups in Britain. A second event, at around 9100 cal BC, saw temperatures drop by an average of 4 degrees for around 100 years at a time when Mesolithic people were present. This event does not though seem to have had a noticeable impact on human settlement, at least in lowland Northern England (Blockley et al. 2018).

The distribution of Star Carr-type sites can be seen in Figure 2.4. They are relatively few in number (at least in comparison with later assemblage types), with the exception of a cluster in the Vale of Pickering. The predominantly easterly distribution indicates groups moving into Britain from Doggerland, either along major river systems or, more probably, along the now drowned coast, as discussed above. Sites in the Vale of Pickering, for example, show a strong connection to the coast, with most of the flint used on sites sourced as beach pebbles, while isotopic analysis of dog remains from Seamer L show a marine signature, indicating this animal spent some of its life on the coast.

Star Carr-type microliths are similar to those used by Ahrensburgian hunters in Northern Germany during the younger Dryas, again reinforcing the suggestion of an eastern origin for these groups, while the similarity between Star Carr-type assemblages and Early Mesolithic assemblages from Southern Scandinavia and Northern Germany has long been noted (e.g. Clark 1932). Clark borrowed the Southern Scandinavian term 'Maglemosian' to describe British Early Mesolithic groups. Shared cultural practises between groups in these areas did not just encompass shared forms of archery equipment, but may have encompassed more fundamental belief systems: Red deer antler frontlets (Figure 2.5), which have been argued below to embody ideas about shamanic transformation (Little et al. 2016) and the spiritual significance of certain animals (Conneller 2004), are so far found at only Star Carr and at three sites in Germany (Wild 2019).

Figure 2.4 Distribution of Star Carr-type sites. (1. An Corran, 2. Kinloch, 3. Sheddon's Hill, 4. Staple Crag, 5. Highcliff Nabb, 6. Morton A, 7. Pointed Stone 2 and 3, 8. South Haw, 9. Seamer L, 10. Seamer K, 11. Seamer C, 12. No Name Hill, 13. Flixton I, 14. Star Carr, 15. VPD, 16. Flixton School, 17. Barry's Island, 18. Manton Warren I, V and Manton Pond, 19. Warcock Hill South/Turnpike, 20. Rushy Brow, 21. Broxbourne 104, 22. Thatcham III (patinated series), 23. Waun Fignen Felen 6, 24. Waun Fignen Felen 8, 25. Daylight Rock, 26. Palmerston Farm, 27. The Nab Head I)

The vast majority of Star Carr-type sites are in Northern England, clustered in particular in the Vale of Pickering, North Yorkshire. Further Star Carr-type sites are also found in upland areas of Northern England: The North York Moors, the Lincolnshire Edge and the Pennines. Further north, in Scotland, are a series of undated, often mixed, assemblages that bear considerable similarities to those of Star Carr type. Perhaps most similar to Star Car is the assemblage from Donich Park. Argyll (Ballin and Ellis 2019) and the material recovered from below the midden at An Corran, Skye (Saville et al. 2012), with large obliquely blunted points and isosceles triangles. Morton A (Coles 1971) and Lussa Bay (Mercer 1969) also have large numbers of Star Carr-type microliths, though mixed with

Figure 2.5 Red deer antler frontlets from Star Carr (copyright Neil Gevaux)

some later material. Other sites with possible Star Carr-type microliths include Lussa Wood 1 (Mercer 1978), Craigsford Mains, Dryburgh Mains, Woodend Loch, Shewalton Moor (Clark 1932; Lacaille 1954; Warren 2001), Kinloch (Wickham-Jones 1990), the Chest of Dee (Wickham-Jones et al. 2020) and Nethermills (Wickham-Jones et al. 2016), though the dominance of isosceles triangles on some of these sites, such as Glenbatrick Waterhole (Mercer 1974), is not typical. None of these have yielded satisfactory radiocarbon dates.

In Southern England, Star Carr-type sites are rare. Only two excavated sites are present, at Broxbourne 104, in the Lea Valley, Hertfordshire and at Thatcham III (patinated series) in the Kennet Valley, Berkshire (see chapter 3). Both these rivers are tributaries of the Thames, which is likely to have served as a routeway into Southern Britain. Given the lack of visibility of sites along the Thames itself (see chapter 3), it is likely that these two sites are a remnant of a more extensive network of sites along the river. However, in comparison to Deepcar assemblages, which have a similar distribution along the Thames tributaries, Star Carr sites are extremely rare, suggesting the nature of settlement in this region during the earliest Mesolithic was relatively small scale. They may represent a failed colonisation of the south, or seasonal visits by groups based in Doggerland.

Star Carr-type sites do not seem to be present in North Wales, but have been identified in the south, in particular at Palmerston Farm and The Nab Head in Pembrokeshire and Daylight Rock on Caldey (David 2007). The latter two have yielded relatively late dates, in comparison with sites in England, belonging to the last centuries of the ninth millennium BC. These assemblages also subtly differ to those from Star Carr-type sites in England, in their elevated numbers of large scalene triangles (forming 43% of complete early types from David's excavations at Nab Head I), and the rarity of isosceles triangles and trapezes (see chapter 1). They may represent groups of similar cultural heritage to those in the east (both also share a penchant for shale beads), but one which has changed over the centuries. They will be discussed in chapter 3.

Sar Carr and the Vale of Pickering

Star Carr has come to dominate discussions of the British Early Mesolithic. There are several reasons for this, not all of them related to the quality of the site's archaeology. The status of the excavator, Grahame Clark (Box 1.2), his innovative interpretation and speedy publication of the site all played a part. But the quality of preservation was also important, representing a step change in knowledge of the material repertoire of the British Mesolithic, both in quantity and range: 191 barbed antler points were recovered in Clark's excavation, whereas only a handful of examples had previously been recovered; antler frontlets, antler mattocks, bone pins and scrapers, types previously unknown in Britain, were also found. For a long time, Star Carr was used as an exemplar of life in the Early Mesolithic, what we might expect of a typical Mesolithic site with organic preservation. We now know the site is unusual, not only in its size and duration, but also in the nature of some of the activities undertaken there.

Star Carr was discovered by John Moore, a local archaeologist, who located a series of Mesolithic sites in the Vale of Pickering, which he surmised clustered along the shores of a Late Glacial/Early Holocene palaeolake that he named Lake Flixton (Moore 1950). Moore recovered lithic material and animal bones from the section of a drainage ditch and sent a sample of this material to Grahame Clark (see Box 1.2) at Cambridge University. Star Carr was excavated by Clark and a team of Cambridge students over three summer seasons between 1949 and 1951 (Clark 1954).

A vast array of Mesolithic remains were recovered, from flint and animal bone, to stone and amber beads, to organic artefacts such as barbed antler points and elk antler mattocks. Most intriguing were 21 antler masks (Figure 2.5), made from modified red deer skulls that had been trimmed, smoothed and perforated. Drawing on ethnographic analogy, Clark suggested these functioned as either hunting aids designed to help hunters stalk deer at close range, or as costumes in ritual dances. Most of the artefacts were found, broadly, in association with preserved wood, including a complete birch tree, which Clark interpreted as a living area on the edge of the lake. Based on this structure and the range of artefacts recovered, Clark interpreted Star Carr as a base camp, the size of the site indicating it would be occupied by only four or five families. The presence of men was determined by hunting equipment; women by the presence of scrapers (based on analogy with Inuit groups); children by the presence of women. The site was suggested to be a winter settlement through the presence of shed and unshed red deer antler (red deer typically being shed in April) and of shed elk antler (elk shedding antler in January), though this was later challenged. Clark's longstanding collaboration with Godwin (see Box 1.2) continued at Star Carr, resulting in a detailed picture of the environment. The platform on which settlement took place was built into the reed-swamp that fringed the lake. Behind this were birchwoods, with pine becoming established. On boggy ground willows stood, while waterlilies grew in the lake waters (Box 2.1).

Clark retired in 1974, and it is perhaps not a co-incidence that it was only then that his interpretations of Star Carr were challenged. Both Jacobi (1978a,) and Caulfield (1978) pointed out the presence of unshed roe deer antler, an indicator of summer seasonality. They also noted that since red deer antler significantly outnumbered post-cranial remains and antler was used as a raw material, it was likely that antler was collected throughout the year and cached, and thus should not be used as a seasonal indicator. Grigson (1981) also pointed out that some of the birds found at the site would only have been present in the summer. To address these issues, Legge and

---

Box 2.1   Plant resources in the Preboreal

Traditional narratives of the Mesolithic have been critiqued for focusing too heavily on the hunting of large game animals (Finally 2000). While this is partly due to author bias, plant remains do not readily preserve, making an under-standing of the extent of their contribution uncertain. Only hazelnuts, whose shells are extremely durable when burnt, appear in large quantities on Mesolithic sites (see chapter 4). The preboreal predates the widespread appearance of hazel in the pollen record. In the Vale of Pickering, the initial appearance of hazel in the pollen record is at around 8500 BC, with the main hazel rise dated to c.8200 BC (Bayliss et al. 2018), well after the main occupation of the site.

Despite a lack of direct evidence for their exploitation, Clark gave serious consideration to the role of plant foods at Star Carr. He pointed out that there was macrofossil evidence for the presence of many plants at the site that could be eaten. These include water-lily seeds and rhizomes and the rhizomes of reeds and bogbean. He suggested that the elk antler mattocks would be useful tools for recovering rhizomes. The diggings sticks recovered during the recent excavations would also be useful in this regard. The leaves of nettle, fat-hen (*Chenopodium album*), hemp-nettle (*Galeopsis tetrahit*), sorel (*Rumex sp.*) and chickweed (*Stellaria media*) could all be gathered. Many of these are salad leaves that can be eaten raw, though nettles and fat-hen are better cooked, the latter being similar to spinach. Many of the plants present also have medicinal uses: Hemp-nettle is used as a decongestant, knotweed can sooth stomach problems, while chickweed has historically been used to treat both skin conditions and pulmonary disease.

The usefulness of plants goes beyond foods. Bast (the inner bark of trees) and reeds can be collected, processed and used to make cord and weave baskets, mats and nets. No direct evidence of such objects has been found at Star Carr, but textiles have been recovered from Late Mesolithic submerged sites in Denmark. These reveal the use of willow bast, grasses and possibly aspen bast to make knotted and looped textiles (Harris 2014; Figure 2.6). There is, however, indirect evidence for these sorts of activities: Use-wear results on flints from Star Carr indicate both the cutting and scraping of reeds. While cut reeds could be used for thatch, scraping of reeds is particularly indicative of craft activities (Little and van Gijn 2017; Conneller et al. 2018a,b), and we can imagine the production of baskets, mats and even clothing (Harris 2019) with elaborate patterns and decoration at the site.

Figure 2.6 Experimental reproduction of Mesolithic textiles. Left: Couched button-hole stitch, Right: Couched button-hole stitch with extra turn (copyright Susanna Harris)

Rowley-Conwy (1988) re-examined the original faunal assemblage, and analysed red and roe deer tooth eruption and wear patterns. This evidence indicated summer occupation, predominantly in May and June, with only a juvenile elk, killed in October, demonstrating occupation beyond late spring/summer. Juvenile reeds and burnt aspen catkins show vegetation was burnt by Mesolithic groups between March and June (Mellars and Dark 1998). More recently, Carter (1997, 1998) used radiography of tooth development in juvenile red and roe deer jaws to argue for occupation earlier in the year, with at least one red deer being killed in the winter. While there has been a tendency for those interpreting the seasonality data from the site to argue for a single season of occupation, in fact the evidence suggests multiple seasons of occupation (Table 2.1) (see also Milner 2006 for a discussion of the problems associated with seasonality indicators). This is unsurprising given the site was (re)occupied over a period of around 800 years (see below).

The second focus of reinterpretation has been site function. Clark based his interpretation of Star Carr as a base camp on the construction of the brushwood platform and the rich inventory of material culture. However, the faunal material recovered from the site does not obviously support this interpretation, as the less meaty elements that might be expected of a processing camp rather than a residential base camp are most common. From the 1970s onwards, interpretations can be divided into those that have prioritised the material culture to interpret Star Carr as a base camp and those that have given precedence to the faunal remains to suggest that Star Carr functioned as a more specialist site, a hunting camp (e.g. Legge and Rowley-Conwy 1988) or even a kill site (e.g. Andresen et al. 1981). The explanation for this discrepancy seems to

Table 2.1 Seasonality evidence from Star Carr, based on Legge and Rowley-Conwy (1988), Figure 2.7 with additional information from Carter (1997, 1998) and Mellars and Dark (1998)

Seasonality indicator	J	F	M	A	M	J	J	A	S	O	N	D
Unshed roe deer antler				background	background	background	background	background	background	background	background	background
Tooth eruption (roe deer)					background	background	background	background	background			
Tooth eruption (red deer)				background	background	background	background	background	background			
Juvenile reeds			background	background								
Charred aspen catkins			background	background	background							
Elk jaw	background	background										
Elk skull, antlers shed									background	background	background	background
Tooth development (red deer)	background	background	background							background	background	background
Tooth development (roe deer)		background	background	background	background							

derive from Clark's recovery and curation strategy: The faunal assemblage was selectively collected during the original excavation, with only the more complete and
identifiable elements retained (Milner et al. 2018). The assemblage thus is subject to
the problems of such collections (see Marean and Kim 1998), where elements that
have been smashed for marrow (often also the prime meaty limb bones) are discarded.
Evidence derived from the original faunal assemblage should thus be treated with
caution.

Suggestions that Star Carr was used for a single function have also become increasingly difficult to maintain, given the evidence for the long duration of occupation.
The complexity of the site was recognised even in early reinterpretations: So while a
single function has been suggested by Clark (1954, 1972), Andresen et al. (1981) and
by Legge and Rowley-Conwy (1988), Pitts (1979) has argued that Star Carr functioned
as a specialised hide working site during the summer months, but was a residential site
in the winter, while both Jacobi (1978a,) and Mellars and Dark (1998) urge caution in
positing a single interpretation for a site that was occupied over a long period of time.
It is now 70 years since it was first excavated; yet, Star Carr continues to be re-
interpreted. Most interpretations have continued to focus on the key issues that Clark
originally established, seasonality and site function. The numerous re-interpretations
of the site indicate the powerful hold it retains over understandings of the period.

Despite the significance of Clark's excavations, no further fieldwork took place
within the Vale of Pickering until 1976, when the Seamer area, only 1 km from Star
Carr, was designated a site for future waste disposal. This precipitated survey and
excavations of the Seamer and surrounding area over a thirty year period (see below).
As part of this work, palaeoenvironmental sampling trenches were excavated at Star
Carr in 1985 in an area that was considered to be some distance from Clark's estimates
of the site boundaries (Cloutman 1988). This trench was extended, and a platform of
hewn aspen timber was uncovered, as well as animal bone and organic and flint artefacts. Clark's work, and subsequent interpretations, had been predicated on the
assumption that the entirety of the site had been excavated. The realisation that Clark
had only uncovered a small portion of the site raised further question marks over past
interpretations.

In 2004, a new campaign of fieldwork was initiated at Star Carr to understand the
full extent of the site and its diversity (Conneller et al. 2012; Milner et al. 2018),
stimulated by the results of fieldwork around Lake Flixton undertaken by Tim
Schadla-Hall. This indicated that, rather than being a typical base camp or hunting
camp, Star Carr was actually unique within its local landscape. None of the other sites
discovered round Lake Flixton had similar rich organic material culture to Star Carr
(Conneller and Schadla-Hall 2003): No further antler frontlets had been found, and
only a handful of barbed points.

The new fieldwork at Star Carr initially consisted of fieldwalking and test pitting,
but from 2007, large open areas of the site were excavated. This encompassed both the
wetland areas sampled by Clark and dryland areas, which had not previously been
investigated. In all, an area of c.55 by 30 m was excavated, stretching eastward from
Clark's trenches and encompassing and extending eastwards beyond the small 1980s
trench (Figure 2.7). This work was accompanied by a programme of radiocarbon
dating and Bayesian modelling, which built on previous work by Dark (2000) to
produce a refined understanding of the history of occupation at the site. This modelling indicates Star Carr was occupied for at least 800 years and offers a remarkable

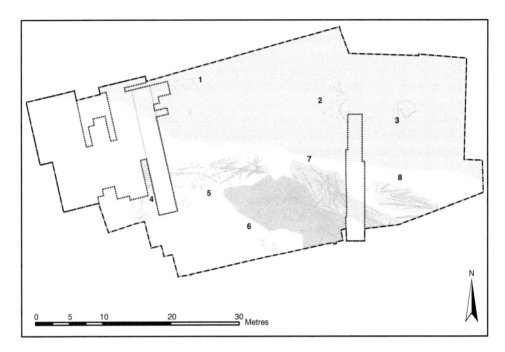

Figure 2.7 Plan of excavations at Star Carr (copyright Star Carr Project)

insight into the development of the site, from a small clearing visited by the first pioneers, to a substantial settlement with a long history. This is currently the only site in Britain where a nuanced historical narrative of occupation can be produced.

Star Carr: A history

At around 9300 BC, the first Mesolithic groups reached Lake Flixton and camped at Star Carr. They were inhabiting a landscape that was still fairly open grassland, though occasional stands of birch were present in the vicinity of the site. Gnawed wood indicates that beavers were active in the area before people arrived. They were just one species of a faunal community that contained red deer, elk, aurochs, roe deer and pine marten. People camped in an area that was free of trees in the central part of the site, and they cut and worked wood probably from a clump of birch trees in the western part of the site. A small post-built structure (the central structure) may belong to this earliest period of occupation; certainly, radiocarbon dates indicate people were active in this area (Figure 2.7, no. 2).

The majority of the evidence for this early use of the site comes from the wetland, immediately to the south of the central structure, where between 9300 and 9000 BC people deposited a range of wooden debris, stone tools and animal remains in the shallow waters of the lake (Figure 2.7, no. 6). Much of the animal material appears to result from selective and patterned deposition. Animal heads are common. The earliest of these heads to be deposited was an elk; patterned deposition of elk remains is a feature of the earliest archaeology of Southern Scandinavia (Jessen et al. 2015, see Box 2.3). This act at Star Carr may be an echo of a common cultural practise.

However, deposition quickly started to focus on red deer, as local traditions became important: The remainder of the skulls in the lake are those of red deer, both an unmodified female cranium and two antler frontlets. Also deposited in this area was the part-articulated remains of a red deer. This deer is represented by four near-complete limbs (two of which are articulated, while the other two lay in anatomical position) and parts of the torso and crania. This animal is certainly not a whole animal that died in this area, either through natural causes or having escaped, fatally wounded, from hunters, as it has been heavily processed. Nor is it a single animal, as it has two left hind legs, and three possible heads (of which two are antler frontlets), the most proximate of which is a female red deer skull. It appears a composite red deer has been reassembled through one or more acts of deposition.

Memory of these events, perhaps subsequently mythologised, may have structured more intensive occupation of the site from 9000 BC. A place that had been an important but relatively small scale and ephemeral focus of action was formalised through modification of the landscape and large-scale construction practises. By this time, birch woodland was well established, so the area of the site may have needed to be cleared of trees, or settlement would take place between them. As the lake began to shallow and reedswamp expanded, burning of the wetland vegetation may have been important for maintaining access to open water in the vicinity of the traditional area for deposition. This phase of intermittent burning in the central area probably continued for two to three generations, and it is probable that one of these episodes cleared the area for the erection of the first large-scale piece of communal architecture at the site, the central timber platform (Figure 2.7, no. 7).

The central timber platform is at least 17 m long (the end was never reached during excavation due to the presence of an active field drain) and is made from hewn aspen timbers. It has three layers, which may suggest episodes of repair, but is more likely to represent a single phase of construction. The platform respects and is on the same alignment as the scatter of wooden debris that was the focus of previous acts of deposition; yet, the timber platform was constructed at least a generation, and more likely two to three generations, after the last act of deposition occurred in this area. The clearance of this area through burning may have memorialised earlier acts of deposition, keeping them alive in people's memory, before access to this area was marked by the timber platform.

The central timber platform was the largest of three such structures established successively on the lake edge between c.8985 and 8755 BC (Figure 2.7, nos. 5, 7, 8). All seem to have fairly short histories of use and were, with a few notable exceptions, kept clear of artefacts and debris. The central platform is the most substantial and the only one that is not parallel to the shore. It also is associated with more artefacts than the others, though most of these appear to have been deposited just off its lakeward edge. The one exception is a small cluster of 57 flint artefacts, most of which had been used in animal processing and were probably deposited in a small bag. This may represent a lost or discarded personal toolkit or, given the previous focus on deposition of animal remains, a toolkit that needed formal deposition as a result of its use in a significant act of animal processing. The western timber platform probably also saw some more formal acts of deposition, in this case associated with its construction: A wild boar mandible and two large flint nodules were found within the structure (Figure 2.8). The function of the platforms remains enigmatic; they may have been routes of access to the lake waters either for launching boats or continued acts of deposition.

(a)   (b)

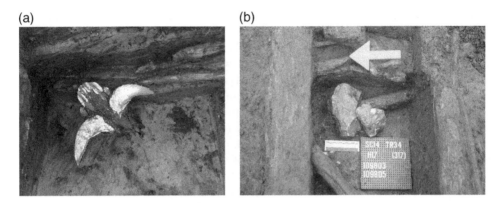

Figure 2.8 Deposition on the western platform. Left: Wild boar mandible, Right: Cache of flint
        nodules (Images: Star Carr project)

As peat began to grow over the central platform in the generations following its
construction, the area remained a continued focus but saw a more varied use: Small-
scale tasks of manufacture and tool use were undertaken, predominant amongst which
was the reworking and resharpening of several small flint axes. This may be related to
construction in the vicinity, with a post-built structure (the eastern structure) erected
on the dryland (Figure 2.7, no. 3) and a new platform (the eastern platform) constructed immediately to the east (Figure 2.7, no. 8). A renewed period of burning at
this time may also be associated with initial clearance of the area for the construction
of this eastern platform. It did not see prolonged use and was covered by a fallen tree a
few decades after it was built.

The dryland was a focus of significant activity at this time, with the building of the
eastern structure (Figure 2.7, no. 3) and activity in the area of the western structure/
midden (Figure 2.7, no. 1). The eastern structure consists of a shallow pit c.2.5 m
in diameter, surrounded by a ring of posts. The pit was filled with organic material,
possibly reeds, bark or branches. The presence of lithics showing working of siliceous
plants suggests the floor may have been covered with matting. Possible evidence
for repair of the structure and the density of finds within it suggest a period of
(re)occupation that was reasonably long in duration. The structure was the focus of
a range of different activities. Food, both large mammals (mainly red deer, but some
aurochs and pig) and fish (both pike and perch), was prepared and cooked, with
the bones of the mammals often split for marrow. An aurochs butchery area to the
northwest may have supplied meat to the structure. The presence of antler and a
fragment of pine marten bone suggest craft activities also took place. Though flint
knapping was not a major activity, tools, particularly burins, were manufactured for
use elsewhere on the site, and personal toolkits, including axes, were repaired and
stored. The structure was cleared out regularly and waste material dumped either
in a midden immediately behind the structure or in an area to the northwest.

Around the same time, possibly slightly later, in the western dryland part of the site,
a large midden was accumulating in an area that may have previously been the site of a
small structure. This structure may have burnt down, as much of the flint (35%) recovered from this area is heavily burnt. Alternatively, hearth debris may have been

Figure 2.9 Deposition in the western wetlands (Image: Star Carr project)

preferentially collected and deposited here. The midden also contains unburnt flint debitage and tools, often highly worn. Fragmentary animal bones are also represented, with a wide range of species present. On the eastern edge of the midden is a cluster of faunal remains, including a pair of calcinated distal phalanges of wildcat. The western midden is some distance from the other structures located in the recent excavations, and it may be that this midden incorporates material cleared from other structures destroyed by the digging of the Hertford Cut (canalised Hertford River) to the north.

Not long after the construction of the eastern platform, wetland activity shifted to the western wetland area (Figure 2.7, no. 4), where an area of shallow water (incorporating the southeastern part of Clark's trenches and an area excavated during 2015) was the focus for intensive deposition over a relatively short time (Figure 2.9). This cannot be described as an off-shore rubbish area, of the type found on many Southern Scandinavian sites, as the material found here has been carefully selected. Flint knapping waste, the main component of the debris found on the dryland, and in the dryland middens, is not present; instead, the lithic material recovered consists mainly of blades and large flakes with macroscopic wear. Undamaged as well as broken barbed points were recovered; yet, both the broken ones and those potentially reusable lacked hafts, having been dehafted before deposition. Antler and woodworking debris was present as well as finished bone, antler and wooden tools, an amber bead and a decorated pendant. Several antler frontlets were recovered (Figure 2.10). These include both finished (and potentially used) examples as well as unfinished frontlets where the face and jaw of the animal had been removed, but the cranial base was still intact.

Large quantities of animal bones were also recovered from this area of deposition. The majority of the remains come from red deer, but roe deer, aurochs, elk and, to a lesser extent, pig are also represented, as are rarer animals: Beaver, pine marten, wild cat, wolf, pike and various waterbirds. A few partially articulated elements are present, mainly bones from the foot, but overall these remains have been heavily processed, with 57% showing evidence for percussion breaks, spiral fractures and cut-marks. There are some significant differences between faunal material recovered from this area during the recent excavations and the selectively collected Clark assemblage. Clark preferentially retained material that was identifiable to species. This has resulted

Figure 2.10 Frontlet from the deposition area in the western wetlands (Image: Star Carr project)

in an under-representation of bones that were heavily fragmented for marrow extraction and body parts, such as ribs, that are not readily identifiable to a particular species. The Clark assemblage lacks ribs, and meaty limb bones are under-represented, leading Legge and Rowley-Conwy (1988) to suggest Star Carr was a hunting camp rather than a base camp. By contrast, ribs were in fact by far the most common element (n = 118) recovered from this area in the 2015 excavations. Meatier humeri outnumber radii and ulnae. Femora are less common than tibia, but there are a large number of unidentified long bones, which have been smashed for marrow, a practise which is likely to have preferentially targeted femora. In all, rather than a faunal assemblage based on the processing of marginal elements, the recently excavated material indicates all elements are represented. The faunal remains represent a range of animal-focused activities: Food consumption waste (ribs, limbs, marrow processing), butchery waste (vertebrae and pelves) and craft waste (both bone and antler).

The material in this wetland deposition area is varied, but specific. Much of it is food waste, and if generated in a short time, as the radiocarbon dates suggest, may indicate feasting, though it includes animals killed in both the summer and winter months. But it also consists of material culture, both 'special' items such as antler frontlets and more mundane objects such as flint blades. Much of this material was used and has a history: The frontlets, for example, come from animals killed in the winter months; barbed points are broken and have been dehafted. It may represent the debris associated with certain key events and acts that needed to be disposed of in a particular way. Alternatively, it may represent material carefully selected from dryland middens (it is not representative of the material on the middens as this is mostly flint debitage), perhaps representing the curation of key elements of an occupation of the site.

The last of the three platforms, the western platform (Figure 2.7, no. 4), was constructed in the 88th century BC, immediately adjacent to this area of deposition. It was almost certainly constructed after deposition had started, but it is possible that deposition continued after its construction. It may have been built to facilitate continued deposition, especially as the character of the lake-edge environment continued to change. Alternatively, it may have been associated with its cessation, marking the place of an important assemblage of spiritually charged artefacts and significant acts for future generations, in the same way that the central platform marked the location of the earliest area of initial deposition.

Box 2.2   Dogs and people in the Early Mesolithic

Before widespread domestication, dogs were the only animals to live with human groups. Dogs were domesticated sometime in the Upper Palaeolithic, with estimates ranging from 100,000 to 15,000 years ago, depending on the criteria used for identification of archaeological specimens or the particular strand of genetic evidence employed (Larson et al. 2014). Recent accounts of domestication suggest that this was a process initiated as much by wolves as by people (Morey 2010). Wolves would scavenge left-over meat from human kill sites, eventually aiding people in bringing down prey. From this, certain individuals began to live with human groups, and over generations developed a more dog-like appearance, smaller in size and with a shorter muzzle. Dogs are ambiguous creatures, living with humans, but not human. This ambiguity is evidenced in the Swedish Late Mesolithic cemeteries of Skateholm I and II. One dog was buried in a rich grave with an antler hammer and a flint blade across its pelvis, analogous to human graves. Another grave at the site featured the burial of a human female, with a decapitated dog placed at the woman's feet (Larsson 1990). At Hardinxveld in the Netherlands, both human and dog remains are found both in graves and disarticulated in the wetlands (Louwe Kooijmans 2003). Grøn (2003, 4) notes that amongst the Siberian Evenk, clever hunting dogs (and bears) are seen as having the same number of souls as humans and thus deserving of similar burial rites. These distinctions may underlie the differential treatment of dog remains at Mesolithic sites. This suggests that some dogs could become persons, perhaps as Grøn suggests, through their skilful participation in group hunting events.

The remains of several dogs dating to the Early Mesolithic period have been found at Star Carr and more broadly in the Vale of Pickering at Seamer N, Barry's Island and Flixton School Field (Clutton-Brock and Noe-Nygaard 1990; Lane et al. in press). The most complete of these was a young (six- to seven-month-old) dog found in an area that would have been shallow lake waters (Knight et al. 2018). The dog remains were found partially articulated and spread over an area of around 1.5 m, suggesting it had been deposited whole and drifted apart as it started to decay in the shallow waters (Figure 2.11). While this may represent a natural death in the wetland, the possibility remains that this was an animal specially selected for deposition, possibly even, given its young age, deliberately killed. Furthermore, two dog skulls were recovered during Clark's excavations, though post-cranial remains were rare (three femora and a tibia) (Schulting and Richards 2009). Skulls of red deer and elk seem to have been specially selected for deposition at the site, and it may be that dogs, too, were a species that demanded special treatment. There are hints at this elsewhere in the Vale. At Seamer L, six articulated cervical vertebrae of dog were recovered, perhaps also suggesting a whole animal had originally been deposited (Clutton-Brock and Noe-Nygaard 1990).

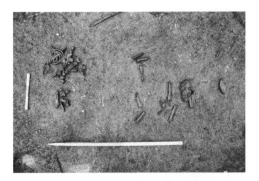

Figure 2.11 The remains of a young dog found in the wetlands at Star Carr (Copyright: Star Carr project)

The close proximity of dogs and humans in Mesolithic societies means that dogs have been used as a proxy for humans in understanding in particular dietary issues. In the absence of human remains from the Vale of Pickering, the isotope signatures of several of the dogs have been analysed. These have uncovered a strong terrestrial signature, with values ranging from -21.1 to -19.0 $\delta^{13}C$ (see Table 2.2). There is, however, one exception – the dog from Seamer N, which seems to have depleted dC13 values at -16.5 to -15.8. While the significance of this has been debated (Dark 2003; Schulting and Richards 2009), one possibility is that at least at some point in the history of the Early Mesolithic occupation of the Vale of Pickering, people spent part of their time on the coast. However, another possibility is that dogs were exchanged between different groups, as has been suggested for the Baltic region (Eriksson and Zagorska 2003).

From the 87th century, occupation of Star Carr appears to have become more sporadic, as fen carr colonised the wetland edge, and the area of open water became smaller. There is evidence for activity on the wetland edge in the eastern part of the site, which is probably associated with nearby knapping activity on the dryland. A burning event is also recorded in the central wetland edge area. In the 86th century, activity took place in the vicinity of the long since abandoned central structure, where a large flint nodule was knapped to produce a range of tools. In these two centuries, sporadic activities can also be noted on the wetland edge to the east of the site, with a dog skull dating to this period (Box 2.2). Craft activities in this area seem to have continued: Resin production, antler working and bead manufacture all took place around a series of small, ephemeral hearths. There is no further evidence for occupation of Star Carr after the 85th century BC.

Several Mesolithic sites and locales have been described as persistent places (Barton et al. 1995). The original use of this term posits that the presence of long-lived structural features, such as good views, attracted intermittent occupation over millennia, without necessarily indicating the place occupied a long-term role in a group's social memory. Star Carr provides some evidence for the nature of persistence.

Table 2.2 Isotope value of dogs from the Vale of Pickering

Site	Cat no	Age	Element	$\delta^{13}C$	$\delta^{15}N$	C:N	Collagen	Source
Star Carr	58.11.15.3	Sub-adult	Cranium	-21.1	9.0	3.5	6%	Schulting and Richards (2009)
Star Carr	58.11.7.168	Adult	R. Femur	-19.8	10.4	3.2	11.1%	Schulting and Richards (2009)
Star Carr	58.11.15.4	Adult	L. Femur	-19.0	11.2	3.5	3.5%	Schulting and Richards (2002)
Star Carr	58.11.15.5	Adult	Tibia	-19.5	11.1	3.4	4.8%	Schulting and Richards (2009)
Star Carr	108261	6–7 months	Rib	-20.4	10.5	3.4	22.5%	Knight et al. (2018)
Seamer N	81.5125	<9 months	Axis	-16.5	12.3	3.4	3.3%	Schulting and Richards (2002)
Seamer N		<9 months		-15.8				Clutton-Brock and Noe-Nygaard (1990)

The site provides many desirable affordances: Proximity to the lake and its resources, a location near to the lake outflow, facilitating movement westwards. However, there is more to Star Carr than this. People were drawn back to the site because of the events that took place there, and while there was change over time in the rhythm and intensity of occupation, memory of past actions structured many later activities at the site. The first of the timber platforms respects the location of the earliest focus of deposition at the site. This long-term route to the lake waters was maintained by burning between the final deposition in this area and the building of a timber platform adjacent to it. The central platform continued to be a focus of activity long after it had been covered by peat. There are also striking similarities between the nature of objects deposited in the lake waters during the earliest occupation of the site, and the rather later western deposition area: Animal heads, frontlets and flint tools, particularly large utilised blades. It may be that the very substance of the earliest activities at the site continued to structure aspects of its use several centuries later.

Star Carr in context

Star Carr is not the only Early Mesolithic site around Lake Flixton. It is part of a broader complex of sites around the shore of palaeolake Flixton and on islands in the middle of the lake (Figure 2.12). Several of these sites were found by John Moore, the

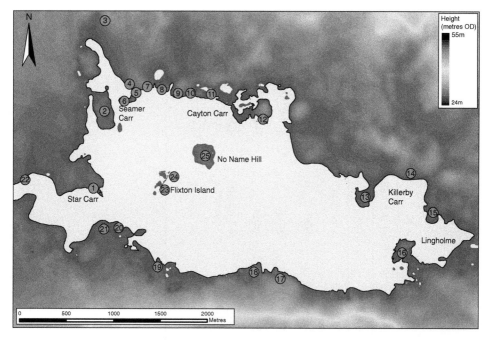

Figure 2.12 1. Star Carr; 2. Ling Lane; 3. Seamer F; 4. Seamer L and N; 5. Seamer K; 6. Seamer D; 7. Seamer B (Rabbit Hill); 8. Seamer C; 9. Manham Hill; 10–12. Cayton Carr; 13. Lingholme Site B; 14. Killerby Carr; 15. Lingholme Site A; 16. Barry's Island; 17. Flixton School Field; 18. Flixton School House Farm; 19. Woodhouse Farm; 20. VPE; 21. VPD; 22. Flixton Site 9; 23. Flixton Island Site 1; 24. Flixton Island Site 2; 25. No Name Hill

discoverer of Star Carr, in his surveys in the 1940s; the remainder were found through the work of Tim Schadla-Hall and the Vale of Pickering Research Trust between 1976 and 2005. In the mid-1970s, the Seamer area was earmarked as a waste disposal site, resulting in a campaign of rescue excavations between 1976 and 1985. The most extensively excavated sites were those located during the rescue campaign of 1976 to 1985 in the Seamer area, with two major areas of excavation focusing on Seamer C and K. Subsequently, fieldwork focused on the excavation of 2 × 2 m test pits along the 24.5 m contour around the ancient lake edge. Some areas underwent further exploration but never on the scale of the Seamer sites (Schadla-Hall 1987, 1989).

Seamer K

Seamer K was situated on the northern shore of Lake Flixton, on a small lagoon known as the western embayment behind the main lake, (see Figure 2.12, no. 5). Here, six major lithic scatters of Early Mesolithic date have been identified in an area where final Palaeolithic occupation is also present (Figure 2.13). These are likely to represent successive reoccupations of the same area. Scatter 5 represents a major focus for a wide range of activities (Table 2.3): Burins were made, used and resharpened; scrapers and awls were used. Microlith manufacture and retooling was also a major task, with microliths and microburins forming a discrete cluster within the southeastern part of the scatter and refitting to two cores made from glacial till flint (see Box 2.5). Burnt flint is very common at 23% and not dissimilar to levels for the eastern structure at Star Carr. No clustering can be discerned, possibly due to disturbance.

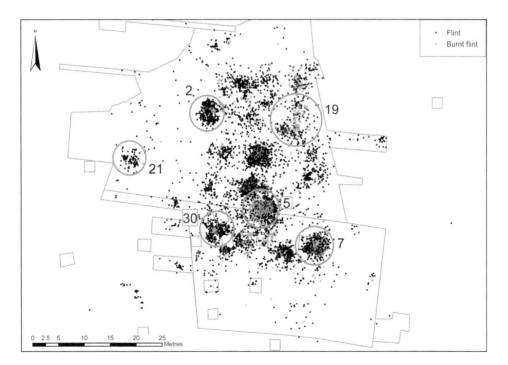

Figure 2.13 Early Mesolithic scatters (circled) at Seamer K (Image: Star Carr project)

Table 2.3 Composition of lithic scatters at Seamer C and K

Site	Seamer K					Seamer C	
Scatter	2	5	7	21	30	H	K
Awl	1	2	1	0	0	0	1
Burin	1	14	5	0	0	6	6
Microlith	2	12	15	1	21	12	8
Scraper	6	24	3	4	0	89	48
Truncation	0	1	2	0	2	2	3
Other tool	3	1	1	0	1	6	5
Retouched/used	12	32	4	1	15	55	46
Axe flake	1	0	0	0	0	0	0
Burin spall	1	36	7	1	0	8	3
Microburin	4	12	6	2	40	8	0
Scraper sharpening	0	1	0	0	0	0	0
Core preparation	10	12	8	3	15	34	29
Blade	81	57	63	11	53	213	259
Flake/fragment	581	2363	993	132	508	3409	2361
Core	26	6	8	3	4	32	29
Total	729	2573	1116	158	659	3874	2797

In contrast, scatter 30 in the western part of the site is highly specialised, focused on microlith production around a small hearth. Here, three cores were imported and used to produce microliths (Table 2.3). Production was intense, with 40 microburins recovered, 11 fitting back into a single core sequence. Twenty-one microliths were also recovered, indicating repair of composite tools as well as production. Other tools are rare: A single notch could be related to haft production, and two truncations could also have served in production of composite tools. This scatter is associated with poorly preserved faunal remains, of which only a red deer humerus could be identified to species. Scatter 7 in the southwest of the site is similarly microlith dominated, though a range of other tools relating to craft activities were also present.

Scatter 2 in the northwest of the site consists of a small knapping scatter to the north of a small hearth involving the reduction of two beach pebbles. To the south of the hearth is a dump/cache of 16 exhausted or flawed nodules and six unmodified nodules that are too small to be worked. Also present are a range of tools and debitage that were not knapped within this scatter (Table 2.3). It is likely that scatter 2 represents a midden where material was cleared from the surrounding area. This scatter contains a worn core made of Scottish southern uplands chert, a rare possible instance of long-distance transfer of raw material (though glacial movement is also a possibility).

More ephemeral activity is also represented at the site. Scatter 21 in the far west represents an isolated area where a small lithic assemblage of 158 pieces was recovered. Here, a single nodule was reduced and tools made both for immediate use (scrapers) and for future use (microliths) (Table 2.3). This scatter does have a range of associated fauna: Within the scatter is a cut-marked goose bone; on the northeastern edge was a large groove and splintered antler and an unmodified antler; to the northwest a red deer tibia and metatarsal. Tool-use task areas can also be identified. In the north, the west and southeastern parts of the site, areas of tool use are indicated by the absence of knapping debris and the presence of tools and large, edge-damage flakes and blades, such as a cluster of three scrapers associated with blades and fragments in the southeastern corner of the site.

Site K is composed of a series of lithic scatters, indicative of a range of different tasks. While scatter 5 represents an area of intense, varied activity, other areas represent specialised workshops; others represent more ephemeral visits to undertake a particular task. There are no obvious refits between the Early Mesolithic scatters on the site, possibly indicating a lack of contemporaneity; we can instead imagine repeated occupation of this area for a variety of different purposes.

Seamer C

Seamer C is only 250 m to the east of Seamer K (Figure 2.12, no. 8). It is also of mixed date with both a Terminal Palaeolithic long blade and an Early Mesolithic component. The Early Mesolithic occupation consists of two large scatters, H and K, and two smaller scatters B2 and G (see Figure 2.14). Radiocarbon dates exist for scatters H, K and G, though the measurements for scatter H and K, obtained in the 1970s, have large standard deviations. Bayesian modelling indicates that Seamer C was broadly contemporary with Star Carr and that it is likely to have been visited on more than one occasion (Conneller et al. 2016a).

Scatter H is composed of two sub-scatters: A northern and a southern one. The southern scatter is 4.5 m in diameter (very similar to the diameter of the Star Carr eastern structure) and has a very pronounced edge, suggesting it was enclosed by a

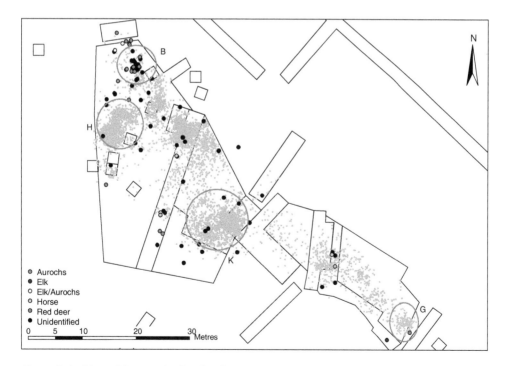

Figure 2.14 Plan of Seamer C, showing faunal remains. The horse remains belong to the Upper Palaeolithic Long Blade occupation

boundary, either a tent or built structure (Figure 2.14). Within this a tight, central cluster of burnt flint can clearly be discerned that is likely to indicate a hearth. Adjacent to this are two clusters of flint likely to represent knapping scatters. This spatial integrity suggests a relatively short-lived structure, in comparison to the eastern building at Star Carr, where material has been cleared out and deposited in surrounding middens. People inhabiting the Seamer structure were focused on the intensive manufacture of scrapers; other tools were less common (Table 2.3). The northern scatter by contrast is almost entirely focused on knapping with only a couple of scrapers and burins associated (Conneller and Schadla-Hall 2003). Fauna is sparse, consisting of a handful of unidentifiable fragments.

Only 4 m to the north of scatter H is a small scatter, B2. Within the northern part of this is a cluster of 20 aurochs bones (most within a 2 m area), with meaty limb bones common as well as mandibular fragments; pieces that might need processing for marrow (Uchiyama 2016). This area also yielded two microliths and a small knapping scatter consisting of the reduction of a nodule(s) of Wolds flint (see Box 2.5), perhaps production of equipment to process this animal.

Scatter K is located in the central part of the site (Figure 2.14). This is an area that has been disturbed, and a number of tree throws were recorded. This disturbance is reflected in the spatial distribution and stratigraphic reversal of radiocarbon dates. The scatter is characterised, as was scatter H, by a focus on scraper production with 36 examples found in an 3 × 2 m area (Table 2.3). The similarity in composition of the Scatter H and K assemblages and the presence of three refits between the two scatters could suggest that they are broadly contemporary; alternatively, people may have returned to use the area for the same purpose. The major difference between the two scatters is knapping quality. Scatter K is produced on extremely poor-quality raw material, possibly by inexperienced individuals. This may be a case of children learning to knap flint.

Finally, at the eastern end of the site is scatter G, another small scatter. This consists of several small clusters of lithic debris associated with occasional scrapers and microliths. Scatters of animal bone were also found here, with red deer, aurochs and elk all identified. There is no evidence to suggest this scatter is contemporary with others at the site, and it appears to represent a series small-scale fleeting visits to the lake shore, perhaps focused on butchery as a cluster of animal bones was found in this area.

Lake Flixton: Smaller sites

Several smaller excavations along the northern shore of Lake Flixton have also located Mesolithic material. Apart from Flixton 1, these sites are known only from small test pits and few have radiometric dates but are potentially contemporary with Star Carr on typological grounds. Seamer L (Figure 2.14, no. 4) is a small lithic scatter of mixed date containing both Long Blade and Early Mesolithic material. The Mesolithic material indicates a task site focused on microlith production and re-tooling. Seamer D (Figure 2.12, no. 6) is another small scatter located on the West Island peninsula consisting of 214 lithic artefacts. Here, flint knapping, including the production of microliths and the use of imported scrapers, took place around a hearth (Table 2.4). To the northwest of the hearth was a cache of flint nodules found placed in a small pile of around 0.4 m diameter (Figure 2.15). All are tested or partially reduced; none are substantially worked. Beyond the Seamer area, to the east at Cayton Carr, Mesolithic material was also encountered, much of this was relatively ephemeral, and the greatest concentration of lithic and faunal material was not in primary context but instead redeposited by a stream.

Table 2.4 Composition of lithic assemblages from sites around Lake Flixton

	Seamer D	VPD	Flixton (Moore exc.)	Flixton I (Schadla-Hall exc.)	No Name Hill
Awl	0	2	9	3	2
Axe	0	0	2	0	1
Burin	0	11	19	8	2
Microlith	1	33	78	21	19
Scraper	4	16	165	11	27
Truncation	1	4	24	1	2
Other tool	2	3	12	3	4
Retouched/used	5	94	185	77	85
Axe flake	0	0	7	3	2
Burin spall	0	25	0	11	3
Microburin	3	34	32	15	6
Core preparation	2	40	169	43	25
Blade	21	255	907	184	146
Flake	166	2061	5958	2026	1043
Core	10	22	131	12	28
Total	214	2600	7698	2418	1395

(a) (b)

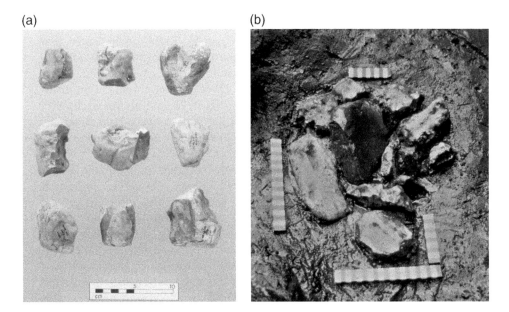

Figure 2.15 Left: Nodules from Seamer D cache (photo: Gwil Owen). Right: The Flixton School cache (photo: Vale of Pickering Research Trust)

Four sites have been located along the southern shore of Lake Flixton, immediately opposite Star Carr. The most westerly of these, VPD, consists of a 20 m² trench and two adjacent 2 m² test pits excavated in 1986 and 1988 (Figure 2.12, no. 21). These excavations located the northern part of an extremely dense lithic scatter, likely to be an area of some significance. A cluster of burnt flint indicates a hearth was located at the southernmost edge of the trench. Fauna was present, of which 33 pieces could be identified to species: Red deer and roe deer are most common, but isolated elements of aurochs, elk, wild boar and wildcat were also present, an extremely diverse range for such a small area. The lithic assemblage is dominated by microliths, though other tools are well represented (see Table 2.4). Tool manufacture seems to have been a major task: Many microburins and burin spalls, the waste from production activities, were recovered. Wolds material and some small till pebbles (see Box 2.5) were worked, but there are also several large blades that seem to have been imported to the site.

Just over 1 km to the east of this area is Flixton School House Farm (Figure 2.12, no. 18). Here, scatters of Early and Late Mesolithic flintworking were present adjacent to a small pool. In the pool aurochs, remains were recovered, consisting of 13 ribs, several vertebrae and part of the pelvis (Overton and Taylor 2018). Rather than these being partly articulated, the patterning of elements indicates that this is a collection of humanly modified material from different parts of the axial skeleton that was deposited into this pool. The small area (less than 30 cm across) within which these remains were found suggests that these were wrapped in a bundle or deposited in a bag.

Box 2.3   Mesolithic animists?

While Mesolithic people have often been portrayed as rational harvesters of resources, even a cursory perusal of ethnographic literature indicates that relationships between hunter-gatherers and the animals that they encounter are considerably more complex. As Lévi-Strauss famously argued, 'animals are not just good to eat, they are good to think' (1966). Ethnographic accounts of animist groups have recently become influential in Mesolithic research, with many anthropologists arguing that animism is a near-universal characteristic of hunter-gatherer groups (Descola 1999; Fausto 2007; though see Porr and Bell 2012).

Animism is an ontology that attributes a soul or other human-like qualities to animals in particular, but also sometimes to plants and certain important objects. The categories structuring human social life also apply to animal groups, meaning that amongst themselves animals indulge in human-like social relations, and see their fur or feathers as clothing, their teeth or claws as weapons. Descola (1992) has argued that hunter-gatherers conceive of relationships between humans and animals as reciprocal or predatory or a mixture of the two. Reciprocity is based on balancing relationships of give and take between species. Animals are often seen to choose to give themselves up to the hunter, or to be a gift from a 'master of animals' but in return need to be treated with respect. Predatory relations are more antagonistic, with humans aiming to capture animals and desubjectify them in order to eat them, while at the same time animals – particularly predators – try to capture human souls.

These accounts of animism are, however, broad, generalised models, drawn from numerous ethnographies that differ considerably in detail. Amerindian cosmologies, for example, do not attribute personhood equally to animals – the emphasis seems to be on those species that perform key symbolic and practical roles, such as the great predators and the principal prey species (Viveiros de Castro 1998). While it might be a truism that hunter-gatherers do not understand animals in the same way as modern westerners, we should not expect Mesolithic worldviews to replicate those of contemporary hunter-gatherers or to remain static over time.

Jordan has argued that animist belief systems have material correlates, as ideas of the necessity of respectful deposition of animal remains are widespread (Jordan 2003). Hallowell, for example (1926), has outlined how amongst northern hemisphere hunter-gatherers bear bones, especially skulls, are cached and protected from dog scavenging to avoid the spirit or spirit 'owner' of the animal from being offended. Most bones are hung in trees or placed around special poles; others are thrown into a river or buried. Similarly, Binford (1978a,) noted shrines amongst the Nunamuit where sheep skulls were displayed. Jordan's own fieldwork amongst the Evenk people recorded that bear bones were deposited in deep pools, while elk bones were returned to the forest.

How then might Mesolithic people have conceived their relationships with animals, and what are the material correlates of these relationships? Most of the evidence we have for the Early Mesolithic comes from Star Carr, where evidence from the wetland suggests formal deposition of animal remains. In addition to the reassembled red deer, made from the remains of at least two animals, animal heads seem to have been specially selected for wetland deposition. In the area of deposition associated with the earliest occupation of the site, a series of cervid heads – both modified and unmodified – encircle the re-assembled red deer. The earliest of these appears to be a juvenile male elk skull, accompanied by two articulating phalanges, which might suggest the skull was wrapped in a hide. This initial focus on elk perhaps echoes depositionary practises amongst the earliest Scandinavian groups, where bundles of processed elk remains were deposited in deep pools (Jessen et al. 2015). The remainder of the skulls deposited into the lake during this early phase of Star Carr were of red deer, with both male and female represented; the male examples had been modified into frontlets.

A similar focus on the deposition of heads can be seen in the slightly later wetland deposit in the area of Clark's trenches. Here, eight red deer and five roe deer heads were found in the 2015 excavation of the baulk between Clark's Cuttings I and II (Elliott et al. 2018, Knight et al. 2018). Most of these were modified in a way that indicates they represent both complete and partially manufactured frontlets (Elliott et al. 2018). Material from the 1949–1951 excavations does not retain detailed spatial information; however, it is likely that the majority of the fauna recovered by Clark also comes from this area. Seven frontlets, one of red deer and one of roe deer, and three red deer and three roe deer crania came from Cutting I (Clark 1949), and at least four red deer fontlets and several skulls of red deer, roe deer and elk came from Cutting II (Clark 1950). These two trenches lie on either side of the 2015 excavation area. In addition, an aurochs skull came from the 1950 excavation. Finally, there is a report that a bear skull was encountered by Tot Lord when investigating Clark's sections following excavation (Jacobi pers. comm.).

Beyond Star Carr, the bundle of aurochs remains from a small pool at Flixton School House Farm suggest depositionary practises were complex and varied between species and over time. The patterning seen at Flixton School, in the presence of ribs, vertebrae and the pelvis, is echoed at Seamer B, though at the latter site these elements were articulated, and a mandible and radius are also present. The Seamer B aurochs seems to have been abandoned in wetland/fen carr, rather than its remains collected and deposited in water. The aurochs dates to the transition between Early and Late Mesolithic, both on the basis of a radiocarbon date of 8210–7590 BC (slight humic acid contamination may be an issue) and its association in a layer with quantities of hazelnuts, whereas the Flixton School aurochs predates the hazel rise. This may suggest a change in ways of dealing with animal remains, from more formal deposition at Flixton School, where the remains were deposited in a bundle into water, to more casual abandonment at Seamer B. Formal deposition of aurochs in the earliest part of the Mesolithic seems to have occurred elsewhere in Northern Europe. In Scandinavia, three Early Mesolithic finds of entire aurochs carcasses have been made at Vig and Prejlerup in Denmark and Önnarp in Sweden. As all were found in close association with microliths, it has been argued that these were wounded animals who escaped the hunters only later to die of their wounds. The Prejlerup aurochs appears to have been shot with nine microliths. Mesolithic groups must have been skilled trackers, and it seems highly unlikely that a seriously wounded 1000 kg aurochs could not have been easily tracked, suggesting this represents a formal deposit.

It may be no co-incidence these incidences of formal deposition appear to have focused on the main prey animals in the Vale of Pickering: Red deer and aurochs for the patterned post-cranial remains, and red deer, roe deer, aurochs, elk and possibly bear for the cranial material. Eating an animal that is conceived of as having a soul or being a person is an area of spiritual concern, and it may be that these were the very animals that needed propitiating through proper conduct in relation to their remains.

In contrast to the treatment of large prey animals, which focused on the deposition of heads or bundles, the representation of small fur-bearers on Early Mesolithic sites is different. Overton (2016) points out that while specialised trapping and skinning sites exist (the Danish Late Mesolithic site of Ringkloster yielded the remains of 41 pine marten with skinning marks, for example), on other sites fur-bearers are represented by single elements only. This patterning, which does not seem to be due to taphonomic issues, may be a result of elements of certain animals being retained as amulets, perhaps worn as pendants or attached to clothing. At Faraday Road in the Kennet Valley (see chapter 3), wildcat is represented by a scapula and a tibia; at Star Carr, there is a badger phalange and humerus. Many of these furbearing animals tend to be solitary, stealthy and often nocturnal and carnivorous or omnivorous, less routinely encountered than the major prey animals. Overton argues that some of these qualities may have been sought after by humans: The ability of the wildcat to stealthily stalk its prey, for example, and that wearing parts of these animals may have enhanced people's ability to act in this way.

The skins of fur-bearers became human clothing. Ethnographic accounts indicate the wearing of animal skins is often a way in which relationships between human and animal bodies are articulated. Ingold (2000) points out that furs from part of an animal's body are often tailored to corresponding parts of the human body. On occasions wearing parts of an animal body can have powerful effects on a human body. The antler frontlets are likely to represent this sort of powerful animal costume. We have seen that much depositionary activity is focused on the head of prey animals – perhaps as heads were seen to represent the essence or soul of the animal (Conneller 2004). The frontlets are thus perhaps a distillation of the essence of an animal, and one that was purposely worn by people as costume, perhaps with the animal skin still attached to the frontlets. This may have allowed certain people to take on animal essences or *habitus*, allowing them to act like, or communicate with, important animals or spirits. Pedersen (2007) describes, in Mongolia, powerful Darhad ritual costumes that allow ritual specialists and spirits to travel between worlds. Similarly, Fienup-Riordan's (1987) study of masks amongst the Yup'ik of Western Alaska suggests they allowed the wearer to see into other worlds.

When Mesolithic people wore animal clothing, they attempted to see the world from the point of view of animals or spirits. When we do archaeology, we attempt a similar exercise, to see the world from a Mesolithic point of view. This may have been a very different world, a world of spirits and animals that could act like people, a world where places and things had intentionality, and where the flow of life-force between people and things was carefully balanced.

Around 250 m to the east, situated on the adjacent peninsula, is the site of Flixton School Field (Figure 2.12, no. 17). Here, a series of test pits yielded dense spreads of Mesolithic material in dryland areas and had wetland portions characterised by tools and larger utilised pieces where animal bone was common. Two caches of raw material were located: One consisting of five cores and tested nodules was located in the wetlands amongst lithic and faunal material; a second cache recovered from test pit PB was found isolated from other finds (Figure 2.15). This cache consisted of 12 extremely large but poor-quality nodules collected both direct from the till and from the beach.

Barry's Island is the most easterly of the southern shoreline sites (Figure 2.12, no. 16). A large assemblage of flint and animal bone was recovered from a series of test pits along the shore of the island, excavated between 1992 and 1996. This site has been reported in the literature as a base camp based on its faunal assemblage (Rowley-Conwy 199; Uchiyama 2016). However, the evidence is very clear that the vast majority of material from this site was redeposited by a stream channel (as previously reported by Conneller and Schadla-Hall 2003). The wide scatter of radiocarbon dates reveals that the stream has redeposited material from a number of sites from a range of different periods spanning the Late Palaeolithic to Late Mesolithic, with the majority of the material dated belonging to the Late Mesolithic. The vast majority of the lithic material is heavily worn, compatible with water action. The only clearly in situ area is the lower contexts of a single trench, where a refitting assemblage reveals decortification of several large nodules and shaping of material into preforms; in other words, a specialist task area located in reedswamp at the water's edge.

There were islands in Lake Flixton: Flixton Island and No Name Hill. Flixton 1 (Figure 2.12, no. 23) was first excavated by John Moore between 1947 and 1948, and further excavations were undertaken by Tim Schadla-Hall in 1986–1987 and 1993. Moore excavated a long trench across the gravel island, locating two areas of high-lithic densities divided by a channel creating northern and southern areas. Several hearths were located within the scatters. Moore noted differences between the microlithic component of the two areas and suggested that the northern one might be earlier. Certainly, the presence of more elongated obliquely blunted points than typical for the area may support the idea of chronological differences. Overall, the assemblage is dominated by scrapers, though microliths are also common, and burins rather rarer, but tools and production debris indicate a wide variety of tasks involving tool production and use (see Table 2.4). Fauna was relatively sparse, though a barbed point was recovered. In all, the impression is of varied activity areas with some temporal depths.

No Name Hill is located to the east of Flixton Island and is surrounded by some of the deepest water in Lake Flixton (Figure 2.12, no. 25). Fieldwalking and test pitting revealed that occupation on the top of the island had been destroyed by ploughing; however, Mesolithic material was preserved along the shore of the island. Of the small 2 m² test pits excavated along the shoreline, most yielded very small assemblages. Unit NC, on the southwest shore, was the only exception, with 385 pieces, a moderate-sized assemblage for this size test pit. Awls, microliths and scrapers were all represented, and burin manufacture and resharpening was undertaken. Test pit BJ seems to represent a small knapping scatter focused on a hearth. Other test pits yielded assemblages that are indicative of more ephemeral tool-use areas, lacking small debitage and burnt flint and characterised by high percentages of utilised pieces and formal tools. Many of these were recovered from the northern shore of the island, near to the water's edge. The evidence indicates that activities on this island were only ever small-scale, focused on low-level flint knapping and tool-use activities.

Star Carr and the Vale of Pickering

Lake Flixton was a major focus of activity in the Early Mesolithic: Sites are numerous; many were revisited. Though we do not have the same temporal resolution as at Star Carr, these sites were occupied over much the same period, and there are similarities between them and Star Carr. We see similar patterns of caching flint nodules, as well as the association of wetland areas with tool-use assemblages. However, there are also differences. Many of these are likely to be amplified by the focus on Star Carr and the large areas excavated there. Star Carr certainly seems different from the large open area excavations at Seamer, but other sites that have had more spatially restricted excavation may be more similar.

Overall, many of the sites around Lake Flixton are characterised by more specialised occupation; for example, the intensive production of microliths or scrapers. Such areas are rarer at Star Carr, present only on the wetland edge: On one occasion axes were reworked; in another area beads were produced. We do not know whether similar specialised areas existed on the dryland and have been elided through repeated reoccupation or whether the dryland archaeology has a 'domestic' rather than specialised character. Star Carr also seems to have more evidence of site maintenance than other sites: The middening of material, the clearance of material from structures and the scavenging of usable flint during later occupations; this is relatively rare elsewhere. There appears to have been a small midden present at Seamer K, scatter 2, though the coherence of material deposited on it argues for a relatively short use. The assemblage from the possible structure at Seamer C, scatter H, has a high level of refits and is coherent, focused on scraper production; it does not seem to have subject to site maintenance activities. Structures are also rarer elsewhere, with the example from Seamer C being the only possible comparator. Neither post-holes nor a central hollow were noted here, suggesting it may have been a lightweight tent-like structure.

It is more difficult to comment on patterns of animal deposition, one of the major features that marks out Star Carr as special (Conneller and Schadla-Hall 2003; Conneller 2004). The artefacts made from antler that are so common at Star Carr are rare or absent elsewhere. No further frontlets are found beyond Star Carr, and barbed points are rare, with three examples found at No Name Hill and one at Flixton Island. There are wetland areas beyond Star Carr that saw the deposition of animal bone such as at Flixton School Field, and there are even instances of patterned deposition of fauna such as the aurochs described for Flixton School House Farm, but thus far the intensity appears much less. However, this is an issue that is likely to have been affected by the sampling strategy of Schadla-Hall's excavations, where the majority of test pitting has occurred at the 24.5 m OD contour, rather than the submerged areas where this material may be concentrated. To date, Star Carr clearly stands out in terms of its longevity and the intensity of deposition of animals and special artefacts; however, this is a situation that may change with further fieldwork around Lake Flixton.

Beyond Star Carr: Pioneers in Northern Britain

Beyond the Vale of Pickering, sites simiar to Star Carr in Northern England are relatively rare, consisting of small groupings on higher ground on the Lincolnshire Edge, the North York Moors (Jacobi 1978ab), the Central and Northern Pennines (Chatterton 2005; Coggins et al. 1989; Howard-Davis et al. 1996) and, Coupland 1925. Several sites are also known in Scotland that are comparable to Star Carr, though these tend to be components in mixed assemblages.

Star Carr in Scotland?

In Scotland, typologically Early Mesolithic material is either undated or has yielded surprisingly late dates. None of these dates can currently be relied upon: For example, the date from Morton A represents a measurement on bulked charcoal from a site with both typologically late and early material. Early Mesolithic groups do not seem to have made formal hearths either in pits or with stone surrounds, and in soils where animal bones only survive in shell-middens, it is unlikely that they will generate material ideal for radiocarbon dating. Several sites in Scotland (such as Morton A, Craigsford Mains, Dryburgh Mains, Kinloch, Woodend Loch, Glenbatrick Waterhole, Lussa Wood 1 and Lussa Bay) have often been compared to Star Carr-type sites; however, many of these are dominated by isosceles triangles, which is not typical for Star Carr industries, where obliquely blunted points are most common. Most of these Scottish assemblages are of mixed date, further complicating typological comparisons. One such site where Star Carr-type microliths are present as a small proportion of a much larger assemblage is Nethermills, where a fragment of a schist bead very similar to those from Star Carr and other Star Carr-type sites was recovered from the ploughzone (Wickham-Jones et al. 2016). The material from Morton A (Box 2.4)), a small, unmixed assemblage from Donich Park, Argyll (Ballin and Ellis 2019), the eroded assemblage from Lussa Bay and the undated assemblage from the base of An Corran in Skye are probably most similar to a typical Star Carr-type assemblage.

The lithic material from Lussa Bay has been found in a derived position on the beach and at the estuary of the Lussa River. It appears that much of the material has been eroded from the area of the estuary, and thus derives from a fairly low level. Relative sea-level in this region has been significantly higher than at present over the last 15,000 years. The only time sea-levels were similar to today was a brief period, centred around 9000 BC (Bradley et al. 2011); if the location of this material could be pin-pointed, a relative date might be obtained. An Corran is a rockshelter site in a small bay (Figure 2.16), the first natural landing spot for some distance along a steep coastline (Saville et al. 2012). The shelter and the presence of a good source of lithic raw material, in an outcrop of baked mudstone immediately adjacent to the site, would have made it a good stopping point for coastal colonisers. These sites might indicate that the earliest pioneers were moving into Britain along the early post-glacial

Figure 2.16 View to an Corran (copyright Caroline Wickham-Jones and Scotland's First Settlers Project)

shoreline as far as the western shores of the British peninsula. There is though also evidence for movement inland: The small scatter from Donich Park, Argyll (Ballin and Eliis 2019) is located on Donich Water, at the head of Loch Goil, a natural route into the uplands. The small assemblage from this site is dominated by microliths with a small number of other tools, perhaps an overnight stop where composite tools were repaired with microliths manufactured elsewhere and routine tasks carried out.

The other sites, where Early Mesolithic types are found as part of mixed assemblages, may, given the dominance of isosceles triangles and the presence of curve-backed pieces, be a bit later, based on typological comparisons with material at Cramond, and more broadly patterns in Southern Britain and on the continent. Though there are coastal sites amongst these potential later groups, for example, floor G1 at Glenbatrick Waterhole (Mercer 1974), these sites appear to have a more fluvial distribution, for example, at Dryburgh Mains and Craigsford Mains in the Tweed Valley. The Tweed was suggested by Lacaille (1954) to be an important routeway between groups moving from east to west, but also as outlined by Warren (2001), an area rich in resources, particularly salmon. The Tweed and the Biggar gap would lead to areas in the west, such as Woodend Loch in the Clyde Basin, and further afield to the Jura sites. A similar pattern can be seen from the Dee. Here, Early Mesolithic microliths have been recovered as small components in much larger scatters. These can be seen at Nethermills near to Aberdeen (Wickham-Jones et al. 2016) and in recent fieldwalking campaigns by the Mesolithic Deeside group, on sites such as East Park, where 18 microliths and several scrapers were recovered amongst an assemblage of mixed Mesolithic and Neolithic date (Wickham-Jones et al. 2017). Their representation extends as far as the river's upland reaches in the Cairngorms at the Chest of Dee (Wickham-Jones et al. 2020).

Box 2.4   Morton A. A pioneer site in Eastern Scotland?

The site of Morton A was located on a rocky outcrop, south of the Tay (see chapter 5 for further discussion). Here, characteristically Early Mesolithic microliths of broad obliquely blunted points and isosceles triangles were recovered amongst an assemblage that included geometric elements indicative of the Late Mesolithic. The significance of these finds has been widely debated. Coles, working in the broadly functionalist approaches of the Cambridge prehistorians of the time, suggested that different microlith styles could represent different seasonal components used by a single group. Other archaeologists, more convinced of a chronological and/or cultural explanation of microlith variation, suggested that these represented an Early Mesolithic presence at a site, where Late Mesolithic occupation also occurred (Bonsall 1988; Lawson and Bonsall 1986; Myers 1988). These authors suggested that the series of broad obliquely blunted points and isosceles triangles were equivalent to Early Mesolithic assemblages in Northern England, such as Star Carr. The earliest radiocarbon date for the site is 7875–6230 cal BC (8050 ± 355 BP; NZ-1191) (Coles 1971, 320). This is on bulked, unidentified wood, taken from an area where six separate occupations, separated by wind-blown sand, were recorded. The material used in the measurement includes charcoal from all six occupations. Given other dates from the site cluster in the last half of the sixth millennium BC, it is likely that some much older charcoal was included in this measurement.

If, on typological grounds, a date of c.9000–8500 BC can be suggested for the occupation, this would correspond to a time of slightly lower sea-level in this region, somewhere between 2 m lower and levels similar to the present (Bradley et al. 2011). Morton would still be close to the coast, as deposits to the east are of more recent origin (Coles 1971). The lowest levels at T46, where the earlier date was obtained, consist of a scoop surrounded by stones of local andesite, within which a hearth was set. A pile of andesite manuports stood next to the hearth. The lithics suggest a small scale-occupation with only 61 pieces of flint recovered. Tools are perhaps what a group might need for an overnight stop: A burin, a scraper, two microliths and a handful of retouched and utilised pieces. Morton A, along with An Corran on Skye, may represent rare remnants of an at least partial coastal economy practised by the earliest Mesolithic groups in the north.

Holderness

Southeast of the Yorkshire Wolds, low-lying Holderness, like the Vale of Pickering, should be seen as an eastward extension of Doggerland. This was a land of lakes and meres, dissected by rivers, and Early Mesolithic groups seem to have been particularly drawn to these sorts of environments. Barbed points have been recovered from several locations in this region (Figure 2.17). The largest collection comes from Brandesburton, where four were discovered in 1953 at Coney Garth Gravel pit during quarrying, and a further two fragments from a nearby pit in 1955 (Clark and Godwin 1957). A further example from Coney Garth Hill came to light in 1965. A second quarry site, a sand pit by nearby Fosse Hill at Milldam Beck, has also yielded a number of points, with four examples recovered between 1968 and 1975. A single point was found at Catfoss gravel pit in 1968. A further example, examined by Radley in the Grantham collection, is also provenanced to the Holderness area (Radley 1969). Beyond the Brandesburton area, a barbed point was recovered from the beach near Hornsea in 1932. Its condition suggests it had only recently been eroded, probably from the mere deposits recorded on the foreshore by Clement Reid (Clark and Godwin 1957). There are also two early finds, one found in reed peat at Hornsea Mere in 1915 (though this location has been disputed, see Clark and Godwin 1957) and one in 1903 from a small infilled mere Skipsea Withow (Armstrong 1922). These, along with a barbed point dredged from the Leman and Ower Bank by the trawler Colinder in 1931, brought home to Clark the cultural and geographical connections between 'Maglemosian' groups in Southern Scandinavia and Britain.

The Leman and Ower point is now known to be of Final Palaeolithic date, as are some other uniserial barbed points once thought to belong to the Mesolithic (see Tolan-Smith and Bonsall 1999). None of the points from Holderness have been dated, and in the absence of direct measurements the possibility that at least some of these may be of Upper Palaeolithic date remains. There has been little evidence for lithic material associated with these barbed points, albeit none have been recovered under ideal conditions. Clark searched spoil heaps and adjacent fields when visiting Coney Garth Quarry and did not recover lithics. The Skipsea barbed point was recovered in association with fauna (including pike) but not lithics (Armstrong 1922), though some lithics of possible Mesolithic age were subsequently recovered from the same silts, and a flake axe was recovered from the beach (Armstrong 1923). More recently, fauna of Early Mesolithic age has been recovered from the mere, though there is no sign of

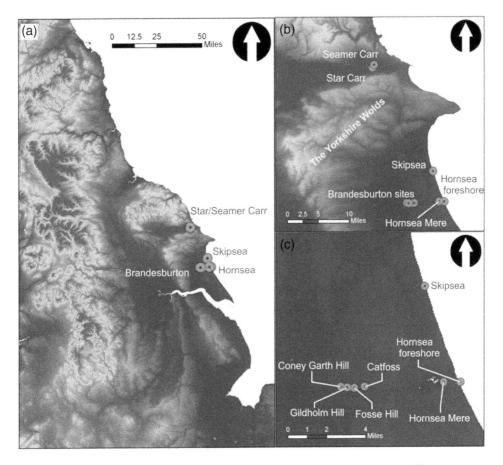

Figure 2.17 Location of barbed point finds from Holderness (copyright Ben Elliott)

human modification (Cadman et al. 2018). The lack of settlement evidence associated with the Holderness barbed points has led to suggestions that these are losses made during the course of fishing activities in the meres and rivers of Holderness.

The North York Moors

In 1972, despite the fact that no Early Mesolithic sites were known from the North York Moors, Clark suggested that the people who wintered at Star Carr followed their prey and spent their summers on these uplands. In the Early Holocene, the moors seem to have been grassy heath, where crowberry was common. In 1978, Jacobi provided support for Clark's hypothesis: The sites of Pointed Stone 2 and 3, located 20 m apart on the eastern flank of Bilsdale Moor East at 410 m OD, excavated by himself and Geoffrey and Sheila Taylor. Both are Star Carr-type assemblages characterised by similar typology and raw material as at Star Carr itself (Jacobi 1978a,). Both sites were completely excavated until no further artefacts were located, revealing a flint scatter of 28 m^2 at Pointed Stone 2 and 39 m^2 at Pointed Stone 3. Site 3 consists of three lithic scatters, each with a central hearth (indicated by a cluster of burnt flint).

There is some clustering of artefacts with a group of microliths and microburins in squares G5 and G6 and a group of cores that were not flaked on site in squares H5 and I5. These are reminiscent of the caches of raw material found in the Vale of Pickering. Site 2 is composed of two lithic concentrations, and a patch of reddened earth may indicate a hearth (Jacobi 1976, V. 3).

Both sites had a high proportion of microliths and microburins, while percentages of other tools were negligible. None of the microburins refitted to the microliths, and the latter were often broken (Jacobi 1976, V. 4), indicating repair of composite weapons. Jacobi suggested, again on the basis of putative red deer movement (for fauna was not preserved on either site), that the uplands would have been primarily exploited in the summer months. Such arguments were linked also to the contrasting composition of the assemblages at Star Carr and the Pointed Stone sites. Large numbers of burins (presumed to be tools for the manufacture of barbed antler point blanks) were found at Star Carr; while only one dubious burin fragment was recovered from the upland sites. Since red deer shed their antlers in April, Jacobi equated the lack of burins at Pointed Stone with a lack of available raw material, thus placing occupation in the summer and so suggesting that the upland sites may have re-presented part of a complementary settlement system with Star Carr. The more open landscapes of the North York Moors, composed of grassy heath with stands of birch, may have aided hunting, while the common occurrence of crowberries, bearing fruit in September, may have added to the attractions of the area (Spratt et al. 1976).

More recent work has located further evidence for Star Carr-type settlement on the North York Moors, at Highcliff Nab near Guisborough, on a small raised spur on the northern escarpment of the Moors, overlooking the Tees floodplain (Waughman 1996). Surface collection (Harbord 1996) and excavation (Waughman 1996) recovered both Star Carr and Deepcar-type microliths, in an area where the presence of several hearths was noted. In common with other upland sites, the assemblage is dominated by microliths.

The Pennines

Mesolithic material has been recovered from the Pennines since the late 19th century, and this rich history of excavation continues to the present day. Unfortunately, much of the Pennine material is imprecisely dated. The area was the focus of Jacobi and Switsur's radiocarbon programme in the 1970s, when archived charcoal from Francis Buckley's excavations in the 1920s was dated (Switsur and Jacobi 1975). Conventional dating at that time required large quantities of bulked charcoal, which often could not be identified to species, so the dates acquired must be considered at best *termini post quos*. As a result, it is impossible to state for certain that the Pennine assemblages are contemporary with Star Carr, though on typological grounds it is highly likely that at least some of them are. The distribution of Star Carr sites is relatively sparse, being only found in the Central Pennines, in the Anglezarke Uplands on the western edge of the Pennines and in Upper Nidderdale and Teesdale in the Northern Pennines. Radley and Mellars (1964) highlighted the use of east coast till flint by Star Carr groups (Radley and Mellars 1964, see Table 2.5). Star Carr groups in the Pennines appear to have avoided Yorkshire Wolds flint, despite it being a component of assemblages in the Vale of Pickering. Recent work indicates that chert played an important role, being, for example, the main material employed at Rushy Brow (Howard-Davis et al. 1996; Poole 2020).

Table 2.5 Raw material use on Pennine sites. * Values for South Haw are based on microliths only from the Collins collection and on microliths and debitage from the excavation by Chatterton (2005)

Site	Wolds%	Till Flint%	Chert %
Rushy Brow	0	3.5	96.5
Turnpike	4.2	80.3	10.2
Warcock Hill South	10.0	85.0	5.0
South Haw*	0	93.4	6.4

Table 2.6 Essential tool frequencies of Central Pennine Star Carr-type assemblages

Site	Microliths	Scrapers	Burins	Axes	Micro-denticulates	Microburin ratio
Warcock Hill S.	61.8	35.3	2.9	0	0	0.43
Turnpike	76.7	16.7	0	0	6.7	1.04
Rushy Brow	100	0	0	0	0	0.4

In the Central Pennines, Star Carr-type sites are known from Warcock Hill South/ Turnpike (Stonehouse 1992), Facit Quarry and Knowl Hill, West Yorkshire (Poole 2020) and at Rushy Brow, Anglezarke Moor, Lancashire (Howard-Davis et al. 1996). At Warcock Hill are the sites of Warcock Hill South and Turnpike. Warcock Hill South was excavated by Francis Buckley, who recovered at least 714 pieces of lithic material. The majority of the material was recovered from an area of 4 m^2, and also small patches near this concentration, though a small group of tools and debitage was located around 45 m from the main site, and Star Carr-type material was also re-covered from exposed surfaces within 400 mm of the site (Buckley 1924). The Turnpike site may represent one of these surrounding concentrations (Stonehouse 1992). Turnpike was excavated in 1973 by Pat Stonehouse, who recovered 1688 pieces from a concentration measuring about 53 m^2. Both Warcock Hill South and Turnpike reveal similar raw material use. Translucent flints dominate, with smaller amounts of Wolds material and black chert (Table 2.5). At both sites, microliths are the most common tools (Table 2.6), though the ratio of microliths to microburins varies dramatically. At Turnpike, microburins outnumber microliths, indicating extensive manufacturing activities. At Warcock Hill South, the ratio is 21 microliths to 9 mi-croburins, whereas at Turnpike figures are more equal (Table 2.6). This may reflect different excavation standards or may be a real pattern, picking up different activity areas along the ridge. Both sites have smaller quantities of other tools (Table 2.6). Scrapers, truncations and mèches de foret are fairly equally represented at Turnpike, while scrapers are more common at Warcock Hill South, though two truncations, two awls and a burin are also represented.

While Warcock Hill South/Turnpike show some variation in activities, the tool assemblage recovered from Rushy Brow is completely dominated by microliths (Table 2.6), while large numbers of microburins indicate manufacture of microliths and repair of composite tools. The site is located on Anglezarke Moor, a western outlier of the Pennine chain, and is situated with unimpeded views over the Southern Lancashire Plain (Howard-Davies et al. 1996). The lithic scatter was associated with a semi-circular stone setting c.1.5 m in diameter, which may represent a windbreak. Though some glacial till flint was used, it represents only 3.2% (13 pieces) of the entire assemblage. Of the till material, seven are microliths and another is a utilised flake, indicating transportation of this material as finished tools. Gearing up and replacement of broken microliths of till flint took place using relatively poor-quality Pennine chert, as indicated by microliths and microburins of this material. Thirteen cores of chert were recovered, all still relatively productive, suggesting either caching or that this material was insufficiently valued to be curated and transported elsewhere. If the Pennine sites and the sites in the Vale of Pickering are part of a single system of mobility (or exchange), it is telling that though till flint is imported to the Pennines, Pennine chert certainly does not return to the Vale. A notable find at Rushy Brow, and one that potentially connects the site to Star Carr, is a shale bead, found in four fragments (see Box 3.9).

On the eastern flank of the North Pennines, in Upper Nidderdale, further scatters of Star Carr-type microliths have been found at South Haw, where Margaret Collins collected material from several areas of erosion. While much of this material was Late Mesolithic, she also recovered 31 Star Carr-type microliths, most of till material, but 6 of chert. Further gridded collection from erosion patches by Chatterton (2005) located a small scatter of knapping debris of till flint in conjunction with seven microliths and three microburins in the western part of the site. This appears to be one of the areas where Collins also located early material. She also recovered early microliths in a cluster in the eastern part of the site, and there also appear to be similar microliths from collections from Great Haw, only 1 km to the west, at Little Haw, just over 1 km to the north, at Peat Pits and Kay Head Allotments, all on the high plateau above Nidderdale, and in the valley at Gouthwaite Reservoir. These finds indicate the sporadic presence of groups with Star Carr microliths more broadly in the area of Nidderdale (Chatterton 2005). All these locations are sites of mixed date, so it is difficult to know whether any other tool types belong with the microliths; certainly, they seem relatively sparse, though the presence of microburins indicates microliths were being produced at South Haw at least. Further north in Teesdale, Star Carr-type material has been discovered eroding from the bank of the Tees. In addition to a variety of different tools made on till flint and chert, a shale bead was recovered (Coggins et al. 1989).

The Star Carr-type sites in the Pennines appear to be relatively small and less dense, at least in comparison to subsequent Deepcar-type sites (see below): Warcock Hill South (at 4 m^2) and Turnpike (at 53 m^2) appear to represent a series of synchronic or diachronic activity areas along a ridge. This pattern is similar to the Star Carr-type sites on the North York Moors and even in the Vale of Pickering (except Star Carr and Flixton I). The pattern of activity, particularly in the uplands, is more typical of small, discrete knapping scatters and activity areas. This distinction is likely to have bearing on the different ways in which lithic-focused activities were organised in the landscape and in relation to occupation sites.

Star Carr settlement in Northern England

The upland sites of the Pennines and the North York Moors have frequently been described as summer hunting camps (Clark 1972; Donahue and Lovis 2006; Jacobi 1978a; Rowley-Conwy 1994; Smith 2002). This originally derives from the work of

Clark (1972), who borrowed the seasonal transhumance models of his Cambridge colleagues to describe Star Carr within its broader seasonal round. Mesolithic people, he argued, would follow their main prey animal, red deer, on its seasonal migration to the uplands. As such, in the following decades upland sites became relegated to specialised satellites of Star Carr.

In the same way that Clark's pioneering work on seasonality and site function focused subsequent interpretations on similar themes, so Clark's model of seasonal mobility has spawned seasonal settlement models of increasing complexity, but all based on the same premise: Mesolithic people were seasonally mobile and replicated a single mobility pattern throughout the entire Early Mesolithic. However, the relationship of upland sites (as well as the remainder of the sites in the Vale of Pickering) to Star Carr very much depends on interpretations of what Star Carr actually represents. For those who saw Star Carr as a winter base camp, small sites dominated by microliths in adjacent upland areas could be interpreted as summer hunting camps to form a neat, coherent seasonal round. Jacobi's (1978a,) observation that the same till flint sources were employed in the Vale of Pickering as well as at Star Carr-type sites on the North York Moors and the Pennines reinforced a sense that these sites were connected.

However, for those who saw Star Carr neither as a base camp nor as a winter settlement, the nature of the upland sites as well as the remainder of the sites in the Vale of Pickering became more problematic. More recent work has also indicated red deer are unlikely to have undertaken upland migration during the Early Mesolithic, and in any case, they were not the dominant meat source at Star Carr (Caulfield 1978; Legge and Rowley-Conwy 1988). Interpreting Star Carr as a summer hunting camp, Legge and Rowley-Conwy (1988) suggest that a relationship with the (presumed) summer sites on the North York Moors is thus less likely, instead hypothesising a relationship between Star Carr, other sites in the Vale of Pickering and the coast. Rowley-Conwy (1994) posited a more complex model following preliminary analysis of the faunal assemblage from Barry's Island. He suggested the existence of different site types in the Vale of Pickering – the 'hunting camp' at Star Carr and a possible winter base camp at Barry's Island (though this is now known to represent redeposited material of different ages). He related these to hypothetical summer residential sites on the now submerged coastline. Movement between the coast and the Vale of Pickering would be undertaken at various times of the year by hunting parties and whole groups. In this model, the role of the upland sites remains unclear.

The most recent attempt to elucidate seasonal settlement systems in Northern England once again suggests Star Carr represents a residential (in this case, summer) base camp (Donahue and Lovis 2006), with a relationship to specialised autumn/winter sites in the Vale of Pickering and to spring/summer residential and specialised extraction sites on the coast. In this scenario, upland sites represent autumn/winter specialised sites.

Various commentators (Donahue and Lovis 2006; Pitts 1979; Rowley-Conwy 1994) have rightly highlighted the potential significant role of the coast for groups occupying Star Carr. It is likely that the early date for the occupation of the Vale of Pickering came about as a result of rapid colonisation by groups moving along the coast. The coast was also the main source of flint for groups using the Vale of Pickering, as well as other items, such as amber, while the canine remains from Seamer L also reveal a marine signature. However, there is unlikely to have been a consistent relationship with the coast throughout the entire time Star Carr was occupied. For example, there are possible indications that beach flint may have been exchanged rather than obtained directly, and this may reflect temporal changes in people's relationship to the coast. The morphology of Doggerland was undergoing rapid change, and the area to the east of Star Carr was undergoing inundation at around this time. It is likely to have been impossible to maintain any form of stable coastal settlement system in such an unstable area, and it is tempting to suggest the long-term focus on Star Carr as a fixed location in the landscape might represent a counterpoint to rapid transformations affecting familiar landscapes elsewhere (Conneller 2000).

Reynier (2005) has suggested that Star Carr groups were characterised by logistical mobility. This is a term coined by Lewis Binford (1980) to characterise groups that 'move resources to people', typically by use of a residential site occupied by the entire group in conjunction with more specialised sites, which are visited by a smaller group of people to extract seasonally restricted resources. This broad system seems to fit the evidence from Northern England. The use of similar flint sources may suggest contacts between groups using the Vale of Pickering, the North York Moors and the Central Pennines. It is reasonable, given similarities in tool forms and raw materials (Jacobi 1978a,), to suggest that the Star Carr-type sites on the North York Moors represent logistical sites generated by groups also visiting the Vale of Pickering. It should be pointed out though that Pointed Stone 2 and 3 appear rather less focused on gearing up for hunting than some sites in the Vale of Pickering. The essential tool assemblage at scatter 30, Seamer K, consists of 100% microliths, and numbers of microburins are nearly double those of microliths. This compares with 94.7% microliths and a microburin-to-microlith ratio of 1:1.75 at Pointed Stone 2 and 83.6% microliths and a microburin-to-microlith ratio of 1:1.04 at Pointed Stone 3. Binford (1978a,b) outlines the huge range of sites generated by a single group in a single season, with hunting occurring (amongst other activities) on a range of short-term and longer term sites occupied by a range of different people: From overnight camps occupied by male hunters to longer term seasonal 'lovers' camps' occupied by young couples. Given the range of tools and the quantities of lithic material on Pointed Stone 2 and 3, it seems reasonable to suggest they represent camp sites of moderate duration. Pointed Stone 2 and 3 are the only excavated sites amongst ten find-spots of Star Carr-type material, suggesting persistent use of the North York Moors. Further excavation may reveal greater variation in use of these areas, as suggested by reports of an extremely large Star Carr-type site near Osmotherley, on the western edge of the Moors, excavated in the 1990s (Lee Cherry pers. comm. 1995).

Star Carr-type sites in the Pennines also reveal variability, with Rushy Brow characterised by microliths and microburins and evidence for a broader range of activities at Warcock Hill South and Turnpike. While use of mainly glacial till material on the two Central Pennines sites suggests some connection with sites to the east, the use of chert at Rushy Brow indicates connections to the north or south, rather than the east. In addition, the site's location so far to the west on a western outlier of the Pennine Chain raises the possibility that this site has connections to the Lancashire coastal plain, the archaeology of which is not well known. Again, this variation may have a temporal dimension.

The current evidence indicates logistical use of the landscape by Star Carr groups, with sites of longer and shorter duration and with greater and lesser degrees of specialisation. Ethnographic accounts indicate northern latitude hunter-gatherers generate a wide range of sites and that seasonal movement varies on a year-by-year basis, and on the basis of personal decisions by individuals and family groups (Jochim 1991).

The variability evident in the Vale of Pickering and adjacent upland areas is likely to reflect the product of a variety of decisions and actions produced by a variety of groups and group members in a variety of seasons and over several hundred years. The evidence indicates archaeologists should not continue to attempt to reconstruct a single, time-averaged seasonal round for the earliest Mesolithic groups in Northern England.

Box 2.5 Flint sources in Mesolithic Northern England

Flint derives from chalk, and chalk deposits outcrop across Eastern England, in the north forming the Yorkshire and Lincolnshire Wolds. Wolds material varies from semi-translucent to opaque bluish grey or grey to white. It is often coarse and of relatively poor quality and contains numerous flaws, pinholes and fossils. The chalk plateau of the Wolds is made up of five different formations: The Flamborough, Burnham, Welton, Ferriby and the Rowe Chalk formations (Hopson 2005). Most are flint-less, but both the Burnham and Welton formations contain a number of siliciferous horizons, the Welton Formation containing nodular flint, and the Burnham Formation mainly tabular and semi-tabular flint (Henson 1982; Hopson 2005). The nodular form is of higher knapping quality, while the tabular form has a tendency to fracture along its natural planes.

Exposures of flint-bearing horizons are likely to have existed through erosion of the Wolds edge, particularly on its eastern side as Doggerland was inundated. Much of the material that can be recovered from the Wolds edge today is heavily frost-fractured and too poor for knapping. Mining for unaffected flint was not an option, even in the Neolithic, because Wolds chalk, unlike the chalk of Southern England, is very hard. One mechanism for obtaining undamaged Wolds material may have been through the erosional action of the numerous springs and streams, which originated on the Wolds edge and glacial action, which moved this material into major river systems, and Myers (1986) has noted that the cortex of Wolds nodules found on Deepcar Mesolithic sites suggests they were obtained from a fluvial source. Wolds flint was used infrequently by Star Carr groups, but was favoured by Deepcar groups in Northern England. It was also used in the Late and Final Mesolithic, where it has a strong association with four-sided microliths and is found as far northwest as Cumbia (Brown et al. in press).

Till flint can be found in the glacial deposits that blanket the east coast. This flint originally derives from chalk sources under the North Sea that have been eroded by glacial action. It varies considerably in colour from translucent brown, to speckled grey or red. It is generally of higher quality than Wolds material. While it can be obtained direct from the till, it often seems to have been collected from a further derived source most frequently as beach pebbles. The sea erodes the soft glacial till at a considerable rate, meaning that large quantities of pebble flint can be obtained from eastern beaches, especially in Yorkshire, though it becomes rarer and pebbles tend to be smaller in size further north. This material was favoured by Star Carr groups, who used it in large quantities, not just on sites close to the coast, but also inland in the Central Pennines. It is widely used in Eastern Scotland and Northeastern England throughout the Mesolithic.

8500 BC: Deepcar groups in the north

Around 8500 BC, microlith forms in Northern England began to change. Obliquely blunted points become elongated and retouch more oblique than previously. Retouch is often more extensive, often extending beyond the mid-way part of the microlith, to produce a partially backed point. Pieces with additional retouch on the leading edge, extremely rare in Star Carr-type assemblage, become more common. Elongated trapezes and large triangles are still very occasionally present (see Figure 1.3). Assemblages to the west of the Pennines appear to lack microliths with retouch on the leading edge (Myers 2020), though obliquely blunted points share a similar very oblique angle. In the course of the excavation of the site of Deepcar, South Yorkshire, Radley and Mellars (1964) noticed that the assemblage from this site was rather different from Star Carr, not simply in the presence of these different microliths forms, but also in terms of raw material. While Star Carr groups in the uplands of Northern England predominantly used east coast till flint, Deepcar groups employed material from the Yorkshire and Lincolnshire Wolds.

Dates for Star Carr-type sites, from the well-dated site of Star Carr, and a handful of less well-dated sites in the Vale of Pickering, fall before 8500 BC. The rather limited dates for sites with Deepcar and similar very oblique angled microliths (at Little Holtby, Windy Hill Farm and Greasby) indicate these broadly belong to the period 8500–8200 cal BC. This relationship is reinforced by stratigraphic evidence from Star Carr, where a handful of very oblique Deepcar-style microliths (though lacking retouch on the leading edge) have been found. Some of these have been found in the wetland, where they can be seen on stratigraphic grounds to belong to the later phases of activity at the site. Thus, while patterns are much more ambiguous in Southern England and South Wales (see chapter 3) in the north, Deepcar types seem to succeed Star Carr types with potentially little overlap.

Deepcar and assemblages with similar oblique-angled microliths are distributed rather more broadly across Northern England than Star Carr types and as far as Northwest Wales (Figure 2.18). In some areas, such as the North York Moors, Central Pennines and Lincolnshire Edge, both types can be found, but Deepcar assemblages are also found in new areas, which currently do not seem to have been favoured earlier: The Vales of York and Mowbray, the Southern Pennines, the Cheshire Plain, the Wirral and North Wales. Unlike Star Carr-type sites, Deepcar material does not seem to be present in Scotland, though it can be found in County Durham and Northumberland, at Hart, for example, near Crimdon on the Durham coast (Weyman 1984).

Little Holtby and the occupation of the Vale of Mowbray

The Vale of Mowbray, a northwards extension of the Vale of York, is one of the areas that was newly settled by Deepcar groups. This is a low-lying area between two adjacent uplands: The North York Moors to the east and the Yorkshire Dales to the west. The valley is carpeted with glacial till, and once held a number of meres and small lakes, relics of glacial meltwater. The Little Holtby site is located on a ridge of sand and gravel, the Leeming moraine, that would have provided a dry route through what would have been a boggy and waterlogged landscape (Speed et al. 2018). Immediately to the west, a lake, around 3 km in length, was once present

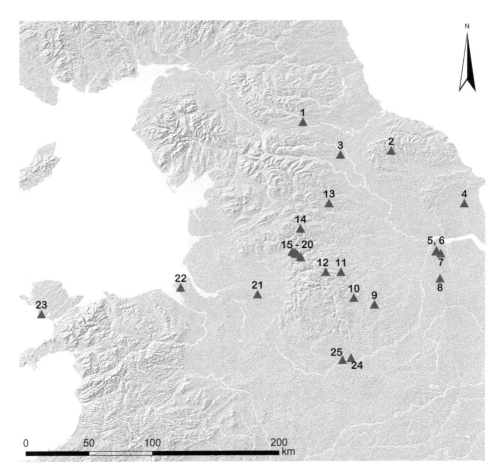

Figure 2.18 Deepcar-type sites in Northern England and North Wales. (1. Towler Hill, 2. Money Howe 1, 3. Little Holtby, 4. Brigham Hill, 5. Bagmoor, 6. Roxby Sands, 7. Risby Warren, 8. Willoughton A, 9. Whaley Rock Shelter, 10. Unstone 1, 11. Deepcar, 12. Mickleden 1–4, 13. Pike Low 1, 14. Nab Water, 15. Pule Hill Base, 16. Warcock Hill North, 17. Lominot 2, 3 and C, 18. White Hassocks 1 and 2, 19. Waystone Edge 1, 20. Windy Hill 3, 21. Tatton Mere, 22. Greasby, 23. Aberffraw/ Trwyn Ddu, 24. Swarkestone Lowes, 25. Potlock)

(Chatterton 2005). Palaeoenvironmental work around 10 km to the south at Snape Mires, a similar lake basin location, suggests closed birch woodlands were being replaced by hazel at the time of occupation, with sedges abundant and ferns growing in clearings (Bridgland et al. 2011).

Two phases of fieldwork have taken place at Little Holtby, both related to road-widening schemes focused on the adjacent A1. The first came in 1994, when trial trenching followed the recovery of lithic material during fieldwalking. In one of the trenches, just over 3000 lithic artefacts were recovered, the majority clustering in a 4 × 4 m area on the edge of a hollow, which was interpreted as a structure (Figure 2.19). Only two spits of this feature were excavated, and the finds were plotted by square metre only, but the steep fall-off between squares was seen to indicate a boundary (Chatterton 2005).

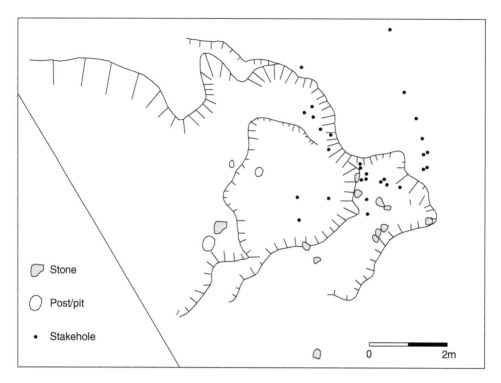

Figure 2.19 Plan of the excavations at Little Holtby (redrawn after Speed et al. 2018)

Further work on the site was undertaken in 2005, when the trench was reopened and enlarged (Speed et al. 2018). During this work, it became clear that the hollow located in 1994 was just one of a series of inter-cutting features. Given the constraints of the road scheme, the entire span of these could not be excavated. As previously, the lithic material was located on the very edge of one of these hollows. Beyond the hollows, the stratigraphic sequence consisted of ploughsoil directly overlying glacial sands and gravels. Mesolithic material was recovered both in the ploughsoil of the trench and during fieldwalking of the two fields nearest the trench. The material in the hollow thus appears to be the only remnant of a much larger site that has been truncated by ploughing. The excavators also uncovered a number of possible stakeholes and a couple of possible post-holes. Though some of the stakeholes formed lines and partial arcs, none were compatible with a structure focused on the hollow (ibid).

The lithic assemblage from Little Holtby was manufactured on Wolds flint, with the nearest chalk source lying 80 km to the south. Chatterton (2005, 111), however, notes that the cortex of the nodules suggest they come from a derived source, probably a river gravel, which given the paucity of rivers draining the Wolds and the direction of glacial movement, could suggest a source even further south. Scrapers (45) and microliths (103) are the main tool types recovered. A sieving programme during the 2005 excavation revealed large numbers of microburins, which outnumber microliths at a ratio of 1.5:1, indicating activity focused on gearing up for hunting. Other formal tools were present but rarer, including awls, burins, notches and microdenticulates; re-touched and utilised pieces were common (Speed et al. 2018).

Given the constraints imposed by the scale of the excavation, the excavators offer a number of possible interpretations for the features, as either a natural hollow, a tree throw or humanly constructed. The distribution of lithic material might suggest a tree throw, given the fact that small clusters form a banana-shaped arc along the edge of the hollow, also associated with a large lump of clay. Similar distributions were noted at Farnham where 'pit houses' are now usually interpreted as tree throws (see Box 4.8). However the possible presence of stakeholes and post-holes might also indicate human modification. Importantly, two radiocarbon dates were obtained, the first in Northern England for a Deepcar assemblage in recent times. Two charred hazelnuts, from the lower and upper fills of the main hollow yielded very similar measurements of 8450–8285 cal BC (9141 ± 31 BP; SUERC-67553) and 8470–8290 cal BC (9173 ± 31 BP; SUERC-67554).

Chatterton's (2005) survey of the Vale of Mowbray shows that Little Holtby is not an isolated site. Fieldwalking of fields on the northern and eastern shore of the lake to the west of the site revealed a number of areas of Early Mesolithic occupation. Three concentrations, associated with Early Mesolithic microliths and the knapping of Wolds flint, were found on the eastern side of the lake, within a few hundred metres of the site at Little Holtby. A fourth site was located on the northern shore of the lake, of mixed date, but also including Early Mesolithic material. Little Holtby thus seems part of a broader complex of sites mainly located on higher, drier ground overlooking a lake.

From the Wolds...

Given their choice of raw materials, Deepcar sites close to the Wolds might be expected, and indeed, several sites are known. Most are collections of lithic material from eroding sands along the Lincolnshire Edge immediately to the west of the chalk: At Manton Warren, Risby Warren 1 and Willoughton A. Another major site is known at Brigham Hill, 8 km south and east of the Wolds, where Mesolithic material was found during gravel extraction (Manby 1966; Radley 1969). Much of the site was removed by quarrying, though lithics were recovered through sieving spoilheaps and a small excavation recovered in situ material. The site was located at 15 m OD on a hill of sand and gravel emerging from the low clay lands of Holderness. The hill commands clear views to the south and west over the wetlands and the river Hull. A moderate-size lithic assemblage of nearly 5000 pieces was recovered, with microliths and scrapers common and smaller numbers of burins. The assemblage is dominated by Wolds flint (92%), with a smaller proportion of good-quality till flint used. The till cores were worked down; the Wolds cores remained relatively large (Manby 1966), and an unworked nodule of Wolds flint was also present. These patterns suggest exploitation focused on local Wolds sources.

Myers (1986, 2015) has studied patterns of raw material use by Deepcar groups across Northern England. His analysis indicates that the patterns at Brigham are indicative of Lincolnshire Edge sites more generally. Proportions of Wolds flint are high, ranging from 81% at Willoughton A to 90% at Risby Warren I. This work also investigated Deepcar assemblages in a range of geographical situations: Misterton Carr close to the river Trent and 40 km from the Wolds; Deepcar itself, on the eastern edge of the Pennines, 70 km away; and a range of Central and Southern Pennine sites, around 80–90 km from the chalk (see below). However, Myers found no drop-off in percentages of Wolds material used at sites a considerable distance from the source. Wolds flint comprised between 80 and 100% of all assemblages analysed, whether they were from sites on the Lincolnshire edge, along the Trent (40 km distant), on the edge of the Pennines (70 km distant) or in the Central Pennines (80–90 km away). Myers did, though, discover some differences in the state in which material was imported to these various sites. At Misterton Carr on the Trent, a series of large cortical flakes were recovered, indicative of the early stages of preparation. A series of large pre-formed cores were also recovered from the site. While not so close to the Wolds itself, this site is located close to glacial till deposits that contain large nodules of Wolds flint. Preformed cores and large cortical flakes are not found amongst the Pennine assemblages, indicating that at these more distant sites cores were imported as prepared or partially reduced pieces. Myers suggests this patterning is the product of a fairly standardised mobility pattern by groups inhabiting this region, suggesting movement from the Trent Valley lowlands into the Pennine uplands.

...to the Pennines

Deepcar-type assemblages are more common in the Pennines than Star Carr sites. Major excavated Deepcar-type sites are represented in the Central Pennines at Waystone Edge, Windy Hill 3, Warcock Hill North (Buckley 1924), Pule Hill Base (Stonehouse 1992) and Lominot sites 2, 3 and C (Spikins 1999) and in the Southern

---

Box 2.6   Deepcar

Located at c.150 m OD on a spur overlooking the confluence of the rivers Don and Porter, the site of Deepcar was excavated in 1962 (Radley and Mellars 1964). Here, three hearths were located, partly surrounded by exotic stones. Water-worn quartzite pebbles formed a line to the north of the hearths, while an arc of rounded gritstone on the edge of a hollow encircled two of the hearths (Figure 2.20). This may represent a dug feature or an elaborated natural hollow. Given that quarrying truncates this possible feature and there are areas of disturbance, it is difficult to understand the significance of this evidence. A series of tent rings with associated stones scavenged to create hearths appears likely, though a dug structure or elaborated natural feature is also possible.

The area of the hollow corresponds with the greatest concentration of lithic material. In all, an extremely dense assemblage was recovered, numbering over 23,000 pieces from an area of 70 m². Activities appear focused on microlith production, with microburins very common (n = 102), as were microliths (68 examples, almost all broken). Other tools are rarer: 37 scrapers, 21 notches and eight burins. Notches were relatively common, which Myers (2015) suggests may be related to arrow shaft manufacture. The assemblage is dominated by Wolds material, indicating connections to the east. All evidence suggests Deepcar is a camp dedicated to gearing up for hunting activities, probably accompanied by hide processing. The lithic densities and arrangement of stones suggest a repeatedly occupied camp.

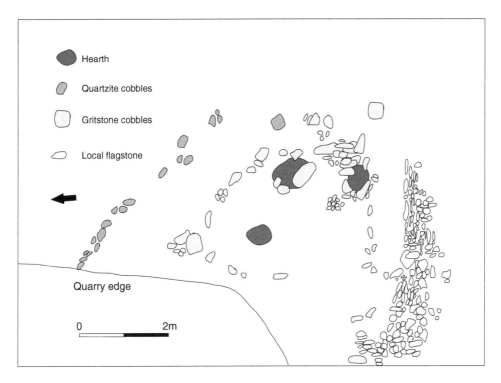

Hearth

Quartzite cobbles

Gritstone cobbles

Local flagstone

Quarry edge

0   2m

Figure 2.20 Plan of excavations at Deepcar (redrawn after Radley and Mellars 1964)

Pennines by sites at Deepcar (see Box 2.6) Mickleden Edge and Pike Low 1 (Radley and Marshall 1965). Several of the Central Pennine sites were excavated by Francis Buckley (see Box 1.1). Lominot 2 and 3 appear to have consisted of adjacent scatters or 'two round emplacements' (Petch 1924), although possibly representing a single occupation. Though microlith dominated, these two scatters also yielded a variety of different tool types, scrapers in particular being relatively common (see Table 2.7), while cores and microburins demonstrate core reduction and microlith production activities. Further small-scale excavation at Lominot (site C) was undertaken by Penny Spikins as part of the March Hill Mesolithic project (Spikins 1999), where a 15 m² trench surrounded by additional test pits were excavated. The material recovered was of mixed Early and Late Mesolithic date, but differences in raw material use mean some Early Mesolithic activities involving microlith production and burin use could be discerned. Raw material quantities appear similar in all three Lominot scatters: Wolds material dominates, with a smaller percentage of clear brown flint. However, chert, which was present in very small quantities at Lominot 2 and 3, is absent from trench C.

Other nearby sites of Deepcar type include Pule Hill Base and Windy Hill, situated roughly two miles south and north of Lominot, respectively. Pule Hill Base was excavated in 1983 by Pat Stonehouse (1992). This excavation yielded a large and dense assemblage of 7439 pieces of flint. Though proportions of the different raw materials (see Table 2.8) were remarkably similar to those of Lominot 2 and 3, activity patterns were rather different. Microliths are most common at Pule Hill Base, though scrapers

Table 2.7 Essential tools from Deepcar sites

Site	Microliths	Scrapers	Burins	Axes	Micro-denticulates	Microburin ratio
Deepcar	58.6	31.9	6.9	0.9	0.9	1.42
Lominot 2	52.5	36.8	10.5	0	0	–
Lominot 3	58.6	41.4	0	0	0	–
Nabb Water	64.4	25.3	1.1	0	9.2	0.25
Pule Hill Base	76.2	16.9	0	0	6.9	0.04
Warcock Hill N.	60.1	32.3	5.1	0	2	0.37
Windy Hill	50.8	36.9	12.3	0	0	0.69

Table 2.8 Proportions of raw materials used at Pennine Deepcar sites

Site	Wolds%	Till Flint%	Chert %
Deepcar	95.9	0.6	3.5
Lominot 2 and 3	92.0	5.0	1.0
Pike Low I	99.2	0.8	0
Pule Hill Base	94.0	4.5	0.7
Warcock Hill North	97.0	2.0	1.0
White Hill I	95.0	5.0	0
Windy Hill	94.0	2.0	4.0

are also well-represented (see Table 2.7). The assemblage is unusual in that though 99 Deepcar-type microliths were recovered, the site yielded only four microburins. The deposition of microliths at the site thus appears unrelated to their manufacture, and if they represent pieces discarded during retooling, the replacement elements must have been manufactured elsewhere. The microliths may well represent cached material.

Windy Hill 3 at 380 m asl on the western edge of the Pennines, with views extending far over the Cheshire Plain (Figure 2.21), was excavated by Francis Buckley in 1922–1923. Here a more balanced assemblage was recovered (Table 2.7). Though microliths are again most common, scrapers are well-represented and burins more frequent than at other Pennine sites. The ratio of microliths to microburins is also more even, indicating on-site microlith manufacture as well as discard. Raw material proportions are very similar to the other Deepcar-type sites (Table 2.6), with Wolds material dominating and smaller amounts of brown translucent flint and minimal quantities of black chert.

Early Mesolithic Deepcar sites are generally much larger in size than both the earlier Star Carr-type sites and the subsequent Late Mesolithic scatters. Pule Hill Base has been estimated at 250 m² (Stonehouse 1992) and appears to represent one super-dense concentration of material. Lithic production appears so frequent an activity at the site that individual knapping scatters have been obscured. Stonehouse (1992) notes that this type of site may not be unusual, as several such sites (e.g. Pule Hill North, White Hassocks I and II and Windy Hill) have yielded lithic artefacts in their thousands. At Waystone Edge, Deepcar-type material has been recovered in erosion patches extending for around 300 m (Poole 2020). Smaller sites are represented: At Warcock Hill North, four scatters each around 3.6 m in diameter were located (Myers 2015), while

Figure 2.21 View from Windy Hill towards the Windy Hill Farm site and to the Cheshire and
South Lancashire Plains below (copyright Brian Howcroft)

in the Southern Pennines, Mickleden Edge sites 1, 2 and 3 were all small scatters
around 3 m in diameter (Radley and Marshall 1965).

Though the Pennine Deepcar sites tend to have more microliths than other tools, their
status as 'upland hunting camps' is not unproblematic. A broad range of other tools are
also represented, and though such incidences are usually explained as 'boredom redu-
cing activities' whilst awaiting prey (e.g. Legge and Rowley-Conwy 1988), the activities
represented in the Pennines appear more varied and the sites more substantial than
other potential hunting camps (e.g. Barton et al. 1995). In general, numbers of microliths at Pennine Deepcar sites are equalled by the combined numbers of scrapers and
burins. As Myers (1986) notes, scrapers and burins can be resharpened and repaired;
microliths cannot. Furthermore, several microliths make up a single tool. If these differential resharpening practises are taken into consideration, most of the assemblages
discussed appear more balanced. Scrapers are particularly abundant at several of the
sites discussed (see Table 2.7) and are also found in large numbers at Pike Low 1
(Radley and Mellars 1964) and Waystone Edge Hassocks site 1 (Stonehouse 1992).
Burins are rarer, with Windy Hill being a notable exception. Though this is the case for
almost all Early Mesolithic sites except Star Carr, it may be particularly true for the
Pennines (Petch 1924, 19). It is worth noting the difference between the Pennine sites
and Money Howe on the North York Moors, which fits much better a hunting site
profile, with 115 microliths but only three scrapers and three burins (Spratt et al. 1976).

The Pennine sites thus appear to represent visits from relatively substantial groups
associated with the procurement and subsequent processing of particular resources,
possibly occurring at a particular season of the year. Jacobi (1978a,) argues that sites

lacking burins may represent summer activities when antler was not available. However, burins are present in numbers at Windy Hill, and a certain amount of variability is present in the manufacturing and depositionary activities represented at the Pennine sites. Myers (1986) offers an alternative suggestion that these sites may be autumn hunting camps, located to take advantage of the concentration of deer in more open areas during the rut. Reynier (2005) has suggested a shift in mobility strategies amongst Deepcar groups. He suggests that rather than having a system of logistical sites tethered to a residential base as was the case for Star Carr groups, people practised what is known as residential mobility (Binford 1980). In this system, people use resources in the vicinity of their residential site, and when these are diminished, all group members move to a new area to establish a new base camp. Reynier relates this new system of mobility to increasing density of woodland, which made animal movements less predictable, leading to a shift from intercept to encounter hunting. This may have been less of an issue in the Pennine uplands, which would have been still open at this time, but it fits the evidence from lithic assemblages in the region, which show a lack of specialisation.

Northwest England

The Early Mesolithic appears to be much rarer west of the Pennine chain. Microlith types differ slightly from Deepcar types, in that they lack retouch on the leading edge and draw on different sources of raw material (Myers 2020). There are a handful of important sites, at Greasby and Thurstaston Dungeon on the Wirral, Tatton Mere in Cheshire, and further north, above Morecambe Bay, two caves: Bart's Shelter and Kent's Bank Cavern (Figure 2.1), the latter yielding the only Early Mesolithic human remains from the north. These two caves now overlook Morecambe Bay, but in the Early Mesolithic the sea may have been up to 20 km to the west (Smith et al. 2013). From Bart's Shelter an assemblage dominated by microliths was recovered (Jacobi archive). Microliths are also present at Kent's Bank Cavern, where a human femur was recently dated to between 8350 and 8245 cal BC (9100 ± 35; SUERC-35295) (Smith et al. 2013). Early excavations recovered 43 fragments of disarticulated human bones from the interior of the cave, most representing fragments of a skull, with five further cranial bones, two humeri, a radius, ulna, femur and phalanx. These seem to represent the remains of a minimum of three individuals: Probably two adults and a child, the latter represented only by a deciduous canine. Given the widespread proclivity for depositing human remains in caves throughout Prehistory, there can be no guarantee that these all date to the same period.

In Cheshire, Tatton Mere was excavated between 1982 and 1985. The site is located in Tatton Park on the edge of an artificial lake, a landscaping feature created by damming a small stream. The waters of the mere had eroded part of the site, but the remainder lay on its northern bank, with one major lithic concentration recorded. The lithic assemblage, at c.8000 pieces, indicates a moderate-sized Mesolithic site, though much of this material comes from ploughsoil/colluvium that overlies the Mesolithic layers and includes some Late Mesolithic microliths. Tools are fairly evenly balanced between microliths (41) and scrapers (45). A small, but broad range of other tools are also present, including awls, microdenticulates, truncations and utilised pieces. One burin appears to be figured, and an axe sharpening flake indicates this tool was once present, while seven microburins indicate tool manufacture (Higham and Cane 1999). On the Wirral sandstone ridge at Greasby Copse, three dates on burnt hazelnuts cluster in the mid-ninth millennium BC (Myers 2017). Greasby, along with Thurstaston Dungeon, is one of two large Early Mesolithic sites in this area. Both seem fairly substantial settlements with lithics found over an area of 200 m², a wide range of formal tools, and the presence at Greasby of stone-lined pits (Hodgson and Brennand 2006, 27). In one of these pits, a cache of three blades and two microliths were found under a band of pebbles (Cowell 1992, 8); other pits were lined with stones. The Early Mesolithic material in Cheshire has a strong association with sandstone ridges, not just on the Wirral ridge but also on the dramatic sandstone ridge at Alderley Edge, and at Hilbre Point, now at the mouth of the Dee. The presence of banded chert at Greasby, Thurstaston and Hilbre suggests connections between sites in Cheshire and North Wales.

North Wales

Several sites of Early Mesolithic type are known from North Wales, and three, Trwyn Ddu/Aberffraw on Anglesey (White 1978) and Rhuddlan E and M, Denbighshire (Quinnell and Blockley 1994), have associated radiocarbon dates. These, which range from 7940 to 6530 BC (see Table 2.9), seem rather too late for the associated microliths. All, however, are on bulked charcoal or hazelnut on sites with significant later activity (David 2007), and thus may represent the aggregate of activities of different dates. While obliquely blunted points are common, including those with retouch on the leading edge (unlike those in Northwest England), all three sites have microliths (curve-backed pieces and lanceolates) that in other geographical contexts indicate Late Deepcar or even Middle Mesolithic activities, meaning that these dates cannot be entirely discounted. However, there is clearly a problem with the Trwyn Ddu measurements; HAR-1194 and Q-1385 are not in stratigraphic sequence, while HAR-1193 had a low collagen yield. The Rhuddlan dates are from two features: BM-691 comes from a discrete lens within a pit, which has been clipped at the edge by a later ditch. BM-822 comes from material collected throughout a pit, which has been extensively disturbed by later activity and is thus more likely to be suspect. These dates are complicated by the presence, just 6 km away of the Prestatyn (Bryn Newydd) site, which has two measurements on fragments of hazelnuts associated with an assemblage containing Middle Mesolithic variably lateralised narrow scalene triangles. The dates from Prestatyn are almost identical to Rhuddlan E, while Rhuddlan M probably post-dates the other two sites (see Figure 2.22). Unless one were to invoke the spectre of specialised coastal and inland groups, each using different microlith forms (a scenario frequently posited

Table 2.9 Radiocarbon dates associated with Early Mesolithic microliths in North Wales

Site	Lab No.	Material	C14 age	Calibrated age (95% confidence)
Rhuddlan E	BM-691	Charred hazelnuts	8739 ± 36 BP	7940–7610 cal BC
Rhuddlan M	BM-822	Charred hazelnuts	8528 ± 73 BP	7730–7460 cal BC
Trwyn Du	HAR-1194	Charred hazelnuts	8590 ± 90 BP	7940–7485 cal BC
Trwyn Du	Q-1385	Charred hazelnuts	8460 ± 150 BP	7935–7080 cal BC
Trwyn Du	HAR-1193	Charred hazelnuts	7980 ± 140 BP	7315–6530 cal BC

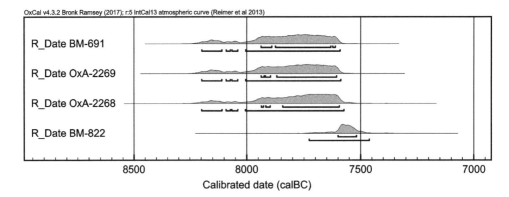

OxCal v4.3.2 Bronk Ramsey (2017); r:5 IntCal13 atmospheric curve (Reimer et al 2013)

R_Date BM-691

R_Date OxA-2269

R_Date OxA-2268

R_Date BM-822

8500   8000   7500   7000

Calibrated date (calBC)

Figure 2.22 Probability distributions from Rhuddlan E and M (respectively top and bottom), plotted against those dating the Late Mesolithic assemblage from Prestatyn (Bryn Newydd) (middle)

but usually later found to be erroneous) these dates suggest the dating of at least Rhuddlan M is flawed.

The Mesolithic evidence at Rhuddlan consists of series of Mesolithic scatters on a bluff on the eastern bank of the River Clwyd at Rhuddlan. These had been extensively disturbed by later activity so that most of the lithic assemblage was recovered from later features. Some remnant patches of an Early Holocene buried soil had survived, and Mesolithic material was recovered from this and a series of hollows. While Mesolithic-age lithics were found at several sites, at only three (sites A, E and M) were Mesolithic features or buried soils located. The most prolific of these sites was site E, where the Early Holocene soil was present, though uneven, through most of the area. Three Mesolithic features were also located within a few metres of each other: Two pits and J104, a hollow measuring 2.40 m by 1.40 m and 0.50 m deep. The hollow contained over 1000 lithic artefacts (Table 2.10) and burnt hazelnuts, which produced a date of 7940 to 7610 cal BC (see Table 2.9). Site M consisted of an evaluation trench, 5 m wide. In the southern part of this, two complex clusters of Mesolithic features were located, cut through a buried soil. The southernmost cluster consisted of a shallow pit or hollow, at least 1.7 m in diameter,

Table 2.10 Assemblages from undisturbed Mesolithic contexts at Rhuddlan

	Rhuddlan A	*Rhuddlan E*	*Rhuddlan M*
Awl	0	6	2
Microlith	8	71	22
Fabricator	1	0	0
Notch	0	4	0
Scraper	3	51	15
Retouched/utilised	2	95	16
Axe flake	0	4	1
Microburin	0	9	4
Cores	0	109	20

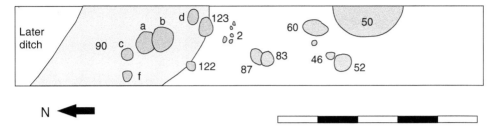

N ◀

Figure 2.23 The southern part of the Rhuddlan M trench, showing Mesolithic features (redrawn after Quinnell and Blockely 1994)

extending beyond the trench edge and filled with reddish, possibly burnt, sand. On its edge was a cluster of pits or post-holes (Figure 2.23). This may be a structural feature. The northern cluster also consists of a larger pit or hollow (M90), at least 3 m wide, which truncated two earlier pits. There were also six small pits or hollows in its base, which contained charcoal. The upper parts of the feature were truncated by a later Prehistoric gulley. M90 contained large quantities of worked flint, an engraved pebble (see Box 2.7) and charred hazelnut shells. A radiocarbon date of 7730–7460 cal BC (see Table 2.9) was obtained for this feature. At site A, the buried soil did not survive, but three Mesolithic pits were located, one of which was over a metre deep and contained 101 pieces of worked flint and chert. At sites S and T, no in situ material was located but lithic artefacts and an engraved pebble were recovered from each. Small quantities of lithics were also recovered at site V (Quinnell and Blockley 1994).

Box 2.7   Engraved pebbles

Rhuddlan is unique for the large number of engraved pebbles found. Six were recovered, across four different sites, and pebbles were only examined systematically following the first discovery, two years into the excavation, meaning further examples may have been missed on two of the larger Mesolithic sites A and E. Only one was recovered from a feature, the possible structure M90 on site M. The others came probably from the buried soil at site E, and later soils or ploughsoil at sites M (1), S (1) and T (2) (Quinnell and Blockley 1994).

The pebbles were recovered from a variety of different contexts. All the Rhuddlan examples were made from water-worn pebbles of micaceous sandstone, most likely obtained from the bed of the Clwyd. All engravings were made on elongate pebbles, using a flint blade, apart from one example from site T, which is made on a trapezoid block, seemingly chosen for its flat surface (Berridge and Roberts 1994). This is the only complete example and shows a techtiform design (see Figure 2.24). Similar designs in Upper Palaeolithic art have been interpreted as hut structures, though this interpretation is controversial. Jacobi (in Berridge 1994) has suggested an alternative: That the design may represent a fish trap.

Figure 2.24 Engraved pebble from Rhuddlan T with techtiform design (copyright National Museum of Wales)

The remaining pebbles, all elongated forms, are broken, meaning that the full design cannot be understood; however, they seem quite varied. SF1 (Figure 2.25) an elongated, square-sectioned pebble carries a series of penniform designs on each of its four faces. SF2 (Figure 2.26) shows cross-hatching, an infilled band and the base of a series of infilled v or w-shaped forms, the tops of

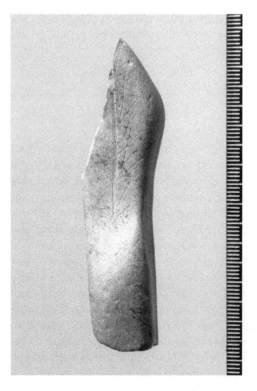

Figure 2.25 Penniform designs on SF1 (copyright National Museum of Wales)

Figure 2.26 Designs on SF2 (copyright National Museum of Wales)

which are no longer present due to breakage of this pebble. These may be the basal parts of infilled lenticular designs. These are found in the Southern Scandinavian Mesolithic, where some of the less stylised examples indicate that these represent human figures. The SF2 pebble is curiously reminiscent of some of the designs engraved in the chalky cortex of an engraved flint nodule from Holmegaard V in Zealand, Denmark. This nodule is similar in shape to SF2 and is engraved with a stylised human figure. The very form of the nodule has been argued to symbolise maleness (Fischer 1974). This flint nodule was knapped into pieces following engraving so that designs, which may have represented secret knowledge, could not be read (Conneller 2012). A similar concern at Rhuddlan may explain the breakage of these elongated pieces, which may have carried designs that were not appropriate for certain people to read. Similar arguments have been made for designs on stone plaquettes made during the Magdalenian at sites such as Gonnersdorf (Bosinski et al. 2001), which were rapidly engraved, then broken and discarded in domestic contexts. Here, the engravings were not 'art' to be admired, but instances where the act of engraving itself was significant. The Rhuddlan engraved pebbles may have had a longer currency, as there appears to be wear, which may represent the passage of time, or an episode of use between the different actions that created the cross-hatched area on SF2. The pebbles may have circulated for some time before being destroyed.

Engraved pebbles are known from other Mesolithic contexts, but are rare. Another example is known from North Wales: A round pebble, engraved on both sites from Llandegai, Gwynedd (Lynch and Musson 2001), a site primarily known for its Neolithic evidence. The only diagnostic Mesolithic elements in this area of the site are Late Mesolithic rather than early. A possible example comes from Trwyn Du, which has eight very faint sub-parallel lines along it, and in form and breakage is almost identical to SF2 from Rhuddlan (White 1978). Further examples with a few parallel lines come from a rather more distant contexts at Camas Daraich on Skye (Wickham-Jones et al. 2004), Portland I and Culverwell in Dorset (Palmer 1977) and Hudder Field, Trevose Head and Poldowrian in Cornwall (Jones et al. 2019, see chapter 5). This group are Late Mesolithic in date and consist of incised elongated pebbles, mostly of a similar range of materials to those used as bevel-ended tools (Figure 5.42). Similar examples are known in Normandy (Ghesquière et al. 2000). There is more of a continuum in this group from incisions due to use to more elaborate patterns of incisions.

Mesolithic groups made extensive use of a local chert (often called Gronant chert) that outcrops either side of the Vale of Clwyd. This comes in a number of forms: A distinctive black-banded chert, a finer black chert, a lustrous grey chert and a white chert. Beach pebble flint was also used, indicating a relationship to the coast. Though chert is more common on the sites, flint was preferred for the production of formal tools. All three sites where in situ Mesolithic material was recovered show broadly similar quantities of formal tools, with assemblages microliths and scrapers most common. Miscellaneous retouched and utilised tools were common at site E, indicating a variety of processing activities (Berridge 1994).

Pit J104 is particularly remarkable in the large lithic assemblage recovered: 1604 pieces came from this feature, with 3626 coming from the buried soil and 3110 from residual contexts on this site. Also found within the pit was a lens of charred hazelnut shells. While this feature could represent a structure, there are no obvious structural elements, such as posts or stakeholes. It may alternatively represent a midden. If so, lithic material is found in rather different quantities than in the buried soil. Microliths outnumber scrapers 3:1 in the pit, whereas in the buried soil the ratio is even. While small elements such as microliths might be expected to be more easily located in a feature than in a buried soil (sieving was not undertaken), the figures for microburins suggest this was not the case. Thus, the waste products from certain activities – perhaps symbolically charged hunting episodes – may have been disposed of in different ways. Microliths were also more common in feature M90, outnumbering scrapers 2:1 (Berridge 1994). This feature is more likely to be structural, but truncation by later features prevents full understanding of the sequence of associated features and how it was used. The material found within it could relate to its use as a structure, or as a midden, post-abandonment.

Trwyn Ddu is further west on Anglesey, though at the time of occupation, sea-level would have been around -20 msl (assuming the actual date of the site is more in the region of 8200 BC). The Menai Straights would have been entirely terrestrial, and Anglesey a peninsula. Trwyn Du would have over looked the valley of the Avon

Ffraw, in a landscape dominated by hazel and birch, with willow in wetland areas (Roberts et al. 2011). Now located on the southwest corner of Anglesey, lithic material has been erroding from a cliff edge overlooking the Aberffraw sands for many decades. Houlder excavated an area along the cliff edge in 1955, including part of a Bronze Age cairn, Trwyn Du, and further work was undertaken by Ireland (Jacobi archive, British Museum). Both located a lithic assemblage in which microliths were dominant, with smaller numbers of scrapers, burins, awls and utilised pieces. Charcoal and charred hazelnuts were present. Further Mesolithic material was located during further excavations of the Bronze Age cairn in 1974 by the Gwynedd Archaeological Trust (White 1978).

Under layer 4, associated with the Bronze Age cairn, was a dark soil containing charcoal flecks, hazelnuts and flint, chert and stone artefacts. Two small pits, which cut into the underlying clay, were located: F16 containing charred hazelnuts, and F17 containing worked flint. A probably natural hollow F13 contained concentrations of hazelnuts and two radiocarbon dates (Table 2.9). Combining the excavations of Houlder and GAT provides a tool total of 163 microliths, of which the majority are obliquely blunted points, 101 scrapers, a burin and two axes, as well as many utilised flakes and blades (Lynch 1970; White 1978; Jacobi archive). Several bevel-ended tools were recovered, of which two appear to have lines faintly incised. One of these is very similar in form and breakage patterns to one of the Rhuddlan pebbles and in form to the Nab Head venus (White 1978, Figure 19.1), though this needs to be confirmed by further study.

Favoured locations for these North Welsh sites seem to be on slightly higher ground overlooking rivers. The Rhuddlan sites are just above the floodplain of the river Clwyd, while Trwyn Ddu lies above the Avon Ffraw. A second Anglesey Early Mesolithic site at Penmon is situated above the water course that would have flowed northeast through what is now the Menai Straits. A similar location was noted for Early Mesolithic surface scatters at Hilbre on the Wirral, just above the Dee, and only 20 km from Rhuddlan (Jacobi archive). The evidence from Rhuddlan shows sites with fairly consistent microlithic assemblages and idiosyncratic engraved pebbles (Figures 2.24–2.26, see Box 2.7) extend across a stretch of land over 300 m in length. This suggests a 'persistent' place, probably repeatedly reoccupied over several decades by a single group or related groups. These occupations would have taken place within a time of social memory, rather than the intermittent reoccupation due to particular structural affordances – by groups widely separated in time, as at many other persistent places (e.g. Barton et al. 1995). Early Mesolithic material has also been recovered in the form of isolated microliths from caves in the region, for example, at Corkscrew cave and Ogof Pant-y-Wennol on the Orme and at Ffynnon Beuno cave, Denbighshire. Early Mesolithic material is also present in open air upland locations, for example, at Brenig 44 (Lynch 1993). In contrast to the larger, denser sites above the rivers, these are likely to represent places of transient visits.

3   The Early Mesolithic colonisation of the South

Deepcar and the Early Boreal Mesolithic 9300–8200 BC

More so than the north, the landscape of Southern Britain was radically different from today (Figures 2.2 and 3.1). While the sea was close to Star Carr, Early Mesolithic groups in Southeast England inhabited a fluvial landscape; the coast was distant, perhaps unknown to many. Throughout the period covered by this chapter, the landscape stretched east, unbroken, as far as Siberia. The Thames flowed into Doggerland, where it was joined by most of the major Northern European rivers. This massive Channel river turned south, crashed through the Dover Gorge and flowed west into a huge marine embayment, which at 9000 cal BC, would have stood, broadly, somewhere south of Kent. By 8500 cal BC, the sea had worked its way eastward of the Dover Straits, creating a narrow marine inlet just east of Norfolk (Figure 3.2). In Southwest England, people would have inhabited an area between two large estuaries: To the south was the Channel embayment, and in the west the bay of the Bristol Channel, the shoreline of which stretched between Tenby and Bude. An initially fairly open landscape was colonised by stands of birch, then by open woodlands of pine, which appear to have played a more important role than in Northern England. This was the landscape of the first settlers; however, much of the Early Mesolithic occupation of Southern England occurred after hazel had become an important component of the local woodland. The vegetation of Southern England also varied across regions: The chalk plateau may have remained fairly open, while in the marshy riverlands that people favoured, reeds, willow and dogwood grew.

People followed the rivers, moving into Southeast England from the marshy lands of Doggerland and the river valleys of now continental Europe, camping on sand and gravel islands in the wetlands. There appears to have been a more gradual colonisation in the south than there was in the north, where the long-term use of the Vale of Pickering was rapidly established. Pioneer groups moved into Southeast England from around 9300 BC. Only a few sites seem to belong to the following half a millennium, and much of this evidence appears relatively ephemeral. What material exists comes from the Thames and its tributaries (Figure 3.3): A scatter of lithic and faunal material at Eton Rowing Course on the Thames, an isolated barbed point from a gravel pit at Waltham Abbey on the river Lea and an episode of enigmatic wetland deposition from a small pool at Thatcham IV/V on the Kennet. This latter is likely to be associated with a residential site, though the nearby dryland areas Thatcham I/III are poorly dated, so the scale of this early occupation is unknown. The patinated series at Thatcham III has been argued to be earlier than the non-patinated series on stratigraphic grounds (Reynier 2005), so it may be related to this early occupation.

DOI: 10.4324/9781003228103-3

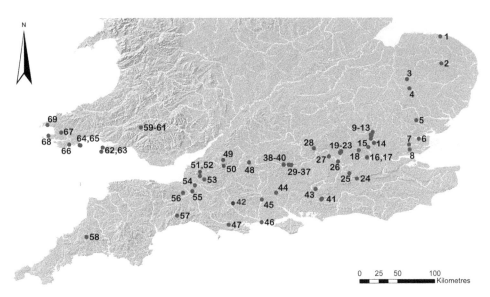

Figure 3.1 Sites discussed in the chapter (1. Kelling Heath, 2. Great Melton, 3. Wangford/
Lakenheath Warren, 4. Lackford Heath. 5. White Colne, 6. Maylandsea, 7.
Hullbridge, 8. Dawes Heath. 9. Stanstead Abbots 2, 10. Broxbourne 106, 11.
Broxbourne 104, 12. Broxbourne 102, 13. Fisher's Green (Waltham Abbey), 14.
Hillwood, High Beech, 15. Ikea Site/Meridian Point, 16. West Heath, 17. B and Q
site, 18. Marlborough Grove, 19. Church Lammas, 20. Eton Rowing Course, 21.
Kimble Farm, 22. Three Ways Wharf, 23. Cowley Mill Rd, 24. Sandstone, Iver,
25.100 Acre Pit, 26. Reigate Heath, 27. Fetcham, 28. Thatcham III, 29. Thatcham
III (patinated series), 30. Thatcham II, 31. Thatcham IV, 32. Thatcham V, 33.
Thatcham I, 34. Thatcham Sewage Works, 35. Greenham Dairy Farm/Faraday Rd.
36. Victoria Park, 37. Marsh Benham, 38. Wawcott XV, 39. Wawcott XXX, 40.
Selmeston, 41. Iping Common, 42. Iwerne Minster, 43. Oakhanger V/VII, 44.
Bossington, 45. Downton, 46. Hengistbury Head, 47. Winfrith Heath, 48. Cherhill.
49. Tog Hill, 50. Hot Spring and Sacred Spring, Bath, 51. Aveline's Hole, 52.
Gough's Cave, 53. Badger Hole, 54. Shapwick, 55. Greylake, Middlezoy, 56.
Greenway Farm, 57. Telegraph Cottage, 58. Dozmary Pool, 59. Waun Fignen Felen
6, 60. Waun Fignen Felen 8, 61. Burry Holms, 62. Worm's Head, 63. Daylight Rock,
64. Valley Field, 65. Freshwater East, 66. Palmerston Farm, 67. The Nab Head I, 68.
Penpant)

It was probably only around 8800 cal BC that the Early Mesolithic occupation
became more fully established, with reliable dates coming from Lackford Heath,
Three Ways Wharf and a series of sites in the Kennet Valley. Settlement was still
primarily focused on rivers in the southeast, but adjacent hills and plateaus were increasingly visited. Dates from southwest England and south Wales, both from settlement evidence and human remains, tend to fall after 8500 cal BC. These western
sites appear in more varied locations, from sandy islands within wetlands to upland
ridges and plateaus. This expansion in settlement location and the association of
particular landscape features with the ancestors appears to represent a shift to the
making of more permanent relationships with place.

The distinction between Star Carr and Deepcar assemblages (see chapter 1) was
based on work in Northern England (Radley and Mellars 1964). Reynier (2005) has

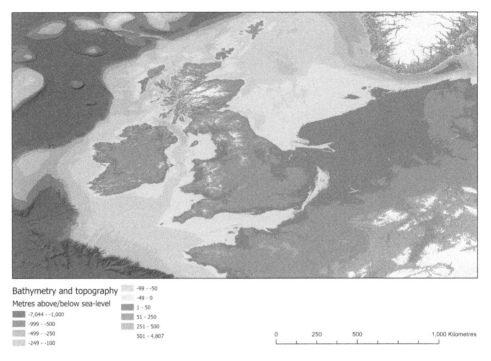

Bathymetry and topography
Metres above/below sea-level

-7,044 - -1,000
-999 - -500
-499 - -250
-249 - -100

-99 - -50
-49 - 0
1 - 50
51 - 250
251 - 500
501 - 4,807

0   250   500   1,000 Kilometres

Figure 3.2 Palaeogeographic map of Britain at 8500 cal BC (Image Fraser Sturt. Bathymetry provided by EMODnet Bathymetry Consortium (2020): EMODnet Digital Bathymetry (DTM). https://doi.org/10.12770/bb6a87dd-e579-4036-abe1-e649cea9881a, Topography produced using Copernicus data and information funded by the European Union (EU-DEM))

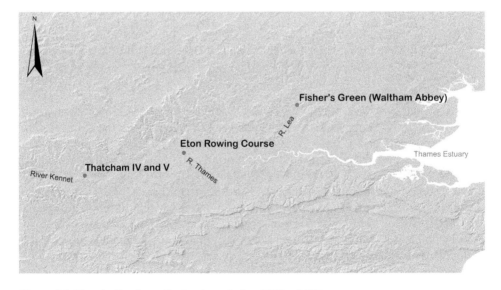

Figure 3.3 Sites in Southern England predating 8800 cal BC

extrapolated this typological division to Southern England. It remains to be seen whether this is justified. Reynier identifies only two Star Carr-type sites in Southern England: Thatcham IIIB (or patinated series) and Broxbourne 104. While microliths from the former are similar to those from Star Carr, those from Broxbourne are rather less so; the presence of elongated scalenes, relatively rare in the north, is more similar to the Welsh Star Carr-type assemblages. Overall, the Broxbourne 104 microlith assemblage is very similar to that from 100-Acre pit, Denham and Three Ways Wharf, categorised by Reynier as Deepcar-type sites. To possible Star Carr-type sites in the south might be added a scatter recently excavated at Fetcham, on the River Mole. This is a small, microlith-dominated assemblage, mainly composed of obliquely blunted points, lateralised fairly evenly between left and right, lacking retouch on the leading edge and accompanied by a trapeze and triangle (Munnery 2014). Thatcham IIIB and Fetcham are undated.

While there are similarities between Northern Deepcar sites and many southern assemblages, there is also considerable variation within these southern sites. The equation of all these with a single static 'type', considered by Reynier to encompass a social or ethnic grouping, perhaps does more harm than good, and elides the temporal and regional variation within these sites. More broadly there appears to be a distinction between sites with large numbers of fairly simple obliquely blunted points (Denham, Thatcham III, Three Ways Wharf) and those that are more elaborated, with greater numbers of partially backed points and occasional curve-backed points (Lackford Heath, Sandstone, Iver). There are also variable quantities of broad triangles, trapezes and rhomboids within these assemblages, some having reasonable amounts, others none at all. Lateralisation also varies considerably, with many assemblages being exclusively left lateralised (Hengistbury Head, Cherhill, Sandstone, Iver, Three Ways Warf), while others (Denham, Three Ways Wharf, Dozmary Pool) are much more mixed.

Jacobi was attuned to the temporal and regional variation within these Southern Early Mesolithic assemblages, seeing variation in microlith types as having both a regional and temporal component. He noted, for example, the presence of curve-backed microliths at Oakhanger V/VII, which has a number of consistent, if imprecise, dates on bulked pine and hazel charcoal, indicating occupation, probably sometime in the region of 8300–7900 BC. Similar types are also present at Marsh Benham, which also saw occupation at this time, suggesting this might represent a temporal development of the Early Mesolithic. Both sites also have reasonable quantities of elongated trapezes and pieces with pointed bases.

In the decades since Jacobi's Mesolithic publications, relatively little has changed to elucidate temporal aspect of variation in Southern England. Probably all that can be said is that the microlith types used by the earliest colonisers were fairly undifferentiated obliquely blunted points, while some of the more elaborate forms, part backed, curve backed, rhomboids and pieces with pointed bases are likely to be later. However, radiocarbon dates are few, and microliths associated with early dates are rare; more work is needed to confirm these observations.

East Anglia

We start on the edge of Doggerland in East Anglia, perhaps not the location of the earliest Mesolithic site in Britain, but certainly the location of the earliest major excavation, at Kelling Heath (Sainty 1924, 1925, 1927). Several large Early Mesolithic scatters exist in the region (Figure 3.4), though most of these have suffered from poorly documented, early excavation/collection. A key feature of these sites is their density and extensive area. Clark (1932) named the Wangford/Lakenheath Warren area as one of the three major concentrations of Mesolithic material in the country. Here, both Early and Late Mesolithic material has been recovered over many generations (Jacobi 1984). At Kelling Heath, the area of the main site was estimated at 56 by 46 m, and some areas were extremely dense (Sainty 1924, 65). At Great Melton, the area excavated measured only 12 × 12 m in area, but 37,786 artefacts were recovered in total, with lithic densities in excess of 1500 pieces per square metre (Wymer and Robbins 1995). At Lackford Heath, a small excavation of less than 9 m^2 yielded over 5000 lithic artefacts in what Todd (nd.) interpreted as a shelter but which may have been a tree throw.

Several of these sites are located in close proximity to rivers, and Billington (2017) has noted more broadly the clustering of Mesolithic sites in river valleys in this region. Most are found on sandy, well-drained sediments, such as a very large scatter on the Greensand at Cottenham or at Great Melton. The preference for these sorts of lithologies has been noted in the southeast (see in particular chapter 4), though considerable biases exist due to the complex geomorphological history of the region. Much of the Mesolithic of the fenland is so deeply buried below layers of peat and marine sediment it will never be uncovered; like the Mesolithic of Doggerland, it is effectively submerged.

By virtue of their sandy sediments, none of the East Anglian sites preserve fauna, and only Lackford Heath is dated, at 8760–8270 cal BC (OxA-2342; 9240 ± 110 BP). The range of microliths present at both Kelling Heath and Great Melton may suggest a slightly later date. These sites are likely to represent 'persistent places' (Barton et al. 1995), located in favoured areas of well-drained sediment close to water-courses. They

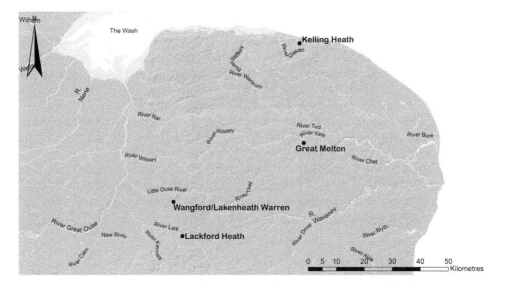

Figure 3.4 Early Mesolithic sites in East Anglia

Table 3.1 Representation of tools at major East Anglian sites. Figures taken from Jacobi (1984), Wymer and Robbins (1995), Jacobi archive and author's observations. The figures from Lackford Heath are based on a remaining sample of 468 pieces from an original assemblage of over 5000 pieces. The assemblage from Kelling is also likely to have suffered attrition

Tools	Lackford Heath	Kelling Heath	Great Melton
Awl	1	5	0
Axe	1	44	22
Burin	0	34	34
Microlith	57	688	320
Notch/denticulate	1	320	0
Microdenticulate	5	51	11
Scraper	54	351	333
Truncation	12	146	0
Retouch/utilised	41	542	223
Total inc. debitage	5000	n/a	786

are likely to have been revisited over generations. As might be expected in this case, their tool inventories show a wide range of activities, a palimpsest of varied and specific tasks, taking place over centuries (Table 3.1).

Riverlands: The Thames and its tributaries

More evidence is available from the Thames and its tributaries, particularly the Lea, Colne and Kennet (Figure 3.5). Though these areas have also suffered from early excavations, more recent work, undertaken mainly in the course of development or through long-standing campaigns by local archaeologists, as well as better organic

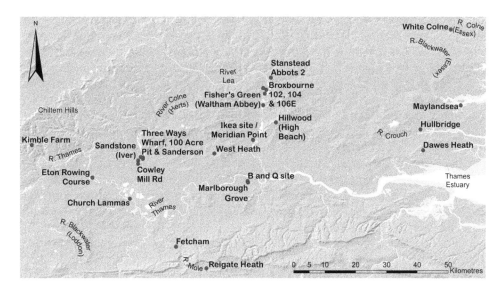

Figure 3.5 Early Mesolithic sites along the Thames and its tributaries

preservation, means these areas provide the greater part of our knowledge of the Early Mesolithic of Southern England.

The Thames rises near Kemble in the Cotswolds, becoming constricted as it cuts through the chalk of the Chilterns at the Goring Gap, but gaining strength as it flows through the Thames Basin as it is joined by the Kennet and its major London tributaries. During the Windermere Interstadial, the Thames was a braided river, with several channels running across an unstable, open landscape. There is evidence that some of these channels were abandoned from the end of this interstadial, as the river began its transition to a meandering form, though its middle stretches at least maintained a multi-channel form during the early part of the Holocene (Sidell et al. 2000).

The Thames is currently a tidal river, but at times of lower sea-level this would not have been the case along its existing course. At c.9000 cal BC, when the relative sea-level was roughly at -45 m, it would have flowed far beyond its current estuary (Figure 2.2), across the marshy and waterlogged landscape of Doggerland, and into a massive delta system where its waters met and mingled with the Rhine, Meuse and Scheldt. This river system, which drained much of Northwestern Europe, is known in this part of its course as the Loberg Channel. The river turned southwest and was constricted into a single powerful channel to crash through the Dover Gorge to a broad floodplain, where it took a lower energy, braided form. Here, it was joined by the Seine and opened up to a broad estuary (Leary 2015; Sturt et al. 2013).

Pettitt has suggested that the Channel River formed a major barrier to colonisation during the Pleistocene, with movement into Britain almost always taking place from the east. As sea-level rose, the Channel River was massively truncated, and new landscape configurations arose (Figure 3.2), which altered both long-standing routes into Britain and areas seen as favourable for settlement within Britain. Some settlement patterns followed those of previous periods: Early Mesolithic sites show a similar focus on the Thames tributaries as those of the Long Blade groups that preceded them. However, new areas were also favoured. Major sites, such as Hengistbury Head, Downton and Iping Common, are also found on or close to north-south river systems that would have run either into the Channel embayment or a much more southerly coastline.

Since the 19th century, Mesolithic artefacts have been recovered from the Thames. Most of these finds consist of flint axe-heads, the so-called 'Thames Picks', but there are also some spectacular organic finds, such as a decorated bone adze from Hammersmith, as well as barbed points from Wandsworth and Battersea. Chatterton (2006) has suggested that these finds may have represented votive offerings; however, this is hard to substantiate on the current state of the evidence. The course of the Thames has migrated during the Holocene, swallowing up Mesolithic sites on its banks (Sidell et al. 2000). Typically, at meanders the river erodes material from the outer banks, whereas material becomes redeposited on the inner bend. Field (1989) has plotted finds of tranchet axes dredged from the Thames that are now housed within the Museum of London. The patterns are clear: Adzes are predominantly located on the bends of the river (Figure 3.6). Others are clustered at junctions with tributaries, particularly the Hogsmill, the Brent and the Wandle, where there once must have been important settlements. These patterns indicate axes are likely to have been eroded from abandoned riverside camps.

While sites along the outer bends of the river have been eroded, those that may have stood in close proximity to the inner side of the bend are likely to have been preserved,

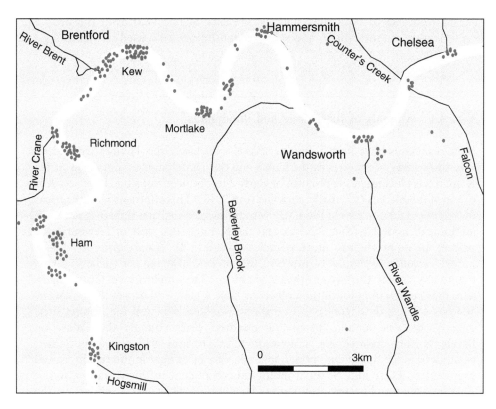

Figure 3.6 Distribution of tranchet axe-heads from the Thames in West London (redrawn after Field (1989) with addition of 'lost' rivers from Barton (1962))

though today may be some distance from the river's current course. Surviving sites in the lower Thames are likely to be deeply buried; Late Mesolithic 'Tibury Man' (see chapter 5) was found 10 m below present ground surface, beneath deep sediments resulting from marine transgressions (Schulting 2013). Some Mesolithic sites have been located in the middle reaches of the Thames but are still relatively rare. At Eton Rowing Course just west of Windsor, a number of channels cut through gravel terraces by a braided Thames during the Late Glacial created gravel islands, which became foci for later settlement. As these channels were abandoned in the Early Holocene, a lake formed. People camped on its banks, leaving behind a series of lithic scatters, which were revealed in three trial trenches. One of these at least is a rare example of a pre-8500 BC Early Mesolithic site in the southeast, with an aurochs sacrum dated to between 9150 and 8750 cal BC (Allen et al. 2013). The lithic material associated with this event shows a range of generalised but small-scale activities involving microliths (3), burins (2) and scrapers (5) and more extensive use of axes, involving both manufacture and resharpening. Evidence for charred bulrush stems and seeds suggests access to the lake was kept open by burning dead vegetation in winter. Undated Early Mesolithic material is also present on the banks of the Bermondsey Lake, which developed in another cut-off meander of the Thames, recovered from the B&Q site and Marlborough Grove (Rogers 1990; Sidell et al. 2002).

These represent small-scale, possibly repeated, activity areas, given the caching of gravel flint nodules at both sites, and the presence of two hearths at the B&Q site. Microliths were manufactured, and scrapers and burins were used in processing and manufacture.

Box 3.1   Animals of the forests and floodplains

Faunal remains have been found at several sites along the Thames tributaries. Overton's study of the sites of the Colne and the Thatcham/Newbury sites of the Kennet has elucidated the reliance of Early Mesolithic groups on either red deer or pig in these areas (Conneller and Overton 2018). This contrasts with the focus on red deer and aurochs in the Early Mesolithic of Northern England. With the addition of material from the Lea and the Kennet sites west of Newbury, the pattern becomes slightly more complex (Table 3.2). Broxbourne 104 has a faunal assemblage similar to those of the north of England. Crucially, this is potentially a Star Carr-type lithic assemblage. The similarity to the northern sites may represent cultural preference, or have a temporal aspect. (Broxbourne 104 has a single date from poorly preserved bulked bone; on the Kennet sites, dates from bone tend to be several hundred years younger than those on hazelnuts.) The undated site of Wawcott XXX (Froom 2012) is also an outlier, as aurochs is the dominant species, and elk, rare elsewhere in the region, is well represented. There may be a chronological component to this variation, too.

A final temporal pattern can perhaps be glimpsed: Sites where red deer are the most common prey animal tend to be slightly earlier than those where pig are most common, with the majority of their distribution tending to fall before 8500 BC, while those with pig post-date 8500 BC. There are, though, many caveats: The number of sites involved are few, and many are clearly places that saw repeated occupation, with insufficient radiocarbon measurements to appreciate their complexity. However, if this pattern is reinforced by additional sites and dates, it could suggest a situation similar to that of Northern France, where Boreal sites are dominated by pig (Seara et al. 2010).

Though never the major species in an assemblage, roe deer plays an important role at both the pig and the red deer focused sites, being the most common 'subsidiary' species. Beaver also seems to have been an important species, and traces of their presence would have been very visible in the river lands, where these sites are found (see Figure 3.7). More rarely represented are fur-bearers: Wild cat, badger, wolf, fox, otter and pine marten. Two waterbirds are represented: Widgeon and Whooper swan, both winter visitors.

Southern groups had different traditions of bone and antler working to those in the north. In contrast with the north, barbed points are rare, consisting of three unassociated finds from the Thames and Lea. Large sites with good faunal preservation, such as Thatcham III, show little evidence for antler working and only a few antler tools. Amongst these, the lame du hache, an unperforated antler axe blade, is more common than in the north, found at Thatcham III and Greenham Dairy Farm (Elliott 2012).

Table 3.2 Faunal assemblages from sites on the Lea, Colne and Kennet

Site	Date (cal BC)	Main prey animal	Secondary species	Moderate presence	Rare presence
Broxbourne 104	8800–8400	Red deer	Aurochs	–	Widgeon
Preferred area 4, Denham	8565–8260	Pig	–	–	–
Sanderson site, Denham	8550–8300	Pig	Red deer	Beaver	Otter
Three Ways Wharf	8750–8250	Red deer	Roe deer	–	Fox, pine marten, beaver, wild cat, swan
Thatcham I	–	Red deer	Roe deer	Pig	Aurochs, fox, pine marten
Thatcham III	8640–8260	Pig	Roe deer	Red deer, aurochs, beaver	Elk, badger, fox, wildcat, wolf
Thatcham II	–	Red deer	Pig	Beaver	Aurochs, elk, roe deer, badger
Thatcham IV	9350–8700	Red deer	Roe deer	–	Elk, dog, pig, beaver, wildcat
Thatcham V	9250–8500	Red deer, pig	–	Roe deer	Beaver
Ufton Green	8740–8340	Roe deer	–	–	–
Faraday Road	8500–8270 7610–7470	Pig	Beaver	Roe deer	Aurochs, red deer, wildcat
Greenham Dairy Farm	8570–8220	Pig	–	Roe deer	Red deer
Marsh Benham	8280–7790	Pig	–	–	Aurochs, beaver
Wawcott XXX	–	Aurochs	Elk	Pig, red deer	Roe deer, badger

Though relatively little remains of the sites that must have once dotted the Thames, much more is known about the occupation of its tributaries. Particularly important amongst these for Mesolithic research are the Lea, the Colne and the Kennet, all of which saw early finds through gravel extraction that alerted researchers to their potential. Many of the Thames tributaries, even relatively large rivers such as the Fleet, around 150 m wide at its mouth (Barton 1962), are now 'lost', transformed into storm drains beneath the expansion of London. However, these also saw Mesolithic occupation, with finds of axes in particular recorded from their ancient courses (Lewis 2000) and small sites such as Three Oaks Lane, located on an eyot in the Neckinger (Proctor and Bishop 2002). Even small streams seem important: The large, scraper-dominated site at Creffield Rd, Acton (Burleigh 1976), lies very close to the source of the Bollo Brook, a tributary of the Stamford Brook, which flows into the Thames at Hammersmith. To the current tributaries of the Thames should also be added a number of rivers in Essex, the Essex Colne, the Blackwater, the Crouch and the Roach, which now flow directly into the sea, but in Early Mesolithic times would have met the Thames in the now submerged area of Doggerland. All have evidence for Early Mesolithic occupation. The Essex Colne has sites excavated by Nina Layard,

Figure 3.7 Tree felled by beaver, showing characteristic gnawing marks (copyright Nick Overton)

including White Colne, where a 'pit-dwelling' (see chapter 4) was found in the 1920s (Layard 1927). On the Blackwater is Maylandsea, on the Crouch is a series of scatters at Hullbridge and on the Roach is Dawes Heath (Jacobi 1980a Wilkinson and Murphy 1995).

The Lea

The River Lea is the easternmost major tributary of the Thames and has the broadest floodplain of any of the Thames tributaries. It rises at Leagrove in the Chilterns and flows broadly southeast for 113 km before meeting the Thames at Leamouth in Poplar. It is joined by several tributaries on the way, including some that were relatively substantial. The now lost Hackney Brook, which joined the Lea a little south of Hackney Wick, is described as 30 m wide at flood along its lower reaches (Barton 1962). In the Early Holocene, the Lea was a braided river, with evidence in places for several channels, separated by gravel islands or eyots, though it was beginning to adopt a single thread meandering form (Corcoran et al. 2011; Warren et al. 1934). As river flow decreased in the Early Holocene, former channels of the braided river would have been abandoned. These low-lying areas would initially have been open pools, before gradually infilling with marl and peat deposits, forming areas of marsh and fen (Grant et al. 2012). While several large meres existed on the valley floor during the Younger Dryas, most of these had probably become infilled by this time, but persisted as wetland areas (Corcoran et al. 2011).

The Boreal vegetation of the Lea was varied. In some areas, there is evidence for a typical succession of denser pine woodlands with some hazel or birch and aspen and dogwood on the wetland margins before 9000 cal BC; elsewhere, pine woodland is only present from 8300 cal BC; other areas remained open wetland with grasses and sedges until relatively late (Corcoran et al. 2011). This variation may be due to poor water-logged soils or to human manipulation of the environment. There is some evidence for burning in sediment cores, both in the area of the Olympic Park and from Temple Mills Lock, in the lower Lea Valley, and further north at Enfield Lock (Chambers et al. 1996), though whether these are anthropogenic or natural fires is uncertain.

In the upper Lea Valley a complex of important Early Mesolithic sites can be found in the Broxbourne area, just to the north of London (Figure 3.5). Here, fieldwork by Warren in the early years of the 20th century, and by Jacobi in the early 1970s un-covered evidence for four Early and two Late Mesolithic sites. More recent developer-funded excavations have provided evidence for Mesolithic sites in the Lower Lea: A small assemblage, including Early Mesolithic microliths, possibly redeposited, was recovered from Meridian Point, Glover Drive, Enfield, while redeposited Mesolithic fauna and flintworking was located in a palaeo-channel at the IKEA site, also on Glover Drive, while flint flakes were recovered from Early Mesolithic age peats at Millmarsh Lane, Enfield (Grant et al. 2012). Mesolithic settlements tend to be found on slightly higher and drier sand or gravel ridges, either the remains of eyots from the former braided river, or gravel bars that accumulated on the edge of meanders. These would have allowed access to the adjacent channels and ponds and wetlands, which formed in former channels. There is some evidence that areas where tributary streams met the Lea were also favoured places. Both Meridian Point and the IKEA site were located near to where a former course of Pymmes Brook met the Lea. Tributaries may have been routes to higher ground, and Mesolithic finds are associated with areas adjacent to former courses of the Saddlers Mill Stream and the Turkey Brook in Enfield. Stray finds of axes and knapping debris are also associated with the former course of the Hackney Brook (Corcoran et al. 2011).

Early Mesolithic occupation has also been recorded on higher ground above the Lea, at 90 m asl on a ridge of Eocene sands at Hill Wood, High Beach, Essex. Here, Early Mesolithic occupation took place near a spring, and only 10 km SSE of the Broxbourne complex and 4 km southeast of the location of the barbed point found at Fisher's Green, Waltham Abbey (Jacobi et al. 1978b, 206) In the early years of the 20th century, Warren (1912a), uncovered lithic material closely scattered in and round a small depression (Clark 1932, 62–3), interpreted as a pit dwelling. Further excava-tions in the area were undertaken in the 1950s by local school children and in 1959, 1961 and 1977 by the West Essex Archaeological group. These excavations recorded assemblages dominated by microliths, with only a handful of other tool types present (Jacobi et al. 1978, 1980a). Most microliths were broken, suggesting repair and discard of damaged toolkits.

The Broxbourne complex

Quarrying for gravel along the Lea floodplain in the 19th and 20th centuries exposed sections of Late Pleistocene and Early Holocene stratigraphy. These gravel pits were monitored from the early years of the last century by Samuel Hazzeldine Warren (1912b). While Warren's interests were primarily focused on the Late Pleistocene se-dimentary sequence, the quarry known as Rikof's Pit yielded important remains of early post-glacial deposits and associated settlement evidence. Warren found evidence for three sites, Broxbourne 101, 102 and 103 (Warren et al. 1934). The material from site 101 was not found in situ, but in a sandy dump, where it had been placed by the quarrymen, though Warren was able to relocate its approximate position. The sandy deposit was sieved to recover even the smallest material. In all, a small assemblage of 117 pieces of flint were recovered. No microliths were found, but a wide range of formal tools was present, albeit in small quantities, with single examples of awls, denticulates and burins, and two examples of both notches and scrapers.

Site 102 was located in leached sand, interpreted by Godwin (letter 11th March 1973, Jacobi archive, British Museum) as a mineral soil, on what appears to have been a gravel bank or mid-channel bar, which formed in a cold climate, braided river system. The occupation seems to have taken place in close proximity to an active channel. Mesolithic material was recovered in situ by Warren. Quarrymen had re-moved the overlying peat, and some of the underlying sand, leaving flint flakes ex-posed on the top of the gravel bar. The area was excavated by Warren, who exposed a concentration of around 4.5 m in diameter, with sparser lithic material extending for a further 3–4 m around this. In all, an assemblage of nearly 2000 lithic artefacts was recovered. Tasks seem particularly focused on the use of notches and denticulates, possibly related to woodworking, a suggestion which is reinforced by the presence of two axes and resharpening flakes. Numbers of utilised blades are also high. The production of microliths and retooling of composite tools and use of scrapers were also important tasks. Only one animal bone was found, and this was too poorly preserved for identification. While a small minority of the flint nodules used at the site came from fluvial gravels, the majority seem to have been obtained from a surface exposure relatively close to the chalk, perhaps from a head deposit (Warren et al. 1934). While the Rikof's Pit sites have not been dated, pollen analysis of the peat overlying site 101, suggests woodlands of pine and hazel, with smaller quantities of elm and oak, suggesting, by comparison with sequences in the lower Lea valley (Grant et al. 2012), a date in the region of 8500–8000 BC. Site 101 must be earlier than this. It is not impossible it derives from a similar time period to the fragment of uniserial barbed point found just 3 km further down the banks of the Lea in spoil at a gravel pit at Fisher's Green, Waltham Abbey. This has been dated to between 9950 and 8835 BC, confirming the presence of pioneer settlers along the river.

In the early 1970s, Roger Jacobi, initially with Tony Legge, undertook new ex-cavations in the area, with a series of small sites excavated on the edge of old gravel workings around 1.2 km to the north of Warren's Broxbourne sites, now part of the Lea Valley Country Park. Three areas, Broxbourne 104, 105 and 106, were in-vestigated, with 104 and 106 dated to the Early Mesolithic, and 105 to the Late Mesolithic (see chapter 5). Relatively little information is available for site 106, where material was located during the cleaning of a quarry section to the west of the railway. A date 9240–8295 BC (9360 ± 150 BP; Q-1146) was obtained on bulked, unburnt hazelnuts from a thin peat layer, which contained Early Boreal pollen. This layer also contained two slender obliquely blunted microliths (Jacobi 1994).

Rather more archive information is available for site 104. Here, an area of c.15 × 8 m was excavated on the edge of the gravel pit; the southern part of the site had been truncated by quarrying (Jacobi archive, British Museum). The lithic assemblage was found within peaty gravel lying on top of a gravel bank (Reynier 2005). Pollen analysis of the peat overlying the implementiferous horizon on the bank suggested the occupation predated the Early Boreal (Reynier 2005), while bulked animal bone was dated to 8880–8300 BC (9350 ± 120 BP, Q-1096) (Jacobi 1994).

Analysis of the distribution of lithic artefacts across the excavated area indicates one major scatter, with an area of nearly 4 m in diameter where lithic densities exceed 100 pieces of flint per square metre. Even though the site was dug by square rather than material being individually plotted, a sharp drop off suggests a barrier effect, possibly indicating the presence of a structure (see Figure 3.8). A noticeable feature of the assemblage is the extremely high densities of burnt flint. In several squares, more than 30% of flint recovered was calcined. While burnt flint is common across the site, densities are generally higher in the area of the potential structure and the area immediately surrounding this. This may represent repeated clearing out of a central hearth, but another possibility is that the structure was burnt down.

Figure 3.8 Distribution of major tool types at Broxbourne 104

The assemblage recovered from site 104 is balanced between a number of different tasks (Table 3.3). Most tools are concentrated within the area of the possible structure, but a number of external activity areas were present. Microlith production appears to have taken place within the possible structure, though microliths were discarded more broadly across the site. Most of these were broken, and almost half were burnt. Scrapers and burins are also concentrated within the structure, though burin use and resharpening took place outside. The presence of both burins and scrapers, the latter commonly used in spaces relatively free of knapping debris (Rozoy and Rozoy 2002), might suggest that tools forming part of personal toolkits were moved into the structure for safekeeping, as seems to have occurred at Star Carr. The majority of the burins (11) are corbiac burins, based on the removal of a burin spall at the end of a flake or blade, transverse to the main axis of the piece, and lacking a prepared platform for the removal. This type is not present in Northern England.

No axes were recovered; yet, axe manufacture seems to have been an important task, focused particularly in the northern part of the site, where two production scatters were located. A total of 56 axe-thinning flakes were identified, with several refitting (Jacobi archive, British Museum). Refits of axe-thinning flakes occur over wide distances across the site (up to 7 m), possibly because some appear to have evidence for use. In contrast, with the axe-thinning flakes, tranchet sharpening flakes and one broken tip were found on the site margins, perhaps reflecting areas of axe usage. Burins were also used within these northern activity areas, particular in the northeast part of the site, where four corbiac burins and two spalls, one of which refits, were recovered. Microliths were also occasionally produced in these northern areas, and notches also cluster in the north and west. Miscellaneous retouched pieces and utilised blades are scattered across the site, though there is a marked concentration of used pieces in the southern part of the potential structure.

Table 3.3 Early Mesolithic assemblages from Broxbourne. Figures taken from Jacobi archive, with additions from Warren et al. (1934). Some collections are likely to be incomplete (some hundreds of flints are mentioned by Warren as coming from site 101)

	Site 101	*Site 102*	*Site 104*
Awl	1	19	1
Axe	0	2	0
Burin	1	2	15
Microlith	0	25	25
Notch	2	34	12
Scraper	1	25	8
Truncation	0	1+	6
Retouched/utilised	3	37	70
Axe flake	0	3	56
Burin spall	0	5	6
Microburin	0	25	31
Cores	5	37	21
Core tablet	0	3+	45
Crested blade	0	3+	80
Blades	66	742	1428
Debitage	37	992	1072
Total	116	1955+	2876

Broxbourne 104 can be characterised as a single occupation site, possibly focused on some form of structure. A wide range of tasks were carried out in the area of the possible structure, involving cutting, the manufacture of composite weapons and the use of burins and scrapers. To the north of this area, axes were manufactured and a range of tasks, including use of burins, notches and microlith manufacture, occurred. Red deer and aurochs remains were brought to site, possibly for tool manufacture, and processed outside the area of the main concentration.

Above the rivers: A Mesolithic site at West Heath Hampstead

Though most of the evidence of Mesolithic occupation of the middle Thames has been buried in the expansion of London, one major site survives, perched high above the river valleys on Hampstead Heath. The heath is part of a sandy ridge of high ground, reaching heights of 134 m asl, stretching from Hampstead to Highgate. The area is known today for its views across London. Good views would have been important to hunter-gatherer groups, but the area may have had special significance for people who followed the rivers: This is an area of springs that serve as the source of several tributaries of the Thames, the Brent and three of London's lost rivers, the Fleet, the Tyburn and the Westbourne (Barton 1962).

The site of West Heath was discovered by Hendon and the District Archaeological Society and excavated between 1976 and 1981 (Collins and Lorimer 1989). It is located at 98 m asl next to the Leg of Mutton Pond, the product of the damming of a small stream that arises around 300 m to the east. The West Heath site is undated. A couple of Horsham points and a handful of small geometric microliths suggest small-scale later occupation, but the majority of the assemblage appears very similar to the large Late Early Mesolithic complex at Oakhanger V/VII (Rankine et al. 1960), characterised by elongated obliquely blunted point, partially backed points and curve-backed points. Like Oakhanger, the site is extremely dense in lithic material: 61,000 lithic artefacts were located from an excavated area of 288 m^2; in several areas, more than 500 pieces were recovered per square meter. The assemblage is dominated by evidence of microlith production and the use of scrapers; other tools, including axes, were present in very low numbers. Like Oakhanger, it probably represents an increase in the scale and intensity of the occupation of local high ground, particularly that connected with springs, as groups began to move beyond the river lands.

A notable find is a piece with engraved cortex. The engraving consists of a series of cross-hatched lines, engraved before the flint was knapped. Initially, a parallel series of lines were engraved spanning top left to bottom right. These were overwritten by a much more extensive and irregular series of lines crossing the piece from top right to bottom left. The purpose of this second set of lines may have been to erase the original image; indeed the purpose of cortical engraving may have been that designs would have been destroyed by subsequent knapping, making them impossible to read (Conneller 2011). Other interpretations exist: Cortical engraving is much more common in the Scandinavian Mesolithic, and one suggestion has been that these were used to remove chalky cortex to produce a white pigment (Karsten and Knarstrom 2003). The repeated incision of lines might favour this interpretation here, though the original study indicates all lines are very narrow (Collins and Lorimer 1989, 59), rather than a broader scraping motion that would be more likely to remove greater amounts of cortex. The presence of material with chalky cortex might indicate some procurement from chalk sources around 15 km away, though some chalky material is also present in glacial till, which can be found within 3 km of the site. The size of the raw material indicates one of these two sources rather than gravel material was used (Collins and Lorimer 1989, 101).

The Colne Valley

The Colne Valley, like the Lea, has yielded a number of important Mesolithic sites, initially as a result of gravel extraction (Lacaille 1963). More recently, developer-funded archaeology has hugely increased our understanding of the Mesolithic occupation of the valley, with material recovered from Three Ways Wharf (Lewis and Rackham 2011), Preferred Area 4 (Wessex 2005) and the Sanderson site, Denham (Halsey 2006).

The Colne rises as a subterranean river on the Chilterns at North Mymms in Hertfordshire; it flows initially northwest, before turning south and meeting the Thames at Staines. It has a number of important tributaries, particularly the Chess, which joins the river by Rickmansworth and the Misbourne, which joins at Uxbridge. Several tributaries provide easy routes to the uplands of the Chilterns. North of Denham, the Colne cuts through the chalk; to the south, the river has cut through Pleistocene terrace gravels, made up mainly of flint. At the confluence with the Thames, the river split into five shifting, braided channels, meandering across a floodplain between 2 and 2.5 km wide (Jones 2013).

Environmental analysis indicates an initial Holocene landscape of open grassland and heath vegetation, with shrubs such as dwarf birch. A situation similar to the Lea seems to have prevailed, with channels of a meandering, braided river cut off, initially persisting as areas of standing water, then becoming filled with peat, and surrounded by wetland vegetation. By the Early Mesolithic, a scrub woodland had developed on the floodplain, of birch, pine and willow and aspen. Tree cover was patchy, with some dense stands, but also areas of wet marshy grassland and fen vegetation with nettles and henbane (Grant et al. 2012). From c.8300 BC, birch and aspen were replaced by hazel, but pine remained an important part of the woodland. Oak and elm were probably present in the wider landscape and open areas of wet grassland, and marshy fen persisted.

Several individuals record finds of Early Prehistoric flintwork from the early years of the 19th century. Inspired by Warren's work in the Lea, and recognising similar deposits in the Colne Valley, Marsden, a local collector, kept a number of gravel pits under observation during the inter-war years, locating flint typologically identical to Broxbourne at Harefield, Middlesex, West Hyde, Herts and, most importantly, Sandstone, Iver, in Buckinghamshire (Lacaille 1963). The latter site lay at the Colne's confluence with the Alder Bourne. Marsden recovered lithics from what was probably an immature soil formation, but also from sand lenses, probably representing the margins of active channels (see Corcoran and Howell 2002) and from the base of peat layers probably in areas of relict channels. These varied sediments lay immediately on top of Late Devensian gravels, which formed bars and ridges, on which occupation was concentrated, a similar situation to the Lea valley, and Three Ways Wharf (see below).

A.D. Lacaille took over Marsden's work on his death, returning to Sandstone, Iver, in 1955, locating the level of Mesolithic finds, and obtaining environmental samples. Mesolithic material was located on top of a sandy/gravel layer developed on the top of the basal gravel. Pollen in the overlying peat was poorly preserved, but of likely boreal age, with the lowest levels dominated by pine, with smaller quantities of birch, hazel and willow and with high quantities of sedge pollen. The absence of elm and oak suggests the lowest part of this peat dates to just before 8300 BC, providing a TPQ for the Mesolithic industry. A small assemblage from the site is preserved, though it is uncertain whether it derives just from Lacaille's 1950s excavations, or from Marsden's work, too. The group of microliths preserved is fairly coherent, consisting mainly of obliquely blunted points and curve-backed pieces. Scrapers, truncations, microdenticulates and retouched blades are present in fairly equal numbers, with other tools being rare (Table 3.4). The recovery of both microburins and axe-thinning flakes shows that tools were manufactured on the site.

Lacaille also carried out work at 100 Acres (Boyer's Pit), Denham, Buckinghamshire, a large gravel extraction pit that was monitored by Kennard and Haward (Lacaille 1963). Haward amassed several thousand artefacts, which were located on a gravel island surrounded by marshy deposits. While the lower part of the gravel ridge was overlain by tufa, the occupation debris was concentrated on the top of the island, overlain by a thick layer of peat. Like Sandstone, microliths and scrapers are most common, with a single axe and burin, and evidence of microlith manufacture and axe sharpening (Lacaille 1963).

Recent discoveries of Mesolithic material have occurred in advance of development. This includes large excavated areas, in particular the sites adjacent to 100 Acres Pit: The Sanderson site, Denham and Three Ways Wharf, but also smaller scale work such as the discovery of refitting Early Mesolithic scatters at Cowley Mill Rd, Uxbridge (Lewis 2000) and Preferred Area 4, Denham (Wessex 2005). The latter was found in alluvium on the edge of a gravel island, near to the confluence of the Colne and the Alder Bourne, and only 250 m to the southwest of Three Ways Wharf. A small stream, the Rusholt Brook, runs through the site. On the western side of a gravel island by the brook a small lithic scatter, of 18 pieces of flint, including an obliquely blunted point and a retouched blade, was located. This was associated with some bones and a tusk of wild boar dated to 8465–8260 cal BC (9131 ± 45; NZA-19005). This appears to be a short-term episode of tool use associated with the butchery of a boar hunted on the wetlands. A second probable Mesolithic scatter was located on an adjacent gravel island close to the Colne (Wessex 2005). Mesolithic activity has also been located along the lower course of the Colne at Church Lammas, on a gravel island between relict channels. Some flint knapping may have occurred, but the area seems more focused on animal processing. An aurochs butchery area appears to be represented, as well as the deposition of animal remains into a hollow (Jones 2013).

More substantial evidence for occupation is present at the Sanderson site, the area of the former Sanderson Factory, erected on the area of 100 Acres Pit and around 300 m to the south of the area reported on by Lacaille. It was excavated by MoLA in 2004, following a watching brief in 2002 (Halsey 2006). The excavations and a borehole survey found evidence for a meandering channel, which had created a gravel bar on which occupation took place. There was evidence for incipient soil formation, as vegetation colonised the bar. The excavations revealed four scatters of flint along the margins of the gravel ridge. The deposits on the top of the ridge appear to have been truncated during the formation of later alluvial clays, but a patch of burnt natural gravel probably indicates the presence of a hearth in this area.

Table 3.4 Composition of lithic assemblages from the Colne

	Sand-stone	100 Acres	Sanderson 1	Sanderson 2	Sanderson 3	Sanderson 4	TWW (C west)
Awl	–	–	0	0	0	0	2
Axe	1	2	0	0	0	0	4
Burin	P	1	0	3	3	3	6
Microlith	15+	17+	1	7	5	23	48
Notch	P	–	0	0	0	0	10
Microdenticulate	–	–	1	2	3	0	0
Scraper	P	14+	0	1	1	8	93
Truncation	P	2+	0	0	0	0	3
Ret./ut.	P	P	6	22	4	3	94
Axe flake	0	P	2	0	1	0	89
Burin spall	–	–	–	–	–	–	13
Microburin	P	P					18
Cores	P	P	56	54	70	59	62
Core prep.	P		12	23	10	20	362
Blades	P	P	197	411	337	377	1935
Debitage	P	P	1698	1224	1562	845	6946
Total	–	–	1706	1747	1996	1935	9544
Burnt	–	–	299	1005	472		

The northernmost flint scatter was an area of intensive knapping where several cores were deposited in a small pile. It is associated with several retouched blades, used blades and microdenticulates, but few other tools. To the north of this scatter is a group of c.30 pieces of flint of which half are cores. This may represent a cache or a midden. The latter may be indicated by the additional presence in this small area of a cluster of animal bone, most of which, apart from a few pig teeth, is not identifiable, but indicates animals killed in the summer or autumn. Immediately to the east of the scatter was an area of tool use, where more utilised blades were found along with a couple of axe sharpening flakes. The large central scatter is also strongly associated with utilised flakes and blades, but also has microburins and microliths, indicating retooling, along with single examples of microdenticulates, scrapers and burins. Single elements of red deer, pig and beaver are associated with this scatter.

Most of the faunal remains are associated with the two southernmost scatters. Faunal analysis (Overton 2014) indicates complete wild boar were probably brought to the site, though some limb bones were subsequently removed. An extremely tight cluster of red deer remains associated with scatter 3 includes both limb bones, probably brought in as joints of meat, and the head of a single individual, including the antler. Both red deer and pig remains indicate a summer and/or autumn season of occupation. The only burins found at the site cluster round this group, suggesting that the skull with intact antlers was imported as raw material for antler working. A scraper and microdenticulated and utilised blades were associated with this scatter. A burnt hazelnut from the area of this scatter returned a date of 8220–7770 BC (9230 ± 50 BP Beta-200075). The final lithic scatter is in the southernmost part of the site, and is composed of a cluster of scrapers in its southwest part and a cluster of microliths and an awl in the southeast part. The only axe recovered also came from this area.

Three Ways Wharf

The site of Three Ways Warf is located on the eastern bank of the Colne on a low gravel bank adjacent to a stream. The Early Mesolithic occupation took place on an area of alluvial gleyed soil, in an environment that was mainly open, but had evidence for woodland in the proximity. Three Ways Warf is best known as a Terminal Palaeolithic Long Blade site, but a large scatter of Early Mesolithic material is present, concentrated in scatter C west, though there is some spatial overlap between the two occupations, which makes it difficult to completely differentiate activities. Scatter C west has been partially truncated by a later Prehistoric ditch, again obfuscating the nature of activities at the site. Radiocarbon measurements on two red deer and one roe deer are consistent with a single period of occupation, which took place some time between 8700 and 8300 BC (Lewis and Rackham 2011).

The Mesolithic scatter is a medium density site (up to 150 pieces per square metre), which Lewis suggests represents a single occupation, probably occurring in the autumn or winter. There is a tight fall off of flint in the scatter, possibly suggesting the presence of an ephemeral shelter, with an entrance to the south facing the adjacent water-course. The presence of higher densities of burnt flint in the southern part of the scatter has been used to suggest the presence of a hearth. Lewis has suggested scatter C West can be broken down into four smaller concentrations: Two relatively high-density southern scatters, one of which surrounded the hearth, and two lower density northern scatters. These two southern scatters seem focused on knapping, with the western one focused on tool production and the eastern one more on tool use. The two more northerly concentrations may be associated with more ad hoc production (e.g. the use of a broken axe fragment as a core to produce a microlith), tool use, particularly for bone working and butchery, and tool discard.

Terrace gravel flint, which could be easily obtained from adjacent water-courses, was the main source employed. Some flint with a chalky cortex was also present, which could have been derived from closer to the chalk. The initial processing of these river cobbles took place at Three Ways Wharf, as indicated by the presence of unworked and partially worked smashed fragments, the result of testing material for flaws. The only hammerstone from C West was found in a cluster with four unworked nodules in the southeastern scatter (Lewis and Rackham 2011, 90).

Scrapers are the most common tool type recovered from C West (Table 3.4). These cluster on the margins of the C West scatter, particularly in the northwest and southwest (Figure 3.9). Microliths are also common, and a production area can be discerned by the presence of several microburins in the southern part of C West. This same area also served as a production area for burins, as several manufacturing spalls are found here. Most of the burins manufactured in these areas appear to have been removed from the site, though some were made here, and others that were perhaps brought in were deposited in two areas, one to the north of C West and one to the south. A cluster of antler in the southeast scatter is associated with tools with use traces of antler working. Corbiac burins are present, a feature of the Early Mesolithic of the region. Retouched and utilised flakes and blades are scattered at low densities across C West; notches are more concentrated in the

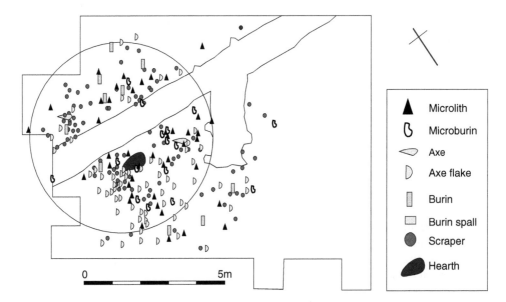

Figure 3.9 Distribution of major tool types at scatter C West, Three Ways Wharf (Redrawn after Lewis and Rackham 2011)

southern part of the scatter. Use-wear indicates use of these tools for butchery (both meat and fish).

The production and use of axes appear more common at Three Ways Wharf than on other sites along the Thames tributaries, with the exception of Broxbourne 104, and use-wear evidence indicates wood working was a major task, involving both axes and scrapers. Several axe-thinning flakes and 15 sharpening flakes were recovered, as were two roughouts and two fragments, which had broken during production, three of which were reused as cores. Axe-sharpening flakes are present in flint colours that are not represented either in thinning debris or by the axes themselves. This is also the case at Broxbourne 104 and suggests that axes were tools that had longer life histories, traveling beyond the sites on which they were made.

The Mesolithic faunal assemblage at the site is dominated by red deer remains, with an MNI of around 15 (Table 3.2). These appear to have been introduced to the site as whole limb elements, which were then processed for marrow and grease extraction (Lewis and Rackham 2011; Overton 2014). Elements of the axial skeleton are almost absent, indicating these have been left at kill sites or butchery camps elsewhere in the area. The red deer remains are strongly associated with the possible structure area of scatter C West and, in particular, with an area immediately to the south of this (Figure 3.10). This has been suggested to represent a midden area, where limb bones were deposited. This midden corresponds to a gap in the flint distribution; the composition of this midden differs from others present in the Kennet Valley and the Vale of Pickering, which do include substantial quantities of flint. Interestingly, this midden is in the same location as a small cluster of reindeer bones belonging to the Long Blade occupation. Given that there seems to be at least one instance of flint from the Long Blade scatter being scavenged during the Mesolithic, it is likely that at least some evidence of this earlier occupation was visible on the ground during the Early Mesolithic. It may be that this midden was established deliberately because of the presence of reindeer bones in this location, or it was considered appropriate to gather up visible reindeer remains and associate them with the Mesolithic midden.

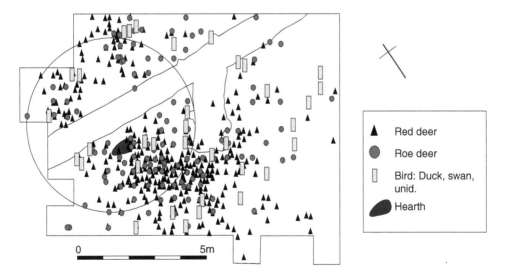

Figure 3.10 Distribution of faunal remains at scatter C West, Three Ways Wharf

Box 3.2   Early Mesolithic axe production

The Colne may be associated with complimentary upland occupation of the Chilterns. A substantial site of Early Mesolithic date was located by Peake (1917) at Kimble Farm, Turville, at c.180 m OD on the high ground of the Chilterns. Peake notes numerous (130) cores, scrapers, 12 obliquely blunted points and several tranchet axes (see also Clark 1932). The presence of several axes is noteworthy, as these are relatively rare on the Colne Valley sites (though common as dredged finds from the Thames). Tranchet axes are also known from Nettlebed, a few hundred metres from a flint source on the southern edge of the Chilterns. Here, axes were found on high ground, close to springs, on a south-facing slope overlooking the large meander of the Thames between Wallingford and Henley. Early Mesolithic material, represented by obliquely blunted points and a range of other tools, predominate in the area (Jacobi 1976), though Late Mesolithic material is also present (Boismier 1995). One possible further example may be Daws Heath, Essex, where 33 axes were recovered from a quarry (Jacobi 1980b). This site is located on a patch of fluvio-glacial sand and gravelgravel, which may have provided raw material. It should of course be noted that all these sites are likely to suffer from collection bias, which results in the under-representation of Late Mesolithic activity, and it is possible that both assemblages of axes belong to the Late Mesolithic, when large-scale production sites appear more common.

Large-scale axe production in the Early Mesolithic seems relatively unusual. Most Early Mesolithic sites on the Thames and its tributaries evidence a small number of axes seemingly produced for personal use, rather than playing any role in exchange systems as in the Neolithic. These, as examples from Three Ways Wharf and Broxbourne 104, hint axes may have on occasion had longer histories of curation. Some, though not all, were removed from the sites of their production.

Kimble Farm's location on clay with flints may point to the presence of a solution hollow, a habitual source of flint material throughout prehistory. It may paint a picture of more habitual axe production in upland areas with abundant flint, which were carried down to the lowland river valleys for further use. There are reports of the use of a small number of nodules with chalky cortex at both Three Ways Wharf and the Sanderson site, suggesting some use of more distant sources, amongst a predominant use of local raw materials.

Roe deer are also present at the site, but in smaller numbers, with an MNI of two. In contrast to the red deer, these seem to have been imported to the site as entire animals. Their remains show a similar distribution to red deer. Other animals are present, but represented by smaller numbers of elements. Remains of beaver, swan, pine marten, wild cat and fox were all recovered from C West.

Settlement on the Lea and Colne

Sites along the Colne and Kennet tend to be small or medium in size. The latter, represented by Three Ways Wharf and Broxbourne 104, are associated with possible tent rings, which may have housed a small group. Tools such as scrapers, burins and axes are better represented on these two sites in comparison with the smaller sites. Smaller sites seem to be short-term camps, where activities varied. Microliths are more likely to be common, but none of these sites seem particularly specialised. Reynier suggests that Deepcar groups moved camp frequently and lacked specialised sites. This broadly fits the pattern along the rivers, but there certainly seems a distinction between length of stay, with perhaps longer-term sites occupied at different times of year. Adjacent areas of high ground were also exploited, seemingly for a range of different reasons; these in contrast to the river sites perhaps had more specialised use. Hillwood, High Beach, seems focused on hunting, while there seems potentially more specialised production on sites located on the chalk and other good sources of raw material. The largest site in the area is West Heath, a site on the higher ground with spectacular views, and near the source of several of the rivers that were so important to Mesolithic groups. This may have made it significant, and the sheer quantity of material may suggest this was a place where a number of small, dispersed groups met.

The Kennet Valley

A marked concentration of Early Mesolithic sites can be found along the middle stretches of the River Kennet, a tributary of the Thames, between Hungerford in the west and Thatcham in the east (Figure 3.11), with only one significant site to the east of this concentration, at Ufton Green on the lower reaches of the river. The large numbers of sites known can be partly seen as a reflection of development in the area – which includes, historically, peat-cutting, quarrying and more recently the expansion of Newbury – and the number of dedicated field workers in the region, in particular Roy Froom and the individuals that made up the Newbury Museum Group. The large

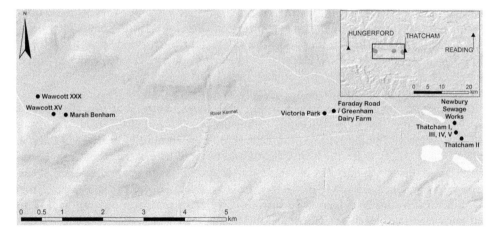

Figure 3.11 Mesolithic sites on the middle reaches of the Kennet (© Crown copyright and database rights 2021 OS 10006404)

number of sites, along with a number of detailed palaeoenvironmental studies (Chisham 2004; Churchill 1962; Holyoak 1980), make the middle Kennet Valley one of the few areas in Britain where the detailed study of Mesolithic landscape archaeology is possible.

The River Kennet rises in the Marlborough Downs and flows eastward for about 40 km before entering the Thames at Reading. Chalk forms the highest parts of the Kennet Valley, and underlies the vast majority of the remainder (Holyoak 1980, 4). The chalk is capped by layers of Eocene clays, which outcrop at the valley margins. Much of the valley is covered by superficial deposits. Clay with flints and chalky head deposits are common on the higher ground and must, like the chalk, have been a valuable source of flint. Terrace gravels are present along the valley margins, and were also important sources of flint at many sites. Along the Colne and Lea, it was gravel bars and eyots that were the focus for Mesolithic settlement. Here, along the Kennet, the youngest gravel terrace, the Pleistocene Beenham Grange terrace, just 1–3 m above the floodplain, was the focus for Mesolithic settlement.

The floodplain was a varied and dynamic landscape in the Early Holocene. The Kennet itself was still a braided river, though lower in energy than during the Late Glacial (Chisham 2004). Small, meandering streams, emanating from chalk springs, flowed through the floodplain to join the Kennet (Barnett 2009). Where these streams became locally blocked by vegetation, tufa or beaver activity, small pools were created. In the Thatcham reedbeds area, an incipient soil developed in the preboreal on the floodplain and adjacent terrace. Peat development also started around this time, spreading out from channel margins to blanket the floodplain. As conditions became warmer and wetter during the boreal and calcareous spring, activity increased; tufa development in these water-courses became more pronounced, and flooding consequently more common as channels became choked with tufa (Holyoak 1980).

Pollen and plant macrofossil evidence indicates the floodplain was covered by herbaceous plants, indicating a relatively open vegetation on the floodplain of grasses, ferns and plants common to wetlands, such as bog-myrtle and meadowsweet. Willow scrub, dogwood, bog-myrtle and aspen also grew in the wetlands, while birch grew in stands on the drier gravel terraces. In the later part of the preboreal, pine became the dominant tree species, at the expense of birch, from c.8700 BC.The floodplain remained relatively open, though drier, allowing the development of stands of willow, while hazel became an important part of the woodland from around 8500 BC (Barnett 2009; Chisham 2004; Holyoak 1980). It is likely that pine covered the higher, drier ground, while evidence from the floodplain indicates a mosaic of herb-rich fen, scrub, and stands of birch and pine.

Early records suggest an area rich in Early Holocene finds. Peat digging was extensive across the area in the 18th and 19th centuries (Froom 2013), resulting in the recovery of finds of potential Mesolithic age. Collet, writing in 1756 (cited in Palmer 1878, 137), recounts that: 'the horns, heads and bone of several kinds of deer, heads and tusks of boars, the heads of beavers … all these things are generally found at the bottom of the peat'. Owen (1846, 193) records bones of beaver, boar, roe deer, red deer and wolf found 20 ft below the surface in a bed of marl resting on gravel. The best known of these early finds is the Ham Marsh aurochs, found some time around 1843. This animal lay 'six feet below the surface enveloped in decayed boughs of trees, amongst which the hazel was readily to be found' (; Palmer 1878; Grey 1839, 141). A set of red deer antlers and the trunk of a very large pine tree was found nearby (Palmer 1878, 133). Early accounts (Palmer 1878, 133) state that a flint flake or microlith was originally found in the nasal aperture, though this no longer survives, and no lesions are visible (Jacobi archive, British Museum). We have no way of knowing the date of these old finds, certainly later material, such as urns and bronze spear heads, are also mentioned in these early accounts. However, peat growth did commence in the Early Holocene, and the tree species mentioned are compatible with those growing in the area during the Early Mesolithic. It is tempting to see these finds as representing off-site activity associated with the major accumulations of archaeological material in the area. If so, they paint a picture of a wooded floodplain landscape rich in fauna.

Thatcham Reedbeds

Just to the south of Thatcham, a 400 m stretch of wetland running from the sewage works to the railway (see Figure 3.11) has been the focus of excavation for more than a century. Mesolithic material was first located by workman from the sewage works in 1920, and the area underwent further investigation by Peake and Crawford (1922), who located the stratigraphic position of the material on the Beenham gravel terrace. Subsequent excavations have demonstrated that this terrace was a repeated focus of occupation for groups camping on dryer ground overlooking the wetland (Figure 3.12). Mesolithic remains are almost continuous along this stretch, and radiocarbon dating

Figure 3.12 Thatcham Reedbeds: View from the terrace to the floodplain

demonstrates repeated visits over several hundred years. The earliest evidence probably comes from the southern part of Thatcham III, where a patinated assemblage, with Star Carr-type microliths consisting of simple obliquely blunted points, squat isosceles triangles and trapezes, was recovered. Activity in the vicinity of a small pool in the wetland below the terrace also seems early, starting at around 9000 cal BC. Intermittent occupation by groups with broadly Deepcar-type microliths make up the majority of the occupation evidence from the terrace, but typological diversity is likely to indicate repeated visits over a long period of time. The presence of a Horsham point at Thatcham II and Newbury Sewage works indicates that visits continued well into the middle part of the Boreal.

Though excavations in the reedbeds area have focused on the gravel terrace, Mesolithic activity also took place on the floodplain itself. Small-scale excavations by Wymer indicate that animal bone and other materials were deposited in wetland pools adjacent to occupation areas. The floodplain was also used for various flint knapping tasks: A microlith tip and lithic debitage was recovered during coring on Thatcham Reedbeds (Barnett 2009). The floodplain deposits also indicate that burning of the wetland vegetation occurred (Barnett 2009). Two small peaks of microcharcoal are present, the latter of the two seeming to result in a drop in pine and peak in birch, which momentarily reversed the broader trend of pine expansion and reduction in birch. These two burning events are probably co-incident with the earliest Mesolithic of the area, at somewhere between 9100 and 8500 BC. More marked evidence for burning can be found in sediments of boreal age, where two major charcoal peaks are evident. The first of these coincides with the hazel rise and probably represents in-termittent firing events over c.130 years centred on 8400 BC. The second probably starting around 8100 BC, lasted in the region of 160 years, and resulted in the decline of pine and expansion of grasses and sedges. In contrast to the small peaks in charcoal belonging to the earliest Mesolithic, which represent short-term fire events, these boreal peaks are considered to reflect a series of events over a decadal to century scale. Barnett argues that these events were relatively small scale, focused on maintaining an open canopy landscape, with Mesolithic people expanding natural openings.

Newbury Sewage Works

Moving from north to south along the terrace, Thatcham Sewage works is the first site to be encountered in the area of Thatcham Reedbeds (Figure 3.11). At 69–70 m asl, it is at a slightly higher altitude than others along the terrace. While Mesolithic material had been found during the construction of the works and in the area immediately to the south (Peake and Crawford 1922), most of our knowledge of the occupation comes from excavations by Wessex Archaeology in 1989, undertaken in advance of exten-sions to the works (Healy et al. 1992). The area can be divided into two parts, se-parated by a relict palaeochannel. The southern concentration is firmly Early Mesolithic, of Deepcar type, with simple obliquely blunted and part-backed points, the northernmost area has a mix of Early, Horsham and Late Mesolithic microliths. Activities in the southern part of the site seem mostly focused on the production of microliths and retooling, with three separate clusters scattered over a 20 m area. The southernmost past of the area south of the palaeochannel saw the most extensive activity, with a large concentration of lithic debitage (scatter 1), within which was a small area focused on microlith manufacture and retooling, and more dispersed activities involving scrapers and a microdenticulate. Use-wear suggests that wood, bone and antler were all worked. Two smaller areas of activity can be discerned; both focused on microlith production and retooling. A small cluster of around 120 burnt hazelnuts associated with one of these smaller scatters, considered to represent snacking, has been dated to between 8565 and 8010 cal BC (9100 ± 80 BP; BM-2744) (Healy et al. 1992, 66).

Thatcham I–V

In the 1930s, a local schoolmaster and member of the Newbury District Field Club, Guyon Bull, relocated the area of Peak and Crawford's excavations and obtained permission to undertake excavations in the area of the sewage works. He was joined by A.H. Collins, and later by the Sheridan brothers, W.A. Barber, P. Hassle and P. Tosdevine (Froom 2012, 132). These individuals (the Newbury Museum Group) were to have a major impact on the Mesolithic archaeology of the Kennet Valley, undertaking a series of excavations in the area. They were not the only people working in the Thatcham area. This was an area noted for its Mesolithic archaeology, and gravel quarrying in the area also created access points at this time; these factors attracted flint collectors who kept little record of the location of their finds.

The Newbury group kept Coghlan, the curator of the Newbury Museum, appraised of their activities, and when lithic material, in conjunction with fauna, was recovered under the peat, in the area later named Thatcham II in 1956, they were directed to John Wymer, who was then curator of Reading Museum (Wymer 1959). Excavations, in collaboration with Wymer, commenced with trial trenching in 1957 and full excavation from 1958 to 1961. It is clear that much of the excavation was undertaken by the Newbury Group in Wymer's absence, with Wymer drawing on their field notebooks, which – in general – provided a detailed record of the stratigraphy and finds recovered from each grid square. This has inevitably resulted in some unevenness of reporting and curation for the site.

Thatcham I and III are contiguous areas of excavation along the gravel terrace overlooking the floodplain. The terrace is covered with a palaeosol (Chisham 2004), within which the vast majority of the Mesolithic artefacts were located. Over this palaeosol, peat developed, while thin layers of tufa over the western parts of both sites indicate periodic flooding from local springs and water-courses. The main period of tufa deposition post-dates the occupation, and seems to have truncated the part of the palaeosol closest to the bluff. A channel divides the main areas of Thatcham I and Thatcham III, and may have been active during the Mesolithic occupation.

Thatcham III was the densest area of occupation located by Wymer and the Newbury Museum group, with up to 700 pieces of flint and 120 faunal remains recovered per square metre (Overton 2014; Wymer 1962). Numerous clusters of burnt flint, pebbles, bone and hazelnuts indicated the presence of hearths and hearth debris (Figure 3.13). Seventeen of these burnt clusters were found in a 180 m² area, suggesting repeated occupation. Faunal remains were also relatively well preserved; the fragile bones of birds and small mammals were recovered here, in contrast to other areas along the terrace.

Thatcham III is composed of two large areas of excavation and a series of smaller trenches. The southernmost trench, box 8/9, named Thatcham IIIB by Jacobi, is associated with the Star Carr assemblage, discussed above. The large northern trench

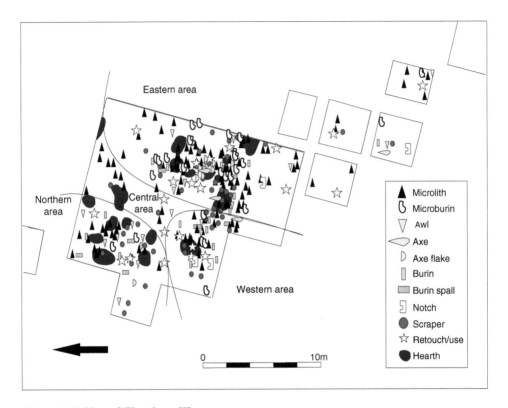

Figure 3.13 Plan of Thatcham III

(Thatcham IIIA in Jacobi's terms) is composed of a series of lithic scatters associated with hearths, sufficiently dense to represent partially superimposed occupations (Figure 3.13). In order to describe the activities at IIIA, the site has been further divided into four areas, and lithic material plotted, based on records from the Thatcham archive (Newbury Museum) and identifications made by Jacobi (Jacobi archive, British Museum). Faunal identifications and distributions are from Overton (2014). Not all of the tools and the fauna retain spatial information. Around 95% of the microliths can be located, but only seven of the 17 axes. Three of these areas are defined on the basis of clusters of hearths and lithic densities; however, there is also a central area, which though characterised by low lithic densities, has concentrations of faunal material.

The eastern area is where both lithics and occupation features are densest. Eight hearths were excavated in a 35 m² area (Figure 3.13). This evidence suggests a series of partially superimposed occupations, with people returning to very specific locations, in a way rarely seen in the Vale of Pickering. This creates some problems for understanding how space was used at the site, as lithic material was undoubtedly scavenged and re-used in successive occupations. There is, however, some spatial patterning to the material that can be glimpsed: Discarded microliths and evidence for microlith production are clustered around all hearths present in this area, as is evidence for production/use of burins, though these latter are at much lower numbers. Other aspects of activities around the hearths varied: An area focused on bone and antler tools was located within the semi-circle of hearths, indicated by finds of burins, red deer antler and two bone tools. An axe and seven axe-sharpening flakes are focused on two adjacent squares in the middle of the hearth cluster, and scrapers are more common around the large western hearth. This feature is associated with a radiocarbon date of 9665 ± 70 BP (Q-1384) (Switsur and Jacobi 1979), though since this estimate was made on unidentified charcoal, this should be considered a maximum age for this feature. Of faunal remains in the eastern scatter, wild boar are most common, which cluster within the semi-circle of hearths. Overton's faunal analysis shows that butchery and discard took place in the northern part of the semicircle, while limb bones, selected as food products, cluster in the southern part, perhaps where meals were prepared. Seven of the nine pigs found here were hunted at the age of 14–18 months, suggesting at least one of the occupations occurred during summer or autumn. An unshed red deer antler from this area suggests an autumn or winter occupation (Overton 2014). To the south of this area a juvenile red deer molar indicates occupation in January/February (Carter 2001). A shed roe deer antler was recovered from the eastern part of the site, though to the north of the main concentration, and would also suggest winter seasonality. There thus seems to be different seasonality evidence for hunting particular species with pig exploited summer/autumn and deer in winter.

The northern area of the site consists of seven hearths in a 64 m² area (Figure 3.13), and also extends into the southern trench of Thatcham I. Here, the varied activities around these hearths can be more readily differentiated than in the eastern area. One hearth is associated with low lithic densities but with a scatter of wild boar remains. Wild boar are relatively rare in the northern area, but are common in the eastern scatter. Two other hearths seem associated with retooling, with several discarded microliths recovered. One of the two hearths is also associated with a concentration of red deer remains and includes an aurochs metapodial, which refits with an example recovered in the central area. Other activity areas seem more varied, with evidence for the manufacture of microliths and the use of burins, awls, scrapers and sometimes axes. Two bone tools were recovered from one of these more varied scatters, a large spear and a small point or awl, while another was associated with the processing of fauna, with a cluster of roe deer and beaver bones.

The western area of IIIA saw less dense occupation (Figure 3.13). A single large hearth is present. While a dense area of flint knapping is located around the northern and eastern sides of this hearth, tool production and maintenance were restricted to the area to the east of the hearth, where microliths were manufactured and retooled, and burin maintenance occurred. Scrapers and awls were also recovered. To the south and west of this hearth is a low-density scatter of flint with large numbers of tools, representing activity areas where tasks were carried out. Different tasks seem to have been undertaken in different parts of this space, with burins around the south and eastern margins of the hearth, a small cluster of notches and retouched blades to the east of the hearth, and a pair of scrapers on the eastern margins of the site. Very little fauna was found in this area.

The central scatter has low lithic densities, but large quantities of fauna. It can be linked with the use of the northern area due to the refitting aurochs metapodials, and the dominance of red deer remains. Beaver remains are also common in this area, though these animals were processed within both the northern and eastern areas.

A single human bone was also recovered from Thatcham III. It is a humerus, lacking articular ends, possibly from an adult female. It was recovered from the base of a layer of tufa that overlies and has partially eroded the peat that covers the Mesolithic horizon. This layer is described by Churchill (1962, 364) as 'derived algal marl', which he presumed derived from flooding of a lake on the floodplain. Due to the enhanced understanding of the Early Holocene environment of the Kennet, following more recent palaeoenvironmental work, it seems likely that this layer represents tufa deposits, resulting from spring action on the edge of the bluff or from overbank flooding of tufa-choked channels winding their way down to meet the main channel of the Kennet. Location information is not recorded for this find, but the layer of tufa is most extensive across the northern and western part of the site. This has been presumed to be of Mesolithic age because all other finds from the tufa layer were compatible with a Mesolithic date (Wymer 1959, 18). Pollen grains derived from 'mud' in the medullary cavity of the femur were suggested to be of boreal age (Churchill 1962, 427), though the number of grains recovered were very few. Isotopic evidence indicates this individual had a diet focused on terrestrial fauna, lacking both marine input and, perhaps more surprisingly, substantial amounts of riverine fish. The isotopic signature is similar to that of a dog from Thatcham IV (Schulting and Richards 2000).

The human femur is just the most recent example of finds of isolated human remains from the area. The majority of these were recovered during peat-cutting in the 18th and 19th centuries. The earliest of these finds is mentioned by Buckland: 'A human skull of high antiquity, has been found in it [the peat near Newbury], at a depth of many feet, at the contact of the peat with a substratum of shell marl. It was accompanied by rude instruments of stone, which lead us to conclude that it was the skull of one of the Aboriginal inhabitants of the Island, who had not the art of working metals' (Buckland 1825, cited in Grey 1839, 146).

A second such find was made at Speen, between Marsh Benham and Newbury, in around 1838. Here, a human calotte was found in association with the teeth of an aurochs, both lying 'deep in the peat' (Grey 1839, 146). Later accounts describe finds of a human skull and red deer antlers at Halfway (Palmer 1878), where the Wawcott complex of Mesolithic sites is located. Obviously, we have no way of being certain that these date to the Mesolthic; however, their contexts and associations are compatible with a Mesolithic date. Both peat formation and tufa deposition commenced during the Early Mesolithic in the Kennet Valley (Chisham 2004; Collins et al. 2006). The context of Buckland's skull, between a layer of tufa and overlying peat, is strikingly similar to the Thatcham III humerus. These finds might suggest similar mortuary practises to Southern Scandinavia, where human remains are found as isolated, disarticulated elements on wetland sites. The association of the Thatcham III humerus and the Newbury skull with tufa may be significant, given the interest Mesolithic people seem to have had in tufa (see chapter 5).

Just a metre to the north of the Thatcham IIIa trench lies the area known as Thatcham I. In general, lithic densities in this area are lower, and fauna was relatively poorly preserved (Wymer 1959, 21). The Newbury Group's transect notebooks, most of which are preserved in Reading Museum, record that 1673 fragments of animal bone were recovered, though in the extant collections from the site only 85 pieces remain (Overton 2014). The highly fragmentary remains of skull, long bones and the axial skeleton of a single red deer were recovered, as were the teeth of beaver, dog, pig and roe deer, the minimal remains of the latter species most likely the result of poor preservation. Marten is represented by the teeth of a lower jaw, and fox by an ulna.

At Thatcham I, three knapping scatters can be discerned (Figure 3.14), associated with hearths, mainly indicated by clusters of burnt flint and charcoal, but in one instance represented by a pit 'surrounded and lined with large flints and pieces of sarsen stone' (Wymer 1962, 333). Distributions are taken from Wymer (1959, 9), augmented by archive records. Scatter 1 in the western part of the site is a low-density knapping scatter associated with microlith production and retooling, the use of burins, scrapers, awls and microdenticulate. This scatter was also associated with two antler tines that had been cut away from the beams and a small bone point. Wymer (1959, 20) suggests that the bone point is similar to ethnographic examples used for hunting birds. The worked bone and antler were recovered adjacent to three burins and three pieces with smoothed edges, which Wymer (1959, 19) suggested had been used to work them. Extant fauna from this scatter consists of red deer, roe deer, aurochs and pine marten.

Scatter 2 in the eastern part of the site is focused on microlith production and retooling and use of scrapers and notches, the latter possibly associated with shaft preparation. Microdenticulates and burins are present but relatively rare. A stump of worked antler had been artificially removed from the base; however, faunal remains are otherwise rare. To the west and north of scatter 1 and the east of scatter 2 were areas with extremely low flint densities, where finished tools are common. These

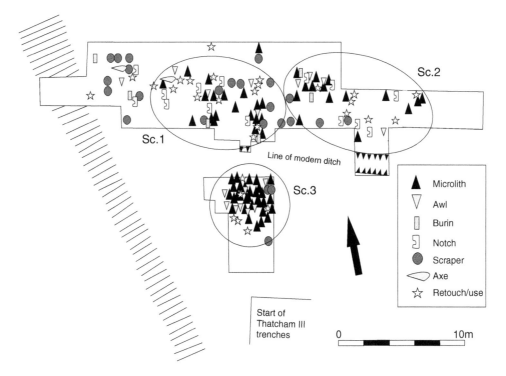

Figure 3.14 Plan of Thatcham I

appear to be areas of tool use, where tasks were undertaken, and tools discarded. The area to the west and north of scatter 1 is dominated by scrapers, probably suggesting an area of hide working; a bone 'hammer' and two axes were also found in this area. There is also a cluster of red deer bones. To the east of scatter 2 were a small cluster of microliths, a utilised flake and a burin. Animal bones are relatively common to the north of this scatter. Pig, red deer, roe deer and fox were found, possibly suggesting a butchery area. Seasonality evidence is available for this scatter in the form of a juvenile red deer, which was killed in January/February (Carter 2001).

Scatter 3, the area of greatest flint densities on the site, is located mainly in the southern trench (Wymer's grid 2). It also probably extends into the northern trench, but is interrupted by the course of a modern ditch. In contrast to the more generalised scatters to the north, and to the south at Thatcham III, activities here appear more specialised and intense, with a concentration of 29 microliths and eight awls in a 12 m² area. Given that microliths seem to have been used as awls on occasion in the Kennet, this could suggest very particular activities focused in this area. Little fauna was associated with this scatter; however, it is bounded to the south by an ancient channel from which the remains of red deer, roe deer and pig were recovered (Overton 2014). This channel may have been used as a dump for faunal remains.

Thatcham IV and V

These two trenches were located on the floodplain. Thatcham IV was initially excavated in 1959, at the instigation of Grahame Clark, who suggested this might reveal important stratigraphic information. A high water-table made this impossible to dig by hand, and it was machine excavated. Despite this, flint, bone, antler and burnt and unburnt wood was recovered from the lower levels of a white marl, which overlay peat. Funding for a coffer dam permitted the hand excavation of Thatcham V, located immediately to the west of Thatcham I, in 1961.

Stratigraphy of Thatcham V was more complex (Figure 3.15): Overlying a basal blue clay was a hard white marl (layer 5), a silt and marl (layer 4) and a peaty calcareous silt (layer 3). These seem to represent marl deposits that formed in a small lake or pool, which was subject to increasing minerogenic input, as flooding became more common, and through erosion caused by human activity on the adjacent occupation site on the terrace. Over this was a layer of what Churchill (1962) described as disturbed marl, but which is likely to be nodular tufa, derived from spring action on the terrace edge (layer 2). Artefacts were recovered throughout this sequence: Material in the upper parts of the sequence may be redeposited, but the lower parts of the sequence, as at Thatcham IV, seem to represent objects deposited into shallow water.

The material deposited is generally similar to that from the dryland, with a few exceptions. The only example of dog from the excavations came from Thatcham IV. More complete cranial material was also recovered in comparison to the dryland – particularly of pig, which is well-represented at both Thatcham IV and V (Overton 2014). Antler also seems common in comparison to the dryland (two antlers were recovered from the small area of Thatcham V compared with four antlers from the entire area of Thatcham III). There are suggestions that articulated joints may have been deposited; however, the lack of precise spatial data precludes an understanding of any potential patterning to this deposition. Artefactual material was also recovered, including an antler spear tip and bevelled antler beam from site IV and a

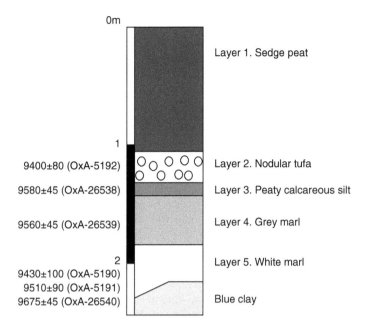

Figure 3.15 Stratigraphy of Thatcham V (redrawn after Wymer (1959) and Churchill (1962) with recent radiocarbon dates added)

worked antler beam, a handful of flint flakes and blades (several with macroscopic edge damage) and a perforated limestone bead at site V. The limestone bead is paralleled by a second example, made on a flat pinkish-cream calcareous pebble, which was recovered from a wetland context at Thatcham VI/Mudhole, a site to the west of Thatcham II. These depositionary practises took place as part of the early occupation of the site. The date range for contexts 4 and 5 span 9260–8770 BC. Churchill notes that hazelnut shells were not found in contexts 4 and 5, though these were plentiful in later contexts, while the pollen from the lower part of context 2 is compatible with the boreal chronozone, with high levels of hazel and the first appearance of elm. This environmental evidence provides additional support for a preboreal date for the lowest layers.

These wetland depositionary practises bear some similarities to those from Star Carr, with which they are broadly contemporary. These include the presence of more complete cranial material, organic artefacts, utilised flint and canine remains. It would be tempting to associate these early activities with the Star Carr-type patinated series from Thatcham IIIB; however, this scatter is some distance away. It is more likely to be related to as yet undated dryland activity in the area of Thatcham I or of Peake and Crawford's trench, both of which are in close proximity to this area. Whether this is a Star Carr-type site or an Early Deepcar one cannot yet be determined. However, the evidence from Thatcham IV and V indicates that some of the earliest Mesolithic activity in the area relates to wetland deposition rather than dryland occupation, a very similar situation to Southern Scandinavia (Jessen et al. 2015).

Thatcham II

Thatcham II is located to the southwest of Thatcham I/III, slightly lower lying than the other two sites, extending from the gravel terrace down onto the floodplain. This is the location originally discovered by the Newbury Museum Group in 1956. Mesolithic artefacts were recovered lying in a buried soil. There seems to have been some later disturbance to the site. To the east was a 1.2 m deep channel filled with tufa. Flooding from this channel had resulted in a layer of tufa deposited over the buried soil on the eastern side of the site. This contained flint and animal bone, presumably eroded by the channel from Thatcham II or an adjacent site. The channel itself also contained quantities of animal bones, and may have been a place where faunal remains were deposited. In contrast to the deep channel, a series of more shallow channels crossed the site, most of which appear to have predated occupation, though some may have continued to be active, and caused truncation of the deposits. Based on the excavation of a hearth and scatter of artefactual debris from a channel, Wymer suggests occupation took place within the depressions of relict channels, which provided shelter from the elements.

The assemblage of microliths from Thatcham II contains forms not present at Thatcham I: Elongated scalene triangles, trapezes and rhomboids and curve-backed pieces, a type considered by Jacobi to date to the later part of the Early Mesolithic, though the site itself is undated. Fauna is relatively sparse, with remains of red deer and boar most common. The rather minimal seasonality evidence present suggests that at least some of the pig were killed in the winter months.

At least four hearths were located, around each of which was a cluster of artefactual debris. Scatter 1 appears partially truncated by later stream action. Activities around the hearth were varied, involving flint knapping, tool production and use. A bone point was also recovered from this scatter. Immediately to the south was a small pile of stones and a handful of microliths. To the west was a more ephemeral scatter where microliths were common.

In the northern part of the site, three hearths were found with only 9 m separating the most easterly from the most westerly. Around the central hearth of the three were burins, microliths and a small axe. To the west was a small hearth associated with a scatter of microliths and a burin, while the easterly hearth had a microlith.

In the eastern part of the site, a pair of inverted red deer antlers, still attached to the skull, were found that 'stood proud of the floor by about a foot' and were associated with an antler hammer and a concentration of waste flakes. While originally interpreted by Wymer (1959, 16) as an anvil for flint knapping, the arrangement is unlikely to have been sufficiently robust for this. The description of this concentration as surrounded by silty shell marl, may suggest that this whole arrangement has been generated by spring action, though tufa springs do seem to have been a focus for deposition (Lewis et al. 2019, see also chapter 5).

East of Thatcham

Immediately to the east of Thatcham II are a series of sites dug variously by local archaeologists but also visited by flint collectors. At the Mud Hole/Thatcham VI, microliths, burins, scrapers and a bead were recovered. At Thatcham VII/ Thatcham Farm/The Spinney, Gordon Wilkins excavated a large hearth, surrounded by burnt flint and bone, a high-density scatter containing large numbers of cores and pig bones, which may represent a midden situated next to a possible dwelling structure (Jacobi 1975). Pig, red deer, roe deer and beaver were all present, as were a small number of more recent domesticates. Further to the west are two sites recorded by Peter Tosdevine, a meticulous excavator (Froom pers. Comm.), at Thatcham Farm/Tosdevine A and B. At site A, both flint and bone were located, the flint clustered in a single main scatter in the southeastern part of the site, with relatively high densities represented. Microliths (35), scrapers (26), burins (8) and utilised pieces (27) were all represented in an assemblage totalling 1834 artefacts (Froom 2012). Site B represents a lower intensity site, with densities not exceeding 50 flints per square metre. A small number of microliths, scrapers, burins and utilised pieces were recovered.

The only significant excavation further east, on the lower reaches of the Kennet, is Ufton Bridge, 13 km distant. Here, the valley floor was characterised by a series of gravel islands and bars interspersed between lower lying ponds and wetland areas. Mesolithic occupation took place on the crest of a gravel rise, close to a palaeochannel. Local woodland was of hazel, oak and elm, while sedge swamp grew on the floodplain. Fieldwalking in 2002 located a small scatter a few metres in diameter, and a 2×1 m test pit located in its centre revealed a small lithic assemblage of 270 pieces, including five scrapers, a microlith and a notched piece. This area underwent further excavation, and a test pit was opened 8 m to the south, where the remains of one or more roe deer were located, with the bones showing evidence for butchery. This is an animal that usually plays a subsidiary role in faunal assemblages from the Kennet. A microlith and two flint flakes were associated with the bones. The occupation has been dated to 8740–8340 cal BC (9311 ± 60 BP, UBA-27302; 9323 ± 28 BP, SUERC-56977) (Barnett et al. 2019).

West of Thatcham

Only 2 km further up the Kennet from the Thatcham Reedbeds, a series of sites have been found in the vicinity of Newbury. Several of these were uncovered in the 19th century, and little information remains: From a section of peat, underlying tufa, exposed at Northbrook St, Newbury, Richards recorded 'neolithic' flints, consisting of 'one axe-like instrument, many scrapers, knives, and needle-like flints, together with wasters in abundance' (Richards 1897, 432). Traces of fire were represented by calcined flints and charcoal. A drilled and ornamented piece of antler was also found. These were associated with the bones of red deer, roe deer, pig, bos, wolf and dog, many of which had been split longitudinally (Richards 1897). More recent excavations provide more detail for two sites: Greenham Dairy Farm/Faraday Road and Victoria Park.

Greenham Dairy Farm/Faraday Rd

Greenham Dairy Farm/Faraday Road is a contiguous spread of debris located on the Kennet floodplain, around 200 m to the north of the river and to the west of its confluence with the Lambourn. The Kennet floodplain is approximately 2 km wide at this point (Ellis et al. 2003). An ancient palaeochannel, filled with light grey silty clay, underlies the site. Above this was a layer of overbank alluvium (a pale grey silty clay), on top of which had developed an Early Holocene soil horizon in which the Mesolithic material was recovered (Ellis et al. 2003, 112).

The site of Greenham Dairy Farm was excavated by the Newbury Museum Group in 1963 during the building of an abattoir (Sheridan et al. 1967). A small area of around 7 m^2 was excavated, and an assemblage of 2495 flint artefacts and one antler pick were recovered (Table 3.5). As Froom (2013, 127) points out, this is a high density of lithic material, compared to other Early Mesolithic sites in the Kennet Valley, where densities are more habitually in the region of around 30 artefacts per metre. The assemblage is dominated by microliths (117 examples), and their production and re-tooling activities appear to have been a major task. Scrapers (27), utilised blades (13) and notches (8), played a more minor role. A small faunal assemblage included pig, red deer, roe deer and aurochs, which are represented mainly by head and foot remains (Jacobi archive, British Museum).

In 1997, the abattoir was demolished, and council offices were constructed at the site (Ellis et al. 2003). Excavations by Wessex Archaeology immediately to the east of the Newbury Group's site uncovered further Mesolithic material, an assemblage consisting of 2367 lithic artefacts (Table 3.5) and 2046 fragments of animal bone. The assemblage recovered is similar to that from Greenham Dairy Farm, in the dominance of microliths (65), with smaller numbers of retouched/utilised blades (55) and scrapers (22) and other tools fairly negligible.

Faunal remains are also similar to GDF, with pig most common and smaller quantities of red deer, roe deer and aurochs. Beaver and wild cat, two species not represented in the GDF excavations, were also recovered. Cut-marks on beaver bones indicate that these were exploited for meat, rather than just for their pelts (Ellis et al. 2003, 118). Pigs are represented by a minimum of 13 individuals and were mainly killed as young animals with about a third killed before their first year, and 90% before the age of 30 months (Ellis et al. 2003, 119).

Spatial analysis indicates two scatters were represented, one in the east and one in the west, with the latter disturbed by a wall foundation trench. In the western scatter, a concentration of microliths and microburins demonstrates microlith manufacture and retooling, and quantities of small flint chips indicates routine flint knapping. Burnt hazelnuts are more common in this part of the site. Patterning is particularly clear on the eastern side of this western scatter, where small clusters of both microburins and microliths can be discerned in close association with smaller numbers of scrapers and truncations. The western part of the scatter appears rather more disturbed. Faunal material is relatively rare in the western scatter.

The eastern scatter was rather different in character. It contained large flint debris, including 25 cores, of which 12 occurred in 1 m^2. Large broken fragments, seemingly the product of core preparation, were also recovered. Scrapers were also reasonably common. Faunal remains are also common in this area, particularly pig, of which a minimum of 12 individuals are represented. This area was interpreted as a midden area by the excavators. Overton's (2014) reinterpretation of the seasonality of the site suggests pig remains were deposited on this midden at more than one season of the year (summer/autumn/winter), perhaps suggesting repeated occupations. The midden's contents are strikingly reminiscent, in the concentration of large numbers of cores and pig bones, of the Thatcham VII/Spinney site, suggesting that the middening of cores and pig bones was a repeated pattern in the region.

Two radiocarbon dates were obtained for the site, both coming from the same square in the eastern scatter. A charred hazelnut shell was dated to 8495–8270 cal BC (9148 ± 60 BP NZA-11038) and pig bone to 7630–7470 cal BC (8510 ± 60 BP NZA-11039). If these dates are reliable, they suggest reoccupation of the same area. While the vast majority of microliths are simple obliquely blunted points, a basally modified form is also present (Ellis et al. 2003, Figure 3, no. 15), which may belong to this later occupation.

Victoria Park

Little information is available about the earliest excavations at the Park. Peake notes that while excavating the boating pond workmen found a tranchet axe and three bladelets in a black peaty soil, resting on gravel (Peake 1934, 50). Additional material is present in the Newbury Museum, including nine microliths, ten scrapers and a burin (Froom 2012). The Newbury Group also undertook small-scale excavations in the area in 1963 in advance of the construction of the A34 bypass. Some records of these survive in the Jacobi archive. An excavation trench of 6 × 4 ft located a small, but dense (up to 390 flints per metre) scatter of material clustered around a hearth. In all, 4447 lithic artefacts were recovered (Table 3.5). The assemblage of tools was fairly balanced between microliths (43), scrapers (33) and microdenticulates (21). While microliths are found distributed fairly broadly across the site, though with a concentration adjacent to the hearth, scrapers and microdenticulates have a more concentrated (and rather similar) distribution around the hearth, particularly clustering immediately to the northeast. The presence of nine microburins and an axe-thinning flake indicates the production of both microliths and axes. Faunal material was recovered, but records of this are not preserved, apart from two worked pieces found in

Table 3.5 Lithic assemblages from Newbury and the Upper Kennet

	Greenham Dairy Farm	Faraday Road	Victoria Park (1963)	Marsh Benham	Wawcott XXX
Awl	0	0	0	0	1
Axe	0	0	0	1	6
Burin	1	2	0	18	18
Chamfered	0	0	0	2	0
Fabricator	2	0	0	0	1
Microlith	117	65	45	30	33
Microdenticulate	5	1	21	32	1
Scraper	27	24	33	93	8
Truncation	0	9	0	21	4
Retouched	6	62	6	38	7
Utilised	13	0	0	14	0
Notch/dent	8	7	0	0	10
Axe flakes	2	0	1	5	8
Burin spalls	0	0	0	11	12
Microburins	47	22	9	12	9
Debitage	2182	2084	n/a	3091	n/a
Cores	85	99	0	109	40
Total	2410	2276	4447	3368	n/a

the eastern part of the site: One was a piece of scraped bone, the other a possible bone point fragment. Parts of the site were observed to be rather disturbed on excavation, and a sheep bone was noted by Jacobi, even in a part of the site thought to be intact.

A more recent 2 × 2 m trench was excavated by Barnett et al. (2019). Here, a Holocene soil, becoming peatier in its upper parts was sealed beneath deposits from canal digging. This layer is interpreted as initially formed of alluvium, which became more stable and organic, but was still subject to periodic flooding. The soil was rich in charcoal and artefacts. Fifty animal bones were recovered, of which only eight could be identified to species: Roe deer, red deer, beaver, watervole and possibly hare. The beaver bone is a tibia that may have been used as a tool, and two further possible bone tools were located. In addition, 489 lithic artefacts were recovered from the trench. Microliths dominate the tool assemblage and indicate both Early and Late Mesolithic occupation at the site. Animal bone was poorly preserved; instead, charcoal from within the trench was dated, none associated with a hearth. These measurements fall into two groups: One in the centuries either side of 8500 cal BC; the other set is more coherent, falling between 7615–7545 cal BC (ibid., 200). As part of this project, charcoals from the 1963 excavation, located between 25–50 m away, were dated and fell into these same temporal groups. If these charred materials were generated by human action, they would be compatible with the Kennet's Early and Middle Mesolithic occupation, respectively.

The Upper Kennet

Further up river to the west lie the Wawcott/Marsh Benham complex of sites, where can be found sites dug by the Newbury group, and those excavated by Roy Froom from the early 1960s. Wawcott XXX is the most extensive of the Early Mesolithic sites investigated by Froom. An area roughly 14.5 by 9 m, located following a programme of fieldwalking, was excavated between 1972 and 1974 (Froom 2012). Archaeological material was located within an Early Holocene soil horizon, which rested on basal gravels and was sealed by a layer of tufa that is likely to represent overbank flooding from local channels, which lie to the south and west of the site. Seven thousand two hundred sixty worked flints were recovered (Table 3.5). The site is unusual amongst those in the Wawcott area in that a faunal assemblage was also recovered, of which 43 elements could be identified to species. The assemblage is also unusual in the wide range of species represented. Pig and red deer, the staples of the Kennet Valley sites (Overton 2014), are relatively rare with six and seven elements recovered, respectively. Elk is represented by eight elements and aurochs by 15, the only assemblage within the Kennet where these species are most frequent. A small number of elements of both roe deer and badger were also recovered. Badger, as is the case with other solitary or carnivorous animals in the region (Overton 2016), is represented by a single element.

Faunal remains are associated with individual lithic concentrations, where there tends to be relatively low species diversity (Figure 3.16). However, there is a cluster north of scatters 5 and 6 where lithic material is rarer, and species diversity is at its greatest, probably suggesting remains deriving from a number of separate hunts. This may represent a faunal processing area, or a midden. A second, but smaller, diverse cluster can be found between scatters 4 and 5.

The unusual representation of faunal remains is echoed by the microlith types re-presented. Other Early Mesolithic sites in the Wawcott area, such as Wawcott XV, are

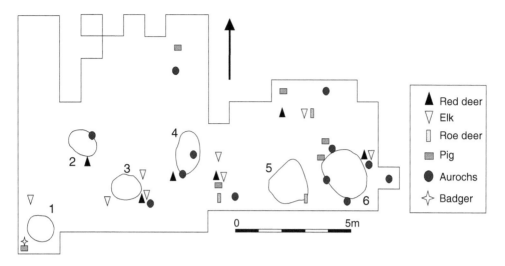

Figure 3.16 Distribution of faunal remains from Wawcott XXX (redrawn after Froom 2012)

characterised by considerable homogeneity, with very oblique points, often with retouch on the leading edge and partially backed points. The microliths from Wawcott XXX, by contrast, are similar to those from Thatcham III and Dozmary Pool in Cornwall, in the dominance of simple obliquely blunted points, with retouch on the leading edge rare, and the presence of isosceles triangles and trapezes. The site may thus predate others in the area. Froom points out the presence of a handful of unpatinated microliths in the western corner of the site, perhaps indicating a later visit. Radiocarbon dating was unsuccessful, yielding two dates incompatible with the assemblage. TL dating, with its large error range, was unable to resolve the issue.

The excavated areas are composed of a series of separate lithic scatters, some of which are likely to represent reoccupation of the same area, others which may be contemporary (Figure 3.17). Froom's (2012) detailed analysis and refitting work makes it possible to reconstruct the different activities that took place at the site and possible connections between the different areas. Scatter 3, though small, is the main area that shows connections to other areas of the site. It seems to be a place where knapping that provisioned other areas and retooling occurred. Cores also seem to have been aggregated here, removed from knapping sequences in the western part of the site. Microlith production and retooling seems to have been a major task, accompanied by smaller scale production of a range of other tools. Two scrapers were recovered, and several burins, or at least blanks for their production seem to have been made at the scatter, though the burins themselves were used in scatter 4. There are also connections to the west of the site where blanks made in scatter 3 were used in an area adjacent to the possible midden.

Though no refits were found, there could also be a connection between scatter 3 and the adjacent scatter 2, as Froom's metrical analysis reveals they are very similar. They are also united by a focus on microlith production, though retooling seems less important at scatter 2 than scatter 3. Tool production for use elsewhere was important at scatter 2, with axe flakes and a burin spall found, but no corresponding axes or burins. Scatter 4 appears

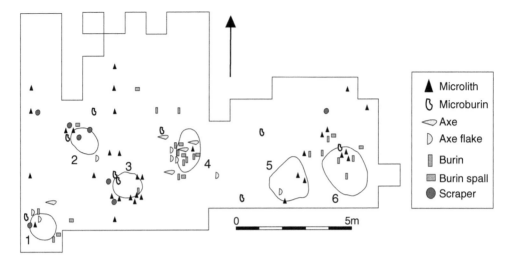

Figure 3.17 Distribution of faunal remains from Wawcott XXX (redrawn after Froom 2012)

focused on axe and burin production: Two broken, but unfinished, axes were recovered here and could be refitted to a number of production flakes within the scatter. The three central scatters 2, 3 and 4 are also united by the fauna recovered. All have yielded a restricted range of species, red deer and aurochs, though elk is also present at scatter 3.

The remaining scatters 1, 5 and 6 are less obviously connected to others. Scatter 1 is very small and focused on the production of a small but broad range of tools, with one or two examples of, or production evidence for, microliths, burins, scrapers and axes. The faunal assemblage of elk, badger and pig also sets it apart from the central scatters. The two eastern scatters, 5 and 6, also seem relatively separate, both from the rest of the site and each other. Both are large in compassion with the other two. Scatter 6 is focused on burin production and use. Scatter 5 has few tools or tool spalls, apart from a few microliths and an axe flake. Cores are relatively rare in both concentrations, and tend to be small and exhausted. These features could suggest that scatter 5, if not scatter 6, might represent southward extensions of the possible midden in the east of the site.

Marsh Benham

The Marsh Benham site is located on a low-lying gravel ridge at approximately 82 m asl on the Kennet floodplain, just to the east of the Wawcott sites. In contrast to the detailed records for the Wawcott excavations, relatively few details of the excavations that took place at Marsh Benham have been preserved. The site was discovered by members of the Newbury Museum Group in the early 1960s, and excavations were conducted around the same time. Few finds remain, and the paper archive provides only a possible indication of one of the three scatters (Reynier 2011, 5). The area was surveyed by Roy Froom when it was under cultivation in 1965, and three concentrations of Mesolithic material were located (Froom 2012, 113 and Figure 3.17). It is not known whether these are the same three scatters noted by the Newbury Group. However, given the temporal proximity of the two surveys, it seems a strong possibility.

In November 1972, Roger Jacobi and the Newbury group undertook fresh excavations at the site. Unfortunately, records do not survive, and only a portion of the finds recovered are in the Newbury Museum. Some information on the site can be gathered by correspondence to Jacobi sent by the group, and by annotated sections in his hand, suggesting he did make a visit to the site.

An initial area was opened, consisting of two adjacent 0.6 m test pits. Under topsoil and a layer of friable peat about 30 cm in depth was a buried soil profile developed over the gravel. Here, a patch of charcoal, burnt hazelnuts and burnt stones around 45 cm in diameter was interpreted as a hearth. A radiocarbon date of 9130–8250 cal BC (9300 ± 150 BP, Q-1129) was obtained from bulked hazelnut shells from this feature. Around this hearth was a scatter of flints, including retouched tools, and animal bones, including a cluster of pig teeth. The excavation then continued from the gravel ridge into the reedswamp. Below brown sedge peat and a thin layer of humified peat was a band of marl or tufa. At the base of this layer was a scatter of blades and cores. Further small-scale excavations were undertaken in December 1993 and March 1994 by Michael Reynier, when 6 m^2 were excavated adjacent to the 1972 trench. Burnt hazelnut shells recovered from this excavation returned a date of 8275–7790 cal BC (8905 ± 80 BP, OxA-5195) (Reynier 2011).

The most accurate count for material from these excavations can be found in the Jacobi archive, which, combined with Reynier's totals, indicates an excavated assemblage of nearly 3500 (Table 3.5). This indicates the unusual nature of the Marsh Benham assemblage, which in contrast to others in the Kennet Valley, is dominated by scrapers (93) and microdenticulates (52), with only modest numbers of microliths (30) and burins (18). Awls are entirely absent, and axes are represented by only a single example. Scraper-dominated sites are rare in the British Mesolithic. Microdenticulated pieces tend to be associated with craft activities focused on plant material, such as basket making. Scrapers have an association with skin working, but have a wider range of functions, depending partly on their edge angle, which include wood working. It is tempting to suggest that this site was a specialised one, focused on preparation of objects made from plant remains.

While Wawcott XXX and Marsh Benham are the major excavated sites in the Wawcott area, further concentrations of material of this date are also present in the area. These include a small assemblage from a trial trench at Wawcott XXVIII, where two microliths and three scrapers were recovered. A mostly fieldwalked assemblage from Wawcott XV extended over a large area c.20 × 75 m, yet yielded a very consistent group of 28 slender, elongated obliquely blunted points. Two microburins, 18 scrapers, a handful of burins, 11 microdenticulates, two truncations and an axe indicate a wide variety of activities were carried out at the site. Early Mesolithic microliths are also present at the 'supersite' Wawcott III (see chapter 4).

Mesolithic settlement in the Kennet Valley

There are some similarities between the structure of settlement in the Kennet in comparison to the Colne and Lea. These sites broadly fit Reynier's assessment of 'collectors' (Binford 1980) or groups that moved residential bases frequently, in that the highly specialised sites seen in Northern England are absent. That said, there does seem to be more specialised activity amongst sites along the Kennet than on the Colne and Lea. Whilst as amongst Deepcar sites more generally, assemblages tend to be characterised by slight fluctuations in the proportions of scrapers and microliths, other tools show more interesting patterns. Microdenticulates are very common at both Marsh Benham and Victoria Park. These tools tend to be related to plant processing, perhaps suggesting more specialised activities at these two sites. Marsh Benham is also characterised by an unusually high number of scrapers in comparison to microliths. Axes, which along the Colne and Lea tend to be associated with the more substantial residential sites, are only common at Thatcham III and Wawcott XXX. While the groups using the Colne and Lea visited adjacent high ground, Barnett (2009) has argued that this concentration of Mesolithic sites on the Kennet floodplain can be considered a real pattern, given that extensive fieldwalking in the adjacent chalk uplands of the Berkshire Downs failed to locate equivalent numbers of sites. It seems likely that there is not a seasonal pattern of visits to local high ground as has been argued for the Early Mesolithic in other parts of the country (e.g. Clark 1972; Jacobi 1978a, 1980a).

South of the Thames

While the Early Mesolithic archaeology discussed thus far in this chapter shows a distribution focused on major rivers, as we move west and south to the Greensand and Chalk regions of South-Central England, a slightly different situation appears to have pertained. Here, we have a series of Early Mesolithic sites on slightly higher ground, often overlooking river systems that drained into the Channel Embayment (Figure 3.18). Lowland sites tend to be found away from an immediate riparian location, instead near springs or streams that drained into major rivers, though there are exceptions: The Early Mesolithic element at Bossington was located on a gravel terrace, adjacent to the floodplain of the River Test, and Downton is on a terrace of the Hampshire Avon, a situation very similar to the Kennet sites. There also appears more specialisation of the activities undertaken on these southern sites than there was along the Thames tributaries,

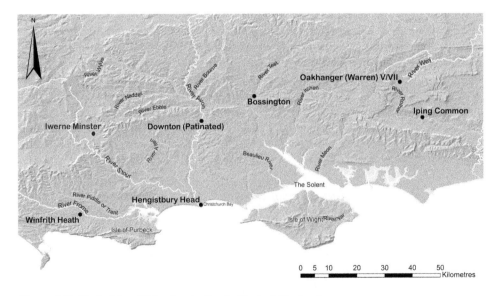

Figure 3.18 Early Mesolithic sites in South-Central England

with processing sites and gearing-up sites represented (Barton 1992; Jacobi 1981), as well as locations focused on the procurement of raw material.

The early occupation of the Greensand

The Mesolithic preference for sites on the Greensand has long been noted (Clark 1932). Many of these are Middle Mesolithic in date, and this area will be discussed in greater detail in the next chapter. However, there are also Deepcar sites in this region, particularly on the Folkstone Formation of East Hampshire, notably the large, dense site of Oakhanger V/VII, concentrations at Kingsley Common and Petersfield Heath (Gardiner 1988; Jacobi 1981). In Sussex, the smaller site of Iping Common is also on the Greensand, as is Selmeston, which though mixed has a large Early Mesolithic component. These sites all share a preference for chalk flint.

A series of sites at Oakhanger, Selborne, Hants, were excavated by W.F. and W.M. Rankine between 1950 and 1958. The area of the Rankines' investigation was bounded by woodland to the east and the Oakhanger stream to the west. It is bisected by a stream that emerges at Oakhanger Ponds and runs into Oakhanger stream. The waters of the stream pass another area of Mesolithic settlement at Kingsley Common before eventually joining the river Wey. The geology is of the Folkstone Formation of the Lower Greensand overlain by blown sand deposits. The area has been Ministry of Defence land, and much of the archaeology excavated by Rankine was uncovered as a result of damage to the sediments occasioned by military vehicles. Site III, for example, was stripped of its vegetation by heavy vehicles, then wind action removed the blown-sand covering, exposing a flint scatter of around 100 m^2, focused around four separate hearths. Similarly, Oakhanger Warren V/VII, the most prolific site, was first encountered in furrows produced by tank tracks sinking into waterlogged ground (Rankine 1953, 22–4). Of the nine Mesolithic scatters located by the Rankines at Oakhanger, only three, sites V, VII and VIII, were excavated; the remainder were surface collections of material exposed by vehicles and wind action.

Oakhanger V was excavated from March 1950 (Rankine 1953). The designation Oakhanger VII was given to a scatter only a few metres to the northwest (Rankine et al 1960), which was excavated in 1957–1958. Oakhanger V and VII thus seem to represent a contiguous scatter of material around 35 m in length. The site showed evidence for intensive occupation. In all, 186,000 worked flints were recovered, with densities of up to 1800 pieces per square metre. The Rankines suggested that three separate artefact horizons were present. The majority of the artefacts related to phase II. Artefacts associated with the lowest level, phase I, were found in small clusters, leading Jacobi (cited in Reynier 2005, 58) to suggest that these were the result of material deriving from layer II that had been displaced by tree falls, dropping into the base of the resulting tree throw. Phase III, the latest represented at the site, is associated with at least three of the six Horsham points recovered (Rankine et al 1960). The stratigraphic location of the others was not noted during excavation, though in a later publication Rankine (1961) suggests all were likely to derive from phase III. The lithic material recovered from layers I and II is of Deepcar type, but with larger quantities of curve-backed pieces and lanceolates than usual. Jacobi linked these types with the relatively late radiocarbon dates from the site to suggest these types are indicative of the latest Deepcar groups. However, the radiocarbon dates, with the exception of one measurement on bulked hazelnuts shells, are all on bulked wood of uncertain longevity, on a site where there is also Horsham activity. Their large standard deviations, spanning 8700 to 7600 cal BC, also mean their significance is difficult to interpret.

Clusters of burnt flint led Rankine to suggest that six hearths, in two groups of three, were present at Oakhanger V, and at least six more seem to be represented at site VII. Densities are too great to discern individual activity areas, but there are general differences between sites V and VII in that microliths are the most common tool type at site V and scrapers at site VII. Microburins are also better represented at site V, suggesting retooling was a more common activity here. Microdenticulates are well represented in both areas. Burins are most common at site V, but there is considerable overlap between the forms of true burins and bladelet cores on flakes, which are common in both areas. Rankine's figures in Table 3.6 are likely to include some of these bladelet cores. Awls are well represented in Jacobi's counts for site VII but not mentioned by Rankine in his assessment of site V. Only three axes were recovered, though axe-sharpening flakes proved that more had been used. Several pebble tools were found at the site, some of which seem to have a southwestern (possibly Cornish) origin (see Box 3.3). Overall, Oakhanger V/VII appears to be a site that saw repeated intensive occupations and where a wide variety of activities were undertaken.

Box 3.3   The movement of stones

While non-flint lithic material has often been overloked on Mesolithic sites, W.F. Rankine devoted some attention to the stones found on sites he excavated across Southern England. He noted a persistent presence of stones originally deriving from the southwest across Southern England (Rankine 1949a,). The movement of Portland chert appears to have started in the Early Mesolithic, as indicated by its presence at Frensham Great Pond, Surrey, and Oakhanger VII (Jacobi 1981). Rankine also records the transfer of slate artefacts, though these appear to be a Late Mesolithic phenomenon (Jacobi 1981), and fine-grained elongated pebbles, which derive from the Palaeozoic of Southwest England (Rankine 1949a, 1956, 55). These latter were moved during the Early as well as the Late Mesolithic, as demonstrated by finds from Oakhanger V/VII, where five siltstone pebbles were recovered. Petrographic analysis indicated a Cornish origin, though they are likely to have been collected as beach pebbles; Rankine (1956, 56) suggests Chesil beach is a possible source. Similar pebbles, with a Devon or Cornish origin, were recovered from Farnham (Rankine 1956) and from the Early Mesolithic site of Kingsley Common, R4 (Jacobi 1981, 20). Sandstone grinding slabs are also known from Oakhanger with possible sources in Kent and Sussex as well as sandstone and quartzite pebbles with likely exotic sources.

Since Rankine's 1949 synthesis, further examples have been uncovered, for example, sarsen stone was used to line a pit at Thatcham I, Berkshire, and a piece of abraded sandstone and quartzite pebble flaked into a disk were recovered from the same site (Wymer 1962, 333). Two pieces of Devon Sandstone, used as rubbers, come from Hengistbury Head, as well as a more immediately local sarsen block (Barton 1992). However, it is likely that exotic as well as utilised stones are often missed, particularly on sites with complex taphonomic histories.

Jacobi (1981, 15) has drawn a contrast between the large varied assemblage from Oakhanger V/VII and the smaller microlith-dominated assemblage from Iping Common, located 16 km to the south. Iping Common is also on the Lower Greensand, near the edge of a marsh that extends down to a pond and a permanent spring. It is only 1 km from the River Rother, a water-course that would have flowed into the Channel River or Channel embayment during the time of occupation; this is in contrast to Oakhanger, focused on the Thames tributaries catchment. This is just one of a series of Early Mesolithic sites in the vicinity of the Common (Jacobi 1981). The site was excavated by the West Sussex Excavation Group in 1960–1961 (Keef et al. 1965), with further excavations by Jacobi in 1976 and 1977 (Reynier 2005). The Mesolithic material was recovered from a darker stained layer, about 7.5 m in diameter, which was interpreted as a buried soil, underlying white, wind-blown sands and an upper layer of peat (Keef et al. 1965). Pollen was recovered from this layer, and while such sandy sediments are prone to the movement of pollen through the profile, the dominance of hazel both in this layer and the layer below might suggest the occupation took place some time in the Boreal, at the transition between Godwin's zone V and VI, and thus would represent a relatively Late Deepcar site.

Jacobi (1981) suggests Iping was focused on gearing up for hunting and Oakhanger on more varied processing activities. Microliths are numerous at Iping (Table 3.6). They are often broken and are outnumbered by microburins. Notches are also very common. Some of these are likely to be unsnapped micro-intermediates; others may relate to haft preparation. Notch spalls are also common. Scrapers and microdenticulates, as Jacobi notes, are rare; however, truncations are extremely numerous.

Table 3.6 Composition of the assemblages from Oakhanger and Iping. Figures for Oakhanger V taken from Rankine (1952), Oakhanger VII from Rankine and Rankine (1960) and Jacobi archive and Iping from Jacobi archive

	Oakhanger V	*Oakhanger VII*	*Iping Common (Keefe exc.)*
Awl	0	178	1
Axe	1	2	0
Burin	180	88	1
Microlith	1281	1014	163
Notch/denticulate	0	0	138
Microdenticulate	444	364	3
Scraper	1052	1760	19
Truncation	0	0	26
Misc. retouched	7	2	107
Axe flake	2	13	17
Burin spall	0	11	4
Microburin	338	148	256
Resharpening spall	0	0	13
Chamfer spall	0	0	2
Core	705	342	177
Total inc debitage	81,338	c.105,000	30,085

Truncations appear to have varied functions. In the Final Palaeolithic, they seem to have been used in the same way as burins to groove bone and antler (de Bie and Caspar 2000). In the Early Mesolithic at Star Carr, they were occasionally used in this way (Dumont 1988, 143), but were more usually used to scrape both bone/antler and wood (Conneller et al. 2018b, 528; Dumont 1988). While these could point to more varied activities at the site, they may, like the notches have been used as woodworking tools in haft and bow manufacture and maintenance.

The assemblage from Iping Common is substantial, however, and it cannot be dismissed as a small-scale hunting camp; rather the Common seems to have been occupied repeatedly in a very similar way, perhaps as a seasonal residential camp, where a lot of the activity was focused on the maintenance of composite tools. The paucity of hazelnuts, in contrast to the processing sites such as Oakhanger, has been suggested to indicate seasonal occupation, possibly in the summer months. The characteristics of the material at Iping Common are in fact very similar to those assemblages generated by people using Horsham microliths that seem to have succeeded Deepcar groups and occupied the Greensand more persistently and extensively (see chapter 4 and Box 4.5). These, too, show evidence of gearing up, and saw repeated reoccupation of the same place (Jacobi 1981). If Iping Common is relatively late, it may suggest continuity in the way these areas were occupied, either through continuity of traditions or the particular affordances offered by the landscape of this time.

South of the Greensand, an area that was a focus for occupation throughout the period has recently been located at Coombe Haven, near Bexhill. In the Early Mesolithic, this was an area of streams that ran through valleys of pine, oak and hazel woodland. Seventeen Early Mesolithic scatters have been uncovered, located along the valley edges and on rises on the valley floor. These include both larger areas of occupation and smaller, more specialised activity areas. Lithic assemblages show significant variation in the manufacture and maintenance of microliths and scrapers and other key tools, indicating complex taskscapes (Champness et al. 2019).

Southwestern Britain

Moving westwards, into the southwestern region, the land changes and becomes more varied. There are still major river valleys, along which Mesolithic sites are clustered, but also upland areas and karstic regions, which offered different affordances for inhabitation. All saw occupation in the Early Mesolithic Figure 3.19. These areas are likely to have differed substantially in their vegetational makeup. Upland areas would have been relatively open still, while the chalkland may have been less wooded, with more varied grasses and shrubs than other areas (French et al. 2003). Lowland river valleys saw the more typical vegetational succession with the pine woods of the late preboreal diversified through the increasing spread of hazel during the boreal, along with the initial appearance of oak and elm. Willow in boggy areas was beginning to be replaced by alder.

Flint is less ubiquitous in parts of the region, though chalk deposits are present as far west as Beer in Devon. Beyond this are areas where Greensand chert can be obtained. Secondary sources exist in river gravels, beach pebbles and glacial till. There is some evidence in this region for sites situated specifically to obtain raw material, perhaps a way to even out the patchy distribution in this region. Sites on the edge of the chalk include Cherhill (Evans and Smith 1983); while in the Blackdown Hills, the site of Telegraph Cottage (Berridge 1985) was located to procure Greensand chert,

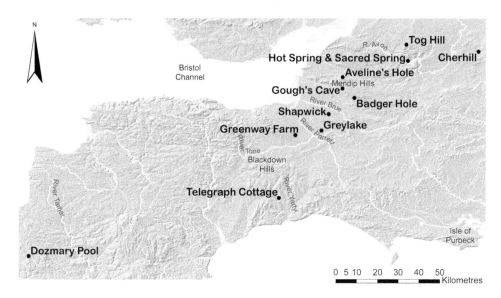

Figure 3.19 Early Mesolithic sites in Southwest England

particularly for axe manufacture. There appears more concern to obtain high-quality, often more distant chalk flint rather than mainly rely on local derived sources as in the southeast.

Though the caves of South Wales and Mendip are filled with fauna, these assemblages are of mixed date, and little material – apart from a beaver found at Gough's Cave – has been dated to this period. Our best evidence for the types of resources people relied on come from the oldest layers of Cherhill. In this assemblage, pig is most common, with smaller quantities of roe deer and red deer. Aurochs, the focus of Late Mesolithic hunting practises in the southwestern region, is rare. As usual, information on plant use is limited, though charred hazelnut shells have been dated to this period at three sites in the region.

A key feature of this region is the prominence of mortuary practises, particularly focused on areas proximate to the now-submerged palaeo-Severn and the Bristol Channel Embayment. This encompasses sites in Mendip, the Somerset levels and on Gower. A variety of practises are represented, but these earlier Mesolithic mortuary sites differ from later ones in the same region in terms of scale. Multiple interments were the norm, with remains from more than 50 individuals recovered from Aveline's Hole.

By contrast, our knowledge of the tempo of settlement in the region is poor. There are few dates that are not on human remains; all come from South Wales (David 2007). The available measurements do not suggest a particularly early date for the colonisation of this region, with little to suggest occupation before 8500 BC. However, with so few dates, a pioneer settlement phase, as we saw in the southeast, is unlikely to be identified.

In the following discussion, the region will be divided into three: The palaeo-Solent and its tributaries, the south-west peninsula and South Wales.

The Palaeo-Solent and its tributaries

In the Early Mesolithic the drainage of South-Central England was dominated by the palaeo-Solent and its tributaries, the Hampshire Avon, the Stour and the Test. The palaeo-Solent, a continuation of the present river Frome, was a major river that initially ran east-west, flowing onwards to the north of the Isle of Wight, where it turned southeast to flow into the Channel Embayment (Momber et al. 2020). As long ago noted by Rankine (1956, 32), this was a major focus for Mesolithic settlement, and several important Mesolithic sites are located in this area: On a terrace of the Hampshire Avon is Downton, overlooking the Stour is Iwerne Minster, above the Frome is Winfrith Heath, on the Test the important, but unpublished site of Bossington and above the palaeo-Solent itself the important site of Hengistbury Head. Evidence for Early Mesolithic occupation has also been found in the present-day intertidal zone, for example, at Cams, Fareham (Rankine 1951a), a location that would have been on the Wallington River, near to its confluence with the palaeo-Solent.

The Powell Mesolithic site at Hengistbury Head provides a rare glimpse of groups who probably spent much of their time in the valleys of the palaeo-Solent. Today, Hengistbury Head is a narrow spit of land that projects into the sea on the southwestern side of Christchurch Harbour. Its situation was very different in the Early Mesolithic, when it was an inland site with the coastline some 20–40 km to the south (Allen and Gardiner 2000; Devoy 1987) The site is located in a sheltered position, just below the brow of Warren Hill, with views that would have stretched over the valley of the palaeo-Solent. Raw material patterns suggest that life for the groups who visited the high ground of Hengistbury was focused on the Solent Valley and submerged land to the southeast. The main raw material employed was river gravel flint, the cortex of which does not match that of the local rivers and which Barton suggests may have derived from the Solent gravels. Some chalk flint was also employed; this may also have had a source close to the Solent either to the east on the Isle of Wight or the west on the Isle of Purbeck, though northern sources along the upper reaches of the Stour are also possible.

The Powell Mesolithic site was discovered by Ronald Powell in 1977, who recorded 3000 artefacts from the area, and excavated by Nick Barton between 1980 and 1983 (Barton 1992). In all an area of 78 m^2 were investigated. The artefacts were found within Aeolian sands, which had also at times been subject to deflation. On these sediments, a brown sandy soil developed in the Early Holocene, indicative of woodland development in the area. The artefacts have been affected by movement down this profile, resulting in a vertical distribution of c.0.5 m; horizontal movement is considered to be less pronounced, but still has caused some blurring of distribution patterns. As a result, patterning is not pronounced; most activity simply focused in the northeastern part of the site.

In all, 36,010 artefacts were recovered from the excavations. Tools are dominated by microliths, with smaller numbers of scrapers, microdenticulates and truncations (Table 3.7). Microburins were numerous, indicating a major task at the site was microlith production. Microliths, which are mainly obliquely blunted points, seem to separate into two types, a more numerous set of large, very oblique Deepcarr types, and a small set of small obliquely blunted points, which in form and size might belong best with a Horsham-style assemblage, indicating repeated visits to the headland.

Table 3.7 Assemblage composition of Palaeosolent tributaries sites

	Hengistbury Head	Downton (patinated)	Iwerne minster	Winfrith Heath
Awl	0	18	0	3
Axe	0	1	28	3
Burin	0	7	2	39
Fabricator	1	0	0	0
Microlith	347	86	156	223
Microdenticulate	64	26	n/a	8
Scraper	85	55	P	86
Truncation	15	0	P	3
Retouched	60	n/a	n/a	98
Utilised	p	50	n/a	n/a
Axe flakes	0	20	32	8
Burin spalls	0	6	0	0
Microburins	273	39	11	78
Debitage	35,671	p	P	18,500
Cores	185	392	888	242
Total	36,701	n/a	n/a	19,326

Further up the Hampshire Avon is the site of Downton, which lies on a gravel terrace, at 7.5 m above the current river. The site was excavated by Eric Higgs in 1957, after initial discovery following trial trenching by Philip Rhatz in 1956. The main area of excavation totalled around 14 by 14 m, with additional test pits located to the southeast. Mesolithic material was recovered from a red clay-silt with sand and stones, which had developed over cold-weather gravel deposits and wind-blown silt and that lay immediately below the modern subsoil (Higgs 1959).

In all, 38,086 lithic artefacts were recovered, an assemblage that is of mixed date with Early and Late Mesolithic and Neolithic material. Higgs argues that the later Prehistoric material is unpatinated and in general found higher in the sequence than the Mesolithic material, which has a blue patina. Later work by Jacobi (Jacobi archive, British Museum) has further separated the Mesolithic material into an unpatinated group consisting of Late Mesolithic microliths and a patinated early group, which constitutes the majority of the material recovered from the site, characterised by Deepcar-type microliths.

The site is of medium size, consisting of a main concentration around 9 m in diameter, but dense, with up to 1800 flints per square metre. Taking patina as an indication of Early Mesolithic date, a picture of a varied assemblage appears (Table 3.7), with almost all major tool types present in large numbers, though burins and axes are rarer. Proportions of microliths and scrapers are more balanced than at other sites in the region. A range of activities are indicated, including the processing of both plant and animal remains and manufacturing activities. Axes are common on the site but mostly unpatinated, suggesting they belong with a perhaps more specialised Late Mesolithic occupation; however, a single patinated axe and several axe flakes are present, indicating these tools were maintained at the site during the Early Mesolithic.

Higgs located a 'Mesolithic hollow' in the central part of the main Mesolithic scatter, which he believed was likely to represent a pit dug to obtain flint nodules from the underlying gravel (see Box 4.8). In fact, the section of this feature suggests it represents a tree throw that post-dates the Mesolithic occupation of the site, though this does not rule out the idea that it was used as a way of collecting flint nodules. Other features were also encountered. An area of stakeholes was located in the northern part of the site, which Higgs related to the Mesolithic occupation. Several of the stakeholes had carbonised wood at the base, which was identified as oak. This tree is unlikely to have been present during the Early Mesolithic, so this activity area seems to post-date the main phase of Mesolithic activity at the site. Finally, a hearth was located in a test pit to the south of the main site. This consisted of a neat pile of 165 fire-cracked flint nodules, from some of which flakes had been struck, overlying four large river pebbles, reddened and blackened on the underside. These in turn rested on charcoal. Higgs states that these were associated with a small scatter of Mesolithic flints, though by type none of these are unambiguously Mesolithic. This is an intriguing deposit, though the presence of later Prehistoric occupation in the vicinity urges caution.

Two further sites in the region have yielded large quantities of Early Mesolithic material: Iwerene Minster and Winfrith Heath. Located at 152 m asl on a patch of clay with flints above the Valley of the Stour is Iwerne Minster, Dorset (Barton 1992; Summers 1941). Its position is likely to be related to the easy accessibility of good-quality raw material. The site was located as a ploughzone scatter, and is likely to suffer from collection bias, as witnessed by the low numbers of microburins recovered; Horsham points and later Prehistoric material are also present in the collection (Jacobi 1975). The assemblage appears to reflect numerous visits to this locale to procure flint for knapping and axe manufacture (as witness to the relatively large numbers of both). Microliths, scrapers and microdenticulates are also common (Table 3.7), indicating varied tasks were undertaken while people camped here, rather than the place simply serving as a workshop.

Finally, Winfrith Heath lies on sandy sediments just below the brow of Whitcombe Hill overlooking a small stream, which flows around to the north of the hill and into the river Frome immediately to the east. The site was excavated in 1971–1972 by Susann Palmer and the Dorset Natural History and Archaeological Society (Palmer and Dimbleby 1979). A large assemblage of nearly 20,000 lithic artefacts was recovered from an area of c.30 × 15 m, which was not itself fully excavated, indicating an area of intense occupation. The vast majority of material was concentrated immediately north of two irregular areas of dark sand and stones, which are likely to represent natural features, probably tree throws. Barton (1992) has suggested that the dominance of microliths may be related to its location on high ground with good views for hunting, though its density and the presence of large numbers of scrapers and other tools, including axes indicate this cannot be categorised as a small-scale upland hunting camp.

Southwest England

Southwestern England and South Wales in the Early Mesolithic was the land of the dead. The dead here were prominent, collected in caves, sometimes in great numbers, or buried on settlement sites. As will be described below, mortuary practises were immensely varied. Much of our knowledge of human lifeways in this region derives from the information provided by the human remains. In contrast, our understanding of settlement in southwest Englandn is poor, though significant fieldwalking programmes have been undertaken (Berridge 1985; Norman 1975). No radiocarbon dates exist for settlement sites, though typologically Early Mesolithic material is present often in substantial concentrations: There are sites above tributaries of the Bristol Avon, associated with springs and springlines, such as at Cherhill, Wilts (Evans and Smith 1980, see Box 3.4) and Tog Hill, Gloucester (Sykes and Whittle 1965), as well as on sandy islands (the Burtle Beds) in the Somerset levels, for example, at Shapwick and Middlezoy (Wainwright 1960) and on the floodplain of the Avon in the Southgate area of Bath (Barber et al. 2015) (Figure 3.19). In some parts of the region, such as the Somerset Levels, Early Mesolithic sites may also be deeply buried by peat and clays from marine incursions (Bell et al. 2015). Further to the west, Early Mesolithic sites are located on Greensand ridges, perhaps partly to exploit this raw material (Berridge 1985), and on high ground, as at Dozmary Pool on Bodmin Moor (Jacobi 1979).

Other types of evidence exist, too. Davis (2012) has outlined how Early Mesolithic lithics recovered from a borehole at the Hot Spring, Bath, must represent deliberate deposition into the spring pipe of this remarkable feature. This small assemblage consists mostly of blades, of which more than half show evidence of utilisation, with utilised flakes also common. This emphasis on utilised pieces echoes the heavy focus on used blades in the deposition areas at Star Carr. It suggests that material was selected for deposition because it was associated with key tasks that may have been particularly meaningful. Similar Early Mesolithic material

---

Box 3.4   Cherhill, a stratified Mesolithic site in Southwest England

Located just above a small stream that flows into the Bristol Avon, but less than 5 km from the headwater of the Kennet, is the site of Cherhill. A rare example of a stratified Mesolithic site, the stratigraphy consists of a Mesolithic buried soil, sealed by a layer of tufa. Above this is a second buried soil, certainly forming in the Neolithic, but possibly by the very end of the Mesolithic. Parts of the site, particularly in the west, have been disturbed by Early Neolithic quarrying and a Late Neolithic ditch. There has been some controversy around the date of the Mesolithic assemblage. Initial reports suggested stratified early, middle and late occupations (Evans 1972), but the site was finally published, on the basis of the lithics, as a coherent Late Mesolithic assemblage (Evans and Smith 1983). Re-examination of the lithic material makes it clear that the initial hypothesis was correct. The material from the 'Mesolithic soil' is a coherent Early Mesolithic assemblage with microliths exclusively composed of obliquely blunted points. Only one microlith was recovered from the tufa. This might be described, broadly, as of Middle Mesolithic date. One Late Mesolithic scalene triangle has adhering tufa, and the assemblage from two possible pits cut into the Mesolithic soil, and containing Late Mesolithic microliths is also substantially tufa encrusted, suggesting the Late Mesolithic occupation(s) also occurred during the tufa formation. Both Early and Late Mesolithic material is found within the later ditches and the Neolithic buried soil as a result of later Prehistoric disturbance, though some of the later Mesolithic pieces within the upper, Neolithic buried soil could conceivably be in situ.

Fieldwork by John Evans and Isobel Smith in 1967 resulted in the excavation of several trenches (Figure 3.20). The western part of the site was extensively

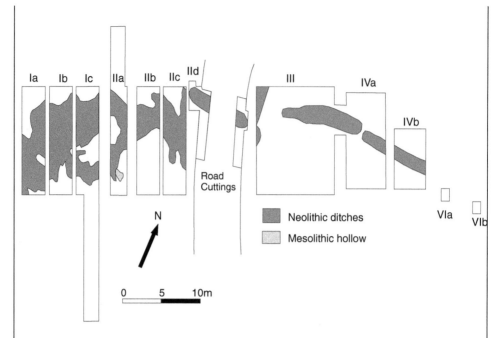

Figure 3.20 Plan of excavations at Cherhill

disturbed by the Early Neolithic quarrying. This was where Middle and Late Mesolithic occupation was concentrated. A couple of early microliths were recovered in this area, but the early occupation was focused in the eastern and northern parts of the site, in trenches IVa, IVb, Vc, VIa and VIb, mostly within the buried soil but also incorporated within later features. By contrast, there was relatively little Late Mesolithic material in this area, with the exception of trenches IVa and IVb, where it is found either within later ditches or the Neolithic buried soil. The later occupation of the site is discussed in chapter 5.

Due to time constraints, individual finds were not plotted. IVb was dug by square metre, enabling some measure of spatial control. VIb was dug in spits; however, no vertical patterning was present within the buried soil. The lithic material appears a single, coherent assemblage. Densities of Early Mesolithic material vary considerably at the site (Table 3.8). The large trench IVa has yielded relatively little material, though some has been displaced by the Beaker period ditch 2. Densities are higher in trench IVb, and spatial information shows an increase in flint densities in the southeast corner, increasing further as we move east into the 1 m^2 trench VIa and remaining high still in the easternmost 1 m^2 trench VIb, suggesting an occupation area of greater than 20 m.

These trenches provide windows into a major area of occupation, which is, however, likely to be made up of several hearths and activity areas. IVb, VIa and VIb all have large quantities of burnt flint, likely to indicate several hearths, or hearth debris; one of these can probably be glimpsed in the southeast corner of trench IVb. A major activity in this area appears to be the processing of faunal material and food consumption (a lot of the animal bone is burnt). Animal bones are highly fragmentary, due to poor conditions for preservation, but indicate a focus on pig

Table 3.8 Composition of the Early Mesolithic lithic assemblage from the buried soil beneath the tufa at Cherhill. Data from Pitts (nd.) and author's own study

Type	IVa	IVb	Va	Vc	VIa	VIb
Microlith	0	5	0	6	1	11
Awl	0	1	0	0	0	0
Burin	0	0	0	1	1	0
Denticulate	0	1	0	0	1	0
Microdenticulate	0	4	0	3	0	5
Scraper	2	2	0	0	7	3
Strike-a-light	0	1	0	0	0	0
Truncation	0	1	0	1	0	1
Retouched/utilised	1	24	1	9	4	9
Microburin	0	0	0	0	0	1
Axe flake	0	0	0	2	0	0
Retouch spall	0	1	0	0	0	0
Core	4	17	0	12	7	2
Crested blade	0	2	2	4	2	0
Core tablet	0	5	0	5	2	6
Blade	4	45	3	123	82	90
Flake/fragment	38	436	5	991	655	612
Burnt flint	0	74	0	19	17	76
Total	49	545	11	1157	762	740

with lesser quantities of red deer and roe deer. There is a suggestion that processing animals for furs was a major task: Hare is represented in two trenches, as well as wild cat, and there are several bones of small and very small mammals (Grigson nd, Table 3.8). Lithic artefacts indicate several areas of knapping, and smaller areas of specialist tool use: Retouched and utilised pieces are concentrated in the northern part of IVb, possibly related to butchery, activities using scrapers occurred in VIa, while discard of microliths and possibly retooling were undertaken in VIb (Table 3.7).

A second concentration of material is found in the northeast of the site, scattered on the small trench Vc. This is an area focused on lithic production, with generally neat, regular cores produced, often on the ends of large, thermally fractured flakes. Refits were noted during rapid analysis of the assemblage, suggesting they are fairly frequent. Flint appears predominantly local, likely to be procured from solifluction or similar deposits. Tools are present in small numbers, indicating a broad range of tasks. Fauna is less common than in the large southern scatter, but pig is represented (Table 3.8). Less is known about the size of this scatter; it appears to extend to the west, with lithic material, including an Early Mesolithic microlith, exposed in the buried soil truncated by the builder's road. Very little burnt material is present.

Snails from the Mesolithic layer indicate this soil formed initially in fairly open conditions, though by the end closed canopy forest was present in the area (Evans 1972). The soil had a damp, marshy surface, and a spring may have been present at the western end of the site. Frog bones and snake teeth were found in this soil; these may be naturally present fauna, though frog bones with cut-marks are present at the site of Blick Mead, only 30 km away, and snake is a known ingredient of Scandinavian Mesolithic fish stews (Larsson 2004). Charred hazelnut shells were recovered from several areas of the site, and yew charcoal from VIb.

Table 3.9 Faunal remains from the early Mesolithic buried soil at Cherhill. Identifications by
Grigson (nd) from the site archive (Wiltshire Museum)

Species	IVa	IVb	Va	Vc	VIa	VIb
Aurochs	0	1	0	0	0	0
Pig	1	35	0	4	27	8
Red deer	0	18	0	0	2	1
Roe deer	1	13	0	0	1	1
Hare	0	0	0	0	1	1
Cat?	0	0	0	0	1	0
Bird	0	0	0	0	0	1
Un-id	8	510	0	6	649	135

has also been recovered from around the Sacred Spring, Bath. This interest in the
hot spring, and particularly in the deposition of material into the spring pipe, indicates a concern with entrances into the earth, which is paralleled in the use of
caves for mortuary practises).

In Southwest England, flint was the preferred raw material at this time. This was
available from a variety of sources: In glacial till deposits, as river cobbles or beach pebbles,
or from sources more proximate to the chalk itself. There appears to be a preference for
chalk flint on many sites, as opposed to secondary sources. At Greylake, for example, 80%
of the flint appears to derive from a chalk source (Scott and Shaw nd), and scatters B and
C at Chedzoy also used chalk flint. West of the River Parrett, at Greenway Farm, chalk
sources were still preferentially used, though flint itself forms a much smaller component of
the assemblage (Norman 1982). Widespread chalk sources are available around 30 km to
the east of Greylake and 45 km from Greenway Farm, or as smaller patches around 25 km
to the south. This may show the size and range of social territories at this time.

Greensand chert was also employed, though still in relatively small proportions
during this period. Norman (1982) has outlined how chert is more common on sites to
the west of the River Parrett, forming 85% (by weight) of the material from Greenway
Farm. It is present in smaller proportions on the sites of the Somerset Levels, composing
just over 20% of Greylake assemblage. Chert cores appear larger than those made from
flint at this site, supporting the suggestion that flint was more valued (Shaw and Scott
nd). An axe made from Greensand chert, found at Greylake, could suggest exchange of
axes in this material, especially given that several of these tools were recovered from the
site of Telegraph Cottage in the Black Down Hills in Devon (Berridge 1985). This site,
on high ground (220 m OD), overlooking the Yarty Valley is in close proximity to a
source of Greensand chert. Six axes from the site were recovered, all in chert. This is still
a relatively small number; thus, any exchange is likely to be small in scale or may
alternatively represent gearing up at a location where raw material was abundant. This
fits with the picture more generally in the Early Mesolithic, with axes tending to be
found in relatively small numbers, likely indicating small-scale use, rather than playing a
role in more elaborate systems of exchange, as was the case for the Neolithic and has
been suggested for the Later Mesolithic (Care 1979). To support this, the assemblage
from Telegraph Cottage does not appear to be specialised. This shows the range of ways
upland sites were used, rather than simply representing hunting camps.

Box 3.5   Dozmary Pool: The end of the Mesolithic world

In the far west, at a height of 270 m asl, Dozmry Pool is the only permanent standing water on Bodmin Moor (Figure 3.21). This lake is associated with many myths and legends and is the supposed resting place of Excalibur. As a rare water source in this area, it attracted Mesolithic occupation. It is likely that the surviving collection from the site, which is scattered across many different museums, and made by many different individuals, derives from more than one area. The largest collection was made by Francis Brent following drought in 1866, when the water levels were much lower than usual. Confirmation that the major area of occupation is now underwater comes from Andrew (Jacobi 1979, 52), who collected flint from below the current water level.

Dozmary Pool is notable for the dominance of scrapers at the site. One hundred fifteen were recovered, in comparison to 60 microliths. Upland sites are generally often small in size and dominated by microliths (Mellars 1976a,). This is the case, for example, for the Waun Figlen Felen, a similar lakeside location in the Black Mountains (see below), which seems to have been repeatedly used for hunting and the repair of microlithic equipment. The use of Bodmin Moor seems rather different in nature: While retooling of armatures did take place, along with a small amount of antler and wood working, activities round the pool appear foused on hide-working, perhaps assisted by the waters of the lake. Lithic material employed at Dozmary Pool is a high-grade translucent flint, which was preferred during the Early Mesolithic of Cornwall in contrast to the opaque grey and black flint and Greensand Chert, which was used during the Late Mesolithic (Jacobi 1979, 54).

Figure 3.21 View across Dozmary Pool (© Mark Eastment/Dreamstime.com)

The Bay of the Dead

Thus far, human remains have been curiously absent from our narrative. In chapter 2, only a single femur from Kent's Bank Cavern has featured, while another femur found in tufa at Thatcham III has an uncertain chronological relationship to the main occupation. By contrast, much of the evidence for the lifeways of Early Mesolithic groups focused in the regions surrounding the Bristol Channel embayment, comes from human remains (Figure 3.22). Mortuary treatment is mainly focused on caves; however, the recent dating of material from Greylake (Middlezoy) to the Early Mesolithic indicates that on occasions human remains were interred at open air cemeteries, a practise more commonly recorded in Southern Scandianvia and the Eastern Baltic. This adds to the diversity of mortuary practises already documented (Conneller 2006), with human remains in caves consisting variously of collective practises focused on several individuals, isolated bodies and disarticulated elements. Deposition of human remains appears to start around or just before 8500 cal BC, occurring on both sides of the Bristol Channel embayment at Badger Hole, Somerset and at Worm's Head Cave in Glamorgan. In the following few centuries, human remains began to be interred on a larger scale at Aveline's Hole and Greylake (Middlezoy), while the isolated inhumation of 'Cheddar Man' took place in Gough's Cave. These practises continue in subsequent centuries in this region, crossing the traditional Early/Late Mesolithic divide based on microlith typology. However, the diversity of practises decreases, limited to the deposition of isolated elements in caves, often through dropping material into shafts in the ground.

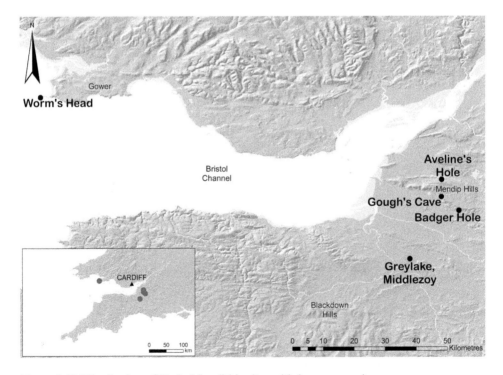

Figure 3.22 Distribution of Early Mesolithic sites with human remains

Aveline's Hole, Burrington Combe

From around 8400 cal BC (Schulting et al. 2019), a narrow cave 40 m long, with an inner and outer chamber, and set within the gorge of Burrington Coombe was used to deposit the remains of several generations of people (Figure 3.23). The human remains were all found in the outer chamber. The inner chamber was empty apart from a lozenge-shaped design engraved onto the cave wall (Mullan and Wilson 2004, Figure 3.24). While initial radiocarbon dating programmes indicated the human remains all belonged to the Mesolithic period (Schulting and Wysocki 2005), recent work has revealed a later presence, with six separate cranial elements dating to the Early Neolithic (Schulting et al. 2019). Unfortunately, due to its early discovery, relatively little is known of the mortuary practises represented at the cave, and relatively little material recovered from the various excavations remains, following the bombing of the University of Bristol Speleological Society (UBSS) Museum in 1941.

The cave was discovered on 9 January 1797 by two men hunting a rabbit. Early accounts vary considerably in detail, but report: 'On the left side of the cavern are a number of human skeletons ... not placed in regular order but lying promiscuously' (Anon 1797). This is reinforced by a letter from Robert Southey, who visited the cave around two weeks after the initial discovery. This states that reports of 'near 50 perfect skeletons lying parallel to each other' (Anon 1805) were exaggerated, and that 'neither was there any perfect skeleton or any apparent regularity in the mode of laying them'

Figure 3.23 Aveline's Hole (© Graham Mullan, University of Bristol Spelaeological Society (CC BY NC SA))

Figure 3.24 Engraving of the wall of the rear chamber at Aveline's Hole (© Andrew Atkinson, University of Bristol Spelaeological Society (CC BY NC SA))

(cited in Boycott and Wilson 2010, 14). In the following 80 years, more than 50 skeletons were removed from the cave (Jacobi 1987), and fragments of human bone were taken by tourists as souvenirs. Several well-known antiquarians also worked there: William Buckland and William Beard both recovered quantities of skeletal material from the cave, and Boyd Dawkins excavated in the inner chamber but found relatively little (Dawkins 1864). The cave underwent further excavation in 1914 and again between 1919 and 1931 by the UBSS, when the outer chamber was effectively emptied, and a further 20 individuals were recovered and described (Davies 1921, 1922, 1923, 1924).

By the time the UBSS came to excavate the cave from 1919, sediments were too jumbled by the efforts of, amongst others, Buckland, Dawkins and particularly the 1914 expedition of the UBSS, to be able to infer much about the original position of the skeletons. However, these excavations did uncover a patch of the original sta-lagmite layer adhering to the right side of the cave. This contained the seemingly disarticulated remains of at least three individuals: Two adults and one child. Tratman (1975) argues that the adults represent the somewhat damaged inhumations of two intact adult bodies accompanied by the dismembered remains of a child. Though there do seem to be most of the body parts of one individual on the right of the stalagmite layer, the anatomical elements are not in the correct order. Yet, these include an articulated femur and patella.

Bodies also seem to have been buried beneath the surface. The 1920s excavations located a double inhumation of intact bodies, though damaged by a rock fall (Davies

1924, 106). The bones of these individuals were stained with ochre; yet, the ground itself was free from ochre, suggesting some aspect of the mortuary ritual may have taken place elsewhere. Perforated animal teeth beads were found with the bodies: Originally mis-identified, these seem to represent red deer and bovid teeth (Jacobi pers. comm.). In addition, 18 unperforated red deer incisors were found scattered amongst the bones, which is at much greater frequencies than they were encountered elsewhere in the cave (Davies 1923). Near the head of one of the individuals, a pile of seven ammonites was discovered. Though no shell beads were found with this burial, perforated periwinkle shells were extremely common finds in the cave; about 60 have been recovered at various periods. A second possible burial was found below the stalagmite layer along the south wall. Items found in association apparently included flint blades, unperforated red deer teeth and the tooth of a young brown bear, as well as the beams of three giant deer bones with the frontal bones still attached (Davies 1924, 112; Schulting and Wysocki 2005, 183). Red deer antlers are associated with Late Mesolithic burials in Brittany (Schulting 1996), while the description of antlers with frontal bones attached is suggestively reminiscent of the Star Carr antler frontlets (though Davies description of these as 'giant' deer could suggest fortuitous association with the rather larger Late Glacial red deer associated with the Magdalenian occupation). The UBSS excavation also recovered many other human bones that had been disturbed by the activities of earlier investigators.

Despite the poor state of the evidence, it is probable that several mortuary practises are represented. Early reports suggest some complete bodies were laid out on the cave floor. The UBSS excavations suggest that some remains were also disarticulated. Whether this was by human agency or simply as a result of disturbance as a result of the dynamic nature of cave environments cannot now be determined. Some intact bodies also appear to have been buried. The double burial found by Davies was relatively far down in the sediment and so appears to have been buried fairly deep. There have been previous suggestions that this burial may be Upper Palaeolithic (e.g. Chatterton 2006); much of the artefactual and faunal remains recovered from the cave belongs to a Magdalenian occupation. However, intact burials from the Magdalenian are extremely rare, and none are known from Northern Europe, the preference being for disarticulation, suggesting this double burial is also part of the Mesolithic use of the cave.

A variety of different mortuary practises has also been noted at two Early Mesolithic cave cemeteries in the Belgian Ardennes (Cauwe 2001). These show some striking parallels to Aveline's Hole and hint at the sort of evidence that was once preserved there. At Grotte Margaux, a spread of disarticulated human elements were found on a stone pavement (a stone pavement was also mentioned in early accounts of Aveline's), while an adjacent pit contained additional disarticulated remains. The nearby cave of Abri des Autours contained the individual grave of a woman as well as a small pit and a surface spread containing disarticulated remains of at least five adults and six children. Many of the human remains were spread along the northern wall of the cave, as at Aveline's, and 32 phalanges were found in a crevice in this northern wall (Cauwe 2001). Based on the representation of skeletal parts, Cauwe argues that bodies were initially laid out on the cave floor at Abri des Autours, and the missing elements were later removed. A similar practise could explain the differing early accounts of Aveline's Hole, with some bodies relatively complete and others more jumbled with elements removed.

Though much of the material from the site and the documentation was destroyed, some was recovered from the ruins of the UBSS museum and was the subject of a recent reassessment. Schulting and Wysocki (2005) list 860 surviving human elements, most very fragmentary. These indicate an MNI of 16, out of an original set of at least 50 individuals. Amongst these are two infants, three young children and two adolescents; more younger than older adults appear represented, though two older adults are present. Both women and men are represented. Analysis provides tantalising glimpses into the lives of these people. Their diet was focused on terrestrial resources, both plant and animal (though different proxies produce different results as to the relative balance between the two). Fish, either marine and fresh water, were not consumed to any significant extent, though marine shells, in the form of beads, were present on the site. Some people suffered seasonal stress as young children around weaning. They squatted, rather than sat cross-legged, used their teeth to prepare cordage and had strong forearms, possibly related to spear-throwing. They were habituated to a mobile lifestyle and may have spent some time at least 50 km to the east on chalk geologies.

During the Mesolithic, Aveline's Hole seems to have been set apart from everyday domestic activities. The faunal material appears late glacial rather than Mesolithic, though relatively little has been dated, and there is only sparse lithic evidence that can be attributed to the Early Mesolithic (a core and three microliths), despite very small chips attesting to the meticulous recovery practises of Davies' excavations (Jacobi 2005). This contrasts with the extensive use of the cave as a repository for the dead. Setting human remains apart from daily life is unusual in a Western European context, where the majority of human remains (including cemeteries) are found within, or at least adjacent to, settlements. This may have something to do with the nature of caves, or at least the significance accorded to caves in the southwest at this time. The people who deposited their dead at Aveline's Hole may well have seen the cave as a mysterious place associated with ancestors, vanished ancient people and extinct beasts. This is because the cave was used during the Upper Palaeolithic as a horse and red deer butchery site. Traces of this previous occupation would be visible, especially if people were, on occasions, digging burial pits. The discovery of strange stone tools, associated with the bones of some larger-than-expected familiar animals and some completely unknown species would certainly give people an impression of the cave as associated with other(s) and augment any status the cave might have had as liminal between living and dead.

Gough's Cave, Cheddar

A complete skeleton of a young man, known as 'Cheddar Man' or Gough's Cave 1 (Box 3.6), was recovered during drainage work at Richard Gough's show cave in the winter of 1903 (Jacobi 198;7 Parry 1928). Though only a single inhumation, this individual has attracted considerably more attention than the rather more significant evidence at Aveline's Hole. The skeleton was recovered from a small chamber to the left of the cave, near the entrance, and appears to have been found in a crouched position. The bones were covered by stalagmite, rather than sediment, in a similar manner to the remains at Aveline's Hole. Cheddar Man may thus have been laid out on the surface of the cave, or just beneath the surface in a shallow burial (Brace et al. 2019). Two radiocarbon dates suggest the individual is contemporary with activity at

Box 3.6   The changing faces of Cheddar Man

Cheddar Man was a young male, though falling 'at the feminine end of the male range of variation' (Trinkaus et al. 2003, 45). He was aged between 18 and 23 years old (ibid). Very little is known of his life history or how he died. A depressed fracture on his frontal has been suggested to be a cause of death, but more recent work suggests this could be the mark of an infectious abscess or even the result of post-excavation damage (Brace et al. 2019). A healed lesion is present on an individual from Greylake (see below), on Tilbury Man (see chapter 5), and healed cranial depressions are present on several individuals in Southern Scandinavia and the Baltic region chapter 5. Thus, while there may have been something that marked him out and led to his unique mortuary treatment, this is by no means a certainty. In contrast to the elusive life of this individual, he has become, in death, a powerful symbol in debates surrounding the genetic history of the populations of Britain.

Research in the 1990s focused on the mitochondrial DNA of the individual. This is inherited through the female line, and thus provides information about maternal lineages. Testing of volunteers from Cheddar found individuals living in the area that shared the same mtDNA haplogroup U5b1 as Cheddar Man (Barham et al. 1999). These people were popularly represented as descendants of Cheddar Man, though any putative descendants would not inherit any mtDNA from a male ancestor. This narrative was popularly used to suggest a long history of local population continuity in Britain, though the U5b1 haplogroup is widespread across Europe (Sarkissian et al. 2013).

In recent years, scientific advances have permitted the study of the entire human genome, and a number of Mesolithic individuals have now been sequenced across Europe. In Britain, genome-wide data comes from six individuals, including Cheddar Man (Brace et al. 2019). These individuals show Western Hunter-gatherer (WHG) ancestry, indicating genetic links to populations in France, Luxemburg, Spain and Hungary. Cheddar Man has the best genetic coverage of any of the human remains analysed, and this reveals clues to his appearance. The evidence suggests his skin was likely to be dark to black, his hair dark brown or black and his eyes blue or green (Brace et al. 2019). A similar appearance has been suggested for a Mesolithic individual from La Braña in Spain (Olalde et al. 2014), though a third individual from Loschbour in Luxemburg was lighter skinned, suggesting a certain amount of variation amongst Mesolithic populations (Brace et al. 2019). Before the sequencing of the La Braña individual, it had been assumed that lighter skin was selected for in Europe amongst the earliest Homo sapiens groups who had migrated into the region from Africa as a response to the cold conditions of the last glacial maximum.

The genetic study of Cheddar Man and the associated reconstruction (Figure 3.25b) generated widespread media coverage and social media comment. While elements of this were positive, negative comments questioned the veracity of the research, seeing it as PC propaganda (Brophy 2018). *The Daily Mail* (2/8/ 2018) reported doubts over the findings of the study, in an article that simply highlights researchers' lack of complete understanding in how different genes are expressed. Many responses in the comments section to this article use their knowledge of human origins to counter these claims. The reaction from others shows a problematic equation between genes, skin colour and race and a belief amongst the far-right in Britain that antiquity provides legitimacy. Archaeologists have not done enough to counter these ideas, and indeed many pander to narratives of both origins and ancestry in representing their research to the media. Many different and unrelated peoples have inhabited Britain over the millennia, and their relationship to contemporary populations needs to be reconfigured in terms of shared histories of dwelling (cf Ingold 1993) rather than genetic relatedness.

A reconstruction of the face of Cheddar Man was undertaken by Denise Smith of the pioneering Manchester University group as part of the 1990s research. This shows an unkept white man who is not wearing his years well (Figure 3.25a). The potential lesion on his forehead is represented and prominent. As is the case for many Prehistoric reconstructions, Cheddar man has wild hair. While few styling tips have been handed down from Mesolithic Britain, later Mesolithic evidence does exist from the Baltic region. The positioning of fans of ochre and beads around the head of some individuals suggests that big hair, reddened with ochre and adorned with beads, was all the rage (at least for the dead). The 2018 reconstruction, undertaken by the Kennis brothers, as is the case with all their work, shows a face full of expression, engaged with the viewer (Figure 3.25b). The possible lesion is represented but is played down, most likely due to the possibility it is post-depositional. There is some evidence for personal grooming, though it is relatively minimal: Someone has taken a flint knife to his fringe, and he shows parallel stripes of pigment on his neck.

(a)   (b)

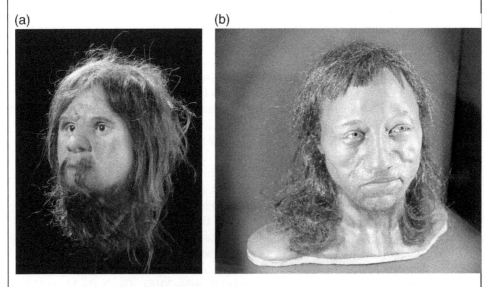

Figure 3.25 Left: Cheddar Man: 1990s reconstruction by Denise Smith (© The Trustees of the Natural History Museum). Right: Cheddar Man: 2018 reconstruction by Adrie and Alfons Kennis (Image: Susie Kearley/Alamy Stock Photo)

Genetic work and facial reconstructions have political effects, and their impact needs to be considered. The emphasis on continuity between Cheddar Man and contemporary populations in the 1990s, based on a misrepresentation of the genetic evidence, was big news at the time, and its working into popular contexts and narratives of 'Britishness' no doubt contributed to some of the reception of the 2018 research, where the opposite findings were put forward.

Aveline's and Greylake and probably dates to between 8465 and 8235 BC. One of the workmen involved in the work recalled finding many human skeletons; Cheddar Man was kept because he was the most complete (Jacobi pers. comm.). Whether this additional skeletal material was Mesolithic or part of the more extensive Magdalenian mortuary evidence at the cave is unknown.

As at Aveline's Hole, the vast majority of the occupational debris dates to the Magdalenian; however, there does seem to have been some small-scale occupation that may well have been contemporary with mortuary activity. In his survey of the surviving lithic assemblage from the cave, Jacobi (2004, 13) records the presence of four microliths, seven microburins and a refitting core sequence; those that are provenanced were recovered from the upper layers (spits 7–11) of the cave. Other bladelets with plain linear butts from these layers may also belong to the Mesolithic. The extant material might suggest a small hunting camp. Though Gough's Cave does not seem to have been so consciously set apart from day-to-day life as Aveline's, it did have elements that may have made it strange. Gough's cave seems to have been the most extensively occupied of all British Magdalenian sites. In the dynamic environment of a cave, some of traces of this earlier occupation are likely to have been visible, including, possibly, cut-marked and engraved human remains (Bell et al. 2015). The awareness of Gough's cave as a place where these remains, as well as the bones of extinct animals (reindeer, horse and antelope), giant animals and ancient tools could be recovered may have made the cave seem an appropriate place for an interment (Box 3.6).

Badger Hole, Wookey

The evidence from Badger Hole is much more typical of mortuary treatment across Western Britain than Aveline's Hole or Gough's Cave, consisting of isolated, disarticulated elements. Badger Hole is a small cave located 10 m above the floor of the ravine, near the large cave of Wookey Hole and less easily accessible than either Gough's or Aveline's. Badger Hole has a large entrance way, with two small passages leading to a large inner chamber with a chimney that leads to the fields above (Barrington and Stanton 1972). Herbert Balch spent 20 years excavating the cave (Tratman 1975) and plotted the location of the material he discovered, though extensive badger disturbance had destroyed most of the original stratigraphy (Campbell 1977; McBurney 1959). The human skeletal material was disarticulated and consists of two mandibles and two skull fragments deriving from a minimum of three individuals: Two children and a young adult. The mandibles are dated to 9120–8305 cal BC (9360 ± 100 BP; OxA-1459) and 8615–7825 cal BC (OxA-679; 9060 ± 130 BP) (Gowlett et al. 1986). Given the extent of disturbance in the cave, it is difficult to evaluate the position of the finds. It is possible that they were washed in through the chimney from the land above, or they could have been dropped through the chimney or brought in as isolated elements through the main entrance. The existing material all derives from the head, but this may be a result of taphonomic issues.

No.1 Sand Quarry Greylake, Middlezoy

While Mendip seems to have been a place where human remains were interred in caves, this interest in the dead in the southwestern region extended into the lower lying river valleys now submerged below the Somerset levels. Little evidence exists for the environment at this time, as sediments have been truncated (Bell et al. 2015). On the hills of sand and gravel that now rise above the levels – presumably once dry islands on the river floodplain – many Mesolithic sites have been found. One of these, at Greylake in the Parrett Valley, was the location of a sand quarry, and here, on the northeast corner of a much larger island, five human skulls and a quantity of post-cranial material were recovered during quarrying in 1928. Of these only seven elements remain; the Royal College of Surgeons was also bombed during the war. Three radiocarbon dates produced a remarkably consistent set of results, indicating that mortuary use of the site took place sometime between 8540 and 8280 cal BC, contemporary with the Mendip sites.

Little evidence remains as to the form of mortuary practise represented. Grey (1928) found human remains two feet below the surface of the sand, suggesting deposition of remains in grave pits. The discovery of a phalanx and metatarsal embedded in sediment within one of the skulls might suggest disarticulation and manipulation of the remains (Brunning and Frith 2012). The two surviving crania are both from adult males, though Arthur Keith identified another skull as female amongst the material that is now lost. One of the existing skulls has a healed lesion, a feature found on Mesolithic Southern Scandinavian skulls (and possibly Cheddar Man) and suggested to relate to conflict or perhaps medical practises.

In contrast to the Mendip sites, a substantial Early Mesolithic flint assemblage was recovered from the quarry. This was collected in the 1930s, and numbers over 7000 pieces. The most common tools remaining are microliths, accompanied by micro-burins, indicating production. The only other tools were an axe and two more amorphous bifacial tools. A number of tranchet flakes indicates maintenance and likely use of these tools. Several burin spalls indicate that burins were made and/or resharpened, though none themselves have been found (Scott and Shaw nd.).

The location of the site, on an island of dry ground on the floodplain, is reminiscent of preferred locations for Early Mesolithic sites in the southeast. Bond (2009a,b) highlights the ubiquity of Early Mesolithic lithic material on the islands of the Burtle Beds, indicating that here, too, these landforms were preferred settlement locations. This is a stark contrast with the treatment of the dead in Mendip, where people were set apart from daily life; here, the dead were interred amongst the places of the living.

Worm's Head Cave, Gower

The last mortuary site in this region is on the other site of the Severn embayment, in what is now South Wales. Here is Worm's Head Cave, located on the tip of the Gower peninsula, at the eastern end of a prominent rock formation jutting out over what then would have been a near coastal valley (Figure 3.26). The site is clearly visible from

Figure 3.26 View of Worm's Head (copyright Rick Schulting)

adjacent Early Mesolithic sites, for example, at Burry Holms on a promontory just to
the north and at Daylight Rock (see below) on the western tip of Carmarthen Bay.

   Human remains were recovered during excavations by Riches in 1923–1924 (Davies
1989), at which time it had already been disturbed. Various finds of human bone
occurred over the following decades, including excavations by the prolific cave in-
vestigator Mel Davies and more recent excavations by Rick Schulting (Schulting
2009). Upper Palaeolithic implements and Pleistocene fauna have been recovered from
the cave (Davies et al. 1989). Various human bones have been collected from the cave,
seemingly embedded in breccia. Even less is known about their arrangement than the
other sites previously discussed, though at least four individuals were represented, and
two further mandibles, labelled 'Mewslade Bay', may also belong to this collection.
What has emerged from Schulting's work is the relatively tight dating of the remains,
which suggest use of the cave some time between 8700 and 8300 cal BC (Meiklejohn
et al. 2011; Schulting 2009). A single outlier may suggest use of the cave several
centuries earlier, but this should be treated with some caution due to a low collagen
yield. Even without this measurement, dates indicatethe dead were interred at Worm's
Head several generations before the mortuary sites in Mendip and the Levels came
into use. The available evidence, albeit sparse, suggests that Worm's Head represents a
short-lived, collective inhumation site, possibly similar to Aveline's Hole.

Early Mesolithic settlement in Southern Wales

The majority of Early Mesolithic sites in Southern Wales cluster in coastal locations (Figure 3.27). This distribution is an artefact of visibility, as sites erode from cliff-lines. In the Early Mesolithic, these sites, though broadly lowland, would have been some distance from the sea. Several other types of locations, such as inland river valleys and upland sites, also saw settlement. Early Mesolithic material has been recovered from under a Neolithic long cairn at Gwernvale at 77 m asl in the Usk Valley (Britnell and Savory 1984). This valley is a routeway between the Brecon Beacons and Black Mountains and would have also afforded access into both upland areas. In the uplands, Early Mesolithic microliths are also known from Cefn Hill on the northeastern ridge of the Black Mountains (Jacobi 1980ab, 193).

The best evidence for upland settlement comes from Waun Fignen Felen in the Black Mountains, where five certain and two possible Early Mesolithic scatters were located along the margins of a lake (Barton et al. 1995). The scatters are small in size, with all but WWF8 yielding fewer than 200 pieces. Microliths are the most common tools in the small scatters, though single scrapers were recovered from both WWF2 and 6. Two mudstone beads, similar in form to those from Star Carr (chapter 1) and The Nab Head I (see below), were recovered from WWF6. WWF8, set back slightly from the lake, is larger at over 600 pieces and has a wider range of tools: Six scrapers, two retouched flakes and a piercer. Seventeen microburins indicate repair of microlithic armatures was a major task at this site. Both Deepcar and Welsh Star Carr-type microliths (see Box 3.7) are present round the lake, probably indicating some temporal depth to the patterns of repeated occupation. A relationship between this site and coastal areas is indicated by the use of beach flint, while Greensand chert, whose nearest primary source is 80 km distant, was also used. The mudstone used for the beads seems to derive from a source 100 km. These figures indicate Early Mesolithic groups ranged widely across the region.

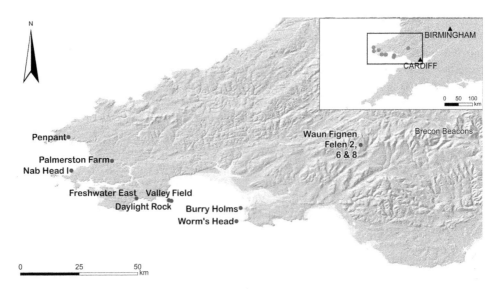

Figure 3.27 Distribution of Early Mesolithic sites in South Wales

Box 3.7   Star Carr groups in Wales?

The presence of differing Early Mesolithic ssemblage types was initially based on observations of material from Northern England (Jacobi 1978a; Radley and Mellars 1976). Further work by Reynier extended this distinction across England and into Wales. Reynier (2005, 86–92) identifies three Star Carr-type sites in Wales: The Nab Head I, Pembrokeshire, Daylight Rock, Caldey and Waun Fignen Felen 8, in the Black Mountains. Assemblages from these sites are characterised by obliquely blunted points and broad triangles. Further assemblages with similar characteristics are noted by David (2007) and David et al. (2015). In Pembrokeshire, these include Llangwm, Valley Field on Caldey Island, Freshwater East, Palmerston Farm and Penpant; Burry Holms in Glamorgan, and Waun Fignen Felen 6 in Brecknockshire. Several of these sites (The Nab Head I, Palmerstone Farm, Freshwater East and Waun Fignen Felen 6) also share Star Carr groups fondness for shale beads (see Box 3.9).

David (2007) is more cautious than Reynier, and rather than attributing these sites to the working of Star Carr 'groups', he simply points out some similarities with Southern English sites, such as Broxbourne 104. There is reason to this, for there are also important differences between the Welsh sites and the Northern English assemblages. The angles of the obliquely blunted points tend to be more oblique than typical for Star Carr assemblages, overlapping with those of Deepcar sites. Trapezes are not present, and isoceles triangles are rare. Instead, the triangles that dominate the Southern Welsh assemblages, often outnumbering obliquely blunted points (David 2007), are scalene in form. As David points out, the dating of these sites is also rather later than typical. While the standard deviations at two sigma overlap with the latest dates from the Vale of Pickering, there is no evidence for an early presence contemporary with the earliest, or even the main, phase of Star Carr. Whether this is a real pattern for this assemblage type, or whether it is simply the result of sampling hazelnut shells to date an assemblage type that in the main predates the hazel rise, remains to be seen.

Many of the sites discussed in this section are now coastal; however, when they were occupied the sea-level would have been significantly lower. When The Nab Head I was occupied, St Bride's Bay would have been mostly dryland, with the site overlooking a coastal plain with the sea around 5 km to the west. Daylight Rock and Valley Field are now on the island of Caldey, but when Daylight Rock was occupied Carmarthen Bay would have been dryland and the coastline some distance away (10–20 km) at 8500 BC, but because of a submarine shelf, flooding of this area would have been rapid, and by 8000 BC, the sea would have been much closer.

Nab Head I

In the far reaches of Southwest Wales, between Milford Haven and St Davids, lies a north facing area of eroding headland known as The Nab Head (see Figure 3.28). To

Figure 3.28 The Nab Head from the air (© Crown: CHERISH PROJECT 2017). Produced with
        EU funds through the Ireland Wales Co-operation Programme 2014–2020. All
        material made freely available through the Open Government Licence

the north the headland slopes down to be truncated by sea-cliffs; to the east is a small
valley, eroded into by the sea. To the south is an area known as 'The Neck', an area of
faulting, resulting in a narrowing connection to the mainland that also suffers from
erosion. The Neck has been known as a place where Mesolithic material can be collected from the 1880s; since then, thousands of flints and hundreds of shale beads have
been removed from the area.

Though several flint collectors and antiquarians are known to have dug here,
knowledge of the site comes through three different excavations. The first of these, by
the Rev Gordon-Williams (1926), does not provide detailed description of the excavations, but recovered some of the better-known evidence from the site: Numerous
shale beads and a shale figurine (Box 3.8), a modified shale pebble with what might be
best termed ambiguous sexual characteristics. Small-scale excavations by Geoff
Wainwright in 1969 found only disturbed soils and very few flints, concluding that the
site had been destroyed by the activities of flint collectors. However, test pitting,
followed by more extensive excavation in 1979 and 1980 by Andrew David and Don
Benson, revealed deposits undisturbed by recent activities (Figure 3.29).

These excavations revealed a sequence of sandy-clay loams overlying solifluction
deposits. The relation of these to an Iron Age promontory fort reveals that the latest
layers post-date this feature. It is likely that this sequence represents a complex history
involving soil development, later Prehistoric ploughing and periods of erosion, indicated by two stone lines. Mesolithic material was recovered throughout this

Figure 3.29 The Nab Head I under excavation in 1980 (copyright Andrew David)

Box 3.8   The Nab Head figurine

The Nab Head figurine (Figure 3.30) derives from the excavations of the Reverend Gordon-Williams in the 1920s. It is a small pebble of black shale, measuring 42 mm in height. While the back is unmodified, the front has been shaped, incised and polished (Jacobi 1980b, 159). The figurine was found under a patch of turf, associated with nine shale beads, and in close proximity to a bevel-ended tool (Gordon-Williams 1926, 88). It was found coated in a 'soapy substance' which was suggested to represent a coating of fat or clay, or the remnants of a skin bag. Gordon-Williams suggested it represented a phallus, but quoted correspondence with the Abbe Breuil, the pre-eminent French prehistorian, who suggested it may have had ambiguous sexual characteristics, representing at the same time a phallus and a stylised female figurine, a description sufficiently anatomically detailed that the Reverend Gordon-Williams did not translate it from the French.

David (2007, 109) cites the opinion of W.F. Grimes, who knew the clergyman, that the figurine may have been a forgery, the motive being the intense rivalry between local collectors at the time. It does perhaps evoke Upper Palaeolithic objects and concerns rather than those of the Mesolithic. Breuil compares it to similar examples from Mezin in the Ukraine (Gordon-Williams 1926, 99), as well as examples from Trasimeno in Italy and Mauern, Germany (Breuil 1953). David (2007, 111) does not find these satisfactory parallels, and both were found after

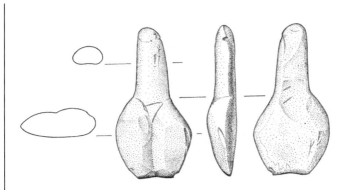

Figure 3.30 The Nab Head 'venus' (Image: Andrew David)

the Nab Head figurine. Perhaps a more pertinent comparison is the Venus of Lespugue. The back of this figurine is very similar to the Nab Head example, and if a non-specialist were trying to carve a similar object from shale, one which might be more suitable for the 'degenerate' pre-Neolithic age, something like the Nab Head piece might result. The Venus of Lespugue was then a very recent find (in 1922) and had been published the year before Gordon-Williams' 'find' (St-Perrier 1924).

Perhaps in favour of the authenticity of the figurine is the possible presence of another, figured by Gordon-Williams (1926, plate 3) as a tool for fabrication. This is an elongated pebble, 57 mm high, with a sharp groove, 7 mm long at the base. Jacobi (1980b, 159) suggests this could be interpreted as 'a second, more "elementary" Venus representation, with the vulva indicated by the incision'. However, David reports that the surface of this piece is too weathered to be sure even whether the incision is humanly made. While there is a tradition of this sort of object in the Upper Palaeolithic, where a continuum of engravings from representational to schematic allow archaeologists to interpret some of the more ambiguous images, such a body of material does not exist in the Mesolithic, making it difficult to comment on the significance of this object.

sequence, but was concentrated in particular in layer 12, possibly a relict B horizon of a truncated early post-glacial soil (David 2007).

David's work at the site confirms earlier research by Jacobi (1980a,b) that there is both Early and Late Mesolithic material represented at the site. The Early Mesolithic component is of Welsh Star Carr-type (see above) and is dated by two radiocarbon estimates, of 8625–8285 cal BC (9210 ± 80 BP; OxA-1495) and 8565–8205 cal BC (9110 ± 80 BP; OxA-1496) on charred hazelnut shells, both taken from context 12, in areas where there were marked clusters of Early Mesolithic material culture. The Late Mesolithic is represented by a series of small geometric scalene triangles, narrow-backed bladelets, sauveterre points, a petit tranchet, micro-crescents and micro-rhomboids. This Late Mesolithic occupation(s) is undated in this area, but radiocarbon determinations from The Nab Head II, around 100 m to the south, which has a broadly similar range of microliths, indicate intermittent visits throughout the Late Mesolithic.

The fact The Nab Head was reoccupied throughout the Mesolithic and the stratigraphic mixing – not to mention the long and problematic history of collection – makes it difficult to unpick in detail the nature of Early Mesolithic activities there. A major discernible Early Mesolithic activity appears to have been the production of shale beads. At least 690 have been recovered from the site (see Box 3.9). Shale can be obtained from local beaches, and it is likely that this was the source of the material used for bead manufacture. That people were visiting the coast is confirmed by the use of beach pebble flint for the manufacture of stone tools. As at Star Carr, these beads were manufactured using meche de foret, of which 44 have been recovered during David's excavations.

Bead manufacture was not the only activity at the site: Microliths were manufactured and discarded. Scrapers were also common (100 from the most recent excavations), and David (2007, 99) suggests, on morphological groundsgrounds, that these belong with the Early Mesolithic occupation. If these scrapers can be associated with the processing of hides, and if beads were sewn onto clothing rather than strung onto necklaces, as seems to have been the norm in early prehistory (Taborin 2004), we might imagine that the production of elaborate clothing was a major feature of the site. Twenty-six burins were also recovered, but were less common (26), and tranchet axes were also represented.

Box 3.9   Early Mesolithic personal adornment

Shale appears to have been the most favoured material for bead production amongst groups using Star Carr-type microliths. The only exception is some use of amber and animal teeth at Star Carr, though as faunal remains of this date rarely survive, the latter are likely to have been more common. Shale is a soft stone, and beads can be made rapidly in very large numbers, using a meche de foret (drill bit) or awl. Experimentation demonstrates that shale beads can be produced relatively quickly. David's experiments using a bow or pump drill indicate that around 100 beads can be made in an hour (David 2007, 105); however, a hand-held meche de foret seems equally effective, with even a novice able to produce a bead in less than a minute (Needham et al. 2018). Shale is also advantageous in that it is easy to procure, at least for groups living in particular parts of the country: At the two sites, The Nab Head and Star Carr, where shale beads are particularly common, shale can be procured on nearby beaches, where people also sourced their flint. At Star Carr, shale may even have been available closer to the site, where stream channels ran through local glacial till into lake Flixton. The shale blanks at both Nab Head and Star Carr are clearly water-worn. Despite a certain economy of effort evident both in ease of procurement and manufacture, selectivity is present in the pieces chosen for perforation. Blanks were fairly regular in shape, oval or sub-circular, and mostly between 2 and 3 cm in size. Two exceptions exist in the two elongated pendants from Star Carr, one of which has surface decoration.

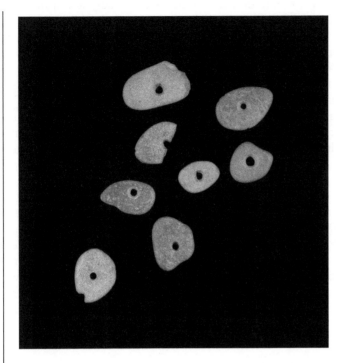

Figure 3.31 Shale beads from The Nab Head I (copyright National Museum of Wales)

The Nab Head I appears to have been the major focus for shale bead manufacture in the South Wales region, with 690 examples known (Figure 3.31) and many more likely to reside in private collections. Numerous awls have been recovered from the site and are likely to have been associated with the production of these objects. A part perforated shale disc has also been recovered, indicating on site manufacture (Jacobi 1980a,b, 160), as have shale blanks (David 2007, 105). Beads produced at The Nab Head may have been exchanged across South Wales (see Figure 3.32), being found as far as Waun Fignen Felen 8 in the Black Mountains. However, as Jacobi (1980b, 160) noted, the vast number of complete beads remaining on the site is curious. He suggested perhaps the site was used as a burial ground, with the dead adorned with richly decorated clothing. Bone does not preserve in the acidic soils, and early collectors are unlikely to have noticed grave cuts. No features that could be interpreted in this way were noted during David's excavations, and phosphate analysis was negative, though one large cluster of 27 beads in a 3 × 2 m area was located amongst a general background scatter on the site.

At Star Carr, bead production also occurred at the site, though not on the same scale as at The Nab Head. Beads cluster in the same wetland fen-edge area in the western part of the site as meche de foret, and microwear studies indicate that at least some of these tools were used in the production of shale beads (Conneller et al. 2018b). Three amber beads, two cervid teeth (one a vestigial red deer canine) and a piece of bird bone were also recovered from the same area as

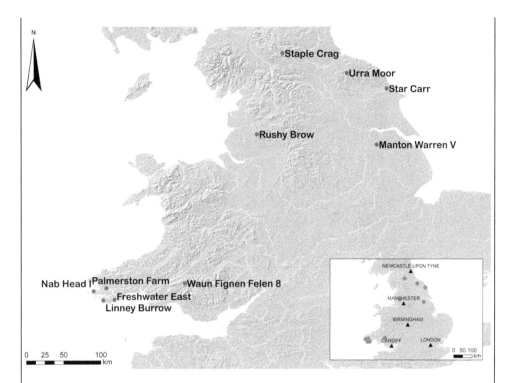

Figure 3.32 Distribution of sites with shale beads

the shale beads, as was a waisted piece of ochre, which may also have been worn. This western fen-edge part of the site seems to have been a craft area where resin was produced, burins used and beads produced around small hearths. As beads are so strongly associated with the awls that made them, they do not seem to have been moved beyond their place of manufacture. Though some beads are broken, most are complete, meaning that these are not damaged pieces discarded during repair of clothing. Two large clusters (of 12 and eight beads, respectively), instead of representing lost necklaces as Clark argued, may represent caches, or perhaps even more formal deposits. One of these clusters also contained an amber bead, which Clark (1954, 165) indicates was in direct contact with a shale bead. This amber bead has a broken perforation, and there are also three broken shale beads that are likely to belong to this cluster, though the remainder are intact (Clark 1949, pl XX).

Though most of the beads were recovered from lake edge fen craft area, three beads must have been placed in the lake waters: An amber bead and probably also a red deer tooth found within the western deposition area, and the decorated shale pendant from the area to the south. There appears to be some temporal depths to bead production. The manufacturing area probably dates to the 88th century, but there appears to have been continued bead production in the western part of the site at least 200 years later. The decorated pendant may predate the manufacturing area, though the probability distribution of the two areas overlap.

Table 3.10 Finds of Mesolithic stone and amber beads

Site	No
The Nab Head I	690
Palmerston Farm	1
Freshwater East	1
Newquay	1
Waun Fignen Felen 6	2
Linney Burrows	1?
Star Carr	37
Rushy Brow	4
Nethermills	1
Urra Moor	1
Staple Crag	1
Manton Warren	1
Thatcham V	1
Thatcham VI	1
White Colne	1

As amongst the Southern Welsh sites, isolated shale beads are also found on Star Carr sites across Northern England (Figure 3.32, Table 3.10). These stretch from Rushey Brow, Anglezarke Moor in the west, to Urra Moor in the east, Staple Crag in the north and Manton Warren V in the southernmost margins of the range of these groups. There is a single example from the far north in Scotland at Nethermills, Aberdeenshire (Wickham-Jones et al, 2018). All these appear to be from single beads with the possible exception of Rushey Brow where four fragments were found. Apart from Rushey Brow, all other isolated beads from both Northern England and Scotland and South Wales are complete, again raising the question of why these were discarded.

While shale beads seem exclusively found on Star Carr-type sites, stone beads have occasionally been found on Deepcar sites. These are not in shale; instead, a range of different materials were used: These include a chalky pebble at Thatcham VI and limestone at Thatcham V.

Beads are rare on British Mesolithic sites, and none have yielded comparable numbers. At Star Carr, 37 have been recovered. These numbers are probably indicative of small-scale production associated with the manufacture and repair of clothing. By contrast, Nab Head appears to have been a major manufacturing centre. Beads that may well have been produced at the site have been found on several sites in the vicinity: At Freshwater East and Palmerston Farm in Pembrokeshire and at Waun Fignen Felen, Brecknockshire (David 2007).

Daylight Rock

Daylight Rock is on the island of Caldey; however, at a time of lower sea-level, it would have been a promontory, cut during an earlier time of higher sea-level, that overlooked dryland to the sea beyond. The site, as so many on Caldey, was excavated by Brother James van Nedervelde, with the encouragement of A.D. Lacaille. His results were reported in Lacaille and Grimes' (1956) survey of the prehistory of the island. Daylight Rock consists of both a small cave where Middle Mesolithic human remains have been recovered (chapter 4) and an area of open air occupation about 10 m from the cave located on a rocky platform and upslope of the cave. Both cave and platform are located along the southern side of a gulley that slopes down to the sea to the east. The platform is sheltered by the southern cliff line of the gulley, in which the cave is located. The occupation took place on top of Pleistocene beach deposits, which were overlain by a greyish-yellow sandy silt and a reddish loam in which the artefacts were recovered, along with limestone fragments from the overlying cliff. The much greater depth of deposits towards the seaward end reported by Lacaille and Grimes (1956, 133) suggests this probably represents colluvium.

Large quantities of artefacts were recovered from outside the cave, originally numbering more than 7000, though most of these, apart from the finished tools, are now lost. The tools recovered indicate an assemblage balanced between a wide variety of tasks. Scrapers (48) and microliths (54) are most common, followed by burins (11), notches (9), truncations (8) and meches de foret (15). Daylight Rock is the only Early Mesolithic site with large numbers of meches de foret but no beads, though we know from microwear of examples from Star Carr that these tools also had other functions. Retouched and utilised pieces are also common, and include occasional microdenticulates. A single axe and ten resharpening flakes were also found. There are reports also of tested nodules present, suggesting flint materials were brought directly to the site from the beach for knapping. As well as flint, adinole was also employed. The assemblage indicates a very broad range of craft activities were undertaken here, as well as manufacture and retooling of composite weapons. A midden recovered from the red loam just outside the cave mentioned by Lacaille and Grimes seems to post-date the Mesolithic, containing molluscs that date to the Roman period at the earliest (Jacobi 1980a,b, 184). This deposit may well belong to a post-Roman Iron Age occupation as evidenced by a 5th century date on human remains from the cave (Meiklejohn et al. 2011, 29).

Further excavations at the site were undertaken by Andrew David in 1988 in order to locate organic material to date the occupation (Figure 3.33). A trench was located upslope from van Nedervelde's excavations, but here the topsoil was extremely thin, and only a small number of artefacts were recovered and no organics. A second trench was therefore opened on top of the cliff immediately above the original focus of artefact finds from the 1950s. This yielded an assemblage, preserved in fissures in the limestone, of around 1500 artefacts, including seven microliths, eight microburins, a meche de foret and an axe-sharpening flake, similar both in typology and pieces represented to those recovered during the 1950s excavations. In addition, charcoal and charred hazelnuts were located. The latter yielded three radiocarbon dates, indicating occupation somewhere between 8485 and 7715 cal BC.

Figure 3.33 Daylight Rock under excavation (copyright Andrew David)

Van Nedervelde also excavated inside the cave, where he located Mesolithic arte-facts, including a large scalene triangle similar to the microliths from the occupation nearby, suggesting these were broadly contemporary. Human remains were also located inside the cave, and one of three mandibles belongs to the Mesolithic, though on current evidence the date of 7580–7500 BC (Meiklejohn et al. 2011, 29) post-dates the Early Mesolithic occupation by at least 200 years.

Life and death in Southwestern Britain

In contrast to the rest of Britain, the dated Early Mesolithic evidence from Southwest Britain comprises human remains rather than settlement evidence. The treatment of human remains in this area during this period is diverse, with collective accumulations of remains in caves, single inhumations and interments associated with a settlement site. Caves, particularly those used for collective interments, were set apart from daily life, and occur in places with abundant evidence for Palaeolithic use. All caves used for the deposition of human remains at this period are west-facing, and when location information is present, there appears to be a preference for the clustering of human remains along the northern wall of the cave. Thus, the dead would be positioned in relation to the setting sun, perhaps suggesting meta-phorical relations between the sun and the life cycle. Worm's Head is particularly notable in this respect, at the westernmost end of a striking rock formation, the last high point of the karstic carboniferous rocks before the land sloped down to the distant coast beyond.

In comparison with the mortuary evidence, settlement is poorly dated in the region. There are no dates for settlement in the southwest, while in South Wales radiocarbon measurements from three sites suggest settlement in the region from c.8500 BC. All dates from these sites are on hazelnut shells, raising the pos-sibility of a less visible earlier occupation that predates the hazel rise. If there is a hidden pioneer occupation (as could possibly be indicated by an early radiocarbon date on unassociated charcoal from Trostrey Castle), the mortuary evidence may represent a shift in the way the landscape was occupied, from an ephemeral pioneer occupation to a concern with forging long-term relationships with places. The de-position of human remains may have been a way of highlighting ancestral links between people and significant places in the landscape.

4 A new way of living

Pits, hazelnuts, places and the ancestors in the Middle Mesolithic, 8200–7000 BC

The Middle Mesolithic (see chapter 1 for definitions) was a time of change. While there is considerable variation both in human lifeways across this period and the sorts of environments people inhabited, several major trends can be recognised. Settlement seems to have expanded into new areas, with some groups making the sea-crossing to Ireland and others, somewhat less dramatically, venturing into the clay lands of the English Midlands for the first time (Figure 4.1). Regions of Britain, such as Northern and Western Scotland and North Wales, where occupation had previously only been inferred on typological grounds, have reliable radiocarbon dated evidence for human presence at this time. Everywhere, there is evidence for people moving beyond the core pioneer areas of coasts, river valleys, lakes and meres, and into a much broader range of environments.

This broader geographical distribution is though partly an effect of the more readily dateable types of evidence these groups left behind: This period sees a huge increase in dug features, both pits and post-built structures, while at the same time, hazel becomes an important part of the early post-glacial woodland community, and sites are often characterised by large quantities of charred hazelnut shells. If any part of the Mesolithic is about 'relationships with hazelnuts' (Bradley 1984, 11), it is this one, and this is particularly the case in the northern half of Britain. The presence of hazelnuts, which produce both reliable and precise dates, and the better preservation of organics in cut features means that this period is much easier to date than the earlier Mesolithic, and therefore occupation of particular areas can be confirmed rather than simply inferred. Of the 255 radiocarbon dates whose probability distribution falls mainly before 8500 cal BC, only 16 (from four separate features) come from cut features, and only two are on hazelnut shells, as these sites in the most part predate the hazel rise. By contrast, of the 284 dates whose distribution falls mainly between 8500 and 7000 BC, 131 come from cut features, and 114 are on hazelnuts. It is important to remember the effects of what is being dated; what may seem like east-west population movement (Waddington 2007, 2015) may simply be tracking the hazel rise.

That said, the increased presence of cut features is important and indicates different forms of engagement with the landscape, perhaps longer stays at particular sites, but certainly new modes of landscape marking. These new practises often included the digging of pits, which were infilled in a variety of different ways (Blinkhorn et al. 2016; Blinkhorn and Little 2018). Particularly important at this time was the deposition of burnt material, often hearth sweepings (Blinkhorn et al. 2016; Chatterton 2006). This may be related to the social and symbolic significance of fire (see Mithen 2019).

DOI: 10.4324/9781003228103-4

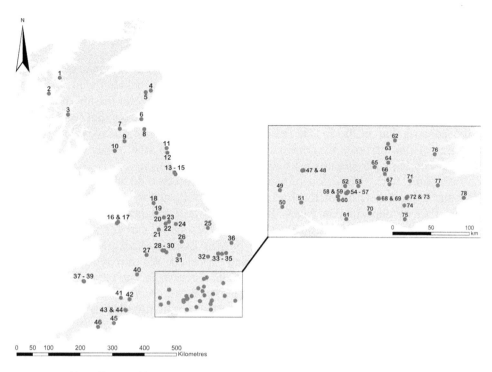

Figure 4.1 Sites discussed in the chapter. (1. Sand, 2. Kinloch, 3. Druimvargie, 4. Miltimber, 5. Warren Field, 6. Fifeness, 7. Echline, 8. East Barns, 9. Manor Bridge, 10. Daer Reservoir I, 11. Howick, 12. Low Hauxley, 13. Flipoke Beacon, 14. Crimdon Dene, 15. West Hartlepool, 16. Prestatyn, 17. Hendre, Rhuddlan, 18. Ickornshaw Moor, 19. Warcock Hill III, 20. Broomhead Moor V, 21. Wetton Mill, 22. Big Moor, Baslow, 23. Blake Acre, 24. Mother Grundy's Parlour, 25. West Keal, 26. Asfordby, 27. Lightmarsh Farm, 28. Over Whiteacre Spring, 29. Over Whiteacre 4, 30. Corley Rocks, 31. Honey Hill, 32. Marlow Ridges, Over, 33. Peaock's Farm, 34. Wangford, 35. Two Mile Bottom, 36. Spong Hill, 37. Potter's Cave, 38. Ogof-yr-Ychen, 39. Daylight Rock, 40. Madawg Rockshelter, 41. Stonehenge Carpark, 42. Parchey Sand Patch, Chedzoy, 43. Aller Farm, 44. Crandon's Cross, 45. Kent's Cavern, 46. Oreston Third Bone Cave, 47. Wawcott III, 48. Wawcott IV, 49. Blick Mead, 50. Downton, 51. Broom Hill, 52. Farnham, 53. St. Catherine's Hill, 54. Devil's Jump Moor, 55. Lion's Mouth, 56. Kettlebury 103, 57. Kettlebury I and II, 58. Oakhanger V/VII, 59. Oakhanger I, 60. Longmoor I, 61. Westhampnett, 62. Broxbourne 106, 63. Thorntons Farm, 64. Addington St., 65. Ham Fields, 66. Orchard Hill, 67. North Park Farm, Bletchingly, 68. Beedings Wood, 69. Old Faygate, 70. Rock Common, 71. Hermitage, High Hurstwood, 72. Selmeston, 73. Hamborough Hill, 74. Fairbourne Court, 75. Saltwood Tunnel)

What seems important in these contexts is fire's part in food production: Ethnographic accounts show that fire plays an important role in transformation. For people who see animals as having souls (see Box 2.3), cooking can be seen as a means to de-subjectify animal remains and turn them into food. Similarly, burning can be a way of respectful treatment of animal remains (see Mansrud 2017 for a discussion). The same may be true for plant remains, which seem an important focus of depositionary practises at this time. At times, these acts of deposition may have been focused on the remains of special meals, related to celebrations or other key events. The proper disposal of hearth debris seems a particular concern in the northern half of Britain; in the southern part, deposition of specially selected lithic material may have been more important.

In some regions, these new practises may have included the erection of wooden posts or the construction of fairly substantial buildings that included wooden posts. The temporality of these houses and monuments extended beyond the life of a single individual. This is a temporal scale more akin to the life of the trees that were central to the construction of both. The evidence from Stonehenge Carpark, where an alignment of pits or posts may have started with a fallen tree, suggests trees were important, perhaps playing a role as social or spiritual beings.

At the same time, deposition of human remains became an increasing concern. While the large cemeteries of the Early Mesolithic fell out of use, isolated remains continued to be deposited in caves. In the southwest, the practise spread a little geographically beyond North Somerset to South Devon and across Cardigan Bay to Caldey. Some of the dead, who are found only as isolated elements, may have circulated with the living before eventually being deposited. We may see an increasing interest in ancestors, and more particularly, in the association of ancestors with particular key landscape locations. Across most of the country, though, finds of human remains are absent, and mortuary practises are as invisible as amongst the early pioneers.

Also appearing in this period are what we might term 'supersites'. These are sites with an extremely high density of lithic material and a broad diversity in the stone tool assemblage. In earlier times, these were termed 'type B sites' and seen as base camps (Mellars 1976a,). Indeed, some of them may have been used in this way, at least on occasions. However, microlith typology indicates that rather than being single events, they are made up of the debris of numerous visits to the same place. Many of these, at least in Southern England, seem to have been initially occupied from around 8000 BC, perhaps earlier in some places. These settlement practises contrast to the Early Mesolithic, where, as Jacobi (1978b) originally noted, several sites with identical microlith types are found in a small geographical area; in the Middle Mesolithic and the Late Mesolithic, people repeatedly returned to a specific place.

This is a different sort of persistence to that seen in the Early Mesolithic, and perhaps one closer to its original meaning as associated with a particular type of landscape affordance (Schlanger 1992). Broom Hill, Hampshire, for example, was revisited for millennia because it combined easy access to good-quality flint with a good view (O'Malley and Jacobi 1978). Its use changed over time; the earlier occupation of the place appears to have been relatively substantial in comparison to later visits to the site. Wawcott III, in the Kennet Valley, by contrast, where over 100,000 lithic artefacts were recovered from a site probably spanning 4000 years, is a lowland, riverine location (Froom 1976). Kinloch (more than 140,000 lithics; dates spanning at least 1200 years) is on Rùm, an island with a source of high-quality and distinctive raw material (Wickham-Jones 1990). These sites are likely to have seen relatively intermittent occupation, though at times there may have been episodes of longer term or more closely spaced visits. These patterns, at the very least, suggest some continuity in the way the landscape was understood over very long periods, but at some of these sites at least, reoccupation may have been guided by memories and stories of previous visits.

A further key feature of this period is increased levels of regionalisation, probably as a result of increased population and lowered mobility, but further evidence, too, of the emergence of long-term commitment to particular areas. Regionalisation can be seen in the appearance of distinctly different lifeways and practises: Island-hopping in the far north; an enduring focus on the dead in the southwest; the love of sandy hazel groves in the southeast; or a preoccupation with pits in the northeast. It can be most obviously be seen in a divergence in the forms of microlith used and broader technological traditions in different parts of Britain: Horsham points in the south and west; Honey Hill points in the midlands, and assemblages with variably lateralised narrow scalene triangles in the north (see chapter 1 for definitions).

These changes, and the period covered in this chapter, span the traditional divisions of the Early and Late Mesolithic, as well as several key 'assemblage types' (see chapter 1). A lot of these changes are gradual, starting at the end of the Early Mesolithic with the use of caves for the deposition of human remains, the appearance of large, extremely dense sites (such as Oakhanger, see chapter 3) and the movement into a broader range of landscapes. These changes continue into the Middle Mesolithic, defined here by assemblages containing basally modified points in the south and midlands of England and assemblages with variably lateralised narrow scalene triangles in Northern Britain (see chapter 1). This chapter will cover Mesolithic sites dating between 8200 and 7000 BC, though in some regions we will delve a little further back in time for narrative sake.

Landscape and environment: Life in the woods

In general, the Middle Mesolithic saw warm temperatures; however, there were also two periods of short-term climatic downturn, one at c.8300 cal BC and another at 7300 cal BC, the latter lasting 100–150 years (Yu et al. 2010). This was a time when sea-level rise had a major impact: By 8000 cal BC, the straights of Dover had been breached, and a large embayment had formed to the east of East Anglia, fed by the Thames and other major rivers (Figure 4.2). Britain remained a peninsula, but Doggerland, particularly in its western part, was shrinking, and a much narrower neck of land joined East Anglia and the Midlands to the continent, while the Dogger Bank was becoming an island. In the period 8000–7500 cal BC, nearly 20,000 square km of Doggerland was submerged, the greatest rate of loss of land during the Mesolithic (Sturt et al. 2013). It has been argued that the shrinking of Doggerland caused massive population movement and the appearance of marine-adapted displaced groups in Scotland and Northern England (Waddington 2007).

This chapter covers the Boreal period, Godwin's pollen assemblage zones V and VI, characterised by the appearance of mixed oak forest (oak-hazel-elm), and ending with the widespread appearance of alder in the pollen record, which heralds the start of the Atlantic (Godwin 1940a,1956, see chapter 1). In the past, it was thought that Godwin's zones would emerge in parallel across Britain; however, from the 1970s, it was realised these were diachronous, and the extent of regional differences became increasingly clearer (Bennett 1988), leading to a focus on local pollen sequences instead (see chapter 1). The term does continue to be used in relation to archaeological evidence, particularly on the continent, where it serves as useful shorthand for Middle Mesolithic adaptions in woodlands with a strong component of hazel.

(a)

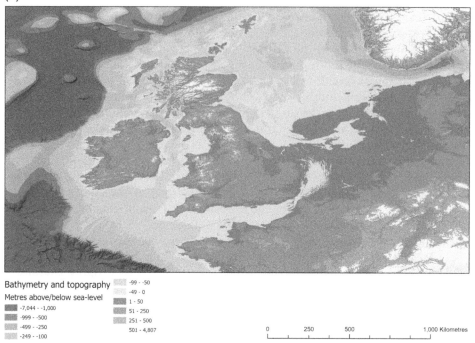

Bathymetry and topography
Metres above/below sea-level

-7,044 - -1,000
-999 - -500
-499 - -250
-249 - -100

-99 - -50
-49 - 0
1 - 50
51 - 250
251 - 500
501 - 4,807

0   250   500   1,000 Kilometres

(b)

Bathymetry and topography
Metres above/below sea-level

-7,044 - -1,000
-999 - -500
-499 - -250
-249 - -100

-99 - -50
-49 - 0
1 - 50
51 - 250
251 - 500
501 - 4,807

0   250   500   1,000 Kilometres

(caption on next page)

Figure 4.2 Palaeogeographic model of Britain at 8000 cal BC (left) and 7500 cal BC (right). (Image Fraser Sturt. Bathymetry provided by EMODnet Bathymetry Consortium (2020): EMODnet Digital Bathymetry (DTM). https://doi.org/10.12770/bb6a87dd-e579-4036-abe1-e649cea9881a, Topography produced using Copernicus data and information funded by the European Union (EU-DEM))

In contrast to many other tree types, the first appearance of hazel before 8500 BC seems fairly synchronous over much of the British Isles. Hazel generally shows an initial emergence, followed by a much steeper rise. It seems that only following this major expansion, when it became common in woodlands as a canopy tree, that it became an important resource for people. Hazelnuts become ubiquitous on Mesolithic sites, but only from around 8400–8300 BC. These were rich landscapes of: 'endless nut groves, a garden of Eden where one could reap without having sown.' (Iversen 1973, 126). While charred hazelnuts are the most common plant food source preserved, charred seeds of fat-hen (Chenopodium), sloes, *prunus*, vetch and sorrel have occasionally been recorded from Middle Mesolithic sites.

From around 8300 cal BC, oak and elm begin to appear in lowland pollen diagrams, though the appearance of these species shows a greater propensity for clinal, time-transgressive distributions (Bennett 1988; Birks 1989). Oak is present in pollen diagrams in large parts of England and Wales by c.8200 cal BC, becoming common in Northern England by 7700 cal BC and reaching by the Moray Firth by c.7500 cal BC. Beyond this, its spread was slow, due to climatic factors which exceeded its natural tolerances. Pollen evidence dating to c.7000 BC from Warren Field, Crathes, suggests that birch/hazel woodland was still present at this time, with areas of more open heathland (Murray et al. 2009).

Oak is more shade-tolerant than birch, meaning denser forests formed, though understorey vegetation still grew. While Boreal forests have been associated with dense vegetation, making animals more elusive and hunting more difficult (Reynier 2005), this does not always seem to have been the case. Simmonds (2016, 315) notes that several pollen diagrams from Southeast England show an increase in herbaceous pollen, indicating these mixed deciduous forests were initially more open than the preceding birch/pine woodlands.

Within these broad vegetational patterns, considerable local variation existed, determined by altitude and soil type. Hazel was still abundant when oak became more dominant. It was still the main tree type on some calcareous soils (Spikins 1999) and formed the understorey of the mixed deciduous oak-elm woodlands. On nutrient-poor sandy soils such as the Lower Greensand, pine woodland seems to have persisted. On base-rich soils, elm was more common, while oak thrived on more acidic soils. Many chalkland areas, though, still seem to have been fairly open (French et al. 2003). In upland areas, such as the Central Pennines, that had previously been grassland or juniper, birch and hazel woodland began to grow (Spikins 1999), though hazel did not reach the Northern Pennines until c.7700 cal BC, and the highest parts of the Pennines were probably still open (Bridgland et al. 2011). On boggy ground, willow grew amongst reeds and grasses, and alder was locally present though did not become dominant in these areas until the end of the period.

From the Tees to the Tay: The coast of Northeast England and Southeast Scotland

Perhaps the most startling evidence for the change in Mesolithic lifeways at this time is that sites in Northumberland and in Eastern Scotland suddenly become visible in the

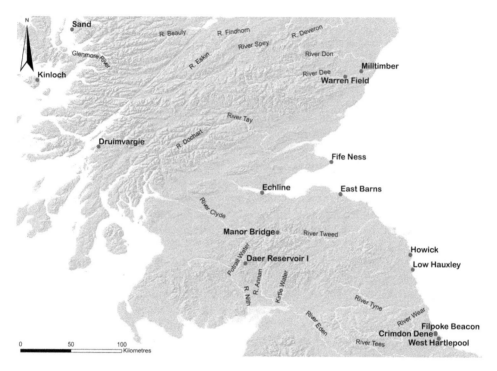

Figure 4.3 Middle Mesolithic sites in Northern Britain

radiocarbon record (Figure 4.3). An Early Mesolithic presence appears likely in these regions on the basis of microlith typology (see chapter 2), but from 8500 BC, human occupation can be traced through radiometric dates, based on the happy co-incidence of the establishment of hazel in the local environment, and a sudden enthusiasm for pit digging amongst Mesolithic groups. Despite accounts of marine-adapted 'narrow blade' wielding refugees from Doggerland (Waddington 2015), the evidence is more supportive of people practising mixed economies.

Bone is rarely preserved on these predominantly sandy-till sediments; only burnt bone occasionally survives. This undoubtedly affects our understanding of the range of species present, with only some being readily identifiable. With these caveats, the evidence from sites in the northeast shows a dominance of terrestrial fauna, particularly pig, and plant remains (Table 4.1). Evidence for use of marine resources is sparse. Admittedly, fish are particularly fragile, but they are recognisable when burnt, found in this state at Star Carr, for example. Fish bones are only present within a small oval structure at Echline, despite wet sieving, often of 100% samples from certain features on many sites in this region; however, equally fragile bird bones have been recognised at several sites. Shellfish also are curiously rare. The only good evidence for marine – or at least shoreline – exploitation comes from two sites, Howick and East Barns, where burnt bones from seals are present. This does not appear a dramatic change from the Early Mesolithic (Waddington 2015); shoreline exploitation is well-evidenced from Star Carr, where almost all flint and material for personal ornamentation was obtained from the beach, and isotopic evidence indicates a probable marine component to the diet of the Seamer dog (see chapter 2), dogs often being used as a proxy for human diets (Eriksson and Zagorska 2003). The predominant coastal distribution of Middle Mesolithic sites in Northern England also appears illusionary, an effect of fieldwork history (Young 2007) and the enhanced visibility of now-coastal sites due to coastal erosion. Patterns in parts of Southeastern Scotland, with an increased input from developer-funded archaeology in the Edinburgh region, may be becoming more robust.

What is clear from the available evidence is that terrestrial mammals, particularly pig, but maybe also aurochs, remained important. The evidence here is slight but a greater reliance on pig during the Boreal has been noted in other regions of Europe (Séara et al. 2009) and possibly also in Southern England at this time. But most ubiquitous of all on these sites are hazelnuts, and their role – given also the prominence of processing facilities on several of these sites – should not be under-estimated (Table 4.1).

The varied focus of these groups can be seen in the location of the two earliest dated sites in the region. At Manor Bridge, Peebles, 35 km from the current coast, a handful of test pits located two hazelnut-rich pits or scoops that indicate, probably, repeated occupation between 8400 and 8200 BC (Warren 2001). This site is located both on and above a rocky outcrop where the Manor flows into the Tweed, an area historically that has been an important place for salmon fishing, gravel pools at the confluence of these rivers serving as resting places for the fish on their migration routes (Warren 2001). The second set of early dates come from Cramond, overlooking the Firth of Forth, where excavations of a small trench, measuring only 4.3 × 1.8 m, located a cluster of pits (Saville 2008). From these come a coherent set of radiocarbon dates, suggesting occupation between c.8500 and 8250 BC (Waddington et al. 2007, 216). While this site would be a convenient location for estuarine resources, bone is not preserved, and the only alimentary evidence is, as ever on these sites, hazelnuts, present in abundance.

Typologically, Cramond demonstrates a transition from Early to Late Mesolithic microlith types, having yielded a unique range of microliths for the Scottish Mesolithic (Ritchie 2010). Saville (2008) noted the presence of a Honey Hill microlith. Beyond this, the assemblage is characterised by curve-backed pieces and isosceles triangles, with a

Table 4.1 Evidence of plant and animal exploitation in Northeast Britain

Site	Faunal preservation	Terrestrial mammals	Birds	Marine mammals	Fish and Shellfish	Plant food
Cramond	None					Hazelnuts
Manor Bridge	None					Hazelnuts
Echline	Burnt bone	Pig, bovid/red deer sized, roe deer sized, canid	Present	None	3 small fragments of fish bone	12,000 hazelnut fragments
East Barns	Burnt bone			Seal		
Howick	Burnt bone	Pig, fox, canid	Present	Seal	81 shells (mainly limpets, dogwelks and periwinkles)	c.200,000 hazelnut fragments
Low Hauxley	None				5 shells (periwinkle)	Present
Filpoke Beacon	Burnt bone	Aurochs, pig, small carnivore	Present			Hazelnuts

small number of obliquely blunted points. The dominance of isosceles triangles, along with obliquely blunted and curve-backed points, link it to the undated assemblages, suggested to be Early Mesolithic on typological grounds, such as Morton A (Coles 1971) and Dryburgh Mains (Lacaille 1954), though the Cramond microliths are smaller in size. The assemblage can perhaps be more usefully thought of in the context of the diversification and regionalisation of forms at the end of the Early Mesolithic, the beginning of a trend that characterises the Middle Mesolithic. Echline may also belong to this group, though very few microliths were recovered from the earliest contexts. From around 8200 cal BC, assemblages in the region are characterised by the typical combination of variably lateralised scalenes, backed bladelets, crescents and obliquely blunted points that characterise the Middle Mesolithic of Northern Britain (see chapter 1).

Possibly from as early as c.8400 cal BC, but certainly from 8200 cal BC, a series of large sunken-featured, post-built structures become visible in this region (Figure 4.4).

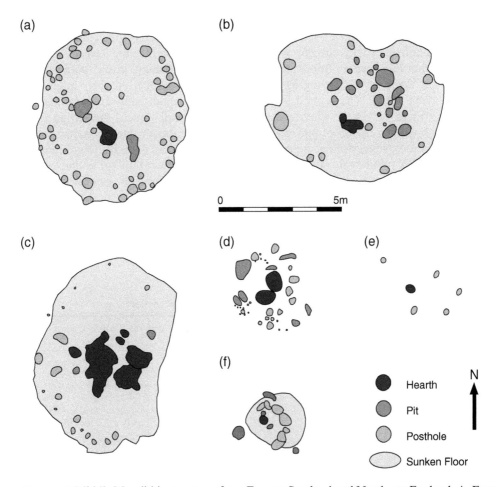

Figure 4.4 Middle Mesolithic structures from Eastern Scotland and Northeast England. A. East Barns, B. Echline, C. Howick, D. Echline oval structure, E. Daer 2, F. Fifeness. (Redrawn after Gooder (2007), Robertson et al. (2013), Waddington (2007), Ward (2012), Wickham-Jones and Dalland (1998))

Examples are known from Echline, East Barns, Howick, and possibly Silvercrest and are discussed in more detail below. These structures are also present to the west, in the Isle of Man, at Cas ny Hawin II, dating from just after 8300 cal BC (Brown in press), and in Ireland at Mount Sandel, dating from c.7800 cal BC (Bayliss and Woodman 2009). It is not certain that the Isle of Man was an island by this time, but it probably was, and Ireland certainly was so. These sites, along with the evidence for inhabitation of the islands of Western Scotland, demonstrates that Middle Mesolithic groups were knowledgeable sea-farers, and these skills are also seen in other Northwest European contexts at this time (e.g. Conneller et al. 2016b).

Sunken-feature structures are known from across Northwest Europe, and Grøn (2003) has discussed the formation of these buildings in some detail, based on some of the better-preserved Scandinavian examples. Occupation does not seem to have taken place on the base of the pit; rather, these sunken features were infilled with branches and other organic material or covered with a bark or plank floor. Through the structure's use, sand would work its way into the pit, infilling the gaps in the organic material. As a result, lithic material tends to be concentrated in the upper layers of the pit, as at Howick, for example.

Also, within these structures are pit hearths and hazelnut roasting pits, while pits dug to be filled with debris from cleaning out hearths are common. The amount of clearance and renewal activities undertaken in relation to these structures is likely to be underestimated. An ostensibly simple structure at Star Carr was discovered, through refitting, to have been cleaned out frequently, with midden material accumulating in the vicinity. This kind of work has not been undertaken on these structures, and most exist only as subsurface features, adjacent occupation debris having been truncated either by ploughing or machining, meaning that their role within a broader settlement cannot be understood.

These large buildings are associated with evidence for long-term (re)occupation. The modelled occupation for the Howick building was between 100 and 300 years (Bayliss et al. 2007, 71). It was then abandoned for between 130 and 280 years, before seeing a probably brief reoccupation of the same place. The same may have happened at Echline, where a structure may have been erected around 8300 BC (Robertson et al. 2013), before being reoccupied around 1000 years later (alternatively, this structure may date to the later phase and have truncated an area of earlier occupation). Cas ny Hawim has a group of mid-eighth millennium pits to the south of the structure, while at Mount Sandel pit digging continued after the structure seems to have fallen out of use. This evidence certainly suggests these larger structures may have marked, or produced, significant places in the landscape that were remembered for some time.

The appearance of large substantial houses at around 8200 BC has been interpreted as a movement towards a more sedentary lifestyle (Waddington 2007), though their spread of radiocarbon dates is also compatible with more intermittent occupation (Mithen and Wicks 2018). Sedentism is hard to demonstrate archaeologically, and the ethnographic record demonstrates that even hunter-gatherer societies who built substantial villages were mobile at certain times of the year (Kelly 1995). The east coast Mesolithic buildings have been interpreted as primarily domestic structures, though Mithen and Wicks (2018) have suggested other possibilities, such as sweat lodges or similar ceremonial functions, should be considered. As far as can be ascertained from the remaining evidence, these structures do appear associated with domestic debris, tasks such as flint knapping, craft activities, food preparation and cooking.

However, the appearance of these structures may perhaps be indicative of broader changes in society. The similarity of these large structures may suggest more rigid rules associated with the inhabitation of space. In other Mesolithic contexts, elaborate houses have been argued to be associated with an increasing emphasis on lineage and ancestry (Boric 2008). There has been increasing archaeological interest in Levi-Strauss' (1982) concept of 'House Societies', in which the house itself, often personified, is the medium through which lineage is reckoned. A role as the source of lineage may account for the long life of the Howick building, the evidence for the later occupation of the same footprint, noted at Howick and at Echline, and (if it is Mesolithic in date) the construction of a similar building at Silvercrest, Lesmurdie Road, adjacent to one erected more than a millennium previously (Suddaby 2007). The structure at East Barns appears to have been burnt down (Gooder 2007), possibly marking the death of the lineage associated with it. These structures may thus be the product of a similar preoccupation with lineages and ancestors during the Middle Mesolithic that manifested itself in Northern Britain through houses and in the southwest through a focus on human remains.

In addition to these large buildings, many sites in the region have evidence for a smaller set of structures. At Echline, a small, oval structure was found, measuring just over 2 m; at Fife Ness, a possible structure of similar dimensions was uncovered (Figure 4.4). Both of these have a coherent set of radiocarbon dates, probably indicating short-term use, possibly, as suggested by Wickham-Jones and Dalland (1998), logistical use, though the lithic assemblage from Echline appears fairly generalised. A seemingly similar-sized structure was located at Daer Reservoir 1, in the Southern Uplands, just over the other site of the watershed from Manor Bridge, on a site investigated by the Biggar Archaeology Group (Ward 2012). This has a single radiocarbon date, indicating occupation sometime between 8550 and 7950 BC, and its location, at 340 m asl, may suggest both a specialised and short-term focus.

Northeast Scotland: The pits of the Dee

Pit digging was a key feature of lifeways in Northern Britain during this period (see below); however, in general these pits tended to be relatively small and usually related to the disposal of domestic debris, particularly burnt material deriving from hearths. In the north of Scotland, at two sites, Warren Field, Crathes and Milltimber on the River Dee (Figure 4.3), pit digging was of a rather different nature. An elaborate pit alignment has been located at Warren Field, while at Milltimber, a rather more eclectic, if broadly linear, arrangement was uncovered (Figure 4.5). These two sites share many similarities: Pits tend to be large, often over 2 m wide and up to 2 m deep; they were left to silt up, rather than backfilled with domestic debris; and they display a number of recuts, some of which indicate reuse in the later Mesolithic and Neolithic. Some may have held timber posts. These are pits that were intended to mark places in the landscape on a scale that extended well beyond a human lifespan and are the earliest Mesolithic monuments in the British landscape. The dates from the earliest pits from both sites are effectively identical, indicating these were first dug between 8200 and 7800 BC, and at both sites the main phase of pit digging seems to span 8200 to 7000 BC. Both also have evidence for very late Mesolithic (mid-late fifth millennium BC) and Early Neolithic recuts.

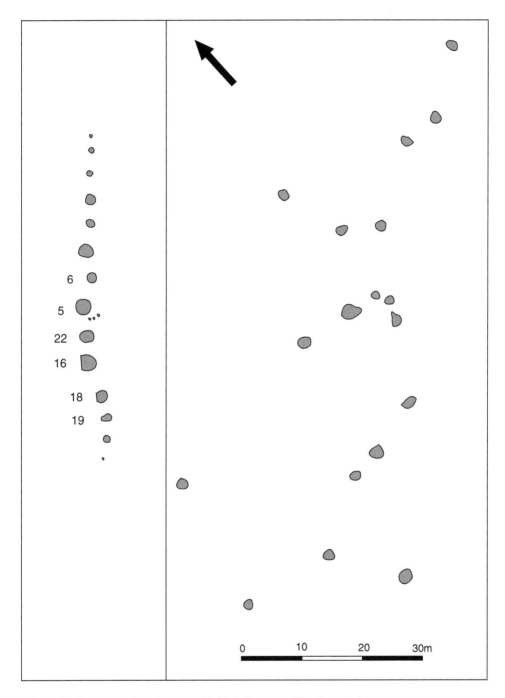

Figure 4.5 Large pits from Warren Field (left) and Milltimber (right)

In 2004, a Mesolithic pit alignment was discovered at Warren Field, Crathes, Aberdeenshire (Murray and Murray 2014). The alignment was located on a gravel ridge, around 600 m north of the River Dee. Pollen and macrofossil evidence suggest that when the pits were dug, the area was open woodland of birch and hazel. The canopy was sufficiently open for grass, ferns and scabious as well as heath plants such as ling, heather and bilberries to grow. Willow may have been present in the damp river valleys when the site was first visited. The presence of light woodland means that the alignment would not be obviously visible from a distance, particularly in the summer months.

The excavation and the majority of the use of the pits spans the period 8200 to 7000 BC. The radiocarbon dates indicate they were not all dug at the same time; instead they were excavated at intervals, seemingly several hundred years apart. Not all of the radiocarbon measurements are on primary fills, and some pits have no dates at all; thus, the sequence of digging cannot be fully determined. Pit 6 is likely to have been dug first, at or before around 8000 cal BC. Between 7970 and 7610 cal BC, pits 18 and 19 were dug, and possibly also pit 22; pit 16, however, was probably dug at least 200 years later than these two. Evidence from pit 5 suggests activity around 7000 BC, though it may well have been in existence before this time.

Rather than acting as containers, it appears to have been the digging of these pits that was important. They were left open, surrounded by visually distinctive mounds of upcast. Pits 5 and 6 also seemed to have contained stakes at one point during their use. Pits 16, 18, 19 and 20 also received deposits as primary or early fills (Murray et al. 2009). As is common amongst pits of this date, these deposits consisted of burnt material: Charcoal from both the surrounding area and possibly also more distant areas, such as damp valleys with willow, alder and spikerush. Also included were burnt foodstuffs, burnt animal bones, hazelnuts, seeds of fat hen (Chenopodium album) and vetch (Vici sp.) (Murray et al. 2009). Some of this may be hearth debris: The deposit in pit 19 consisted of charcoal, burnt stones, burnt animal bone and a bunt seed of fat hen. The chemical signature of several of the charcoal fills suggested the presence of ground-up minerals, possibly from the Pass of Ballater around 40 km from Warren Field. This was found in the charcoal-rich primary deposit in pit 16 and in charcoal-rich recuts of pits 5 and 6, as well as in inwashed upcast material in pit 5. The date of these fills spans several hundred years, suggesting that use of rocks from this source may have been a recurrent activity.

Most of the fills in the pits consists of silting events, as material from the mound of upcast slipped back into the pits. Some of these silting fills include charcoal, indicative of fires set in the area around the pits. Pit 5 contains a handful of abraded flint flakes in one of these slip layers, showing use of lithic material in the area surrounding the pit and its incorporation in the mounds of upcast. The ancient landsurface surrounding the pits had been destroyed by ploughing. In the first year of excavation, the ploughsoil was sieved for artefacts; only one flint flake was recovered, indicating minimal activity involving lithic artefacts and that those lithics that were present seem to have been deposited on the mounds of upcast, perhaps indicating these functioned as middens.

Recently, it has been argued that the pit alignment represents a calendrical system, with the central and earliest pit (6) marking a location for viewing the mid-winter sunrise between the Slug Road Pass and the pits themselves marking divisions in a lunar system of time-reckoning (Gaffney et al. 2013). The different size of the pits, they suggest, relate to the waxing and waning of the moon: 'a symbolic view of how observers saw the lunar cycle overall'. However, this does not seem to fit well with the extended period over which the pits were dug. Only five of the pits have dates, but of these only two could have been excavated at the same time, and the digging seems to encompass several hundred years. The evidence from the more extensively dated pits suggests that each pit was a focus of activity for a relatively short time, before becoming partially silted up with upcast material. There was an episode of stabilisation and soil development visible in the upper fills, though the pits must have been visible as shallow depressions, as several of them were recut in the Early Neolithic. Furthermore, as the excavators point out, the mounds of upcast surrounding the pits appears to have been highly important, and their position needs to be considered.

More broadly though, the Warren Fields pit alignment, is perhaps in the same tradition as the Stonehenge pits or the Star Carr platform, a relatively short-term (decadal?) use of a feature, which was allowed to decay/silt up/become covered, before a very similar feature is erected in the immediate vicinity.

More recently, 30 pits have been located at Milltimber (Dingwall et al. 2019), a site 12 km further down the Dee from Warren Field. These consist of both large, steep pits (22 are over 2 m in diameter) and shallower, often smaller pits. The large, steep pits and many of the small shallow ones are very similar to Warren Field, in that they appear to have been infilled through natural silting processes and include periods of soil stabilisation. Shallower pits seem more likely to contain some occupation debris and possible posts, though one of the larger pits contains a substantial lithic assemblage that may represent the clearance of a knapping floor. Some of the material may be specially selected, such as ten rock crystal flakes found in the upper fill of pit AMA09–2064, unique in the Scottish Mesolithic; however, formal deposition seems the exception rather than the rule. Most were simply left open to gradually silt up, some on occasion being recut.

While pits are found across the area of excavation, there is a concentration of these on the break of slope just above a gravel terrace, where they form two rough arcs. The rather imperfect alignment of Warren Field pits, argued to have an astronomical basis, is in some way echoed by the even less linear arrangement here. In contrast to the astronomical/monumental interpretation of the Warren Field pits, it has been suggested that the pits from Milltimber might represent animal traps (Dingwall et al. 2019). While this is certainly an explanation worth entertaining, it is perhaps not entirely compatible with the temporal and geographical patterning to pit digging at either site.

Fewer radiocarbon measurement have been made on these features than at Warren Field, so understanding of sequence is limited. The earliest dated pit, at 8210–7820 BC (SUERC-68106), is located in the northern part of the site, and is not part of the two arcs. However, the second date within the sequence of 7712–7852 BC (SUERC-680896) comes from the northernmost pit in the northernmost of the two arcs. Two other dates for the pit arc fall in the later part of the eight millennium BC, while a further pit in this arrangement dates to the mid-fifth millennium BC. Of the 11 measurements on these pits, only two pairs could have been excavated during the same occupation. It is clear that, as at Warren Fields, people revisited Milltimber over a very long time period to add to an existing arrangement of pits, an arrangement that must have changed over time as some pits infilled with material and became less invisible.

Around 10 m southeast of the pits was a spread of silty sediment within which several lithic scatters had been preserved. These scatters are dominated by microliths with smaller numbers of scrapers and retouched and utilised pieces. Small pits and a tree throw in this area have yielded two dates – one similar to the earliest pit dates, the other belonging to the very end of the Mesolithic. It is thus uncertain to what extent this large spread of material, numbering over 10,000 pieces, is contemporary with the large pits. If it is this would represent a very different situation to Warren Field, where the pits appear isolated from contemporary settlement and industrial activities.

Southeast Scotland

In Southeast Scotland, pits are smaller, and both large and small structures are known. Three key sites are present: Echline, East Barns and Fifeness. The site at Echline is at 35 m OD on land sloping down towards the Firth of Forth, a series of Mesolithic features were located during work in advance of the Forth replacement crossing (Robertson et al. 2013). Amongst these were two Mesolithic structures, and a number of pits that have yielded Mesolithic dates, indicating settlement commenced on the site around 8300 BC. Amongst these features is a large sunken feature building, similar to examples from East Barns, 60 km east along the Firth of Forth, and from Howick, Northumberland (see below).

This sunken feature building is composed of a large, shallow pit, 6.96 by 5.92 m and 0.55 m in depth, surrounded by a ring of nine post-holes, slightly angled towards the centre of the structure (Figure 4.4). The entrance of the structure may have faced toward the west. The southern part of the base of the pit feature was cobbled, possibly the remnants of a platform as has been found associated with several Southern Scandinavian examples (Gron 2003). An inner ring of post-holes encircled a couple of hearths in the centre of the structure, forming an oval 2.9 × 2.2 m. Single measurements on charred hazelnuts from the fills of one external and one internal post-hole returned almost identical dates of 8319–8240 BC (9075 ± 35 BP; SUERC-39764) and 8302–8238 BC (9060 ± 35 BP; SUERC-39769). Sixteen small shallow pits were located within the central part of the structure, most of which contained burnt hazelnuts, burnt bone and burnt flint and thus were seemingly used to dispose of material cleared out from hearths. One of these pits has a single radiocarbon date of 8452–8283 BC (9145 ± 30 BP; SUERC-42918) (Robertson et al. 2013).

The internal features were sealed by a layer of charcoal-rich silty sand and gravel, which was determined by micromorphological analysis to be an *in situ* occupation floor. While one early date was obtained from this floor, three other measurements spanned 7350 to 7050 BC. This raises interesting questions as to the nature of the structure. It is unlikely that a structure built around 8300 BC was still sufficiently preserved for occupation a millennium later, and no evidence for rebuilding is present. This does raise the possibility that the majority of the building dates to this later period, and it has truncated a location of earlier activity, with the date from the external post-hole residual.

The only faunal material comes from this later occupation floor, consisting of pig, probably roe deer, a red deer/aurochs sized animal, birds and a canid. Lithics were not systematically collected during excavation and come only from samples. Within this rather limited assemblage, microliths and scrapers dominate. The raw materials used were flint and southern uplands chert, both of which can be obtained from local beaches.

Evidence for the decay of the building is present, with a ring of organic sediment around the margins of the pit and over this redeposited sands and gravels that may have formed a bank, shoring up the walls of the structure. This very obvious evidence for decay demonstrates a contrast with the similar structure at East Barns (below) that may have been deliberately fired.

Around 20 m to the north of the large building at Echline, a second, smaller structure was located. This belongs, more securely, to the earliest phase of occupation of the site and has only yielded dates in the range of 8400–8200 BC. This is an oval structure composed of a small ring of 11 posts measuring 2.95 by 2.10 m (Figure 4.4). The structure contained two large hearths, one of which was dated, as was one of the post-holes. A series of stake holes and pits also clustered around the structure. Burnt bone from one of these pits has been identified as belonging to fish, birds and small mammals. The small lithic assemblage from the oval structure was made on southern uplands chert and is fairly balanced between microliths and scrapers. The oval structure appears to have been associated with a fairly large scatter of occupation debris, now only preserved in the fills of subsurface features. This scatter seems to have extended to the west (with lithics recovered from slots of later ring and groove structure) and to the north, recovered as residual elements from a series of probably later pits that formed a large arc. Pits within 4 m of the oval structure have moderate quantities of lithics (between 14 and 32 pieces), while those beyond this tend to have only one or two. This suggests an area of working or middens adjacent to the oval structure and an area of more ephemeral tasks extending at least 15 m to the north. Residual lithics in these later features provide a rare glimpse into the nature of activities outside these Southern Scottish and Northern English buildings on sites where surrounding evidence has been truncated.

East Barns, Dunbar overlooks the Firth of Forth; here, a large sunken-floor dwelling was located in 2001 by AOC in advance of quarrying (Gooder 2007). A series of deposits were preserved within a hollow. This, as well as protecting the structure from ploughing, partly preserved an occupation horizon and a number of external pits. The sunken floor of the building measured 6.8 × 6.2 m and was surrounded by around 30 post-holes, between 25 and 55 cm in diameter (Figure 4.4). This makes it larger than the Howick structure (see below), and with more substantial evidence for the post-built superstructure. The majority of the posts were slightly tilted towards the centre of the structure. A gap in their distribution suggests a doorway to the south, facing inland away from the Firth of Forth. Artefacts from in and around the structure include a large chipped stone and coarse stone assemblage. Analysis of the microliths shows some were impact damage from use as projectiles while a couple were employed in hide-working activities (Evans 2009). Also present were the ubiquitous hazelnuts and a small quantity of burnt bone. Of the latter, only a seal could be identified; this species is also known from Howick. East Barns is probably slightly earlier than the Howick structure; three radiocarbon dates span 8300 to 7650 BC.

Substantial evidence for burning was present, with burnt material in the upper part of the post-holes and as a curving, burnt organic deposit following the walls of the structure. These suggest the structure burnt down at the end of its life. Given the difficulty in firing such structures (Stevanović 1997), this may have been a deliberate act.

Further up the coast, at Fife Ness, a coherent set of radiocarbon dates have been obtained on a series of intercutting pits and occupation debris (Wickham-Jones and Dalland 1998), indicating the site was occupied around 7500 BC (Waddington et al. 2007). The Mesolithic occupation appears preserved in a dip in the topography, and while the site has been characterised as a small, specialist occupation, it may also be the case that this is all that remains of a larger site that has not been preserved.

The features located consist of seven inter-cutting pits, forming an arc just over a metre in length (Figure 4.4). In the shelter of this arc was a layer of reddened sand, which may have represented a hearth. These pits initially appeared to be covered by a layer of occupation material that overlapped the arc, but the relationship could not be discerned in section, due to the effect of soil processes. Though no post-pipes were seen, the semi-circular form of the pit arrangement suggested to the excavators they may have functioned as post-holes for a windbreak; however, the content of the pits in the eastern end of the arc is rather different from that of the occupation layer, suggesting that they functioned as containers for particular types of deposits, at least at the end of their lives. Beyond this arc of pits and layer of occupation debris were four further pits, one very large, measuring 2.5 by 2.2 m.

A relatively small assemblage of stone artefacts, numbering just 1518 pieces, was recovered. The chipped tool assemblage, made on local beach pebbles, is dominated by microliths, with a smaller number of scrapers. A hollowed stone, just over 5 cm long, which could have been used for grinding food or pigments was also recovered. The microlith assemblage is characterised by curve-backed/crescentic microliths, only ever small components of microlith assemblages on other sites during this period, but supporting an interpretation of this site as short-term and possibly specialised. Suggestions for its use include a fishing camp or a bird-hunter's hide (Wickham-Jones and Dalland 1998).

While the nature of the arc of pits and occupation layer remains enigmatic, this site, which certainly has some indicators of a short-term stay, is notable for the large number of pits represented. It demonstrates just how central pit digging had become to the way people occupied the landscape at this time. Several of these pits seem to represent ways of disposing of waste material (Table 4.2). The large pit to the southwest of the pit-arc contained 38% of the stone tool assemblage from the site. Several of the pits within the arc seem to have been used specifically to deposit hearth material, with three adjacent pits in particular containing heavily burnt flint, burnt hazelnuts and charcoal. Quantities of burnt flint are much higher than within the layer of occupational debris, indicating that burnt material was specially selected for deposition within the pits. Cultural rules regarding the disposal of different kinds of materials appear to have been in operation, and these acts connected people to certain places in the landscape.

Northumberland and County Durham

Further south, the archaeology of sites in Northumberland and County Durham share considerable similarities with the Scottish east coast sites, in the presence of pits and large structures. The initial impetus for research in this area comes from the holidaying habits of Francis Buckley (see Box 1.1), whose wife Bebba's family lived in the area, and Coupland who located important sites at Filpoke Beacon and Crimdon Dene in County Durham (Young 2007). More recently, sites have also been located

Table 4.2 Content of the Fife Ness pits (data collated from Wickham-Jones and Dallard 1998)

Pit	Lithics no	% burnt lithics	Charcoal
F41 (large external pit)	574	15	Burnt hazelnuts
F61 (external pit)	120	52	Burnt hazelnuts
F70 (external pit)	19	21	Burnt hazelnuts
F46 (occupation layer)	367	31	Burnt hazelnuts, hazel, birch, willow and oak charcoal
F67 (pit arc)	7	14	
F82 (pit arc)	2	50	
F84 (pit arc)	38	32	Burnt hazelnuts
F86 (pit arc)	150	56	
F72 (pit arc)	50	66	
F65 (pit arc)	49	80	
F63 (pit arc)	72	33	Burnt hazelnuts
F68 (hearth)	1	0	
F74 (internal pit)	0	0	
F76 (internal pit)	3	0	
F78 (internal pit)	12	8	
F80 (internal pit)	9	11	
F88 (internal pit)	5	40	
F94 (internal pit)	0	0	

through the effects of coastal erosion, in particular through monitoring work undertaken by John Davies. Two of Davies' sites have seen more extensive excavation projects, at Howick and Low Hauxley.

The structure at Howick is now on the edge of a sea-cliff, and its eastern side is eroded (Figure 4.6). There are problems reconstructing sea-level rise due to a lack of sea-level index points predating 7000 cal BC in the region; however, models suggest that at 8000 cal BC relative sea-level would have been around −20 m, making Howick around 3 km from its contemporary coastline (Shennan et al. 2012). More locally, the Howick Burn, a deeply incised stream, is located around 100 m to the south.

The building took the form of a large pit around 5.5 m in diameter, partly encircled by a series of pits and post-holes, and has been interpreted as having four separate phases of use and rebuilding (Figure 4.7). Howick is probably similar to the structures described by Grøn (2003), with the floor covered by organic material, and occupation taking place on top of this. Howick appears to have three such floor layers, as the structure was modified and rebuilt over time, with the features from the first and then the second occupation area sealed by sand, which may have been brought in (as it was on occasions on Southern Scandinavian sites).

In comparison with Echline, there is relatively little evidence for a substantial superstructure at Howick, and the evidence that exists is mainly associated with the first phase of occupation. This is not unusual in comparison to the European evidence, and Grøn (2003, 688) points out that even relative substantial structures, such as log cabins, may leave relatively little evidence for the superstructure. At Howick, the first phase is associated with the large sunken pit and a series of post and stake holes along its southern and western border, and in the north, linear features that may have had a structural purpose. (The eastern part of the structure has been eroded.) The pit and post-holes were first dug in 7970–7760 cal BC (95% probability)

Figure 4.6 Footprint of the Howick structure (copyright Clive Waddington)

(Bayliss et al. 2007, 71). The first phase of occupation appears extremely intensive and is associated with a series of intercutting pit hearths and charcoal spreads (Figure 4.7), with reddened sand indicating in situ burning. It also seems to have lasted longer than subsequent phases, extending between 40 and 160 years (68% probability). Food processing activities were a particular focus, with burnt hazelnuts common and burnt bone also present. Several pits were recorded, some of which were used to dispose of hearth material, while the function of others is more enigmatic. Five thousand nine hundred fifty-nine lithic artefacts and nine bevel-ended tools made from local sandstone derive from this phase, attesting to a wide variety of activities. Over 800 fragments of burnt bone were recovered, most from hearths or pits containing hearth refuse. Some could be identified to species: Fox (2 elements), canid (1), seal (2), pig (2) and bird.

Phase 2 is separated from phase 1 by a layer of sand, containing much occupation debris, that seals earlier features. This change in the form of the structure was initiated in 7800–7700 cal BC (95% probability) (Bayliss et al. 2007, 71). There is nothing to indicate the presence of a superstructure in phase 2, raising the possibility of a change of function, though the area still remained a focus with a couple of hearths being set and two hazelnut roasting pits (one containing more than 7000 charred hazelnuts) recorded (Figure 4.7). Indeed, the proximity of one of the hearths to the putative walls of the structure suggests none were present. This phase lasted between 10 and 80 years (68% probability). Two thousand seven hundred twenty-two lithic artefacts were recovered, with a broadly similar assemblage composition, though microliths are more common than in phase 1.

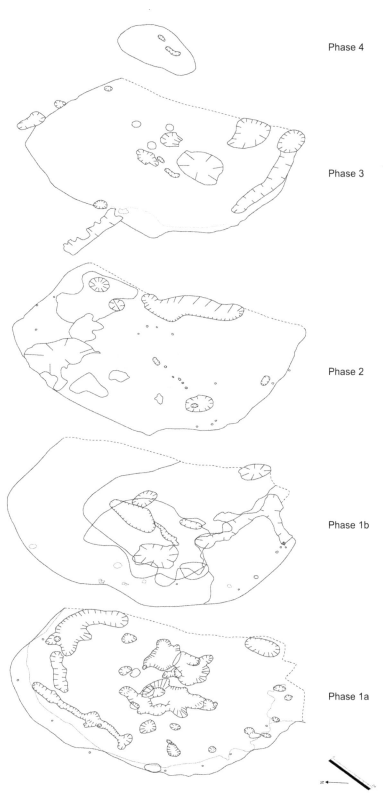

Phase 4

Phase 3

Phase 2

Phase 1b

Phase 1a

(caption on next page)

There is more structural evidence associated with phase 3, when a handful of post-holes were located along the edge of the sunken feature (Figure 4.7). This rebuild took place in 7750–7630 BC (95% probability) (Bayliss et al. 2007, 71). Based on the number of features, activity appears perhaps shorter term than previous phases: A single hearth and a cooking pit are present, while three pits appear to contain cleared out hearth debris. This impression of shorter-term activity is reinforced by the Bayesian modelling that indicates it lasted between 1 and 60 years (68% probability). However, a respectable 4245 pieces of worked flint and hundreds of charred hazelnuts indicate a range of activities took place within this structure. The large number of lithics, despite the shorter occupation, is likely to mean that in contrast to other phases less clearance and maintenance took place.

An ephemeral fourth phase of occupation – not associated with any superstructure – has been recorded, consisting of a burnt spread and a couple of shallow burnt features (Figure 4.7). This occupation took place between 130 and 280 years after the Howick sunken feature building was abandoned. That this short-term visit to the site focused on exactly the same area as the central hearth in all previous occupations suggests it remained a known place, perhaps, given the potential association of these structures with lineages, associated with ancestors.

Any lithic scatters surrounding the structure at Howick have been removed by ploughing. Only a small number of pits were located to the southwest of the structure, which may be Mesolithic. Relatively few lithics were recovered from the ploughsoil or subsoil, where it was examined, except in the immediate vicinity of the structure. If this is a real pattern, rather than taphonomic, this would be a stark contrast with earlier structures, such as Star Carr, which was located amongst dense lithic scatters, consisting both in situ knapping, butchery and craft activities and middening (Box 4.1).

Just 15 km down the current coastline from Howick, further evidence for occupation of a similar date comes from Low Hauxley. The site was also exposed by coastal erosion, and rescue excavations have been undertaken by a number of different archaeologists over the past few decades, resulting in the recovery of Mesolithic and later Prehistoric evidence (Waddington and Bonsall 2016). The focus of the occupation was a low hillock of till and glacial outwash sands and gravels, lying to the north of a small stream, the Bondicarr Burn.

The Mesolithic material has been recovered from a buried soil, preserved by overlying dune formation of Early Iron Age date. Excavations have revealed a series of pits and shallow hollows that may have served as footing for tents or foci for middening (Figure 4.9). Portions of two potential circular features were located at the edge of excavation, one of which (occupation area 1) was associated with large stones and a gulley. Neither has been dated, but both yielded Mesolithic flintwork. More extensively excavated was a large, shallow scoop, 6.7 by 7.1 m and 20 cm in depth, known as occupation area 2 (Figure 4.10). This contained a higher density of lithic material than the surrounding palaeosol, as well as charcoal and hazelnuts. There is no evidence for any post-holes that would indicate use as a structure, and lithic distributions seem to cross-cut its boundaries; instead it may have been used for the deposition of midden material. A large pit cut within it contained charcoal but no evidence for in situ burning. Lithic distributions show a focus of activities in the

Box 4.1   Bevel-ended tools

In the Middle Mesolithic, bevel-ended tools make their appearance in the archaeological record and continue to be used throughout the remainder of the period. The earliest dated examples, at Howick, are of stone, but bone andantler examples appear from c.7500 BC at both Sand and Druimvargie Rock Shelter. These tools consist of elongated pebbles or bone or antler, with a bevel, formed at one end (see Figure 4.8). Of the organic examples, bone was used more commonly than antler, and when species and element can be determined, red deer metapodials seem to be the preferred blank, though other species such as roe deer and cetacean were employed on occasions (Saville et al. 2012). The ends of the bone examples, made on split ungulate long bones, often seem to have been flaked into shape before being polished (Hardy and Wickham-Jones 2009), though there is some debate about whether the polish derives from production or simply from use. Jacobi (1980b) noted the strong association of these tools with coastal sites along rocky shore, suggesting they were used to process marine resources, possibly the seals that would favour these areas.

Suggestions as to their function have included limpet scoops (Bishop 1914), limpet hammers (Anderson 1898; Lacaille 1954), tools for the removal of whale or seal blubber (Lacaille 1954), or related to hide processing (Anderson 1898; Connock et al. 1991; Finlayson 1996). Experimental work undertaken as part of the Scotland's First Settlers Project tested bone and antler bevel-ended tools on a variety of different materials (Hardy and Wickham-Jones 2009). They proved ineffective as limpet scoops, and bone examples performed poorly when used as limpet hammers. Antler examples were more effective, but caused jarring in contrast to the stone examples, which seemed best suited for this task. A small-scale experiment by Barlow and Mithen (2000) also found that stone bevel-ended tools were effective limpet hammers. This might suggest that bevel-ended tools made from different materials, despite their morphological similarity, were used for different tasks. Certainly stone bevel-ended tools seem to have rather different use traces from organic ones, including percussive events that might indicate use as hammers. Bone and antler examples performed well in woodworking and plant working, but these activities did not generate the types of polish seen on archaeological examples. While they were not well suited for working with wet hide, experiments using dry hide were more productive. Use of bone and antler softened this material and made it more pliable; this task also generated the same type of polish seen on archaeological examples. While experiments were carried out on wild boar skin, Waddington (2007) suggests the association with coastal and near-coastal sites might indicate the processing of seal skins, perhaps for use as lightweight boats. However, seal remains are not present at Morton, where bevel-ended tools were found in large numbers.

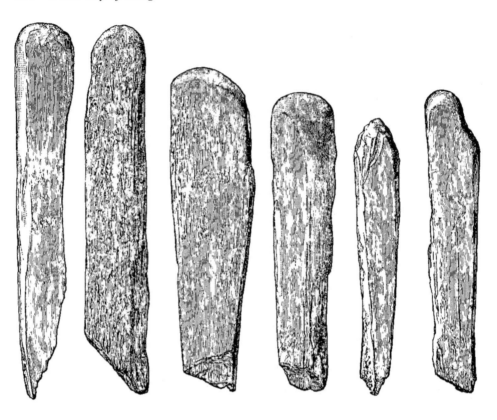

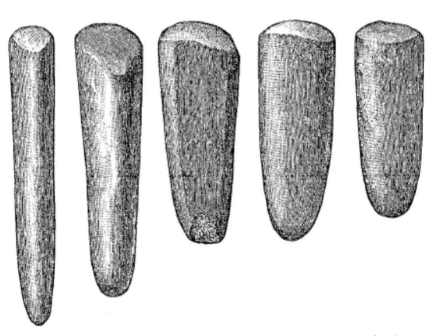

(caption on next page)

Figure 4.8 Above: Bone and antler bevel-ended tools from Druimvargie Rockshelter. Below: Stone bevel-ended tools from Casteal nan Gillean (Anderson 1898)

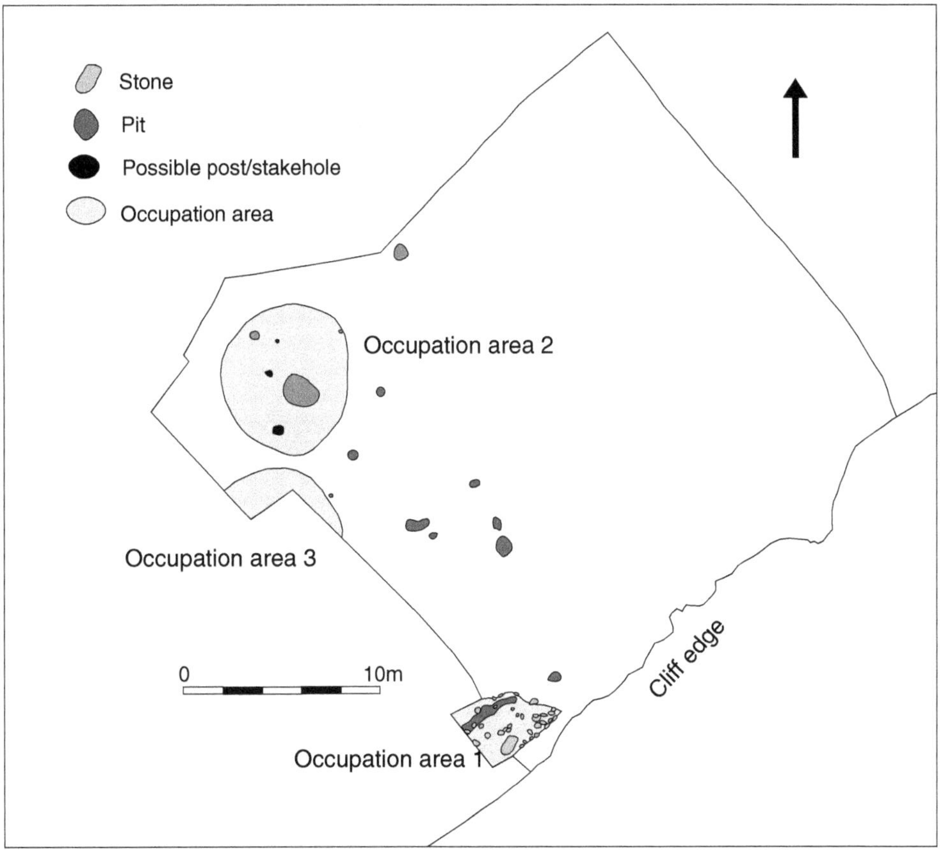

Figure 4.9 Plan of excavations at Low Hauxley (Redrawn after Waddington and Bonsall 2016)

vicinity of the scoop, with retouched and utilised pieces, microliths, awls and scrapers all clustering in this area. Bevel-ended tools and ochre are found more broadly scattered across the excavated area, though several examples come from in and around the scoop.

Several pits were found, mainly to the southeast of the scoop. These all contain a combination of lithics, charcoal and charred hazelnuts. The ubiquity of hazelnuts in these features is noteworthy, given these have a seasonal aspect. One pit, only 0.63 by 0.37 m in diameter and 17 cm deep, contained 1305 fragments, and only two of the 11 pits had none, both containing only lithics.

Radiocarbon dating indicates intermittent occupation of the hillock. Bayesian modelling indicates this started in 8155–7810 cal BC and ended in 7410–7050 cal BC (95% probability). The scoop has some of the earliest evidence for occupation at the

Figure 4.10 Occupation area 2 at Low Hauxley under excavation (copyright Clive Waddington)

site, but certainly contains the debris of more than one occupation. Pit digging also seems to have taken place on more than one occasion. Though some of the pits were dug fairly early; in general, more pits were dug during later visits to the site.

While this site has been linked to groups with specialised coastal economies, there is relatively little evidence for this at Low Hauxley. The scoop contained only five shells, of which only two are of a size to be edible. Only one pit contains shells, three periwinkles. This does not suggest a focus on shellfish at least. Fauna is unfortunately not preserved.

A final site where a structure or large pit has been excavated is Flipoke Beacon in Southeast County Durham. 'The Beacon' is located around 1 km to the south of Blackhall, on a small, sandy plateau, overlooking to the south the valley of Crimdon Dene; to the east is the current coastline, though it would be some distance during the time of occupation. The location is in many ways reminiscent of Howick.

Lithic material was noted in an adjacent sand and gravel quarry, and excavations were undertaken by George Bennett Gibbs and George Coupland in 1937, the latter returning to excavate again in 1946 (Coupland 1948). The quarry face was excavated around 3 m back until the edge of deposits were reached. The stratigraphy consisted of topsoil overlying a sandy subsoil with occasional flints and hazelnut shells. Below this was located the majority of the Mesolithic material, in a black sandy layer, rich in charcoal and burnt hazelnut shells. This overlay a 'white layer' composed of bone ash, fragments of bone and presumably sand. Coupland suggested (1948, 1) these remains lay within a hollow or pit, though he was unable to discern any boundaries to this feature. This seems extremely likely, given the concentration of the material.

Jacobi suggests this may have been a rubbish pit, but Coupland (1948, 2) reports evidence for in situ burning. It may be that this represents a structure that was burnt down, or alternatively, given that Coupland does not record measurements of the burnt area, this may have been a hearth or roasting pit within a larger structure. Radiocarbon dates on burnt hazelnuts were obtained by Roger Jacobi. These indicated occupation between 8235 and 7586 cal BC (8760 ± 140 BP; Q-1474) (Jacobi 1976, 71).

Faunal remains, mostly burnt, recovered from the lower layer were examined by Dorothea Bate, and found to represent aurochs, pig, an unidentifiable bird and a small carnivore. The remainder were too fragmentary to identify, but appeared to be small mammals, none larger than pig. The lithic assemblage consisted of 1887 pieces of flint, all sourced as beach pebbles. The assemblage is dominated by microliths, with 73 examples recovered, though only one microburin was noted. Sieving does not seem to have taken place, meaning that both microliths and microburins are likely to be under-represented. Scrapers are also relatively common, with 26 examples. Retouched and utilised blades and flakes were present, while cores (28), hammerstones (5) and debitage were also recovered.

Unlike Howick, which seems curiously isolated, there is evidence for considerable Mesolithic activity in the vicinity. Site B, a surface site a few metres to the north, yielded 190 flints, including similar microliths, while a few hundred metres to the south, considerable quantities of Mesolithic material derive from surface collections at Crimdon Dene. This site is on a spit of glacial till on the northern site of the burn (Raistrick et al. 1936). Lithic material, numbering more than 9000 pieces, was recovered as surface collections, eroding out of a thin grey sand on top of the glacial clay, possibly representing an episode of soil development. While the assemblage contains later Prehistoric material, most appears Mesolithic and was recovered from two scatters, measuring a few metres across. The assemblage contains microliths, microburins, truncations and scrapers. The microlithic assemblage is characterised by narrow-backed bladelets and scalene triangles, very similar to Filpoke Beacon, suggesting a complex of sites of similar date in the area.

Early settlers of Western Scotland

It is likely that there was an early occupation of the west coast: The last Upper Palaeolithic groups are known to have reached Colonsay (Mithen et al. 2015), and there are typologically Early Mesolithic microliths known from several sites in Western Scotland (see chapter 1), though these have no reliable associated radiocarbon determinations. Towards the end of the Middle Mesolithic, evidence for occupation is confirmed in these areas through radiocarbon dated material. On the western shore of Loch Lomond, a series of pits and hearths have been dated to 8000 cal BC (MacGregor 2009). A single estimate exists on a bone bevel-ended tool a midden at Druimvargie Rockshelter of 7570–7175 (OxA-4608) (Ashmore 2004), though this is 500 years earlier than two other, consistent dates on material from this old excavation. Two dates, from a hearth and a post-hole, are also available from the Creit Dubh on the Isle of Mull, suggesting initial occupation between c.8320 and

Figure 4.11 Kinloch and Loch Scresort (copyright Kinloch excavation project)

8230 cal BC of a site that dates in the main to the first half of the seventh millennium (Mithen and Wicks 2018). Importantly, this is an island, indicating sophisticated marine voyaging skills were present, as demonstrated by the fact that groups made the crossing to Ireland and the Isle of Man at this time. Mid-eighth millennium dates from the Chest of Dee, in the uplands of the Cairngorms, also show an inland, upland presence and suggest rivers were being used as routeways between east and west (Wickham-Jones et al. 2020).

More substantial evidence comes from Kinloch on Rùm (Figure 4.11), excavated by Caroline Wickham-Jones between 1984 and 1986, where a series of radiocarbon dates show repeated occupation, between c.7500 and 6500 cal BC (Wickham-Jones 1990). Two Bayesian models of the site (neither unfortunately taking account of a 1988 re-counting exercise that revised the radiocarbon dates) suggest broadly two phases of occupation – one possibly representing a single episode, the other representing longer-term revisits on a fairly continuous basis (Waddington et al. 2007; Waddington and Wicks 2017). The site is located on the east coast of the island, just above Loch Scresort, a marine inlet into which feeds two major rivers and a number of smaller streams, one of which crossed the eastern edge of the site. At a time of higher sea-level, the waters of Loch Scresort were in very close proximity to the site. Pollen evidence suggests that vegetation was still relatively open at the time of occupation, with grasses and heathers growing. In sheltered locations grew stands of birch and hazel and ju-niper shrub, though hazel increased throughout the period of occupation, gradually forming a closed canopy woodland in sheltered areas. By the loch was an estuarine salt-marsh, fringed with reeds, but also edible plants such as sea plantain, purslane and crowberry (Hirons and Edwards 1990).

The Kinloch site shares many similarities with the east coast sites. Pits are common, many intercut, and show a focus on the deposition on hearth material. The earliest dates come from areas AD and AJ in the southwest of the excavated area. AJ consists of three highly truncated pits, but more has survived in area AD, where a complex of pits and hollows was located. A natural hollow, around 2 m in diameter, was modified to create a flat base, then infilled with a mix of lithic material and burnt hazelnut shells. Later, a second hollow was excavated, through the fill of which was cut two pits, then both were deliberately backfilled at the same time. Finally, two further pits were dug, both c.90 by 80 cm and 50 cm deep. AD5 was back-filled with charcoal-rich sediment containing burnt lithic material. Two post-pipes were visible in the fill. At the top were a cache of pebbles, some showing signs of use (Figure 4.12). AD6 was very similar, though with a single post-pipe. These posts may have marked out the site as a significant place and marked this place out as a lo-cation for future occupation. Two radiocarbon dates (both recounted in 1988, with slightly different results) come from AD5, suggesting the digging of these final two

Figure 4.12 Pit AD5 containing cache of pebbles (copyright Kinloch excavation project)

pits dates to c.7500 cal BC. This is, however, the latest of the events in this area, some of which seem to have a long currency. This is likely to indicate that the first phase, rather than a single occupation, was similar in nature to the later phase; there may also be occupation earlier than that indicated by the radiocarbon date, though the presence of carbonised hazelnut shells in the earliest of the cut features makes the hazel rise a TPQ for the start of this sequence of features.

The second phase of occupation was located further to the west in the largest trench BA. Here another series of intercutting pits and hollows was located in the east and a series of more isolated pits in the west. This area has radiocarbon measurements spanning a millennium. These had the usual fill of flint, burnt flint and hazelnuts, but one contained a series of refitting burnt slabs, which seem to represent a deposited hearth setting. A similar deposit was found in a nearby pit. This confirms suggestions that these pits served as foci for the deposition of material cleared from hearths. In the broader area concentrations of burnt flint that might indicate hearths were not found (Wickham-Jones 1990, 161); instead, burnt flint was spread across much of this area. This might suggest that hearths were routinely dismantled and much of the material incorporated into pits.

The sequence of pits and hollows in the west of the trench was more difficult to determine. It consisted of four hollows, cut by a linear pit and a later field drain. These contained lithic debris, large stones and carbonised hazelnut shells. The two radiocarbon measurements from this are not consistent and indicate this complex is the product of more than one occupation. Four semi-circular arrangements of stake holes, which may represent windbreaks or the reinforced ends of tent structures were found in this area.

Bloodstone Hill on Rùm is the source of a crypto-crystalline silica forming in lavas of tertiary age, and known as Bloodstone (Box 4.2). This was used in good quantities at the site, and this resource, plus the affordances offered by the sheltered estuarine location, may be amongst the reasons why this site was so persistently occupied. Bloodstone and local beach flint were used in fairly equal quantities at the site. More cortical flakes and unmodified nodules are known from flint, which might suggest that while this material was imported to the site as complete nodules, bloodstone underwent initial preparation elsewhere, possibly at a procurement site closer to its source. Smaller quantities of agate, quartz, silicified limestone and volcanic glass were also used. These are present on adjacent islands, but the small quantities used might suggest they were collected as pebbles on local beaches.

An extremely large quantity of lithic material was recovered from the site coming both from the plough zone and from excavation. This numbers 138,043 pieces, a vast quantity considering the material from the ploughsoil was only sampled (10% was recorded). These figures reflect the repeated, intensive use of the site over a long period of time. The assemblage is dominated by microliths, with 1155 examples recovered, these consisting of fairly equal quantities of variably lateralised scalene triangles and backed bladelets, with smaller numbers of crescents. A small number of larger obliquely blunted points probably indicate an Early Mesolithic occupation, which may have been accompanied by some of the classic examples of *meches de foret* recovered. Other tools are present, but less frequent: Scrapers, awls, *pieces ecailles* and miscellaneous retouched pieces, though as this is repeatedly occupied site, their use may have been important on occasions. Coarse stone tools are relatively common, and their use appears varied. Bevelled-pebbles (see Box 4.1) and hammerstones were most common, but several anvils were also present.

Box 4.2 Bloodstone

Bloodstone is a crypto-crystalline silica, a jaspar, associated with lavas of tertiary age. The silicas were deposited within cavities within the lava flow through hydrothermal solutions. The stone ranges in colour, from red to both light and dark green and purple. Historically, the term 'Bloodstone' has been reserved for the fine-grained dark green nodules, shot through with red, that were used in jewellery. However, more recently the term has been extended to include a broader range of material from this source (Wickham-Jones 1990, 51)

Bloodstone is found at both Bloodstone and Fionchra Hills on the west of Rùm. It can most easily be recovered today as pebbles on local beaches, and archaeological samples show this was the usual way it was procured in the past. However, Ballin (2018, 244) has noticed a rough outer surface on bloodstone artefacts from Loch Doilean, Ardnamurchan, suggesting on occasions it may have been procured direct from a primary source.

Bloodstone was used extensively by both Mesolithic and later Prehistoric populations on Rùm (Wickham-Jones 1990, 150) and was a major component of the assemblage from Kinloch (Figure 4.13). It has been found on some of the large sites discussed elsewhere in this book, Camas Daraich, Sand and Sheildaig, and it seems to be present too amongst the Early Mesolithic assemblage at

Figure 4.13 Lithics from Kinloch, Rùm, which include a substantial portion of Bloodstone (copyright Kinloch excavation project)

An Corran (chapter 2) (Ballin 2018). It is also found in a range of Prehistoric assemblages up to 80 km from the island, and occasional finds are much more distant, from Lewis in the north (c.150 km from Rùm) to Oronsay in the south (112 km) (ibid, 248). There has been debate as to whether some of this distribution might reflect the presence of glacial erratics or beach pebbles in the broader landscape; however, surveys suggests that this material, though very occasionally present on some more distant beaches, is not common and usually absent (Wickham-Jones 1990, 154; Wickham-Jones et al. 2004). A human input is likely, which might represent direct procurement from the island, or is evidence for exchange of an aesthetically desirable or cosmological significant material. Ballin (2018) suggests that these patterns might be explained through gifts of small amounts of bloodstone from people visiting Rùm (or even controlling the source) to neighbouring groups, creating ties of alliance and obligation.

On these more distant sites, Bloodstone usually occurs as debitage, though in some instances cores or retouched items were most common. At Sand, Applecross, 60 km from Rùm, occasional cores of Bloodstone were recovered (Wickham-Jones et al. 2004) and the piece of bloodstone found at Barabhas on Lewis is also a core though not necessarily of Mesolithic date (Ballin 2018). Amongst the bloodstone debitage at Sand, cortical flakes were rare, indicating material was imported as prepared or part-worked cores and blanks (Hardy and Wickham-Jones 2009); the same pattern is present at Camas Daraich on the south coast of Skye, 25 km from the source (Wickham-Jones et al. 2004). The rarity of cortical flakes of bloodstone at these more distant sites might support the evidence from Kinloch that suggests that nodules underwent preparation at the source; however, it could also reflect the distance of these locations from Rùm, with core reduction occurring at as-yet-undiscovered sites between the two (Wickham-Jones 1990).

The Pennines

While Deepcar sites were both relatively common on the Pennines and relatively large, there is less obvious evidence for substantial settlement of the area in the Middle Mesolithic. This may be a simple issue of visibility, in that assemblages of this date are less typologically distinctive than those of Deepcar, and at the same time seem to lack the stone-built hearths and cooking pits that characterise the latest Mesolithic of the region and permit radiometric dates. Four Pennine sites have radiocarbon dates falling within the period 8250 to 7000 BC: Broomhead Moor V in South Yorkshire, Big Moor, Baslow, Derbyshire and Ickornshaw Moor and Warcock Hill III in West Yorkshire (Figure 4.14). Of these, the date from Warcock III is on a bulked sample taken from three adjacent firepits. All firepits are said to be associated with lithics of a distinctive grey chert (Switsur and Jacobi 1975); however, a bulked sample from an area where Early Mesolithic settlement is known should be treated with some caution.

Broomhead V, excavated by Jeff Radley, is one of ten sites on Broomhead Moor revealed by peat erosion and, in the case of site V, the excavation of a trench for shooting butts (Radley et al. 1974). A small trench 8 × 3 m was excavated, which

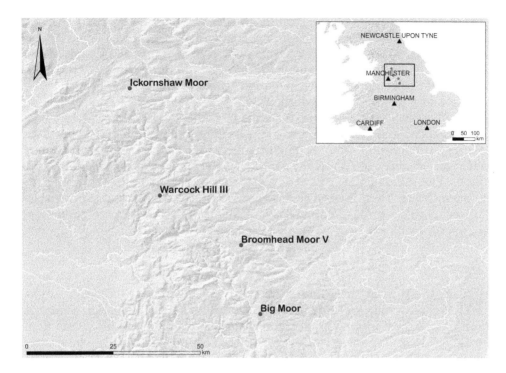

Figure 4.14 Pennine Middle Mesolithic sites

revealed several stakeholes argued to represent a small shelter that appears to have been burnt down at the end of its life, though this appearance of a layer of charcoal may be a product of subsequent peat erosion (Garton 2017). Three patches of charcoal and burnt flint represent either hearths or hearth debris; charcoal from these provided a radiocarbon date of 7960–7445 cal BC (Q-800) (Switsur and Jacobi 1975). The tools assemblage is dominated by microliths (37), with a small number of scrapers (4). The microliths are mainly scalene triangles with two sides retouched, which grade into isosceles triangles. A few crescents are present. The microliths are relatively large, with lengths between 31 and 11 mm, with an average of 17 mm (Radley et al. 1974, 3). If this radiocarbon measurement can be trusted, this appears to be the one site where a broadly left lateralised set of scalenes has a pre-7200 cal BC date.

The assemblage was made on black chert, a material that is present on Deepcar-type sites, but never common (see chapter 3). Icornshaw Moor and Warcock III, the other radiocarbon dated Pennine assemblages belonging to this period also appear to employ mainly chert, much more so than the scalene triangle assemblages of the first half of the fifth millennium BC, which will be discussed in the following chapter. This shift in raw material use parallels that seen in Southeastern Scotland, where chert use also became common in this period. The use of cherts and other poor-quality raw materials in the Late Mesolithic has been seen by Myers (1986) to reflect an increased focus on local raw material in the context of a shift from a combination of intercept and encounter hunting in the Early Mesolithic to encounter hunting only in the Late Mesolithic.

If variable lateralisation can be considered a Middle Mesolithic feature in this region, then the site at Piethorn Brook can be included in this list. This site, at 300 m asl, lies in a sheltered valley close to the current course of a small stream, and the occupation area was focused on a natural hollow. Here, an arc of stakeholes, measuring around 3.5 m in diameter, was recorded (Poole 1986), a rare example of structural evidence in the Pennines. Lithic material was scattered over 45 m^2, but there were few artefacts within the arc of the stakeholes. Instead, knapping debris surrounded a hearth on the open edge of the arc. A second hearth was found a few metres to the south. The lithic assemblage is most indicative of a hunting camp; it is microlith dominated (89 scalenes), with 11 microburins, and refitting microliths indicating production and repair of composite tools. Only four utilised flakes indicate other activities. Flat stones that may have served as anvils, seats, or tables were associated with the structure. These are known from other Pennine sites: Buckley, for example, reports an anvil stone found on the north of March Hill, showing pitting from use, and associated with a scatter of lithic debitage (Spikins 2002).

North Wales

Early dates for narrow geometric microliths are also present in North Wales from the sites of Prestatyn and Snail Cave rockshelter. At Prestatyn, Mesolithic activity is known from a small area discovered during the building of a housing estate, Bryn Newydd, in the 1920s. The architect Gilbert Smith was a keen antiquarian who recovered various Prehistoric remains. The Mesolithic material was recovered during the excavations for the foundation of manhole access for a sewer. The area of the housing estate consisted of a basin filled with tufa deposits, produced by a nearby stream, fed from a spring on the edge of the limestone. Within the basin were three areas of higher ground, plateaus of sand and clay that may have had a fluvial origin. Mesolithic settlement took place on the smallest of these plateaus and was subsequently covered by tufa. The site seems small: 'half a dozen square yards' (Smith 1926) and the presence of refits indicate it is likely to represent a short, single episode occupation. It cannot be determined whether tufa was forming in the lower lying areas during the time when people camped on the hillock. Clark (1939, 201) reports that the hazelnut shells from the occupation were spread into the surrounding tufa, but this could be the result of later erosion by flooding.

At the time of occupation, Bryn Newydd was not a coastal site. Bell (2007, 309) suggests the sea may have been as far as 14 km to the north. However, around 5 km north of the current coast is a deep channel that may represent a palaeochannel of the river Dee, which would mean that riverine and possibly estuarine resources were within reach for the inhabitants of the site.

The Mesolithic scatter was found in a thin, dark palaeosol, sealed by over half a metre of tufa (David 2007). Smith recovered an assemblage dominated by microliths. It consists of 27 variably lateralised scalene triangles, 12 slender obliquely blunted points, two backed bladelets and two basally truncated, obliquely blunted points. Microburins indicate microlith manufacture and retooling; 18 scrapers and steeply retouched pieces suggest processing activities (Jacobi archive, British Museum). Apart from one microlith in opaque grey flint, the assemblage was made on local chert, which outcrops 2.5 km from the site (Bell 2007), mostly fine black and banded tabular blocks, but some shiny grey. Debitage in some material is present without a core, and a blade of blue flint has no associated debitage, indicating movement of raw material (Jacobi archive). In addition to lithic artefacts, a perforated oyster shell was recovered, along with a bone awl and a red deer antler tine. Burnt hazelnuts and burnt bone fragments were recovered, indicating food preparation. Two of the burnt hazelnut shells were dated to 8200–7590 cal BC (8730 ± 90 BP; OxA-2269) and 8200–7575 cal BC (8700 ± 100 BP; OxA-2268) (David 2007).

The second site of this date in North Wales is on the Great Orme at Snail Cave. This is a rockshelter on the eastern side of the Orme around 25 m long and 2 m deep. The floor is fairly flat but falls away beyond the rock shelter in a steep slope of periglacial scree. A small trench 3 × 1 m was excavated in 2011. The deposits had been disturbed by animal burrowing, and a cowrie shell bead was recovered from the surface of the shelter. The deposits contained animal bones, shells and 146 pieces of flint, mostly in the lower levels. Tools consist of microliths, an awl and retouched blades made from both pebble flint and local cherts. Most of the lithic pieces that are diagnostic are Mesolithic, with only a single awl belonging to the Late Neolithic/Early Bronze Age. There is certainly, however, a component of later Prehistoric material present, represented by pottery, domesticates and 4th century radiocarbon dates. This makes it difficult to understand which occupation much of the faunal and shell material belongs with. The only clue comes from the radiocarbon measurements, which give Neolithic dates for the shells and a roe deer mandible, but Mesolithic dates for three charred hazelnuts and a teal/garganey bone. These four dates are all remarkably consistent, spanning 8220–7725 cal BC (Smith and Walker 2014).

An undated site that may belong with this group is Hendre, Rhuddlan, where microliths include variably lateralised scalenes. Hendre is on the river Clywd. If this site does belong to the eighth millennium, the sea would have been some distance at the time. At Hendre, an assemblage numbering just over 1000 pieces on flint and chert was found in two large excavation trenches around 50 m apart. Material was densest in trench 2, though tool densities were highest in trench 4. A pit was located in trench 2, and charred hazelnuts were found throughout the sediments, though as these are accompanied by evidence of cultivated crops, these are not necessarily Mesolithic in date. The assemblage is dominated by microliths (26). Scrapers (7) were also present, as were microdenticulates (5), piercers (4) and miscellaneous retouched pieces.

Defining a Middle Mesolithic in Southern Britain: Basally modified point assemblages

The old typological distinction between Early Mesolithic (with 'simple' or 'broad' microliths) and Late Mesolithic (with 'geometric' or 'narrow' microliths) has always worked less well in certain parts of the country, where assemblages with basally modified microliths appear to fill a broadly intermediate period between early and late (Jacobi 1984; Reynier 2005). Basally modified microliths, the appearance of which seems to relate to improvements in hafting technologies (Reynier 1997), are found from Southern England to Scotland. In some of these areas, such microliths are very rare; in others, they are more common and found in association with a restricted range of other microlith types. In these latter cases, assemblage types have been defined (Reynier 2005). Foremost amongst these are Horsham assemblages, characterised by asymmetric hollow-based points, associated with obliquely blunted points and iso-sceles triangles (Clark 1934; Jacobi 1978b), and Honey Hill assemblages, defined by symmetrical inversely flaked microliths, with rounded or pointed bases, obliquely and straight-backed pieces and lanceolates (Jacobi 1984; Saville 1981a) (see Figure 1.4). The heartlands of these assemblage types are Southeastern England and the Midlands/ East Anglia, respectively; however, their type fossils occur more widely. Horsham points span Devon to the Humber, while Honey Hill types are found from Sussex in the south, to Denbighshire in the west and Edinburgh in the north.

Basally modified points are widespread across Northwest Europe, where they take a variety of forms, such as the *pointes de Tardenois*, a symmetrical point with straight basal truncation, a type also found in Britain (see Figure 1.6, 10b). Horsham points are occasionally present in France, for example, at Saleux in Picardy. Honey Hill points have been compared with *feuilles de gui* (mistletoe points) of Northern France and Belgium dated to between c.7200 and 6600 cal BC (Ghesquière 2012); however, Honey Hill point seem rather earlier, appearing around 8000 cal BC. Basally modified points are very good chronological indicators, being very distinctive and, unlike many microlith forms, having a restricted temporal span. Often in Europe, they are used to define the local 'Middle Mesolithic' stage. More detailed investigation of particular combinations of microlith types have also yielded useful results for constructing typo-chronologies: Assemblages with Tardenoisian points, obliquely blunted points and curve-backed pieces, collectively known as the Northern Beurronian A, span 8300–7700 cal BC (Ducrocq 2013).

Basally modified points have the potential to be similarly important chronological indicators in Britain, but a paucity of radiocarbon dates means our understanding of their span is currently imperfect. Secure dates for Horsham industries are available for only two sites, suggesting a span from 8200 to 6800 cal BC. This span is also compatible with less securely associated dates from North Park Farm, Bletchingly, where Horsham and Late Mesolithic microliths are both present. A single well-dated Honey Hill site exists, at Asfordby, Leicestershire (Cooper and Jarvis 2017), which was occupied between 8200 and 7500 BC. This is broadly contemporary with the earliest dates for Horsham sites. A second probable date for this assemblage type comes from Spong Hill, where several Honey Hill microliths were recovered from a tree throw containing charcoal dated to 7515–7125 cal BC (8280 ± 80 BP; HAR-7063) (Bayliss et al. 2012, 212). Honey Hill-type activity may also be dated by two measurements on charred hazelnuts from the lowest levels of Stratford's Yard, Chesham, of 7780–7600 cal BC (8700 ± 26 BP; OxA-38836) and 7675–7575 cal BC (8603 ± 27 BP; OxA-38837). This is a site of mixed date (see chapter 6), but the oldest lithic material seems to consist of curve and partially backed points, lanceolates and inversely retouched microliths with a pointed base, though no classic Honey Hill points were recovered. The measurements for Spong Hill just predate the latest dates for Horsham industries and is likely to suggest that rather than having a chronological relationship as previously suggested (Reynier 2005), these are regional manifestations of the same phenomenon: Technological innovations in hafting practises (Cooper and Jarvis 2017; Reynier 1997).

The midlands and Honey Hill points

Settlement of the midlands, particularly the clay lands of the east midlands, may have taken place slightly later than the rest of Britain (Cooper and Jarvis 2017). It is only

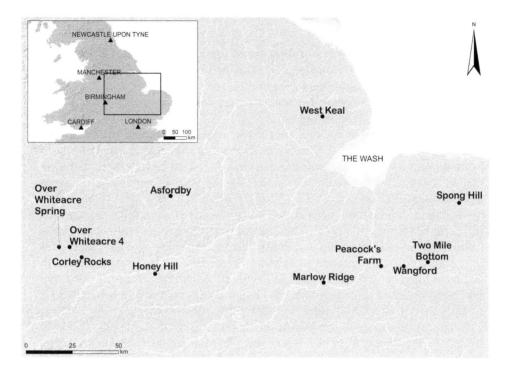

Figure 4.15 Distribution of Honey Hill sites discussed

with the appearance of Middle Mesolithic, or Honey Hill assemblages, that there is good evidence for a widespread Mesolithic presence. Classic Honey Hill sites – those with a combination of microliths with invasive inverse retouch, obliquely blunted points, curve and straight-backed pieces and lanceolates – are found from the coast of East Anglia to the West Midlands and as far north as the Humber (Figure 4.15). Isolated examples of Honey Hill points are known as far north as Cramond in Edinburgh (Saville 2008), and west as Cwm Bach I in Pembrokeshire (David 2007), while to the south they are found in some Horsham assemblages, for example, at Beedings Wood (Jacobi 1978b).

Little evidence exists for the animal and plant resources used at Honey Hill sites. Faunal remains were only preserved when burnt at Asfordby (see Box 4.3), but pig and deer could be recognised. Eighth millennium dates on a bovid tooth and a large mammal rib with embedded flint fragment from Mother Grundy's Parlour indicate hunting of aurochs. The Mesolithic assemblage from Mother Grundy's Parlour includes two Honey Hill points (Jacobi archive, British Museum), but their relationship to the fauna is unclear. In addition to the dates on faunal remains, three samples of charred hazelnuts from the site indicate at least two visits in the late ninth and first half of the eighth millennium BC, contemporary with known Honey Hill dates. Red deer, pig and brown bear are present in the same squares as the dated aurochs and hazelnuts, though their age and association with human activity is uncertain, as all come from the talus slope of the cave, a mixed deposit that includes Upper Palaeolithic lithics and a Pleistocene fauna of horse and reindeer.

Box 4.3   Asfordby

A rare example of an excavated Mesolithic site in this region, Asfordby was located in advance of development and excavated by ULAS (Cooper and Jarvis 2017). The site is on the southern spur of a hill, overlooking the river Wreake. A spring is nearby. The Mesolithic remains were found in a sandy-loam buried soil, overlying silty/clay head deposits.

The lithic material is focused round two hearths, indicated by scatters of burnt flint and burnt bone: The larger eastern hearth, which may have been located within a tent structure, and a smaller western hearth. Several radio-carbon dates have been obtained, indicating the start of occupation between 8220–7840 cal BC and ending at 7960–7530 cal BC (95% probability). The modelling of radiocarbon dates at Asfordby gives us an important glimpse into the periodicity of 'persistence'. This suggests at least five separate occupations (more may be hidden within a radiocarbon plateau). The eastern hearth was in use first, probably between 8100 and 7730 cal BC, while the western hearth probably dates to 7760 to 7540 cal BC. Despite an overlap in distribution, the modelling indicates there was likely to have been a temporal gap between these two occupations, and both were probably fairly short-lived.

A large assemblage was recovered, made on local till flint, possibly collected from tree throws or from the River Wreake (Cooper and Jarvis 2017, 56). Microliths are the most common tool type, and microburins are also present in good numbers, suggesting retooling was a major task. Though many of the microliths display wear or breakage consistent with use as tips and barbs of arrows, they were also used for other activities, for butchery, working plant material or bone/wood. Other formal tools, such as scrapers and burins, as well as utilised pieces confirm a broad range of activities, were undertaken. The scrapers showed use on both fresh and dry hide. Evans (2017, 73) notes that the presence of dry hide has been argued to be indicative of a residential site, but considers microliths with impact evidence to indicate strong evidence for a focus on hunting and carcass processing. Little evidence remains for the prey, as bones only survived when burnt and heavily fragmented. Only three can be identified, one as pig and two as deer.

The differing evidence for the site being either residential or related to hunting may be a factor of its repeated occupation. Cooper and Jarvis argue for a more substantial initial occupation, focused around the eastern hearth within a tent structure where composite tools were repaired, food prepared and craft activities undertake. This may have been a 'fixed facility site' (Reynier 2005), where long-term investment in fixed resources led to repeated visits.

Both Saville (1981a) and Cooper and Jarvis (2017) have noted a preference for Honey Hill sites to be located on free-draining geology and on hill tops, plateaux edges and slopes, often with views over the surrounding countryside. Water can usually be found close to these sites, with springs common, and many in close proximity to small tributaries of the major rivers of the region. West Keel, Lincolnshire, is a typical example: Located on Greensand, on a projection of the Lincolnshire Wolds, with extensive views over the low-lying fenland to the south, and also to the west and north. Numerous springs still rise along the edge of this hill (Clark 1932). Similarly, Honey Hill itself is on a sandy hill at 210 m asl, next to a spring (Saville 1981b). Caves and rock shelters are also known to have been visited: In addition to Mother Grundy's Parlour, Honey Hill points are present in the lower layers of Thorpe Common Rock Shelter in Staffordshire, and a Horsham Point was recovered from Wetton Mill Minor in the Southern Peak District. Jacobi (1976) suggests that Wetton Mill Minor and other microlith-dominated caves and rockshelters southwest of the Peaks may have served as short-term transit camps.

Biases obviously exist: Caves and open sites on higher ground, now ploughed fields, are likely to be more visible to collectors than lower-lying sites, potentially deeply buried by colluvium or alluvium; however, low-lying sites do exist, particularly in Cambridgeshire, where the favoured landscape location was in close proximity to rivers (Billington 2017). Marlow Ridge, Over (Evans et al. 2016) and Two Mile Bottom (Jacobi 1984), near Thetford, are located on the banks of the Great Ouse, Cambridgeshire and Little Ouse, Norfolk, respectively. Both sites incorporate material of mixed date, making it difficult to understand whether there were any functional differences in lowland tool assemblages in comparison to those recovered from upland sites. Better evidence is available from Wangford, where Dixon Hewitt, amongst others, collected and Jacobi undertook small-scale excavations in 1972. The assemblage from Jacobi's excavations shows scrapers slightly outnumbering microliths, and scrapers are also common amongst the earlier collections from the site (Jacobi 1984). This might suggest lowland assemblages were more balanced between major tool types, with people at these sites focused on a range of processing activities. However, microliths are common at the lowland site of Peacock's Farm (see Box 4.4), while the evidence from Asfordby (see Box 4.3) indicates a range of activities were taking place even at small upland sites dominated by microliths. Both these sites were revisited over a long period.

Box 4.4   Peacock's Farm, Shippea Hill and the Mesolithic of Fenland

The pioneering work of Harry Godwin, Grahame Clark and other member of the Fenland Research Committee in the 1930s did much to elucidate the complex history of the fens and underline the difficulties of understanding the Mesolithic of this area. The Committee excavated deep sondages, which have not been subsequently repeated, recovering Mesolithic and Neolithic material from great depth at Plantation Farm and Peacock's Farm. At Peacock's Farm, where more substantial traces of Mesolithic occupation were found, excavations extended from the top of long sandy hillock, rising to a height of -1 m asl, down into the fen. Here, a potentially Mesolithic core was recovered at 4.5 m depths in a 'black band' within peat, which may represent desiccation resulting from a lowering of the water table. At the top of this lower peat was Early Neolithic pottery; above this was over 2 m of fen clay, evidence of a Bronze Age marine transgression that submerged the fens (Figure 4.16).

Figure 4.16 The deep stratigraphy of Fenland at Shippea Hill: The Mesolithic levels are to be found by the knees of Grahame Clark, towards the base of the trench (labelled Tardenoisian). (Reproduced by permission of University of Cambridge Museum of Archaeology & Anthropology (LS.14103.GCLK))

More substantial evidence for Mesolithic occupation was found on the sandy hillock, where microliths of both Honey Hill and Late Mesolithic type were recovered along with the remnants of a Neolithic occupation. The hillock was located close to a roddon, representing a relict channel of the Little Ouse. Radiocarbon dates for the black band were obtained through fresh excavations in 1960 (Clark and Godwin 1962) and in 1984 (Smith et al. 1989). It was suggested these dates indicated the timing of the occupation of the sand ridge, given the high sand content in the black band, considered to represent erosion of the sand ridge through trampling. It is now clear, given better knowledge of microlithic technology, that the assemblage on the higher ground is the product of more than one occupation. Furthermore, Bayesian modelling of the sequence of dates for the black band suggests it formed over a period of at least 1200 years, between 7520–7060 BC and 5880–5320 BC (Healy et al. 2011, 264).

A radiocarbon measurement from near the base of the peat indicates peat development is likely to have started in the late ninth millennium, most probably before the Honey Hill occupation. This suggests occupation of the hillock started when it began to offer a dry camping spot as the valley bottom became increasingly boggy. Far away, sea-levels were rising, rivers became backed up and the water table rose. The pollen from the lower part of the peat shows these changes happened in a heavily wooded landscape of hazel, with pine and oak also common and a little elm and birch, while a sluggish channel or pond, gradually infilling with wood-peats, lay immediately to the south of the site (Smith et al. 1989). There is evidence for some change in the woodland makeup, possibly initiated at the time of the Honey Hill occupation when a small opening in the forest was made. Subsequent more radical transformations, which saw a dramatic reduction in first hazel, then pine, are likely to be related to subsequent Late Mesolithic occupation of the area.

Excavation by Whittle and colleagues in 1984 (Smith et al. 1989) revealed more about the occupation of the hillock. Several hollows, many of which are likely to be tree throws, yielded flint, burnt flint and sandstone and charcoal. Also present were burnt seeds of fat hen (Chenopodium album), Black Nightshade (Solanum nigrum) and dock/sorrel (Rumex sp.). These features returned radiocarbon dates that clustered in the late eighth and early seventh millennium BC. While the earlier of these may be compatible with Honey Hill occupation, as measurements on bulked charcoal, taken from a repeatedly reoccupied site, the likelihood these represent aggregated activities from a mixture of Middle and Late Mesolithic occupation is high. However, the discovery of Mesolithic activity on the sandy ridge, 60 m from where Clark and Godwin excavated, emphasises that this was a favoured place, revisited over a very long period. Jacobi (1984, 62) suggests it may have been a fishing camp, where people stopped for a while in the summer months.

Though most Honey Hill sites are known through surface collection, several seem large, with hundreds of microliths recovered (Saville 1981a). Collections of material from Two Mile Bottom were made over an area of 100 m by 30 m. Many major sites also seem to be located at ecotonal boundaries (Cooper and Jarvis 2017), where a range of different vegetation types and their resources might be exploited. Similar landscape preferences have long been noted for Horsham sites and are discussed below. Little structural evidence is present on Honey Hill sites. At Asfordby, concentrations of burnt flint indicate hearths, but these lack associated stones or pits. There are perhaps hints of the deposition of lithic material: At Spong Hill, lithic material was found in a tree throw, while at South Acre, a concentration of lithic material, including several microliths and a high proportion of blades (50%), was recovered from a pit (Wymer 1996). While residuality is certainly a possibility, the structure of the lithic collection from South Acre suggests deliberate selection.

Cooper and Jarvis (2017) have suggested that Reynier's settlement model for Horsham sites may also apply to those of Honey Hill. Reynier had suggested that as hunting became more difficult in deciduous forests, people became invested in fixed resources, such as traps and areas of hazel trees. Settlement would encompass residential sites, fixed resources and specialist extraction camps, with greater territoriality emerging as a consequence of tethering to particular resources, leading to long-term commitments to an area. The flint used by Honey Hill groups was predominantly local, usually glacial till or gravel flint, possibly also indicating ties to local areas.

Southern England: Defining Horsham assemblages

In 1934, Clark noted the distinctive nature of Mesolithic assemblages found in the area surrounding the town of Horsham, West Sussex, based on his analysis of nearly 4000 microliths amassed from five sites by local collectors, Thomas Honywood in the 1870s and C.J Attree and E.J.G Piffard in the early decades of the 20th century. While recognising the overall dominance of simple obliquely blunted points in these assemblages, Clark drew attention to the presence of a series of distinctive basally modified microliths (Clark 1934, 64). Prominent amongst these were asymmetric, hollow-based points, now known as Horsham Points (Figure 1.4). These hollow bases could be produced through retouch on either the dorsal or the ventral side of the piece. Also present in these assemblages were symmetric basally modified points (Tardenois Points), and pieces with rounded or pointed bases and flat, inverse retouch (now known as Honey Hill Points, see above). Clark's survey of the British Mesolithic suggested that these asymmetric hollow-based forms were restricted to parts of Sussex, Surrey and Kent, and he compared them to similar points from Belgium.

Further work was undertaken on these assemblages by Roger Jacobi in the 1970s and 1980s. Jacobi reanalysed these large collections, excavated new sites, and undertook cluster analysis on his data. Sites with large numbers of Horsham points clustered as a group, distinguished by a range of basally modified pieces, obliquely blunted points, isosceles triangles and rhomboids (Jacobi 1978b). Jacobi noted that while isolated Horsham points can be found on Mesolithic sites across England, it is only assemblages with the combination of short obliquely blunted points, Horsham points and isosceles triangles that should be categorised as Horsham sites (O'Malley and Jacobi 1978). Jacobi also suggested that some of the variation noted by Clark might have a temporal component, with Old Faygate and St Catherine's Hill (characterised by large numbers of obliquely blunted points and a smaller number of Horsham points) possibly earliest, dating by comparison with continental assemblages to around 9000 radiocarbon years ago. At Beeding Wood, Halt and Colgate microliths with flat and pointed retouched bases were also common, suggesting they might be later. He also recognised that some of these assemblages were of mixed date, Beedings Wood, for example, containing also Deepcar material (Jacobi 1982b). Jacobi also excavated, in collaboration with Hazel Martingell, two Horsham sites: Longmoor Inclosure I and Kettlebury 103 (see below).

Michael Reynier (2005) provided a detailed study of technological features of three assemblages with Horsham points, as well as looking more broadly at the environmental setting of Horsham sites. By investigating three sites (Longmoor I, Kettlebury 103 and St Catherine's Hill) with no trace of earlier or later activity, he was able to refine knowledge of these assemblages (see Box 1.3). Within the common tool assemblages of these sites, scrapers are well-represented, with smaller numbers of truncations, notches and a tool type that is perhaps unique to Horsham assemblages:

The chamfered piece. This type consists of a flake whose distal end has been removed by a transverse blow from the ventral surface. Other tools: Burins, core tools and microdenticulates are present, but rare. Reynier (2005) also notes a greater presence of orthogonal cores and platforms lacking preparation in comparison to other Early Mesolithic assemblage types.

Horsham sites have been difficult to date, as relatively few excavations have been undertaken, and settlements were preferentially located on sandy sediments, which are often disturbed and lack faunal preservation. Measurements have been obtained on burnt hazelnuts from two sites – Longmoor I and Kettlebury 103 – which show few signs of later activity (Table 4.3). These suggest a long duration for Horsham industries, with dates spanning a millennium. This duration is reinforced by dates from recently excavated sites from Bexhill that contain basally modified points (Champness et al. 2019). There are additional dates for some other sites that have Horsham-type microliths, but the associations are less secure. At North Park Farm, Bletchingly, Surrey, a hearth in area 6 has slightly inconsistent, but temporally close, measurements, suggesting occupation in the second half of the eighth millennium BC. Around this hearth were found inversely retouched points, curve-backed pieces and isosceles triangles. However, backed bladelets are also present in some number, and the broader picture of this site is of a major palimpsest, on sandy, disturbed sediments. It has proved difficult to date (Jones 2013). A single Horsham point was probably recovered from the same level as the dated material at Broxbourne 106, but the association is not close (Jacobi archive). At Westhampnett, West Sussex (Fitzpatrick et al. 2008), the assemblage from area 4 appears to be a Horsham one, characterised by an atypical tanged Horsham point (common at St Catherine's Hill), obliquely blunted points, a convex-backed point and a rhomboid. Two rather different dates come from an L-shaped feature, though both would be compatible with other Horsham dates. No microliths were recovered from this feature, and no connection can be made between this feature and the Horsham assemblage.

Table 4.3 Secure dates from Horsham sites (top) and dates from sites with Horsham microliths where the association between material dated and Horsham settlement are less certain (below)

Secure dates Site	Lab no.	C14 years	Calibrated date (95.4% confidence)
Kettlebury 103	OxA-378	8270 ± 120	7555–7050 cal BC
Kettlebury 103	OxA-379	7990 ± 120	7195–6600 cal BC
Kettlebury 103	OxA-6395	7990 ± 90	7140–6665 cal BC
Kettlebury 103	OxA-3696	7890 ± 80	7040–6600 cal BC
Longmoor I	OxA-376	8930 ± 100	8295–7750 cal BC
Longmoor I	OxA-377	8760 ± 110	8210–7515 cal BC
Possible dates			
Broxbourne 106	Q-1583	8780 ± 150	8255–7785 cal BC
North Park Farm	SUERC-13955	8275 ± 40	7480–7170 cal BC
North Park Farm	OxA-16905	8275 ± 40	7480–7170 cal BC
North Park Farm	OxA-17596	8170 ± 45	7330–7050 cal BC
Westhampnett	OxA-4170	8880 ± 100	8280–7715 cal BC
Westhampnett	OxA-4171	8300 ± 90	7530–7125 cal BC

Settlment in Southeastern England

The sites that Jacobi termed 'Horsham' or 'Wealden' sites – characterised by a combi-nation of obliquely blunted points, isosceles triangles and Horsham points – are mainly found in Southeast England (Figure 4.17). While these are more common on the sand-stone geologies of the Lower Greensand and High Weald (see Box 4.5), they are also found across a range of geographical zones. Orchard Hill, for example, is on vestigal Thanet Sands, overlying upper chalk at the foot of the dip-slope of the North Downs. The site overlooks Charshalton Ponds and the spring line that gives rise to the river Wryse that flows into the Wandle, a Thames tributary (English et al. 2018). This site seems to have been attractive throughout the Mesolithic for its water, views, routeway and local flint source. Several Horsham sites are also known from the banks of the Thames and its tributaries, such as Ham Fields, located on a gravel bar by the Thames (Lacaille 1966), and various sites at Addington St Lambeth, located on an eyot (Powell and Leivers 2013). The assemblage from Addington St (ADD95) is relatively small, consisting mainly of microliths and a handful of other tools. Microburins are rare in contrast to sites on the Weald. This site seems to represent a short-term stop-over, with tools discarded and some knapping using local gravel material taking place for immediate needs. Horsham sites tend to be situated close to a source of raw material (Reynier 2005), and this appears true also of sites beyond the classic Wealden locations. A similar small Mesolithic scatter, including Horsham material at Addington St (WSC90) and possibly also at 29 Addington St (WSB90) (Sidell et al. 2002), suggests this riverine location may have been re-peatedly used for short-term visits by groups using Horsham points.

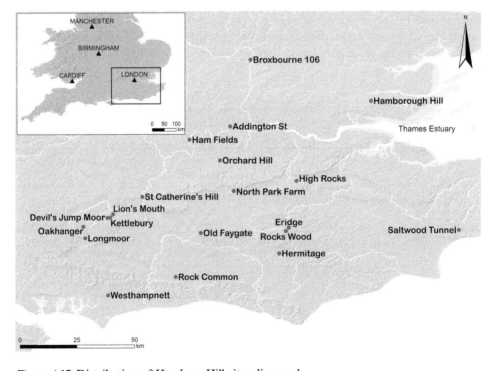

Figure 4.17 Distribution of Horsham Hill sites discussed

Box 4.5   The Mesolithic and the Lower Greensand

The Weald is the land between the two parallel chalk strips of the North and South Downs. It encompasses part of Kent, all of Sussex, Southern Surrey and the easternmost part of Hampshire, running from Petersfield in the west, to Folkstone in the east. On the northern and southern edge of the Weald is the Greensand Ridge, in places rolling downland, elsewhere forming conspicuous scarps, rising up to a height of 220 m asl. In the centre of the Weald is the sandstone High Weald, characterised, like the Greensand, by sandy, well-drained soils. In the west of this area, rockshelters formed in outcrops of Tonbridge Wells Sandstone. Between the Greensand and the High Weald lie areas of Wealden clay. These different geologies, giving rise to different environmental and topographical affordances, have been argued to have had a major effect on human settlement of the region.

The Lower Greensand holds a special place in Mesolithic studies. In 1932, Grahame Clark, in the publication that defined the Mesolithic period in Britain, noted the frequent representation of Mesolithic sites on the Greensand and other sandy sediments of Southeast England in comparison with clays and the chalk. Clark (1932, 88) suggested that well-drained sandy soils would be most favourable for living sites, while the relatively light woodland vegetation on these soils facilitated hunting and the presence of springs and water-courses added to their attractions. Nearly 50 years later, Mellars and Reinhardt (1978) revisited the issue. Since Clark's work there had been an increase in Mesolithic findspots on other types of geology. Clark, for example, recorded only a single site on the Wealden Clay; yet, in Mellars' and Reinhardt's analysis, Mesolithic sites were slightly better represented here than the regional average. However, findspots on the Lower Greensand (particularly the Folkstone Beds) were still dominant. The explanation, they suggested, lay in the types of vegetation that grew on each soil type. Dry oak forests on well-drained soils were relatively free of understorey vegetation, while damp oak forests were characterised by dense growth of shrubs, particularly hazel. These latter, they argued, hindered mobility and enabled animals to conceal themselves, decreasing hunting success.

Yet, it is clear that while primarily located on the Greensand, the sites plotted by Mellars and Reinhardt are preferentially located on the boundary between different underlying geologies. As Jacobi (1978a,b) notes, while settlement may be on the Greensand, the areas surrounding these sites that people would have moved through during hunting and gathering activities were actually varied: The well-drained, more open woodlands, the damp oak forests of the clay, where hazelnuts were aplenty, and – forming the boundary of the area – the chalk, which may still have been fairly open, and an important source of flint. These areas would encompass both upland areas with views and more sheltered river valleys; areas of springs and water-courses; and drier landscapes.

The effect of landscape history and collection needs also to be taken into consideration (Evans 1975, 103). The acidic podzolized soils of the Greensand form heathlands, often used as commons, which are relatively accessible and where a high level of activity by rabbits, or erosion by footpaths or vehicles, makes Mesolithic material easy to locate. Areas with high concentration of Mesolithic sites, such as Oakhanger (Slab Common), Longmoor, Kettlebury (Hankley Common), are all open, relatively accessible and crossed by footpaths. Billington's (2017) study of the effect of land-use history on the visibility of Mesolithic scatters has made it clear how important this factor is. Billington's work in East Anglia considered the Bedfordshire Greensand, an area with a very different landscape history to the Weald, where the tying up of this land in large estates meant that little early work took place. However, more recent fieldwork suggests that the Bedfordshire Greensand did indeed see a concentration of Mesolithic occupation in comparison to other areas.

In the southeast, current HER data does suggest continued high representation of sites along the lower Greensand Ridge, but there is also stronger clustering of sites along river valleys than was previously obvious. Important sites are also present on the clay, Ellaby's Final Mesolithic pit site of Charlwood (Ellaby 2004), for example (see chapter 6). More finds have also been found on the Weald Clay in the Horsham area (Ellaby 1987, 58). A detailed analysis of the HER data from Surrey by Simmonds (2016) shows sites are three times more common on the Lower Greensand than expected from a purely random distribution. This over-representation also encompasses sites close to this geology, with double the number of sites within a kilometre of the Lower Greensand than expected. There was also a greater number of sites on the Thanet Sands, Lambeth Group and clay-with-flints than expected, while the Wealden Group, London Clay, Bracklesham Group, peat and alluvium all had fewer finds than expected, the last two undoubtedly due to issues of visibility. An older survey by Gardiner (1984, 17) breaks down sites by typology to a greater extent and indicates that while later Mesolithic sites are found in a variety of areas, Early Mesolithic sites do show a preference for the lower Greensand. More systematic sampling is needed, but it does currently seem that a high density of Mesolithic sites can been seen in certain regions of the Greensand ridge in particular.

Few Mesolithic sites on the Greensand have radiocarbon dates, the product of collection histories and the types of sediments represented. However, examination of microlith forms of a sample of 78 Mesolithic sites on the Greensand and the sandy sediments of the High Weald show some temporal patterns. Deepcar-type Mesolithic sites are present in small numbers (ten). Many of these appear to be potentially Late Deepcar sites, as at Oakhanger V/VII (Rankine and Rankine 1960, see chapter 3), with increased numbers of curve-backed blades, and rhomboids. Horsham sites are most common with 39 examples, while Late Mesolithic sites number 29. There are also patterns within this distribution, with Deepcar sites found only on the Greensand, while both Horsham and Late Mesolithic sites are found both on the Greensand and the High Weald. Given the much longer time span of the Late Mesolithic, the preferential location of Horsham sites on the Greensand seems clear.

Recent fieldwork has also filled in some gaps in areas of the Greensand that previously had not recorded evidence for Mesolithic occupation. Three large scatters of Mesolithic material have been located near Petworth, in the Rother

Valley, West Sussex, during fieldwalking that has covered 69 ha (David and Kowalski 2019). The Mesolithic elements of these scatters were composed almost exclusively of Middle Mesolithic material. One scatter had a Late Mesolithic component, but there was no definite Early Mesolithic presence. This random sample of an area of Greensand is perhaps more broadly indicative of the temporal patterns of its use.

The nature of Horsham sites on the Greensand varies, but in general they seem to represent reasonably substantial, seasonal residential sites. They seem to be characterised by multiple hearths, charcoal spreads, pits and possibly episodes of middening, indicating longer-term use.

Horsham sites, as opposed to isolated examples of Horsham points, do not seem to be present (or at least common) north of the Thames. Horsham material has been found at West Heath, Hampstead (see chapter 3), on high ground overlooking London, though seemingly only as a small element amongst a mixed, but mainly Early Mesolithic assemblage. Other possible Horsham sites north of the Thames include Hamborough Hill on the river Crouch in Essex (Reader 1911) or a very small cluster of material from Broxbourne 106 on the river Lea (Jacobi archive), where a scatter of wild boar remains associated with a radiocarbon date of 8255–7785 (8780 ±150 BP; Q-1583) (Jacobi et al. 1978) may possibly be associated with a hollow-based microlith. All seem small-scale. Instead, north of the Thames Honey Hill assemblages are more common.

To the south of the Weald, at Bexhill, a rapid marine transgression changed what had been a landscape of streams and woodland dramatically, as the Coombe Valley developed into a tidal inlet with saltmarsh extending across the valley floors (Champness et al. 2019). Horsham sites are relatively few in number compared with both Early and Late/Final Mesolithic activity. Those that are present show a wide variety of activities were carried out (Champness et al. 2019). Three of the four Horsham sites were located on a vantage point at the meeting of two valley systems, while estuarine resources were close. This location thus may fall into a broader Horsham pattern of site location close to different ecotonal zones (Jacobi 1978a,b).

There appear to be some contrasts between sites in different environmental zones. The Thames sites seem relatively small, short-term stops where the emphasis is on production for immediate use. Further small sites are found in the rock shelters of the High Weald. Sites such as Hermitage (Jacobi and Tebbutt 1981), High Rocks (Money 1960), Rocks Wood (Harding and Ostoja-Zagórski 1987) and Eridge (Greatorex and Seager Thomas 2000), though characterised by assemblages of mixed date, contain distinctive Horsham points or similar forms, and have been suggested to represent short-term hunting camps. Larger sites are found on the Lower Greensand ridge, often close to springs or streams. Those that are excavated, or at least comprehensively collected, show a dominance of microliths and, particularly microburins, suggesting gearing up for activities using composite tools, probably hunting. Refits between microliths and microburins are relatively common; this is unusual on Mesolithic sites. Microliths were mobile tools that were rarely discarded. Refits suggest a site of some duration where composite tools were made, used in the wider landscape and then brought back for repair. At some sites (e.g. Kettlebury II), tools other than microliths were rare. Usually, however, moderate quantities of non-microlithic tools were used in varying proportion: Scrapers are common at Kettlebury I (Rankine 1949b) and Longmoor I, for example; awls and scrapers at St Catherine's Hill (Gabel 1976); truncations at Rock Common (Harding 2000); scrapers, notches and truncations at Hesworth (David and Kowalski 2019) and scrapers and chamfered pieces at Kettlebury 103. All these sites have moderate quantities of retouched and utilised blades as well as small quantities of other tools, indicating groups undertaking a variety of activities, perhaps taking advantage of the varied affordances offered through the location of sites on the boundary of different geological and topographical zones. Horsham sites cluster in certain areas (Kettlebury Common, Longmoor Inclosure, Oakhanger, Lion's Mouth and Devil's Jump Moor), as noted by Jacobi (1981), suggesting repeated use of a favoured area, a similar pattern to the Early Mesolithic.

The Middle Mesolithic sees the first evidence for widespread settlement of the sandy geologies of the High Weald (Gardiner 1988). Many sites on the High Weald, particularly those around Horsham, appear rather more extensive than those on the Greensand, though as these are selectively collected assemblages, their composition cannot be analysed in the same way. Jacobi (1978b, 20) has noted that some, such as Old Faygate (with 200 microliths), appear to have been made up of multiple large scatters, perhaps suggesting these larger occupations, as with other types of Horsham sites, were tethered to particular places.

The High Weald landscape is characterised by small streams cutting deep gorges between sandstone ridges. Gardiner (1988, 279) notes the preferential presence of clusters of Horsham sites on some of the flatter ridges, or just above the springline with the Wealden clay. Reynier (2005, 93) suggests Horsham sites are preferentially located on valley sides and plateaus in between valleys; however, this observation is based on relatively few (nine) unmixed assemblages. More striking, as Gardiner suggests, is their close proximity to, or situation overlooking, springs or streams. This differs from the predominant location of Deepcar sites, which are more frequently focused on major river valleys, though later Deepcar sites and those in the southwest echo more closely the Horsham pattern.

Reynier (2005, 101) correlates Horsham sites with the appearance of thermiphilous forests of oak and elm, with a thick understorey of hazel. These woodlands, as has previously been noted (Mellars and Reinhard 1978), created increased cover for animals. Woodland species also tend to be more dispersed; these two factors may have made hunting more difficult in comparison to earlier period. As a consequence, Reynier argues for an increased investment in fixed resources, such as traps and gardens (e.g. areas where hazel trees clustered), and a resultant increase in territoriality. Short-term settlement strategies would incorporate long-term base camps, fixed resources and a few specialist extraction camps, while long-term settlement would be tethered to a particular territory.

There are certainly signs of long-term connections to places, the repeated occupation of favoured areas, and a strong coherence in terms of distinctive regional microlith types, which might suggest 'signalling' of a shared identity between local groups. However, with the possible exception of the large sites on the High Weald, Horsham sites do not seem to be sufficiently dense to represent long-term camps; instead, Horsham groups seem to have moved residential sites relatively frequently.

Site structure does not seem dissimilar to Deepcar groups, with relatively little variation between assemblages. The main difference between sites appears to be in the representation of microburins – that is, some sites that appear longer term were used for gearing up; other shorter-term sites perhaps indicate short-term extractive visits where microliths were deposited.

Horsham groups seem to have shared the Middle Mesolithic interest in pit digging, though they are not present to the same extent as the north. Pits were noted at both Longmoor I and Kettlebury 103 (Jacobi archive, British Museum). A particularly intriguing deposit was recovered during developer-funded work at the Saltwood Tunnel in Kent. Here, eight large Horsham points were found deposited in the upper fill of a pit-like feature (McKinley et al. 2006). No associated material was recovered, leading excavators to suggest they may have been buried in a bag. Several had broken tips, suggesting they had been used. The lack of associated barbs suggests patterned deposition.

A tale of two sites: Longmoor I and Kettlebury 103

Much of the work on the Wealden Mesolithic has focused on these broader patterns of land use. This is partly as a result of the nature of the evidence, most of the sites in this region consist of unexcavated surface finds. Two excavations permit an examination of settlement in more detail: Longmoor I, dating to the start of the Middle Mesolithic in this area, and Kettlebury 103, dating to the end.

Longmoor I is located near Liss, Hampshire, on the Lower Greensand at the very edge of the Weald. The site is located in a shallow valley through which flowed a stream, one of the headwaters of the Rother (Reynier 2005). A number of important Mesolithic sites can be found in the vicinity: It is 5 km from Oakhanger (see chapter 3); 6 km from West Heath Common, where Early Mesolithic material has been recovered and radiocarbon dates broadly contemporary with Longmoor come from unassociated charcoal; and around 9 km from the Early Mesolithic site of Iping Common (see chapter 3). The site was discovered by Hazel Martingell and excavated by her, Roger Jacobi and members of the Haslemere Archaeology Group between 1977 and 1982. This work located a number of Mesolithic sites at Longmoor, at least two others of which were Horsham sites (Jacobi 1978b, 13), though site I was the only one that underwent full excavation. The site is important as a relatively large, dense Horsham site with minimal evidence for later activity. Three radiocarbon dates suggest the site was occupied around 8000 cal BC; it thus presents the earliest evidence we have for groups using Horsham points.

Below a dark organic top soil, covered in places by recent dumping of sediment, was a dark grey sand A-horizon, underlain by a silvery grey sand-leached illuviation horizon, itself underlain by the soil's B-horizon. As is common in sandy sediments, lithic material was found throughout the profile, but was most common in the upper 25 cm of the silvery grey sand. An area of around 14 × 14 m was excavated (Figure 4.18). Several hearths were located, both dug hearths in pits and more ephemeral clusters of charcoal. The number of hearths, often in close proximity, is likely to be the result of multiple visits to the site, though, given the coherence of the lithic assemblage, probably over a relatively short period of time. There is some evidence for a very small-scale later Mesolithic occupation. Charcoal from a hearth higher up in the sequence yielded a radiocarbon date of

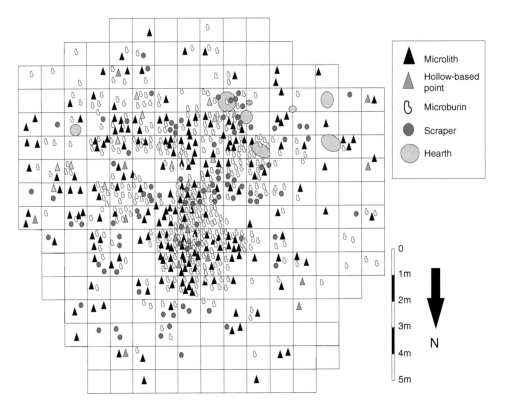

Figure 4.18 Plan of excavations at Longmoor I

4900–4850 BC (5830 ± 80 BP; HAR-5356), and there are a handful of geometric microliths, mostly scalenes with three sides retouched, which may belong with this later visit.

Longmoor I is characterised by high lithic densities, of up to 900 flints per square metres. No faunal remains were recovered from the sandy sediments, but burnt hazelnut shells were present. The site is dominated by evidence for microlith manufacture and retooling; 387 microliths have been recovered and 346 microburins. Nearly half the microliths are burnt, perhaps suggestive of rules regarding their deposition.

All microliths are lateralised to the left. Of these microliths, short obliquely blunted points are most common. Basally modified microliths are also well-represented. Many of these are classic Horsham points: Asymmetric hollow-based points. At Longmoor, the retouch that forms the base is almost always direct rather than inverse, which contrasts with other Horsham sites, such as Kettlebury 103.

Beyond microliths, a wide range of tool types are present, but in general in very low numbers (Table 4.4). Only scrapers are well-represented. Burins are rare and in general poorly developed transverse examples, which grade into chamfered pieces. Chamfered pieces, tools characteristic of Horsham assemblages, consist of flakes whose distal end has been removed by a transverse blow from the ventral. Wear damage and morphology suggest they were used as scraping tools.

Table 4.4 Longmoor I and Kettlebury 103: Composition of the lithic assemblage

Tool type	Longmoor I	Ketttlebury 103
Microlith (total)	387	99
Obliquely blunted points	97	28
Oblique with retouch on leading edge	7	6
Part-backed	2	0
Curve-backed	0	4
Rhomboids	19	1
Isosceles triangle	10	21
Hollow-based	44	15
Tardenois point	1	0
Lanceolate	1	2
Unidentified fragments	106	22
Scraper	95	19
Chamfered piece	7	16
Awl	3	2
Burin	4	4
Denticulate	5	0
Microdenticulate	3	0
Notch	14	19
Truncation	0	10
Retouched	33	23
Utilised	8	21
Tool spalls:		
Burin spall	5	8
Chamfer spall	16	31
Microburin	346	198
Retouch spall	11	34

The site can broadly be divided into two large scatters, a northern and a southern one, though these partially overlap (Figure 4.18). A series of smaller scatters are found around the margins of these two larger concentrations. The lithic material from the northern scatter does not cluster around the hearths, but rather to the northeast of them. It may be a midden. Middening is also suggested by the refit of microlith production waste products 7 m apart. Both lithic concentrations show retooling was a major activity: Microliths are common, and the number of fragmentary (and burnt) microliths is high. Scrapers cluster between the northern and southern scatters. The number of hearths in close proximity suggests repeated occupation of the area, primarily for repairing composite tools and processing hides.

Kettlebury 103 was discovered by Hazel Martingell in the mid-1970s, one of ten surface scatters she located on Hankely Common, West Surrey. Site 103 is located at c.95 m asl on the lower Greensand Folkstone Beds, on a plateau between three small hills (Reynier 2005, 7) and close to a spring-fed stream that runs into the river Wey. To the north the plateau rises, then the ground falls down to the valley of the Wey. High ground can be found to the west, with the small hills of the Devil's Jumps offering good views over the surrounding landscape (Figure 4.19).

In the 1930s, Hankley Common was first investigated by W.F. Rankine, who located and excavated two scatters (Rankine 1949b, 31–33), Kettlebury I and II. Site II (and probably also site I) was also a Horsham site; site II was focused on microlith

Figure 4.19 Views from the Devil's Jumps (©Simon Burchell (CC-BY SA 3.0))

production, site I on scrapers (Rankine 1949b, 33). Kettlebury II is probably very close to site 103. A number of other sites are in close proximity: Lion's Mouth I and II, are 1.5 km to the northeast, while two more scatters at Frensham Great Ponds are 3 km to the east (Rankine 1949b).

Kettlebury 103 was excavated between 1977 and 1978 by Martingell, Jacobi and the Haselmere group. An area of nearly 9 × 4 m was excavated. The site was re-located by Reynier and the Surrey Archaeological Society in 1995, and a further 6 m^2 excavated. In all, an assemblage of around 6000 lithic artefacts were recovered. The stratigraphy of the site consisted of a dark grey humic sand A-horizon, underlain by a light grey leached sand and an eluviated sticky white sand at the base of which was an iron pan. Lithic material was found throughout the sequence, but was concentrated in the 15 cm that formed the base of A-horizon and top of the B-horizon (Reynier 2002).

Microliths dominate the tool assemblage (Table 4.4), and all are lateralised to the left. As at Longmoor, 1000 years earlier, obliquely blunted points dominate, though the points at Kettlebury are slightly smaller. Isosceles triangles are more common than Longmoor, while rhomboids, a major type at Longmoor, are almost absent. Hollow-based microliths are well-represented, but in contrast to Longmoor, where all but one have retouch on the dorsal, the concave truncation is always formed by inverse retouch. Whether this variation represents chronological differences, regional styles or personal idiosyncrasies has yet to be determined. While other tools are less frequent

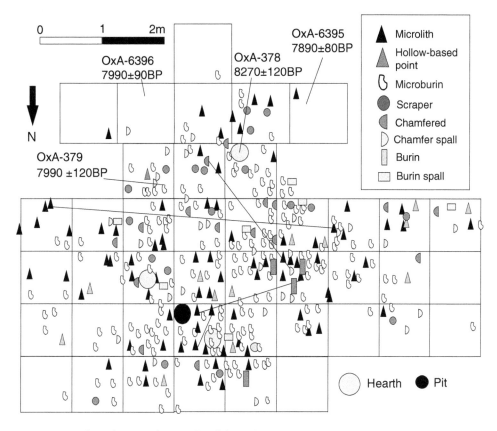

Figure 4.20 Plan of excavations at Kettlebury 103

than microliths, a very wide range are present, with scrapers and chamfered pieces particularly common around the southernmost hearth.

Four radiocarbon measurements were made on hazelnuts from the site: Two from the Jacobi excavations, and two from Reynier's trench. All come from the southern area of the site (Figure 4.20). While three of these measurements are consistent at 95.4% confidence, the other is not and appears earlier. This, combined with evidence for numerous Horsham scatters in the vicinity, suggests groups favoured this location, returning to camp in the area over generations.

The Middle Mesolithic in the southwest

Over the past decades, a series of sites with basally modified points have been discovered to the west of the classic Horsham areas of the Weald (Figure 4.21). While some of these simply represent isolated occurrence of Horsham and others basally modified points within larger assemblages, often of mixed date, others represent more substantial concentrations. These sites are not dated, but the strong typological similarity suggests they belong to the same period as the dated Horsham sites of the southeast. Particularly noticeable is the presence of Horsham points and other basally

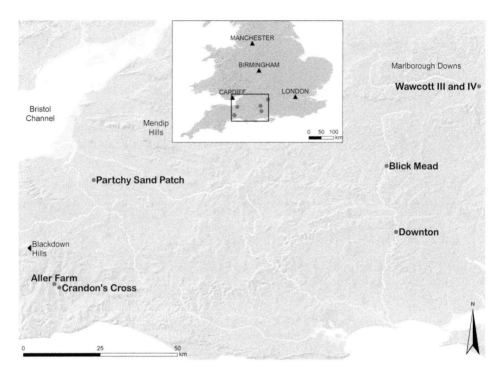

Figure 4.21 Distribution of sites with basally modified microliths in Southwest England

modified microliths in the Kennet Valley. Horsham and/or Tardenoisian points are present at Thatcham Sewage Works (Healey et al. 1992), Wawcott IV (Froom 2012, 86) and Faraday Road. At all these sites Deepcar and sometimes also Late Mesolithic material is present; it is thus difficult to understand the extent of the Horsham occupation. A mid-eighth millennium date on pig at Faraday Road (Conneller et al. 2016a) is likely to belong with the basally modified material. Wawcott IV has fauna of red deer, aurochs, pig and elk, but whether these belong with the Middle Mesolithic microliths is unknown.

Of the Kennet sites with basally modified microliths, Wawcott III has by far the largest quantity, with 27 examples. Most are Horsham points, though a Honey Hill type is also present (this contrasts with Wawcott IV, where Honey Hill-like forms are more common). Wawcott III is another site of mixed date, through Froom demonstrates there is some level of stratification present, albeit with a certain amount of mixing. The Horsham material clusters mainly in spits F-I and is characterised by short obliquely blunted points, some with retouch on the leading edge, isosceles triangles and asymmetric basally modified points with inverse retouch. It is very similar to the material from Kettlebury 103 in the large number of triangles, rarity of rhomboids and the inverse retouch of the Horsham points. In contrast to the sites on the Thames, the Horsham occupation of Wawcott III seems substantial, or at least repeated. It is clear that Wawcott III was a 'persistent place' (Barton et al. 1995), where the presence of specific affordances resulted in occupation over millennia.

Assemblages with basally modified microliths are also present further to the west, where they can be traced as far as north Devon. They are present as a component of almost all large palimpsest sites in these regions: For example, at Broom Hill, Hampshire (O'Malley and Jacobi 1978), Blick Mead (Jacques et al. 2018) and Downton (Higgs 1959), both Wiltshire.

A distinctive Middle Mesolithic phase in Southwest England has been identified by Chris Norman (2001). He has located several sites with basally modified material, including a large scatter at Parchey Sand Patch, Chedzoy (see Box 4.6). While this site is of mixed date, several classic Horsham points were recovered, as well as a single Honey Hill point. Norman groups these with a series of obliquely blunted points, isosceles triangles and pieces with rounded bases. A number of lanceolate points may also belong with the Middle Mesolithic assemblage, given their presence in Honey Hill assemblages, such as Asfordby (Cooper and Jarvis 2017). Bond (2009b) has also argued for the presence of a distinctive Middle Mesolithic phase in this area.

Box 4.6   A Middle Mesolithic site on the Burtle Beds: Parchey Sand Patch, Chedzoy

In the previous chapter, we saw how small hills of sand and gravel (the Burtle Beds), rising above the Somerset Levels, were significant places in the Early Mesolithic. Though the levels are now a wetland area, this is the result of more recent sea-level rise. During the Middle Mesolithic, the Burtle Beds would have been small hillocks, rising a few metres above the floodplain of the River Parrett. In the Early Mesolithic, these were not just convenient settlement sites, but places for the burial of the dead at Greylake, Middlezoy. These locations continued to be sought out for settlement during the Middle Mesolithic. On a low sandy rise, known as Parchey Sand Patch, located on the eastern edge of Chedzoy Island, a large concentration of lithic material has been recorded by Chris Norman (2001). Three scatters were noted, of which the largest and most southerly (scatter A) contained all of the hollow-based points. Late Mesolithic microliths are represented in fairly equal numbers to those that appear of Middle Mesolithic date, limiting what can be said about Middle Mesolithic lifeways. Scrapers were the most common tool recovered, with large numbers of miscellaneous retouched pieces, indicating varied processing activities.

Most of the assemblage was made from Greensand chert, which, from the condition of its outer rind, appears to have been obtained relatively close to its source. The range of colours appears different to that obtainable from the Blackdown Hills to the south. Norman (2001, 16) suggests an exposure on the western edge of Salisbury Plain, some 40 km to the east, is more likely. Flint nodules with relatively fresh cortex as well as a gravel flint were also used. Middle and Late Mesolithic microliths are made from fairly similar proportions of these materials, suggesting continuity in raw material procurement strategies over the two periods. More broadly, they reflect an increasing use of Greensand chert over time, noted by Bond (2009b).

Middle Mesolithic material is also present to the west of the River Parret in the Blackdown Hills. Two major, coherent fieldwalked assemblages come from Aller Farm and Crandon's Cross in the Upper Yarty Valley in Devon (Berridge 1985). Both sites are on the floor of a valley that cuts through a ridge of Greensand. The assemblage from Crandon's Cross, which lies just above the floodplain of the River Yarty, is characterised by obliquely blunted points with smaller numbers of rhomboids and symmetrical basally truncated pieces. The assemblage from Aller Farm, a site along the edge of what was once a permanent pool, is smaller, contains obliquely blunted points, with small numbers of curve-backed and lanceolates and a classic Horsham point. Crandon's Cross is focused on axe production, not usually a major activity on Horsham sites. The scale of manufacture, with 23 of these tools, may suggest something more than simply gearing up for personal consumption, possibly the exchange of axes across the broader region.

Box 4.7   Monuments of the Middle Mesolithic

The Middle Mesolithic in the far north has been characterised by the presence of monumental pit alignments, with suggested astronomical significance (Gaffney et al. 2013). In the south, monumental markers also become visible at this time. Here, they take the form of large pits or posts, best known from the alignment at Stonehenge but present on a number of sites in the region.

At Stonehenge, three large pits and a tree throw were located during excavations in 1966, with a fifth feature found in 1988 (Figure 4.22; Allen and Gardiner 2002;Vatcher and Vatcher 1973). GPR survey located two possible additional examples around 100 m to the south, though these remain unexcavated (Bowden et al. 2015). The pits were substantial, measuring between 1.5 and 2 m across and c.1.2 m deep. Pits A-C are argued to have contained post-pipes and wedging material, indicating the presence of large pine posts that rotted in situ (Vatcher and Vatcher 1973). There was no sign of a post-pipe associated with WA 9580. Calculations based on the width and depth of surviving post material indicated they may have stood up to 3 m tall. Pollard (2017) has argued that these features were not post-holes at all, but rather pits with complex episodes of infilling, silting and recutting. The splayed edges of the features suggest they were left open for some time, while the darker lenses, interpreted as wedges by their excavators, may represent episodes of stabilisation. Furthermore, the shape of the dark fills interpreted as post-pipes are conical and do not extend to the base of the pit; they are thus likely to represent recuts infilled with a dark sediment.

The features were dug in clearings within a fairly open landscape with areas of pine-hazel woodland (Allen 1995; French et al. 2003; Scaife 1995). Radiocarbon dates come from three of the pits (Figure 4.23) and indicate they were not dug at the same time. Particularly noticeable is the gap of several hundred years between adjacent pits A and B. Pit 9580 is around 100 m from the group found in 1966. The radiocarbon dates from this feature come from a recut, meaning that the digging of the original pit and pit A could be broadly contemporary. Modelling suggests the Mesolithic activity represented at the site

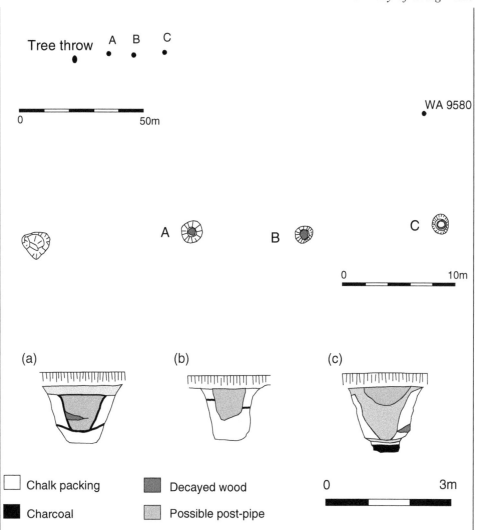

Figure 4.22 The large pits from Stonehenge Carpark. Redrawn after Vatcher and Vatcher (1973) with additions from Allen and Gardiner (2002)

took place over a span of between 300 and 1600 years, with the events occurring between 8500–7650 cal BC and 7500–6700 cal BC (Bronk Ramsey and Bayliss 2000, 30). In this, they are similar to the large pits in Aberdeenshire, that appear to have been dug successively. At Stonehenge, the pits may have been dug to commemorate particular events, and if they did contain posts, a new pit may have been dug when an earlier post may have been partly decayed, or even fallen. All pits appear to contain a basal fill, that predates any putative post (Vatcher and Vatcher 1973). These fills may have been related to the events commemorated, or signal connections to other places, as the inclusion of exotic minerals may have in the Warren Fields pits (Murray et al. 2009). Material of potential significance, including charcoal and burnt bone, has also been found within other pits (Vatcher and Vatcher 1973). Given the lack of evidence for

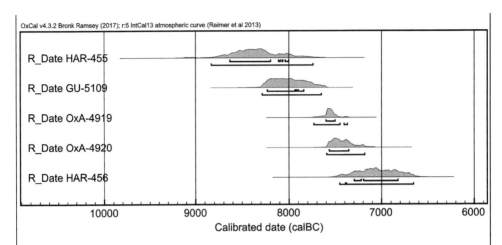

Figure 4.23 Probability distributions of radiocarbon dates from three of the Stonehenge pits. HAR-455 comes from pit A, HAR-456 from pit B and GU-5109, OxA-4919 and OxA-4920 from pit 9580

Mesolithic activity in the immediate vicinity, these may be related to the events surrounding the digging of the pits.

The Mesolithic pits are not in exact alignment, with pit B lying off the line of the 1966 features by about 0.6 m. The 1988 pit is around 100 m away, around 30 m off the 1966 alignment and curving in the opposite direction. Loveday (2012, 344) has noted that the alignment of the 1966 group is broadly that of the Stonehenge cursus, arguing these share a long-standing focus on a spring-autumn celestial alignment calculated on a combination of solar and lunar observations. Pollard has also highlighted a potential relationship with the Avenue, which is now known to be a partially modified natural feature of three ridges, fortuitously aligned on the solstice, produced by differential erosion of the chalk. Pollard (2017) has argued that these may have been seen as important to Mesolithic groups, with the pits broadly aligned with the northwest end of the ridges. Similarly, Parker-Pearson (2013) has suggested possible Mesolithic interests in natural alignments of both periglacial ridges and natural mounds in the vicinity.

During the original excavations of the 1966 pit group, the fourth feature, lying at the westernmost end of the group, was argued to be a tree throw, since its form was more irregular and rather different from the three pits (Vatcher and Vatcher 1973, Figure 4.22). McInnes (2015), following the interpretation of the pits as post-holes, has argued that the sequence may have started with an important tree, perhaps associated with myths or seen as a significant being in its own right. She suggests its fall was marked by the erection of a post within its footprint, and following the post's decay, with the creation of new post-pits. These posts of pine, she suggests, may have been seen as living trees, and the long gap between episodes of construction a recognition of the supra-human lifespan of trees.

The Stonehenge pits are not an isolated example; other such monuments are present in the area. At Boscombe Down, a large pit, with possible traces of a post-pipe, was uncovered (Allen and Gardiner 2002). Though this feature was not dated, it contained charcoal of birch, pine and willow/poplar, suggestive of Mesolithic vegetation. Another possible example is three pits or post-holes beneath the Neolithic barrow on Thickton Down, Dorset, again associated with pine charcoal (ibid.). Radiocarbon dates have been obtained for two pits on Hambleton Hill; while one is smaller than the Stonehenge examples, the other is 2 m across. They have a similar span of dates to Stonehenge, ranging between 7945 and 7465 cal BC, and were dug at different times (Bayliss et al. 2012). Two further pits at the site may belong to this group. These pits are in a dramatic location, on the edge of the chalk and overlooking the Stour (Pollard 2017). In a similar scarp-edge location is a pit on Urchfront Hill. This has three dates on charcoal, all falling into the second half of the eighth millennium (Roberts et al. 2017). Within its fills were calcined bone and flint, showing a similar concern with burnt materials as the Stonehenge examples.

Narrow geometric microliths in the south and west

In areas where basally modified points were favoured, people adopted narrow geometric microliths relatively late. Horsham and Honey Hill industries extend to around 7000 cal BC, if not a little later. Ellaby (1987) makes a strong case for assemblages characterised by narrow-backed bladelets representing the earliest traditional Late Mesolithic in the southeast. The earliest radiometric date for narrow geometric microliths belongs to the second half of the eighth millennium from Tolpitts Lane B101 and is associated with narrow-backed bladelets and scalene triangles; however, as a bulked date on unidentified wood, it should be considered a TPQ for the occupation.

Further west, beyond the core Horsham and Honey Hill areas, there are earlier dates for narrow geometric microliths, at Broom Hill in Hampshire (see below), at Madawg Rockshelter in Herefordshire and at Lightmarsh Farm in Worcestershire (Figure 4.24). The dates from Broom Hill, in particular, were key for Jacobi's understanding of Mesolithic chronology (O'Malley and Jacobi 1978). Three measurements were made on bulked, unidentified charcoal from the base of pit 3, a possible structure, and one from the top, while a final date was made on bulked hazelnuts from a layer above the structure. These dates were all in correct sequence. The three basal dates have a weighted mean of 7610–7210 cal BC (Waddington et al. 2007), while the upper layer of the pit is dated to 7040–6390 cal BC. Microliths from the fill of pit 3 consist of obliquely blunted points, backed bladelets and a small number of variably lateralised scalene triangles. As representing a rare instance of a Mesolithic stratigraphic sequence, the sequence of dates was hugely significant at the time; however, today elements would be considered less than ideal. The presence of large obliquely blunted points could suggest some mixing, in what is a complex feature, and the dates on unidentified, bulked charcoal should be considered a TPQ for occupation.

A single date from Lightmarsh Farm on hazelnuts of 8210–7617 cal BC (8800 ± 80 BP; OxA-4327) comes from a banana-shaped feature, which may represent a pit or a tree throw, from which lithic material was recovered (Jackson et al. 1994, 1996). This feature contained 421 pieces of flint, of which more than a third had been burnt, and 170 charred hazelnut shells. Seven microliths, including narrow scalene triangles and

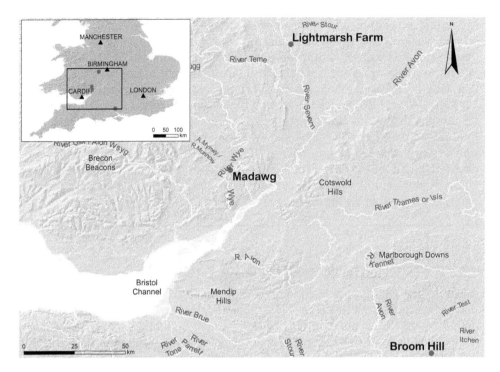

Figure 4.24 Distribution of the earliest dated sites with narrow scalene triangles in the southwest

backed blades, were recovered from the feature, along with three scrapers. The broader site has been suggested to represent a hunting camp. It is situated at c.100 m asl, on a spit of land overlooking the River Severn, around a kilometre away, and microliths are common. However, scrapers and retouched pieces are also well-represented, and the presence of a number of pits and post-holes might suggest something more substantial. The excavation area, though, is very small and narrow, and part of the archaeology was destroyed by the pipeline; little is known of the date range represented by the uncovered features.

The final date comes from Madawg Rockshelter, located high above the river, in the Wye Valley Gorge. This material comes from a shallow depression, which may represent material washed in from elsewhere (Barton 1997). The depression contained charcoal from ash, oak, elder, pine, yew and hazel in the upper part and of pine and yew in the lower part. Two dates come from the lower part: One on a sloe stone of 7970–7585 cal BC (8710 ± 70 BP; OxA-6081), the other of 5675–5480 cal BC (6655 ± 65 BP; OxA-6082) on charred hazelnut shells. The lithic assemblages are small: Only ten pieces were recovered, of which six were microliths. Barton and Roberts (2015, 192) have recently suggested that the microliths belong with the later occupation (see chapter 5).

Taken together, the dates from Lightmarsh Farm and Broom Hill probably suggest people adopted narrow geometric microliths in the west midlands from around 8000 BC, at a time when people in the east midlands were still using Honey Hill points, and around 7500 BC in South-Central England, when people around 50 km to the east were still using Horsham points. This pattern might account for the rather fewer sites with basally retouched points in the southwest; however, dated sites are few, and more work is needed to resolve this issue.

Broom Hill, Braishfield, Hampshire

Broom Hill is a tract of high ground on the end of a spur extending to the southwest from the chalk of the South Downs, forming the watershed between the rivers Test and Itchen (O'Malley and Jacobi 1978). The Mesolithic site lies on the southern end of the hill at 101 m asl, a location that commands splendid views in all directions, except the north. The underlying geology is the Reading Formation, here consisting of gravels and sands overlying clay. Chalk outcrops a couple of hundred meters to the north, as do areas of clay-with-flints. Several chalk solution hollows are present in the vicinity, as are a number of springs and ponds. Around 100 m to the west of the site is a permanent spring, whose waters erode the chalk of a swallet hole, exposing flint nodules.

Mesolithic material was identified as a surface scatter by Michael O'Malley, and excavated by him and a small team throughout the 1970s (Figure 4.25). O'Malley was meticulous in many ways: He set up a site grid aligned with OS grid and ex-cavated the site by square metre; he sieved all material through a sieve with a quarter-inch mesh, the standard mesh size for excavations at the time (though even many professional excavators did not sieve); and when it became apparent that smaller material was falling through the sieves, he redesigned these to a 1/8th inch mesh. The recovery of Late Mesolithic microliths, in particular, is hugely affected by whether sieving has taken place, and mesh size. Recovery of microliths improved by 325% at Broom Hill following the introduction of sieves with 1/8th mesh. O'Malley's innovations allowed detailed distribution plotting of artefacts across the site, which by the end extended to 179 m².

During his excavations, O'Malley encountered four features, labelled pits 1–4. Of these, pit 3 was the largest and interpreted as a Mesolithic dwelling structure. O'Malley's interpretations were disputed at the time. Part of this simply seems to be the product of unfounded prejudices against amateurs, but also this was a time when the earlier finds of Mesolithic 'pit-houses' (e.g. Clark and Rankine 1939; Layard 1927) were being re-interpreted as tree throws (Newell 1981, see Box 4.8). It does seem fairly clear that pits 1, 2 and 4 are tree throws; they display the familiar banana-shaped plan and irregular profile. However, pit 3, is rather different, as O'Malley himself outlined. This is a larger and more regular-shaped structure, measuring c.5 × 4.5 m in diameter and surrounded by 14 post-holes, reinforced on two sides by a series of stakeholes. The site's photographic archive shows a clear edge to this pit and the presence of at least some of the surrounding post-holes. Sections of a handful of these post-holes exist, and most look convincing. It is not beyond the bounds of possibility that the pit itself may represent a modified tree throw: It is more irregular to the southeast, and in this area there are also reports of three areas of clay mounds (see O'Malley 1982; Broom Hill Archive), which could represent underlying sediment caught up in, and dropped from, the rootwad. There is increasing evidence that tree throws, modified or otherwise, were used in the Mesolithic (see Box 4.8 and 5.7). A second possibility for a natural origin of pit 3 is as the remnant of a solution hollow in the underlying chalk. O'Malley's contour plans for the site show that pit 3 lies within a larger depression,

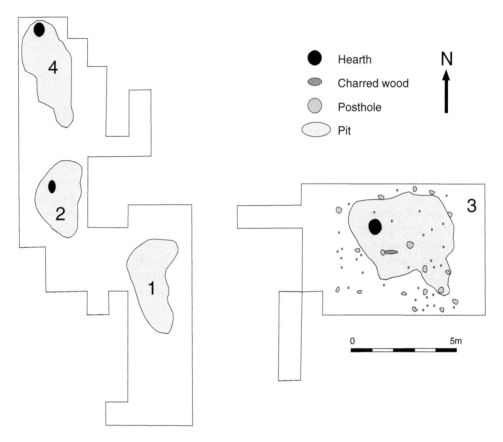

Figure 4.25 Plan of excavations at Broom Hill. Redrawn after O'Malley (1982) with additions from the site archive (Hampshire Museums) and the Jacobi archive (British Museum)

which seems to have a clay base, but which was infilling with wind-blown sand (de-rived presumably from the sands of the Reading Formation), both prior to and during the occupation. However, even if it originated as a tree throw or dissolution hollow, pit 3 has certainly been extensively modified. It contains considerable quantities of cultural material and clear pits or post-holes (both on the edge of and cut into pit 3) are visible in the photographic record.

Part of the difficulty of understanding pit 3 lies in the way in which O'Malley dug the site in 1 m^2 segments (which he called 'transects'). This, effectively a test-pitting technique, makes it difficult for the excavator to see they are in a larger feature. O'Malley became aware in 1973 that some transects were deeper than others and that the white sand that represents the basal artefact-bearing layer of the site contained considerable quantities of charcoal. Material from this year is not separated by con-text. In subsequent years, more consideration of stratigraphy was made, with material from the infill separated from overlying artefacts, and transect 23/27 was dug in 1.5 cm spits. Long sections of the area of pit 3 were drawn, though these lie beyond the edge of the pit (the very edge of it may be present on the edge of the 27E section).

Box 4.8   Farnham and the Mesolithic pit dwellings

When Clark wrote the *Mesolithic Age in Britain* (1932), structural evidence was limited. The only settlement remains discussed were Buckley's finds of small firepits associated with his sites on the Pennines; these scatters, Clark suggested, 'probably represent the floor space of huts of which no trace remains' (Clark 1932, 23). In 1933, Clark visited Selmeston, Sussex, with Eliot Curwen, who had been collecting material from the working edge of the Selmeston sand-pit. On the visit, Clark noted a pit in the section, which he interpreted as a dwelling. This, and a further two pits, were excavated by Clark in 1933. In his discussion of his finds, he compared the Selmeston pit dwellings to a similar feature at the site of Hassocks, Sussex, discovered by H.S. Toms. Following his work at Selmeston, it is clear that his interest in the phenomenon was piqued. A report by W.F. Rankine (1936) of several pits at Farnham led Clark to renew excavations at the site, in collaboration with Rankine in 1937–1938.

The Farnham publication contains an extensive discussion of pit dwellings, or semi-subterranean houses (Clark and Rankine 1939). Clark traced the history of such features, from Upper Palaeolithic mammoth bone dwellings of the Russian Plain to ethno-historical examples from Siberia. It may have been the knowledge of these analogies that gave him the confidence to interpret his finds as similar dwellings. Clark suggested that the pit dwellings would have represented winter houses, a counterpart to flimsy summer structures, such as those represented by Danish Maglemosian structures by lakes, and small discrete scatters of flint surrounding firepits discovered by Buckley on the Pennines. He drew on the presence of burnt hazelnuts in the pits at Farnham and Selmeston to suggest that people occupied the pit dwellings from the autumn to the following spring.

Clark's work at Farnham cemented the idea that pit structures were a feature of the Mesolithic of Southern England. However, even at this time, not all such features were interpreted in this way. Higgs, for example, suggested a pit at Downton, Wiltshire might represent a quarry for the procurement of flint nodules. From the 1970s, doubt began to be more explicitly expressed about the nature of these finds, with Newell (1981) suggesting they are in fact tree throws. Tree throws are characterised by banana-shaped, crescentic or oval depressions, caused by the roots being ripped out of the ground when a tree is uprooted. These roots carry with them clumps of soil and bedrock, which gradually fall back within the pit (Figure 4.26). Depending on the size of the tree, the depression can range in size between 0.5 and >4 m and is irregular in profile. Fills may show stratigraphic inversions, as material falls from the rootball, and silt lines, as the depression fills up (Bonischen and Will 1999).

Where data are available, the southern pit dwellings generally fit this profile. Plans record characteristic forms: Clark's Farnham pits are all crescentic to ovoid in plan, and the irregular sections he depicts (with one slope steep the other gradual) are also characteristic of tree throws (Figure 4.27). The pit at

Figure 4.26 Fallen tree, showing sediment caught within the root-wad and associated infilling depression to the right

Abinger Common is very similar (Leakey 1951). Selmeston pit 1 is also oval, though the section drawn is rather more regular in profile, as is Farnham pit II. Some stratigraphic detail also suggests tree throws: The 'ridge of undisturbed gravel' in Farnham pit II may represent subsurface material caught up in the rootball, which has subsequently dropped back into the pit, and there is a similar mass of sandy upcast at Abinger. A line of pebbles was also observed, which Clark suggested represented evidence of silting (Clark and Rankine 1939, 67).

If the 'pits' at these sites are tree throws, what are we to make of the large quantities of artefacts that are found within them? Both Clark and Rankine highlight the great concentration of artefacts in the pits, in comparison with the surrounding sediments – 6600 pieces of flint were found in Selmeston pit I, for example. There are certainly some obvious taphonomic reasons for this phenomenon: Tree throws are capture points for artefacts in landscapes where early Holocene soil horizons may be disturbed or truncated by ploughing, colluviation and alluviation, and thus may preserve evidence that has been lost in the surrounding area. However, we need also to consider cultural reasons for artefact concentration, at least in some cases, and to investigate this issue a consideration of the timing of Mesolithic activities in relation to the tree-fall event is key.

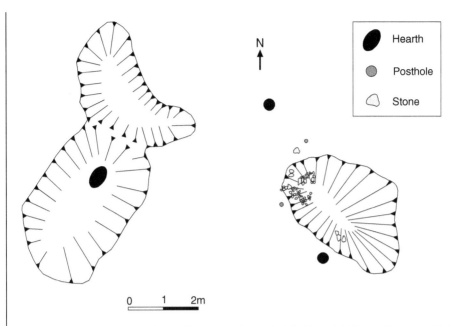

N

Figure 4.27 Plans of two pit dwellings: Farnham pit 1 (left) and Abinger Common (right). (Redrawn after Clark and Rankine (1939) and Leakey (1951))

It is clear that in many instances at least Mesolithic activity predates tree-fall and that occupation material has subsequently silted into the pit, or fallen from sediments caught up in the rootwad. This is clearly the case for Farnham pit II, the pit for which we have the most detailed description and information on artefact distribution. Clark and Rankine (1939, 67) state, 'the impression given was that the bulk of the flints had silted into the pit from the edge after its abandonment'. Artefacts were distributed uniformly throughout the fill, and microliths suggest an admixture of material of different dates.

However, there are also indications that some of the pits were contemporary with the Mesolithic occupation and that some may have been modified. Clark and Rankine (1939) report the discovery of hearths in pits 1 and 3, respectively, indicated by tight concentrations of charcoal and burnt flint. A potential post-hole was also reported from pit 2. Evans et al. (1999) have suggested that pit 2 may have been extended by the Mesolithic inhabitants of the site. Other examples of this practise have been noted. Two post-holes were associated with the pit at Abinger Common (Leakey 1951). At Streat Lane, Sussex (see chapter 5), what appears to have been a partially silted-up tree throw was subsequently used for deposition of material, including large quantities of burnt flint, some of which was found in specific clusters, suggesting dumping from containers. The northeast quadrant was also modified by a series of post-holes, suggesting the area may have been used as a shelter (Butler 2007, 13). A range of utilised, and possibly modified, tree throws have also been reported from Bletchingly (Jones et al. 2013, 3) and at Broom Hill (see above) with a hearth and a post recorded in pit 1.

A second interpretation of these features demands serious consideration: That is, Higgs' (1959) suggestion, based on his excavations at Downton (see chapter 3), that such pits could be used to procure raw material. Downton is located on river terrace gravels, and Farnham has a very similar situation; the pits cut through gravels, derived from an old course of the Blackwater River, and this was the source of the raw material used on the site (Clark and Rankine 1939, 61). The solid geology underlying the site is chalk, and a solution hollow was also recorded at the site, a possible alternative source of raw material. Care (1979, 94) has suggested the Farnham pits may have been dug to access flint, noting a concentration of tranchet axes in the Farnham area. Fifteen adzes and similar core tools come from the site itself, including one to which two flakes refit (Clark and Rankine 1939, 70). Other early finds of pits dwellings, as at Nina Layard's (1927) sites at White Colne, are also on gravel, though others, such as Selmeston and Abinger Common on the Greensand (Clark 1933; Leakey 1951) and High Beech on the clay-sand Claygate Beds (Jacobi 1980b), are not.

It is likely that the various pit dwellings located in the first half of the 20th century represent many different things. Some, such as Broom Hill pit 4, are tree throws undoubtedly post-dating Mesolithic occupation. Others (Broom Hill 1, Farnham 1 and 3) are tree throws that seem to have been used by Mesolithic groups, with modifications, as shelters. Some (Streat Lane) may have been used for the deposition of midden material; others as means of obtaining raw material. Others may have been deliberately dug, either as structures, as some of the more elaborate examples with surrounding posts, or as quarry pits. The Farnham pits may have had more than one origin and purpose. The site has yielded large numbers of artefacts, with 39,675 pieces of worked flint. Microlith typology reveals the site was visited over an extremely long period, with both a Horsham-type assemblage and a very late Mesolithic assemblage, characterised by micro-tranchets and Bexhill points. While fresh tree throws would be useful as sources of flints, partly silted and overgrown examples may have been modified as shelters.

It is evident that the archaeology of pit 3 was complex. Sections adjacent to pit 3 show large areas of disturbance, with rabbit activity a major issue and a number of more recent features and tree throws also present. However, the material within pit 3 appears to date almost exclusively to the Mesolithic period. Only a single fragment of pottery was found, and this appears to result from an episode of section collapse. This contrasts with the other pits excavated by O'Malley: A moderate sized assemblage of later Prehistoric pottery was recovered from pit 4, for example (Broom Hill archive), and Late Neolithic and Early Bronze Age lithic material was present in the upper levels of the site (O'Malley 1982). That pit 3 does have stratigraphic integrity in places at least is also confirmed by the coherence of the radiocarbon dates (see Table 4.5).

The stratigraphy of pit 3 consists of a feature cut into underlying clay, which seems to have had a fairly irregular base. Depressions within the base were infilled with white sand (Jacobi archive, BM box 12). Above this was a firm white sand stained black in

Table 4.5 Radiocarbon dates from Broom Hill. Charcoal dates are on unidentified, bulked charcoal so should be understood as providing a TPQ for the use of the structure

Lab no.	Pit	Material	Location	Measurement	Calibrated date range BC
Q-1192	3	Charcoal	Base of pit 3 infill (−1.31 m), transect 22/29	8540 ± 150	8160–7190 BC
Q-1528	3	Charcoal	Base of pit 3 infill (−1.31 m), transect 23/27	8515 ± 150	7600–7040 BC
Q-1383	3	Charcoal	Base of pit 3 infill (−1.31 m), transect 24/27	8315 ± 150	7960–7180 BC
Q-1460	3	Charcoal	Top of pit 3 infill (−1.03 m), transect 25/26	7750 ± 120	7040–6390 BC
Q-1191	3	Charred hazelnuts	Brown sand 5 cm above pit infill (−0.98), 25/26	7220 ± 120	6380–5810 BC
Q-1128	2	Charcoal	Hearth (−1.4 m), transect 8/30	6535 ± 125	5710–5230 BC

places with charcoal. Post-holes on the perimeter of pit 3 were visible at the top of the infill. Post-holes within pit 3 itself were stated by O'Malley only to be visible at the lowest layer of the infill, and definitely not visible in the overlying white sand (layer D). Post-holes, he suggests, were dug into the white sand (F) at the base of fill and into the underlying basal clay. However, the photographic record reveals one post-hole at least is clearly cut through the infill. The cut of pit 3 is extremely irregular in this area, and photographs suggest that there may be a series of intercutting pits here, which cut pit 3, and through which post-hole G is cut.

Taken together, the site archive and the radiocarbon dates indicate successive use of pit 3 over a long period of time. Post-holes were erected around the edge of pit 3. Some of these post-holes contained post packing of sandstone, and in one case, a flint adze. Two large features are present within the pit. The first of these consists of a hearth or cooking pit, measuring around 60 cm in diameter, with a clay and charcoal fill (O'Malley 1982); its perimeter was encircled by pebbles. Immediately to the west was a post-hole, which may be dated by Q-1192 (Letter from O'Malley to Jacobi, n.d., Jacobi archive, British Museum). The second major feature has been reconstructed from the site archive and consists of a pit cut into the clay, with a mid-grey sandy fill. This contained large quantities of charcoal, particularly in its upper part, burnt hazelnuts and possible a *prunus* seed. It may also, as O'Malley suggested, have contained a post-hole. This feature is probably dated by both Q-1383 and Q-1528 (Jacobi archive, British Museum). Above this feature is what O'Malley saw as a clay platform, described as 15 cm above this hearth/pit. The fill of pit 3 is described as heavily stained with charcoal, possibly indicating additional features.

In addition to the post-holes, O'Malley uncovered a series of 38 stakeholes. These appear to have a slightly different footprint to pit 3 and its post-holes, with the stakehole footprint around 1 m to the west and cutting into clay in the west. In the east, the stakeholes seem to cut through the pit fill. This could mean that there were two phases of structure: A probably earlier, more substantial one, focused on pit 3 and surrounding post-holes. O'Malley suggests this structure may have burnt down, based on the presence of what he interpreted as charred posts within the infill of the structure. If this was the case, a more light-weight structure may have been built on a slightly different footprint. A date of 6645–6105 cal BC (7750 ± 120, Q-1460) was obtained from the top of pit 3; infill indicates subsequent activity in this area.

Activities taking place within pit 3 when the infill was accumulating were varied. Hearths indicate cooking, and some hazelnuts and a *prunus* seed indicate plant processing/ consumption, though hazelnuts, it should be noted, are present in much lower quantities than higher levels of the site. Tools and tool spalls that are recorded belonging to the pit infill include 20 microliths, microburins, a core tool and several sharpening flake, two scrapers (one burnt, recovered from the hearth), two micro-denticulates, a truncation, a knife and 13 retouched or utilised pieces. Blades were common, and cores and knapping debris were also recovered. Blades are well-prepared, and there are a number of neat, regular, opposed platform blade cores. The microliths from the infill are a varied bunch, including large obliquely blunted points (mainly left lateralised), straight and curve-backed blades, rods and scalene triangles. This variability suggests this assemblage accumulated over some time. A slate knife, whose source may be as far away as Cornwall (Jacobi 1981, 20), was found just to the northwest of the hearth, while a second example was found a few metres to the west of pit 3. While relatively few tools can now be associated with the infill, the extant sample suggests a focus on craft activities, possibly food processing and tool repair.

Above the charcoal-stained pit infill was a layer of white or light sand (layer D) that is alternately described as 'containing many implements' (O'Malley and Jacobi 1978, first page) or 'sterile' (O'Malley 1982) and 'sealing the pit' (Jacobi 1981, 17). However, there does appear to be material associated with this layer, particularly in the upper part. As these are sandy sediments, where material may move through the profile, this may be material that derives from the overlying light brown sand (C), or represents material in pits cut from above. At the top of the white sand (or the very base of the brown sand) was found a cluster of over 200 burnt hazelnuts (O'Malley and Jacobi 1978; O'Malley 1982, 39), from which a radiocarbon date of 6380–5870 cal BC (7220 ± 120 BP; Q-1191) was obtained. This appears to have been a small pit, cut from the overlying layers. Flint, burnt flint and pebbles were also present at this level. The only tools that can be matched to this layer were microliths (four examples), part of a group of 80 lithic artefacts recovered in a 3 cm spit.

O'Malley plotted the location of tools across the site, though since context was not noted, these could belong to any phase of occupation. However, there is a strong association of adzes and sharpening flakes with the area of pit 3. Sharpening flakes cluster in the southern area of the structure and just to the northwest. Adzes are found in the eastern area of the structure and immediately to the south. Examination of material from the area of pit 3 revealed additional core tools, strengthening the association of this area with heavy duty tool use.

The remaining pits 1, 2 and 4 in the western part of the site (Figure 4.25), though clearly tree throws, appear to have rather different histories. There are relatively few records for pit 1, but details of pit 2 are recorded, suggesting the presence of a hearth and a post-hole. Charcoal from this feature was dated to between 5710 and 5295 cal BC (6535 ± 125 BP; Q-1128). This date comes from bulked, unidentified charcoal and thus should be treated with caution, as it could represent mixed material of both Mesolithic and Neolithic date. However, taken together, this evidence might suggest some Mesolithic modification and use of this feature. Pit 4, by contrast, clearly seems to have post-dated the Mesolithic occupation, as it contains both Mesolithic material and later Prehistoric pottery throughout the sequence (this feature was dug in spits).

The microlith assemblage from pit 4 is, however, very coherent, consisting almost entirely of elongated, narrow scalene triangles, with mainly three sides retouched, suggesting this area was not so frequently reoccupied as the area of pits 2 and particularly pit 3.

O'Malley's artefact plots reveal that adzes were also very common in the western part of the site, with at least 15 examples recovered, and a cluster of six examples immediately to the south of pit 2. Sharpening flakes were also common, with at least 57 examples recovered and several clusters visible. This reinforces the evidence from the eastern part of the site, where adzes, core tools and resharpening flakes were also found in large numbers. Adzes across the site appear in a variety of conditions, from fresh, large and unfinished, to very small, worn and heavily used. The ready availability of flint in the area makes this a likely place for an axe manufacturing site, where tools were made for transport or exchange to other areas. It is clear though that axes were also being used here: Some were made expediently for immediate use, but others had longer histories and had been used, repaired and reused before finally being discarded at the site.

Jacobi has previously drawn attention to the large number of axes at Broom Hill. These, he suggests, form a group with other sites on the edges of the South Downs, where large numbers of axes can be found amongst old collections, for example, at Beachy Head, Seaford, Alfriston, Cissbury, East and West Dene, Exeat and Selmeston (O'Malley and Jacobi 1978, 24). These may be areas where axes were manufactured for broader distribution. Axe-sharpening flakes at Broom Hill tend to be larger than the axes found at the site, suggesting axes were removed from Broom Hill. Similar arguments have also been made for a second Hampshire chalk site, at Wallington, where axes production may be associated with the procurement of flint nodules from solution hollows (Hughes and ApSimon 1977, 34). Beyond just axes, Jacobi (1981) has suggested that Broom Hill and other sites on the chalk may served as sources for the production of cores, blades and finished tools for use in non-flint areas of Southeast England, such as the Weald, where during the Late Mesolithic, knapping debris is very small, and cores and rejuvenation flakes rare.

Dealing with the dead in the Middle Mesolithic

In the previous chapter, we saw the emergence of mortuary practises in the southwest that created more permanent relationships between people and certain places. The Early Mesolithic saw varied but substantial mortuary practises, with caves being particularly important. Over 50 individuals were interred at Aveline's Hole, though smaller-scale practises focused on disarticulated elements from a small number of individuals perhaps also occurred. In the Middle Mesolithic, caves continued to be repositories for the dead, but practises were less varied and always small-scale, involving only certain individuals rather than the entire community.

Human remains from six sites date to this period (Figure 4.28): Ogof-yr-Ychen, Potter's Cave and Daylight Rock on Caldey Island; Oreston Third Bone Cave and Kent's Cavern in Devon; and Totty Pot on Mendip. Totty Pot is in the same region (Mendip) that saw extensive earlier Mesolithic mortuary practises, lying on the plateau above Gough's Cave. Caldey Island is only 25 km across Carmarthen Bay from Worm's Head, the Welsh Early Mesolithic mortuary site. Finally, the two Devon sites are in a region that had not previously seen evidence for mortuary

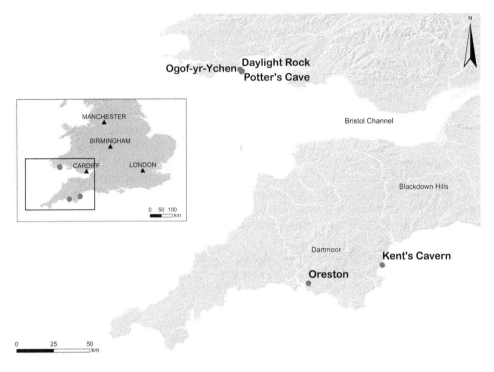

Figure 4.28 Distribution of Middle Mesolithic sites with human remains

practises; both sites, around 50 km apart, face towards open sea, which had encroached along the Channel embayment.

The dead of Caldey

Three caves were used to deposit the dead of Caldey – Daylight Rock, Potter's Cave and Ogof-yr-Ychen – can all be found along the northeastern limestone coastline of the island, facing not towards the rapidly encroaching sea, an important source of food in this area, but inland. The entrances to all face north, away from the sun, and the human remains were found well away from the entrances; at Ogof-yr-Ychen the majority of human remains appear to have been dropped down a shaft into the darkness (Conneller 2006). This is a change from the earlier preference for west-facing caves, orientated towards the setting sun, and may suggest changing understandings of, and metaphors for, death.

The Early Mesolithic settlement evidence from Caldey was discussed in the previous chapter. Fieldwork by Andrew David at Daylight Rock suggests settlement took place between c.8400 and 7800 cal BC, and while this is the only site on the island with radiometric dates, all other sites are dominated by Early Mesolithic microliths (David 2007). Dates for the human remains on the island, by contrast, mainly span 7600 to 6500 cal BC with a single outlier at Ogof-yr-Ychen dating to around 5600 cal BC. Caldey, once an area for settlement activities, seems to have become a place for the dead, where knowledge that it was used by past generations may have resulted in it becoming dedicated to the ancestors.

The most extensive collection of human remains comes from Ogof-yr-Ychen, excavated between June and December 1970 by Brother James van Nederveld. The cave is relatively inaccessible, with its mouth opening onto a vertical cliff face, though access that may have existed in the Early Holocene may have been removed by quarrying and the encroaching sea (David 2007). The cave consists of consists of four chambers (Figure 4.29), two accessed on the horizontal plane (though a chimney may also exist) and two accessed through a vertical shaft. Disarticulated remains of at least six individuals were recovered, most of which come from chambers 1 and 3, the shaft (van Nedervelde et al. 1973). Only individual C may have entered through the horizonal opening (David 2007, 39), though the dispersal of their remains across chambers 2 and 4 might also suggest they were dropped in from a chimney above. The span of dates indicates extremely long-lived practises focused on the shaft, extending across at least a millennium and a half (Meiklejohn et al. 2011). This practise is echoed at Potter's Cave, though this is not a shaft into the darkness but a very narrow cave unsuitable for habitation (Davies 1989). Here, the remains of two individuals were

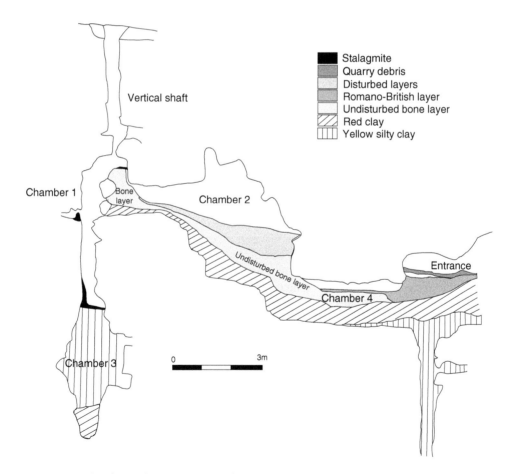

Figure 4.29 Ogof-yr-Ychen. (Redrawn after van Nedervelde et al. (1973))

found, represented by 'scattered' elements (Lacaille and Grimes 1956), an ulna and a metacarpal (Meiklejohn et al. 2011), their deposition separated by 1000 years. Daylight Rock cave is also extremely narrow (Lacaille and Grimes 1961); currently only one Mesolithic individual is known from the cave, though not all the human material has been dated (Meiklejohn et al. 2011). A few skull fragments, three mandibles and two vertebrae have been reported, though one mandible has a Romano-British date (Lacaille and Grimes 1956; Meiklejohn et al. 2011).

Rapid excavation and poor recording prevent a proper understanding of mortuary practises on Caldey. The position of the remains in the shaft at Ogof-yr-Ychen and the demonstration that these are isolated elements of different individuals is likely to indicate a multi-stage process of dealing with the dead, with defleshing/excarnation, possible circulation and final deposition down the shaft. Such complex and multi-stage processes have been recorded at sites on the continent such as la Chausee-Tirancourt (Ducrocq et al. 1996) and Grosse Ofnet (Orschiedt 2005). At Potter's Cave, Lacaille and Grimes (1956) report that the bones 'were scattered as the remains of other warm-blooded forms throughout the site'. Some however, seem to have been cemented in a stalagmite layer towards the back of the cave. Whether these are disarticulated elements or disturbed burials cannot be determined. At Daylight Rock the presence of the more robust skeletal elements and perforated cowrie shells (also found at the earlier cemetery site of Aveline's Hole) could suggest a ceremonial burial.

In south-west England, the site of Totty Pot, on the plateau above Gough's Cave, has a chimney and a north facing entrance. Two radiocarbon measurements on a femur and a humerus are very similar, suggesting they may derive from a single individual, probably an adult male. The nature of the excavation, and the subsequent destruction of many of the remains by the Leicestershire constabulary precludes any further understanding of mortuary practises at this site.

The first mortuary sites also appear on the southern coast, at Kent's Cavern and Oreston Third Bone Cave. Very little is known about the latter from which a human clavicle (dating to between 7900 and 7500 cal BC) was found amongst faunal material collected by workmen during quarrying in the first half of the 19th century (Pengelly 1872). More is known of Kent's Cavern, despite its early excavation, due to the meticulous work of Pengelly. The cave has two entrances, though unlike the other sites of this date both broadly face east. Two Mesolithic elements are now known from the cave, both recovered from the Vestibule, which was also the main focus of Upper Palaeolithic activity at the site. An ulna was recovered from this layer, the 'black band' (Schulting et al. 2015) and a maxilla from the overlying granular stalagmite (Meiklejohn et al. 2011). Both date to between c.7200 and 6900 cal BC. The ulna is distinguished by the presence of cut marks, made by a stone tool, and peri-mortem breakage, similar to the sort of fractures used to break bones for marrow. This confirms previous arguments that isolated elements in British caves dating to the Mesolithic do on occasions at least represent evidence for intentional practises of disarticulation (Conneller 2006). What exactly this practise represents though is difficult to understand. Evidence exists in the Mesolithic record both for funerary processing as part of a multi-stage mortuary ritual (at la Chausée-Tirancourt) and cannibalism (at Grotte des Perratts) (Boulestin 1999; Ducrocq et al. 1996). Given that cave environments often erode the surface of human bones, cut-marks may be under-represented.

Human remains from the Middle Mesolithic show continuity with previous prac-tises, but there are also new elements. While our data-set is obviously limited by reason of taphonomy, caves as far as can be ascertained remained a preferred location for the dead. Most caves employed have evidence for Pleistocene fauna, if not also earlier human occupation. There is less focus on the interment of large numbers of individuals, and instead, single bodies or isolated elements, which may have under-gone secondary processing, were inserted into caves or shafts into the ground. Death many have been a multi-stage process, and parts of some humans may have circulated with, or been consumed by, the living. Intriguingly, there may have been a shift in understandings of dead, with a move away from the west-facing caves of the Early Mesolithic that may have been connected with the setting sun and metaphors of the cyclical nature of life. In the Middle Mesolithic, caves mostly faced north, away from the sun, with some remains deposited into shafts, into the darkness.

5   The forgotten people

The Late Mesolithic, 7000–5000 BC

Just as Star Carr has (erroneously) come to be seen as representative of the way of life of the earliest Mesolithic groups, so the midden sites of Oronsay have come to stand for the adaptions of the Late Mesolithic. This too is misleading. The lives of people over the last three millennia of the Mesolithic were extraordinarily diverse. There is increasing evidence for marine adaptations the west coast of Scotland, where the last centuries of the Mesolithic mark a concern with new practises of ostentatious middening; in the east, rivers and estuaries were important for salmon fishers and whale-hunters. But in many other areas, people probably had little to do with the sea. The greatest densities of Mesolithic sites in Northern England come from the Pennines (Figure 5.1). These were probably connected to lowland sites through river systems, and human remains from the Trent indicate a fully terrestrial diet with no evidence for marine protein. In the south, people moved along the Thames and its tributaries as they had for millennia, skeletal remains showing little evidence for a marine diet, even near its estuary; small hunting groups camped in the rock shelters of the high Weald. In the southwest, people evinced a fascination with colourful springs.

In this book, the Late Mesolithic has been divided into two. This chapter deals with the period 7000–5000 BC; the following chapter looks at the changes associated with end of the Mesolithic. In many ways, the period 7000–5000 BC is the hardest to characterise. It lacks some of the unifying features of the preceding periods as regional trajectories become increasingly divergent. It is not so typologically distinctive as previous periods, which makes undated sites more difficult to place.

While its people remain elusive, this was a time of major shifts in climate and landscape, some relatively short in duration, others more permanent. Sea-level rise was particularly acute on a human scale in the seventh millennium BC, with around 36,000 km^2 of Doggerland inundated over this time and the full severing of Britain from the continent (Sturt et al. 2013). In the same millennium a short-lived climatic deterioration occurred, known as the 8.2 event (8200 cal BP or 6250 cal BC) (Alley et al. 1997). There have been suggestions that populations declined, at least in more marginal areas of Britain, in response (Wicks and Mithen 2014). Towards the end of the 8.2 event, a second disaster struck: The Storegga Slide tsunami at c.6200 cal BC, which would have devastated coastal communities and groups who camped along the lower reaches of rivers in the northeast. The tsunami is likely to have killed many, as waves more than 5 m high swamped coastal sites in the northeast and reached as far as Norfolk.

The severing of Britain from the continent has long been seen as marking a period of isolation (Jacobi 1976); Britain lacks the trapezes and transverse arrowheads and

DOI: 10.4324/9781003228103-5

the new technologies of regular blade production through indirect percussion that swept across the continent and arrived in Northern France and Belgium at around 6200–6000 cal BC (Marchand and Perrin 2017; Perrin et al. 2009). While Western Britain continued to be characterised by sophisticated sea-faring skills in this period, the devastation wreaked on eastern coastal communities by the tsunami may have had an impact on marine voyaging in the east. These eastern groups were the people who had cultural connections with continental Europe in the Early and Middle Mesolithic and may have voyaged between the archipelago of islands that were the last remnants of Doggerland. With these people and skills lost, perhaps coupled with a newfound mistrust of the sea amongst eastern groups, it may have been many generations before continental connections were reforged.

Vegetation and climate

Following the expansion of alder, and the arrival of the slow-spreading species ash and lime, vegetation across the country was varied. In the south and east, dense lime forests gradually replaced oak from around 6500 cal BC (Bennett 1989). Lime woods, with their dense canopies, support relatively little understorey growth which is important browse for deer. Fewer plant and animal resources may have made these areas less important foci for people (Spikins 1999). Mixed oak woodlands remained important over much of the rest of the country south of the Tay. These, apart from the densest, included understorey plants, which were attractive to animals, though some

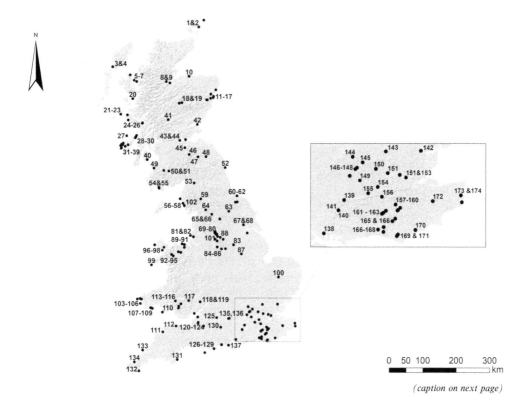

(caption on next page)

Figure 5.1 Sites discussed in the chapter (1. Long Howe, 2. Links House, Stronsay, 3. Northton, 4. Traigh a Teampuill, 5. An Corran, 6. Loch a Sguirr, 7. Sand, 8. Tarradale, The Black Isle, 9. Castle St, Inverness, 10. Silvercrest, Lesmurdie Rd, 11. Sands of Forvie, 12. Sandingstones, 13. St Paul Street, Aberdeen, 14. Garthdee Rd, 15. Milltimber, 16. Nethermills, 17. Warren Field, Crathes, 18. Chest of Dee, 19. Caochanan Ruadha, 20. Camas Daraich, 21. Fiskary Bay, 22. Criet Dubh, 23. Ulva Cave, 24. Druimvargie, 25. Raschoille, 26. MacArthur Cave, 27. Staosnaig, 28. Lussa Wood I, 29. Lealt Bay, 30. North Carn, 31. Kilellan Farm, 32. Newton, 33. Gleann Mor, 34. Rockside, 35.Coulererach, 36. Aoradh, 37. Kindrochid, 38. Bolsay Farm, 39. Rubha Port an t-Seilich, 40. Auchareoch, 41. Ben Lawers, 42. Morton A, 43. Inveravon, 44. Castlandhill, 45. Garvald Burn, 46. Manor Bridge, 47. Rink, 48. Springwood Park, 49. Littlehill Bridge, Girvan, 50. Starr, 51. Smittons, 52. Low Hauxley, 53. Stainton West, 54. Low Clone, 55. Barsalloch, 56. St Bees, 57. Drigg, 58. Monks Moor, 59. Wickers Gill, 60. Upleatham, 61. Urra Moor, 62. White Gill, 63. Topcliff on Swale, 64. Kingsdale Head, 65. Malham Tarn, 66. Blubberhouses Moor, 67. Holme on Spalding Moor, 68. Risby Warren, 69. White Hill North, 70. Red Ratcher, 71. Rocher Moss, 72. Dean Clough, 73. Rishworth Drain 2, 74. Dan Clough, 75. Pule Bents, 76. Windy Hill, 77. Readycon Dean, 78. Broomhead Moor V, 79. Grange Farm, 80. Harry Hut, 81. Formby, 82. Lunt Meadows, 83. Thorpe Common, 84. Beeley Moor, 85. Stoney Low, 86. Lismore Fields, 87. Staythorpe, 88. Dunford Bridge A, 89. Splash Point, Rhyll, 90. Gop Cave, 91. Fynnon Beuno, 92. Brenig, 93. Llyn Aled Isaf, 94. Cwm Penamnen, 95. Roman Bridge, 96. Capel Eithen, 97. Newborough Warren, 98. Porth Ruffydd, 99. Ynys Enlli (Bardsey), 100. Two Mile Bottom, 101. Badger Slacks, 102. Williamson's Moss, 103. Nab Head II, 104. Llanuwas, 105. Poinzcastle, 106. Penpant, 107. Ogof-yr-Ychen, 108. Potter's Cave, 109. Lydstep, 110. Fox Hole, Paviland, 111. Westward Ho! 112. Hawcombe Head, 113. Waun Fignen Felen, 114. Pant Sychbant, 115. Craig-y-Llyn, 116. Cwm Selsig, Mynydd Ystradffernol, 117. Gwernvale, 118. Madawg Shelter, 119. King Arthur's Cave, 120. Goldcliff, 121. Birdcombe, 122. Gorsey Bigbury, 123. Totty Pott, 124. Langley's Lane, 125. Cherhill, 126. Portland I and Culverwell, 127. Blashenwell, 128. Christchurch Harbour, 129. Mother Siller's Channel, 130. Blick Mead, 131. Little Darmouth Farm, 132. Poldowrian, 133. Trevose Head, 134. Gwithian, 135. Wawcott III, 136. Avington VI, 137. Bouldner Cliff, 138. Fort Wallington, 139. Farnham, 140. Oakhanger III, 141. Oakhanger VIII, 142. Eton Rowing Course, 143. Hengrove Farm, 144. Misbourne Viaduct, 145. Tolpitts Lane site B101, 146. Stratford's Yard, 147. Low Farm, Fulmer, 148. North Park Farm, Bletchingly, 149. Tank Hill Rd, 150. Fetcham, 151. Canning Town Eyot, 152. Orchard Hill, 153. West Heath, 154. Broxbourne 105, 155. Tilbury, 156. Langford, 157. Stonewall Park, Chiddingstone, 158. High Rocks, 159. Rocks Wood, Withyham, 160. Eridge, 161. Stone Hill, Rocks, 162. Tilgate Wood, Balcombe, 163. Chiddinglye Rocks, 164. The Hermitage, High Hurstwood, 165. The Rocks, Rocksfield, 166. West Hill, Pycombe, 167. Streat Lane, 168. Falmer Stadium, 169. Selmeston, 170. Bexhill, 171. Alfriston, 172. Finglesham, 173. Westcliff, 174. Beechbrook Wood, Westwell)

upland areas such as the North York Moors seem to have still been relative open with areas of birch woodland and grassland (Albert and Innes 2015), and the chalk landscapes of the Wolds too may have remained fairly open (Bush 1988). Further north, rich oak/hazel/birch woodlands flourished in the lowlands and pine woods in the uplands. In the far north, birch still held sway (Tipping 1994).

Within this broad picture, there was considerable variation, with soil types and altitude producing important differences in the makeup of woodlands. Alder, for instance, thrived in damp peat of river valleys (Figure 5.2) as sea-level rose and rivers backed up, but could not out-compete oak and elm in other areas unless disturbance was a factor (Bennett 1986). Chalk areas may have been less densely wooded (French et al. 2003).

Figure 5.2 Alder carr at Rostherne Mere, Cheshire. This vegetation type became more common as alder expanded and wetlands increased (copyright Barry Taylor)

Ash thrived on calcareous soils, where it began to replace hazel (Bennett 1989), and pine lingered on the limestone of the Northern Pennines long after it had been outcompeted elsewhere in the country (Simmons 1996). Local factors are likely to have been significant, with beaver activity, local tree falls, lightning strike, disease and disturbance by humans (see below) creating unique combinations of woodland species that have no modern analogues. In these woodlands, clearings and paths would have been important. Brown (1997) highlights the importance of clearings created by tree falls in creating human spaces, and the tree throws themselves were often used as foci by the people who inhabited these spaces (see e.g. Bishop 2008). Whether created by tree fall or human burning practises (Simmons 1996) clearings became foci of human action (Davies et al. 2005), and paths created spaces through routinized action.

These woodlands provided plant food. Hazelnuts were still very common, though there have been some suggestions of a reduction following 6000 cal BC (Ashmore 2004). Of other plants, we have rare glimpses. Crab apples were eaten in the autumn. Lesser celandine bulbs were collected and roasted at Staosnaig and Northton (Bishop et al. 2013). Hawthorn berries were eaten in both England and Scotland (Bishop et al. 2013; Palmer 1999), and sloes are found on three sites in England and Wales. Elder and Dogwood seeds from Goldcliff (Bell 2007) may suggest these berries, too, were eaten. Vetch seeds can be roasted and eaten, and fat hen can be made into flour. Both have been recovered in Scotland (Bishop et al. 2013).

The natural woodland succession was disrupted by two events during this period. The first was climatic: The 8.2 event (at 8200 cal BP or 6250 cal BC) was a severe but short-lived climatic downturn. First glimpsed in the Greenland Ice Cores (Alley et al. 1997), this was the most severe climatic deterioration of the Holocene, with a suggested temperature change of around 40% of that of the Younger Dryas. This appears to have been caused by a pulse of melt-water from the North American Laurentide Ice Sheet, which disrupted the thermohaline circulation system, a mechanism that results in warmer temperatures for Northwest Europe (Alley and Agustdottir 2005). Data from the ice cores suggest the 8.2 event lasted around 160 years, with a 69-year period in which climate was consistently colder (Thomas et al. 2007). It is difficult to gauge both how the effect of events recorded in Greenland played out in Britain and to produce a precise correlation between this ice core date and terrestrial records. Some evidence, for example, suggests an extended period of cooling in Northwest Europe of greater length than the 160 years suggested by ice core data (Thomas et al. 2007). In some areas of Northwest Europe, there is evidence for a reduction in thermipholous vegetation in the later part of the seventh millennium BC, with data from the west of Ireland suggesting contraction of hazel and oak and expansion of birch and pine (Ghilardi and O'Connell 2013; Huang 2002). In Western Scotland there is evidence of the expansion of herbaceous pollen on Mull (Edwards 2004) and Coll (Wicks and Mithen 2014). In other areas, this event may have been of insufficient duration and severity to have a marked effect on vegetation.

Melting of the Laurentide Ice sheet seems also to have caused significant surges in sea-level at this time. A single jump of between 2.5 and 4.7 m was recorded in the Ythan estuary in Eastern Scotland between c.6500 and 6200 cal BC (Smith et al. 2013). In Southwest Scotland three episodes of accelerated sea-level rise were noted, the first an increase of between 0.24 and 0.45 m between 6810 and 6690 cal BC, the second of between 0.67 and 0.73 m at 6545–6515 cal BC and the last of between 0.37 and 0.43 m between 6370 and 6285 cal BC (Lawrence et al. 2016). The time scale of these pulses is likely to be several months or a year (Weninger et al. 2008). The presence of episodes of rapid acceleration in sea-level rise is likely to have made this process perceptible on a human scale, particularly in the low-lying area of Doggerland, which was rapidly shrinking at this time (Sturt et al. 2013). Models vary, but the narrowing land that connected Britain to the continent was probably breached around 7000 cal BC, initially leaving a narrow stretch of water to cross, before Doggerland was transformed into an archipelago of islands, many connected at low tide, extending from Norfolk to the Netherlands (Figure 5.3). To the north lay the larger area of Dogger Island, which may have still maintained populations at this time (Weninger et al. 2006). By around 6000 cal BC, probably only Dogger Island remained, and this was submerged over the course of the following centuries (Sturt et al. 2013). Sea-level rise may have also led to an event that had catastrophic effects across the region, the Storrega slide tsunami (Smith et al. 2013) (see Box 5.1).

Northeast Britain

Settlement during the Late Mesolithic in Eastern Scotland and Northumberland is concentrated along rivers and estuaries, with locations for salmon fishing favoured and showing long histories (Figure 5.4). Evidence for small-scale but repeated visits to the high uplands increases; many of these sites are located on important routeways between east and west. Estuarine sites were important, with some shell-middens dating to this period. Coastal occupation seems to have consisted of small-scale but repeated

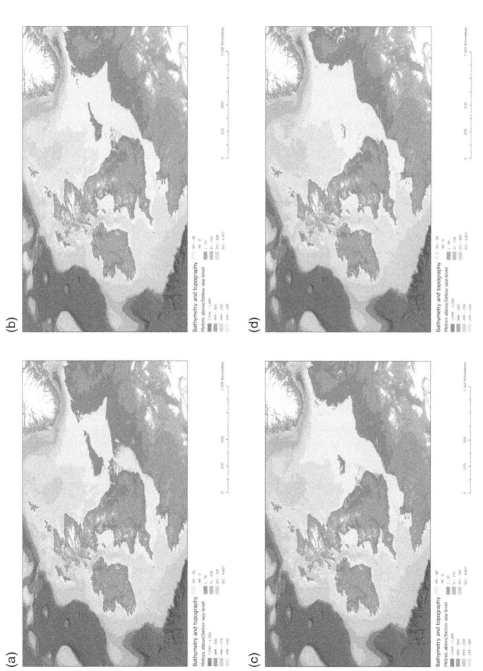

Figure 5.3 The inundation of Doggerland: 7000 BC (top left), 6500 BC (top right), 6000 BC (bottom left), 5500 BC (bottom right) (Image Fraser Sturt. Bathymetry provided by EMODnet Bathymetry Consortium (2020): EMODnet Digital Bathymetry (DTM). https://doi.org/ 10.12770/bb6a87dd-e579-4036-abe1-e649cea9881a, Topography produced using Copernicus data and information funded by the European Union (EU-DEM))

Box 5.1 The Storegga slide tsunami

Around 6150 cal BC, a submarine shelf off the coast of Norway collapsed. This was one of the largest submarine slides ever recorded, affecting an area of 95,000 km^2 and a sediment volume of between 24,000–32,000 km^3 (Haflidason et al. 2004). The collapse caused a wall of water to surge through the North Sea. Estimates of run-up (the height above msl that the water reaches on land) suggest 25 m on Shetland and 5 m on mainland Scotland (Smith et al. 2004). Thick layers of sand laid down by the wave have been recorded within estuarine sediments or peat from Norway, the Faroes, and Northeastern Britain (Dawson 1994; Dawson et al. 1988). The effects of the tsunami have been noted as far south as the southern North Sea (Gaffney et al. 2020). Local impact would have been highly variable dependent on topography, but the morphology of certain valleys may have led to the wave being channelled far inland (Walker et al. 2020).

For Mesolithic groups, probably concentrated in coastal areas, with larger sites close to productive estuaries, the effects would have been catastrophic. This would not simply encompass the casualties of the initial wave; equipment and fixed fishing facilities would have been destroyed and shellfish beds covered by sand. There are suggestions that the tsunami may have happened in late autumn; stored foods, prepared for the winter may have been lost, leading to famine (Weninger et al. 2008). Above all, familiar coastal and estuarine landscapes would have been reconfigured. Weninger et al. (2008, 16) suggest the tsunami caused either total submergence of Dogger Island, the last remnant of Doggerland, or that loss of population and resources may have led to its final abandonment. More recent work suggests Dogger Island itself at least may have survived the event (Figure 5.3, Gaffney et al. 2020). There may, though, have been a loss in faith in an area, at a time of rapid jumps in sea-level, when a tsunami might be interpreted as a malevolent supernatural force and as the affordances of familiar landscapes changed. The repeated occupation of a sheltered gulley at an estuarine location at Castle Street, Inverness (Wordsworth 1985) did not continue above tsunami deposits (Dawson et al. 1990), perhaps suggesting people configured new ways of inhabiting these landscapes.

visits to the shore, with small shelters excavated at Morton A, Fife and small shell-middens at Low Hauxley in Northumberland (Figure 5.4).

Traditions of building changed: The large, uniform pit houses of the Middle Mesolithic were no longer erected; instead a variety of smaller post-built structures, lightweight shelters and larger irregular-shaped structures are found. Only at Silvercrest, Lesmurdie Rd, may something similar to the Middle Mesolithic buildings found. Here, the later of the two structures (discussed in chapter 4), a circle of seven posts 4.6 m in diameter may date to between 6200 and 6000 cal BC. Its location, next to a similar structure build over 1000 years earlier perhaps indicates an interest in ancestral places, though the possibility that the Mesolithic dates are residual elements

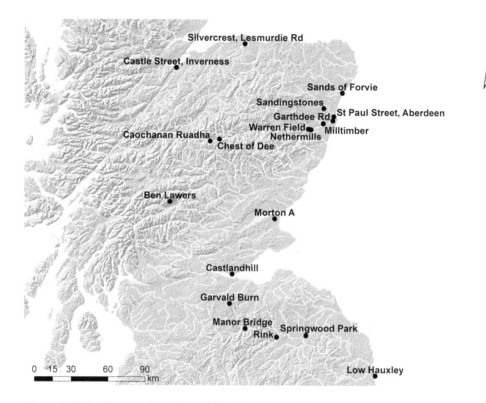

Figure 5.4 Northeastern Late Mesolithic sites discussed

incorporated within a later structure remains. However, a concern with the past is evident at other sites of previous activity in Northeast Scotland. At both Warren Field and Milltimber, large pits continued to be excavated during the first half of the seventh millennium BC and the sixth millennium BC.

The compositions of woodlands in this region was varied as several species reached their latitudinal tolerances. At 7000 cal BC, much of the southern part of the region was characterised by birch-hazel woodland, but by 6750 cal BC elm and oak began to colonise the Tweed Valley at the expense of birch, though this persisted in lake edge and fen communities (Tipping 2010a). By the end of the Mesolithic, oak woodlands with significant representation of elm and hazel covered the lowlands as far as the Great Glen (Edwards et al. 2018), with birch and pine at higher altitudes. Alder started to spread into damp valleys by the end of the period.

Much of the uplands is likely to have had tree cover at this time. Estimates for altitude of the tree-line in Northern England and Southern Scotland are varied, but may be up to 750 m (Turner and Hodgson 1991), with Tipping (1997) suggesting even oak grew at 620 m in some areas, while there are records for pine at 930 m in the Cairngorms (Edwards et al. 2018); fossil tree stumps, preserved in peat have been found at up to 790 m (Bennett 1996). In the high uplands, a shrub landscape of juniper, hawthorn and willow grew (Tipping 2010a).

Along the rivers

Early Mesolithic pioneer groups had camped along the rivers during their first incursions in the north, but from the Late Mesolithic these sites multiply. Extensive lithic scatters have been found along many rivers in the east, with the Dee in particular seeing extensive occupation: From its upland tributaries as at Caochanan Ruadha (Warren et al. 2018, see below) to sites near the mouth of the river at Garthdee Rd, where a small lithic scatter and a pit packed with oak and hazel charcoal and sealed with stones dates to 5630–5380 cal BC (Murray and Murray 2014). Along the middle regions of the Dee, extensive lithic scatters have been recorded, and structural evidence has been found at excavated sites (Wickham-Jones et al. in press). Mesolithic evidence is extensive along several other rivers, and the estuaries of the Forth, Avon and the Ythen seem particularly important.

Nethermills Farm, Crathes exemplifies these large, dense sites on the Dee. This is located on the Camphill Terrace of the river, which by the time of occupation was a dry area, rarely subject to inundation (Wickham-Jones et al. in press). Here, several campaigns of fieldwalking, from the early 20th century onwards, have recorded evidence for extensive occupation. In the 1970s, Grieve collected Mesolithic material from five adjacent fields that stretch for 2 km along the banks of the river. A recent fieldwalking campaign between 2008 and 2012 by the North East Scotland Archaeological Research Society recorded nearly 10,000 lithic artefacts, while excavations by Kenworthy yielded around 30,000 artefacts (Wickham-Jones et al. 2016). Kenworthy's excavations between 1978 and 1981, when an area of 110 m^2 was excavated, also located structural features. These included a circle of pits c.4.5 m in diameter into which posts had been cut, which he compared to the house then recently excavated at Mount Sandel (Woodman 1985).

Reassessment of the archive and renewed radiocarbon dating has not been able confirm the integrity of Kenworthy's structure (Wickham-Jones et al. 2016), though, given the recent finds of similar sized structures in northeastern Britain, it cannot be discounted. The features have been heavily disturbed, both by ploughing and by animal burrowing. Radiometric measurements on bulked wood undertaken at the time of excavation confirm this disturbance, and the new dating programme has been hampered by the discard of the most suitable samples. The possible structure has returned a wide variety of dates from the Mesolithic to the Bronze Age. The two securely Mesolithic measurements, both on oak, fall into the mid/late sixth millennium BC. A second potential structure was also identified to the south of the first, less substantial and subcircular in form. A series of pits, post-holes and stakeholes were also located across the site. Many features include lithic material, burnt hazelnut shells and wood charcoal, particularly oak that seems to have been used for the posts.

A recent test pitting exercise undertaken by the Mesolithic Deeside project excavated 102 2 × 2 m test pits and a larger 12 × 3 m trench (Wickham-Jones et al. in press). Four hundred thirty-three pieces of worked flint were recovered during this exercise, mainly from the ploughzone. While considerable disturbance from agricultural activities had occurred, a small number of cut features were recorded. Two determinations on willow and birch charcoal from a shallow pit was dated to 6830–6640 cal BC (7868 ± 31 BP, SUERC-93093; 7887 ± 31 BP, SUERC-93097). The picture from Kenworthy's excavations and the more recent fieldwalking and test pitting exercises is of a significant place that was revisited over a long period.

Warren (2001) has highlighted the riparian focus of Late Mesolithic settlement in the east, with numerous lithic scatters found along the terraces of several rivers. A number of surveys have noted that Mesolithic artefacts are found within 100 m of the river banks while later Prehistoric material was scattered more broadly across the landscape (Bradley and Batey 2000; Kenney 1993). There may be biases at work here, and the more recent surveys of the Biggar Archaeology Group, further south, have located sites well away from major water sources (Ward 2017). However, both Wickham-Jones (1994) and Warren (2001) note that many Mesolithic sites do seem to cluster in good areas for fishing. Several concentrations in the Banchory/Crathes area (including Nethermills Farm) are at the junction of the Dee and the Water of Feugh, an important salmon river. Further south on the Tweed, at Dryburgh, where Early and Late Mesolithic material has been recovered, and Manor Bridge with Middle and Late Mesolithic microliths, are now a series of shallow pools where salmon can be easily caught. Springwood Park and Rink, large scatters of Mesolithic material on the Tweed (30,000 lithic artefacts have been collected from Rink) are also located close to the junctions of important salmon rivers (Warren 2001). Noticeable is the persistent presence of Early Mesolithic microliths at many of these sites suggesting they re-presented key foci for millennia. They may represent true persistent places (*sensu;*Schlanger 1992), that by virtue of certain structural affordances, such as the presence and facility for catching migratory fish, were repeatedly revisited.

Warren (2001, 143) has enumerated the sheer quantity of salmon in these rivers: In the early 19th century, around 125,000 salmon were caught every year on the Tweed. On the Tay, annual figures were in the region of 100,000, and fish of 22–27 kg were frequently caught. Even small rivers could yield large numbers. Salmon migrate upstream to breed, and on this journey, they often rest in small pools, as at Dryburgh and Manor Bridge. Migration times vary between rivers, and some migration takes place throughout the year, but spring and early autumn are important. Also migrating through these rivers were trout and eels; the latter can reach up to a metre in length. None of these sites preserve faunal remains, and fish bones are particularly delicate; however, these migratory fish and the presence of plants and animals and birds also drawn to these area may explain their persistence. Waisted pebbles, which may have been used as net weights or line sinkers, are a common find in these areas, with a particular cluster known at Dryburgh Mains (Warren 2001). These rivers are also likely to have formed important routeways, particularly in the Late Mesolithic as dense forests made lowland areas less easily traversable.

Into the uplands

New evidence is emerging of the extent of exploitation of upland landscapes. While upland evidence is known from the Middle Mesolithic in Scotland from sites such as Daer Reservoir at c.350 m asl, the extent and altitude of occupation increased. A series of sites have been found in the Cairgorms, including Caochanan Ruadha, located at 540 m asl (Warren et al. 2018). This is an area that may have been close to the tree-line with light woodland of pine and probably birch in sheltered areas and open grass and heathland on slopes. As Warren and colleagues note, visits to this inhospitable area took place at around the same time as the 8.2 ka event (Figure 5.5).

Two small trenches located Mesolithic material at Caochanan Ruadha. In trench 5, a series of charcoal spreads were located; short-lived charcoal of birch and alder

Figure 5.5 Excavations at Caochanan Ruadha (copyright Graeme Warren, UCD school of
        Archaeology)

(the latter unlikely to have been common locally) gave radiocarbon dates with a
weighted mean of 6073–6008 cal BC. A more substantial fire-setting was present in
trench 4, a pit hearth. Two dates on yew twigs from this feature combine to indicate
occupation between 6211 and 6061 cal BC. The radiocarbon determinations from the
different trenches are not compatible and indicate a gap of occupation of between −4
and 87 years (68.2% confidence). Repeated occupation in the same location indicates
this was a familiar place and that routes through this landscape were well-known
(Warren et al. 2018).

Quantities of lithic material from Caochanan Ruadha were small, 16 from trench 5
and 132 from trench 4. These seem to have been heavily curated, with cores and some
tools retained when people left the area. Of the 28 pieces sampled, nearly half show
wear-traces, showing high levels of use of the material available. The lithics in trench 4
cluster round the hearth and show a very sharp fall-off, indicating the ghost of a small
oval shelter, measuring 3 m by 2.2 m, that has not left any structural remains (Warren
et al. 2018). The lithic assemblage within this structure is dominated by microliths,
some with evidence for use as projectiles, with microburins also present, indicating
retooling round the hearth. Micro-wear analysis shows the hunting and processing of
animals, but also a craft signature, with working of siliceous plants and hide perhaps
relating to the repair of clothing or transportation equipment, such as bags and
basketry.

A second area where exploitation of the high mountainous regions has been un-covered is on the slopes of Ben Lawers at 630 m asl, on a bank of moraine above Edramucky Burn, overlooking Loch Tay (Atkinson 2016). Mesolithic material was located at two separate areas along the stream. The larger assemblage came from trench P16, in an area disturbed by later activity, where 988 pieces of lithic material were recovered, mostly quartz, but small quantities of flint were present too, the latter imported as finished tools. A pit was found, which contained a cache of unworked and tested quartz nodules and a few quartz flakes, indicating people intended to return, and that like Caochanan Ruadha, this area was a regular routeway. Charcoal from this pit came from birch, heather, hazel, shrub willow and sorbus sp. (the latter probably rowan, given the altitude), painting a picture of local scrub woodland. The birch charcoal gave a date of 7200–6700 cal BC (OxA-8967).

The more substantial evidence from Ben Lawers is echoed by that from excavations at the Chest of Dee, 8 km to the east of Caochanan Ruadha (Wickham-Jones et al. 2020). Here, a series of hearths and pits were found along the banks of the Dee close to its confluence with Geldie Burn. While Early Mesolithic microliths were found at the site and there are a couple of Middle Mesolithic dates from a fire pit, the majority of the radio-carbon dated features belong to the Late Mesolithic. Amongst these there appears to have been a particular concentration of activity in the first half of the seventh millennium BC, with only occasional visits thereafter in the later seventh and later fifth millennia.

Occupation was concentrated on the northern bank of the river, stratified within alluvial silts (Figure 5.6). While test pitting and trenching sampled a c.500 m stretch of the bank, occupation dating to the first half of the seventh millennium was con-centrated in area F, an area being actively eroded by the river with pits and occupation

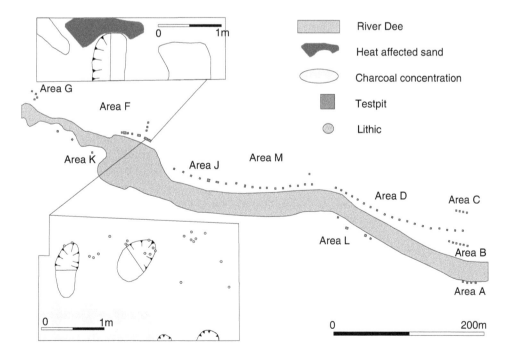

Figure 5.6 Excavations at the Chest of Dee

horizons exposed in section. Charcoal evidence indicates that by the start of the seventh millennium there had been a shift from the open birch woodland exploited for firewood during the Middle Mesolithic to pine forests. Despite being an upland area, the site would be well below the tree-line.

Area F was densest both in lithics and occupation features. In the seventh millennium, levels of one of the small (4 × 2 m) trenches in this area five charcoal spreads were exposed in close proximity, surrounded by a moderate-sized scatter of lithic material of nearly 600 pieces comprising both flint and a substantial assemblage of rhyolite. This latter material may be relatively local and was knapped to produce blades. Tools were used in this area and indicate varied tasks: A scraper, an awl, three microdenticulates and several retouched pieces. A large cooking pit, measuring nearly a metre across which dates to this period was located in a nearby trench. This contained pine charcoal and burnt stones and seems to have been used at least twice. These features, used for food preparation, are common in the Late and Final Mesolithic, particularly in the uplands. Several seem to show signs of reuse, suggesting they came to represent fixed points in the landscape and foci for subsequent reoccupation.

The evidence from the Chest of Dee shows many contrasts with that from Caochanan Ruadha (Wickham-Jones et al. 2020). Features are more common at the former and the lithic assemblage is larger and with evidence for use in a wide range of activities. By contrast the assemblage from Caochanan Ruadha is small, dominated by microliths and lacking cores, all indicating of a brief stopover, probably in the context of hunting activities. The Chest of Dee appears a repeatedly used, seasonal campsite, perhaps a base from which more remote areas such as Caochanan Ruadha were visited.

Other upland Mesolithic sites are known, though at lower altitudes than Caochanan Ruadha, Ben Lawers and the Chest of Dee. Most of this evidence comes further south in the Southern Uplands, as a result of the work of the Biggar Archaeology Group: Daer Reservoir 1, where Middle Mesolithic occupation was recorded, also shows evidence for visits in the Late Mesolithic between 5880 and 5630 cal BC (AA-47770); a second site at the reservoir dates to 7175–6695 cal BC (AA-30355). Another BAG site at Weston Farm at c.240 m asl, a large complex lithic scatter with several features, has dates from the first half of the seventh millennium BC (Ward 2017). This work emphasises the persistent use of the Southern Uplands during the Mesolithic. All these sites have good quantities of lithics as well as pits and other features, indicating more substantial occupation of these areas, in contrast to the ephemeral evidence and small, curated assemblage from Caochanan Ruadha.

Further north, at 150 m asl, is Standingstones on the western slopes of Tyrebagger Hill, overlooking Aberdeen and to the sea beyond, though views at the time of occupation may have been obscured by the birch-hazel woodland that grew in the Dee-Don uplands (Dingwall et al. 2019). At this site, located close to a spring, whose waters drain into the Don, a series of pits were discovered, arranged in a semi-circle around 3.5 m in diameter. The arrangement of features recalls Fife Ness (see chapter 4), though the diameter of the pits is rather larger: The pits overlap with a hollow, though the relationship between the two could not be determined. There is a similar ambiguity as to what the pits represent: Their arrangement suggests a structure, but no post-pipes were noted, and the fills of the pits are rich in lithics (often burnt) and burnt hazelnut shells, possibly midden material or hearth sweepings, given the presence of refits between the pits and the hollow. All pits have a layer of charcoal in their basal fills. The hollow also holds burnt material, hazelnut shells and burnt flints. Five radiocarbon dates from the pits, and the hollow indicate occupation probably took place in the first two centuries of the seventh millennium. A single radiocarbon date on a hazelnut shell from the hollow is an outlier and might indicate later visits between 6740 and 6600 cal BC (7825 ± 30 BP; SUERC-57937). The lithic assemblage, made on beach pebble flint, is dominated by microliths and more particularly by evidence for their production. Fifty-nine microburins have been recovered, two microlith preforms and 57 microliths, most of which are broken; this appears to have been a site where gearing up and repairing of composite tools was a major task. Six scrapers and a couple of truncations indicate processing activities also took place. This range of tools and the presence of pits probably indicate a short-term residential site used as a base for forays into the wider landscape.

More specialised activity is present in the far north, at Oliclett, near Wick in Caithness (Pannett and Baines 2006). Here, a number of small natural mounds rise above the wetland, just to the north of Loch of Yarrows. The mounds were foci for small-scale visits, with the assemblage from mound A, in particular showing evidence for repeated episodes of microlith manufacture and retooling. In the Late Mesolithic, this was an area of springs, streams and lakes with areas of open woodland or scrub of hazel, birch, rowan and willow, as well as areas of grassland and fen. These seem small, specialised camps, representing logistical forays for fowling and hunting into wetland areas on the edge of the uplands.

While upland sites have invariably been interpreted as hunting camps, the activities in this region appear more varied and include structural evidence. Only the highest upland sites such as Caochanan Ruadha seem ephemeral camps. They may also have been located on important routeways: Caochanan Ruadha, The Chest of Dee, Ben Lawers and the Biggar Gap sites are on or close to obvious valley paths and watersheds. The Biggar Gap was initially suggested by Lacaille (1954) to be an important Mesolithic routeway between the two sides of the country and the work of the Biggar Archaeology group which has focused on addressing this issue (Ward 2012, 2017) has successfully demonstrated this is the case.

And down to the sea: Coasts and estuaries

Coasts and estuaries were dynamic landscapes: Sea-levels rose and fell, estuaries shifted positions and dune systems developed, creating salt marshes, back-swamps and mud-flats. These processes affected how people understood and inhabited these regions, but also impacted on the preservation and visibility of sites. Seventh millennium coastal sites may have been drowned by rising sea-levels, and the destructive impact of the Storega Slide tsunami at around 6200 cal BC (see Box 5.1) This may also have dented faith in coastal occupation in some areas (Weninger et al. 2008).

Sixth millennium sites should be less affected by these issues and coastal sites of this period have been recorded but remain rare. Morton is the best-known example (see below), and this site seems to represent numerous, small scale visits (Coles 1971), as do the small accumulations of shells at Low Hauxley in Northumberland (Waddington and Bonsall 2016). Estuarine sites, or sites along what would have been marine inlets at times of high sea-level, such as the Forth, are more common, though less visible in estuarine areas now masked by urban conurbations. As outlined above, Mesolithic sites are numerous along the Dee, but few are known from Aberdeen. These all appear small, as at St Paul Street, where a small scatter with a possible hearth seems to represent a single episode of occupation (Kenworthy 1982). In other urban areas, the opposite has occurred; more is known of the Mesolithic of the Edinburgh region due to development-funded excavations.

Some estuarine sites in the region seem to have attracted repeated occupation. The generation of the large shell-midden at Inveravon (see chapter 6) seem to have started in the sixth millennium, while further north, the earliest dates from what appears to be a large midden at Tarradale on The Black Isle in the Beauly Firth belong to the seventh millennium (Grant 2018). At Castle Street, Inverness, several lenses of grey silt and sand seemed to indicate several visits in the late seventh millennium (Wordsworth 1985). The assemblages are all microlith dominated, and only one hearth was located. Occupation of this favoured place ceased following the Storega Slide Tsunami (Dawson et al. 1990). Further to the west, at the estuary of the Ythan, numerous scatters of lithic material have been collected and excavated from the Sands of Forvie (Warren 2001). Some of these lithic scatters seemingly represent small, discrete areas; others are more substantial, but may represent palimpsests. One major activity at Forvie seems to have been the procurement of beach flint, but Warren also highlights the rich resources of this area, with access to migratory fish, sea-fish, shellfish and water birds. The results of the micro-wear also indicate the importance of plant processing (Warren 2006). Most of these northern estuarine sites seem small-scale, often areas of repeated occupation and varied in their focus. They appear similar to coastal sites, as at Morton (see below), where repeated, ephemeral visits seem to have occurred (Coles 1983).

Further south, estuaries, particularly sheltered inlets may have seen more sub-stantial evidence of occupation. Structural evidence is present at on non-midden sites at Castlelandhill, where a series of pits and shelters were excavated on a terrace at 20 m asl above the Firth of Forth (Robertson et al. 2013). The site was intermittently visited for a long period, with radiocarbon dates spanning 1500 years, from the early seventh to the mid-fifth millennium. The main post-glacial transgression occurred around 5000 cal BC in this region, during the occupation of the site, when relative sea-levels were at around 10 m (Sturt et al. 2013), making the site much closer to the water. Much of the activity at the site appears to date to this time of high sea-level.

The earliest date from Castlelandhill of 6820–6605 cal BC (7860 ± 35 BP; SUERC-39750) comes from one of a series of pits, some containing substantial quantities of lithic debitage and smaller quantities of charred hazelnut shells and burnt bone, which surrounded an undated oval structure, measuring 4.7 m by 3 m. The dated pit contains a core and several scalene triangles; while a series of intercutting pits contained 579 lithic artefacts including 30 tools. Several metres to the north of this structure, a large pit containing layers of oak charcoal was dated to 5290–5050 cal BC (6200 ± 35 BP; SUERC-39751). Several of the pits in this area seem to be associated with posts that may have served as markers (Robertson et al. 2013).

In the western part of the site, three partly superimposed pit-hearths were ex-cavated, and an adjacent pit contained burnt material, probably cleared from one of the hearths. Two of the hearths have similar mid-fifth millennium dates. Pine, oak, hazel and birch, indicative of the mixed and mosaic woodlands surrounding the site at this time, were all used as fuel. The narrow rings in the branches of hazel suggest it formed an understory in mixed oak forest, while the wide rings in the birch wood, suggests fairly open birch woodlands were also present in the area. A sub-circular post structure, measuring 4.2 by 3.3 m was located in the same area. It appears later than the hearths as one of the post cuts these features. It is undated; Mesolithic lithics were recovered from the posts nearest the hearths, but these may be residual.

Though the post-built structures at Castlelandhill are undated, there appears very little artefactual evidence for later activity at the site, suggesting these, too, belong to the Mesolithic. This would suggest a broad range of different structures in the region during the later part of the Mesolithic. While the Castlelandhill structures are oval and sub-circular, a circular post-built building may have been present at Silvercrest, though the Mesolithic material within structure may be residual. These structures have maximum lengths of between 4.2 and 4.7 m, and their varying shapes contrast with the more uniform Middle Mesolithic structures. A series of varied, more ephemeral stakehole structures are present at Morton (see below). These indicate increased variability in settlement practises over the period, with the more traditional form of structure seen in the Middle Mesolithic potentially built only at Silvercrest a site where an earlier example may be present, perhaps conscious mimicry or remaking of an older, ancestral form.

Coastal sites are also known from Morton and Low Hauxley in Northumberland. The sites at Morton were originally located as a ploughzone scatter, now well inland, in 1957 by Reg Candow. Excavation followed at Morton A between 1963 and 1971 and Morton B was excavated by Coles and Candow between 1967 and 1971. The site is located on a rocky outcrop of lava, rising above the surrounding sand and measuring 200 m by 80 m. It is covered by a thin layer of windblown sand that had already begun to accumulate during the Late Mesolithic as the sea moved closer (Coles 1971); this windblown sand separates occupation episodes in several places, with seven superimposed activity episodes recorded in one area.

Radiocarbon dates from Morton A are mainly on bulked wood, with material from a number of squares and contexts. On what was a repeatedly occupied site, where Early Mesolithic lithic material is strongly represented, these should be treated with caution (Bonsall 1988). Potentially the most reliable dates from Morton A (though old wood may be an issue) come from two consistent measurements on a hearth and a single date on wood from an arc of stakeholes, which indicate occupation in the second half of the sixth millennium BC. This would put the occupation at or just before the time of the main post-glacial transgression, at a time when relative sea-level would have been around +8 m (Bradley et al. 2011), meaning that site A, located on the highest part of the outcrop would have been very close to the shoreline. At this time, the site would have been an intertidal island, cut off from the coast at high tide (Coles 1971, 286). Some of the Late Mesolithic occupation probably does predate this. A bulked measurement from the southwest of the site comes from two superimposed levels (levels 2 and 3), separated by windblown sand. Though bulked, this date of 6750–5325 cal BC (6790 ± 210 BP; NZ-1192) suggests that layers 2 and 1, at least, probably predate the late sixth millennium cal BC occupation.

At Morton A, the archaeology in some areas had been truncated by the plough and during the early years of excavation, the assemblage was mainly recovered by sieving, with no features recorded. However, in the final seasons of excavation, a series of hearths, scoops and stakeholes associated with scatters of lithic material, and fragments of bone and shell were located. While overall densities in some areas are moderate, at around 200 piece per square metre, the excavations revealed these denser areas represent series of small-scale superimposed occupation layers, interspersed by wind-blown sand: T44, for example, with 170 pieces per square metre is made up of six separate occupation episodes. Other areas show evidence for a single occupation only; these too are small-scale and ephemeral. T53, the area with the hearth dated to the late sixth millennium is a typical example. The hearth itself consists of a compact layer of charcoal, burnt bone and burnt pebbles; lithic material extends for half a metre around it; only 77 pieces were recovered, most adjacent to the hearth. Two microliths and a retouched piece were the only tools recovered. The area was sheltered by the presence of a natural bank of volcanic material 2 m to the east. Only 7 m to the south another occupation was sheltered by the bank, but here the bank was used in conjunction with an arc of stakeholes to form a rectangular structure around 2 m by 1.5 m across. Outside the structure was a hearth, sheltered between an angle in the lava bank. This area is associated with 218 pieces of flint scattered within and outside the structure. Formal tools consist of six microliths (and a microburin), a burin and a scraper. Retouched and utilised pieces are common and a piece of haematite was recovered.

Two areas reveal evidence for the episodic nature of the occupation. In area T46, seven superimposed, small-scale occupations were recorded, separated by wind-blown sand. A similar sequence was evident in the southwest of the site, where occupation initially took place in a scoop or natural hollow. When this had almost entirely filled with wind-blown sand, a small structure was erected, consisting of 19 stakeholes forming an area of 2 m by 1.2 m, with an external hearth. A dark spread of occupation debris was found both within the structure and externally, against the eastern wall, which may represent middening, suggesting a slightly longer episode of occupation. An assemblage of flint of 363 pieces (still small but larger than most at the site), and two deposits of bone and a hazelnut shell were associated with this deposit. After this came another small occupation associated with a windbreak, and three superimposed occupations lacking any structural evidence, all with small lithic assemblages of between 297 and 69 pieces.

A notable feature of the site is the high proportion of retouched pieces associated with these small occupations. While some knapping took place, using beach pebble flint and a variety of local knappable stones, such as chert, chalcedony and silicified limestone, intense use was made of the pieces that were knapped at the site. Many unused nodules of material were recovered, perhaps stores of raw material for people to use on future visits. Some heavy-duty stone tools were recovered, mostly hammerstone, but also a stone used for grinding material.

Coastal occupation is also known further south in Northumberland. At Low Hauxley, a small hill buried by dune sands (see chapter 4), small piles of shells (mainly periwinkle and limpets, up to 50 cm across), flint, animal bones and teeth, were discovered eroding from the cliff during initial monitoring work. Shell from the largest of these piles indicated a date of 6170 to 5790 cal BC (Waddington and Bonsall 2016, 23). Over the following centuries the environment surrounding the hill changed as sea-levels rose; the land became wetter in response to the rising water-table and peat development started c.5400 cal BC. The top of the peat, which is dated between 5300 and 5050 cal BC, shows impressions of human and animal footprints. The humans – both adults and children – seem mainly to have been travelling along the coastline, though occasional trails towards the sea have been recorded. Two fragments of split oak timber may indicate an attempt to stabilize the boggy ground. Animals footprints include those of red deer and wild pig, and a possible identification of bear has been made at similar peat exposures at the southern end of Druridge Bay. Human and animal prints are present in fairly equal numbers, suggesting this was an area that both visited, intermittently; the human presence not sufficiently substantial to discourage animals visiting to drink from nearby Bondicarr Burn, or from fresh water pools. Relative sea-level was around −1 m, with the site sheltered by a dune system gradually migrating inland. The vegetation was characterised by the presence trees and shrubs, with alder carr dominating the local waterlogged ground. On the drier ground, oak and hazel were important, with birch and elm present and lime and ash appearing (Innes and Tipping 2016, 227). Beyond the dunes was the beach, where flint, and shellfish, could be collected. The rocky terrain of this landscape means that several islands would have been in sight of the shore, where, as today, seals would have basked.

Western Scotland

Mesolithic groups in Western Scotland become much more visible in the archaeological record after c.7300 cal BC. Previously only Kinloch on Rum and possibly Criet Dubh on Mull had evidence for sustained occupation in the Middle Mesolithic, though single dates on bone and antler tools indicate that groups were present more widely on the coast at Druimvargie near Oban and on the Isle of Skye at Sand (chapter 4). From 7300 cal BC, there is radiocarbon evidence for expansion of Mesolithic activity in a much broader range of places, particularly islands, with occupation across the Inner Hebrides, the west coast and inland areas (Figure 5.7). There is also evidence at this time, though of a more limited nature, for visits to the Outer Hebrides (at Northton on Harris) and Orkney. This process of expansion started in the late eighth millennium BC, with occupation at Fiskary Bay on Coll and Rubha Port an t-Seilich on Islay (Mithen et al. 2007, 2015).

A decline in occupation in the region, as measured by radiocarbon dates, in the late seventh and sixth millennia BC has been noted and related to abandonment of the area in response to the 8.2 (cal BP) event (Wicks and Mithen 2014). However, this picture may partly be due to issues of visibility and preservation, as well as the problems of using radiocarbon dates as population proxies. Many coastal sites predating the main post-glacial transgression would have been destroyed; those coming after would be preserved. On the west coast and Inner Hebrides, the highest sea-levels would have been at around 5000 cal BC, but in the Outer Hebrides, these would have occurred only around 2000 years ago which may account for the rarity of Mesolithic sites in this region (Bradley et al. 2011). The effects of sea-level rise are reflected in the distribution of radiocarbon dates in the region. Twenty-six radiocarbon dates come from the period 6000–5000 cal BC, before the transgression; 60 date to between 5000 and 4000 cal BC.

Also affecting this patterning is the role of shell-middens. These are visible in the landscape, leading to preferential investigation of these contexts, and for the aforementioned reasons tend to belong to the final millennium of the Mesolithic. Several middens are also found in caves, also preferred areas for archaeological investigation. Both middens and caves preserve organic material for radiocarbon dating which would not survive in other contexts. Of the radiocarbon measurement for this region, falling into the last three millennia of the Mesolithic, 59% come from middens.

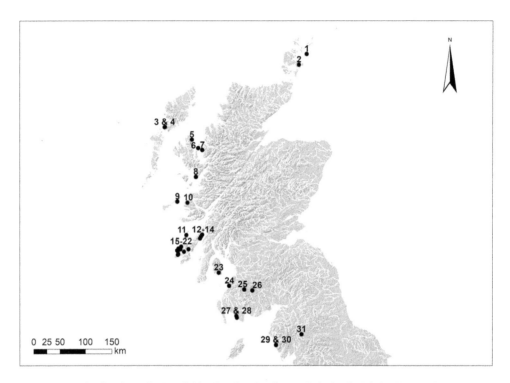

Figure 5.7 Distribution of Mesolithic sites in Northwest Britain (1. Links House, Stronsay, 2. Long Howe, 3. Traigh a Teampuill, 4. Northton, 5. An Corran, 6. Loch a Sguirr, 7. Sand, 8. Camas Daraich, 9. Fiskary Bay, 10. Criet Dubh, 11. Staosnaig, 12. North Carn, 13. Lussa Wood I, 14. Lealt Bay, 15. Rockside, 15. Rubha Port an t-Seilich, 16. Coulererach, 17. Newton, 18. Gleann Mor, 19. Kilellan Farm, 20. Bolsay Farm, 21. Aoradh, 22. Kindrochid, 23. Auchareoch, 24. Littlehill Bridge, Girvan, 25. Starr, 26. Smittons, 27. Low Clone, 28. Barsalloch, 29. Monks Moor, 30. Williamson's Moss, 31. Wickers Gill)

Thus, the radiocarbon dates track cultural choices to generate shell-middens and times and places when these will be preserved. With these caveats in mind, the huge increase in radiocarbon dates in this region probably suggests some increase in population in comparison to the Middle Mesolithic, but using radiocarbon dates as a proxy for population is by no means straightforward.

As well as radiocarbon dated sites, the broader archaeological record is also dominated by coastal and near coastal sites (Wickham-Jones 1990). This is a result of both site visibility and probably also cultural preferences, both of Prehistoric groups and archaeologists seeking attractive fieldwork sites. The larger open-air middens and sites in caves have long histories of investigation and have attracted further research in these areas, while individuals, such as Mercer on Jura, have undertaken extensive work in particular areas. In addition, two major survey projects, the Southern Hebrides Mesolithic Project and the Scotland's First Settlers Project have focused on the west coast and islands, though both projects have been important in discovering sites in the hinterland of islands. In those few areas where extensive inland surveys of the mainland have been undertaken, particularly in Dumfries and Galloway, along the

Dee, the Ken and Loch Doon, Mesolithic sites are relatively common. The focus on river systems in these regions is similar to the pattern both in Eastern Scotland and in Northwest England (see below).

The people at the end of the world

Seventh millennium Mesolithic campsites have been found on islands across the region, from Orkney in the North to Arran in the south, from Mull in the east and Harris in the west. The people who left these traces were sophisticated maritime voyagers, travelling between islands and the mainland. In these potentially dangerous waters, knowledge of tides and currents, submerged hazards and safe harbours was key (Sturt 2006). These people have been described as island-hoppers (Hardy and Wickham-Jones 2002), ranging over not landscapes but seascapes (Warren 2001).

Most formidable of these journeys were those made to the furthest islands: To Orkney and the Outer Hebrides. Mesolithic sites on these islands are so far rare, though evidence from pollen diagrams for sustained burning episodes suggests rather more occupation than is currently known (Edwards 2004; Piper et al. 2018). In the Outer Hebrides, sites would normally be deeply buried under thick deposits of peat and machair (Edwards 1990). However, coastal erosion surveys in 2011 have revealed the presence of Mesolithic activity on both Harris and Lewis. Excavations have taken place at Northton on the Toe Head Peninsula on Harris (Figure 5.8), where several layers of buried soil associated with organic refuse and a pit have radiocarbon dates spanning the seventh millennium (Figure 5.9, Bishop et al. 2012; Gregory et al. 2005). These layers contain accumulations of faunal remains from hare, otter, Great Auk, fish bones and plant remains such as hazelnut shells and lesser celandine, the two latter also staples at Staosnaig on Colonsay (see below) (Bishop et al. 2013). Similar to the 'Obanian' sites (see Box 6.3), microliths and formal tools were absent at Northton. The small lithic assemblage was made mainly on quartz, and no artefacts were found in the lowest layer (Gregory et al. 2005). A similar range of organic remains was located within a buried land surface during smaller scale excavations at Traigh a Teampuill, a site close to Northon, where fish and mammal bones and carbonised hazelnut shells date to the mid-sixth millennium BC. This organic horizon was cut by a scoop, rich in marine shells and ash, also interpreted as a midden deposit (Piper and Church 2012).

On Orkney, several Mesolithic lithic scatters are known, but the only two dated sites, as in the Outer Hebrides, also belong to the start of the seventh millennium BC. At Long Howe, East Mainland, Mesolithic lithics, including microliths, and charred hazelnut shells were found in pockets of sediment preserved in fissures in the bedrock beneath a barrow (Wickham-Jones and Downes 2007). Links House, Stronsay is a more complex site, with a range of truncated features, charred hazelnut shells and a microlithic assemblage that may suggest some longevity (Bates et al. 2013; Farrell et al. 2014; Lee and Woodward 2009).

Settlement on Skye, Raasay and the Inner Sound

In the seventh millennium BC, two sites on the Isle of Skye, An Corran and Camas Daraich, one on Raasay, Loch a Sguirr, and Sand, on the adjacent shoreline of the

Figure 5.8 Northton and Tràigh an Teampuill (Temple Bay), Harris, looking south (copyright Peter Rowley-Conwy)

Figure 5.9 Top of the midden surface revealed at Northon (copyright Peter Rowley-Conwy)

Figure 5.10 View across the Inner Sound (copyright Scotland's First Settlers Project)

Inner Sound (Figure 5.10), saw their main periods of occupation. Sand, Camas Daraich and Loch a Sguirr were excavated as part of the Scotland's First Settlers project between 1999 and 2004, which focused on survey of Skye and the Inner Sound, locating at least 13 new Mesolithic sites, most of which were open-air lithic scatters (Hardy and Wickham-Jones 2009).

Sand is a small rockshelter, sheltered by an overhang today only 3 m deep, at the top of a small bay at 27 m asl (Figure 5.11). The floor of the rockshelter was eroded down to bedrock but a platform extended beyond it on which a midden was located. The midden measured 8 m by 8 m across and up to a metre in depths, though two slumping episodes have been recorded, indicating it was originally higher. Lack of sediment or soil horizons within the midden suggests it built up relatively quickly. The midden is composed of shell, mainly limpets, and fish, birds and animal bones (Figure 5.12, Tables 5.1–5.3). No structural remains, such as hearths, stone footings, or stakeholes were located, but large quantities of heat-fractured rock indicate cooking was a major activity. A series of modelled radiocarbon dates indicate the midden started to accumulate by 6990–6540 cal BC and ended by 6600–6470 cal BC. Activity represented by this assemblage of material can be estimated to have lasted 130–450 years (Elliott and Griffiths 2018). The earlier dates come from the southern area of the midden, the later ones from the northern part, suggesting the focus of middening shifted over time. There seems to have been a gap in occupation at the site before renewed visits in the mid-sixth millennium BC associated with an organic, shell-free midden in front of the old shell-midden, suggesting a shift in the nature of activities at the site.

Charcoal from the midden gives a picture of the local vegetation, though one perhaps affected by human preferences and the likely use of driftwood. Birch was most common, with hazel (and hazelnuts) and heather also well-represented. Other species

Figure 5.11 The rockshelter at Sand (copyright Scotland's First Settlers Project)

Figure 5.12 Digging the midden at Sand (copyright Scotland's First Settlers Project)

Table 5.1 Animal and bird remains from sixth and seventh millennium middens. Some sites have later admixture

Species	Northon	Sand	An Corran	MacArthur Cave (lower midden)	Druimvargie
Red deer		++	++	+	+
Roe deer		+	++	++	
Pig		++	+	+	+
Bovid		+	+	+	
Canid		+	+		
Fox		+			
Badger		+		+	
Otter	+	+	+	+	+
Pine Marten					
Wild cat			+	+	
Bear			+		
Hare	+		+		
Common seal		+			
Whale		+			
Frog/toad		+	+		
Cormorant/shag		+	+		+
Gannet			+		
Gull			+		
Skua			+		
Razorbill		++			
Guillimot		++	+		
Great Auk	+	++	++		
Little auk		+			
Puffin			++		
Thrush		+	+		
Willow-tit			+		
White-tailed eagle			+		

are rarer: Alder, pine, prunus (blackthorn or cherry), maloidiae (probably rowan or hawthorn), ivy and honeysuckle (Austin 2009). The overall character of the assemblage suggests open birch woodland with hazel scrub and areas of heath. This picture is confirmed by pollen work in the area, which shows fluctuating, but dominant frequencies of birch and hazel pollen (Green and Edwards 2009).

The midden contains a substantial quantity of worked stone. A total of 16,000 pieces were recovered from 95.5 m^2 of excavated area. The main lithic concentration was found immediately outside the rockshelter and in areas beyond the midden. In contrast to many Scottish midden sites, microliths were common, with 159 recovered. A wide range of other tools, particularly scrapers and retouched pieces, indicate a wide variety of tasks were undertaken at the site (Wickham-Jones 2009). This is in contrast to the relatively restricted coarse stone tool types, consisting mainly facially pecked pebbles, similar to rather small anvil stones, which might suggest more specialist activities at the site. Relatively little flint was found within the midden itself, suggesting flint was not routinely disposed of in the same way as food waste, though what lithic material there was appeared similar to the remainder of the assemblage. Beyond the midden, small-scale episodes of knapping and tool use occurred, with concentrations of awls, notches and microliths noted in different areas.

Table 5.2 Fish remains from sixth and seventh millennium middens. Some sites have later admixture

	Northon	Sand	An Corran
Tope		+	
Dog fish		+	
Ray		+	
Elasmobranch		+	
Herring	+	+	
Eel		+	++
Conger eel		+	
Saithe		++	++
Cod	+	++	++
Pollock		++	
Haddock		+	
Whiting	+	+	
Mackerel	+	++	
Sea-bream		+	
Wrasse	+	++	++
Rockling	++		
Butterfish		+	
Plaice		+	++
Dab			+
Salmon/trout			++

Table 5.3 Shellfish and crustaceans from sixth and seventh millennium middens. Some sites have later admixture

Molluscs and crustacea	Sand	Loch a Sguirr 1	An Corran	Druimvargie
Limpet	+++	++	+++	+++
Edible Periwinkle	++	++	++	+
Flat periwinkle	+		+	
Rough periwinkle			+	
Dog whelk	++	++	++	
Whelk				+
Mussel	+			
Oyster				+
Scallop	+		+	+
Cockle	+			
Topshell	+		+	
Razor clam				+
Crab	++			

A variety of lithic raw materials were used; some collected from primary sources, others as beach pebbles. Prominent was a baked mudstone, which can be obtained from Staffin Bay on Skye. This regular, fine-grained material flakes very well, but is liable to disintegrate in geological contexts away from its source, so is likely to have been obtained on Skye. Bloodstone was also used; this may have been procured directly from Rhum, 60 km to the south. Relatively few cortical flakes of baked mudstone or bloodstone were found on site suggesting these were imported as prepared cores. Also used was chalcedonic silica (encompassing flint, chert, agate and jaspar, all local to this area and difficult to distinguish), which can be found in the same area, but also in till and as beach pebbles. Quartz and quartzite are poor quality, but are the easiest of these materials to obtain from local beaches. These materials highlight the marine mobility of Mesolithic groups in these areas.

Fifty-three bone and antler tools were also recovered from the site, and small fragments of waste material indicates that tools were being made as well as used here. Most were bevel-ended tools (42) mainly made from ungulate long-bones, though a few were antler (Hardy and Birch 2009). No bevel-ended stone tools were recovered from the midden, despite these being common in similar contexts along the western coastline. Simple bone points and a harpoon fragment were also recovered. Several fine bone points were recovered, one made from bird bone, which may have been used as winkle-pickers. The bone and antler tools were concentrated within the body of the midden itself; this is likely to be related to preservation. Shells were also used as tools, with the sharp edges of broken scallops showing traces of wear. Shells were also personal ornaments and a series of perforated cowries, similar to examples from Oronsay (see chapter 6), were also recovered from the midden, as were two fragments of haematite and limonite, both of which showed exploitation for pigment.

Animal bones found in the midden are mainly red deer and pig (Table 5.1), both represented mostly by lower limb elements which may have been bought in to be exploited for use as tools, or as a result of activities focused on hide processing. Rare elements of roe deer, dog/wolf, otter, fox and whale were also found (Parks and Barratt 2009). Seabirds, particularly razorbill and guillemot, but also shag/cormorant and great and little auk, are well represented. The representation of elements suggests they may have been exploited for their feathers. Fish are common, and were mainly from the cod (mainly saithe and pollock) and wrasse families Table 5.2). The small size of the fish suggests deep water fishing did not take place, and the presence of species that probably represent incidental catches suggest that stationary traps and nets were used in the inshore waters of the Sound. Only a single element of seal was found, and this in the topsoil. It seems here, as at Morton, and in contrast to the Oronsay middens, seal was not exploited. Shells in the midden were mainly limpet, though periwinkle (both edible and flat perwinkle) and dogwelk, were also well-represented (Table 5.3). These are all species of the rocky shore and would have been available close to the site (Milner 2009).

As well as Sand, a second Mesolithic site located by the Scotland's First Settlers Project was dated. On Raasay, Loch a Sguirr 1 consists of a midden within one of a pair of rockshelters. These are located within a distinctive outcrop, now 20 m asl, with good views. Two small test pits located a small shell-midden, dominated by periwinkle and dogwhelk, three bone bevel-ended tools and a small lithic assemblage. Two radiocarbon dates indicate intermittent occupation of the rockshelter in the second half of the late seventh millennium BC (7620 ± 75 BP, OxA-9305; 7245 ± 55 BP, OxA-9255), though there was also some evidence for later disturbance (Hardy and Wickham-Jones 2009).

There are two important sites on Skye itself: An Corran and Camas Daraich. An Corran is, like Sand and Loch a Sguirr 1, a rockshelter (Figure 2.16). The rockshelter overhang extends out 6 m, though may have been greater in the past, and would have provided shelter from westerly winds. The site was excavated over 15 days in November and December 1993 by necessity an extremely rapid rescue excavation in advance of road-building that destroyed a portion of the site (Saville et al. 2012). The lowest layers of the site (contexts [41] and [40]) consist of an ancient soil horizon that contains Early Mesolithic material (see chapter 2), though radiocarbon dates indicate the site has seen some disturbance, perhaps as a result of the use of the midden for the deposition of human remains in the Neolithic (Hellewell 2015). All layers above [40] are anthropogenic, and all but the lowest part of the overlying context [36] contain layers of shell that have led to good organic preservation in the Late Mesolithic layers. The majority of the dates indicate an occupation probably between 6600 and 6250 BC, though two bevel-ended tools reveal sporadic visits to the site at the end of the sixth and end of the fifth millennia BC. Charcoal samples indicate a nearby woodland of hazel (including hazelnuts), birch and willow. Pomodiae (probably rowan) and blackthorn were also represented, a picture confirmed by pollen work on the island, which also indicates areas of open grassland.

The midden layers are associated with a small microlith assemblage of scalene triangles, and crescents; microburins indicate these tools were manufactured at the midden (Saville et al. 2012). Mudstone and chalcedony were preferentially used, the former outcropping just above the site, the latter available on nearby beaches. Organic bevel-ended tools are common in the midden layers, though no stone examples were recovered. Most are made from red deer metapodials, though one is on cetacean bone, one on roe deer and one on antler.

Amongst the faunal remains, red deer and roe deer are most common with small quantities of pig, aurochs, hare, wild cat, otter, brown bear and canid (Table 5.1, Saville et al. 2012). The bear and canid are represented by phalanges, perhaps forming parts of skins, while a third of the red deer remains were metapodials, indicating many of the red deer bones were brought in for tool manufacture; though a wider range of elements of both red and roe deer show joints of meat were also imported. Many bird species are present, mostly seabirds, of which puffin and great auk were most common. Given that later Prehistoric material is intrusive in the lower layers, not all of these mammals and birds may be Mesolithic. Of the faunal remains, red deer, bovid and pig have returned Mesolithic dates. Fish are common in the midden layers and include cod, whiting, saithe, wrasse, plaice and dab (Table 5.2). In contrast to Sand, migratory species salmon, trout and eel are also present. As is typical amongst the west coast middens, shells are dominated by limpets. Other species are relatively rare, with only edible periwinkle, dog-welk and common mussel present in double figures.

In contrast to the other major sites in the area, Camas Daraich on the southernmost part of Skye is an open-air site, located just below the crest of the late glacial raised beach at 20 m asl (Figure 5.13). The sea lies over the crest to the south, while the site faces north, inland to a small peat-filled basin. Lithic material was recovered eroding from a track. This was gridded and collected and a small number of test pits were excavated. This located a black organic layer than seems to have been a midden, which infilled two shallow scoops, with two dates on hazelnut shells, suggesting it was generated in the course of repeated occupation dating to the first half of the seventh millennium BC. An adjacent hearth has two compatible dates, suggesting it was used in 6470–6240 cal BC (Wickham-Jones et al. 2004).

The lithic raw materials consist of a range of chalcedonic silicas that can be obtained from nearby beaches and areas of glacial till. Also available from beaches was quartz and quartzite. Two materials were transported over greater distances: Bloodstone is common and can be procured from Rum 25 km away; rarer is mudstone

Figure 5.13 View over Camas Daraich (copyright Camais Daraich excavation project)

whose nearest source is Staffin, 70 km away on the north east coast of the island. Fewer cortical flakes of these more exotic materials are present, and there is little knapping debris associated with the mudstone and no cores. This suggests mudstone was imported in the form of blanks and tools; by contrast bloodstone seems to have been imported as partially-reduced cores. Tools consist of a range of microliths, scrapers and retouched pieces.

The west coast and the western Isles

Further south, Mesolithic groups ranged across the seas, generating small coastal midden sites found in caves on the mainland and large settlements with varied foci on the islands of the Inner Hebrides. On the mainland a number of small shell-middens were found in caves during the expansion of Oban in the 19th century. Several were reportedly destroyed before any excavation (Pollard et al. 1996), and records for excavated examples remain sparce. Originally seen as belonging to a discrete culture that lacked microliths, the Obanian (see chapter 6), these sites are now known to span several millennia and are contemporary with local microlithic sites. Druimvargie and Raschoille have seventh millennium dates, and Raschoille and MacArthur Cave were visited in the sixth millennium (Table 6.2). There are also seventh millennium dates from a more recently excavated cave midden from the island of Ulva which has 'Obanian' material culture, though a microlith is also present (Bonsall et al. 1989).

In comparison with the large Final Mesolithic middens of Oronsay and Colonsay (see chapter 6), the middens around Oban are small, constrained by the size of the caves in which they were located. Of the Oban caves, MacArthur's Cave measures

7.5 by 6 m; Druimvargie 4.5 by 3 m; Distillery Cave 3.5 by 2.7 m (Anderson 1898; Turner 1895). To the north, Ulva Cave, is much bigger at 17 by 15 m, though the midden itself is 8 m across and only 0.35 m thick (Bonsall 1996; Bonsall et al. 1989). MacArthur Cave, the best recorded of the early excavations, contained a midden of a metre in height, with two phases separated by storm beach gravels related to the post-glacial maximum transgression, which may have truncated the lower midden (Anderson 1898). One hundred and forty bevel-ended tools and seven biserial barbed points were recovered, but only 20 flint artefacts. Eighteen bevel-ended tools come from Druimvargie along with two uniserial points. At the other sites, no organic artefacts were recorded, though this may be a result of recovery methods, with material only incidentally collected as the caves were destroyed during quarrying. Many of the cave middens contained human remains, but all those with radiocarbon measurements post-date the Mesolithic, and the presence of pottery and domesticates at some confirm further post-Mesolithic use. This means that shell and faunal remains cannot be certainly regarded as Mesolithic. Of all Obanian sites, only the Oronsay middens Cnoc Coig and Caisteal nan Gillean II have confirmed human remains of Mesolithic date (see chapter 6).

Jura

The Mesolithic of Jura is known through the extensive fieldwork by John Mercer, who excavated several sites, mainly along the coast of this mountainous island. Mercer obtained some of the first radiocarbon dates for the Mesolithic of Western Scotland in the 1960s and 1970s. Unfortunately, as was necessary for the time, these are mainly made on bulked charcoal from what appear to be sites of mixed date, rendering the measurements of little utility. The Jura sites are notable for their large numbers of Early Mesolithic forms of microlith (see chapter 2), and these bulked radiocarbon dates were used in the past as an argument for their later persistence in Scotland (Woodman 1978, 82). Instead it is more reasonable to consider that many of the sites are persistent places, with intermittent occupation at different dates.

Typologically Late Mesolithic material is present on Jura in some quantities. Lussa Wood 1 is located close to the River Lussa, the island's largest water-course, near to where it drains into Lussa Bay (Mercer 1970). Narrow-backed bladelets and left lateralised scalene triangles dominate at the site (Mercer 1978), and show a similar range to those from mainly seventh millennium BC assemblages excavated by the Southern Hebrides Mesolithic Project on Islay and Colonsay (Mithen 2000, see below). These were found mixed with some Early Mesolithic microliths in a fine gravel. While Mercer interpreted this gravel as related to the main post-glacial maximum transgression, as Bonsall (1988) has pointed out, the site is too high to relate to this event. This gravel is likely to derive from slope-wash, which has incorporated material of different dates, including charcoal, charred hazelnut shells and burnt bone.

To the north, at Lealt Bay, Mercer excavated vast quantities of late Mesolithic material, mostly on what is probably a late glacial raised beach at 15.5 m asl, close to a small stream (Mercer 1968). Here too, much of the assemblage appears to derive from colluviated or eroded deposits. The assemblage is dominated by microliths (scalene triangles, backed bladelets and four-sided pieces) with smaller numbers of scrapers. Beach pebbles and quartz were the main raw materials used; quartz is more common here than amongst the sites of Islay and Colonsay, which are closer to sources of beach pebble flint, though this patterning may be affected by the presence of later Prehistoric material at Lealt Bay. A third Late Mesolithic site at North Carn, 4 km to the north is noted by Mercer (1972) as very similar to Lealt Bay; it is located at a similar height on a terrace, with similar raw material and tool representation; as at Lealt Bay, the condition of the lithics suggests most of the assemblage is not in primary context.

Islay

Considerable evidence for Mesolithic occupation comes for Islay. A major project on the island, the Southern Hebrides Mesolithic project (SHMP) located 22 sites (Mithen 2000) and subsequent work by Mithen, Pirie and Wicks has located two further sites on the island. The earliest Mesolithic dates on Islay come from one of these more recent finds, Rubha Port an t-Seilich, where in addition to terminal Palaeolithic evidence, occupation dating to the late eighth millennium BC has been located (Mithen et al. 2015). This site also has a seventh millennium date, and it was at this period, tailing into the start of the sixth millennium that the vast majority of sites on the island were occupied.

In the seventh millennium, when relative sea-levels were higher, Islay may have been split in two, with the low-lying land between Loch Indall to the south and Loch Gruinart in the north submerged. In contrast to the treeless landscape of today, pollen cores from the island indicate a vegetation of birch and hazel with smaller quantities of oak and elm. The woodland is likely to have varied considerably with more open areas in the west of heath and shrub, and denser, mixed oak woodlands in sheltered areas to the east. There is evidence of woodland disturbance during this period when hazel levels fell and birch and grasses increased. This may represent small-scale human impact through burning (Edwards 2000). Today Islay, unlike the smaller islands, supports a similar range of mammals to the mainland and this is likely to have been the case in the Mesolithic. As well as marine resources, the inland waterways support a range of different fish and the island is attractive to migratory birds, meaning a wide range of resources would have been available to Mesolithic inhabitants (Mithen 2000).

Prior to the SHMP work, two Mesolithic sites had been excavated on the island. The first, at Kilellan Farm, was uncovered during excavations of a Bronze Age midden; a refitting lithic assemblage, a pit and stone spreads were found sealed beneath a layer of windblown sand (Ritchie 2005). More intensive occupation is present from a site at Newton, on the edge of the floodplain of the river Sorn in the central part of the island. Here, a shallow depression was uncovered, filled with burnt hazelnuts, lithics and burnt bone, and which dates to the first half of the seventh millennium (McCullagh 1988). This feature was not fully excavated and thus remains somewhat ambiguous, but it appears to have been a structure. In the centre was a pit filled with fire-cracked stones and charcoal. Three angled posts were located within a gulley on its southwestern edge. The central pit was overlain by several fills, some of which showed evidence for further hearths. It seems that these represent several successive floors of this feature. Fifty percent of a substantial lithic assemblage of 10,000 pieces was found in the uppermost layer. This suggests that lithic material may have been partially cleared from previous floors, with only the full assemblage from the final occupation remaining, alternatively the hollow may have been used as a midden once abandoned. Lithic material was found in the surrounding buried soil and silts on the edge of the terrace indicating activity, possibly including middening, in the surrounding area.

The SHMP work mainly focused on the southwestern part of the island, an area of rocky uplands area with small sheltered sandy bays; to the north is an area of extensive dune formation. Occupation sites appear to have been preferentially located in places with good views and proximity to flint sources. Survey of beaches on Islay and surrounding islands (Marshall 2000) has revealed that along the west coast of Scotland flint is restricted to the western beaches of Islay, Colonsay and Iona. As the island with the longest shoreline, Colonsay is therefore the most significant for these flint sources, and this seems to have been an important factor both in encouraging Mesolithic occupation and in making sites more visible to archaeologists. Coulererach, in particular, seems to have been a site focused on flint procurements and initial preparation. Large cortical flakes are common on this site and contrast with the small mainly tertiary flakes and heavily reduced cores from sites such as Rubha Port an t-Seilich, Criet Dubh and Fiskary, which are located much further away from flint sources (Mithen et al. 2019). Most of the sites excavated by the SHMP have yielded unmodified flint nodules. Some of these may be caches for future exploitation (as at Coulererach where ten tested pebbles were found in a 2 m area), but some are too small to be usable. They may have been collected by children unaware of the parameters for successful knapping. Coulererach has most of these unusable nodules, this is also where Finlay and colleagues have noted the potential presence of children's knapping sequences, though the presence of well-made blades indicates experienced knappers were also present to provide guidance (Finlay et al. 2000). The focus on raw material collection and lithic production at this site may have made it particularly appropriate for teaching children these skills. Amongst groups of this date, children may have participated in or even been responsible for the collection of local lithic material, something that perhaps took place hand in hand with shellfish collection on the local beaches.

Six main sites – Glean Mor, Rockside, Coulererach, Aoradh, Kindrochid and Bolsay Farm – were excavated by the SHMP between 1989 and 1993, all on the western side of the island. Aoradh and Coulererach are close to the coast, Bolsay Farm and Gleann Mor are inland and upland, with the others occupying intermediate positions. Most, apart from Bolsay Farm, were sampled by extensive test pitting with only smaller areas of open excavation. Most were subject to greater or lesser extent some form of colluviation, though in cases colluviated sediments preserved buried soils with evidence for Mesolithic occupation. Rockside and Coulerach yielded smaller assemblages, but other sites are characterised by extremely large and dense lithic assemblages, ranging from 29,000 pieces at Kindrochid and 31,000 pieces at Gleann Mor to 320,000 at Bolsay Farm; these are likely to indicate repeated visits to these areas, and given that radiocarbon dates from these sites are relatively few, they may incorporate visits both earlier and later than their current date range, which clusters in in the second half of the seventh millennium and the start of the sixth. Several sites have features, though none are substantial, from three small pits/post-holes at Aoradh, patches of burning, stakeholes and a pit at Kindrochid. At Kindrochid, lithic material appears to have been dumped into a hollow on the edge of boggy ground.

Lithic assemblages excavated by the project were to a greater or lesser extent dominated by microliths (Table 5.4), with scalene triangles most common, apart from Aoradh, where backed bladelets were dominant. At all sites a range of associated processing tools were also recovered, with scrapers particularly common. While the dominance of microliths on a site has often been seen to represent hunting (Mellars 1976a), Myers (1989) has argued we need to consider patterns of tool use and repair.

Table 5.4 Characteristics of assemblages excavated by the SHMP

Site	Assemblage size	Scraper: microlith ratio	Microlith: All retouched/used
Gleann Mor	31,243	1:5.6	1:0.9
Rockside	10,827	1:5.7	1:0.8
Coulererarch	4197	1:10.5	1:1.1
Aoradh	6332	1:2.6	1:0.9
Kindrochid	29,082	1:21	1:1
Bolsay Farm (Tr I)	66,281	1:8.5	1:0.5
Bolsay Farm (Tr II)	253,752	1:33.1	1:0.3
Staosnaig area A	61,217	1:6.3	1:0.5
Staosnaig F.24 [17]	49,153	1:12.6	1:0.3
Staosnaig area D	6707	1:3	1:1.4

While many microliths would be used to make a single composite tool, other artefacts such as scrapers represent tools in themselves and moreover ones that could also be used and resharpened. Sites such as Coulererarch and Kindrochid, where there appears to be a balance between numbers of microliths and other tools, are actually likely to indicate a stronger focus on activities that did not involve microliths. Furthermore, microwear studies indicated that microliths recovered from the site of Gleann Mor had a range of functions, not simply as projective points, but also as knives, and as borers.

The largest of the SHMP excavations on Islay took place at Bolsay Farm, a relatively sheltered site located on a plateau below Bein Tart a'Mhill, the highest of the Rinns, close to a stream that led from Loch a'Bhogaidh to the coast at Loch Indall. Test pitting in 1989 located an extremely dense, microlith-rich lithic scatter, which underwent further investigation in 1990 when a 7 × 4 m trench (Trench I) was opened and in 1992 a 20 × 15 trench (Trench II) was excavated (Figure 5.14). In Trench I, a scatter of five stakeholes was located, with no particular patterning, and an extremely dense lithic assemblage of 66,281 pieces, amongst which microliths were common. Trench II also contained vast quantities of flint and was associated with several small pits and a couple of stakeholes. Seven of the pits contained flint, most of which was burnt. Some broad spatial patterning is present in trench II with both primary knapping and microlith manufacture and discard in the northwest part of the trench. Debitage, including microdebitage, may also have been dumped into boggy ground on the edge of the site. Comparison with other sites on the island (Table 5.4) demonstrates that Bolsay Farm is much more focused on microlith production and discard with other activities involving the use of lithic artefacts relatively rare.

Charcoal from the site indicates extensive use of hazel, both as fuel and food, while pomoidiae (probably rowan) was also frequently used in hearths. The excavations indicate that a spring and pool of standing water was once present at the site, which made it a focus for Mesolithic and later Prehistoric groups over a long period of time: Radiocarbon dates provide evidence for Mesolithic occupation in the second half of the seventh millennium and the first half of the sixth. While large assemblages such as Bolsay Farm are often seen as base camps, the lack of tool diversity and spread of radiocarbon dates suggests it was repeatedly revisited, probably as a base for hunting and fowling around Loch a'Bhogaidh, by people attracted by the presence of the spring.

Figure 5.14 Excavations at Bolsay Farm, Islay (Copyright Steven Mithen)

The other sites excavated by the SHMP are interpreted as have been used in a different way to Bolsay Farm; at Coulererach, close to flint-rich beaches, tested pebbles underwent initial reduction to produce blades; Rockside may have been a stop-over point as it is located on a logical routeway between Sanaigmore Bay and Loch Gorm; Gleann Mor with good visibility and near to Loch a'Bhogaih may have been a place to monitor animal movements; Aoradh had views over the Gruinart-Loch Indal tidal strait. Mithen notes that potential settlement elements may be more difficult to locate or, in the case of coastal sites destroyed during marine transgression. However, he suggests the lack of a classic base camp or of truly specialised sites indicates that the people on Islay were, in Binford's (1980) terms, 'foragers' rather than 'collectors'. Collectors are characterised by the logistical organisation of residential and specialist camps seen amongst Star Carr groups (see chapter 2); foragers, by contrast, move their main residence frequently, generating small sites with fairly homogenous assemblages. That said, some sites show more of a focus on microliths, and others are more focused on processing activities (see Table 5.4), while on Colonsay a specialist plant exploitation site exists at Staosnaig (see below). It is notable that the larger sites excavated by the SHMP are microlith dominated. It may that there was more stability in landscape use for certain specialist sites, whereas the location of more generalised camps may have been more varied.

On Colonsay

Twelve kilometers from Islay is the much smaller island of Colonsay, only 13.5 km long and 5 km wide. At low tide, it is joined to the even smaller island of Oronsay (see chapter 6). It is lower lying than many of its neighbours, with a few rocky peaks and inland lochs. Along the coast are several large bays and smaller inlets, and major dune systems in the west and north. In the first part of the seventh millennium BC, the island hosted birch-hazel woodland. Fauna is more restricted than on Islay: Deer do not seem to have been present in the early post-glacial period. Marine mammals were likely to have been abundant: Seals bask on nearby rocky islets, and whale beachings are not uncommon.

Only one major site from this period has been excavated on the island, but it is an important one that gives a rare glimpse into the extent of the use of plant foods in the Mesolithic. Staosnaig (Figure 5.15) was excavated between 1989 and 1995 by the Southern Hebrides Mesolithic Project (Mithen 2000). Following extensive test pitting and trial trenches, two major areas were excavated: Area A, an area of around 16 m by 15 m, excavated in 1994, and the smaller area D, measuring around 9 m by 5 m and dug in 1991. A moderate-sized lithic assemblage, low in tools, was recovered clustered around three small hearths. This assemblage is less microlith focused than others in the region (Table 5.4), indicating a range of processing activities taking place around the hearths.

More extensive occupation was evident in the larger area D, where several features were located. Most significant was the largest: F.24 a sub-circular pit measuring 4.5 m across and 0.28 m deep (Figure 5.16). The feature contained a vast quantity of artefacts and food waste: 49,356 pieces of chipped stone, 45 bevel-ended tools (see Box 3.1), anvils, pumice, pigment and burnt bone fragments. However, it is the quantities of plant remains found within the feature that are most remarkable. Most of these were hazelnut shells: 3 kg were recovered

Figure 5.15 Excavations at Staosnaig, Colonsay (copyright Steve Mithen)

Figure 5.16 F24 at Staosnaig under excavation (copyright Steve Mithen)

(estimated to represent between 30,000 and 40,000 individual nuts) along with 400 fragments of tubers of the lesser celandine and 24 fragments of crab apple seed. This intensive hazel harvesting may have had such an impact that it is seen in local pollen profiles (Mithen 2000). The charring of crab apple indicates they may have been dried to increase sweetness. Lesser celandine is toxic and needs cooking to be edible. It can be roasted on hot stones or boiled and has been eaten historically as well as being favoured by modern wild food enthusiasts. It is best collected after the plant has flowered from summer onwards. The presence of apples and hazelnuts indicates late summer/autumn activity, though drying and storage mean that this cannot be certain. Indeed, it is unsurprising that a site that lacks bone, and where seasonality evidence is limited to plant foods, suggests this. Other seasons of occupation are unlikely to be represented by the evidence available.

Most of this material was concentrated in a dark organic fill of F.24, known as context 17. Micromorphology indicates a substantial component of unburnt organic material, whose decay caused collapse of what originally had been a much thicker layer. This unburnt material, which remains unidentified, has been hypothesised to represent unburnt hazelnut shells, as experiments suggest that only a small proportion of nut shells are charred following roasting. Context 17 was interpreted as midden material that was deposited into the footings of a small hut following its abandonment (Mithen 2000). This pit seems to have been repeatedly used for the deposition of hazelnuts, occuring during at least four of the minimum of six occupation events represented (Mithen and Wicks 2018).

However, another possibility could exist, that context 17 represents a wooden floor of a pit house and its associated living debris which has collapsed into the pit. The presence of possible wooden planking used as flooring for Scandinavian pit-houses has been noted by Grøn (2003). The sand component of this layer would have been brought in on footwear or clothing when it was used as a floor. This scenario of collapse would be a plausible interpretation for the spatial patterning, which shows in general the highest densities of various classes of lithics on the eastern edge of the feature in spit 1, on the southern, northern or western edges in spit 2 and only in the centre in spit 3 (see Mithen and Finlay 2000, Figures 5.2.27–32). The spread of radiocarbon dates suggests some longevity for this feature; it may have been imperfectly cleared out, and fresh matting laid on the remnants of previous occupations. This may have on occasions preserved material: A lens of microdebitage within context 17 may have been preserved as another layer of matting was added. The interpretation of this as a collapsed floor obviously does not preclude the feature subsequently being used for middening.

Just over a metre away from this feature was a large stone lined pit, 3 × 1.25 m in size, that seemed to have had several phases of use. This has been interpreted as a cooking pit or hazelnut roasting pit, perhaps the source of much of the burnt material found in F24. Unlike the smaller Pennine examples which were used to cook foods other than hazelnuts and which were probably reused as rubbish pits, this pit seems to have been abandoned with most of the stones in their original arrangement. This cooking pit seems to have had several phases of use, and was filled with charred hazelnut shells, small flint debitage, course stone tools and a fragment of bone. A smaller pit had a stone lining on its western edge and may have functioned as a hazelnut roasting pit. Several smaller pits which just contain lithic material were also found in the vicinity.

The lithic assemblage from the site was mostly made on flint (98.9%) with small quantities of quartz, rock crystal, pitchstone and siltstone. The microlith assemblage is characterised by backed bladelets, in contrast to the scalene triangle assemblages of Islay. The excavators have suggested this is a functional difference, associated with specialised plant processing. The presence of further plant processing equipment has been noted on the site in the coarse stone assemblage: Stone bevel-ended tools (suitable for crushing hazelnuts), anvils and pounders.

Coll, Mull and Arran

While the islands of Islay, Colonsay and Oronsay have dominated understanding of the Late Mesolithic of the Western Isles, more recent fieldwork projects have begun to fill in the gaps. On Fiskary Bay, Coll, lithic artefacts, fish remains (of wrasse, whiting, saith and pollock) and hazelnut shells have been recovered from raised beach deposits. No remains from terrestrial mammals were found, perhaps indicating their absence from the island (Mithen et al. 2019). Dates span the late eighth and seventh millennium BC, and modelling of dates suggests at least three visits to the site (Mithen and Wicks 2008; Mithen et al. 2019). The narrow inlet of the bay has made it suitable for fish weirs and traps in more recent time, and its excavators argue that this topography may have also been attractive to Mesolithic groups (Mithen et al. 2007). Mithen et al. (2019) note that the voyage to Coll in small boats would have taken several hours and while this is a good fishing location, similar places were present on the mainland; thus, purely economic reasons for these repeated visits cannot be invoked.

Criet Dubh on Mull is on the shores of Loch a' Chumhainn, an estuarine location. The site lies in a sheltered gully between two rocky outcrops and close to a small stream. Excavations have revealed a complex arrangement of features, including stone-lined hearths, post-holes and stakeholes. Twenty-six dates from the site span the first half of the seventh millennium BC, apart from two earlier outliers discussed in chapter 4, and suggest a minimum of five separate occupations (Mithen and Wicks 2018). These features appear to be related to at least one structure, made up of posts and stakeholes, with internal pits and hearths (Figure 5.17). The footprint of this, at up to c.6 m in diameter, is similar in size to the large Middle Mesolithic structures (see chapter 4), though unlike these and the earlier structures from Star Carr, the Criet Dubh examples lack an internal pit. Within this structure were a series of overlapping hearths and a series of stakholes that might represent racks (Mithen et al. 2019). While microliths are most common, a broad range of other tools was recovered, concentrated in capping deposits and a small number of features. The restricted range of the assemblage may suggest a specialised function for the building such as a smoke-house, though other non-economic interpretations such as a sweat-lodge were also considered (Mithen and Wicks 2018).

On Arran, Mesolithic material has been recovered from Auchareoch. This site lies inland, 4 km from the current coast and at 165 m above sea-level and was located on a kame deposit on the edge of a small basin. Lithic material was recovered from quarry workings which had severely damaged the sites (Affleck et al. 1988). Two quarries had been excavated and the main area of Mesolithic occupation located was on a platform on the southern edge of the northern quarry. Here over 4000 lithics, in three concentrations, and a series of pit-hearths were excavated. Analysis of the

Figure 5.17 Complex arrangement of features at Criet Dubh (copyright Steve Mithen)

assemblage indicates that beach pebble flint was favoured; less than 10% of the material is of Arran Pitchstone, despite this being a favoured material for Neolithic groups in the region (see Box 5.2). This material is available as rolled nodules from the kame deposit. The tool assemblage is dominated by microliths, both scalene triangles and backed bladelets, while microburins indicate microlith production and retooling. Two dates are available from the platform area, one from hazelnut shells recovered from one of the hearths of 6375–6015 cal BC (7300 ± 90 BP; OxA-1599). A measurement on oak from an adjacent hearth is around 500 years earlier, but this may be a result of the old wood effect. However, earlier occupation is certainly present, as a pit containing charcoal and burnt bone excavated by Peter Strong in the face of the southern quarry has a date of 7307–6690 cal BC (8060 ± 90 BP; OxA-1601) (Hedges et al. 1989). This is likely to indicate that Auchareoch was a favoured place for repeated occupation.

Box 5.2   Arran Pitchstone

Pitchstone (Figure 5.18) is poor man's obsidian, a volcanic glass, arising from the rapid cooling of silica-rich magmas, but without the extreme lustre that has made obsidian widely attractive to human groups across time and space. Pitchstone has a higher water content and more phenocryst (crystalline inclusions) than obsidian, though some of the finer material on Arran has similar flaking qualities. Work by Williams Thorpe and Thorpe (1984) highlighted that much of the pitchstone exported beyond Arran is the high-quality homogenous aphyric type that they suggested was procured from the Corriegills outcrop on the east coast of Arran. Ballin and Faithfull's (2009) survey suggested that other sources may also have been used, though aphyric pitchstone was preferred in the Early Neolithic.

Pitchstone is used in Mesolithic contexts on Arran, as at Auchareoch (see above). Here, both the high-quality aphyric and the less good-quality porphyritic forms were employed, though both seem to have been procured from local gravel rather than a bedrock source (Affleck et al. 1988). An extensive survey (Ballin 2009) indicted widespread exchange of pitchstone in the Early Neolithic but little use beyond Arran during the Mesolithic. Since this survey, new evidence has emerged to modify this position. Pitchstone has been recovered from two features with Mesolithic radiocarbon dates at Dunragit, Dumfries and Galloway and at Succoth, near Arrochar, Argyll and Bute, both between 70 and 75 km from Arran. Microliths in pitchstone are also known from Tayvallich in Argyll c.60 km from Arran. This is a multiperiod site with dates in the sixth millennium BC (Ballin et al. 2018). Pitchstone is also known further south from Stainton West, Carlisle. Here, it was imported in small packages, used for blade production and worked to exhaustion (Brown et al. in press). Ballin et al. (2018) suggest that exchange of pitchstone may have started in the Mesolithic, but became more formalised and ritualised in the early Neolithic when its networks of distribution seem much more extensive.

Figure 5.18 Pitchstone (copyright Graeme Warren, UCD School of Archaeology)

The Western borders: Ayrshire, Dumfries and Galloway and Cumbria

In Dumfries and Galloway and Cumbria late Mesolithic sites are known from areas of coastal erosion. Large surveys of these areas by Cormack in Dumfries and John and Peter Cherry in Cumbria have revealed much Late Mesolithic evidence. Most of these are surface scatters, but excavations have taken place at Low Clone a site located by Cormack on cliffs above Luce Bay (Coles 1964; Cormack and Coles 1968), while in Ayrshire late Mesolithic sites are known through commercial excavations.

Low Clone lies on top of a 15 m asl cliff on the east side of Luce Bay, above the post-glacial raised beach and near to a stream with views over to the Isle of Man. Excavations in 1965 and 1966 revealed a large, disturbed depression 14 by 4.5 m in-terpreted as one or a series of dug features. These were associated with stone settings, charcoal flecks and a small lithic assemblage. This included some narrow microliths (along with some earlier material), burins, scrapers and awls.

Similar enigmatic hollows have been located in more recent developer-funded work in the area. At Littlehill Bridge, Girvan, in Ayrshire, on a site just above the margins of the maximum marine transgression, a series of scoops measuring 4–6 m by 4 m were located. These may represent the remains of structures, though no post or stakeholes were noted (MacGregor and Donnelly 2001). Fills of these features include ashy de-posits and dumps of hearth material. Two contexts were noted in the most extensively excavated feature, the upper part of which contained greater quantities of worked flint, as well as charred hazelnut shells with a late seventh millennium date. This pattern, indicative of a raised floor, is compatible with other sunken feature structures, such as Star Carr. As well as hazelnuts, other charred seeds recovered were sun spurge (*Euphorbia helioscopia*), charlock (*Sinapis arvensis*) and chickweed (*Stellaria media*). The latter two can be eaten, the former is an irritant; the excavators suggest a possible use as a medicine or poison. Littlehill Bridge is just one of a series of Mesolithic scatters in the Girvan area, which include the site of Gallow Hill (chapter 6). At a time of higher sea-level, this would have been a rich area of lagoons and estuaries (Donnelly and MacGregor 2005).

While initial work in this region suggested a coastal focus for Mesolithic occupation, subsequent survey of inland areas, particularly as a result of the work of Tom Afleck, revealed a persistent Mesolithic presence along rivers systems and the shores of lochs, particularly the Ken and Dee and Loch Doon. In contrast to Cormack's coastal sites where flint dominates, these inland sites employed significant quantities of chert which can be obtained locally. Of these inland sites, two have undergone more significant excavation. Smittons is located on a gravel ridge close to the Water of Ken (Edwards 1996). The assemblage employed both flint and chert, and several charcoal concentrations and a stone setting were located. Two dates on burnt hazelnut shells show occupation in the second half of the sixth millennium BC, as well as during the last centuries of the Mesolithic. At Starr on the southwestern shore of Loch Doon, lithic material was recovered from several trenches spread across a 100 m stretch of shoreline. The lithic material came from an old soil horizon that was buried by peat in the Iron Age. Several features were located including a stone-built heath within a gully, and a series of stakeholes associated with pits and hearths. Only one radiocarbon date was obtained: This was almost identical to the late sixth millennium date from Smittons (Edwards 1996). Both sites are microlith dominated, though microwear demonstrates these tools were used differently: At Starr, microliths were used as knives and piercers, while at Smittons they had a projectile function (Finlayson 1990).

The evidence from Cumbria echoes the findings from Southwest Scotland. Initial work indicated a coastal focus, but more recent evidence underlines the importance of rivers. Key amongst this is the Stainton West site, excavated by Oxford Archaeology North between 2008 and 2011 (Brown et al. in press). The site lies on the northern bank of the river Eden, and activity took place around a palaeochannel, subject to both episodes of higher energy with overbank flooding and slower flowing phases. Here were clearings and areas of hazel scrub in an oak-elm woodland; beneath the trees and in the clearings grew bracken, wood sorrel and creeping buttercup. The earliest occupation took place at the start of the sixth millennium BC, when a small tent-like structure (structure 1), marked by lithic debris was probably erected. This is associated with a pit with burnt stones that may represent a cooking pit and an external hearth. Two additional pits (one within, one outside the structure) contained lithic material. This structure is close to a midden, which seems to have had a long duration and may have been first used by those who used structure 1. Beneath this is another group of undated features, a hearth and stakeholes which may be contemporary or even predate structure 1. Brown and colleagues suggest that if this is the earliest occupation of the site, the emplacement of the midden may reference this initial episode of occupation.

A few centuries after this visit, the channel was colonised by beavers who constructed a dam (Figure 5.19) made from trees dendrochronologically dated to the 56th century cal BC. One of the oaks used in the construction of the dam and which also died in the 56th century was charred, another showed a series of scratches, possibly made by a young bear or a lynx, while a handful of pieces of wood found in and around the dam showed charring or marks of stone tools. In the sixth millennium, Stainton West was a landscape of co-habitation and a place that at different times was a focus for the activities of humans, beavers and other animals; it is only in the fifth millennium that humans became the primary inhabitants.

Figure 5.19 The beaver dam (left) and lodge (right) in the main palaeochannel at Stainton West (copyright Oxford Archaeology Ltd.)

On the Cumbrian coast, a major fieldwalking project by John, Joyce and Peter Cherry investigated a stretch of coast 40 km long, extending from Whitehaven to Silecroft. Significant concentrations of lithic material were located at St Bees, Sea Scale, Drigg and Eskmeals (Cherry and Cherry 1983). A series of Late Mesolithic scatters were located both immediately north and south of St Bees. These are microlith dominated, but some also show significant quantities of scrapers. Small nodules of beach flint dominate, though black chert and tuff were also used. The greatest concentration of Mesolithic material came from the Eskmeals area, where many scatters were located at Monks Moor, Eskmeals Pool and Williamson's Moss at Eskmeals dating to the sixth and fifth millennia (Cherry and Cherry 1986). In comparison to the other sites from this survey that are located on coastal cliffs, the Eskmeals sites are lower lying, located around the 8 m contour on ridges above waterlogged areas around a sluggish stream known as Eskmeals Pool, which drains into the river Esk. A hearth from Monks Moor dates to the first half of the sixth millennium BC, a time when environmental evidence suggests estuarine conditions (Tooley and Huddart 1972).

Inland, there has been less work in Cumbria. Late Mesolithic material has been located on the eastern edge of the Cumbrian mountains, at around 250–300 m asl, through the excavation of a pipeline near Shap (Cherry and Cherry 1987).

Several scatters were located close to Wickers Gill, a stream that drains into the river Lowther, and to the north of Shap at Windrigg Hill. The assemblages were mostly made on black chert, with varying quantities of tuff and flint. While many of these sites are microlith dominated, with microburins indicating manufacture, other tools are present, particularly at Wickers Gill 2, where scrapers and awls were also recovered. Several further sites were located to the east at a similar altitude on the edge of the limestone uplands, indicating a persistent presence of Late Mesolithic activity in the region.

Northern England and the Midlands

In Northern England and the Midlands (Figure 5.20), the best known, and most of the well-dated sites come from the Pennines where over a century of excavation and collection have produced a relatively detailed picture of Mesolithic life, particularly during the last millennium of the period. To the east of the Pennines, Mesolithic sites are poorly dated and there is a much shorter history of research. However, scatters with Late Mesolithic microliths are common, particularly on the North York Moors. Here Radley (1969b) has noted that most scatters are small and

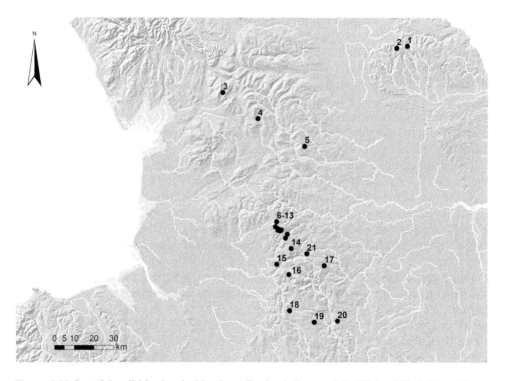

Figure 5.20 Late Mesolithic sites in Northern England discussed (1. White Gill, 2. Urra Moor, 3. Kingsdale Head, 5. Malham Tarn, 6. Rishworth Drain, 7. Windy Hill, 8. Readycon Dene, 9. Dean Clough, 10. Dan Clough, 11. Badger Slacks, 12. Pule Bents, 13. Rocher Moss, 14. Red Ratcher, 15. Grange Farm, 16. Harry Hut, 17. Broomhead Moor, 18. Lismore Fields. 19. Stoney Low, 20. Beeley Moor, 21. Dunford Bridge A)

dominated by microliths, which he suggested represented hunting camps. However, larger sites with more diverse toolkits are also represented: At the two large scatters at Upleatham on the edge of the uplands, where scrapers are as common as microliths; at Mauley Cross where a spread of flint spanned 400 by 250 m (Spratt et al. 1976); and at Snilesworth Moor where large quantities of lithic material were located close to a spring (Simmons 1996). Late Mesolithic sites are usually found in prominent positions on the high moorland plateau (though rarely above 400 m asl), on or below the spring line, just below the crest of the watershed (Simmons 1996; Waughman 2017).

Charcoal within pollen profiles has been argued to represent evidence for vegetation management and thus a proxy for human presence in both the Pennines and North York Moors during this period. While much evidence for burning dates to the fifth millennium (see chapter 6), a charcoal peak has been recorded at around 7000 cal BC at Robinson's Moss (Tallis and Switsur 1990) and two burning phases in the seventh and sixth millennium at Soyland Moor (Williams 1985) both Pennine sites, while charcoal in the lowest layer of peat at White Gill on the North York Moors indicates activity during the second half of the sixth millennium (Innes and Blackford 2003).

In other areas of Northern England and the eastern midlands, high ground and high points in lower lying areas also seem to have been favoured, with sites on the Lincolnshire edge, and high points overlooking the rivers Nene and Welland (Myers 2006). Caves also saw occupation at this time, at Creswell Crags and in the Upper Dove Valley. Thorpe Common Rockshelter has provided three Mesolithic dates with large standard deviations that span the sixth and seventh millennium. Here three thousand artefacts, including 64 Late Mesolithic microliths, mainly recovered from the upper layer indicate a fairly substantial or repeated occupation, with two hearths and a linear arrangement of stones. Faunal remains in the cave consisted of mainly red deer and pig, though it is unclear if these were accumulated by human agency (Mellars 1976a, Richards 1989).

Two main chronological grouping of Late Mesolithic sites have been suggested in the north of England (Radley et al. 1974; Switsur and Jacobi 1975). These have assemblages either characterised by left-lateralised scalene triangles (March Hill type assemblages) or those consisting of 'rod' microliths (straight-backed bladelets). Triangle sites show variability in raw material use and the frequencies of other microlith types present (usually backed bladelets and crescents). 'Rod' assemblages are characterised by the absence of chert, and narrow straight-backed bladelets are the only microlith type represented. These date to the Fifth millennium and will be discussed in chapter 6. Late Mesolithic sites with other forms of microlith are also present. Four-sided microliths have been suggested by Jacobi to have a chronological significance: In the north the sites of White Hill North (Switsur and Jacobi 1975), Red Ratcher (Stonehouse 2001) and Rocher Moss F (Preston 2012) in the Central Pennines and Beely Moor in Derbyshire are characterised by trapezoids (though Red Ratcher also has small scalenes), while rhomboids have been found at Dean Clough (Myers 1987). Small crescents are found at Rishworth Drain 2, and make up a small component in many assemblages. Pear shaped microliths are rare, found in the Pennines only at Dean Clough, and to the east in northwest Lincolnshire at Risby Warren and Holme-on-Spalding Moor, East Yorkshire (Jacobi 1975).

The Mesolithic of the Pennines

Just as upland routeways and watersheds saw concentrations of Mesolithic material in Scotland, the Marsden/Saddleworth region has long been known for finds of Mesolithic flint artefacts (Figure 5.21). This area is the narrowest point of the Pennines and connects the headwaters of streams that drain into the Mersey, Ribble and Humber basins, an obvious routeway between east and west. Clark noted this area as amongst the three most widely known of English microlithic sites (Clark 1932, 32). As long ago as 1882, Law and Horsfel commented 'flints are so scattered on this elevated moorland that in almost every case where an opportunity was offered for an examination of the subsoil, one or more could be found'. Stonehouse (2001) notes the presence of 111 Mesolithic sites in 9 km^2 in this region. The use of the watershed as a routeway has been seen for a long time as a possible explanation for the high density of Mesolithic sites on this desolate stretch of moorland (Buckley 1924), and Mesolithic sites line natural routes across the area (Preston 2012).

In the Late Mesolithic, woodland would have covered the entire Pennines, with the possible exception of some of the very highest areas. Oak and hazel woodland would have been present on the slopes, with birch and pine in higher areas. Open birch woodlands and hazel-oak woodlands in the early stage of succession encourage understorey vegetation that is attractive to animals and humans (Spikins 2002). Human manipulation of these woodlands through managed burning would have also introduced clearings and areas of new vegetation growth (Jacobi et al. 1976; Mellars 1976b; see Box 6.5). These factors may have made this region more attractive than the densely wooded, unproductive lime-oak forests of the lowlands. The lighter wooded uplands may have also represented easier routes to traverse north-south in comparison

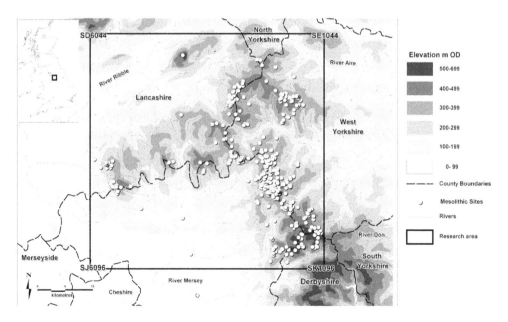

Figure 5.21 Density of Mesolithic sites and findspots in the Central Pennines (copyright Paul Preston)

to movement though the lowland forests; and north-south transfers of raw material do seem to be important in the region (see Box 5.3).

In the previous chapter, the paucity of dated Pennine Mesolithic sites belonging to the eight millennium BC was noted. The same is true of the seventh and much of the sixth millennium. While most sites are undated and may well belong to this period, sites that do have dates belong almost exclusively to the fifth millennium. While this may be taphonomic, related to preservation or a fashion for built hearths, this evidence may suggest the upland areas of the Pennines (and perhaps also the North York Moors) became much more important foci in the final millennium of the Mesolithic, perhaps following, as Spikins (2002) argues, the choking of lowland areas with dense, unproductive woodlands. In this chapter, the few sites dated to the sixth and seventh millennium will be discussed, along with a more general discussion of undated Late Mesolithic sites.

There are only two dated seventh and sixth milleniums sites in the Central Pennines and both – Rishworth Drain 2 and Dean Clough 1 – are measurements on bulked, unidentified charcoal. Dean Clough 1 is a small scatter 3–4 m wide, though truncated by erosion to the south, around two fire patches. The radiocarbon date of 6770–6100 cal BC (Stonehouse 1986) was made on bulked charcoal taken from three separate grid squares, one related to one of the concentrations interpreted as hearths, the other squares closer to the second potential hearth. The lithic assemblage contains small scalene triangles; however, Early Mesolithic microliths are also present raising the possibility that this measurement may combine evidence of activity of different dates. As well as microliths, a series of small straight and oblique truncations were present in the tool assemblage, and a variety of flint types and a small quantity of cherts were used. The date from Rishworth Drain 2 comes from a charcoal stain, adjacent to a lithic scatter where small crescents were manufactured. The entire assemblage was made from Derbyshire chert, a source 50 km to the south (Myers 1986). The presence of charcoal clusters, rather than built hearths on these two sites may indicate that the low visibility of Mesolithic groups in the seventh millennium is due to a lack of the dug features that more readily preserve material for dating.

More reliable evidence for Mesolithic occupation is found in the Northern Pennines, where work by the Ingleborough Archaeology Group has uncovered a Mesolithic site at Kingsdale Head on the western edge of the Dales (Melton et al. 2014). Here a large cooking pit 1.5 m in diameter was found. Hawthorn charcoal from the base gave a radiocarbon date of 7025–6645 cal BC (SUERC-11499). Two measurements from a recut suggested this pit had a later period of use between 6220 and 6070 BC. A second smaller pit, filled with charcoal at its base and sealed with a layer of stones was found close to the cooking pit and dated to 6600–6440 cal BC (SUERC-33528). Such cooking pits are often described as 'earth ovens' and are well-known both in the archaeological and ethnographic record (Black and Thorns 2014). They consist of a pit, the base of which is often lined with stones, then covered with fuel and large stones; the fire is then lit. Once it is smouldering, food is added, sandwiched between packing of green plant material, then an earth plug is added. A second fire may be lit on top, as seems to have occurred at Kingsdale. Ethnographically these earth ovens have a strong link with plant processing, though they were also used to cook meat in northern latitudes (Black and Thorns 2014, 209). The presence of burnt bone in an earth oven from South Haw (Chatterton 2006) indicates that at least on occasions meat was cooked on the Pennines. Earth ovens were often reused, remaining visible for centuries (Black and Thorns 2014). Their presence would thus encourage reoccupation and the emergence of a 'persistent place' (Schlanger 1992). The range of

Box 5.3   Raw material use in the Pennine Late Mesolithic

Myers (1986) has highlighted a major shift in raw materials use between Early and Late Mesolithic in the Pennines. Deepcar assemblages in the Pennines and lowland areas to the east were characterised by the predominant use of Wolds flint (see chapter 2). The late Mesolithic sees a much broader use of raw materials: Translucent brown pebble flints, grey or white flint and a wide variety of cherts. These nodules range in size, but are often smaller than those of the earlier assemblages. This shift in material has been linked by Myers to technological strategies to deal with changes in the post-glacial vegetation, with denser woodland resulting in a shift from intercept of migratory animals to encounter hunting of solitary beasts. While it is no longer though that red deer herds migrated in lightly wooded early post-glacial landscape, these woodlands did become denser, and it may have been more difficult to locate animal prey. The ability to draw on a more diverse range of materials was coupled with the use of composite tools with increased numbers of smaller elements that, unlike the barbed points and single-barbed arrows of the Early Mesolithic, would still be usable if elements were damaged (Myers 1987). With a ready supply of small raw material packages, these composite tools could be repaired whenever time permitted, rather than jeopardising a hunting event.

The Pennine cherts range from relatively good quality shiny black material, through brown, grey or blue of moderate quality, often vesicular chert, to very poor material in a variety of colours which tends to angular rather than conchoidal fracture along bedding planes (Figure 5.22). These cherts are extremely variable, even within a single nodule, which makes discussions of types and sources problematic, though geochemical sourcing work has been able to distinguish between material from the Northern and Southern Pennines (Evans et al. 2007, 2010). Their poor quality means they are often dismissed as 'local' (Howard-Davies et al. 1996), but Hind (1998) persuasively argues their distribution may be the product of long-distance systems of movement and exchange.

The best known, and best quality, of the Pennine cherts is the shiny black chert which derives from the Monsal Head limestone of North Derbyshire (Radley 1968). Both Poole (1986) and Hind (1998) point out that fine black chert can also derive from the Yordale series of the northern Pennines, as it simply represents the finer quality end of a broad spectrum of variability amongst the Pennine cherts. While the original location of all these cherts is the limestone of the Northern or Southern Pennines, they can also be found in a range of derived contexts in glacial tills and fluvial systems. Chert is found in waterways draining the central Pennines, though recent surveys suggest this material is rarely of knappable size or quality (Poole 2020). Another possible source of chert is Merseyside to the west (Hind 1998) or even the banded chert of North Wales, which was used in the northwest lowlands (Cowell 1992). Radley (1968) suggests poor quality vesicular chert, which is common in the assemblage from March Hill Carr trench A, is local to the Central Pennines; it is certainly present as small, generally unknappable elements in local till deposits

(a)

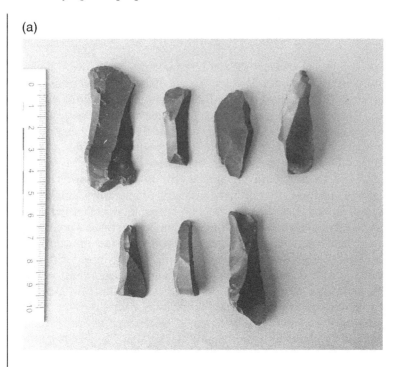

(b)

Figure 5.22 Pennine cherts: High-quality Derbyshire chert (top), poorer quality vesicular chert (bottom) (copyright Stephen Poole)

(Poole 2020), but its original source is unknown. A blue/grey banded material may be rhyolite (Poole 1986). The nearest source of rhyolite is the Borrowdale volcanic series, but this differs in appearance from the Borrowdale material (P. Cherry pers. comm.). This blue-grey material appears to be more common on sites on the west side of the Pennines than the east (Jacobi 1975). At Piethorn Brook, for example, it is the most common material used (Poole 1986).

The March Hill Carr assemblage (see chapter 6) reveals numerous different materials of varying colours and qualities. In contrast, many other sites show dependence on a single material type. The Late Mesolithic material from Lominot C, was manufactured almost entirely from brown translucent flint, while nearly all the artefacts recovered from Broomhead V and X were made from black Derbyshire chert (Radley 1968). The frequency of a particular material in an assemblage appears to be unrelated to the distance from its source (Hind 1998; Myers 1986), with chert assemblages found both close (Broomhead V) and distant (Rishworth Drain 2) from the Derbyshire lime-stone, while sites with relatively little chert (Harry Hut) can be located close to this source. Recent geochemical sourcing studies show that Mesolithic groups at Lismore Fields, Derbyshire, and Malham Tarn, North Yorkshire, used southern chert and northern chert, respectively (Evans et al. 2007, 2010). If these small-scale studies can be extrapolated, it may be that groups in areas with abundant chert sources procured them locally, but chert was moved longer distances into the Central Pennines.

Refitting of chert from Badger Slacks, another site where Derbyshire chert was used and over 40 km from its source, indicates that the chert was brought in as unmodified small blocks, while Stephen Poole's refitting of material from Dan Clough indicates the same was also true for flint (Myers 1986). This contrasts with the Early Mesolithic in the region, where cores in Deepcar assemblages are heavily reduced in comparison to those found nearer the source (ibid.). A feature of the Pennine Late Mesolithic appears to be a technological strategy designed to make efficient use of small nodules of good quality material. Amongst the material excavated by the March Hill Project (Spikins 2002), composite tools, in particular scraper/burins are relatively well represented. Use has also been made of the sturdier core preparation flakes as tools – several examples exist of crested blades or plunging flakes being used as awls, and even scrapers and burins.

Fine-quality flint material appears to have been specially selected for the manufacture of microliths. This is true of the March Hill Carr complex (see chapter 6) and also of other Pennine sites. At Harry Hut, Derbyshire (Pierpoint and Hart 1980), only 11% of the entire assemblage was of flint, in comparison with 76% of the microliths. At Piethorn Brook, the rhyolite-like material makes up 54.2% of the assemblage but 64% of microliths were made from chert and 24.7% from flint, materials that make up 28.1% and 15.7% of the overall assemblage (Poole 1986). Raw material patterning is also likely to be a reflection of individual, sub-group and group mobility and prevailing networks of associa-tion and obligation. These ties appear to have stretched both to the northern and southern ends of the Pennine chain and to the coastal plains to the west, and on occasions to the Yorkshire Wolds in the east (Preston and Kador 2018).

dates from Kingsdale Head indicate that this place was indeed revisited over a period of several hundred years.

Lithics from Kingsdale Head indicate a broad range of activities with microliths (30), scrapers (16), awls (5), burins (3), notches (6), truncations (3) and miscellaneous retouched/utilised pieces (44) all present. While Late Mesolithic sites on the Pennines have been characterised as small hunting camps (Donahue and Lovis 2006; Smith 2002), it is clear that often this is not always the case. Kingsdale is in many ways typical of sites which have undergone more extensive excavation. These show repeated occupation, several built features in close proximity and lithic assemblages that are rather more than simply microlith dominated. The initial use of the pit at Kingsdale was prior to the 8.2 cold event, while the later recut may be contemporary with the event but most likely just post-dates it. This does not suggest any significant disruption in landscape use in the Northern Pennines at this time, despite its effects being severe in this region, as evidenced by loess-derived colluviation (Vincent et al. 2010).

Late Mesolithic industries in the Pennines are heavily microlith dominated (see Table 5.5). This has led to the assumption that the Pennine sites represent hunting stands (Smith 2002). Microwear studies over the last few decades have made it clear that microliths had a varied function, not simply as projectile elements, though this was undoubtedly an important role, but also as piercers and knives. As small elements in composite tools their whole *raison d'etre* may be this flexibility (see chapter 1). Beyond the difficulty of equating forms with particular functions, a consideration of the dynamics of use and resharpening reveal further problems As Myers (1987) has noted (see Box 1.4), Late Mesolithic technologies involved the use of larger numbers of microliths in composite tools than in the Early Mesolithic, thus frequencies of microliths in assemblages are not strictly comparable between the two periods, and discussions of site function need to take this into consideration. As single elements in composite tools, microliths represent only part of a tool, whereas burins and scrapers, as the only lithic part of a tool, represent a tool in themselves. Furthermore, burins and scrapers can be re-sharpened and re-used, whereas microlithic elements would have been discarded and replaced (Myers 1987). As a result, microliths are likely to have much higher representation and other tools much lower representation than the frequency of activities related to their use. If this is taken into consideration, variation is more apparent in the Pennine industries, though even so, at some sites activities requiring the manufacture, maintenance or deposition of composite tools using microlithic elements seem to have been a major focus.

Table 5.5 Formal tool frequencies from selected Pennine Mesolithic sites

Site	Microliths	Scrapers	Burins	Awls	Truncation
Badger Slacks 2 (Myers 1987)	3	9	2	0	0
Blubberhouses Moor (Davies 1963)	5	108	5	2	0
Dean Clough 1 (Stonehouse 1986)	22	0	0	4	19
Dean Clough C (Stonehouse 1987)	53	5	1	0	0
Dunford Bridge A (Radley et al. 1974)	41	0	3	0	0
Harry Hut, Derbyshire (Pierpoint and Hart 1980)	19	2	0	0	0
Pule Bents (Stonehouse 1997)	93	0	0	0	0
Rishworth Drain 2 (Myers 1987)	30	1	0	0	0

Perhaps only sites where microliths are the only tool, or sites with only one or two other tools can properly be considered as purely focused on hunting. One such site may be Pule Bents, on the southern flank of Pule Hill, overlooking the Colne Valley. Here 93 microliths were recovered spread across a 4 by 4 m area in association with only 10 pieces of debitage (Stonehouse 1997). However, this small group of material could also represent a cache, and Myers (1989) has suggested that the isolated groups of microliths found on high ground in the Pennines and North York Moors and usually interpreted as hunting losses could in fact on occasions represent caching of material for future use (see Box 1.4 for a full discussion of these finds). Preston (2012) has suggested that cores too were cached on occasions, on sites such as Windy Hill F.

In contrast to these isolated microlith groupings, other sites show a much more varied range of activities (Table 5.5). Blubberhouses Moor, at 250 m asl (a lower altitude than many other Pennine sites) is dominated by scrapers, with microliths uncommon (Davies 1963). Hazelnuts shells (rare on Pennine sites despite the presence of hazel wood in hearths) have also been recovered, perhaps suggesting a different seasonality to occupation compared to the more upland sites. Scrapers are also common at Badger Slacks 2 at 420 m asl. On higher altitude sites, burins are frequent, as at March Hill Carr, Buckley's March Hill excavations (see chapter 6) and Dunford Bridge A, while truncations are common at Dean Clough 1 (Stonehouse 1986), Dean Clough C (Stonehouse 1987) and Harry Hut, Derbyshire (Pierpoint and Hart 1980). Rather than being characterised by evidence for hunting activities, if functional morphology and tool maintenance practises are taken into consideration, many of the Pennine assemblages appear more balanced between retooling and processing, while others display evidence of functional variation in favour of tasks involving the use of microliths, burins or scrapers. Today these moorlands can be rather bleak, encouraging interpretations that suggest they were only visited out of necessity (usually presumed to be hunting), but in the Late Mesolithic they would have been oak and hazel woodlands, favoured places for collection of plant foods and for animal browse. The post-glacial thermal maximum of the sixth millennium BC, meant these areas are likely to have been warmer than the present (Wanner et al. 2015). The evidence for varied activities, taken in conjunction with the presence of built hearths and cooking pits, suggests that some Pennine Late Mesolithic sites are something more than simple hunting camps.

Despite the ubiquitous presence of hearths on these sites, evidence for other features or structures is rare. An arc of stones may define a tent ring at Rishworth Drain C (Preston 2012). Flat stones that may have served as anvils, seats, or tables are also reported from several sites, though this is an area in which such stones also occur naturally. Several are associated with the structure at Piethorn Brook (see chaper 4), and other examples were found on Dunford Bridge A (Radley et al. 1974) and Linsgreave Clough C (Preston 2012). Buckley reports an anvil stone found on the north of March Hill showing pitting from use, and associated with a scatter of lithic debitage (Spikins 2002), while a 65 cm long stone at Readycon Dene was associated with a hearth (Stonehouse 1986). Further south, at Stoney Lowe in Derbyshire, Radley (1968) has suggested that a small alcove in an outcrop of carboniferous limestone might have been roofed. A linear arrangement of stones may have been used to weigh down the edge of a tent. Relatively few lithic artefacts have been recovered, indicating this would have been perhaps an overnight camp. Rather more substantial evidence may be present on the lower flanks of the Pennines, areas that have traditionally seen less archaeological survey. Recent work by the Tameside Archaeological

Society at Grange Farm has located an area of complex pits and hearths that appears to have been a focus for occupation over a long period. Charred hazelnut shells from one feature were dated to 6620–6470 cal BC. This site is located in one of the major valley routeways between the uplands and the lowlands to the west (Myers 2020).

Lowland Northern England

While Late Mesolithic evidence is common in the uplands, dated sites are rare in adjacent lowland areas of Northern England and the Midlands despite an increase in Mesolithic finds in recent years spanning sites on all types of geologies (Myers 2006). Seventh and sixth millennium activity has been recorded at Flixton School House Farm, in the Vale of Pickering (Taylor pers. comm.). By this time, Lake Flixton had shrunk into a series of pools and the occupation took place in an area of hazel woodland leading down into fen carr (Taylor and Gray Jones 2009). Late Mesolithic material is relatively common more broadly in the eastern end Vale of Pickering, found at sites both on the northern (at Seamer B, Rabbit Hill, Lingholm Farm) and southern margins (Barry's Island) of the area of fen carr covering the former extent of Lake Flixton. Late Mesolithic material tends to be found on slightly higher ground, which would have formed islands and peninsulas into the wetland.

Beyond the Vale of Pickering, radiocarbon dates on charred hazelnut shells also come from two separate pits from Kirkby-on-Bain in Lincolnshire. One pit was dated to the start of the seventh millennium, a second pit was found to date to more than a millennium later (Griffiths 2011). A third dated site is Staythorpe (see Box 5.4) in the Trent Valley, a find that indicates the significance of fluvial settings in the region; this has been echoed by undated sites in this area, where small rises in lower lying areas, and high points overlooking rivers seem to have been favoured (Myers 2006).

Rivers seem important settings for Late Mesolithic sites in both Northern England and the Midlands. This encompasses sites in the north of the region, such as Topcliffe on Swale (Chatterton 2006; Cowling and Strickland 1947) to those on the Trent to the east of the Pennines, such as Staythorpe (see Box 5.4), and Lunt Meadows on the River Alt to the west. At Lunt, excavations have located structural evidence and arrangements of colourful stones (Cowell 2018). On the west coast, survey by Alison Burns (2014, 2021) has revealed ephemeral evidence for the use of the saltmarsh areas at Formby. Here, both human and animal footprints are represented, with dates spanning the late Mesolithic. As in other inter-tidal areas, children are well-represented, suggesting they may have played important roles in checking traps and gathering shellfish.

Further south in East Anglia, similar patterns have been noted, though separating out Early and Late Mesolithic evidence is difficult. Billington (2017) has noted the strong clustering of Mesolithic sites along river systems in the Breckland, with sites along the Lark and the Little Ouse. Away from the rivers in East Anglia, sites on the interfluves are rarer and those that have been located are often clustered around lakes and meres (Billington 2017). While sites themselves are undated, charcoal in environmental profiles at some of these meres has been seen as produced by hearths from nearby Mesolithic campsites. At Hockham Mere, charcoal is present throughout much of the Mesolithic, while at Quidenham Mere, charcoal increases during the last two millennia of the period (Bennett et al. 1990). Occupation at Quidenham Mere

Box 5.4   Human remains from Staythorpe

Mesolithic findspots show some clustering along the river systems of Northern England and the midlands, and while new evidence is emerging for their importance in the west of the region, relatively little is known of those sites to the east of the Pennines. Evidence from Staythorpe near Newark in Nottinghamshire hints at the significance of riverine sites in this region too. Here, two palaeochannels were located, which had been active in the mid-late sixth millennium BC. The channel margins were fringed with a wetland vegetation of willow, aspen and alder. There were areas of open grassland, while oak, elm and lime grew on the terraces beyond. Animal bones were recovered from the palaeochannels, including the remains of roe deer, aurochs and otter, some with cutmarks (Davies 2001).

From one of the channels a well-preserved human femur was recovered. This individual was probably female, and isotope evidence suggests a reliance on terrestrial protein, with no evidence for marine protein and apparently relatively little contribution from either plant resources or riverine fish (Schulting 2001). It is unclear whether the femur was intentionally deposited in the channel, or whether it derives from an eroded occupation or grave site. However, it remains one of the few instances of human remains from the period that do not come from either caves or middens. The only other human bone from a similar context is the undated humerus from Thatcham III (Wymer 1964). This was found in tufa deposits that overlie, and partly truncate the site; it may be a redeposited element that derives from the Early Mesolithic occupation or contemporary with tufa deposition and thus slightly later. As with Staythorpe, it may be associated with water or derive from an adjacent settlement.

took place on the edge of a shallow lake, fringed with reeds and sedges and surrounded by mixed deciduous woodland (Pelgar 1993).

Continuity of occupation appears a strong feature of many of the East Anglian sites. The Middle Mesolithic occupation at Peacock's Farm by an ancient course of the Little Ouse seems to have continued into the Late Mesolithic. Two dates belonging to the first half of the seventh millennium are on charcoal from small features containing burnt material, which may represent hearths (Smith et al. 1989). Further up the Little Ouse, Late Mesolithic occupation continued in the vicinity of Two Mile Bottom, where Dixon Hewitt's site XXII evidenced Middle Mesolithic occupation (Jacobi 1984, see chapter 4). Late Mesolithic microliths have been recovered from the broader area collected by Haward and Dixon Hewitt. More recent work around 500 m to the northwest of site XXII was undertaken by the Norfolk Archaeological Unit in 1995. This located three irregular hollows, which seem to represent tree throws. One of these (feature 108) seems to have been intensively used by Mesolithic people, though all yielded some flint. Feature 108 contained a cluster of burnt flint which may be the remnants of a hearth and a large assemblage of 4554 lithic artefacts. Of formal tools the assemblage was dominated by microliths (n = 16), mostly narrow-backed blade-lets, but there were also large numbers of miscellaneous retouched and utilised pieces indicating a range of activities (Robins 1998). Three or 4 km south of the Little Ouse, the extensive spread of material in coversands between Wangford and Lakenheath, also consists of a mixture of Middle, Late and Final Mesolithic occupation evidence.

North Wales

Sites in North Wales dated to the period 7000–5000 cal BC are relatively rare and the significance of those that exist are difficult to interpret. Several of the Mesolithic-age dates for the region come from charred materials found during excavation of later sites: They could represent hearths, burning of the vegetation by people, or simply natural fires or lightning strikes. They are found in a variety of topographical contexts: In the lowlands at Capel Eithen and Bryn Celli Ddu on Anglesey; on the edge of the uplands at Llandegai; and in the heart of Snowdonia at Cwm Penamnen. The date from Llandegai may be related to small, widely dispersed Mesolithic scatters in the area, partly captured in later features both at Houlder's site, where a possible engraved Mesolithic pebble was also recovered (Lynch and Musson 2001) and at the more recently excavated Parc Bryn Cegin (Kenney 2008). Potentially more significant are early sixth millennium dates on pine charcoal from two post-holes at Bryn Celli Ddu, which were located at the entrance to the Neolithic tomb. These come from older excavations in a complex area of the site and are part of a group of several post-holes variously represented in the site archive as a line of five or a tri-angle of eight posts (Burrow 2010, 255). While this charcoal may be residual, the use of pine and potential linearity of these posts raises obvious comparisons to the earlier Stonehenge posts, though in contrast to this site, the two dates from Bryn Celli Ddu are likely to be contemporary, suggesting at least two would be upstanding at the same time.

Coastal occupation is indicated by the find in 1910 of an antler beam adze at Splash Point, Rhyl, in a blue clay which is likely to represent estuarine sediments, which lay below a layer of peat. This has been dated to 5635–5360 cal BC (6560 ± 80 BP; OxA-1009). Below the estuarine sediments is a lower layer of peat, which may have been the location for finds of Mesolithic flint (Smith 1924, 120, cited in Bell 2007, 306). More substantial evidence for use of coastal resources comes from Garreg Hylldrem (Robinson 2013), a rockshelter 10 m long at 20 m asl, overlooking the estuary of the Avon Glaslyn (Figure 5.23). Here, the remnants of what may have been one large midden or several smaller middens were recovered. The largest preserved area of middening is in a shallow hollow and dominated by periwinkle, with limpet, mussels, oysters and cockles also represented. Fish bone and terrestrial fauna were recovered, but unidentified to species apart from a tentative suggestion of cervid. A small lithic assemblage, much of it burnt, was found within the midden. The lowest layer of this midden and patches of shells attached to the rock-shelter wall date to the seventh millennium, but there is also a late sixth millennium date on shell from the upper layers and from another small area of preserved midden, suggesting brief visits over a long period of time.

Undated Late Mesolithic flint scatters are also known from coastal locations in Anglesey at Newborough Warren and Porth Ruffydd, and along the Lleyn Peninsula,

Figure 5.23 View from Garreg Hylldrem over reclaimed land that would have been in the Mesolithic a wide estuary (copyright Gary Robinson)

where due to the steep coastline sites would be close to the sea, even a times of lower sea-level (Smith 2005; Smith and Walker 2013). These include significant quantities of lithic material from Ynys Enlli (Bardsey) (Edmonds et al. 2009; Kenney and Hopewell 2016). Ynys Enlli was an island at this time, indicating the successful use of boats for marine navigation (and Bardsey Sound is particularly difficult to navigate), perhaps in the context of seal-hunting.

Caves and rockshelters were used for brief stopovers. Mesolithic material has been recovered from the caves and rockshelters of the Orme, for example, at Corkscrew Cave which gave views to the sea beyond. The caves of the Clwydians were also visited, for example, at Gop Cave and Fynnon Beuno (Figure 5.24). Both sites are notable for their excellent views across the surrounding landscape. A single microlith has also been recovered from Pontnewydd Cave just to the west, overlooking the river Elwy, suggesting it also falls into this pattern. What distinguishes this site is the presence of human remains, in this case, a mandible fragment of a child of around 12 years old. This was uncovered from a 20th century spoil heap generated when the cave floor was levelled for use as a munitions store during WW2 and has been dated to 6390–6110 cal BC (7420 ± 90; OxA-5819) (Aldhouse-Green et al. 1996). Two further elements also found within this spoil heap have been suggested to be Mesolithic, though these are undated and Middle Palaeolithic and Neolithic human remains have been recorded from the site. One element is a molar, which may derive from the child's mandible; the other is a fragment of vertebra that belongs to a second individual (Meiklejohn et al. 2011).

Figure 5.24 Fynnon Beuno cave

Perhaps surprisingly, relatively little Mesolithic evidence has been recovered from the major river valleys of the region. On the Ystrad, a tributary of the Clwyd, near Denbigh, Mesolithic lithics have been located during limited excavations of alluvial silts and palaeochannels, in the course of work on a later Prehistoric site at Tandderwen (Brassil et al. 2014). This area may have still held the remnants of a glacial lake at the time of occupation. Little Mesolithic evidence has been found in the Conwy Valley, with the exception of a series of scatters in the valley of an upland tributary, the Lledr, at Boncyn Ddol, Roman Bridge near Dolwyddelan where people camped on a flat knoll extending into an ancient lake. Several scatters with both Early and Late Mesolithic microliths indicate a place repeatedly revisited. The assemblage is mainly flint but a handful of chert and rock crystal artefacts were found (Smith 2005).

Several of the open-air sites in the uplands seem more substantial, and like Pontnewydd, date to the late seventh millennium – at a time when it has been argued that marginal areas of Western Scotland saw a crash in population due to climatic deterioration. The evidence from North Wales supports that from the Cairngorms and the Pennines, where sites of this date are present. Between the valleys of the Clwyd and the Conwy, is an upland area known as Mynydd Hiraethog. Several Late Mesolithic scatters have been recorded in this area at Llyn Aled Isaf. A radiocarbon date from one of these scatters suggests occupation in the late seventh millennium BC (Smith and Walker 2014).

Only 7 km away from this lake is Brenig, a small, upland valley within this moorland, drained by the Afon Brenig and its tributaries, which flow southwards to join the Dee (Lynch 1993). Brenig 53 is located on a flat promontory overlooking the river at around 360 m asl. Though a limited area was excavated, the scatter may have been extended over more than 6000 m^2 (Healey 1993, 23). Here, a series of small firepits, earth ovens, pits and lines of stakeholes were discovered in association with 1600 pieces of lithic material, which was formed several distinct clusters. While several of these features yielded Neolithic dates, a series of large, intercutting pits (F19), which seemed to re-present a succession of hearths and earth ovens, date to the Mesolithic. Within these pits, layers of stones and burnt stones interspersed with layers of earth were recorded. A pile of stones was located adjacent to this complex, cached perhaps for future use of this facility. Two radiocarbon dates made on bulked hazel, hawthorn and oak from these pits indicate activity in the late seventh millennium BC. Lithic material used was a mixture of beach pebble flint and banded chert. The assemblage was dominated by microliths (58), with left lateralised scalenes and backed bladelets dominating. Microburins (16) indicate these tools were manufactured at the site. Burins (14), scra-pers (14), truncations (5), microdenticulates (4) and a denticulate indicate a wide range of activities were undertaken. Immediately to the north, the contiguous site of Brenig 45 also produced Mesolithic material, much of this in the turf mound of a barrow or on the pre-barrow surface, but also sealed beneath a nearby ring cairn. On the other site of the valley, a pit produced a Mesolithic radiocarbon date of 6650–6385 (5700 ± 80; HAR-565), though no contemporary lithic material was recovered.

The Thames and its tributaries

As sea-level rose, the character of the Thames changed. Developing wetland choked channels and brackish water seeped into the region, as the Thames estuary en-croached on and, from c.7000 BC, exceeded its current position. Peat and alder carr expanded across much of the area, and reeds and wetland grasses were common. As Doggerland drowned, the lowest reaches of the Thames became flooded as marine influences worked their way across areas that are now low-lying marshes of the Thames estuary (Bates and Stafford 2013). Two transgressions are recorded at Tilbury at 7200–5850 BC and 4900 BC, interspersed by an episode of fen carr development (Devoy 1979).

At Swanscombe, a freshwater marsh was succeeded by tidal mudflats in the second half of the sixth millennium, then high saltmarsh in the last centuries of the Mesolithic. Estuarine contraction saw the area return to organic sedimentation and the regrowth of alder carr around the Mesolithic/Neolithic transition (Bates and Stafford 2013). These are likely to be landscapes rich in wetland resources. Stable isotope evidence from 'Tilbury Man' indicates some contribution of freshwater protein sources, such as fish and wildfowl, though the majority of this individual's diet came from terrestrial sources. Alimentary remains from Late Mesolithic sites along the Thames and its tributaries also emphasise terrestrial fauna (Table 5.6). A range of the main prey animals are present. Though numbers are small, aurochs may have played a more important role than previously, being dominant at Stratford's Yard and the only fauna at Broxbourne 105 (admittedly a single kill site). Otter is the only fluvial species, with no fish remains recovered; the birds at Stratford's Yard could not be identified but are small in size, rather than larger water-birds that might have been targeted.

As outlined in previous chapters, sites on the Thames, particularly along its lower reaches, are rare (Figure 5.25). Considerable depths of deposits mask Early Prehistoric archaeology: Tilbury Man (see Box 5.5), for example, was found below 10.5 m of peats and clays. Holocene sediments thicken considerably downriver, from less than 2 m at Tower Bridge to a depth of 25 m at Canvey Island (Marsland 1986). The erosive potential of the river for sites on its banks has also been noted. The flint axes and picks recovered from the river in great numbers probably have a wide temporal range, but are likely to include Late Mesolithic material. More securely Late Mesolithic are antler beam mattocks, whose dating spans 7000–4000 cal BC (Elliott 2012; Tolan-Smith and Bonsall 1999). Around 18 of these objects have been recovered from the Thames, with a distribution stretching from Battersea in the east

Table 5.6 Faunal remains from sites along the Thames and its tributaries (D = dominant, P = present)

Site	Aurochs	Pig	Red deer	Roe deer	Other
Eton Rowing Course	P	P	P		
Broxbourne 105	P				
Misbourne Viaduct	P	P	P	P	Lynx, otter, badger
Stratford's Yard	D	P	P	P	Frog, birds
Wawcott XXIII	P	P	P		Human

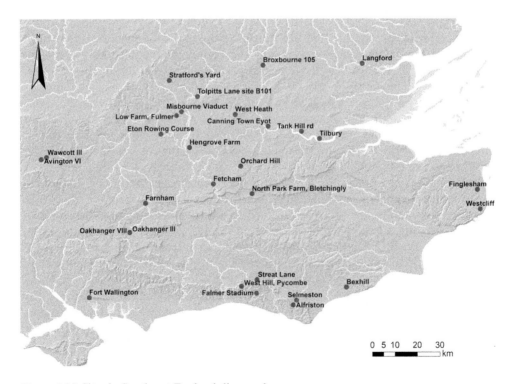

Figure 5.25 Sites in Southeast England discussed

Box 5.5   One burial and a cremation

The rarity of human remains the last two millennia of the Mesolithic away from
the small island of Oronsay in has previously been noted (Blockley 2005;
Conneller 2006); however, this picture has begun to change. Recent dating
programmes indicate that the intermittent deposition of isolated human
elements in caves in western Britain continued, while new research has revealed
the presence of two sets of human remains in Eastern England, the first such
evidence from this region. Both are in Essex: The burial of a man by the Thames
at Tilbury and further north a cremation at Langford. Langford is also by a
river, in this case, the Chelmer, a river which joins the Blackwater at its estuary.
Both belong to the first half of the sixth millennium, hinting at a diversity of
mortuary practises at this time, in a region that could conceivably be the
territory of a single group. The femur from Staythorpe (see above) also belongs
to this period, perhaps suggesting varied mortuary practises focused on rivers
taking place across Eastern England.

'Tilbury Man' (Figure 5.26) was an early find, whose attribution to the
Mesolithic has only recently been confirmed (Schulting 2013). In 1883, at a

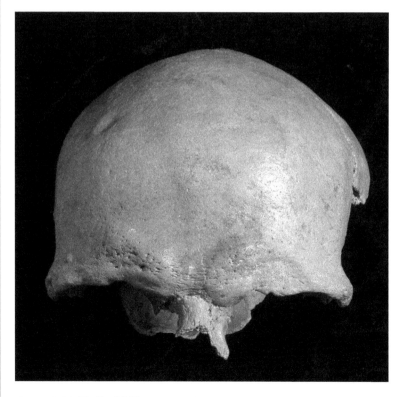

Figure 5.26 Skull of Tilbury Man (Natural History Museum PA SK9) showing healed
lesion (Photo: Rick Schulting)

depth of 10.5 m, below alternating layers of peat and estuarine clays, a human skeleton was uncovered by workman extending Tilbury Dock. Though no records of the position of the body or the presence of grave goods were made, the presence of small bones probably means that the entire skeleton was once present (Schulting 2013, 23). Surviving remains indicate an older adult male. Two healed lesions were noted on the skull. These have also been found associated with Late Mesolithic individuals from Southern Scandinavia, at sites such as Tybrind Vig (Andersen 1985), where these injuries have been related to ritualised conflict resolution. The skeleton seems to belong towards the end of a marine transgression in the region, a few generations after the estuary had migrated east from this area and when saltmarsh and then reedswamp were beginning to develop on areas that had previously been submerged (Andersen 1985, 29).

The cremation at Langford was discovered in a 90 by 81 cm pit, 26 cm deep. The calcined human bone was in the basal fill, a charcoal rich sandy silt. This was capped by an upper fill very similar to the surrounding sediment, probably indicating that the pit was rapidly backfilled with the spoil generated in its excavation (Gilmour and Loe 2015). The relatively small quantity of cremated remains indicates that the pit was filled with a sample of the pyre debris rather than the cremation itself. The remainder of the cremated remains may have been collected up and disposed of elsewhere: In another pit, for example, or the nearby river. There does not seem to have been any particular selection of skeletal elements for the pit. Rather than being a formal disposal of an individual, the material in the pit seems part of a broader pattern of the deposition of burnt material, noted by Blinkhorn et al. (2016). This may indicate a broader interest in transformed material that encompassed both ostensibly domestic debris, such as hearth debris or food material, and more overtly ritual practises involving the transformation of human bodies.

One or more individuals may be represented; all that can be said is that an older child or an adult was present (Blinkhorn et al. 2016), someone who had been brought up in this region (Schulting et al. 2016). Included in the fill were two blades and a flake, while the wood of the pyre included oak. Environmental evidence comes from the Blackwater estuary, which experienced an episode of regression at this time, and where a Late Mesolithic presence is in evidence. Woodlands of lime and hazel were present with oak becoming more important, with ferns and herbaceous plants also well represented (Wilkinson and Murphy 1995).

to Boveney Lock in the west. These objects are likely to represent material eroded from sites along the banks of the river (see chapter 3), though more formal acts of deposition may also be represented.

Beyond the tidal reaches of the Thames, more evidence is preserved. At Runnymede Bridge in the Late Mesolithic, brief and small-scale visits took place on the alluvial silts of the floodplain, on the higher bank of a palaeochannel that was fringed with sedges (Needham 2000). The area was subject to over-bank flooding, though the frequency of these events decreased over the centuries. The floodplain was an area of open grassland with patches of alder carr. Alder became denser along the flood plain, while on drier ground lime and ash were common. The earliest date on charcoal falls into the centuries around 7000 BC, though this does not certainly relate to human activity. More certain evidence in the form of *prunus* charcoal from an isolated post-hole belongs to the last centuries of the seventh millennium. A cluster of eight straight-backed bladelets is likely to indicate a lost or discarded composite tool, perhaps indicative of hunting activities. Low-density lithic debris and an unfinished microlith indicate that manufacturing activities took place here at times. Mid and late fifth millennium dates indicate intermittent, small-scale visits over a long period of time.

Late Mesolithic activity is represented further up river at Eton Rowing Course, Dorney (Allen et al. 2013), in a landscape of elm, pine and hazel woodlands on the dryland, with alder carr becoming more common on the wetlands towards the end of the period. Isolated finds of animal bones indicate these landscapes were inhabited by red deer, pig and aurochs. In contrast to the large Early Mesolithic assemblages from this area (see chapter 2), Late Mesolithic activity consists of low-density finds of microliths on the floodplain, perhaps indicative of hunting or plant processing activities, as well as a few small knapping scatters. An isolated antler beam mattock also derives from the floodplain. On a nearby gravel island two tree throws contained small concentrations of up to 136 lithics, including small debitage from knapping and evidence for microlith manufacture, while residual material is present in other such features on the island. Knapping appears to have been geared to production for use elsewhere in the broader landscape. A lack of refits, even though material appears to have been knapped from a small range of cores, indicate that most useable material was removed (Anderson-Whymark and Durden 2013, 83). Evidence for seasonal flooding indicate short-term, perhaps seasonal visits.

A similar pattern of occupation – of seasonal, ephemeral use of the flood plain and more concentrated, but still extremely small-scale occupation of adjacent gravel islands – appears a common feature of Mesolithic sites of the Thames and its tributaries. Small scatters on the floodplain have been dated to the sixth and fifth millennium in the Ebbsfleet Valley (Bates and Stafford 2013, 162) and to the late seventh millennium at Broxbourne 105 on the Lea (see below). Undated Late Mesolithic material from what may have once been a more extensive site has been recovered the banks of the Thames at 41–42 Kew Bridge Rd, Brentford (Bishop et al. 2017) and adjacent Gasworks site (Bishop 2002). Material recovered from a palaeochannel included burnt flint, indicating hearths in the proximity, while two pits may also belong to the Mesolithic. More extensive occupation can be found on gravel islands, or similar low rises, overlooking the river floodplain. One such site can be found at Tank Hill Road, Purfleet, close to the Mardyke (Bates and Stafford 2013; Leivers et al. 2007), where the densest area of lithic material is centred on a hearth in a shallow pit, associated with large quantities of burnt flint. Here, microliths were produced and retooling occurred; scrapers were also present. An area where tranchet axes were manufactured and maintained was located to the west. Similar types of evidence may also be present on a terrace of the Mole at Fetcham (Munnery 2014) and on a slight rise at Hengrove Farm, Staines near the Colne (Poulton et al. 2017), where the remnants of likely more extensive and varied Late Mesolithic activity, including a high proportion of burnt flint, was preserved in hollows, tree throws and later features. While these sites suggest repeated, usually small-scale occupation of similar locales, a site at Canning Town, on an eyot in the floodplain close to the confluence of the Lea with the Thames, yielded a fairly coherent assemblage of mainly single-edged backed bladelets possibly suggesting a single occupation around a series of hearths. Activities here included microlith manufacture, and the use and repair of burins and scrapers, all manufactured on locally available gravel flint (Nicholls et al. 2013). Several Late Mesolithic lithic scatters are also present along the Beam river in Dagenham (Champness et al. 2015).

Small-scale Late Mesolithic activity is also present on sites at higher elevations focused on springs that fed the Thames and its tributaries. Sites such as Orchard Hill at the headwater of the Wandle and West Heath, Hampstead had much longer and more extensive Mesolithic histories (see chapters 3 and 4), but also saw occasional visits in the Late Mesolithic. Similarly, further up the Thames, at Nettlebed, Oxfordshire, on a south facing elevated site, small-scale Late Mesolithic activity took place in an area where early material is much more common (Boismier 1995; Peake 1915).

The Lea

Along the Lea, the ponds and meres of the early Holocene shrank as they became choked with vegetation. A peat developed across the valley floor between them, which gradually began to dry out. Subsequently increased water-logging, at least partially caused by rising sea-levels impeding drainage, led to increased overbank flooding of channels and meres and ponds expanding in size (Corcoran et al. 2011). Woodlands were composed of elm and hazel with pine from c.7000 cal BC, while alder carr became common from c.6000 cal BC, seemingly in response to these wetter conditions, though there was considerable local variation. Alder was accompanied by lime and ash, and pine remained common in the lower Lea, despite being crowded out by alder in other regions (Bates and Stafford 2013).

Late Mesolithic evidence from the Lea is relatively rare (Figure 5.25): A small site on an eyot at Canning Town near the river's confluence with the Thames and a small site much further up river at Broxbourne. The extensive excavations associated with the Olympic Park on the lower Lea failed to reveal any Mesolithic evidence (Powell 2012).

Broxbourne 105 is located less than 100 m to the east of the Early Mesolithic site of Broxbourne 104 (see chapter 3). It was excavated by Roger Jacobi in the same campaign that uncovered sites 104 and 106. A relatively small trench measuring c.6.5 × 4.5 m was excavated. This was in an area of quarrying, and most of the upper crumbly oxidised peat had already been removed before excavation. Below the oxidised peat was a reed peat. At the top of this was a small Mesolithic flint scatter. In the southern part of the trench a small sondage of around a metre was excavated deeper, revealing a wood peat underlying the upper reed peat and, below this, two lower layers of reed peat (see Figure 5.27). A Mesolithic hearth was encountered at the base of the wood pit. A date either on charcoal from this hearth or waterlogged wood (possibly pine) from this level indicated this feature was in use between 8260 and 7490 cal BC (8700 ± 170 BP, Birm-343). This measurement has a large standard deviation and spans the Early/Late Mesolithic boundary. There does not seem to be any lithic material associated with this feature that might elucidate the nature of this occupation. A pollen sample taken from immediately below this level indicates this was an area of fen carr with willow present, while oak, pine, elm and hazel grew on drier ground. Pollen counts were low so certain taxa may be under-represented.

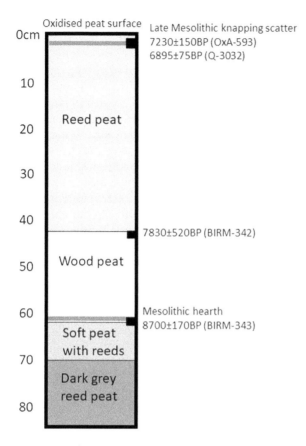

Figure 5.27 Stratigraphy of Broxbourne 105 (redrawn from Jacobi archive, British Museum)

More information is, however, available on the upper, Late Mesolithic scatter. This scatter was distributed over a 1 cm vertical range (Jacobi 1975) and has an excellent refitting rate, indicating a high-resolution, short-term occupation. Its location in reed peat on the floodplain of the Lea and the small, specialised assemblage recovered indicate a short-term task site. The occupation appears to have taken place in a more open wetland landscape than the setting of the earlier occupation at Broxbourne 104 (see chapter 3). By this time alder had replaced willow as the local tree of boggy ground, with drier woodland of oak and elm, with lime appearing at the expense of pine.

A small group of people halted at the site, probably in order to butcher an aurochs they had killed on the river bank. Bone is not well-preserved, but six aurochs teeth were recovered within close proximity, all that remains of a more extensive butchery episode. Around seven flint pebbles were gathered from an exposure of gravel, probably on the edge of the river, and these were knapped to generate sharp flakes to butcher the animal. These pebbles were extremely poor quality, tending to shatter when struck, but people seem to have been familiar with this type of material and exploited it, using shatter fragments as cores to produce sharp flakes, removing these

at very oblique angles without further preparation. Rather than put effort into platform maintenance, cores were rotated and alternative locations exploited for flake
removal. This is expedient production for immediate need: Utilised flakes are common
and most likely used to process the aurochs carcass.

Refitting (undertaken by Roger Jacobi) and the distribution of plotted material and
micro-debitage indicate two areas of activity (Figure 5.28). Most tasks appear to have
taken place in the central part of the site, to the southwest of a patch of charcoal that
may indicate a hearth. Here, large quantities of microdebitage, a broken hammerstone
and cores and refitting debris indicate the main flint knapping area where the small
pebbles were smashed and exploited. The scatter of aurochs teeth and five flakes that
refit to cores were also found in this area. Immediately on the edge of this activity area
is a concentration of microliths, with 15 found in a 30 cm square area, and 26 in total
coming from this broader activity area. These are all, with one exception (an elongated
rod), micro-scalene triangles, none exceeding 1 cm in length. Of the cluster of 15
microliths, several of the scalenes were found in a line, topped by the rod, perhaps
suggesting a broken or abandoned composite tool. Another possibility is that this
represents a cache of microliths stored for future use, as Myers (1987) has suggested
occurred in the late Mesolithic of the central Pennines.

The second activity area is in the northernmost part of the site, immediately to the
north of the potential hearth, where moderate quantities of micro-debitage and three

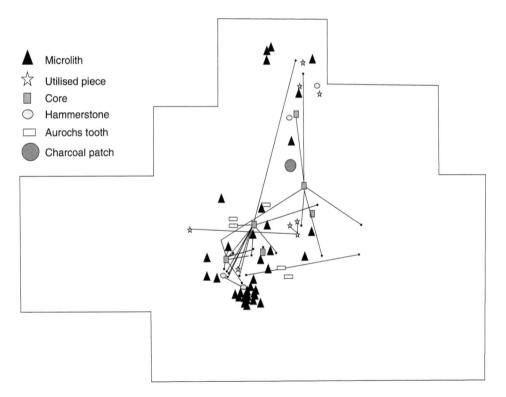

Figure 5.28 Distribution of tools, cores, animal bone and refitted material at Broxbourn
(redrawn from two plots in Jacobi archive, British Museum)

hammerstones indicate in situ knapping, though on a lesser scale than in the main knapping area. Three utilised and retouched flakes indicate some other tasks were also undertaken. There are refits between the two areas, and the northern area also contains the same distinctive micro-scalenes, indicating contemporaneity.

The site has two radiocarbon dates. One was obtained on an aurochs tooth, the other on peat from immediately below the level of the occupation. The former yielded a date of 6420–5835 cal BC (7230 ± 150 BP, OxA-593) (Gowlett et al. 1986, 119), the latter 5920–5645 cal BC (6895 ± 75 BP, Q-3032) (Jacobi archive).

The Colne

In contrast to the Lea, the Colne (noted in chapter 3 for the presence of Early Mesolithic sites) continued to see significant occupation in the Late Mesolithic (Figure 5.25). Three important radiocarbon dated sites are found along the Colne or its tributaries: Tolpits Lane B101 on the Colne, Stratford's Yard on the Chess and Misbourne Viaduct on the Misbourne. The latter two have broadly fifth millennium dates and will be discussed in the following chapter. Many smaller sites are known, such as Low Farm, Fulmer, a low-density scatter of microlith, axes, truncations and debitage, on a gravel peninsula in wetland at the source of the Alderbourne (Farley 1978).

While Early Mesolithic material is concentrated along the broad floodplain of the lower Colne, the upper reaches of the river and its tributaries seem to have been more of a focus during the later period. One exception on the lower Colne is at Heathrow Terminal 5, where a huge landscape project recorded a small ephemeral background scatter of Mesolithic flintwork (of diagnostic pieces just two microliths and a micro-burin). More notable, by a small stream running into the Colne, were a cluster of pits containing a few pieces of worked flint and large quantities of burnt flint, dated by thermoluminescence to the seventh millennium. The latter was natural flint, rather than worked pieces, perhaps suggesting material used in cooking activities, and in general the material in the pits resembles a possible midden assemblage (Cramp and Leivers 2010). This pit cluster was located in boggy ground that may been a small clearing, possibly a meeting place for more than one small group (ibid). Boggy ground is found more widely in this region, and the reduction of settlement evidence in the lower Colne may be as a result of rising water tables on the floodplain and the expansion of sedge swamp (Lewis and Rackham 2011, 206) during the last two millennia of the Mesolithic (Grant et al. 2012). At King William's Flour Mill, adjacent to Three Ways Wharf on the lower Colne, the environmental sequence from c.6500 cal BC shows the growth of peat with remains of bulrushes and plants indicative of large expanses of shallow water, followed by the development of sedge swamp interspersed with episodes of overbank flooding. Hazel and elm became more common in local woodland from c.6500 cal BC, with a decline in woodland as the area became wetter, and sedges more dominant. Other contemporary sequences show a representation of elm and lime, with willow carr locally important (Jones 2013). The black clays of the sedge swamp contain several bands of fine charcoal and charred organic matter, which appear to represent deliberate burning of the wetland vegetation, perhaps to maintain open areas and encourage animal browse. This evidence indicates continuing Late Mesolithic presence in the lower Colne, though the lack of large sites suggests the area was being used in new ways, while more 'domestic' activity is focused on the upper reaches of the river and its tributaries.

Further up the Colne, Tolpits Lane site B101 is one of several Mesolithic sites located by the archaeology society of the Merchant Taylor School in the 1960s, of which a key member was a young Roger Jacobi. The Society located Mesolithic flintwork from a number of sites in the vicinity of the school at Sandy Lodge Farm, Hampermills and various sites on Moor Park Golf Course, indicating the widespread presence of Mesolithic activity along this section of the river. The Tolpits Lane site was discovered in a section in a gravel quarry, just behind the school's playing fields. Several trenches were excavated by the school's archaeology society in 1965, and work started at site B in 1966 with the excavation of the eastern trench; in 1972, Jacobi extended the excavations to the west (named B101) as part of his doctoral work (Jacobi archive, British Museum; site archive Rickmansworth Museum) (Figure 5.29).

These excavations exposed a cut-off meander; lithic artefacts were found both within the channel and at the top of it. At the base of the channel, red deer bones and a single Early Mesolithic microlith were recovered. The channel was partly infilled with peat, and then covered by alluvial clays. The main Late Mesolithic scatter was within this alluvium. Charcoal was common at this level and was identified as oak and maple (or possibly birch). Five pits were also located; two post-dated the Mesolithic occupation, and two were in the area excavated by the MTS Archaeological Society, in an area where Neolithic material is present and the possibility of intrusive features was not considered; a radiocarbon date on bulked material from this area (6330 ± 80 BP; Q-1099) is thus unreliable. More securely Mesolithic is pit 1, located in the 1972 excavations, where the sections show no evidence of an intrusive feature from above the Mesolithic layer. This pit has two separate fills; the lowest seems to represent hearth debris, consisting of sand, burnt flint and charcoal, but no evidence for in situ burning. Several blades were found resting on the base of the pit. The upper layer includes tips of midden material, including bands of burnt stone, clusters of lithic debitage and bands of charcoal, burnt seeds and hazelnut shells. Clusters of cores and microburins were also noted. The quantity of material in the pit contrasts with its relative scarcity in the immediate surrounding area (Jacobi archive, British Museum). A single radiocarbon date on bulked wood was obtained from this pit of 7570–7045 cal BC (8602 ± 120 BP; Q-1147) (Jacobi 1994, 195).

There are refits amongst the lithic material, including between two core fragments in pit 1, which join to a third core fragment in the adjacent square, suggesting that some of the material in the pit derives from clearance of the adjacent landsurface. There may also be elements of more formal deposition: Of the four cores found in the pit, one includes a large and sparkling crystal geode fragment. This is possibly evidence of a broader interest in unusual stones at the site. Both an echinoid and a piece of pyrites were also recovered from the Mesolithic horizon around 2 m from the pit.

An assemblage of just over 2000 pieces was recovered from Jacobi's western trench, an area that encompassed just under 14 m^2 (Table 5.7; Figure 5.29). A mixture of chalk and gravel flint was used, with chalk flint being most common. The chalk outcrops only 2 km to the east and seems to have been easily accessible to the inhabitants of the site; many cores remain large and still workable. The assemblage is microlith dominated, with scrapers, burins and awls rare, and a single tranchet axe recovered. Single notches are common: Some are perhaps unsnapped microburins, others could have been used in the manufacture of hafts. Tool spalls, mostly

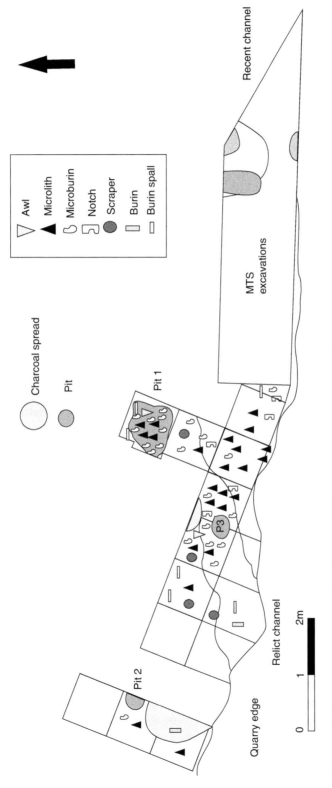

Figure 5.29 Plan of excavations at Tolpits Lane B101 (redrawn from material in the Jacobi archive)

Table 5.7 Composition of the key assemblages from the Lea, Colne and Kennet

Tool/tool spall	Tolpits Lane B101	Broxbourne 105	Avington VI
Awl	3	0	0
Axe/pick	1	0	1
Axe flake	2	0	0
Burin	2	0	4
Burin spall	7	0	0
Microlith	24	26	59
Microburin	23	0	36
Notch/denticulate	23	0	0
Scraper	4	0	8
Truncation	0	0	15
Retouch/utilised	81	8	17
Cores	53	6	86

microburins and notch spalls, also indicate a focus on microlith production. Jacobi (2005, 274) notes this site is one of the earliest where small scalene triangles with three retouched sides have been recovered, though it should be noted that only a scalene with two retouched edges, a backed bladelet and two fragments of oblique truncations were recovered from the dated pit. It is not known whether the material surrounding the pit is the product of single or multiple occupations.

Tools and tool spalls, as well as being concentrated in pit 1, cluster in the south-eastern part of the western trench, to the south of a charcoal spread (Figure 5.29). Microliths, microburins and notches dominate the eastern part of the cluster, while more varied tools and tool spalls are found to the west, perhaps indicating activity zones. A variety of core reduction strategies and levels of skill are in evidence, including a series of well-produced elongated pyramidal cores on split nodules and occasionally thermal fractures.

B101 sits within a wider landscape of Mesolithic activity. Immediately to the west of B101 are two further MTS excavations where Mesolithic evidence was recovered. At Site 1, flint knapping took place, microliths were manufactured, burins used and axes resharpened. At site 2, axe production took place near to a small hearth. Rather than being located on sand or gravel islands, as in other areas, Mesolithic activity at B101 and elsewhere is concentrated on the floodplain. This activity encompasses both small-scale tool use and isolated charcoal scatters to more extensive flint knapping stations as at B101 and site 1. With the growth of extensive woodlands in the area, the floodplain appears to have become relatively stable, with soil development recorded at site 1.

The Kennet

From around 8000–6000 cal BC, tufa became a key element of Middle-Late Mesolithic sequences in the Kennet. Following dissolution of the chalk in the upper reaches of the river, tufa formed in shallow, possibly seasonal pools on the surface of the peat. Later, as temperature and precipitation both seem to have increased, granular tufa formed in a number of channels that migrated across the floodplain. The damp meadows of the Middle Mesolithic floodplain were gradually replaced by alder carr. Beyond the immediate environs of the river, lime may have been more important on the chalk, with oak more common on acidic soils and alder in boggy areas (Collins et al. 2006).

The significance of the middle Kennet in the Early Mesolithic was outlined in chapter 3. Slightly fewer Late Mesolithic sites are present in the area (Figure 5.25), but some of these are extremely extensive. Wawcott III is particularly substantial with over 100,000 lithic artefacts recovered from a c.9 × 3 m trench and 19 0.9 m test pits excavated between 1962 and 1970 (Froom 1976, 2012). Densities reached up to 6500 pieces per square metre, with averages of c.3500, indicating intensive occupation, albeit spread over millennia. The assemblage encompasses material of a range of dates from the early to the latest Mesolithic. Though obliquely blunted points and related Early and Middle Mesolithic forms are dominant, a substantial Late Mesolithic element is present, likely to be the product of many visits.

The band of fine sands on which Wawcott III is located would represent well-drained higher ground on the edge of a floodplain increasingly covered by peat, and as such would represent an attractive area for seasonal settlement. While there appears to be some stratification of the sands, with fewer early and more late forms in the upper spits (Froom 2012), there is certainly some mixing as material has moved through the profile, and some areas have been disturbed by pits and tree throws. If the upper spits are taken as a broad indicator of Late Mesolithic activities at the site, these seem to have included microlith production and retooling, use and resharpening of axes, use of scrapers, microdenticulates and fabricators. A number of features were located. Pit 1 was circular and around 1 m in diameter, while a second pit was smaller, measuring 40 by 20 cm. All these features contained flint.

Late Mesolithic activity is also present just 1200 m to the east at Wawcott XXIII. This site has a Final Mesolithic date and microlithic component and is discussed in more detail in the following chapter, but Late Mesolithic certainly seems present, too. Further, Late Mesolithic activity on the Kennet has been located at Avington VI, with mean densities of lithics of 149–216 pieces per square metre (Froom 2012). Avington VI has a relatively coherent microlith assemblage, which probably indicates a single main period of occupation. One hearth was located in the 35 m^2 excavated. This took the form of a small pit, 40 cm in diameter that contained charcoal and burnt stones. Surrounding this hearth were three probable pits around 20 cm in diameter, densely packed with flint nodules that may have acted as post-packing. Two larger pits were located but not fully excavated.

South of the rivers

South of the Thames, Late Mesolithic sites are numerous. A change in the focus of settlement can be seen from the generally larger Early and Middle Mesolithic sites located predominantly on the Greensand to smaller sites on a broader range of geologies in the late Mesolithic (Gardiner 1988). The lessening of the significance of the Greensand, particularly in the Western Weald, can be illustrated by the Oakhanger region, focus of extensive Early Mesolithic occupation: Late Mesolithic sites are rare and much smaller. Early Mesolithic Oakhanger V/VII covers 420 m^2 (see chapter 3); Late Mesolithic Oakhanger III and VIII were only 7.5 m^2 and 100 m^2, respectively. Oakhanger III is a small task site, where burins and microliths were most common, with activities centred around a single hearth. At Oakhanger VIII, a more varied toolkit of microliths, microdenticulates, scrapers burins and truncations was found in association with four hearths (Jacobi 1981). It seems that even sites where toolkits have a more residential signature are smaller and/or were less frequently revisited than their Early Mesolithic equivalents. As Jacobi (1981, 13) notes, many of the areas of the Western Weald that were favoured places in the Early and Middle Mesolithic were abandoned or rarely visited in the Late Mesolithic, indicating a major shift in settlement.

In Central and Eastern Weald, many sites are still located on the Lower Greensand, or other sandy geologies, particularly in the region of the Ashdown Forest (Gardiner 1988). Some sites, such as Selmeston, that saw Early and Middle Mesolithic occupation were also frequented in the Late Mesolithic (Clark 1934), though as at Oakhanger, late microliths are less common. The reverse though is the case at both North Park Farm, Bletchingly and Rock Common (see chapter 4), where a greater intensity of Late Mesolithic occupation is in evidence (Harding 2000; Jones 2013). Bletchingly represents a typical location for the Early/Middle Mesolithic, close to a spring and a varied range of geologies, including the chalk; however, microlithic assemblages from most excavated areas are characterised by narrow-backed bladelets. Ellaby (1987) suggests these types are indicative of the earliest Late Mesolithic industries in the area, and this is probably supported by the Bletchingly radiocarbon dates. These fall into the eighth and seventh millennium, but are often statistically inconsistent, and given the superimposition of occupation of different dates, difficult to relate to particular strands of occupation. The excavators argue that some of the eight millennium dates relate to Middle Mesolithic basally modified points, but backed bladelets are common also in these areas and in areas where seventh millennium dates were obtained.

Around half a kilometre from the Greensand, on a spread of gravel laid down by an old course of the Blackwater, another persistent place records long-standing occupation. Farnham, close to Bourne Mill spring, whose stream ran into the Wey, saw extensive occupation in the Early and Middle Mesolithic (see chapters 3 and 4), that continued into the Late Mesolithic (Clark and Rankine 1939). Narrow-backed bladelets and scalene triangles make up a significant proportion of the assemblages. Here, the presence of a spring, gravel flint easily accessible through tree throws, and close proximity to the range of resources afforded by different geologies made this place attractive for several millennia.

A third major centre of Mesolithic activity in the region and one that was also a focus for occupation from Early to Late Mesolithic, is at Bexhill. In the Late Mesolithic, the area was rapidly changing. The start of the Late Mesolithic overlapped with the end of a period of marine transgression; after 6000 cal BC, the landscape became more stable, changing from saltmarsh to fen. Late Mesolithic sites tend to cluster along this wetland edge, and the area is likely to have remained close to the shore, though this was beyond the excavated area (Champness et al. 2019). At the start of the Late Mesolithic, occupation seems to have been intermittent, before increasing in intensity once the landscape stabilised, a trend that continued into the Final Mesolithic, when the area seems to have become an important focus (see chapter 6).

Sites on the chalk, previously rare, became more common. Many of the larger flint scatters are on or close to the chalk, or to flint-bearing superficial deposits (Gardiner 1988). Rivers rising in the Weald cut through the chalk and develop wide gravel terraces below the chalk escarpment. The large complex at Farnham is located on such a deposit (Care 1982). A similar site is at Woodbridge Rd, Guildford, where the Wey cuts through the North Downs. Here, a large assemblage of 52,606 pieces seems focused on lithic production and tasks involving microliths. Eleven pits were located in the excavation: Most are relatively shallow (usually 20–30 cm), and between 1 and 2 m in length, though two measure more than 2 m across. These may have been extraction pits, with people digging through the sand to get to the flint gravels below (Bishop 2008). Pits also seem to have been used as middens, with some recording large quantities of lithics and burnt flint.

Many of these material-rich sites show extensive production evidence, either in the form of core shaping or axe production. At West Hill, Pyecombe (Butler 2001) survey and excavation produced 5500 flints and recorded axe roughouts and preparation flaking. This is one of several sites in the region that seem specialised in the production of axes. At Alfriston, Sussex, 49 tranchet axes have been recovered (Jacobi and Wessex Archaeology 2014). Though few are well-provenanced, Alfriston is located at the point the river Cuckmere cuts through the chalk, resulting in easily accessible raw material. Eleven axes come from Mile Oak, Brighton, and six just to the northeast at Sadlescome on areas of the chalk cut by dry valleys (ibid.). Concentrations of tranchet axes are also known along the flanks of the South Downs at Beachy Head, Seaford, Cissford, East and West Dean, Exceat and Selmeston. Most of these axe sites are surface scatters, with some uncertainty as to their date, though where microliths are present these seem mainly to be Late Mesolithic (O'Malley and Jacobi 1978).

An excavated example of an axe production site comes from Finglesham, Kent. This site is located on alluvium, at the foot of the chalk slope, which rises up to the southwest. At Finglesham, lithic material was recovered from the base of a soil sequence mostly truncated by ploughing and from the ploughsoil itself. Though no microliths were recovered, nine TL dates were obtained on burnt flint. Though these have large error ranges, two broadly fall in the sixth millennium BC (including a tranchet flake) and two fall sufficiently early in the fifth millennium that they are unlikely to be Neolithic. The remaining four dates could be either Mesolithic or Neolithic. Eleven axes (including 4 roughouts), 33 tranchet flakes and 44 finishing flakes have been recovered from an assemblage of 1499 pieces. The early stages of production also seem to be present (Parfitt and Halliwell 2014). Though none of the tranchet flakes could be refitted to any of the recovered axes, some may belong to earlier stages of use. It is clear that many of the tranchet flakes come from axes not recovered, either deposited in other areas of the site, or transported (or exchanged) for use elsewhere. Much of the flint used in production is chalk flint. The lower slope of the chalk is covered with clay-with-flints, pocked with solution hollows, an excellent potential source of flint.

Solution hollows seem potentially important sources for flint to make axes. At Westcliff, at least 25 core tools have been recovered from a site on clay, capping chalk (Parfitt and Halliwell 2014, 255), an area where solution hollows are also known. Further west, at Fort Wallington in Hampshire, Mesolithic flint work, including axes, is associated with an area of solution hollows, and solution hollows are also present at Broom Hill. This site has been extensively discussed in chapter 4 and the high number of axes (85) noted.

Such sites on or close to the chalk perhaps show an increased emphasis on large-scale production – both of axes and preformed cores – in the Late Mesolithic. Some sites, such as Beechbrook Wood, Westall, on the Greensand (see below), have assemblages with few cortical flakes (Brady 2006), suggesting that these were the sorts of places where these prepared cores were brought. While there have been some suggestions of long-distance exchange in the Mesolithic, these procurement and production sites do not seem to be operating in quite the same way as the more specialised production sites of later Prehistory. Axe production seems to be taking place amongst a range of other activities. There is nothing to suggest both axes and cores were habitually made for consumption beyond the group that made them. Instead, there seems more of a concern to incorporate procurement within seasonal movement for use away from the chalk. The axes on the Weald often show sign of repair, and there are increasing numbers of axe-sharpening flakes with increasing distance from the chalk (Care 1979), suggesting reuse and repair of these objects as people moved round the landscape.

The radiocarbon record for Southeast England comes mainly from sites with pits. At Streat Lane, East Sussex, four large pits and a possible shelter were located (Figure 5.30, Butler 2007). This site is located on Gault Clay, though immediately adjacent to the Folkstone beds of the Lower Greensand and close to a stream, which runs into the river Ouse. Local alluvial and head deposits provide sources of flint, with the latter favoured. Pit 1 is a probable tree throw that has undergone some modification with a ring of possible posts recorded. This feature began to infill with silt and residual debris, but was used in a later phase as a dump for debris, mainly burnt flint, charcoal and worked flint. It has been suggested that pits 2 and 3, which are deep and irregular, represent quarry pits accessing flint-bearing head deposits (two collections of

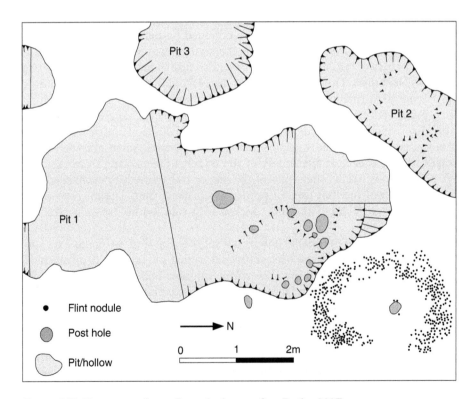

Figure 5.30 Features at Streat Lane (redrawn after Butler 2007)

unmodified flint nodules have been collected from pits 1 and 3). There are also suggestions that these may be tree throws. There is not necessarily a conflict between these two hypotheses, since tree throws are likely to have been a source of raw material, and could be modified to collect additional nodules. These pits then were used as dumps for refuse, particularly burnt material, during subsequent visits to the site. Pits 1 (upper fill) and 3 date to the second half of the seventh millennium BC.

A possible shelter was also excavated, consisting of a post-hole surrounded by a c.3 m wide ring of flint nodules, which may have weighed down the edges of a tepee-like structure. This area lacked lithic debris and seems to have been deliberately kept clean. Knapping areas were located amongst the pits, some of which had been cut by these features (Butler 2007). The microliths from the site suggest that much of the assemblage predates the radiocarbon dates. There are, though, a handful of scalene triangles and narrow-backed bladelets that are likely to be contemporary with the use of the pits for the deposition of burnt debris, and thus with the shelter also, as this seems to have been the focus of maintenance activities. The mixed nature of this assemblage makes it difficult to understand which activities belong to the Late Mesolithic occupation and which were contemporary with the earlier use of the site.

The radiocarbon dates indicate that burning activities belong to the Late Mesolithic occupation. These seem extensive: 108 kg of burnt flint were recovered from excavated contexts and 72 kg from the ploughsoil. Charcoal consisted of oak, hazel and pomoidiae (possibly hawthorn). Prunus charcoal (possibly blackthorn or wild cherry) was present, but rarer. This site shows two interesting features of the Late Mesolithic: An occupation site on the Gault clay, and an occupation that appears small in scale in terms of the lithic assemblage, but was of sufficient importance for site maintenance activities to be undertaken and for, at the very least, some modification of tree throws to occur.

Late seventh millennium dates have also been obtained from Falmer Stadium, where pit digging was also a major activity (Garland and Anderson-Whymark 2015). Here, at least 15 Mesolithic pits were located, containing large quantities of lithic debris. Fourteen of the pits were located in four clusters of three to five pits across an area 25 m in diameter. This appears to be the area of a larger scatter that has been partially truncated by the plough. Quantities of lithics in the pits range from three pieces to 543 pieces, with an average of 99 pieces per pit. Burnt flint is present, but not in high levels, and a couple of pits contain isolated hazelnut shells. Material in the pits does not seem to be specially selected, rather a sample of debris generated by on-site activities.

Tree throws may have been used in similar ways as pits: At Beechbrook Wood, Westwell Kent, a site on the Greensand in the Great Stour valley, a tree throw contained an assemblage of 1393 pieces of worked flint (Brady 2006). The collection included 58 microburins and 30 microliths, indicating the manufacture and repair of composite tools. Cortical flakes were rare, suggesting preforming of cores elsewhere in the landscape, perhaps at some of more specialised procurement sites, such as Finglesham and West Hill, Pycombe (see above). The deposition of material within the tree throw has been argued to represent middening, though the description of the feature may be more compatible with silting episodes from an adjacent landsurface. Residual Mesolithic material was also recovered from later features on the site, suggesting a more extensive scatter of material. Residual charcoal from a ring ditch close to the tree throw may suggest an early sixth millennium date for this activity.

Wealden Rockshelters

Much of the dated evidence for Late Mesolithic occupation in the southeast derives from the rock shelters of the High Weald. Several such sites are known scattered across ridges of the Ardingly Sandstone in Sussex and Kent, often close to springs or streams (Figure 5.31). Mesolithic material has been recovered from Stone Hill Rocks (Gardiner 1988), Stonewall Park, Chiddingstone in Kent (Jacobi 1982c), High Rocks (Figure 5.32, Money 1960), Happy Valley Rocks (Money 1960), the Rocks, Rocksfield, Uckfield (Figure 5.33, Hemingway 1980), the Hermitage, High Hurstwood (Jacobi and Tebbutt 1981), Rocks Wood, Withyam (Harding and Ostoja-Zagórski 1987) and Eridge (Greatorex and Seager Thomas 2000) in East Sussex and Tilgate Wood, Balcombe (Clark 1934) and Chiddinglye Wood Rocks (Allen et al. 2008) in West Sussex. While substantial assemblages of Mesolithic material have been re-covered from some of these sites (c.10,000 from The Rocks for example), many on excavation show considerable levels of disturbance (Greatorex and Seagar Thomas 2000). Despite these problems, some, such as the Hermitage and Stonewall, preserve hearths and post-holes, sealed within in situ soil horizons.

Radiometric dates from these sites range from c.7000 cal BC (at Stonewall), but mainly fall within the sixth millennium (Jacobi 1982c; Jacobi and Tebbutt 1981). The bulked fifth millennium dates from High Rocks come from a layer associated with both Mesolithic flintwork and Ebbsfleet pottery (Money 1960) and should thus be discounted. Given these are mostly bulked charcoal samples and these shelters are often characterised by disturbed sediments, some caution should be exercised.

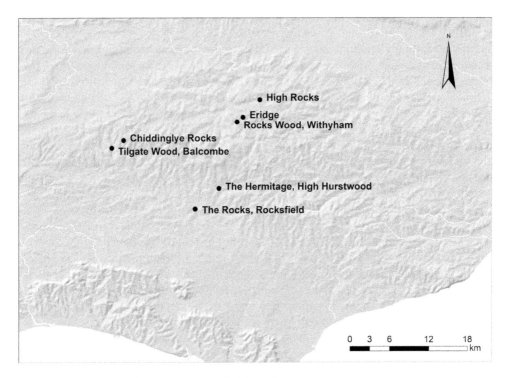

Figure 5.31 Location of the Wealden rockshelter sites

Figure 5.32 High Rocks (copyright Matt Pope). Photograph taken with kind permission of the owner of High Rock

Figure 5.33 The Rocks, Ucksfield (copyright Matt Pope)

However, the dates from Stonewall and the Hermitage come from discrete features, so are more likely to be reliable, though it should be noted that not all the Stonewall dates are stratigraphically consistent (Jacobi 1982c). At the Hermitage, a small number of obliquely blunted points and basally modified points indicate Middle

Mesolithic occupation, though most of the material belongs to the Late or Final Mesolithic (see below). This is fairly typical of the microliths from the larger assemblages, indicating small-scale initial occupation in the Early or Middle Mesolithic, with more repeated visits during the Late Mesolithic.

Though of mixed date, these sites appear dominated by microliths and their production debris (see Table 5.8). Other tools, apart from notches and truncations, are rare; Jacobi (1982c) suggests that the size of the notches indicates they may be related to arrow-shaft maintenance. Burins are more common than scrapers, which apart from Stonewall B are rare or absent. These sites also tend to have a low ratio of cores to debitage, indicating cores were removed. Burnt flint is common, indicating the repeated lighting of hearths, many of which no longer survive. Though these assemblages are the result of repeated occupations, their affinity suggests similar sorts of occupation: Short overnight stops in the context of seasonal hunting expeditions. However, there are hints that they may have had more important roles, as marked persistent places.

Jacobi (1981) draws attention to the large numbers of *pieces émoussées,* or rubbed-end pieces, from Stonewall B; amongst the retouched/utilised group are more than 65 examples. Six examples are also known from the Hermitage (Jacobi and Tebbutt 1981). These are artefacts with extensive wear that seem to have been used on stone. Jacobi suggests these tools may have been used to engrave the rockshelter, though the designs themselves would be long lost due to the erosion of the soft stone. A fallen block within the Mesolithic layers in front of the Stonewall B shelter displays deeply engraved lines and may provide some support for this hypothesis. Further credence comes through work in Northern France, where large numbers of *pieces émoussées* have been recovered from the rockshelter sites of the Fontainbleau sandstone (Île de France). Over 2000 often elaborately decorated sandstone shelters are known in this region (Lesvignes et al. 2019), and recent microwear studies indicates that *pieces émoussées* were used to produce the engravings found on these sites (Guéret and Bénard 2017).

Table 5.8 Assemblage composition of Wealden rockselter sites (data from Jacobi and Tebbut 1981; Greatorex and Seagar Thomas 2000; Jacobi 1982c)

Tool/tool spall	The Hermitage	Eridge	Stonewall A	Stonewall B
Awl	4	0	1	2
Axe/pick	0	0	0	2
Axe flake	3	0	0	4
Burin	18	3	3	9
Burin spall	17	0	1	0
Microlith	141	5	14	95
Microburin	46	1	2	36
Microdenticulate	0	0	0	1
Notch/denticulate	35	0	4	8
Scraper	4	0	2	12
Truncation	31	0	7	20
Retouch/utilised	318	59	29	88
Cores	49	5	–	–
Total inc debitage	4329	513	–	–

Drowned valleys, lost landscapes

While not quite achieving the rates of the Early Boreal, sea-level rise continued to have a significant impact along the south coast. Sturt et al. (2013, Figure 7) estimate that nearly 4000 km^2 were lost in the Channel region in the 500 years from 7000 BC. The period 7000–5000 cal BC differs from earlier times in that there is more immediate evidence for these lost landscapes and details of the process of inundation. This is particularly clear in intertidal and submerged areas between the Hampshire coast and the Isle of Wight. In the Early Holocene, the hills of the Isle of Wight formed a spine of chalk drained by rivers that ran down to coastal cliffs. The Solent flowed to the east of the Isle of Wight along the Eastern Solent Valley, while the area to the northwest formed a sheltered valley (Western Solent Valley). From around 6200 BC, rising seas began to work their way into this northwestern valley; by c.6000 BC, the sea was at −10.7 msl, and the valley began to change from fen to a brackish environment as a lagoon developed (Momber et al. 2020).

Rankine (1951a) collected Mesolithic artefacts from Cams Bay, Fareham, and additional finds have been located in intertidal areas in the region by Draper (1951) and Jacobi (1981). Known finds extend from Selsey in the east to Christchurch Harbour in the west (Hey 2014). As Jacobi (1981, 21) notes both Early and Late Mesolithic sites are represented. While most of this material represents chance finds, more systematic survey towards the eastern end of the area at Langstone Harbour revealed several isolated small-scale Late Mesolithic activity areas, occasionally including animal bones (Allen and Gardiner 2000). Further west, similar small scatters, containing both early and late microliths and focused on hearths, were uncovered from the intertidal zone of Christchurch Harbour at Mother Siller's Channel (Palmer 1972). Significant quantities of Mesolithic archaeology, particularly tranchet axes, have also been recovered during dredging in the Solent area (Momber et al. 2011).

The most vivid picture of the drowned landscapes of the Solent comes from underwater survey and excavation undertaken in the area of Bouldnor cliff, off the northwest shore of the Isle of Wight, once part of the Western Solent Valley. Here, at the base of an eroding marine cliff, was a peat shelf, under which were alluvial sediments and old soil horizons associated with Mesolithic archaeology. Monitoring of this shelf revealed three areas of in situ Mesolithic archaeology. At the time of the Mesolithic occupation this was a river valley, and the site was located on the edge of the floodplain (Momber et al. 2011). Sediment cores in other regions of the Western Solent give a picture of a rich wetland, dissected by several small rivers and their tributaries, and including freshwater lakes. Given inundation of this area occurred only a few centuries after occupation, the sea must already have been close.

At BC-II occupation took place on a sand bar on the margins of the river or lake, which around 6200–6000 cal BC became sufficiently stable to be colonised by vegetation. At this time, alder carr with oak and hazel grew on the wetter areas of the floodplain, while drier ground held a forest of pine, oak, elm and hazel. Ferns grew in areas of open ground and bulrushes along the edge of the channel. Part of a scatter of flint and burnt flint was located, associated with oak charcoal, a single burnt hazelnut shell and a waterlogged dogwood seed. Over 1000 worked and burnt pieces of flint included two axe fragments, a truncation, a possible burin spall and one microlith (a fragment of scalene triangle or backed bladelet). Both chalk flint and beach pebbles were used to produce these tools (Momber et al. 2011, 2020). A single pike vertebra was associated with these sediments (Momber et al. 2011, 52), while an aurochs astragalus was subsequently recovered from the site (Smith et al. 2015, 1000). Bayesian modelling of radiocarbon dates suggests this occupation dates to around 6000 cal BC. The site was subsequently covered with peat as rivers backed up and conditions became waterlogged before the development of saltmarsh and finally marine inundation.

Subsequently, sedimentary DNA analysis was carried out on samples from the palaeosol at this site (Smith et al. 2015). This work added some detail to the picture of the vegetation provided by pollen analysis, showing woodland populated by oak, willow/aspen and a member of the pomoidiae (apple, pear, hawthorn, rowan) and the presence of grasses. Animals were represented by aurochs and canids (dog or wolf). The most remarkable find was that of cereal DNA from the ancient wheat einkorn from the lower layers of the buried soil. Native species were excluded, and many of the sequences most closely resembled the early domesticated wheat, einkorn. There is no evidence that this was grown here, and no macrofossils were present, leading Smith et al. to suggest the exchange of flour between agriculturalists and hunter-gatherer groups. This would be an unusual location to find traces of this, associated with small-scale activity on an area of floodplain subject to inundation. The date of this find is at least 500 years before Neolithic groups were present in the neighbouring areas of northern France. The veracity of the discovery has been challenged, with contamination seen to be a likely issue (Weiß et al. 2015). However, this find may add impetus to older debates surrounding the presence of cereal-type pollen in Mesolithic contexts (see chapter 6).

A few hundred metres from BC-II, a pit, filled with charcoal, burnt stone and burnt flint was found in the eroding cliff section, marking site BC-V (Momber et al. 2011). The pit has a similar date at around 6100–6000 cal BC (derived from three modelled radiocarbon dates) to the activity at BC-II. BC-V was also a floodplain location covered by sedges and reeds that became colonised with alder as it dried out. Above the floodplain on higher ground was hazel and oak woodland with elm. Close to the pit was a spread of burnt flint and organic material within a grey silt, which may represent part of a second cut feature. Several collections of worked wood were recovered, including parallel timbers that may represent a platform (Figure 5.34). One part of a large oak plank from a nearby area has been dated to c.6100 cal BC.

Figure 5.34 Wooden platform from Bouldnor cliff (© Maritime Archaeology Trust)

This overlies patches of charcoal and burnt flint within an organic silt also containing worked and burnt flint. Analysis by Maisie Taylor indicates evidence for wood-working in the form of both tangential and radial woodchips, trimmed roundwood and the tangentially split plank. The trees selected for woodworking were almost exclusively oak and alder. Another important find from this area was several pieces of string (Momber et al. 2011).

The final site to produce archaeology is BC-IV, where a small collection of worked flint (debitage and a few utilised pieces) was recovered eroding from sediments. BC-IV was also a floodplain site but located in an area where the floodplain had stabilised sufficiently to allow soil development. Dryland vegetation consisted of oak-hazel woodland that lime was starting to infiltrate, clearings where ferns grew and areas of wet fen. This is a site at a higher elevation than BC-II and V, with the old land surface submerged rather later at c.5300 cal BC, showing the diachronic effect of sea-level rise in the Western Solent.

The Southwest: Middens and springs

The association of Mesolithic sites and tufa deposits in the Kennet Valley was noted earlier. This is more pronounced in the southwest, where tufa springs and other springs with unusual, often colourful, features seem to have been a special focus. These sites are associated with faunal remains, particularly aurochs, and where the context of deposition can be discerned, these springs seem to have been the focus of formal practises. Davis (2012) notes the transformative and ambiguous properties of tufa, part of bodies of water, but creating a stone-like material when dry. The 'petrifying' properties of tufa are likely to have been seen as remarkable as they are today.

This association was first recorded at Blashenwell near Corfe Castle. Here, tufa deposits extended for 600 by 200 m and were nearly 4 m thick, occupying a depression in a narrow valley (Arkell 1947; Preece 1980). A calcareous spring flows from the Purbeck ridge, through the tufa deposits, to join the river Corfe. The tufa, as exposed in a quarry pit, was investigated in the 19th century by Clement Reid, amongst others (Damon 1884; Reid 1896). Molluscan analysis indicates the presence of marshy fen with boggy pools when the tufa was forming; grey lenses indicate drier episodes. The area appears wooded (Clement Reid noted the leaves of oak and hazel preserved in the tufa), with a later episode of disturbance, perhaps attributable to human activity (Preece 1980).

Reid (1896, 71) recorded the presence of numerous marine shells, dominated by limpet with smaller numbers of periwinkle (both common and flat varieties), top-shell and peppery furrow shell. Apart from the last, which has estuarine habits, these are species of the rocky shore. The present-day shoreline is more than 3 km from the site. A perforated periwinkle shell was also recovered (Jacobi archive, British Museum). Reid mentions a seam of charcoal, extensive enough to turn the tufa black. Flint flakes, charcoal and the bones of pig, red deer, roe deer and aurochs were stated by Damon (1884) to be found throughout the tufa layers, though Reid (1896, 70) notes these as being more common in the middle of the deposit and associated with flint and charcoal. Initial reports from Reid suggested no retouched pieces among the 400–500 pieces of flint he recovered, but he later noted three microliths (Reid 1897). Only one of these was present when Clark

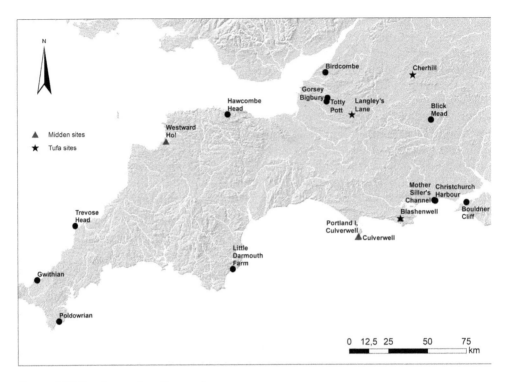

Figure 5.35 Southwest sites discussed

examined the assemblage; this was a triangle fragment, though three microburins and two mis-hits were also noted (Clark 1938). An axe was later found by Rankine and a further microlith during environmental sampling (Preece 1980). Flint appears to have been obtained from local beaches (Clark 1938), and three blades of Portland chert are also present in the collection (Jacobi and Wessex Archaeology 2014). Three dates on fauna (one a bulked sample), none with location data, span the last 1500 years of the Mesolithic.

Better evidence is available from recent excavations at Langley Lane, in the Wellow Valley, near Midsommer Norton in Somerset (Lewis et al. 2019, Figure 5.36). Mesolithic activity took place in a boggy clearing surrounded by woodland, where an active spring began to generate tufa, eventually resulting in a mound 20–30 m in diameter and 0.5 m in height. Aurochs remains from the initial phase of the occupation are mostly head and foot bones, which have been interpreted as evidence for a kill and primary butchery site. The bones include a cut-marked aurochs metacarpal dated to the second half of the seventh millennium BC (7558 ± 49 BP; UBA-20293). Some aurochs remains were found on the dryland, but many (35) were deposited within the waters of the spring and seem to represent an act of formal deposition. Activity at the site thus seems to have started with the killing of a young female aurochs; the act of formal deposition of the remains of this animal, as at both Star Carr and Flixton School some three millennia earlier (see chapter 2), seems to have guided subsequent activity at the site.

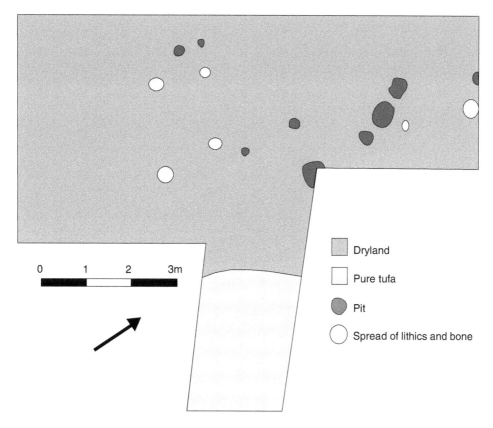

Figure 5.36 Plan of excavations at Langley's Lane

Also found within the tufa were 12 lithic artefacts. The lithics were all sourced from the chalk, in contrast to the remainder of the assemblage from the site, where derived sources dominate. The chalk flint may originate from the Wiltshire Downs, 30 km distant, and thus may have merited special treatment. Lewis and colleagues have noted that many lithics were coated with tufa, which itself resembles chalk cortex, which may mean that chalk flint was appropriate for deposition in the tufa spring. The recoating of flint with 'cortex' may have been a metaphor for rejuvenation, and several dryland pit contexts on the site contain flint coated with tufa, suggesting this rejuvenated material was retrieved from the spring.

On the dryland margins of the spring were five discrete clusters of flint and animal bone and nine shallow pits, ranging from 0.5–1 m in diameter. Eight of these included artefacts: Most had lithics and colourful small stones, one contained fossil belemnites and two contained hand-moulded balls of tufa (Figure 5.37). These pits seem to have been dug and rapidly backfilled. The stones found in the pits come from a variety of different geologies (sandstones, quartz, ironstone, limestone, mudstone, coal), which can be found between 400 m to 10 km from the site. One of the tufa balls, which had disintegrated, was found to contain lithics, animal bone including pig and small stones; the mingling of animal remains and rejuvenating tufa may have created an object that was perceived as animated.

A second Late Mesolithic phase is marked by a slight drying out of the deposit, the

Figure 5.37 Moulded ball of tufa in a pit at Langley's Lane (copyright Jodie Lewis)

basal part of this layer is dated to 5990–5810 cal BC (7003 ± 32 BP; UBA-20199). This layer also contains lithic artefacts and aurochs bones, which continued to be deposited in the tufa wetland, perhaps memorialising the initial aurochs hunting episode.

A third site where Mesolithic activity is associated with tufa can be found at Cherhill; the Early Mesolithic material, sealed beneath layers of tufa, was discussed in chapter 3. A radiocarbon date for an organic layer low down within this tufa deposit (representing one of several periods of drying out) indicates it probably started forming in the eighth or seventh millennium BC (Evans and Smith 1983). Rather than associated with running water, the Cherhill tufa formed in a series of low pools within an open area surrounded by woodland. Blue-green algae has been found preserved within the tufa suggesting at times, the pools were brilliantly coloured, contrasting with their usual murky white hue. These colourful properties may have marked out these pools as significant.

Significant quantities of flint and animal bones were recovered either from the tufa or covered with tufa within the extensive Neolithic ditches that cross the site. Evans and Smith (1983, 52) suggest this material may have been eroded from higher ground as the waters rose, or that they may have been deposited in the white waters. Microliths from within the tufa are either Middle or Late Mesolithic, while the majority of the occupation at the site is Early Mesolithic; no Early Mesolithic microliths are known from the tufa, which one might expect if material had been incorporated within it through erosion. This would suggest that at least a portion of the material from the tufa represents depositionary practises. Two scalene triangles made from Portland chert (Box 5.6) were recovered from the site. One, in a redeposited context truncated by a later ditch, was coated in tufa, indicating its initial context of deposition. The deposition of exotic material in tufa echoes Langley's Lane, and given the contrast of black chert with white tufa, may be related to the interest in colours evinced at these sites.

As at Langley's Lane, the faunal remains in the tufa are dominated by aurochs (Grigson in Evans and Smith 1983). Sixteen elements were recovered that were identifiable to species, in comparison with five of pig and six of red deer. This represents a major contrast with the pig-focused Early Mesolithic occupation, again suggesting that the remains in the tufa derived from Middle and Late Mesolithic depositionary practises. More than 66 aurochs bones were recovered from the Neolithic ditches, and Grigson has suggested these are likely to be Mesolithic. The similarity of species representation in these features echoes that from the tufa, though the microliths from the ditches (15 Late Mesolithic: 5 Early Mesolithic) indicate these also contain some Early Mesolithic material.

Two relatively amorphous Mesolithic 'hollows' were located, probably pits that were cut into the tufa as it dried out. In the original report, these were stated as sealed by and thus earlier the tufa, but each was filled with lithics coated by tufa, indicating they are likely to have been dug from a higher level. These also contain Late Mesolithic microliths, supporting this later date. These are the only Late Mesolithic microliths from contexts originally thought to be below the tufa, and their presence has resulted in considerable confusion over the dating of the site and the typological sequence of the Mesolithic in Southern Britain more broadly. The presence of pits cut into the tufa echoes the evidence at Langley's Lane, and here, too, may have been intended to rejuvenate lithic material, perhaps associated with a significant event. The pit digging may be associated with one of the drying out episodes recorded in the sequence.

The first pit appears to have contained large quantities of material. Forty-six faunal elements include a pig's tooth and aurochs long bones, the size of unidentifiable fauna suggests much of this derives from aurochs. Lithics include two scalene triangles (with two sides retouched) and an unfinished scalene, a burin, a truncation, nine retouched and utilised flakes, a Krukowski microburin, 327 waste flakes and 23 cores. There were also 12 pieces of sarsen. The second feature, truncated by a later ditch, underwent less extensive investigation but includes a microlith (a scalene with three sides retouched) and 22 pieces of lithic debitage.

Blick Mead

Blick Mead is located on the edge of the floodplain of the Bristol Avon, close to where the valley sides begin to rise. Pleistocene gravels provide relief, with gravel rising gradually to the north across the site, and the highest densities of archaeological material are located just below this rise in an area of the site that is now waterlogged in the area of a spring. The archaeological material is located in unit H3, a sediment generated through episodes of alluviation and colluviation (Young et al. 2018, 62). The deposit model suggests the silts at the base of unit H3 in which the Mesolithic material was found are were laid down in still or slow-moving water, the product of rare flooding events (Young et al. 2018, 60–1). The site is close to the

Box 5.6   Portland Chert

Portland chert is a high quality black or grey chert from the Late Jurassic Portland Beds. It varies in quality from fine to courser grained, though much material that is found in archaeological contexts is high quality. Chert seams outcrop extensively on the Isles of Portland and Purbeck. It is available in vast quantities on Portland: From cliff-edge exposures and as beach pebbles along the coast of the island and across Chesil beach; it is also present in raised beaches and in head deposits (Palmer 1970). Care (1979, 99) has suggested quarrying during the Mesolithic for this chert, though any evidence for this is likely to have been destroyed by more recent large scale quarries in the region. Stewart (2017) has argued that the liminal nature of the island of Portland may have made this a special place in the Neolithic, suitable for the manufacture of arrowheads. Whether this was the case in the Mesolithic, too, is more difficult to ascertain. That the material was seen as special might be indicated by its distribution patterns beyond the island, being found from Cornwall to Surrey. It may be significant that three of the materials with the broadest distribution patterns in the Late Mesolithic – Rhum Bloodstone (Box 3.2), Arran pitchstone (Box 5.2) and Portland chert – are all found on islands.

Extensive use of the chert is attested in surface scatters and excavated assemblages across the island of Portland. A characteristic tool produced from this material is the 'Portland Pick', made from coarser cherts and associated limestones (Palmer 1970). These are crude tools with a pointed end, their body generally retaining the rod-like or tabular shape of the raw material. Occasional more adze-like forms, sharpened with a tranchet blow, are found. More than 1000 have been recovered from an area of around a square mile in the area of Portland Bill (Palmer 1970). The long-distance transport of Portland Chert was first noted by Rankine (1951b) and seems to have started in the Early Mesolithic. It is present at Oakhanger VII, Hampshire (Jacobi 1981) and at Frensham Great Pond, Surrey, a bladelet core has been recovered (Palmer 1970). More commonly, Portland chert is associated with Late Mesolithic sites, where it may have been part of a broader interest in strong colours. Care (1982) suggests that distribution is sufficiently broad that this material was exchanged.

While Portland chert is often found as debitage, on occasions this material may have travelled as finished tools, or as blanks for tools: Two microliths are known from Poldowrian in Cornwall (Smith and Harris 1982, 33), two scalene triangles were recovered from Cherhill, while scalenes are also known from Farnham (Rankine 1951b, 94) Chaldon Down, Dorset (White 1974) and a backed bladelet from Broomhill, Hampshire (Jacobi 1981, 19). A tranchet axe-sharpening flake was recovered from Windmill Hill site 4, indicating an axe in this material was curated (Draper 1968). More frequently, though, it seems to have been imported as cores and blanks (Care 1979) into sites where it is present as debitage, for example, at Mother Siller's Channel on the Christchurch Harbour, or at Blashenwell (Palmer 1970).

spring line, and insect evidence does suggest the local presence of water, such as pools or streams, and coring has picked up traces of tufa deposits in one area. The deposit model is based on relatively few boreholes, meaning that smaller bodies of water might be missed.

Given this ambiguity over depositional context, the significant disturbance of the alluvial unit from later landscaping, and the interim nature of current publication, it is difficult to understand how the large quantities of archaeological material arrived in the area of the site that is now waterlogged. The excavators see the material in the wetland as indicative of formal deposition into areas that were standing water at the time of occupation, perhaps marking feasting events (Jacques et al. 2014, 2018). The area is close to the spring line and the deposition of material into springs has been noted at Langley's Lane and probably Cherhill; there is also a tradition of depositing midden material into stagnant pools and waterlogged hollows (as at Westward Ho! and Culverwell, see below), so this would be consistent with regional patterns. However, colluviation is also a possibility, especially given the very large quantity of burnt flint recovered. The evidence that the archaeological material is in situ comes from study of the lithics, of which the majority were relatively fresh. However, around 5% are more extensively abraded, indicating some has a colluvial origin. It is antici-pated that further research will resolve this issue, and clarify the relationship between wetland and dryland deposits, which are currently uncertain (David 2019a; Jacques et al. 2018). It may be that the material in the lower lying area has input from several sources, especially given the time-depth represented: Deposition in wetland pools, seasonal activity on the floodplain and colluviation. Any or all would be compatible with the geomorphology of the site and our knowledge of Mesolithic practises at this time. The presence within present-day springs around the site of an algae that stains flint pink has been noted; it is not known if this was a component of the Mesolithic landscape, but it would be compatible with the interest in unusual colours evidenced at other spring or tufa sites.

However, archaeological material arrived in the waterlogged areas; the sheer density of material indicates a site of some significance. Eleven thousand seven hundred twenty-seven pieces of flint and 2058 animal bones were recovered from trench 19, measuring 6 × 3 m , while reasonably high quantities of materials were also recovered from trenches 22 and 23. In all, around 30,000 lithic artefacts have been recovered, from a relatively small area.

The lithics include large amounts of burnt flint, probably indicative of the presence of hearths on dryer ground. The usual range of Mesolithic tools and debitage are present. Microliths dominate the tools and are likely to be hugely under-represented, given that relatively little sediment was sieved (95 microliths were recovered from the c.4 m^2 of trench 19 that were sieved, but only 14 from the 9 m^2 that were not sieved). The microliths from the site span the Middle Mesolithic (obliquely blunted and basally modified points), the Late Mesolithic (left lateralised scalenes) and the Final Mesolithic (micro-tranchets). This is confirmed by the radiocarbon dates, which mainly span the mid-seventh to early fifth millennium BC, though some early eighth millennium evidence is present. Vertical plotting of finds did not take place in the wetland areas, with the exception of a small area in trench 19. Dates from this area do not seem to be in stratigraphic order, again suggestive of a colluvial input; however, only three measurements come from this sequence, and more material would need to be dated to confirm this.

Tables 5.9 Total number of identified fragments (when available) or presence of major species at tufa or spring sites

Site	Aurochs	Red deer	Roe deer	Pig	Other
Blashenwell	P	P	P	P	
Blick Mead (eighth–fifth millennium)	155	46	8	23	Elk, dog
Cherhill tufa layer	16	6		5	
Langley's Lane (main phase 1c, late seventh millennium)	31			4	
Langley's Lane 1d (early sixth millennium)	2	1			
Langley's Lane 1e (fifth millennium?)	4				

Blick Mead, as is the case with other Late Mesolithic sites in the region, is dominated by aurochs remains. It is unusual, however, in its much wider representation of species than other sites (see Table 5.9). Part of this may simply be by virtue of the much larger assemblage, though the wide spread of dates is also likely to be a factor. Red deer and pig, which are present in reasonable numbers at Blick Mead, are dated or phased to the Late Mesolithic at Blashenwell, Cherhill and Langley's Lane. There are also late seventh millennium to early fifth millennium dates on samples from these species at Blick Mead, confirming that these two animals played a subsidiary role in Late Mesolithic subsistence practises in this region. Roe deer, present in small numbers at Blick Mead, are also found at Blashenwell, though these elements have not been dated. The presence of elk at Blick Mead is unusual, given its rarity in Southern England; its remains have only been found in Early Mesolithic contexts in the Kennet Valley, and are only present in reasonable quantities at Wawcott XXX (Froom 2012, see chapter 3). The elk at Blick Mead is undated, but could indicate an Early Mesolithic presence at the site.

In the quantity of flint recovered and the broad span of occupation, Blick Mead, like similar floodplain sites in the Kennet such as Wawcott III, can be considered a 'super-site' (see chapter 4). These sites have evidence of occupation from the Early or Middle Mesolithic onwards, and seem to have offered particular affordances that made then attractive for a long period. For some, though by no means all, this was the presence of abundant raw material. The similarity between Blick Mead and Downton in the large quantities and temporal span of the lithics has been noted (Bishop et al. 2013, 114). Blick Mead shares a similar landscape position to Wawcott III and Downton. Downton appears to have been important for its raw material sources, and it is possible that at Blick Mead, too, availability of raw material was important: Possible caches of flint nodules have been recorded at the site (Bishop 2018, 77). The flint used on the site appears to have been obtained both as river cobbles and from head deposits; tree throws were located on the dryland area, which would have given access to the gravel below. A favoured place for hunting, given the large numbers of microliths and faunal remains, is another possibility.

Southwest Shell-middens

Shell-middens are usually seen as a feature of Scottish Mesolithic archaeology, but middens are also known from Southwest England and Wales (see below). Four middens have been excavated in the southwest: Blashenwell, Portland I, Culverwell and Westward Ho! (Figure 5.35). All share common features that set them apart from the Scottish middens, revealing differing cultural practises guiding the generation of midden material. They are all associated with large quantities of lithic material including microliths, the latter notoriously absent from the Scottish west coast middens. A further contrast is in their landscape location: The Scottish west coast middens are located in caves or on the strandline, the southwest middens are set back from the sea. It is difficult to understand with any precision the location of contemporary shorelines in relation to these sites, but Blashenwell is today 3 km from the sea, and Culverwell was probably around 1 km from the shoreline at the time of occupation. All middens appear to have accumulated in clearings within woodland, and all seem associated with water: Culverwell and Westward Ho! seem to have accumulated in wet gulleys or small pools, and Blashenwell is associated with tufa deposits.

The midden at Blashenwell has already been discussed above. Very little is known of its extent and associations, or even whether it is fully Mesolithic, though the lithics recovered are of this date, and Reid (1896) noted the association of animal bone (subsequently dated to the last 1500 years of the Mesolithic) with the shell layer. Less than 30 km to the east of Blashenwell are middens at Portland I and Culverwell on the Isle of Portland. Portland I has seen limited excavation and sampling, but appears to represent a large lithic scatter of Mesolithic aspect and a smaller area of thin (5–7.5 cm) midden material. Microlith types suggest a large Early or Middle Mesolithic component to the scatter, and the assemblage includes a number of core tools ('Portland Picks'). No dates have been obtained for the midden material and later Prehistoric evidence is also present (Palmer 1999).

The midden at Culverwell, a few hundred metres from Portland I and on the southern margins of the island, is 270 m to the west of a spring, which flowed as a small stream down to the sea. The stream shows evidence for a period of tufa development. The midden lies towards the bottom of a steep slope, in an area modified by medieval strip lynchets. It is now a few hundred metres back from the edge of sea cliffs; the sea would have been further away in the Mesolithic but still close, probably within a kilometre. Access to the sea is likely to have been easier than today as head deposits, now eroded by the sea, would probably have sloped down from the solid geology of the cliff. Snail evidence suggests the site was wooded at the time of occupation, and this is likely to have made this location more sheltered than it is today. Charcoal indicates the presence of oak and hazel woodland, with ash, privet, *Prunus sp.* and a member of the pomodiae.

Culverwell is a low midden, 35 cm in height, comprised mainly of edible periwinkle, limpets and topshell, with dog welk also very common. However, a broad range of species were recovered (Table 5.10), mainly indicative of the rocky shore. Species preferring sandy/or muddy sediments are more common in the lower layers, perhaps indicating changing coastal morphology as sea-levels rose. There are suggestions that shellfish gathering was intensified in the upper layers of the midden. There seems to have been a seasonal basis to shellfish exploitation, with collection in autumn and winter indicated (Mannino et al. 2003). Only two fish bones were recovered in the lower midden, both identified as whiting, and the only fauna identifiable to species amongst the fragmentary remains were wild pig. Large quantities of burnt stones were common, indicative of a strong focus on food preparation and cooking. Many of the periwinkles and topshells were intact indicating use of boiling water to extract them (Mannino and Thomas 2001, 1109).

Table 5.10 Composition of the southwest middens

Species	Blashenwell	Culverwell	Westward Ho!
Limpet (Patella sp).	++	++	+
Edible Periwinkle (Littorina littorea)	+	+++	+
Flat Periwinkle (Littorina obtusata)	+	++	+
Thick topshell (Monodonta linneata)	+	++	
Purple topshell (Gibbula umbilicalis)		++	
Dogwhelk (Nucella lapillus)		++	+
Sting winkle (Ocenebra erinacea)		+	
Whelk (Buccinum undatum)		+	
Needle Welk (Bittium reticulatum)		+	
Netted dog welk (Hinia reticulata)		+	
Thick-lipped dog welk (Hinia incrassata)		+	
Common mussel (Mytilus edulis)		+	++
Cockle (Cerastoderma edulis)		++	++
Carpet shell (Venerupis sp.)		++	++
Peppery furrow shell (Scrobicularia plana)	+		++
Scallop (Pecten maximus)		+	
Oyster (Ostea edulis)		+	
Razor shell			+
Crab		++	+

The stratigraphy of the site is complex. Above the shells are colluviated deposits, and it is likely that the upper layers of the midden, too, have been reworked through colluviation (Mannino and Thomas 2001); thus, the dating of some of the features associated with the upper part of the midden are uncertain. There has also been some difficulty in relating stratigraphic layers between the trenches and test pits that were excavated over many years; subsequent radiocarbon dating indicates that similar contexts often had different histories. Nor were finds usually 3D plotted (Palmer 1999), which might have permitted reconstruction of the taphonomy of the midden, though on the couple of instances when they were (in trenches 40 and 4, near the base of the midden), lithic refits were achieved.

The available evidence suggests the midden initially began to accumulate at around 6000 cal BC in a natural gulley or hollow in the southwest part of the site that was waterlogged for at least parts of the year (Figure 5.38). As the southern part of the gulley infilled, the northern part began to be used, deposition here starting several hundred years later in the second half of the sixth millennium BC. A few metres from the gulley to the north and east were a series of hearth and pit features. Hearth 1 is broadly contemporary with the lowest layers of the midden in the gulley, though its stratigraphic position indicates it was constructed after the midden had begun to accumulate. It consists of an artificial scoop about 1.5 m across, cut through the lower layers of the midden and the clay below; the clay itself has been baked. It is associated with burnt stones and small bone fragments, some of which could be identified as pig. A cluster of large core tools, unmodified pebbles, steep scrapers, knapped flint and shell beads were associated with the hearth (Palmer 1999, 23–4). Hearth 4 is the largest on site with a diameter of 2 m and is situated within a depression. A cache of 11 picks and roughouts were located on the southeastern edge of this hearth, as was a small paved area of flat stones. Two smaller hearths were also located, one of these is also

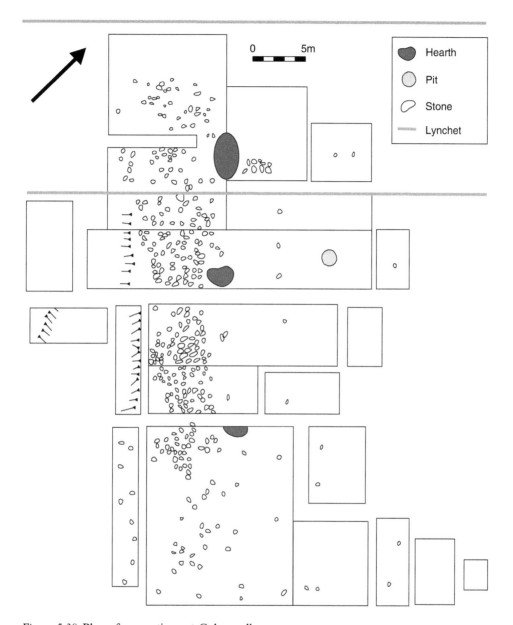

Figure 5.38 Plan of excavations at Culverwell

associated with a cluster of picks. A large pit, a metre wide and deep, was dug through the midden and into underlying head deposits. The pit contained midden material, including large stones, flint and chert, a perforated shell, a charred hazelnut shell and some bone fragments, but the presence of fragments of Prehistoric pottery in the uppermost 30 cm could suggest this is of later date.

Palmer (1999) reports a stone floor or pavement laid across large areas of the midden (Figure 5.38). It seems from context descriptions that this sealed the intact areas of the midden: Midden material below the platform is described as compact, while above is lose and likely to be part of colluviated deposits. While Palmer sees the floor as a Mesolithic working area, this is by no means certain, given the layers above the platform, seen by Palmer to be in situ Mesolithic material may well be colluvium. Given the fact this area seems to have been wooded in the Mesolithic, it seems more likely that the colluvial layers are a product of post-Mesolithic land clearance. Possible ard marks have been noted cutting into the top of the midden, some Prehistoric pottery has been found, and a barbed and tanged arrowhead has been found at the base of a post-hole cutting into the midden, a transverse arrowhead was also recovered; the platform may relate to this later use of the area. However, it is certainly a possibility the platform is contemporary with the midden; Mesolithic groups have been recorded as importing stone for structural purposes since the Early Mesolithic (at Deepcar, see chapter 3), and recent work in Portugal at Cabeco de Amoreira shows this midden was given a stone capping (Bicho et al. 2011).

Lithic artefacts were recovered in some number within and around the midden, though a full analysis is yet to be undertaken. Local grey or black Portland chert (Box 5.6) was used for the majority of the assemblage, though beach flint is also present, and some of the larger core tools, such as axes and picks, were of cherty limestone. The lithic assemblage appears varied, with large numbers of microliths, scrapers and core tools (Table 5.11). Scalene triangles dominate the microlith assemblage, though the large numbers of obliquely blunted points and partially backed points could suggest an Early Mesolithic component not represented by the radiocarbon dates. Microburins outnumber microliths, indicating a focus on manufacturing tools for use elsewhere. Pebble tools are common: These include bevel-ended tools, hammerstones, anvils and countersunk pebbles. Spatial information on artefact distribution is limited, but microliths are more commonly associated with the south and east of the site rather than the deposits of the gulley. Picks and unmodified pebbles are found throughout the site but cluster particularly round the hearths. Items relating to clothing and personal decoration are well-represented. A number of perforated shell beads have been recovered from the site, mostly of periwinkle (28 examples), but

Table 5.11 Data compiled from Jacobi archive, Jacobi and Wessex Archaeology (2014), Palmer (1999), and Balaam et al. (1987). Totals from Westward Ho! Refer to material provenanced from Area 3 (Jacobi coll. and Central Unit excavations)

Tool/tool spall	Blashenwell	Culverwell	Westward Ho!
Axe/pick	2	Numerous	
Awl			1
Burin		Present	
Burin spall			
Microlith	3	573	12
Microburin	5	683	45
Microdenticulate		Rare	
Notch/denticulate	1		2
Scraper		Common	5
Truncation			2
Retouch/utilised		Numerous	6
Cores			22
Total inc debitage			1138

individual examples of dogwelk, cockle and oyster are also known. Ochre is common, including three or four crayons. A number of small highly coloured pebbles were also found (Palmer 1999). While these may have been imported unintentionally on seaweed or by birds, colourful pebbles are present at other Mesolithic sites in the region, such as Langley's Lane (see below).

The huge quantity of material recovered from Culverwell, the varied range of activities, including an emphasis on food production suggests this is a significant site of some longevity. It was located in a shelter clearing, close to a spring and with easy access to the shore. Seasonality evidence suggests it may have served as an autumn or winter camp-site for at least parts of its history.

The third midden in the region at Westward Ho! is further west and, in contrast to the previous middens, is on the northern coast, in an area of Barnstable Bay that is now within the inter-tidal zone. A submerged forest was first noted by Pengelly as far back as 1863, and records of the midden and associated flint scatters were made over the subsequent decade. Collections continued during the following century of material from at least two middens, one Roman, in the inner part of the beach, the other Mesolithic, located further out in an infrequently exposed intertidal zone (Balaam et al. 1987). In the 19th century, reports suggested the midden was fairly large and at least 0.6 m thick. By 1980, it was substantially eroded by marine activity, with a remaining thickness of only 15 cm; reports of its truncation led to survey and sampling by the Central Excavation Unit (Figure 5.39). The midden is only visible and accessible after scouring followed by spring tides. At −2.2 asl, fieldwork was limited to two–three hours per day over a maximum period of four–five days (Figure 5.40). In January 1983, storms

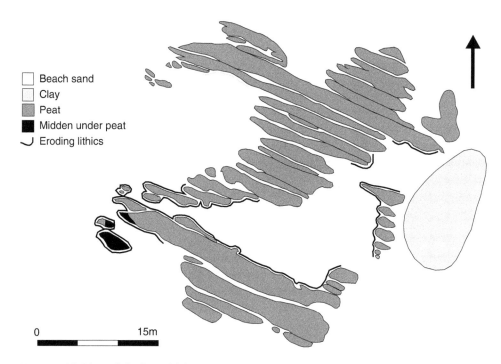

Figure 5.39 Plan of the intertidal area at Westward ho!

Figure 5.40 Excavations of the midden at Westward Ho! (copyright Martin Bell)

exposed the midden and permitted two days of fieldwork at the site and the removal of three large blocks (50 × 80 × 30 cm) for laboratory excavation.

The midden lies on a layer of blue silt that probably represents estuarine sediments and within a slight depression, possibly artificial (Balaam et al. 1987, 178), that may have represented a stagnant pool. The silt and the midden itself are overlain by fen peat. At the interface between these two sediments are various flint scatters that extend up to around 20 m from the midden. Radiocarbon measurements obtained for the midden itself span the sixth millennium BC: Two samples obtained by Jacobi in the 1970s date to the first half of the sixth millennium, while both (bulked) samples from the upper and lower part of the midden obtained in the 1980s fieldwork date to the second half. If sample problems can be discounted, this might suggest shifting foci of deposition over time. Fen peat began to form in the area while the midden was in use, eventually covering it some time during the mid-fifth millennium BC.

Evidence from the 1980s fieldwork provides a rich picture of the local environment. It is clear that the midden was not located on the strand line as previously suggested by Churchill and Wymer (1965) but in a clearing within a fen woodland of oak and hazel, with elm and ivy. In this varied woodland there were areas of willow carr growing by seasonal pools and meadowsweet, nightshade, hemp agrimony and sedge in damper woodland areas. Stands of ash grew on drier ground. During the later life of the midden, willow, birch and ivy became more important around the site. Beyond the woodland and closer to the sea there may have been extensive dune systems (Balaam et al. 1987).

The midden is composed of highly fragmentary marine shells, amongst which mussel (Mytilus edulis) and peppery furrow shell (Scrobicularia plana), unusually for a Mesolithic midden, dominate. These species indicate exploitation of the local rocky shore and estuarine areas, the furrow shell probably coming from the Taw/Torridge estuary, which at a time of lower sea-level would have run to the north of the site (Balaam et al. 1987). Fish were present but rare: Only three fish vertebrae, possibly from a single individual of the goby family, were found in the Central Unit excavations. Jacobi reports a salmonid vertebra and a skate bone from early collections (Jacobi 1979, 85), while he himself recovered a fragment of hake dentary from the midden (Balaam et al. 1987, 220). The remains of slow worm and frog were found, indicators of damp woodland, but also known to have been food resources in Southern Scandinavia and in Britain.

Terrestrial fauna were represented by red deer, roe deer and aurochs, with aurochs more common in the Central Unit excavations, but red deer most common from some of the older collections (Levitan and Locker 1987). Antler from the older collections is mainly shed antler (Jacobi 1979; Levitan and Locker 1987), perhaps suggesting a seasonal element to the occupation. Antler can, of course, be curated for tool manufacture, but the near-absence of unshed antler must have some significance, and may suggest the midden was not visited in the winter months (Jacobi 1979, 85). Plant remains were represented by carbonised hazelnut shells and a hawthorn stone, and the uncarbonized stones of sloes, hawthorn and dogwood. All can be eaten and have been consumed in more recent periods. Hawthorn stones have been found at two Scottish sites (Ailsa View and Chapelfield), reinforcing the idea they were eaten in the Mesolithic (Bishop et al. 2013). Blackberry seeds were ubiquitous, and wild strawberry is preserved in the peat above the midden (Balaam et al. 1987, 239). The beetles that are most common in the midden are Ptiliidae, which are associated with compost and dead vegetation (Vaughn 1987, 241), most likely indicating a substantial plant component to the midden.

Reasonable quantities of lithic artefacts come from the midden (Table 5.11). Jacobi (1979) recorded 1859 artefacts from various collections, though not all are from the midden, as various exposures are known along the beach, and the exact provenance of many artefacts is uncertain. The Central Unit excavations recovered a further 1138 pieces, 886 of which were recovered from erosion gulleys in the peats surrounding the midden, and from the midden itself. Raw material used was mostly flint with small quantities of greensand chert; both seem to have been obtained as beach pebbles close to the site. Microburins were common at the site and indicate the manufacture of composite tools (Table 5.11), though microliths themselves are rarer and most were fragmentary. The remainder of the tools indicate a wide range of tasks were carried out, with small numbers of most major types. Burins are absent but present in older collections from the site. No bevel-ended tools were recovered. This may relate to the absence of two species – limpets and seals – whose processing has been associated with these objects (Anderson 1898; Jacobi 1980b).

Uplands, coasts and estuaries in the southwest

Beyond the shell-middens and tufa sites, dated Late Mesolithic activity in the southwest is rare. Most evidence is found relatively close to the current coastline, though some such sites, for example, Hawcombe Head, on Exmoor at 415 m asl are upland. Jacobi (1979) suggested seasonal movement between lowland coastal and estuarine sites and the uplands, and more recent work has provided some support for this, though seasonality evidence is still lacking. In North Somerset, for example, Gardiner (2009) has suggested a relationship between lithic finds in submerged areas of the Bristol Channel, with findspots on the limestone Failand Ridge. Between these two extends the Birdcombe Valley, and here, close to two springs, evidence for Mesolithic activity has been recovered. While radiocarbon dates indicate late fifth millennium visits, the range of microlithic types, spanning early, middle and late, suggest that Birdcombe may have served as a stop-off point for groups moving between the submerged landscapes of the Bristol Channel and higher ground over a long period of time.

Similar relationships may have pertained in Mendip (Gardiner 2009). Several sites, both caves and open air, are known on the north and west sides of Mendip, where the Rivers Yeo and Axe would have provided access to the lowlands of the Bristol Channel. In addition to a location where human remains were deposited (see chapter 4), lithic material has been recovered from Totty Pott on the Mendip plateau. Lithics were found both within the cave when it was originally emptied, and around the entrance shaft during more recent excavations by Paula Gardiner (2009, 2016). Of the 38 pieces recovered during these excavations, 22 were microliths. These indicate the site was primarily used for the discard and immediate repair of hunting equipment. The range of types suggest these derive from several visits over the course of the Late Mesolithic, rather than a single occupation associated with the deposition of the human remains. Wild pig is well-represented amongst the fauna from the site. Some of this material shows evidence for human modification, though it is undated and the site dated evidence for occupation from the Mesolithic to the Bronze Age. A mid-sixth millennium date on aurochs from the site may give an indication of when at least one of the Mesolithic visits occurred (Schulting et al. 2010). Microliths have also been recovered from a spur overlooking a small tributary leading down to Cheddar Gorge at Gorsey Bigbury (Jones 1938). Small-scale Late Mesolithic use of Rowberrow Cavern and Haywood cave is noted by Rosen (2016). There is also evidence for Late Mesolithic microliths and small-scale knapping activities at Aveline's Hole (Jacobi 2005), though any use of this cave must have recognised the presence of human remains, many of which were distributed across the cave floor.

To the west in the Levels, though not on the same scale as the Early and Middle Mesolithic activity (see chapters 3 and 4), Late Mesolithic microliths have been recovered from the sandy Burtle islands of Chedzoy and Shapwick. By this time, the environment of the Levels had changed radically. A marine transgression led to rising water-tables and extensive peat formation from c.6500 cal BC, and an estuarine phase of mudflats and saltmarshes between 5500 and 4500 cal BC, followed by a slowing of sea-level rise and the development of extensive areas of reedswamp (Bell et al. 2015). The ephemeral evidence for the Late Mesolithic suggests the Levels were used in fishing and fowling, in a manner that did not generate much lithic evidence.

In contrast to the ephemeral traces of upland hunting in Mendip and fowling on the Levels, more substantial evidence for occupation comes from the site of Hawcombe Head on Exmoor. This is an extensive area of Late Mesolithic activity, which contrasts with the generally small lithic scatters and individual stray finds known from the moors. Hawcombe Head is an upland watershed, with springs either side. To the east, the water from the stream flows via Hawk Combe, providing easy access to the coast at Porlock Bay, where a submerged forest of Late Mesolithic date is known and lithics have been recovered (Gardiner 2007). To the west, the spring at Venn Combe runs into the East Lyn river and finally to the coast 13 km away (Gardiner 2009). A relationship between the coast and upland is indicated by the use of beach flint. The site has been known and collected for decades, and lithics numbering in their thousands have been recovered as surface finds and through excavations between 2002–2003 and 2008–2011. Excavations around Venn Combe in particular have revealed a clay floor, hearths, post-holes, stakeholes and shallow pits. Three radiocarbon dates indicate occupation in the mid-seventh millennium around the Hawkcombe spring and late seventh and late sixth millennium occupation around Venn Combe (Gardiner 2009; Gardiner et al. 2011). Charcoal evidence indicates local woodland of hazel, oak and hawthorn (Gardiner 2007). A wide variety of tools have been recovered from the area: Scrapers and retouched pieces were most common in the 2011 excavations, with microliths, microburins, awls and microdenticulates well represented (Gardiner et al. 2011), and scrapers and bevel-ended tools known from previous work (Gardiner 2009). This evidence for varied activities, combined with structural evidence, indicates the area was intermittently used for longer stays over the Late Mesolithic. This was a time when sea-level dramatically transformed the lowlands to the north; yet, Hawcombe Head remained a persistent place when other aspects of people's landscapes changed.

Mesolithic sites in Cornwall and South Devon are concentrated in coastal sea-cliff locations, particularly along the north coast and around Land's End, with patchier representation along the south coast (Berridge and Roberts 1986). These coastal locations are subject to erosion and thus are more archaeologically visible than other areas. Inland sites are also known, particularly on Dartmoor. As well as sharing similar locations many of the coastal sites have a similar range of microlith forms, characterised by lanceolates and curve-backed points with rounded bases, with numbers of obliquely blunted points and scalene triangles. This range of microliths is likely to represent multiple visits throughout the Mesolithic. It is as yet unknown whether the lanceolates and curve-backed points with rounded bases are chronological markers.

On the south coast of Devon, at Little Dartmouth Farm, just over a kilometre from the mouth of the river Dart, a huge pit, 3.8 m wide and 1.8 m deep, was located in advance of development (Green et al. 2012). The pit contained nine different fills: Some appear to be natural silting events, but others, which include clusters of burnt stone and clear charcoal lenses, seem to represent deliberate episodes of infilling (Figure 5.41). Two recuts are evident. Radiocarbon dates from early fills indicate the initial pit cut started to infill in the middle of the sixth millennium, while the fills associated with the second recut date to the early fifth millennium. Fills from the first phase contain relatively little archaeological material, though the last of these yielded 11 pieces of worked flint, chert and quartz, a bevel-ended tool and burnt stone. Charcoal from the middle fills is mainly oak, while those from the latest recut contained oak, hazel and ivy. Thirty-six pieces of flint and chert came from the thickest of the fills associated with the second recut, while 90 pieces came from the uppermost context. Amongst the latter was a single-backed bladelet (Green et al. 2012). It is uncertain to what extent this feature was part of a larger site; the area was machined to natural. Lithics and 14 bevel-ended pebble tools were recovered from later Prehistoric features. While there were no obviously Mesolithic elements amongst the chipped stone assemblage, blades are present, suggesting perhaps a larger occupation area.

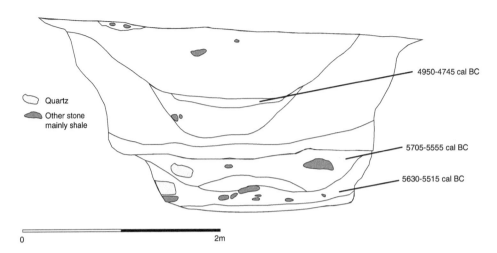

4950-4745 cal BC

Quartz

Other stone
mainly shale

5705-5555 cal BC

5630-5515 cal BC

0   2m

Figure 5.41 Section of large pit at Little Dartmouth Farm (redrawn after Green et al. 2012)

There may be relationships between near-coastal sites such as Little Dartmouth Farm and the numerous lithic scatters known from the granite uplands of Dartmoor. Three Holes Cave occupies an intermediate position between the two areas, located in limestone cliffs within a deep valley, next to a stream that runs into a tributary of the Dart. Environmental evidence indicates this area was heavily wooded at the time of occupation. Late Mesolithic material has been located during three separate excavations, the earliest in the mid-19th century, the most recent completed in 1992 (Barton and Roberts 2015). A Late Mesolithic assemblage, made on beach pebble material, was recovered from a discrete layer of talus outside the cave. This was associated with the cut-marked remains of red deer, roe deer and pig, probably only a single individual of each represented. Also present were 30 marine shells: 20 periwinkles, 9 cowries and a single dentalium shell. Barton and Roberts (2015, 196) note the delicate shells are relatively intact, contrasting with the trampled nature of the faunal assemblage and suggest they may thus belong to the final phase of occupation.

Late Mesolithic radiocarbon dates from Cornwall are rare. A mid-seventh millennium date comes from a pit at Penans Farm, Grampound (Jones 2016), and a late sixth millennium radiocarbon date is available from Poldowrian on the Lizard (Smith and Harris 1982). Some question marks exist over the latter as it is based on a bulked sample from all hazelnut shells found in the main occupation layer of a site, where both earlier Mesolithic and Neolithic material is present. However, the microlith range does indicate Late and probably also Final Mesolithic activity.

Poldowrian is located on a knoll beside a small valley with a spring-fed stream (Smith and Harris 1982). It was excavated as part of a collaboration between the Cornwall Archaeological Society and the Central Excavation Unit, focusing on the Lizard peninsula which located several Mesolithic sites. The site at Poldowrian is now only around 100 m from the edge of the sea-cliff. In addition to food resources, the coast was the source of pebble flint and chert used at the site. The lithic assemblage is

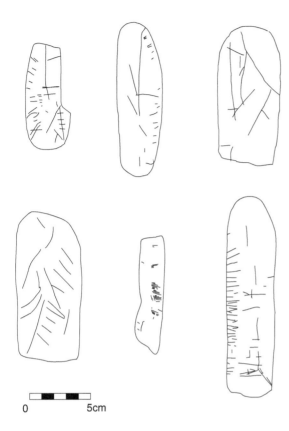

Figure 5.42 Incised pebbles from Cornwall. 1–4. Hudder Field, 5 Trevose Head, 6. Poldowrian. Redrawn from Jones et al. (2018), Jones (2015) and Smith and Harris (1982)

heavily dominated by microliths (791), though these are outnumbered by microburins and other manufacturing biproducts and unfinished microliths are common. Scrapers (39), denticulate scrapers (22) and miscellaneous retouched pieces (53) were also re-presented, but other tools, apart from core tools and pebble tools, were rare, re-presented by single examples. Pebble tools are abundant, and 358 were recovered, including bevel-ended tools, chopping tools and hammerstones. One elongated pebble has a series of inscribed parallel lines (Figure 5.42). The stone used (schist, slate, gabbro, quartzite and granite) can be found with radius of 10 km, though most are not available on immediately local beaches.

The topographic location of Poldowrian recalls the situation of similar south-western sites along the south coast, Culverwell and Little Dartmouth Farm, as well as others located by the Lizard project, such as Beagle's Point or Black Head. Data from the Lizard Project make it clear that all large Mesolithic sites are located next to a stream, and almost all are close to the current coastline, as is also the case in South Wales (see below). Though sea-levels would have been lower, the steepness of the coast in this region means the position of the sea would not have been too distant (Smith 1987).

In contrast to the more patchy record in Southern Cornwall, Mesolithic scatters are extensive along the north coast (Berridge and Roberts 1986). On the north coast of Cornwall, the site of Trevose Head is in a similar location to Poldowrian, close to a stream and set back from the current cliff edge (Johnson and David 1982). This is just one area where more systematic collection has occurred along an area of coastline where Mesolithic material is common. Here, a large assemblage of several thousand pieces, located through gridded fieldwalking, was recovered in two large clusters. While Early Mesolithic material probably dominates, Late Mesolithic microliths and a similar range of tools to Poldowrian were recovered, including denticulated scrapers that grade into cores, bevel-ended tools and pebble choppers. Even an elongated pebble with incised parallel lines (Figure 5.42), very similar to the example from Polowrian, has been found (Jones 2015).

A similar concentration of Mesolithic material can be found further to the south along the North Cliffs at Hudder Field, near Camborne (Jones et al. 2018). Four main scatters have produced thousands of lithic artefacts, though all have later Prehistoric components. Three scatters are located along the cliff close to the spring line, while a fourth is in a sheltered valley by a stream. While all scatters contain coarse stone tools, mostly made from local greywacke, at scatter HU/NE they are particularly abundant and varied, with around 360 recovered. In addition to bevel-ended tools, hammerstones, anvils and choppers, a range of countersunk pebbles were recovered. There are much higher proportions of unmodified pebbles at this location, suggesting a specialist manufacturing centre (Jones et al. 2018). As at Poldowrian and Trevose Head, incised pebbles (in this case, four examples) have been recovered, indicating this is a widespread feature of the Cornish Mesolithic.

South Wales

In the last three millennia of the Mesolithic, the landscape of the Severn estuary was transformed by rising sea-levels. It is estimated that the Severn saw a reduction in length of 46% during the Mesolithic (Bell 2007, 335). At around 7000 BC, sea-levels were at −20 m (Sturt et al. 2013), and the mouth of the estuary lay between Cardiff and Weston-super-Mare. The Severn flowed through the dryland valley that stretched to the northeast, joined along its route by its tributaries, the Usk, Yeo and Bristol Avon. Sea-level rise was extremely rapid between 7000 and 5000 cal BC, but slowed in the following millennium and by the end of the Mesolithic was a few metres below current levels. The tidal range of the Severn Estuary today is nearly 15 m, the second highest in the world. Though its range in the Late Mesolithic is not known, as the estuary was not too dissimilar from its current configuration, it must have approached that of today. These landscapes would be dramatically different at low tide, with a vast stretch of flat, featureless land exposed, with shifting water-courses the only guide. People's lives would be guided by the rhythms of the tidal regime from the cycle of low and high tides and longer scale of neep and spring tides.

The Severn Estuary has seen considerable palaeoenvironmental work, which paints a rich picture of a landscape that was rapidly changing over the last millennia of the Mesolithic. There is widespread evidence for people's activities within this landscape, particularly through sites where human footprints are preserved in estuarine muds, at Magor Pill and Uskmouth, and through evidence for burning of the vegetation.

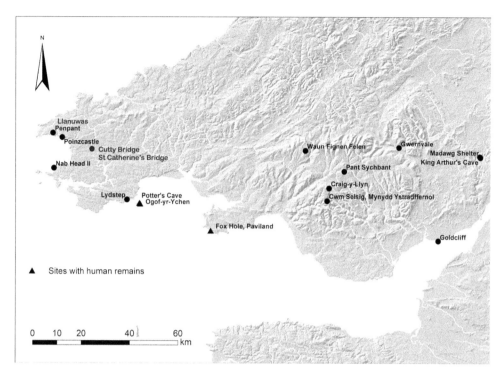

Figure 5.43 Late Mesolithic sites in South Wales

Artefactual evidence is rarer in this wetland, with the exception of the major landscape project at Goldcliff (Bell et al. 2000; Bell 2007, Figure 5.43), and a number of isolated finds such as a red deer antler adze at Uskmouth (Aldhouse-Green and Housley 1993; Elliott 2015).

Two campaigns of excavations took place in the intertidal landscape at Goldcliff (Figure 5.44), where a bedrock island formed a base for Mesolithic groups (Figure 5.45). Fieldwork took place to the west of the island in 1992–1994 when the site of Goldcliff W was excavated, while a second project between 2001 and 2003 investigated palaeoenvironments and archaeological evidence to the east of the island. These excavations were undertaken in difficult conditions, within a small intertidal window, with some of the lower lying sites, such as B and D, only accessible for an average of 1.7 hours during around seven days each spring tide. At sites A, B and D, blocks of sediment were lifted for excavation elsewhere. In addition to concentrations of artefactual debris and faunal remains, Goldcliff is known for its range of human and animal footprints, which show people, and especially children, active in areas of saltmarsh.

Goldcliff island and its flanking superficial deposits provided a dryland area suitable for settlement as wetlands encroached due to rising sea-levels. Now a small area, measuring 350 by 150 m, much truncated by the sea, its original extent is marked by Ipswichian beach deposits, suggesting it extended to 1 km by 450 m in the last interglacial, probably not too dissimilar to its area in Mesolithic times. During the Early Holocene, the island was a hill whose flanks were a focus for the more

Figure 5.44 View of the intertidal zone at Goldcliff (copyright Martin Bell)

substantial Mesolithic occupations in the area (Figure 5.44). Beyond the island on lower ground was a palaeosol, forming a fairly level surface at c.-4 m asl, rising to 1.4 m as it developed on the head deposits on the flanks of the island (Figure 5.46). Woodland – the Lower Submerged Forest – grew on this landsurface. To the east of the island flowed a palaeochannel, located between sites E and I. By 5900 cal BC, Goldcliff had probably become an island at high spring tide, as sea-level rose and saltwater poisoned the trees of the Lower Submerged Forest. This is when the first dated evidence for human occupation has been recorded; as Bell (2007, 321) notes, the area seems to have become attractive to people through this new configuration of land and sea, and they were drawn to the area during a period of dynamic environmental change. As the sea briefly regressed, apart from brief incursion, surfaces stabilised, and a short-lived reedswamp developed by 5650 cal BC, before a marine transgression, lasting around 1000 years, deposited layers of silts, and saltmarsh developed. These layers covered the lower-lying sites and reached the flanks of Goldcliff island, covering part of site J.

Goldcliff W is only site to the west of the bedrock island, and was located during the 1992–1994 fieldwork. Most of the archaeological remains were recovered from a buried soil, which had developed on the head deposits flanking the island. Excavations each year focused on an eroding shelf of peat and underlying sediment, resulting in an area of excavation around 20 m long and (apart from an exploratory trench) only a few metres wide. Within this area one main scatter of

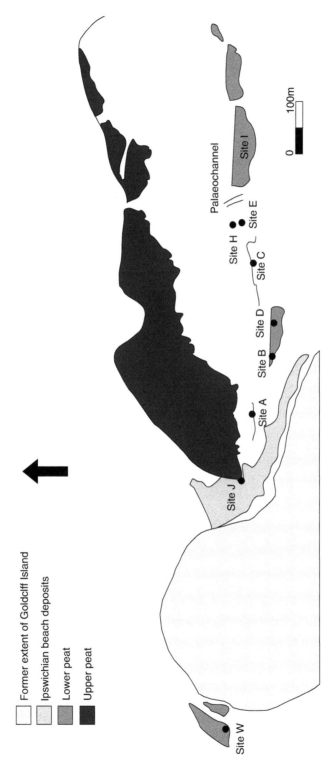

Figure 5.45 Plan of Goldcliff area

Figure 5.46 Exposed sediments at Goldcliff showing Pleistocene head and the old land surface (copyright Martin Bell)

debris and several smaller less dense areas can be discerned. Two concentrations of charcoal, burnt flint and bone indicated that hearths were present, and a single post-hole was located. Activity on the site dates to between 5700 and 5200 cal BC. A small lithic assemblage of 633 pieces was recovered, with further material collected from the eroding surface over the previous decade. Tools are relatively rare in the assemblage comprising just three microliths, a scraper and ten retouched flakes. As on other sites the lithic material used was a mixture of small flint and chert pebbles, with occasional use of tuff, all likely to derive from local marine and fluvial gravels. The closest source may have been the gravels of the river Usk, around 6 km to the east. Some coarse stool tools – hammerstones and rubbers – made from quartzitic sandstone had been imported to the site.

Faunal remains were more common than lithic artefacts, with 1000 pieces recovered. The faunal assemblage is larger than those of other sites in the area and differs in its composition. Across the Goldcliff area, red deer is dominant (Table 5.12), a contrast to the predominant focus on aurochs across Southwest England, noted above. On sites east of the island, aurochs played an important but subsidiary role, but this species is absent from site W, where pig is in the subsidiary role. These two species seem to have been treated differently, with the red deer butchered, cooked and consumed on the site but the pig processed for consumption elsewhere. There is also a wider range of species represented at W, though this is

Table 5.12 Faunal remains from the Goldcliff sites (Bell 2007)

Site	Red deer		Roe deer		Aurochs		Pig	
	elements	NMI	elements	NMI	elements	NMI	elements	MNI
W old land surface	87	4	4	1	0	0	27	3
A old land surface	12	1	2	1	3	1	6	1
A estuarine silts	1	1	1	1	0	0	0	0
B old land surface	3	1	0	0	0	0	0	0
B peat	4	1	1	1	1	1	0	0
J old land surface	28	3	6	1	24	3	11	2
J estuarine silts	4	1	0	0	1	1	0	0

likely to be partially a function of its greater size. Otter is present, and a canid which is probably wolf. These are the only fur-bearers from the Goldcliff sites. Their presence could be related to the seasonal rhythm of tasks: Site W has evidence for occupation in winter, which contrasts with the primarily summer and autumn evidence for the sites to the east. Birds were represented by duck. Fish remains were also common; most were eel, and a similar pattern of dominance was seen at site A, the only eastern site with numerous remains. The second most common species at W was goby, which contrasts with the subsidiary use of bass at site A. Smelt, stickleback and flatfish were also present in small numbers.

Most sites lie to the east of the island, with site A situated on its flanks. This was exposed through marine erosion as a layer of charcoal and flint. Though site A is the greatest such concentration of material, similar exposures can be found up to 150 m west, indicating these higher areas were used regularly and at times intensively, especially in comparison to the lower-lying wetland sites discussed below. At site A, the occupation is associated with the old soil horizon; a single hazelnut shell suggests that at least some of the activity here dates to 5630–5480 cal BC (6629 ± 38; OxA-13928). At this time, the site seems to lie just at the limit of the high tide. There is a marked concentration of lithics, which combines cores and debitage, including evidence for decortification, and a number of retouched tools. Microliths are common with 31 examples recovered, mainly crescents and left lateralised scalenes; 36 microburins indicate a manufacturing area. Other formal tools are rare, but miscellaneous retouched pieces, two denticulates and a notch were present. Some burnt bone and burnt flint suggest the presence of a hearth.

Fish bones are particularly well-represented on site A, where they are mainly associated with the lithic concentration. Eel dominates with 415 bones recovered; bass are also reasonably common. These species are associated with brackish water, indicating they were obtained from local sources. Eels migrate from rivers to seas to spawn, with the young eels (elvers) clustering in estuaries until they reach maturity. The size dimensions of the eels recovered suggest around 25% were adults caught during the autumn migration, but most are smaller, immature individuals who would be present in the estuary all year round. The small size of the eels and bass suggests the use of traps or nets. The rare examples of other species found (salmon, bib, sand eel, mullet) were probably incidental catches using these methods. Some shells were also found at the site, indicating a wider range of resources exploited, though the sediments were mostly decalcified. Species identified were crab, cockles and welks.

Animal bones, mainly deer, were found just to the west of the main concentration. Young piglets suggest the site was visited in the spring. There is some evidence, too, for the use of plant resources, with charred hazelnut shells, a burnt sloe stone and dogwood seeds. Elder seeds were also present, and berries may have been consumed, though the seeds were rarely charred. The impression is of a short-term residential stay associated with microlith production and retooling, cooking and butchery. Microwear indicates siliceous plants were also processed. Much of this activity may have taken place within a small tent structure 2–3 m across (Bell 2007, 62). Two smaller concentrations were also located to the east of the main concentration, which contained a high proportion of tools, one with three scrapers, animal bones and some knapping activity, the other with two microliths and a scraper but which lacks microdebitage, suggesting this was primarily an area of tool-use. These may represent specialised activity areas associated with the main occupation, or evidence of separate visits.

Beyond the dryland area of the island flanks, several sites expose evidence for activities on lower lying ground. These show rather different forms of activity to the short-term camps of A. At site B, occupation also took place on the old landsurface, in hazel woodland with an understorey of ferns. As waterlogging increased, peat developed, on which grew reeds and some trees. Charcoal evidence suggests the wetland vegetation was periodically fired, as was hazel at the woodland edge. Artefacts were found both on the old land surface and the base of the peat, though in both contexts they were few in number, with only 43 pieces of flint recovered. On the old landsurface, a small cluster consisting of a core and a few flakes indicates some limited flint knapping, but most of the material seems to represent tool use activities, which also included the use of coarse stone. One of these stones is incised with parallel lines and, though broken, is similar in shape to The Nab Head venus discussed in chapter 3 (Bell 2007). Burnt microdebitage and some burnt stones may indicate a hearth was present. A radiocarbon date on a burnt hazelnut shell indicates some at least of the activity on the old landsurface dates to 5990–5790 cal BC (7002 ± 35 BP; OxA-13927).

In the peat above, lithic artefacts are rarer, but two clusters of bone and burnt bone were identified. The bone indicates the butchery and cooking of red deer and other foodstuffs, such as fish. The presence of human intestinal parasites indicate use as a toilet area. A few red deer prints were also recorded at the base of the peat. The inception of peat formation has been dated to 5840–5670 cal BC (6871 ± 33 BP; OxA-12359).

Site D is 50 m from site B; this area, too, is a window into ephemeral 'off-site' activity. Relatively little of this area was excavated, and only a single flake and a chip of debitage from the old land surface were recovered. Bell (2007, 47) suggests these may even have been carried into the area on people's feet. The occasional find at a similar level along adjacent peat exposures suggest intermittent use of this area for small-scale tasks. At this time, site D was an area of oak and hazel woodland. Trees died as sporadic marine flooding affected the site, but stabilisation and peat growth followed around 5700 cal BC, and the area became covered by reeds and grassland with shallow pools or sluggish channels. Hazel woodland persisted on the higher, drier ground. Charcoal evidence suggests burning of the local wetland vegetation in August/September. At this time, site D probably lay close to a palaeochannel, which subsequently migrated east towards site I. Evidence for human activity associated with the peat is confined to two episodes of burning and, as at site B, the presence of human intestinal parasites. More ephemeral activity was noted at site I, west of site D and west of the palaeochannel, where the occasional flint was noted in the peat exposures.

This lower lying landscape of sites B, D and I was inundated by a marine trans-gression at around 5650 cal BC, which lasted about 1000 years and which deposited a thick layer of estuarine silts. In several areas these were laminated, with fine bands of alternating sands and silts. These appear to represent seasonal input events, which provide a microstratigraphy for the numerous human and animal footprints exposed on the surface of and stratified within these silts. These show repeated use of these saltmarshes by human groups. It is estimated that the 61 human footprints at site C span 16 years. The main clusters of footprints suggest activity in and around the palaeochannel. The channel was also associated with several pieces of worked wood, which might represent remains of fish traps or other fishing facilities. A part of a plank was also recovered, and a woodchip shows woodworking took place on the banks of the stream. An unstratified antler object was found at site C, which has been inter-preted by Elliott (2012) as debitage from the production of an antler beam adze.

Many of the footprints recorded are of children and adolescents. The two main groups represented are children aged 3–6 (67%) and adolescents aged 11–14 (25%). Younger children were often accompanied by older children: At site E the footprints of a child of about 4 are close to those of an 11-year-old. A second set of tracks shows an 11-year-old and a 6-year-old. These perhaps indicate older children played a role in childcare. Other tracks include the trail of an older child (age 10–12) at site H walking parallel to the sea and heading towards Goldcliff Island. At site E, four adolescents aged between 12 and 16 seem to have walked together, heading towards the estuary, and pausing, perhaps while tracking or fowling (Figure 5.47). These footprints suggest a particular role for children in exploring the marshlands, perhaps gathering plants or setting and checking fish traps and snares for water birds.

The footprint trails also reveal the overlapping movement of humans and animals, through this landscape. The four adolescents at site E crossed the tracks of a red deer. Aurochs tracks were noted elsewhere in association with human tracks. Red deer prints were also found on higher ground at sites A and J, showing that when people moved on, these areas were once again roamed by animals. Overall, red deer dominate the animal tracks, with aurochs also common, and a few roe deer tracks present. A wolf or dog, perhaps, like people, hunting in the wetlands, was also noted. Traces of pig, represented in the faunal remains at sites A and J, were not found, suggesting these animals were killed elsewhere, though the pattern of faunal representation suggests they were butchered at Goldcliff and meaty bones moved to other sites. Waterbird tracks were numerous in the rich wetlands: Crane and heron were plentiful, while gulls, oyster catchers and terns were also found. Cranes and terns are summer visitors; humans, too, seem to have particularly frequented the saltmarsh in the summer months.

Beyond Goldcliff, Jacobi (1980a) has suggested that Late Mesolithic mobility pat-terns in South Wales were characterised by a similar winter lowland/summer upland pattern as he proposed for both Northern and Southwest England (Figure 5.43). Large winter base camps are not currently evinced, with the coastal/estuarine areas at Goldcliff seeming to be small-scale temporary campsites at the most; however, small sites are present in the uplands, indicating areas of activity at higher altitudes. A plot of HER data for the Welsh Mesolithic (Lillie 2015, figure 3) shows a major con-centration of findspots in the foothills of the Brecon Beacons, north of the Rhondda

Figure 5.47 Footprints of four adolescents walking together at site E (copyright Martin Bell)

(this density a product of fieldwork by H.N. Savory and the Forestry Commission) and extending, at a lower density, into higher areas of the Beacons and the Black Mountains immediately to the north and northeast, respectively (Stanton 1984). These scatters lack radiometric dates, but the majority appear to be Late Mesolithic (Jacobi 1980a). A particular concentration of microlith-dominated Late Mesolithic material has been located around a lake, Craig-y-Llyn, at 400 m asl at the head of the Rhondda Valley, where several large surface scatters have been located (Savory 1961). Smaller late Mesolithic concentrations are present in the area, too. Jacobi (1980a) notes a clustering to the south and on the ridge southwest of the llyn. This second cluster of sites includes Cwm Selsig, where a couple of cores and retouched pieces were found in association with eight microliths, and Mynydd Ystradffernol, where seven microliths and 38 pieces of knapping debris were found (Lillie 2015). These suggest brief halts for retooling and other tasks. This upland area seems to show the same patterning of larger and smaller task related sites as lowland areas, such as Goldcliff.

Further north, Mesolithic scatters have been located in the Brecon Beacons at Pant Sychbant (Burke 1966). To the west in the Black Mountains, Late Mesolithic evidence is also known from Waun Fignen Felen (see chapter 3) around an ancient lake located on a limestone plateau at 485 mOD (Barton et al. 1995). The initial Late Mesolithic vegetation was a mosaic of heath, grassland and hazel copses with occasional stands of birch. This landscape may have been kept open and maintained as heathland through regular firing of the landscape (Smith and Cloutman 1988). In the late sixth millennium BC, areas of alder carr developed, and wetland areas of reedswamp were replaced by blanket peat. This peat growth blocked the lake's outflow and led to it infilling with peat. These changes seem to have led to the abandonment of an area that had been repeatedly revisited for millennia; all Mesolithic material, apart from a single chert blade, is sealed below the peat. Five areas of Late Mesolithic activity were located (Barton et al. 1995). At WWF/9 14 microlith fragments were uncovered over a 5 m area, isolated from any other debris. These seem to represent a composite tool: Several pieces refit, and it is likely that between six and nine microliths were originally represented. These are elongated scalene triangles with two sides retouched. Both left and right lateralised pieces are present, suggesting this is likely to date to the eighth millennium BC. A second probable composite at WWF/1 consists of 12 left lateralised scalenes with three sides retouched scattered over an area of 12.5 m^2. The remaining Late Mesolithic sites do include debitage, but are low-density and diffuse, with a small number of artefacts scattered over large areas. The largest assemblage has 68 pieces, and the only tools present are microliths. No cores or refits have been found. The impression is of perhaps removal of one or two pieces from cores for immediate use, or perhaps use of already prepared blanks. No equivalents of the small, refitting knapping scatters known from the Early Mesolithic have been located, suggesting the landscape was used in a different way. Evidence for burning of the vegetation seems clearest in two levels dating to the late seventh millennium BC, suggesting firing of the heathland and grassland communities that had developed at this time. These practises may be related to improving animal browse rather than opening up any woodland to increase visibility.

Bell (2007) has suggested that sites such as Gwernvale and the Wye Valley caves may represent overnight camps on routeways between coastal areas and the uplands. The Wye Valley Caves are around 25 km as the crow flies from the Severn Estuary, and people could follow the river into the Brecon Beacons. At Symmonds Yat, the Wye is deeply incised, and the landscape is of high limestone cliffs and rocky towers (ApSimon et al. 1992). There are three caves where Mesolithic occupation has been recorded in this area: A single late Mesolithic microlith at Huntsham Hill; a small lithic assemblage from Madawg Shelter; and a larger lithic and faunal assemblage from King Arthur's Cave (Rosen 2016). Shell beads have also been recovered from the last two of these sites (Barton and Roberts 2015).

Madawg is a rockshelter located high above the river and more difficult to access than the other caves; activity was restricted in an area to the northern part of the shelter. Much of the material was found in a small depression around 30 cm deep, filled with a charcoal-rich sediment (Barton 1997). Within this depression lay ten pieces of flint, almost all tools and mostly microliths (Rosen 2016), 11 pierced cowries and two flat periwinkle shells (Figure 5.48; Barton and Roberts 2015). The shells may, given the seemingly ephemeral nature of the Mesolithic occupation, represent a cache or votive deposit. Two dates come from the lower part of the hollow: One on a sloe stone of 7970–7585 cal BC (8710 ± 70 BP; OxA-6081), the other of 5675–5480 cal BC (6655 ± 65 BP; OxA-6082) on charred hazelnut shells. Barton and Roberts (2015, 192) have recently suggested the younger date is, on typological grounds, more likely to provide a date for the geometric microliths and shell beads.

King Arthur's Cave is 350 m to the northwest of Madawg and by contrast is a good-sized cave, which is easily accessible. The cave overlooks a small, dry valley leading down to the Wye (Rosen 2016). The site has had a long history of excavation with work by Symmonds and Boyd Dawkins in the 1870s and by the University of

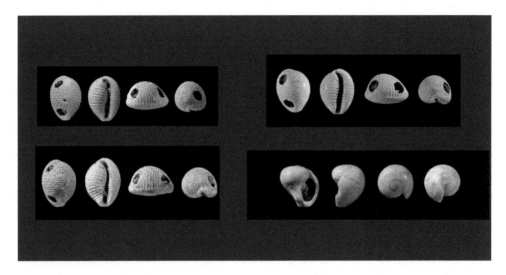

Figure 5.48 Perforated cowries from Madawg (left); perforated cowries and periwinkles from King Arthur's Cave (right) (Copyright Institute of Archaeology, Oxford; Photo by Ian Cartwright)

Bristol Speleological Society in the 1920s. An assemblage of lithics and faunal material was recovered from immediately outside the cave, associated with the 'First Hearth'. Much of this is likely to be Mesolithic, but it is undoubtedly mixed with both earlier and late material. Horse, based on its condition seems intrusive, and later elements are represented by sheep. What remains is an assemblage comprising red deer, aurochs and pig with small amounts of roe deer, all showing evidence for processing and fragmentation, indicating intensive butchery (ApSimon et al. 1992). A lithic assemblage of 361 pieces survives from around the First Hearth, including both knapping debris and tools. The tools are varied, consisting of mainly retouched and utilised pieces (57), microliths (30), scrapers (5) and burins (2) (ApSimon et al. 1992, Table 14; Rosen 2016, appendix 3), indicating a wide range of activities seem to have been carried out at the cave. Three perforated cowries and two periwinkles were recovered from a niche in the second chamber further back in the cave. While this area had been disturbed by early excavations, these are likely to have derived either from this niche or from nearby deposits in the second chamber, where no flint artefacts were recovered (Barton and Roberts 2015, 194). This spatial separation from other areas of Mesolithic activity may similarly indicate caching or formal deposition.

The Mesolithic site at Gwernvale may play a similar role for groups moving between the coast and uplands. Here, a scatter of lithic material lies beneath the Neolithic long cairn on a gravel terrace 5 m above the floodplain of the river Usk. The site is located at 70 m asl, but the land rises immediately to the north to reach 500 m asl within 3 km of the site (Britnell and Savory 1984). The place is thus at the same time on a routeway and a convenient location for logistical forays into the high uplands. The lithic material is concentrated in the eastern part of the site, along the edge of the gravel terrace, concentrated in two main scatters that also include Final Palaeolithic, Early Mesolithic and Neolithic material. A larger and more diffuse scatter of lithic material is also present in the southern part of the site. The only dated Mesolithic feature is to the north, away from any lithic material. This was an earth oven, a pit with charcoal at the base, overlain with stones. From this feature comes a date of 5980–5645 cal BC (6900 ± 80; CAR-118). While the mixed date of the lithics precludes a precise understanding of the nature of Late Mesolithic activities at the site, there appears to be a combination of microliths and small scrapers, and probably also burins and truncations. This assemblage shows a wide variety of activities not typical of the characteristics of an upland hunting camp. The evidence here, in the Wye Valley at Goldcliff and in the Western Cleddau Valley (see below), suggests a broader pattern of small, relatively short-term residential sites, with small-scale, more specialist activities in the immediate area.

The second area in South Wales that shows a major concentration of Mesolithic findspots is the coastal area of Pembrokeshire (David 2007, Figure 7.1), where large surface scatters are nearly ubiquitous. Excavated and dated sites are unfortunately rare, limited to The Nab Head, a location already discussed in chapter 3 as an important site for the Welsh Early Mesolithic. It was also a focus for Late Mesolithic settlement, both at The Nab Head I and at a second, less disturbed site, The Nab Head II, set further back from the narrow promontory on which site I lies (see Figure 3.28). The Nab Head II was excavated by Andrew David in 1981–1982 and 1986; in all, 195 m^2 were excavated (David 2007). The site consists of a large scatter composed of several coalescing foci of activity and radiocarbon dates indicating intermittent, small-scale visits over a long period of time. Three dates are available: The first on oak charcoal, unassociated with any feature, dates to 7305–6700 cal BC (8070 ± 80 BP; OxA-1497). The second measurement of 6415–6060 cal BC (7360 ± 90 BP; OxA-860) comes from a shallow pit on the southern edge of the site filled with packed stones, burnt soil and charcoal, which may represent a hearth or pit for deposition of hearth sweepings. The final date comes from a concentration of charcoal, which probably represents a hearth at the centre of a lithic scatter and dates to 5370–4935 cal BC (6210 ± 90 BP; OxA-861). The only surviving organic remains were small charred wood fragments and hazel nutshells; identifications of these suggest oak, hazel, blackthorn and pomoideae were locally present in the late seventh millennium.

The distribution of lithic material indicates at least three or four denser areas of lithic material encircling an emptier space. Several concentrations of charcoal were noted that may represent hearths or hearth debris. The northernmost scatter has at its heart the charcoal concentration that dates to the late sixth millennium, though the late eighth/early seventh millennium date comes from the very edge of the same scatter. This scatter is associated with a cluster of bevel-ended pebble tools and a variety of microlith types. The southerly scatters, associated with the late seventh millennium pit, are dominated by left lateralised scalene triangle microliths, and denticulated scrapers are also common. Bevelled pebbles are scattered throughout this cluster. A feature of this site is the presence of three ground stone axe-heads (Figure 5.49). These near-unique pieces (a few other examples are known from other Welsh sites) are made from igneous rocks from West Wales that could also be found on local beaches (David 2007, 2019b). These elongated pebbles were pecked and ground at one end and have a distinctive flange that distinguishes them from both contemporary Irish Mesolithic axes and Neolithic examples. This is not the only example of this sort of technology as a ground stone perforated disk was also recovered from the excavations, and two further perforated disks are present in older

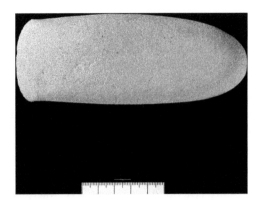

Figure 5.49 Ground stone axe from The Nab Head (copyright National Museums of Wales)

collections from the headland. These have been loosely termed 'maceheads', but their function is unknown.

Most stone used on site was obtained from the beach. Knapped stone was mainly flint beach pebbles, but small quantities of greensand chert and igneous material (also available on the shore) were used. Cores are relatively small, with an average height of 28 mm, and are mainly single platformed; the form is generally driven by the nature of the material. Occasional bipolar, anvil cores are also present, again permitting efficient exploitation of small pebble material, though these have recently been suggested to indicate later Prehistoric activities (David 2019b).

While most Late Mesolithic material is concentrated at site II, there is also a distinctive presence close by at The Nab Head I. This is most clearly demonstrated by the presence of 53 complete and 57 fragments of narrow microliths. These display a similar range of forms to site II: The dominance of left lateralised scalenes, with some crescents, lanceolates and backed bladelets. Probably associated with this material are a number of denticulate core/scrapers and bevel-ended tools. This material reinforces the impression of frequent, small-scale visits to the general area of the present-day headland in the Late Mesolithic.

The Nab Head is in many ways typical of the Late Mesolithic evidence from Southwest Wales; it only differs in that our knowledge of it is enhanced by the excavation. Mesolithic sites elsewhere in the region are numerous but consist almost entirely of surface scatters. Some detail on the location of these sites and the composition of their assemblages is available through fieldwork by Andrew David and others, mainly on the St David's peninsula, which has located and explored 40 such sites. Many of these assemblages are very large; the scatters at Pointzcastle, for example, cover 60,000 m^2 (David 2007, 174); Llanuwas, 10,000 m^2 (David 2007, 171). The coastal plateau in this region is dotted with springs and drained by streams that have incised narrow valleys that lead down to small coves. David (2007, 162) has noted that Mesolithic sites are often associated with these small water-courses and close to the current position of the sea, though some such as Poinzcastle and Penpant are set around 1 km back from the coast by valley heads or by springs. A particular density of Mesolithic findspots have been recorded on the south side of St David's peninsula, where a south-facing aspect, with routes down to the sheltered St Bride's Bay, seems to have been considered particularly favourable for settlement.

These surface scatters are generally made on small beach pebbles and show a similar range of tool types. Microliths are present, though as surface were also found on the river floodplainthese are likely to be under-represented. They consist of left lateralised scalenes and a range of other forms. Denticulated core/scrapers, notches, truncated pieces, large convex scrapers, awls and bevel-ended tools are common at most sites, though there is seemingly some variation in representation and therefore presumed associated activities. Some large scatters, such as those at Penpant, Solva, have a broad range of tools; others are perhaps more specialised: Cwm Bach I, Newgale, Pembrokeshire is a large scatter, spanning 35,000 m^2, encircling a small stream. It has large numbers of burins and truncations, as well as a varied range of coarse stone tools, including a countersunk pebble (David 2007). Llanunwas, close to Penpant, but nearer the cliff top is heavily dominated by denticulated scrapers (David 2020).

Until recently, inland sites have been rare; however, extensive survey by Tim Painter in the Western Cleddau valley has revealed extensive Late Mesolithic surface scatters. A series of low-density sites were located on the river floodplain and on higher ground overlooking the river and its tributary valleys. Two large, dense scatters, St Catherine's Bridge and Cutty Bridge, were also found on the river floodplain, and may be part of a single agglomeration (David and Painter 2014). This is a location where a valley bottom that is generally wide throughout its middle reaches narrows, and thus may have been a good place to set fish traps. Both assemblages display a similar range of Late Mesolithic tools known from the near coastal sites and use beach flint as raw material. At both sites, distinctively utilised pieces outnumber formal tools, which may be indicative of specialised activities associated with the river. Both sites share larger quantities of utilised pieces, end retouched pieces and notches than coastal sites (ibid, 84). Two bevel-ended tools, thought of as predominantly coastal pieces, were also found in the valley, as was a single example of a ground stone axe-head and a stone ring similar to examples from The Nab Head II. These large sites are likely to indicate the importance of the river, which was likely to be rich in migratory fish, such as salmon, sea-trout and eels. These rivers are also routeways into the uplands, though there remains a lack of evidence for Mesolithic activity in the Preseli Hills, with the exception of vegetation disturbances (Bell 2007, Figure 21.1) and a series of radiocarbon dates (most Early and Middle Mesolithic, also spanning the seventh to fifth millennium) from excavations focused on apparent Neolithic quarrying sites (Parker Pearson et al. 2019).

These sites of the coastal plateau and valleys leading down to the sea are likely to have some relationship with finds of small groups of Mesolithic material associated with the old land surface, or overlying peats, on the Pembrokeshire foreshore. Material is known from Abermawr, Newport, Amroth, Frainslake (David 2007) and Lydstep (Murphy et al. 2014). At Frainslake, Gordon Williams (1926, 108) located a scatter of worked flint and stone, including bevel-ended tools in peat, seemingly associated with the remains of a shelter made from gorse, birch and hazel. A second scatter in the bay consisted of worked flint, stone bevel-ended tools and a single bone bevel-ended tool, unique for this area. He also noted the presence of two small shell-middens, though recorded little on their location or composition that might indicate their date. The impression is of repeated occupation on the coastal plateau and small-scale visits to wetland and intertidal areas on the coastal plain below. The significance of these coastal sites is reinforced by isotopic evidence from the latest individuals at Ogof-yr-Ychen and Potter's Cave, on Caldey, and the sixth millennium individuals from Fox Hole, Paviland (Schulting and Richards 2002; Schulting et al. 2013). The latter people had a marine component of 45–60%, while the late individuals from Ogof-yr-Ychen have a similar range. The individual from Goat's Hole, Paviland, had a lower marine contribution, indicating the importance of inland hunting, as implied by the location of some of the more recent finds in the region.

Mortuary practises in Southwestern Britain

Throughout this book, the southwest – encompassing Southwest England and Southern Wales – has provided the vast majority of all known evidence for Mesolithic mortuary practises: From the varied practises of the Early Mesolithic, sometimes involving numerous individuals, to the deposition of single elements in caves, probably as part of extended mortuary treatment in the Middle Mesolithic. In the Late Mesolithic, the situation changed, and a pattern that had extended throughout the Mesolithic came to an end. The period 7000–4000 BC saw relatively little evidence for mortuary treatment in the region, and none at all in Southwest England. In South Wales, deposition of isolated human elements continued intermittently at Ogof-yr-Ychen and Potter's Cave in the seventh millennium and into the first half of the sixth. The practise then ceased, marking the end of the use of Caldey for the deposition of human remains. Sea-level models (Bradley et al. 2011) and bathymetric maps suggest that Caldey is likely to have become an island around this time, and the cessation of the deposition of human remains suggests reconfiguration of relationships with the coastal landscape features.

A new geographical focus for the deposition of human remains emerged instead, that shifted back to the Gower peninsula, a key location for Early Mesolithic mortuary practises. Just 30 km from Caldey, Foxhole, and the better-known Goat's Hole, Paviland, became the focus for deposition in the sixth millennium BC. The two caves are less than 200 m apart. Goat Hole is a large, dramatic and visible feature, now at the foot of a sea-cliff, and was likely to be similarly prominent in the Late Mesolithic as sea-level approached that of the present day. Best known for the Mid-Upper Palaeolithic burial of the 'Red Lady' (Paviland 1), an isolated human humerus (Paviland 2) dated to 5460–5295 cal BC (based on two combined dates; Schulting et al. 2013) was recovered from the cave during Sollas' 1912 excavations (Aldhouse-Green 2000).

Foxhole lies on the western side of the dry valley leading down to the Goat's Hole (Figure 5.50) and is small in comparison: A relatively wide (6 m) entrance opens to a 4 m long outer chamber and a low, narrow, inner chamber mapped for 20 m (Schulting et al. 2013). Small-scale excavations have recovered several isolated human elements. Four of these, two teeth (both from children) and two adult vertebrae, have been dated to the sixth millennium BC. Based on their dating and stable isotope values, the vertebrae may belong to the same individual; the child remains are earlier, and their dating suggests they come from separate individuals. Other human material is Neolithic or later. The sediments are disturbed, and the small-scale nature of the excavations makes it difficult to determine whether the remains were disarticulated as part of mortuary practise, or whether these are the scattered remnants of disturbed burials.

Figure 5.50 Foxhole Cave (copyright Rick Schulitng)

While relatively little can be said about the practises that generated either set of remains, the caves' orientation (broadly south for Paviland and southeast for Foxhole) suggests earlier apparent concerns with alignments no longer pertained; instead, the close proximity of the two sites may suggest the dry valley, Foxhole Slade, was significant. As is usual for Mesolithic burial caves, associated lithic artefacts are minimal, suggesting these spaces were set apart for the dead (Conneller 2006). The final act of deposition in this area, at Paviland, between 5460 and 5295 BC, is the last in Southwestern Britain that can be dated to the Mesolithic. In fact, as has previously been noted (Blockley 2005), there is a gap of around a millennium between the last dates in Gower and the scattered human remains found on the Oronsay middens (see chapter 5).

6 The last hunters

The Final Mesolithic, 5000–4000 BC

The Final Mesolithic in Britain is a story of both continuity and change. Many favoured locations that had been used for millennia remained important (Figure 6.1). At the same time, in some areas new ways of engaging with the landscape appeared. On the small island of Oronsay and the estuaries of the east coast of Scotland, people accumulated shells to produce middens on a monumental scale; on Oronsay, these were associated with the deposition of human remains. In the Pennines, there appeared a greater intensity of occupation in the fifth millennium, at least as far as radiocarbon dated sites indicate. In this region, in the final centuries of the period, there were further changes, as new microlith types emerged and new material sources were used; these may indicate shifting mobility patterns or the emergence of new social contacts. New forms of material culture appeared, often referencing distant places. T-axes (Box 6.4), the type fossil of the Southern Scandinavian Ertebølle, are found in Scotland (Elliott and Griffiths 2018). Polished axes in Cumbria may suggest contact across the Irish sea (Brown et al. in press). New microlith forms are found across Southern Britain, South Wales, and as far north as Cumbria and County Durham (Figure 6.2). Amongst these are micro-tranchet microliths, which are similar in concept to the trapezes and transverse arrowheads of Late Mesolithic continental Europe but rendered through a lens of traditional British Late Mesolithic microlithisation,

It may be pertinent to ask to what extent these changes in Britain were stimulated by developments on the continent. By c.5000 cal BC, Neolithic groups had reached the Northern French coast. Populations and ideas were shifting. Long-distance east-west maritime voyaging has recently been identified in the Channel (Anderson-Whymark et al. 2015; Conneller et al. 2016b); it seems unlikely that north-south travel did not also occur. The bones of domestic cattle dating to 4495–4195 cal BC (Woodman and McCarthy 2003, 33) have been found at the Mesolithic site of Ferriter's Cove on the southwest coast of Ireland, suggested to represent gifts of meat from Neolithic groups far to the south in continental Europe. While no domesticated animals have thus far been identified in Britain, claims have been made for the small-scale cultivation of cereals in the last centuries of the fifth millennium (Albert and Innes 2020). The changes that can be seen in Britain at this time may suggest new fusions of cultures and ideas.

Sea-level rise and vegetation change in the fifth millennium

By 5000 cal BC, Britain was approaching its current form (Figure 6.3). A handful of small islands in the Doggerland archipelago perhaps remained. The shoreline of

DOI: 10.4324/9781003228103-6

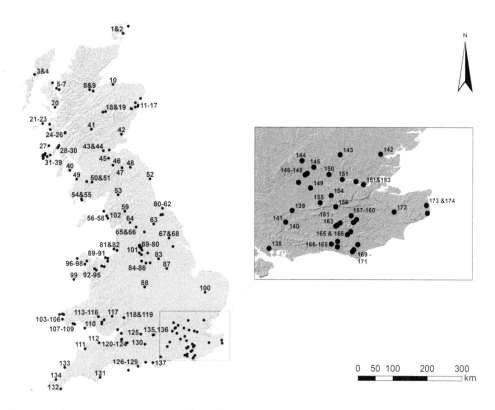

Figure 6.1 Distribution of sites with fifth millennium radiocarbon dates (1. Canal Rd. Muirtown, 2. Tarradale, The Black Isle, 3. Skilmafilly, 4. Milltimber, 5. Nethermills, 6. Spurryhillock, 7. Risga, 8. Carding Mill Bay, 9–12. Caisteal nan Gillean I and II Cnoc Coig, Priory Midden, Cnoc Sligeach, 13. Morton B, 14. Airthrey, 15. Blair Drummond, 16. Braehead, 17. Causewayhead, 18. Meiklewood, 19. Inveravon, 20. Mumrills, 21. Polmonthill, 22. Kilrubie Hill, 23. Wide Hope Shank, 24. Flint Hill, 25. Burnetland Hill, 26. Low Hauxley, 27. Stainton West, 28. South Haw, 29. Slynedales Culvert, 30. Rocher Moss, 31. March Hil Top, 32. March Hill Carr, 33. Lominot Site 2, 3 and C, 34. Dan Clough, 35. Parc Bryn Cegin, 36. Nant Hall, Prestatyn, 37. Dunford Bridge B, 38. Rough Close, 39. Lydstep, 40. Goldcliff, 41. Ascott-under-Wychwood, 42. Manor Farm, 43. Stratford's Yard, 44. Misbourne Viaduct, 45. Tolpitts lane, 46-8, Wawcott I, III, XXIII, 49. Langley's Lane, 50. Blick Mead, 51. Coneybury Anomaly, 52. Fir Tree Field Shaft, 53. Blashenwell, 54. Little Dartmouth Farm, 55. Poldowrian, 56. Windmill Farm, 57. Charlwood, 58. Bexhill, 59. Falmer Stadium)

Southern Britain extended further than today, particularly in the region of the Wash, where it is likely to have been tens of kilometres further east (Walker et al. 2020). The end of the period is marked by a climatic downturn, the 5.9 ka event. The effects of this are seen in European lake sequences from about 4000 cal BC (Florescu et al. 2019). Tipping (2010b) argues that lower sea temperatures and increased storminess between 4500 and 3500 cal BC may have altered movements of migratory fish and changed the form of coastal landscapes through erosion and increased dune formation. More storms may have increased the risks involved in maritime travel (Tipping 2010b), though their

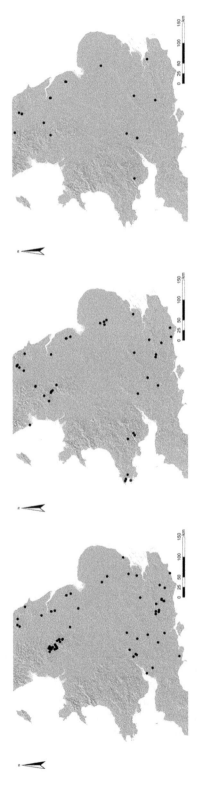

Figure 6.2 Distribution of sites with likely fifth millennium microlith types: Four-sided microliths (left); asymmetric microtranchets (centre) and symmetrical micro-tranchets (right)

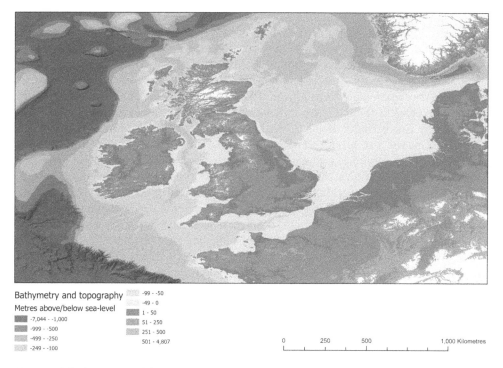

Bathymetry and topography
Metres above/below sea-level

- -7,044 - -1,000
- -999 - -500
- -499 - -250
- -249 - -100

- -99 - -50
- -49 - 0
- 1 - 50
- 51 - 250
- 251 - 500
- 501 - 4,807

0   250   500   1,000 Kilometres

Figure 6.3 Palaeogeographic model of Britain at 5000 cal BC (copyright Fraser Sturt)

effects are likely to have been more pronounced in the North Sea in comparison to the western seaways (Garrow and Sturt 2011).

While all major tree species were present in Britain by 5000 cal BC, the slower-spreading late arrivals, ash and lime, continued to expand, and other species moved towards their natural limits. As sea-levels rose, rivers backed up, leading to increasing development of wetlands and the boggy ground favoured by alder. Peat seems to have increased in the uplands, and here, too, human activities seem to have had an impact, with burning used to create clearings, favour certain species, such as hazel, and even create open heathland in the Pennines and North York Moors.

Northeast Britain

The settlement pattern in the Late Mesolithic was characterised by sites on rivers, and these are likely to have remained important in the Final Mesolithic. A late date of 4325–4055 cal BC (Poz-69104) may indicate continued Final Mesolithic occupation at Nethermills, Deeside (Wickham-Jones et al. 2016; see chapter 5); this is on oak, though, so it could conceivably fall into the Early Neolithic due to the old wood effect. Estuarine sites seem particularly important in this period, with shell-middens dating mainly to the last millennium of the Mesolithic preserved on raised shorelines along the western edge of the Firth of Forth in particular. Coastal occupation is also in evidence, consisting of small-scale but repeated visits to the shore and the generation of small shell-middens at Morton B (1971). Occupation also continued in the uplands:

In the Cairngorms, the Chest of Dee, an important halting point in the seventh millennium, also has fifth millennium dates (Wickham-Jones et al. 2020). Further south in the Southern Uplands, Biggar Archaeology Group's site at Weston Farm also has late dates (Ward 2017). Daer 3 and 84 date to the end of the fifth millennium BC, as does the quarry site at Burnetland (see Box 6.1). At Garvald Burn, at 375 m asl, a series of pits has three dates in the fifth millennium BC (Ballin and Barrowman 2015). Further to the west, occupation continued around Loch Doon at Smittons T3 in the late fifth millennium, close to the late sixth millennium site of Smitton T1 (Finlayson 1990).

Continuity can perhaps best be seen at Milltimber, where pits had been dug for millennia. This site also has fifth millennium dates; similar ways of engaging with this place seem to have stretched across millennia. Post-holes associated with pits were also in evidence in the central areas of the site; the only radiocarbon measurement from these post-holes is between 4895 and 4710 cal BC (SUERC-39748) (Dingwall et al. 2019). This focus on erecting post-holes at a time of rapid sea-level change may indicate an increased concern with marking actual physical places, the whereabouts of which might become disguised in the face of moving ecotonal zone.

The digging of large pits also commenced at new sites without these long histories. On the flanks of a small hill 30 km north of Aberdeen, at Skilmafilly, a large pit, measuring 3.2 m by 2.8 m and 1.4 m deep was excavated (Johnson and Cameron 2012). As with the large Middle Mesolithic pits in this region, it was left to silt up naturally, before twice being recut. Both the initial digging of this pit and the recuts were undertaken in the late fifth millennium BC. At Spurryhillock, 20 km south of Aberdeen, a large truncated pit measuring 2.3 by 1.8 m, and surviving to a depth of 1.3 m, silted up with alternate layers of charcoal and sand (Alexander 1997). Oak charcoal from the lowest fill indicates it was dug in the early-mid fifth millennium BC, but the old wood effect means it may be broadly contemporary with Skilmafilly.

Box 6.1   Mesolithic quarrying

In previous chapters, several locations have been identified as places for the procurement of lithic raw material. In Southern England, Mesolithic groups have been argued to exploit solution hollows and tree throws as means to access flint nodules (Care 1982). Broom Hill, located close to the chalk, where known solution pipes exist, is such a site, and the large lithic assemblage containing a substantial quantity of axes supports this interpretation. The material recovered from two solution pipes near Fort Wallingford during construction of the M27, and also associated with large numbers of axes and cores, could be interpreted in a similar way (Hughes and ApSimon 1977). A case has also been made that some of the so-called pit houses, excavated in the first half of the 20th century, may also have been quarry pits (see chapter 4). Higgs (1959) has suggested the pit at Downton was cut to exploit gravel flint, and similar arguments could be made that some of the Farnham pits were used to procure flint. More recently, it has been suggested that amorphous pits at Streat Lane, Sussex (Butler 2007), London Road, Beddington (Bagwell et al. 2001), and Woodbridge Road, Guildford (Bishop 2008), may have been dug to quarry flint from Head and terrace gravel deposits, respectively. At both London Road and Woodbridge

Road, it has been suggested that tree throws may have alerted people to the presence of flint in the underlying gravels.

While earlier procurement sites are focused mainly on secondary flint sources, in the Final Mesolithic quarry sites associated with the exploitation of primary chert deposits seem to appear. Survey by the Biggar Archaeology Group located at least eight quarry pits and associated spoil heaps on the southwest flank of Burnetland Hill in the Scottish Borders, a known source of Southern Uplands chert. The largest of the depressions were around 5 m across with spoil heaps 1.5 m high. Excavations of one of these revealed it was excavated against the edge of a number of seams of radiolarian chert, of the blue-grey sort favoured in prehistory. A number of large stone pounders were found, used to remove material from the seams. Knapped chert, including bladelet production, was recovered from the quarry pits. Measurements on hazel charcoal recovered from the base of the trench suggested a very late Mesolithic date for quarrying of 4225–3960 cal BC (5220 ± 35 BP; SUERC-17876) (Ward 2012).

Quarry pits of similar size are known from three further sites in the Upper Tweed Valley, located through surveys undertaken by Bob Knox at Flint Hill, Kilrubie Hill and Wide Hope Shank (Warren 2001). Additional survey by Warren recorded around 57 quarry pits across the three sites, with a range of 2–10 m in size. Excavations of one of the pits at Wide Hope Shank (Figure 6.4) revealed a very similar type of archaeology to Burnetland, with large quantities of shattered chert and similar, though fragmentary, hammerstones recovered (Warren 2001). People appear to have been cutting back the poor quality, frost-fractured surface exposures to reach better quality material. Some burnt chert might indicate the use of fire in quarrying, but no charcoal was found. These three quarries remain undated, and only undiagnostic material was associated with the spoil heaps, though blade debitage was found close by. The dating of Burnetland reinforces suspicions that some of these quarry pits are of Mesolithic date. Warren (2001, 218) points to the presence of chert, with surfaces indicative of procurement direct from an exposure at several Tweed Valley sites, including, Manor Bridge, Peebles, dated to the second half of the ninth millennium BC, indicating this practise may have some antiquity.

In the Late Mesolithic, the chert sources of Northern and Southwest England were increasingly used, but evidence for quarrying is more ambiguous. Jeff Radley notes 'chert diggings in Kirkdale below Seldon', suggesting that he may have located evidence of quarrying, though this is undated (Radley archive, notebook 2, cited in Myers 1986, 368). Surveys by Hind (1998) have failed to locate any such evidence. There have also been suggestions that Portland chert was quarried (Care 1979, 99), but there is currently no evidence remaining to support this, though this may have been destroyed by later quarries.

There have also been claims for Mesolithic quarrying of meta-mudstone at Carn Menyn (Darvill and Wainwright 2014). Four Mesolithic-age radiocarbon dates have been obtained from the primary fills of a quarry pit. These suggest two phases of activity: One in the first half of the seventh millennium BC, and a second at the end of the sixth. There is as of yet, though, no evidence for the use of meta-mudstone on Mesolithic sites in Wales (David pers. comm.), raising the possibility that the charred materials are residual.

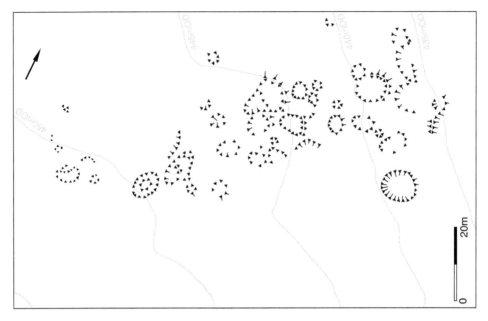

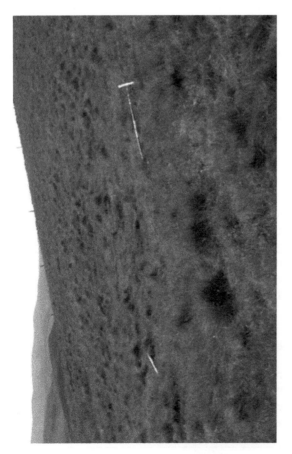

Figure 6.4 Quarry pits at Wide Hope Shank (copyright Graeme Warren, UCD School of Archaeology)

Eastern middens

Shell middens have in general been associated with Mesolithic lifeways on the west coast, but they are present in the east too and not simply at the better known but rather atypical middens at Morton B (see below). Most other middens were estuarine, occupied at a time of much higher sea-level, and now far inland. Several cluster around the inner Forth estuary and tend, unlike Morton, to comprise mainly oyster shells. Others are found overlooking the Beauly and Moray Forth. Most of these are early finds that are poorly dated, and few have undergone systematic excavation. A tendency to be located on raised shorelines has led to the suggestion that they are Mesolithic; however, several have Neolithic evidence in the form of pottery or radiocarbon dates, suggesting a more complex situation, and it is likely that many accumulated during both the Mesolithic and the Neolithic, as is the situation on the west coast.

Several of these large estuarine middens do have Mesolithic dates, and while some earlier examples are known, most do seem to date to the fifth millennium BC, though this may be an issue of preservation, rather than changing practises. A recent survey and excavation programme by the North of Scotland Archaeological Society has located eight middens at Tarradale on The Black Isle, overlooking the northern shore of the Beauly Firth (Grant 2018). A midden (site 2D) on the 17 m asl raised beach dates to between 6630 and 6000 BC (Waddington and Wicks 2017), the earliest recorded in the east. It was accumulated at a time of high sea level, slightly before the maximum post-glacial transgression. A second midden (2B) has a series of radiocarbon dates (4782–3643 cal BC) spanning most of the fifth millennium and into the Neolithic (Grant 2018) and is located on the 9 m asl raised beach, a few metres above a sea that was beginning to retreat. Found within this midden were a biserial antler point and two antler T-axes (Box 6.4, Figure 6.5), both artefacts also associated with middens in the west of Scotland. Stone settings were also located, and possible structural evidence. This may indicate a similar pattern to Cnoc Coig, with midden deposits building up around a dwelling structure. The midden has a range of shellfish (oyster, mussels, cockles and periwinkles), fish, birds and terrestrial fauna, though the range of species reported, including domesticates, indicates that it is of mixed date. A third midden (2 A) similarly spans the centuries of the Mesolithic-Neolithic transition and indicates continuity of occupation and the form of activities across this period (Grant 2018).

On the southern shore of the Beauly Firth, a date of 4650–4345 cal BC (GU-1473) comes from the basal layers of a midden at Canal Rd, Muirtown, one of three known from Inverness (Myers and Gourlay 1991), though the measurements were made on possibly mature oak timbers and could thus belong to a Neolithic occupation. This midden, no more than 0.6 m thick, extended intermittently for around 100 m along the ancient shoreline. The midden was mainly composed of oyster, though mussels, cockles and winkles were found in small concentrations, and fragments of crab shell were noted. While a hearth was present, no lithic material was recovered.

In the Forth Valley at the time of the main post-glacial transgression at around 5000–5500 cal BC, relative sea-level was at c.12 m, with mean spring tide level at c.14–16 m, turning the Forth Valley into a large marine embayment with estuarine conditions at the western end (Bradley et al. 2011; Smith et al. 2010). Areas of mudflats and salt marshes increased as relative sea-level fell (Smith et al. 2010). In the

Figure 6.5 T-axe from midden 2B at Tarradle, on The Black Isle (copyright Tarradale Through Time; photo by Michael Sharpe)

western end of the Firth of Forth Mesolithic dates have been obtained from a midden at Inveravon, on the southern shore of the estuary, now on the north bank of the river Avon. The midden stood nearly 3 m high and stretched for 120 m. It was composed mainly of oyster shell, with some bones observed (Deveraux and Sloane 1983). Five measurements, one on charcoal and four on shell, suggest it began to accumulate during the sixth and fifth millennium cal BC, with the upper layers being Neolithic (MacKie 1972; Sloane 1986). The midden had the remains of hearths set amongst the shells, but no artefacts were found. Only small sections of this midden were investigated when it was disturbed by a pipe trench in 1971 and 1983.

A second midden in the same area, Mumrills, just 3 km from Iveravon, has radiocarbon dates on shells from the base of the midden belonging to the late fifth millennium BC (Ashmore 2004), though the upper layers here, too, were Neolithic. Also close to Inveravon, on the south bank of the Avon, a third, undated midden at Polmonthill was reported to have been 150 m long, 32 m wide and around a metre in height. Both Polmonthill and Inveravon were composed mainly of oyster with occasional mussel, cockle, periwinkle and whelk (Lacaille 1954). All three middens were located on the 15 m contour, around 3 m above the sea-level of the time of the maximum transgression. Around 15 km to the northwest at the most westerly point of the estuary at the time of occupation, a fourth small midden at Braehead, composed mainly of oysters, but with scallops, winkles and mussels, was dated to the second half of the fifth millennium cal BC (Ashmore and Hall 1996).

The whale hunters

In the 19th century, several finds of whale skeletons associated with artefacts of red deer were made around Stirling. Clark (1947) associated these with deposits called carse clays: Intertidal and sub-tidal deposits from a time of higher relative sea-level. He suggested that these were animals that had swum up the Firth of Forth and become beached, before being exploited by human groups. The best known, and the only dated example, comes from Meiklewood. This whale was associated with an antler T-axe (Elliott 2012, Box 6.4), which has been dated to 5000–4590 cal BC (5920 ± 80 BP; OxA-1159) (Bonsall and Smith 1989, 36). This was found 'resting upon the front of the [whale] skull, lying vertically in the blue silt' (Turner 1889, 791). However, a recent date on a vertebra of the associated whale (a rorqual) at 7590–7190 cal BC (8400 ± 80 BP; Beta-158485) (Smith et al. 2010) is much earlier than the date of the mattock. Given the broader pattern of whales associated with antler tools, this association is unlikely to be a coincidence, suggesting one of these measurements is wrong, probably affected by either organic or inorganic conservation media. Dates for antler mattocks across Europe suggest the measurement on the whale bone is erroneous. The other whales and associated artefacts are undated, though their stratigraphic position, in the carse clays but usually resting on the underlying peat (Smith et al. 2010), suggests they are also Mesolithic in date. The only other surviving antler object, from Causewayhead, appears a more informal tool, consisting of part of the beam and an attached tine (Lacaille 1954). However, the original descriptions of the finds suggest that the now-lost antler tools recorded may have been T-shaped antler axes. At Blair Drummond, 'a piece of perforated deer's antler with traces of a wooden handle' was found, while a hole had been bored in one of the two antlers found at Airthrey (Turner 1889, 790). Turner (1889) suggests these implements would have been used as blubber mattocks.

These whales have rarely been identified to species. The Airthrey animal is reported to have been a 22-m-long blue whale, while the find from Meiklewood was a species of rorqual (Clark 1947). The most common modern strandings on British coastlines are porpoises and dolphins, with an average of 540 reported per year over the past 5 years, most of these as a result of injuries from nets and trawlers (Deaville 2016). Whale strandings are rarer (Table 6.1). Sperm whales average at around six per year and are well-represented in Scotland, particularly in the northern and western islands. Many animals are washed up dead, but live strandings, both singly and en masse, are not uncommon, and there have been

Table 6.1 Strandings of rorquals 2011–2015 on UK beaches (data from Deaville 2016)

Rorqual species	Average strandings per year 2011–2015
Minke whale (Balaenoptera acutorostrata)	15
Fin whale (Balaenoptera physalus)	3
Humpback whale (Megaptera novaeangliae)	1
Sei Whale (Balaenoptera borealis)	1
Blue whale (Balaenoptera musculus)	0 (last reported stranding in 1957)

suggestions that the North Sea functioned as a sperm whale trap (Scottish Agricultural College 2000). The quantity of resources that could be obtained from such a beaching event cannot be over-estimated. Males can be up to 20.5 m long and were hunted in historic times for spermaceti and blubber (used in oil lamps and to make candles), and the flesh was sometimes eaten. A large whale could provide as much as 500 gallons of spermaceti. Olaus Magnus in the 16th century estimated that a single whale could provide 250–300 waggons full of usable products, with meat for salting, blubber for heating, small bones for fuel, and large bones for building (cited in Clark 1947, 90).

Clark (1947) notes that the majority of Prehistoric whale finds are rorquals. This group consists of several species, of which five have been washed up on British beaches. The largest of these is the blue whale, which can be up to 30 m in length, while even the smallest, the Minke whale, is up to 9 m in length. Apart from Minke whales with an average of 15 strandings per year, these are rarely found on British beaches. Most Minkes died from entanglement in commercial fishing gear, and this was also a factor in the death of several of the rarer whales. Whale populations have been decimated by hunting, driving several species to near extinction; numbers are only beginning to recover. Even so, a stranding in the Mesolithic would probably have been a relatively rare event, blue whales, in particular, a once-in-a-lifetime encounter with a perhaps fabled species.

The whales stranded on inter-tidal mud flats, the middens along the shoreline behind, offer a vivid picture of life in this estuarine inlet in the fifth millennium BC. Around a quarter of finds of whales have associated artefacts, and other examples may have been over-looked during early discoveries, indicating Mesolithic people were routinely present in these areas, and whale sightings may have been monitored. The excess in resources from a stranding could have been the occasion for feasting and gifting, creating ties of obligation between local groups.

Box 6.2   Life on the Coast: Morton B

At Morton B, on the eastern side of the same former small rocky island as the earlier site of Morton A (see chapters 2 and 5), excavations uncovered a shell-midden around 30 m long, 3.5 m wide and up to 70 cm deep in places, but more typically between 10 cm and 45 cm in depth. Dates on bone artefacts from the midden probably suggest intermittent occupation on a number of different occasions during the fifth millennium BC, which would have been just after the time of the maximum transgression, when sea-levels would have been around 7–8 m asl (Bradley et al. 2011). A raised beach at 9.7 m asl has been recorded, and the midden built up on top of beach deposits of cobbles and shingle. Land snails from the base of the midden indicate that a heavily shaded, dry woodland would have been present nearby (Coles 1983).

The midden was composed of shells, stones, fish, birds and animal bone. Faunal remains were highly fragmentary, and only a small percentage could be identified to species, but red deer, roe deer, aurochs, pig and hedgehog were all recovered. Birds were common, particularly guillemot and gannet, but include fulmar, cormorant, shag, razorbill, puffin, back-backed gull, kittiwake, thrush and crow. Many of these favour cliff ledges, and suitable rock formations (also a possible source of the lava used on site) can be found around 1.5 km from the site. Of fish remains, cod were most common, but haddock, turbot, sturgeon, salmon or sea-trout also were represented. The presence of cod has been suggested to be indicative of deep-water fishing (Coles 1971, 353, but see Pickard and Bonsall 2004). Only a small sample of the shell material was examined, but this revealed 40 different species were present. Most were marine shells, of which cockle, Baltic clam and striped venus clam were most common, and limpet, common and flat periwinkle, dogwelk, common welk and ocean quahog were well-represented, but brackish water species were also present, indicating use of estuarine resources. Plant remains were present in small numbers; all species known to have been eaten historically, such as fat hen, iron root, knotgrass, corn spurrey and chickweed. A notable absentee from the middens is seal (Coles 1983, 12), particularly given the probable presence of rocky islands in the area. Seal bones are present at some of the Middle Mesolithic sites in the region and argued to have been an important component of Late Mesolithic diets (Waddington 2007).

Distinct dumping episodes of shells could be discerned in places, as could periods of abandonment, when the surface of the midden began to erode. Localised deposits of flat stones and boulders were noted, including an area where the midden appeared to have been levelled, then covered with stones. Also, within the midden were stone-set hearths, posts and stakeholes. None of these were arranged in a way that might suggest shelters of the form observed at Morton A.

In some of the areas of the midden, discrete episodes of activity or deposition could be noted: For example, a deposit of four bone tools, three poorly worked cores and a handful of flakes on a variety of material types, associated with the bones of red deer, cod, haddock, guillemot, cormorant and thrush. Several of these short-term events were recorded, but one area seemed to have undergone more extended occupation. Here, around a hearth setting, 285 bones of mammals, birds and fish were uncovered, as well as a wide variety of shellfish (limpet, periwinkle, pelican's foot, necklace shell, dog whelk, common mussel, prickly cockle, venus shell, Baltic tellin, trough shell, common otter shell), including a pelican's foot shell with a double perforation. Four bone bevel-ended tools were found and a small assemblage of 72 stone tools, including manuports, a core, chopping tools and flakes. Thirty-five of these were unworked nodules of chalcedony, 17 of which were scattered over the area of a square metre and may represent a cache.

Further evidence for intermittent use of the midden comes from seasonality studies (Deith 1983). These suggest the majority of the shells were collected during the winter, but there was occasional summer activity and rarer late summer/autumn visits. Shellfish gathering may have been embedded within trips to procure lithic material along the beaches (Deith 1986).

Western Scotland

Understanding of fifth millennium life in Western Scotland has been dominated by the evidence from the Oronsay middens, particularly Cnoc Coig. Until recently, there has been relatively little to compare with this, the large surveys of the Southern Hebrides Mesolithic project, for example, failing to locate any substantial contemporary Mesolithic site (Mithen 2000). This has begun to change in recent years with dating of small middens at cave sites in the region of Oban (see Box 6.3) and on Ulva (Bonsall 1996) and renewed excavations at Risga (Pollard et al. 1996). Recent fieldwork has also located sites of this date on a number of other islands. In the north, on Lewis, dates of 4400–4000 BC have been obtained from Tráigh na Beirigh 1. This site is a shell midden (Figure 6.6), overlying a buried soil, which also preserves evidence for Late Mesolithic activity (Church et al. 2012; Piper and Church 2012). Further south, new sites have also been located on Colonsay and Islay. These are all islands where Late Mesolithic evidence has been recorded. In the far north, visits to Shetland, dating to the last century or so of the Mesolithic have been recorded from West Voe, where a midden, that continued to be visited in the Neolithic, first began to accumulate. The lowest layer of the midden is composed of oysters, with an overlying layer comprising of limpets, seal and sea-birds belonging to the period of the transition (Melton 2009).

Figure 6.6 Eroding section at Tráigh na Beirigh 1 prior to excavation (copyright Peter Rowley-Conwy)

Box 6.3 The 'Obanian' sites

In the last decades of the 19th century, several shell middens were excavated on the small island of Oronsay and in caves and rockshelters on the mainland in the vicinity of Oban (Figure 6.8). These sites were associated with bone and antler artefacts, in particular biserial barbed points (Figure 6.7) and bevel-ended tools (Figure 6.8), some of the latter were also made from stone. Small flaked stone assemblages were present, but microliths, and often retouched pieces more broadly, were entirely lacking. Given their close association with the beaches of the post-glacial maximum transgression, this combination of artefacts was seen as indicative of a geographically restricted, temporally discrete cultural grouping. It was named the 'Obanian' by Movius (1940), who compared it with the non-microlithic Late Mesolithic in Ireland, known as the Larnian.

The concept of the Obanian has been dismantled in recent years, as suggestions that the differences in material culture between Obanian and microlithic assemblages may be functional rather than cultural have gathered momentum (Bonsall 1996). Radiocarbon dating programmes focused on organic artefacts have revealed that the midden sites do not occupy a discrete temporal span, but in fact include some of the earliest dates from the west coast (at Druimvargie) as well as some of the latest (Cnoc Coig and Carding Mill Bay). At the same time, dates became available for sites with microliths in the same region, indicating these were contemporary with the Obanian. Excavations at Lón Mór, for example, revealed microlithic sites and shell

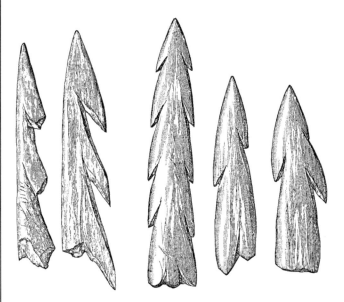

Figure 6.7 Barbed points from Druimvargie (1–2) and Caisteal nan Gillean I (3–5) (Anderson 1898)

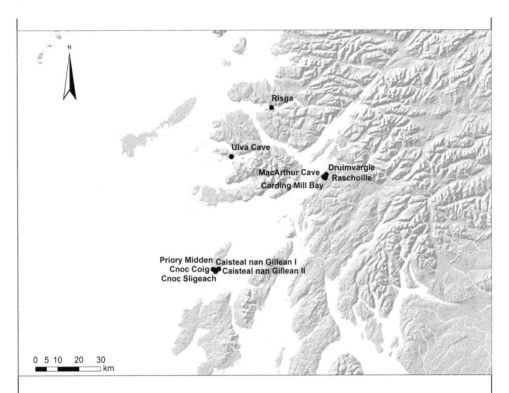

Figure 6.8 Distribution of Obanian sites

middens along the margins of a former marine embayment and dates that span the late seventh to late fifth millennium; yet, Lón Mór is less than a kilometre from Carding Mill Bay and Rascoille (Bonsall 1996; Bonsall et al. 2009). Furthermore, excavations at Risga, a geographic outlier but described by Lacaille (1954) as an Obanian site, have revealed a rich lithic assemblage in which microliths were well-represented (Pollard 2000), while blade debitage and a single microlith have been recorded at Ulva Cave (Bonsall et al. 1994).

Amongst the 'Obanian' sites, the cave site middens in the Oban area and Ulva Cave to the north have a wider date range than the Oronsay middens, mainly spanning the late eighth millennium to the end of the sixth millennium and are discussed in the previous chapter. Only Raschoille and Carding Mill Bay may have very late Mesolithic dates (Table 6.2), one from the latter centring on 4000 BC on an antler bevel-ended tool (Ashmore 2004). Both sites show Early Neolithic activity, and some of these potentially very late Mesolithic dates could reflect the activities of the earliest Neolithic inhabitants of the region.8

Beyond Oban, there is good evidence for fifth millennium activity on other sites previously seen as Obanian, where recent excavations have also taken place. These excavations, at Ulva and Risga, have also been instrumental in showing the association of microliths with Obanian sites. At Ulva Cave, on Ulva Island, just off Mull, a midden 8 m across and 0.35 m thick was located in a large cave measuring 17 by 15 m (Pickard and Bonsall 2009; Russel et al. 1995).

Table 6.2 Radiocarbon dates for 'Obanian' sites

Site	Date range	Mesolithic age radiocarbon measurements
Druimvargie	7570–6465 cal BC	7570–7175 cal BC (OxA-4608; 8340 ± 80)
		7040–6660 cal BC (OxA-4609; 7890 ± 80)
		7030–6465 cal BC (OxA-1948; 7810 ± 90)
Ulva Cave	6650–6265 cal BC	6650–6390 cal BC (GU-2600; 7655 ± 80)
	4770–4180 cal BC	6640–6265 cal BC (GU-2601; 7615 ± 80)
		4770–4455 cal BC (OxA-3738; 5750 ± 70)
		4705–4360 cal BC (GU-2602; 5685 ± 80)
		4545–4180 cal BC (GU-2603; 5525 ± 80)
Raschoille	6650–6020 cal BC	6650–6370 cal BC (OxA-8396; 7640 ± 80)
	5720–5010 cal BC	6590–6330 cal BC (OxA-8397; 7575 ± 75)
	4040–3780 cal BC	6440–6250 cal BC (OxA-3895; 7495 ± 50)
		6470–6215 cal BC (OxA-8398; 7480 ± 75)
		6350–5990 cal BC (OxA-8535; 7265 ± 80)
		6225–6020 cal BC (OxA-8439; 7250 ± 55)
		5720–5010 cal BC (OxA-8538; 6460 ± 180)
		4040–3780 cal BC (OxA-4838; 5115 ± 55)
MacArthur Cave	5730–5490 cal BC	5730–5490 cal BC (OxA-1949; 6700 ± 80)
Risga	5205–4555 cal BC	5205–4705 cal BC (OxA-2203; 6000 ± 90)
		4905–4555 cal BC (OxA-3737; 5875 ± 65)
Carding Mill Bay 1	4235–3655 cal BC	4235–3795 cal BC (OxA-3740; 5190 ± 85)
		3965–3715 cal BC (GU-2796; 5060 ± 50)
		3940–3655 cal BC (GU-2797; 4980 ± 50)
Casteal nan Gillean I	5320–4730 cal BC	5320–4940 cal BC (Q-3008; 6190 ± 80)
	4545–4000 cal BC	5290–4840 cal BC (Q-3007; 6120 ± 80)
		5205–4730 cal BC (Q-3009; 6035 ± 70)
		4545–4045 cal BC (Q-3010; 5485 ± 110)
		4500–4000 cal BC (Q-3011; 5450 ± 110)
Cnoc Sligeach	5220–3775 cal BC	5220–4055 cal BC (Gx-1904; 5755 ± 250)
		4770–3775 cal BC (BM-670; 5426 ± 220)
Priory Midden		4880–4595 cal BC (Q-3001; 5870 ± 50)
		4960–4450 cal BC (Q-3000; 5825 ± 110)
Caisteal nan Gillean II	4725–3805 cal BC	(OxA-8004; 5470 ± 45)
		4455–4070 cal BC (Q-1355; 5460 ± 65)
		4725–3805 cal BC (Birm-347; 5450 ± 195)
Cnoc Coig		(OxA-8004; 5470 ± 45)
		4680–4370 cal BC (Q-3006; 5675 ± 60)
		4650–4335 cal BC (Q-3005; 5650 ± 60)
		4765–4265 cal BC (Q-1353; 5645 ± 110)
		4830–3965 cal BC (Q-1354; 5535 ± 195)
		4550–4045 cal BC (Q-1351; 5495 ± 110)
		(OxA-8014; 5495 ± 55)
		4690–3810 cal BC (Q-1352; 5430 ± 180)

The midden was composed predominantly of limpets and to a lesser extent periwinkles, with dogwelk also present. Limpets were gathered from the middle and lower reaches of a rocky shore. Crabs were exploited for food and may have been collected in the summer months (Pickard and Bonsall 2009). Mammal and fish bones, along with the occasional hazelnut shells, were also incorporated (Bonsall et al. 1994; Russel et al. 1995). The midden seems to have had a long duration, with the lower layers accumulating in the mid-seventh millennium and the upper layers in the mid-fifth, with evidence too for early fourth millennium and Early Neolithic activity. Organic artefacts include an antler bevel-ended tool and a perforated cowrie, though these appear much rarer than at other middens (Bonsall 1996). A single microlith was recovered amongst a small lithic assemblage.

Northernmost of the 'Obanian' sites is a midden on the island of Risga, a small rocky outcrop in the middle of Loch Sunart, excavated in the 1920s with minimal records. The midden was on a rocky platform at 9 m asl. At the time of occupation in the fifth millennium BC, this would be not far above the spring high tide mark (Bradley et al. 2011). The midden was 30 cm thick, and in the centre, a layer of burnt stones and several hearths was recorded (Pollard et al. 1996). In contrast to the middens in the Oban area, a large lithic assemblage was recovered during the 1920s excavations. The midden seems to overly a 'sooty layer' and there have been suggestions that there was an earlier occupation focused on microlith production, followed by an 'Obanian' midden lacking these tools (Woodman 1989). However, examination of records of the 1920s excavations suggests greater stratigraphic complexity and that the midden and sooty layer probably accumulated through a number of different events. At times, the debris of activities taking place in the 'sooty' layer may have been discarded in the midden (Pollard et al. 1996).

The midden was dominated by limpet, with fish and birds well-represented and a variety of terrestrial and marine mammals (Lacaille 1954) (Tables 6.4–6.7) exploited for food, fur and raw materials. A wide variety of organic tools were recovered, including bevel-ended tools, barbed points, simple bone points and a T-shaped antler axe. Stone bevel-ended tools were recovered, as was a large assemblage of over 18,000 lithic artefacts, made mostly on quartz, but with quantities of flint and bloodstone (Pollard 1990). Perforated cowries and pigment add to the range of material recovered (Lacaille 1954, 233). A range of relatively amorphous tools were present, including heavy-duty picks. Further excavations by Banks and Pollard in the 1990s discovered further occupation beyond the midden, including several hearths, pits and curvilinear slots, accompanied by a lithic assemblage with numerous microliths (Atkinson et al. 1993; Banks and Pollard 1998; Pollard et al. 1996).

Dates from a bevel-ended tool and the T-shaped axe indicate occupation in the first half of the fifth millennium BC. These late dates are probably representative of the Mesolithic use of the midden; any earlier occupation is likely to have been destroyed during the maximum post-glacial transgression. Neolithic pottery is also present (Pollard 1990), and without further dates, the extent of activity of various periods cannot be determined.

On Oronsay

The large shell middens found on the small island of Oronsay (Figure 6.9) have been seen to typify fifth millennium settlements on the west coast, though in many ways, at least until the location of a similar-sized midden at Port Lobh on Colonsay (Finlay et al. 2019), they seemed rather unique. It has been suggested that Oronsay

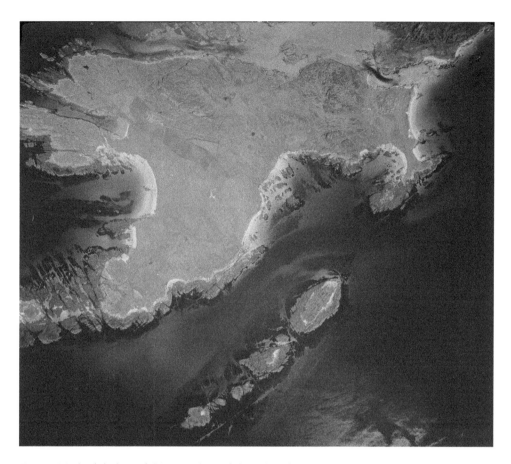

Figure 6.9 Aerial view of Oronsay (copyright NCAP/ncap.org.uk)

was occupied by sedentary, marine-adapted hunter-gatherers (Mellars 1987); however, even the findings of the original excavation indicated that the people visiting Oronsay were sea-farers who travelled widely, and more recent work has further emphasised the complex settlement pattern in the region. While today the island can be reached at low tide from its neighbour Colonsay, in the Late Mesolithic, with higher relative sea-level, boats would have been needed. Estimates of the size of the island at the time of occupation suggest it would have been only in the region of c.4 km^2 (Mellars 1987).

The Oronsay middens are considerably larger than the small cave-middens of the mainland (see Table 6.3) and appear even more prominent because of deep deposits of wind-blown sand (Warren 2007). In the Mesolithic, these accumulations of gleaming white shells would have been visible markers when approaching the island by boat (Finlay 2004). These large mounds attracted the attentions of antiquarians who excavated at Caisteal nan Gillean I between 1879 and 1882, at Cnoc Sligeach in 1884 and 1913 and at a third site Cnoc Riach, whose location is now unknown, but may possibly be Cnoc Coig. Cnoc Coig also underwent excavation in 1913 (when it was known as Druim Hastell, or the Viking Mound). Further work was carried out in the 1970s,

Table 6.3 Features of west coast middens

Midden	Location	Type	Length (m)	Breadth (m)	Height (m)
Sand	Applecross	Rockshelter	8	8	1
MacArthur Cave	Oban	Cave	<7.5	<6	0.9
Druimvargie	Oban	Cave	4.5	3	1.2
Distillery Cave	Oban	Cave	<3.5	<2.7	?
Risga	Loch Sunart	Open air			0.3
Caisteal nan Gillean I	Oronsay	Open air	45	45	2.4
Caisteal nan Gillean II	Oronsay	Open air	15	15	0.6
Cnoc Sligeach	Oronsay	Open air	90	50	1.7
Priory Midden	Oronsay	Open air	25	25	0.8
Cnoc Coig	Oronsay	Open air	25	20	0.7
Port Lobh	Colonsay	Open air	30	25	0.45

when Paul Mellars undertook extensive excavations at Cnoc Coig and more limited testing of the other middens.

Most middens are on the eastern side of the island, facing towards Jura. Cnoc Sligeach is northernmost and Caisteal nan Gillean I southernmost. Only the Priory Midden is on the western part of the island, facing the empty expanse of the Atlantic Ocean. The shell middens represented a fixed point in a shifting, tidal landscape, albeit one threatened by spring tides and storm surges. Tony Pollard (1996) has drawn out the temporality of activities on these shorelines. The rhythms of low tide brought people down to the sea strand to harvest shellfish and check fish traps at times dictated by the pull of the tides rather than the movement of the sun. On a broader scale, travel between the islands was affected by the seasons and patterns of weather. Reading the seascape was an important skill, particularly as it seems the last centuries of the Mesolithic represented a period of increased storminess (Garrow and Sturt 2011).

The excavated middens share a number of common features. They are composed of shells, amongst which limpets dominate; edible periwinkle are common and dog welk well-represented (Table 6.4). Fish bones, often saithe, are common (Table 6.5). Seasonality evidence, derived from the study of saithe otoliths, suggests fishing activities took place at different times of the year at the different middens (Mellars and Wilkinson 1980). At Cnoc Coig, where sampling was most extensive, fishing, both during a pre-midden occupation and during the accumulation of the midden itself, seems to have taken place mainly in the autumn, though occasional mid-summer and winter events were also recorded. At Cnoc Sligeach the evidence suggests summer, and at Priory Midden and Caisteal nan Gillean II, winter, though it should be noted that these results come from a single column sample taken from very large sites.

Sixty percent of the mammalian remains at Cnoc Coig come from seals, almost all grey seals (Table 6.6). Grey seals – both adults and pups – were most likely killed in the autumn when they hauled themselves onto rocks to calve. Entire seal carcasses seem to have been brought to the middens by boat. The remains of whales and dolphins or porpoises were also found. A worked whale bone was re-covered next to a hearth at the Priory Midden (Mellars 1987), and a whale bone point was recovered from Caisteal nan Gillean I (Lacaille 1954). Otter bones were

Table 6.4 Shellfish from fifth millennium middens

	Risga	Caisteal nan Gillean I	Caisteal nan Gillean II	Cnoc Sligeach	Priory Midden	Cnoc Coig	Port Lobh
Limpet	+++	+++	+++	+++	+++	+++	+++
Edible Periwinkle	+	+	+	+	+	+	+++
Flat periwinkle				+			+
Cowrie		+		+		+	
Dog whelk		++	+	++	+	+	
Whelk	+	+		+			+
Mussel	+	+		+		+	+
Oyster				+		+	+
Scallop	+	+		+		+	+
Cockle	+	+		+		+	
Topshell				+			+
Razor clam				+		+	+
Crab	+	+		+		+	+
Sea urchin						+	

Table 6.5 Fish remains from fifth millennium middens. Full details are not available for all sites

	Risga	Caisteal nan Gillean I	Cnoc Sligeach	Cnoc Coig	Port Lobh
Tope	+		+		
Dog fish	+	+	+		
Ray			+		
Angel-fish			+		
Skate	+	+			
Conger eel	+		+		
Saithe				+++	+++
Cod					+
Haddock	+				
Sea-bream			+		
Black bream	+		+		
Wrasse		+	+		
Mullet	+	+			
Norway pout					+

Table 6.6 Mammalian remains from 5th century Scottish middens

Species	Risga*	Caisteal nan Gillean I	Caisteal nan Gillean II	Cnoc Sligeach	Priory Midden	Cnon Coig	Port Lobh
Red deer	+	+	++	+	+	++	+
Pig	+	+		+		++	
Badger	+						
Otter		+	+	+	+	++	+
Pine Marten	+	+					
Common seal	+	+		+		+	
Grey seal		+	+	+	++	+++	
Whale	+	+			+		
Dolphin		+		+			

common, outnumbered only by seals. Otters were brought to the site complete for skinning; they do not seem to have been eaten; instead, their bodies seem to have been thrown on the fire (Grigson and Mellars 1987, 278), perhaps a culturally appropriate way of dealing with a significant animal. Terrestrial mammals are restricted to red deer and pig, both seemingly more important as raw materials than food. Red deer remains consist mainly of antler, imported to make tools such as mattocks, bevel-ended tools and awls. Lower limb elements of both red deer and pig are well-represented: These, too, seem related to the production of bevel-ended tools (Grigson and Mellars 1987).

An extremely wide range of birds have been recovered from the middens, particularly Cnoc Coig (Table 6.7). These are mostly pelagic sea birds, particularly the great auk, which makes up 15% of the birds at Cnoc Coig. As auks, puffin, guillemot and razorbill only come ashore to breed, this indicates focused fowling in the summer months, though there are also a small number of winter visitors, such as the little auk (Best and Mulville 2016). Waterbirds such as duck, geese and swans are well-represented, and a small number of moorland and woodland birds are present. Plant foods are represented by large quantities of charred hazelnut shells (Mellars and Wilkinson 1980).

The middens were places focused on cooking and processing: Burnt stones, small pits and hearths are extremely common. Large quantities of tools have been found on the more extensively excavated middens (see Table 6.8): At Cnoc Coig, 436 bone and antler and 359 stone bevel-ended tools were found (Nolan 1986); on

Table 6.7 Bird remains from fifth millennium middens

	Risga	Caisteal nan Gillean I	Cnoc Sligeach	Cnoc Coig
Swan		+		++
Goose	+		+	++
Duck				++
Red-breasted Merganser	+		+	
Cormorant/shag	+		+	++
Gannet	+		+	++
Plover			+	
Tern	+		+	+
Gull	+		+	+
Razorbill	+	+	+	++
Guillimot	+	+	+	++
Great Auk	+	+	+	+++
Little auk				+
Puffin				++
Water Rail	+		+	+
Curlew				+
Sparrowhawk				+
Buzzard				+
Quail				+
Snipe				+
Woodcock				+
Blackbird				+
Raven				+

Table 6.8 Material culture from 'Obanian' midden sites

Site	Bone/antler bevel ended tool	Stone bevel ended tool	Barbed point	Antler mattock	Lithics
MacArthur Cave	140	0	7	0	20
Druimvargie	18	4	2	1	
Risga	P	P	P	4	18,000
Caisteal nan Gillean I	150	210	10	9	90
Cnoc Sligeach	36	150	7	3	Rare
Cnoc Coig	436	359	2	11	

Caisteal nan Gillean I, 150 organic bevel-ended tools, 10 biserial barbed points (see Figure 6.7, 3–5), numerous simple points (including one made from whale bone) and eight T-shaped antler axes. In contrast, chipped stone is less common than typical on other Mesolithic sites: Assemblages consist mainly of small flint flakes, detached mainly using the bipolar (anvil) technique. Some middens are associated with larger assemblages than others, but retouch is rare in each case: Retouched pieces are absent at Cnoc Sligeach, with only a handful recorded at Caisteal nan Gillean I (Lacaille 1954). At Cnoc Coig, bladelet debitage occurred, particularly in the later phases of the midden, and some formal tools are present (Pirie et al. 2006). Shells were not just food waste but material culture, with perforated cowries worn as beads, scallops used as scoops and larger shells used as containers: A cache of 16 unperforated cowries were found in the shell of a prickly cockle (Mellars 1987).

A feature of three of the middens is the presence of human bone. Fifty-five human bones were recovered, the majority (49) from Cnoc Coig, five came from Caisteal nan Gillean II and a single phalanx from the Priory Midden. The majority of these are hand and foot bones, though 16 represent other elements, mostly bones of the torso. Of limb bones, only a single tibia fragment was found. The bones range in age from those of a child to an adolescent, to those fully adult, and both men and women seem to be present, suggesting age and gender were not a factor in the nature of funerary treatment. A minimum of seven individuals are represented (Meiklejohn and Denston 1987). The unusual patterning of elements has led to suggestions that human remains were excarnated on the middens (ibid.). Bodies may have been laid out on the middens themselves or scaffolding above it, with the larger parts disposed of elsewhere – perhaps into the sea (Pollard et al. 1996) – and the smaller parts overlooked. However, analysis of the spatial location of the human remains suggests that rather than being forgotten, they played a more active role on the site (Meiklejohn et al. 2005). A cluster of hand and foot bones seem to have been placed on a seal flipper (Finlayson 1996; Nolan 1986). Several human elements seem to be associated with the two structures on the site, suggesting some were curated. Nolan (1986) also notes the similarity in skeletal part representation between humans and red deer and pig, all three of which are represented by lower limb elements. This pattern in the animals has been explained through the use of lower limb bones for tools, and it should be noted that while finger and toe bones are common, the larger human limb bones, of suitable size for tool manufacture, are absent.

Cnog Coig is the site where the most extensive fieldwork has taken place; here, 196 m^2, around 70–75% of the entire midden, were excavated during the 1970s excavations (Figure 6.10). The site has been the subject of extensive spatial analysis (Nolan 1986) and is also the best dated (Wicks et al. 2014). As such, the archaeology of the midden is worth exploring in some detail to understand the process of midden accumulation and how this product of ephemeral activity and discard practises emerged as a social space; perhaps even, as has been suggested, as a symbolically charged Mesolithic monument (Pollard 2000; Pollard et al. 1996; Cobb 2005).

At the time of occupation, Cnoc Coig would have been close to a receding sea, lying on an area of dunes. Sedimentological analysis suggests the midden lay close to the junction of the beach and the dune system. A bank of sand to the north would have provided shelter, and a similar bank may once have existed to the south also. Before the midden started to accumulate, there is evidence that people had already visited the location. A layer of debris was recorded on a weak soil horizon, indicating the dune system underwent a period of stabilisation during which vegetation grew. This early occupation in the northern area of the site, in the lea of the land bank, was small, spread over a 5 m by 4 m area. It consisted of two adjacent hearths, only 3 m apart, marked by the presence of burnt stone, burnt shells and charcoal. Small piles of shells surrounded the hearths. Beyond these, shells were sporadic, but there were patches of fish bone, all young saithe. Artefacts consisted of an anvil stone, three bevel-ended tools and the base of a shed red deer antler (Mellars 1987). This occupation, which Mellars suggests was a single event (Mellars 1987, 232) probably occurred sometime in or after the 46th or 45th century BC (Wicks et al. 2014).

Above this episode of pre-midden activity, 20–30 cm of sterile wind-blown sand accumulated, indicating the resumption of dune formation. Within this was a thin palaeosol, indicating some gap between this early occupation and the start of midden accumulation, though wind-blown sand can accumulate rapidly, and a palaeosol may develop with a few years of stabilisation. The earliest dates on the midden are very similar to those from pre-midden activity, albeit all have large standard deviations and are on bulked, unidentified wood, so should be considered *termini post quos* for these events.

The extensive excavations at Cnoc Coig and the detailed spatial analysis of the midden undertaken by Nolan (1986), give an insight into the accumulation of the midden and how its spaces were produced. As McFadyen (2006) argues, in the Mesolithic it is activities and the deposition of the *generata* of ephemeral activities that make space, and nowhere can this be seen more clearly than at Cnoc Coig. Activity seems to have started with a small semi-circular structure, marked out by stakeholes (structure 1), with a diameter of 3–3.5 m (Mellars 1987, 238). A midden (the phase 1 midden) began to accumulate as food waste and hearth debris from the structure was piled up behind it and propped against it. This midden was also a focus for activities with three hearths found at different levels within it. Midden material also began to accumulate slightly further to the south (the midden in this area is known as the phase 2 midden). Refits of human bone between the structure and the lower part of this midden suggest it was also accumulating while the structure was in use, and this lower part (2a) may be contemporary with the phase 1 midden (Mellars 1987, 226).

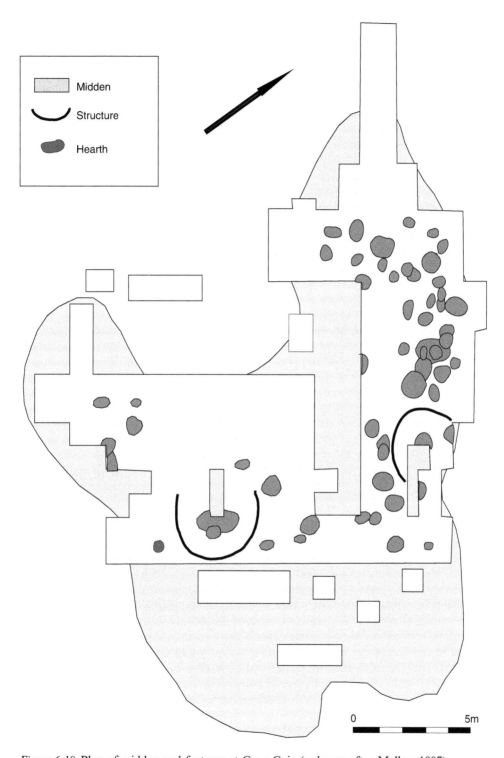

Midden

Structure

Hearth

0   5m

Figure 6.10 Plan of midden and features at Cnoc Coig (redrawn after Mellars 1987)

In the centre of structure 1, a pit was dug, which contained a bevel-ended tool and a red deer bone, which may represent a foundation deposit (McInnes 2015; Nolan 1986). A hearth was laid on top of this pit. McInnes (2015) has drawn attention to the importance of hearths and the transformations enacted by fire at Cnoc Coig. She notes particularly the significance of this hearth as a central focus, which was repeatedly cleared out and remade in the same spot: Mellars (1987, 238) records the presence several superimposed layers of burning, as well as dumps of burnt material in the surrounding midden. In addition to the feature underlying it, the hearth was surrounded by a number of enigmatic pits containing midden material: As Mellars states: 'The interpretation of these in functional terms remains problematic' (Mellars 1987, 238). Two of these pits contained burnt stones – these 'stone holes' were a common feature of the midden architecture. These were not post-holes with post-packing, but instead seem to be related to cooking and heating (ibid 240). They echo the Late Mesolithic pattern of incorporating burnt and transformed materials, often related to particular acts of food preparation, into pits. Burnt material, cleared from hearths, was also found as layers in the midden.

The structure is associated with the deposition of both animal and human remains. The only two barbed antler points from the site were both found on its edge. Near the base of the structure were four human phalanges (Nolan 1986). One of the phalanges refits with another found in the phase 2 midden (Meiklejohn et al. 2005). In total, a grouping of 16 human bones, mainly phalanges and metacarpals/tarsals, have been found in this area of the site, with at least three individuals represented. This group is found in three main areas: In the lowest 10 cm of the phase 1 structure, relatively high (30–40 cm) in the phase 1 midden, and at mid-level (25–30 cm) in the phase 2 midden, below a sand lens that is an important stratigraphic marker in this area (Nolan 1986). While it is possible that the human bone within the structure has slumped in when walling collapsed or was removed and thus derives from excarnation on the midden, it could also suggest curation and circulation of some of the human remains from Cnoc Coig.

The pattern of human bone deposition suggests the earliest parts of the phase 2 midden, located just to the east of the phase 1 structure, are contemporary with the phase 1 midden. However, deposition into the phase 2 midden continued above a sand lens that marks the end of the phase 1 midden. This phase 2 midden started with the deposition of cetacean bone. It also contained clusters of seal bones and a scatter of human bones found close to the remains of red deer, otter and a second cetacean (Nolan 1986, Figure 6.7). Bird remains are common in the phase 2 midden and include discrete clusters of quail, goose, teal, duck and swan bones, which are rare elsewhere on the site. Bevel-ended tools were also found throughout this midden.

The western area of the site was not used for middening during the early phases of occupation. This instead seems to have been a place where activities took place around open-air hearths. A major hearth, one of several at the lowest levels in this area, was associated with clusters of burnt stones and a number of 'stone holes', perhaps indicating large-scale cooking activities (Mellars 1987, Figure 14.18). Antler is also common in these lower levels (Nolan 1986), perhaps indicating that this area was also a focus of craft activities.

Phase 3 marks a shift in the spatial focus of the use of the site, which moved several metres to the south. This involved the building of a new structure, very similar in form to that of phase 1: A semi-circular arrangement of stakeholes, approximately 3.5 m in diameter and with a central hearth. This hearth similarly showed evidence for many superimposed firings with a thickness of 25 cm (Mellars 1987). Antler working seems to have taken place around the hearth (Nolan 1986). Ochre is also common within the structure. Middening recommenced, with the main focus immediately to the northeast (in an area previously associated with cooking fish) and also to the east and south of the structure; the midden, as in phase 1 encircling the structure and perhaps eventually merging with/forming its walls. This phase 3 midden may also have included material redistributed from the earlier phases (Meiklejohn et al. 2005); it may have been important that the new structure was surrounded by evidence of past events, connecting people to the activities of past generations.

A second major cluster of 18 human bones comes from the area of the phase 3 structure, most found between c.10 and 30 cm from the base of deposits, which is at broadly the same level as the main hearth associated with this building (Meiklejohn et al. 2005; Nolan 1986). This cluster may even lie below the hearth (Nolan 1986, 254) and thus might represent a foundation deposit. The human remains are strongly associated with a cluster of ochre. There are refits between this group and two outliers, found in midden material to the south of the structure. Two radiocarbon dates are available for human remains in this cluster: 4250–3840 cal BC (OxA-8014; 5465 ± 55, marine correction applied) and 4330–4000 cal BC (OxA-8019, 5615 ± 45, marine correction applied). This group also consists predominantly of bones from the hands and the feet and represents at least three individuals. A collection of these bones was found immediately above a cluster of bones from a seal flipper. The fact that both major groupings of human bones are strongly associated with the only two structures on the site may be significant. It is difficult to be completely certain whether these are contemporary with the use of the structure or date to the period following their abandonment, though from their stratigraphic position the former seems much more likely. If this is the case, there remains the possibility that the buildings themselves were mortuary structures, or that the parts of the dead, ex-carnated on the middens were brought within the domestic sphere to co-exist with the living.

The phase 3 midden deposits contain three well-defined extensive dark layers, comprising burnt shells, fish bones and charcoal, which seem to represent debris cleared out of hearths, probably from the adjacent structure. Deposition commenced with two cetacean bones, and the upper levels contain the remains of otter, pig and red deer. Oysters are well-represented in comparison with other areas of the site. Antler waste material and foetal and young seal bones are particularly common in the midden to the southeast, and three antler mattock fragments were found in the midden to the east of the structure.

The western area seems to have seen lower levels of use throughout the time Cnoc Coig was visited. After being used as an area for activities focused around hearths, shells began to be accumulated, but at low levels, interspersed by sand. The emplacement of hearths and antler working continued in this area during this phase, and bevel-ended tools are also common. Mellars has suggested that much of the shell accumulation in this area seems to be fairly late in the sequence, equivalent to phase 3, or even later. This has been confirmed by a recent radiocarbon measurement on pig, the only one from this area, which yielded a date of 3980–3805 cal BC (OxA-29937, 5122 ± 30 BP) (Charlton et al. 2016). This time period would traditionally be associated with the presence of Neolithic groups, at least in other parts of Britain. During the later occupation of the site, the area seems to have been used for specific tasks, particularly involving processing of animals: Much of the seal bone from the site clusters in this area, and there are several small scatters of otter, pig and red deer bone in the upper levels.

While less is known about the generation of the other middens on the island due to the smaller scale of excavations at these sites, there are hints of similar processes. At Caisteal nan Gillean II, a hollow 30–40 cm in depth was noted below the midden layers, associated with a post-hole to the east, which may have represented a structure (Mellars 1987). This may suggest that here, too, the midden built up around a structure. A large pit was also recorded at the Priory Midden. At Cnoc Sligeach, the largest of the Oronsay middens, material seems to have accumulated in two or three distinct centres, which, over time, merged to create a single mound, as at Cnoc Coig (Mellars 1987, 195). Two distinct layers were noted. The earliest was characterised by low-density shell debris associated with wind-blown sand, giving the impression of slow, sporadic accumulation of shells. This contrasts with a higher density of shells and occupation debris, including much burnt material, probably cleared from hearths elsewhere on the site, indicating different rhythms and intensities of occupation.

Tony Pollard (1996, 203) argues that these middens may have been liminal places, located just beyond the margins of the tide, where the resources of both the land and the sea were processed. He points to the presence of marine mammals on the middens, animals that belong to both land and sea. The presence of the dead on the middens may also support ideas these were liminal spaces. Excarnation is a process of liminality, transforming known individuals into clean bones. Cobb (2005), however, argues that liminality may be a less useful concept for the strandloopers and marine voyagers who habitually traversed these zones, preferring to see the middens as places of transformation, where people were remade into ancestors, and fish and shellfish into food (Cobb and Jones 2018; Pollard et al. 1996).

Key transformations were enacted at Cnoc Coig, which may have made the middens powerful accumulations. They reflect a long-standing interest shown by Mesolithic groups in differential treatment of hearth debris and other things transformed by fire. They were places where fish, shellfish and marine mammals were transformed into food and the dead transitioned from people to bone. The dead may have undergone further transformations: The similarity between certain seal and human remains in death was recognised by those that visited Cnoc Coig and placed human phalanges on top of a seal flipper (Conneller 2006; Nolan 1986). If the majority of the human bones from people excarnated on the midden were deposited in the sea, as suggested by Pollard (1996), this similarity may be more pronounced. Perhaps the seals were understood carry the souls of the dead, like the selchies seen as lost human souls in Scottish oral tradition; Radovanovic (1996) has made a similar argument for the role of migratory sturgeon at Lepenski Vir. She suggests they were seen to carry the souls of the dead downstream in the autumn, returning in the spring. The occupation at Cnoc Coig coincides with the season when grey seals come to shore to give birth, perhaps conceived as the return of human souls, in a continuing cycle of life.

Tony Pollard (1996) makes the point that as places of excarnation the middens may have played the same role as Neolithic chambered tombs (see also Thomas and

Tilley 1993). This would also extend to a role as a landscape marker; they would be visible as gleaming white mounds to those approaching the island by boat, memorialising past activities (Finlay 2004), including perhaps significant events such as feasts (Thomas and Tilley 1993). Their location may have been a way of broadcasting ancestral connections between Mesolithic groups and a place that was also important for access to the sea (Pollard et al. 1996).

What relationship the people who made the middens had to sites beyond Oronsay has been the matter of some debate. Mellars, perhaps influenced by a prevailing interest in complex hunter-gatherers, for whom a key indicator was sedentism, linked the varied seasonality indicators from the different middens to suggest people were present on the island throughout the year (Mellars and Wilkinson 1980). Isotopic analysis of the human remains was seen to support this, as five samples of human bone from Cnoc Coig indicated a diet focused almost entirely on marine resources (though a single sample from Caisteal nan Gillean II showed a mixed diet) (Richards and Mellars 1998). However, Grigson's faunal analysis showed people had access to red deer, which were unlikely to be present on such a small island as Oronsay (Grigson and Mellars 1987). Two sizes of red deer were represented: Larger animals, probably obtained from the mainland, and smaller-sized animals, which were likely to be have been adapted to the more restricted resources of one of the larger nearby islands. Such evidence, as well as increasing knowledge of the Mesolithic of nearby islands, has led others to argue that visits to Oronsay were more sporadic and that the island was just one of a network of places visited by hunter-gatherers who focused on marine resources but also exploited the flora and fauna of adjacent areas (Mithen 2000; Mithen and Finlayson 1991; Wicks et al. 2014). While the surveys of the Southern Hebrides Mesolithic project failed to locate any sites contemporary with Cnoc Coig, more recent work has uncovered fifth millennium sites on both Colonsay and Islay, showing a variety of settlement forms in the region (Finlay et al. 2019; Wicks et al. 2014).

Box 6.4   T-axes

Over the past few decades, several dating programmes, combined with typological study, have elucidated changing technological traditions of antler tool production (Elliott 2015; Smith et al. 1989). Elliott has noted that two main types of antler digging or chopping tools, termed 'mattocks' by Smith et al. (1989), were in use during the fifth millennium. These axes are tools made on the beam of the antlers of red deer (elk, whose antlers were used for Early Mesolithic mattocks were seemingly extinct by this time). The initial associations of these tools, for example, at Meiklewood (see above), suggested they may have been used as blubber hammers for exploiting whales (Clark 1947). Smith et al. (1989), following Clark's interpretations of the much earlier elk antler examples from Star Carr, suggested they could have been used for digging, leading to their association with plant exploitation (Zvelebil 1994). Elliott (2015) suggests they may have played a more diverse role, with woodworking and animal butchery also possibilities.

The first of Elliott's two Late Mesolithic mattock groups can be defined as having a perforation through the beam itself; they have a longer currency, appearing first around 7000 BC, with dated Mesolithic examples extending to the end of the period. Amongst the second group the perforation is made through the stump of the removed trez tine, giving them, when perforated, a T-shaped profile (Elliott 2015). These T-axes are much more temporally restricted: Two, from Meiklewood (Figure 6.11) and Risga, have direct dates and belong to the first few centuries of the fifth millennium (Tolan-Smith and Bonsall 1999). A third comes from the Priory Midden on Oronsay and is undated, but the midden itself has dates falling into the second half of the fifth millennium (Wicks et al. 2014). Two new finds from Tarradale (Figure 6.5) come from a midden with fifth millennium dates.

These Scottish T-axes are part of a class of objects that have a widespread distribution across Europe, from the Iron Gates in the east, through Central Europe to the Baltic coast, where they are classically associated with the Southern Scandinavian Ertebølle. In continental Europe, they extend as far west as Belgium (Elliott 2015 Figure 6.11). In these contexts, too, they tend to have fifth millennium dates and, as such, are associated variously with Mesolithic groups and pottery using hunter-gatherers. Mesolithic Britain has for a long time been seen as isolated following the inundation of Doggerland (Jacobi 1976). The connection of the Scottish finds with this broader group suggests this is not the case and that parts of Britain at least were caught up in wider networks of marine voyaging.

HLA 3 Meiklewood

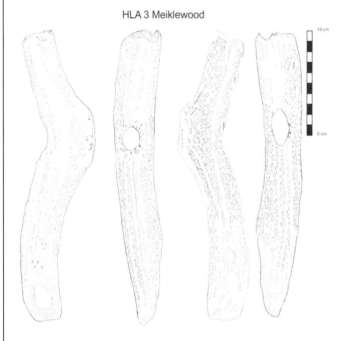

Figure 6.11 T-axe from Meiklewood (copyright Ben Elliott)

Colonsay and Islay

Until recently, there was little trace of occupation from the last 1500 years of the Mesolithic on either Islay or Colonsay, the location of extensive seventh and sixth millennium Mesolithic occupation (see chapter 4). This changed with the excavations of a late fifth millennium shell midden at Port Lobh on Colonsay (Finlay et al. 2019) and an occupation site at Storakaig on Islay, which has a series of radiocarbon dates spanning the second half of the fifth millennium BC and the first half of the fourth (Wicks et al. 2014). The midden at Port Lobh (Figure 6.12), measuring 30 by 25 m, demonstrates that large shell middens in Western Scotland are not confined to Oronsay. The shells would have stood at around the level of the main post-glacial transgression, a few metres above the reach of high tides, on what would have been an extensive lagoon and estuary. This is a sheltered area, close to a freshwater stream. Charcoal is compatible with a local vegetation of birch-hazel scrub, with willow and alder fringing the margins of the lagoon and patches of oak woodland on drier ground.

Six small test pits were excavated into the midden (Finlay et al. 2019). Though truncated by later activity, the midden still stood 0.45 m deep in places and was composed of shell, charred hazelnut shells, burnt and unburnt bone, flint and fire-cracked rocks (Figure 6.13). Limpets are the most common shell recovered, followed by periwinkle. These can be gathered from rocky shorelines close to the site.

Figure 6.12 Port Lobh from the southeast (copyright Nyree FInlay)

Figure 6.13 Midden deposits at Port Lobh (copyright Nyree FInlay)

The large numbers of immature limpets suggest they may have been gathered as fishing bait, rather than for direct consumption; mature periwinkles are more common, suggesting they were eaten. Though rocky shore species dominate, the more fragile-shelled sandy shore species are present in small numbers and include oyster, razor shell and mussel. Saithe are the dominant fish, with smaller numbers of cod and a single otolith of Norway pout, which was probably an incidental catch. Measurements of saith otoliths suggest autumn or winter fishing. These young saith were probably caught from rod and line fishing from the shore or with line or nets in shallow water. Larger cod suggest some offshore fishing.

Radiocarbon dates indicate at least two phases of activity, one centred on the 43rd century cal BC and the other on the 42nd century, though the midden could also be the product of a larger number of small-scale intermittent visits. In places, two phases can be discerned, suggesting changing activities: A lower layer was associated with the processing and cooking of large cod. Hazelnut shells were absent, and the only charcoal was Maloideae. The upper layer, the main midden, has only small cod and debris from a more varied suite of activities.

More ephemeral occupation evidence is also present on Colonsay, located away from the coast. At Staosnaig, a single large pit with stones, lithics and charred hazelnut shells has a very late Mesolithic date of 4360–4055 cal BC (5415 ± 60 BP; AA-21621). This is associated with a microlith assemblage dominated by straight-backed bladelets, raising the intriguing possibility that Final Mesolithic 'rod' assemblages (see chapter 1) may also be present in Scotland, though there are suggestions that the lithic material in this feature may be residual (Finlay et al. 2019).

A more extensive inland occupation has been located on Islay, underlining that Final Mesolithic sites in the region were not exclusively located on the coast. A site at Storkaig, at 110 m asl, in the centre of the island, consists of a dark organic horizon containing lithics, charred hazelnut shells and burnt bone around 18 × 13 m in extent and sealed by peat (Wicks et al. 2014). Though burnt, some of the bone been identified as red deer, roe, pig, badger and a small dog or fox. Bird, amphibian and fish remains are also represented. This appears to represent an organic midden deposit that spans the Mesolithic-Neolithic transition, and this continuity in occupation echoes the evidence from the small shell middens of Raschoille and Carding Mill Bay.

Southwest Scotland/Northwest England

In Southwest Scotland and Cumbria, there are a handful of sites dated to the fifth millennium. Those that do exist come from locations previously occupied during the Late Mesolithic, perhaps suggesting some continuity of landscape practises. Only 600 m from the late seventh millennium site of Littlehill Bridge in Ayrshire (see chapter 5) is Gallow Hill, where a charred hazelnut shell from a pit containing lithics and charcoal has been dated to 4800–4550 cal BC (5835 ± 35 BP; GU-9806). This pit is one of two associated with lithic scatters, indicating repeated occupation during the Mesolithic, focused on a small pool fringed with alder. The lithic assemblage includes a small amount of Arran pitchstone; Gallow Hill is close to the coast, and a 26 km journey to Arran by boat (Donnelly and Macgregor 2005). In Dumfries, Barsalloch, like Low Clone (see chapter 5), is on Luce Bay and sited on a late glacial raised beach (Cormack 1970). In a layer of sandy material below the topsoil were a series of stone settings and five pits forming an arc, some of which were filled with flint or stones and which have been interpreted as hearths. A small assemblage of 461 flints was recovered from the small excavation, which includes eight microliths and several retouched pieces. A single radiocarbon date from unidentified charcoal probably indicates some of this occupation took place in the early fifth millennium BC. As at Low Clone, all flint was obtained from local beaches, and Cormack (1970, 78) noted the dominance of flint in this region of the coast, in comparison to sites to the east around the river Nith, where flint, chert and quartz were all used.

In the uplands of South Ayrshire around Loch Doon, Smittons T3 (see chapter 5) dates to the late fifth millennia BC (though this date may not be reliable), close to Smittons T1, a late sixth millennium site (Finlayson 1990). Further south at Eskmeals, a place used in the sixth millennium, fifth millennium BC activity is present at Williamson's Moss. By this time, the landscape had changed: A marine transgression created a gravel ridge, which allowed a pond to form. This became the focus for Final Mesolithic occupation activity, particularly in the later part of the fifth millennium (Bonsall et al. 1989).

The best evidence for the region comes from Stainton West (Figure 6.14) on the river Eden in Cumbria (see chapter 5), where there seems to have been a gradual increase in the frequency of occupation, culminating in the development of an intensely occupied and highly structured site by the middle centuries of the fifth millennium (Figure 6.15). At the end of the sixth millennium, organic deposits began to

Figure 6.14 Excavations at Stainton West, showing the palaeochannels (copyright Oxford
    Archaeology Ltd.)

form in the main palaeochannel, as the flow slowed and the water grew more stagnant.
Here, the remnants of the mid-sixth millennium beaver dam still seem to have had an
effect on the hydrology as organic sediments built up around it, leading to ponding
behind the structure. This seems to have attracted a family of beavers, who constructed a lodge made from wood of oak, hazel, elm, alder and blackthorn in the first
two centuries of the fifth millennium.

The late sixth/early fifth millennium organic deposits around the old beaver dam
contained both lithics and worked wood, indicating human activity in the vicinity of
the palaeochannel. A cluster of cores, flakes and pebble tools was found around the
beaver lodge. Similarly, a small quantity of worked wood is also broadly contemporary with the beaver lodge, including a possible wooden artefact. Brown and
colleagues (in press) suggest the clustering of material in the vicinity of the lodge may
indicate it was re-used by people as a focus for activity, perhaps a launching spot for
boats, or as bridge to cross the channel (Coles 2006). The evidence for activity in the
channel is matched by evidence from the dryland area dating to the very end of the
sixth millennium and the first three centuries of the fifth. A date of 5210–4930 cal BC
(SUERC-42591) comes from charcoal associated with lithics in a later tree throw. Two
further tree throws indicate occupation of the dryland in the first three centuries of the
fifth millennium. One of these contains a significant amount of lithic material and thus
may have been used for the deposition of midden material, though natural infilling is
also possible. A number of small lithic scatters, often associated with burnt flint that
may indicate hearths, and often focused on microlith production and retooling, may

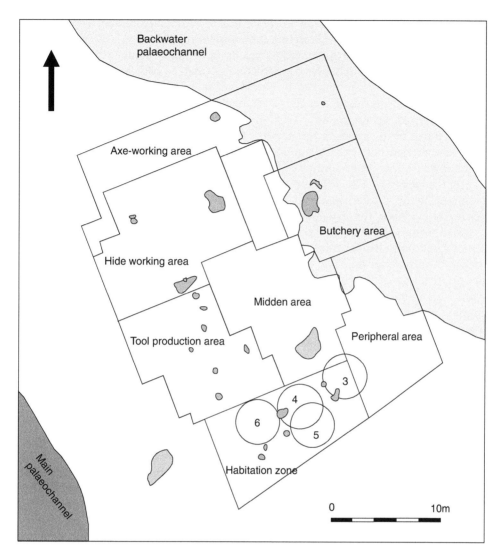

Figure 6.15 Plan of excavations at Stainton West (copyright Oxford Archaeology Ltd.)

also belong to this phase. While this is still seemingly, as it had been in the sixth millennium, a place intermittently inhabited by humans and beavers, human visits now appear more frequent.

Greater intensity of occupation is evident in the mid-fifth millennium, and the vast majority of the occupation, which generated 300,000 lithic artefacts, seems to belong to this phase, dated to between 4690 and 4490 cal BC. At this time, use of space at the site seems to have been highly structured, a characteristic of longer-inhabited settlements (Binford 1978b), with hearth features, dense areas of lithics and coarse stone tools and use of ochre. Lithic analysis has indicated a variety of more specialised areas (see Figure 6.15). In the inhabitation area, three stakehole structures were erected on slightly higher ground of the floodplain lying between the main palaeochannel and a cut-off meander, which would have been a pool or boggy area. The first of these structures (structure 3) is defined by the pattern of debitage surrounding a space of c.4 m in diameter and seemingly respecting the adjacent midden. It is associated with a similar arrangement of hearth and earth oven as an earlier structure at the site dating to the sixth millennium (chapter 5). Structures 4 and 5, two features with partly overlapping footprints, are marked by arrangements of stakeholes. These were sub-circular features also around 4 m across. These may also be associated with a similar hearth/cooking pit arrangement.

To the north of the inhabitation area lay the site midden, an area seemingly with a long history that may have begun during the sixth millennium occupation of the site (chapter 5). Here were dumps of lithic material and burnt stone, the remnants of activities cleared from adjacent areas. There are some spatial patterns in the accumulation of midden material. The southern part of the midden has more microwear evidence for dry hide working, processing of wood and plants and discarded armatures. This is likely to reflect material dumped from the adjacent area of structures. By contrast, the northern area of the midden has evidence of butchery and bone and antler working. This is likely to reflect dumping of tools used in the adjacent butchery location. The tool production area is characterised by more complete knapping sequences than found in the midden. Microliths were common, and a wide variety of other tools, such as awls, scrapers and retouched pieces, were represented; it seems that tools were brought to this area for repair. To the northwest of the midden was another specialised area associated with a small number of hearths and a hollow. While a variety of activities were under-taken here, hideworking seems important, particularly in the vicinity of the hollow. This area is also adjacent to the channel, and Brown and colleagues (in press) suggest this may have been an area for the manufacture and repair of small boats made from hide.

A final phase of Mesolithic activity at the site dates to the 45th and 44th centuries. This consists of the building of a circular structure (structure 6), its position defined by knapping debris. Knapping sequences are more complete in this area, indicative of a late phase of occupation that underwent less subsequent clearance. Probably con-temporary with this structure is a cooking pit, hearth and spread of burnt spread. These are associated with a dense knapping spread, which included the production of microliths in Southern Uplands chert. Tasks here were focused on the working of bone, antler and wood, with some butchery and hide working. A large number of microliths show impact damage, indicating repair of projectiles.

Lithic sources provide an understanding of the broader reach of the people who camped here. Eighty percent of the material used was beach flint and cherts that could be obtained over the course of a seasonal round that ranged from the Solway Firth to the upper reaches of the Eden Valley. More distant materials were also represented: Pitchstone from Arran, Southern Uplands chert from Southern Scotland, Northern Pennine cherts, tuff from the Southern Lake District and even flint from the chalk of the Yorkshire or Lincolnshire Wolds. Brown et al. (in press) suggest that the Solway Firth area may have been a place where groups from more distant regions met up. Scottish lithic materials may have been exchanged with groups whose range extended up the west coast or into the interior of the Southern Uplands; other groups may have moved south up the river Caldew and into the Lake District. Chalk flint from Yorkshire may have been obtained through exchange with groups from the east, with people meeting in the Pennine uplands. There may also be evidence for contact across the Irish Sea. Broken polished axes and reworked axe fragments made from Lake District tuff, including Langdale sources, have been recovered from Mesolithic contexts on the sites. One complete example is similar in form to polished axes common in the Irish Mesolithic. Ground stone axes are also known from West Wales (for example, at The Nab Head II, see chapter 5), though these are rather different in form.

Further south in Lancaster, evidence for fifth millennium occupation has been found at Slynedales Culvert, on a slope above the valley of the Howsgill Brook and next to a small palaeochannel (Bradley and Howard-Davies 2018). Here, a series of amorphous, possibly natural, features were sealed by a localised soil horizon [3087] containing Mesolithic lithic scatters, [3087] in turn was covered by a layer of colluvium. Mesolithic material was associated with the group of amorphous features sealed by [3087]. Small quantities of lithic material were recovered from two of these four features, and all contained small amounts of burnt material, including in one pit hazelnut shells. One of these features has a radiocarbon date of 4650–4460 cal BC (5703 ± 30 BP; SUERC-68590). In the overlying layer [3087], three discrete Mesolithic lithic scatters were located, comprising in total 1475 pieces. The northernmost of these three scatters is the largest and associated with a cluster of burnt flint that may represent a hearth. The discard of microliths took place in the southern part of this scatter, but there is little evidence for their manufacture, and overall across the site numbers of tools are low. A flake from a group VI axe was recovered from the southwestern scatter, associated with a lithic assemblage that otherwise appears Mesolithic (Bradley and Howard-Davies 2018, 36) This may reinforce the evidence from Stainton West for the use of this source during the Mesolithic, though it should be noted that Neolithic features are present on the northern margins of this scatter.

Further south still at Formby, footprints in contexts dating to the mid and late fifth millennium indicate people continued to move through the intertidal mudflats (Figure 6.16). Both adults and children, including very small ones, are represented at Blundell Path C (Burns 2021). Children seem to have been actively involved in tasks, often accompanied with an adolescent or young adult, perhaps following tracks, checking traps, fishing, fowling or playing. Burns' studies paint a vivid picture of life on the salt marsh, of paths and routeways alternately traversed by people and animals, red deer, roe deer and pig, and where cranes and oyster catchers alighted. The animals seem to have visited the area early in the morning, people later in the day, often walking towards the sea.

The end of the Mesolithic in the uplands of Northern England: The Pennines and North York Moors

From the end of the sixth millennium BC, radiocarbon dated sites in the Central Pennines become more prominent (Figure 6.17), and it seems likely that this area played a more important role in peoples' lives, shifting from an area of small temporary camps, to one that was at times more residential, though perhaps still only on a seasonal basis. The clustering of fifth millennium sites on long-established routeways between east and west – such as the March Hill-White Hill-Windy Hill route (Preston 2012) – suggests these continued to be used, or at least places established through this

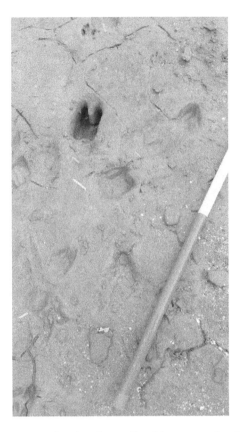

Figure 6.16 Overlapping trails of human and animal footprints at Blundell Path A, Formby
(copyright Alison Burns)

historic use continued to be maintained. There may also have been more occupation
on the North York Moors, though Mesolithic settlement is poorly dated in this region.
In the final millennium of the Mesolithic, dated evidence for human activity in the
uplands comes from two sources: First, evidence from occupation sites, particularly
from the stone-built hearths and earth ovens that seem to be particularly prevalent
during this period, and second, from zones of high concentration of charcoal particles
within environmental profiles, interpreted in many instances as evidence for human
management of the landscape through fire (Box 6.5).

In both the Pennines and North York Moors, evidence for burning of the landscape becomes prominent (Box 6.5). This is partly due to the timing of peat development, which makes identification and dating of these events possible; however,
data from North Gill on the North York Moors, which has longer sequences than
many other sites, shows a greater frequency of firing events in the fifth millennium
(Simmons 1996, 99). In the Pennines, peat began to develop in the deepest basins and
around spring heads in the mid-seventh millennium, with a second phase of development from the mid-fifth millennium (Tallis 1975), though recent work reveals peat
development in many areas was of later date (Garton 2017). The fifth millennium
phase is perhaps broadly co-incident with the clustering of burning events at around

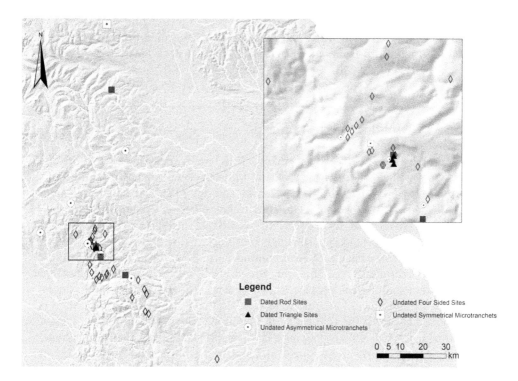

Figure 6.17 Pennine fifth millennium Mesolithic sites

4600 cal BC, noted by Albert and colleagues (2021). In certain areas, fifth millennium firing practises seem to have been sufficiently persistent to trigger long-term landscape changes (Albert et al. 2021).

In the Mid-Holocene, the tree line in the Pennines was probably around 500 m asl, and tree stumps, preserved in peat, have been found on some of the highest peaks. In the fifth millennium, the Central Pennines seem to have been characterised by a variety of vegetation types. Much of the higher upland areas were oak and alder woodland with an understory of hazel and some areas of open grassy heath (Tallis 1991; Tallis and Switsur 1990). In other places, elm seems more important, and lime and birch were also present (Bartley 1975), with perhaps more trees clustering in the more sheltered cloughs. In the Final Mesolithic, Rishworth Moor, an upland plateau at c.420 m asl, was covered with hazel and alder scrub, with areas of grass and heather heath, while sedge fringed basins of marshy or open water. Trees (oak, elm and lime) probably grew on the plateau edge. The area saw three major episodes of firing between 4700 and 4100 cal BC. This seems to have been targeted at rejuvenating calluna scrub, which had itself been established and maintained through burning practises (Albert et al. 2021). The longevity of burning practises may have been sufficient here and elsewhere in the Pennines to effect a long-term transformation of the landscape, as well as encouraging peat development.

The highest point on the North York Moors, at Urra Moor, is 454 m asl, meaning that deciduous woodland probably extended across the entire upland plateau in the Late Mesolithic. Pollen records indicate woodlands of pine and birch with oak and elm, with alder becoming locally important from the mid-fifth millennium (Simmons 1996). On the Moors, too, records of burning suggest extensive Final Mesolithic activity in the area, with dated fifth millennium burning events recorded at North Gill, Bonfield Gill Head, Bluewath Beck Head and Botany Bay (Innes et al. 2012) (Box 6.5).

Box 6.5   Mesolithic 'firestick farmers'

From the 1970s onwards, palaeoenvironmental researchers began to note the persistent presence of micro-charcoal in Mid-Holocene pollen profiles (Tallis 1975). While the causes of this charcoal can only be inferred rather than demonstrated, early explanations noted correlation between charcoal and reduction of tree cover and related this to records of 'firestick farming' (human management of the landscape through burning) in the ethno-historical record (Jacobi et al. 1976; Mellars 1976b; Simmons 1975). Other explanations for these patterns are certainly possible, and Brown (1997) points out that charcoal accumulation and pollen profiles showing clearance and regeneration can be generated by a number of alternative factors. Charcoal from adjacent campfires is one possibility, given the frequency of Mesolithic occupation in many of these areas (Bennet et al. 1990). Tipping (1996) has highlighted the role of climate, suggesting that a synchronous rise in burning events around 7000 cal BC in Scotland is related to a shift to drier conditions rather than human action. Natural fires are likely to have played a role: Pine burns more readily than other native arboreal species and was an important component of upland forests (Brown 1997, 135), though by contrast the damper Atlantic forest were less likely to burn (Simmons 1996). Lightning strikes, the main cause of natural fires, seem to have been more common at this time (Brown 1997, 135). Brown also notes the variable relation of fire to episodes of reduction in arboreal pollen: Some of these episodes are not associated with charcoal, while others show charcoal associated with post-clearance profiles, possibly indicating fire at times played a role in preventing natural clearings caused by tree-fall from regenerating.

Burning of woodland had been noted to increase the availability of plant foods, such as hazelnuts, which were exploited by humans; however, much of the early emphasis was on the increased production of browse that might attract animals to predictable locations in the landscape as well as increasing their number and condition (Mellars 1976b). The presence of fungal spores deriving from animal dung immediately following burning episodes supports the idea that herbivores were drawn to these areas (Innes and Blackford 2003; Ryan and Blackford 2009). These practises, it has been suggested, could have led to incipient domestication (Jacobi et al. 1976, 317) and potential corrals have even been suggested from evidence for clearance at Soyland Moor (Williams 1985).

Burning practises have also been linked to the production of clearances for small-scale garden agriculture, based on the presence of cereal-type pollen in these sequences (Albert et al. 2021; Albert and Innes 2020). Cereal-type pollen have been dated from c.4600 cal BC at sites such as Black Heath (Ryan and Blackford 2009) and Soyland Moor (Williams 1985). However, the pollen of cultivated cereals and some native grasses are near-identical in morphology, leading to a scepticism over claims for Mesolithic cultivation. Recent work has suggested that the pollen of a primitive form of barley (*Hordeum vulgare*) can in fact be distinguished from the two native wild grasses with overlapping pollen morphology (*Glyceria maxima and Glyceria fluitans*) (Albert and Innes 2020). On this basis, Blackford and Innes identify the presence of cultivated barley in sequences dating to the last two or three centuries of the fifth millennium at Dog Hill, Rishworth Moor in the Central Pennines. They also suggest barley is present in sequences from Cat Stones, also on Rishworth Moor, as well as at Esklets on the North York Moors. Barley may have been cultivated rather than wheat as these are marginal areas for agriculture. Barley's role in the production of alcoholic drinks may also have been an attraction (Albert and Innes 2020, 378), particularly if the Pennines was a place where widely dispersed groups met.

Pollen sequences following burning show a typical sequence of an initial phase of melampyrum and ruderal weeds, followed by a phase of heather, hazel and willow scrub, followed by woodland regeneration (Innes and Blackford 2003). Burning seems to have been used at times for different purposes. Early Mesolithic burning seems focused on wetland contexts (Chisham 2004; Mellars and Dark 1998), while Boreal and Atlantic burning became focused on woodland (or the prevention of woodland development), often seemingly focused on its margins (Bush 1988; Simmons 1996). This would encourage browse for animals and was perhaps also focused on increasing hazel (which is relatively fire-resistant) at the expense of other arboreal elements (Smith 1970). At North Gill on the North York Moors, some burning phases increased hazel, others open patches of grassland (Simmons 1996). In the Final Mesolithic of the Pennines, there are examples of burning used to regenerate open heathland.

Burning also creates social spaces, small openings in the canopy that were used by people, where hearths could be built and earth ovens dug. The temporality of these openings may explain the clustering of features with a similar date at March Hill, and relate to the timing of woodland regeneration. Evidence from areas where more extensive surveys have been made, such as North Gill on the North York Moors, where fire cleared places along a stream, suggests areas of disturbance were in the region of tens of metres across (Simmons 1996, 86). Burning also signals the presence of people in the landscape to distant groups, useful perhaps if these were places where different groups aggregated. Nor should we ignore the symbolic significance of woodland and particular tree species and the impact of these broader ideas on the manipulation of woodland (Moore 2003).

At Black Heath in the Central Pennines, the evidence suggests a natural opening in a woodland of hazel, alder and birch attracted animals, but that this clearing was subsequently maintained by people through burning over the following c.250 years (Ryan and Blackford 2009). Peaks in charcoal suggest local firing occurred every 18–36 years, a slightly longer interval than the figures for optimal productivity of 5–15 years cited by Jacobi et al. (1976). Other areas show a variety of temporalities of firing events: At North Gill, a series of sampling points close to a spring show both shorter (ten years) and longer intermittent firing intervals lasting hundreds of years, though these latter may represent composite incidences (Simmons 1996).

The microliths accompanying dated Pennine sites fall into two groups: Those dating to the first half of the fifth millennium are characterised by left lateralised scalenes and narrow-backed bladelets, made in flint and chert. The second assemblage type contains only narrow, steeply straight-backed bladelets (known as rods) made only in flint and dating to the last few centuries of the Mesolithic (Griffiths 2011; Switsur and Jacobi 1979). Four-sided microliths and micro-tranchets may also belong to this period but are poorly dated in Northern England. There has been an inconsistent approach to the identification of four-sided pieces (see discussion in Preston 2012), but using Roger Jacobi's identifications for consistency (Jacobi and Wessex Archaeology 2014), assemblages with four-sided pieces extend across the Pennines, but are rarer on the North York Moors (Figure 6.2). Sixty percent of four-sided pieces are made on Wolds flint or similar white flint sources; the remainder seem to be made on east coast till, with only two examples made on chert. This seems to indicate eastern connections and may be a sign of groups from different regions aggregating in the Pennines. Microtranchets, both symmetric and asymmetric varieties, are more common on the North York Moors. They may be dated by an early fifth millennium measurement on oak charcoal from White Gill, though this site is complex (Carter 2014). This date would, though, be compatible with those from Southern England for this microlith type.

There has been near absence of dated sites on the North York Moors, though work by Spencer Carter is beginning to change this picture, with fifth millennium dates not just at White Gill but also at Esklets (Carter 2016). Beyond dated sites, microtranchets and other novel forms can perhaps provide potential clues to life in the region at the end of the Mesolithic (see Figure 6.2). At Esklets, Late Mesolithic occupation clustered around two spring-fed pools in a woodland of alder, oak, elm and hazel (Albert and Innes 2020). Site ECW1a was undated but composed of three small scatters, of which scatter B has two microtranchets, amongst nine microliths, retouched blades, an awl, a scraper and a burin. Thirteen cores may represent a cache (Carter 2016). Activity leading to the discard of a single micro-denticulate at Botany Bay, East Bilsdale Moor, also belongs to the fifth millennium (5956 ± 51 BP; Wk-15138), through a date on the peat that encased it (Innes et al. 2012). This is an indicator of off-site activity, perhaps related to harvesting or processing of the plant material that grew on this boggy ground.

By contrast, on the Pennines, there are a number of fifth millennium radiocarbon dates for archaeological sites. Particularly notable are the cluster of dated features on March Hill, Dan Clough and Lominot. These sites are all in close proximity. There are around 120 m between March Hill Top and March Hill Carr, around 250 m between March Hill Carr and Dan Clough and around 400 m between Dan Clough and Lominot. All these sites are dated to the fifth millennium BC. Stonehouse (1987) has previously highlighted the similarity of lithic assemblages from sites in close proximity in this region. He notes, for example, the similarity of the microliths (medium sized scalenes) and raw material use (around 20% black chert) on seven adjacent sites at March Hill South. Similarly, three sites with micro-scalenes have been found on the south site of Dan Clough, and 'pears', a rare type, are found on several sites on Dean Clough. These, he suggests, may represent broadly contemporary occupations. This is echoed by the patterning of the radiocarbon dated sites at March Hill Carr, which suggest a number of hearths either used during a single visit, or more likely representing a history of repeated returns to the same place by a single group over a number of years. Given that many of these areas lay below the natural tree-line in this region, this probably represents activity in clearings and areas of woodland clearance that were maintained for decades and served as foci for repeated visits. The construction of stone-built hearths and earth ovens, some of which have evidence for repeated re-use, served as fixed points in these locations, with more temporary structures probably erected in relation to these. Modelling of radiocarbon dates from Black Heath indicates that the clearing was maintained for around 250 years with refiring roughly once a generation (Ryan and Blackford 2009). This may give some clue to the longevity of these upland site complexes and indicates concerns with maintaining places over many generations.

The earliest dates from the March Hill area come from March Hill Mesolithic Project excavations on Lominot in 1996 (Spikins 2002). Three dates from a stakehole provide *termini post quos* for its infilling of 4990–4740 cal BC (Griffiths 2011, 155). Both Early and Late Mesolithic archaeology was found in this trench. The Late Mesolithic assemblage is fairly distinctive, made on flint only, and showing use of the bipolar anvil technique, which is not common in the Pennines. Only three microliths were recovered, all scalene micro-triangles. A second date on bulked, unidentified charcoal of 4765–4235 cal BC (Q-1189) is available for Lominot IV, a site excavated by Francis Buckley; its exact location is unknown. An almost identical measurement of 4770–4455 cal BC (GrN-12278) (Stonehouse 2001) has been obtained on oak charcoal from a small stone-lined hearth excavated by Stephen Poole at Dan Clough, located between Lominot and March Hill. This excavation, as well as an extension of this trench dug by the West Yorkshire Mesolithic Project, found an assemblage of 16 almost identical small scalene triangle microliths as well as other tools, including several truncations (Conneller 1999). The homogeneity of the microliths probably argues in favour of a single occupation.

The greatest intensity of settlement in this landscape is at March Hill Carr, a flat plateau at 430 m asl on the southern flank of March Hill (Figure 6.18). This is an area with a long history of excavation. Petch (1924) recorded four major 'workshop sites'. Most relevant is Buckley's hearth site, which appears to have been located in this area. Here, two radiocarbon dates of 4930–4520 cal BC (Q-788) and 5490–4540 cal BC (Q-1188) come from one or two cooking pits (Buckley's notebooks are ambiguous) around 30 cm deep (Switsur and Jacobi 1975). Since Buckley's excavation, March Hill has continued to be a magnet to both archaeologists and collectors. Local archaeologist J.L. Turner recorded in his notebooks in 1964: 'March Hill, the mecca of all true flint addicts….is in absolute turmoil being slashed, hacked and torn to pieces in a most sacrilegious way' (cited in Spikins 2002). Pat Stonehouse recorded at least eight sites on March Hill Carr during his work in the area (Griffiths 2011).

Between 1993 and 1995, the March Hill Mesolithic project undertook excavations at March Hill Carr (trench A) (Spikins 2002). This may be adjacent to Buckley's site, where one or two cooking pits were located (the adjacent area has been previously excavated, and there were marks of an entrenching tool). In trench A, which measured only 4 by 5 m, four features were located (Figure 6.19). All have dates in the 48th and 47th centuries cal BC (Griffiths 2011), and all (and indeed Buckley's hearth) could have been in use at the same time. Alternatively, the place could have been reoccupied over several decades. Of the four features, two were stone-built hearths, and one a cooking pit or earth oven, measuring 50 cm wide and 20 cm deep (Spikins 2002). This was filled with charcoal and burnt stones. Black and

Figure 6.18 View from March Hill, looking towards Pule Hill

Thomas (2014) argue that on upland plateaux (such as March Hill Carr), earth ovens would have remained visible for centuries, and thus encourage reoccupation and the emergence of a 'persistent place' (Schlanger 1992). The visible presence of this facility may account for the quantity of features, with similar radiocarbon dates, that surround it.

The final feature at Trench A was a small pit crammed with burnt, worked flint and charcoal. The flint was white and heavily fragmented. While this may represent an exercise in heat treatment that went wrong (heating improves flint's flaking quality), there is no evidence that any of the remainder of the lithic assemblage has been heat treated (Conneller 1999). This may represent a more formal act of deposition with lithic material associated with a particular event intentionally destroyed. Burning flint transforms it, making it appear similar to burnt bone, perhaps representing death. More evidence for depositional practises can be found in material in the earth oven, which has not been left with the basal layer of charcoal and stones intact; instead, it seems to have been reused for midden material, including charcoal and burnt stones and worked flint. Charcoal within all four hearths consisted of oak and hazel, likely to be indicative of the local vegetation of the uplands at the time. More rarely represented in the hearths are hawthorn, *Sorbus sp.* (probably rowan) and *Prunus sp.* (probably blackthorn). All but one of the five hearths excavated during the project contained either hawthorn or blackthorn, both useful kindling species (Spikins 2002).

(a)

(b)

(caption on next page)

Figure 6.19 Trench A and associated features

The lithic assemblage indicates that a wide variety of activities were undertaken with large numbers of retouched and utilised pieces. Formal tools are dominated by microliths: Of 62 complete microliths at Trench A, 51 were triangles. March Hill Carr, not unexpectedly, thus fits well into Jacobi's 'March Hill type' site (Switsur and Jacobi 1975), characterised by small, narrow scalene triangles with lower numbers of other geometrics, mostly backed bladelets. Microburins are relatively rare but more common in a small trench (73) a few metres to the east, possibly indicating different activity zones. Small, neat truncation burins are another feature of the assemblage, and March Hill has long been known for the quantity of burins recovered – 29, for example, from March Hill 2 (Buckley 1921; Petch 1924; Stonehouse 1987). These are less common elsewhere in the Central Pennines, though several are known from Dean Clough G and Badger Slacks 2 (Stonehouse 1987). Burins were common elements in Star Carr-type assemblages, but decreased in importance in Deepcar and particularly Middle Mesolithic toolkits. This renewed interest in burin manufacture might be related to the renewed production of bone and antler tools. With the exception of bevel-ended tools and an Obanian style uniserial barbed point from Druimvargie, these were not common between c.8000 cal BC (when Star Carr style uniserial barbed points fell out of favour) and c.5500 cal BC. After this time, both T-shaped antler axes and biserial barbed points were relatively common (Elliott 2012; Tolan-Smith and Bonsall 1999). While burins are not needed to work antler (a snapped blade will work just as well), an increased role for antler tools may have led to the reintroduction of a more formal toolkit for their production.

Much of the lithic distribution at March Hill Carr appears to focus on the northeast side of the hearths. The highest lithic densities are here as well as concentrations of microliths, retouched and utilised pieces, blades, core maintenance flakes and chips. These indicate that activities involving routine core reduction, the replacing of elements of composite tools and cutting activities centred round the four hearths, possibly allowing for prevailing wind direction. The cutting activities may represent food preparation, as these are found next to the earth oven. Moderate lithic densities are represented – up to 275 pieces per square metre. However, this is a landscape where lithic material is not readily available, and some curation is likely.

The variability in Pennine Mesolithic assemblages, usually characterised as microlith-dominated hunting camps, has been discussed in chapter 5. Sites from the fifth millennium show a similar dominance of microliths, but apart from Rocher Moss South 2, all have numbers of other tools, and given the uncertainties around microlith function and impact of resharpening practises, the general picture is of very varied activities (Table 6.9). There is perhaps less evidence for more specialised activities than the Pennine sites discussed in the previous chapter, but there is some variation: Burins are frequent at March Hill Carr and South Haw, while scrapers are well-represented at Dunford Bridge B. The evidence for varied activities, taken in conjunction with the density of stone-built hearths and cooking pits at sites such as March Hill Carr, reinforces the suggestion that Pennine Final Mesolithic sites are something more than simple hunting camps.

Table 6.9 Essential tool frequencies for fifth millennium Pennine sites

Site	Microliths	Scrapers	Burins	Awls	Truncation
Scalene triangle sites					
Dan Clough 2	15	2	1	1	3
March Hill Carr	91	3	8	1	0
Rod sites					
Dunford Bridge B	19	6	2	0	2
March Hill Top	15	0	1	0	0
Rocher Moss 1	30	2	1	0	0
Rocher Moss South 2	35	0	0	0	0
South Haw RA1	42	2	5	1	0
South HawTP1	23	2	4	0	0

Late/Final Mesolithic sites have been traditionally considered to be smaller in size than Early Mesolithic examples. Both Petch and Buckley noted that 'there is seldom found an indefinite scattering of flint over a wide area' (Buckley 1921, 1924; Petch 1924), an observation confirmed by Mellars (1976a) While the Late Mesolithic scatter on Lominot appears small and localised, the March Hill Carr site appears rather different. March Hill Carr, though damaged by collectors and early excavations, could once have extended to 214 m² in area. Earlier digging activities make it difficult to discern the patterning of this activity beyond trench A, but the recovery of one or two cooking pits at Buckley's March Hill 2 site suggests the density of features continued. The series of hearths and the similarity of the radiocarbon dates from two of these features suggests that March Hill Carr saw fairly intensive use over a short period of time, perhaps a regular camping site, perhaps, given the presence of hazel wood but lack of hazelnuts recovered, one with a seasonal basis. A summer aggregation site is a possibility, and the presence of several cooking pits spread over a small area might indicate a place of feasts and celebrations.

Large spreads of Late Mesolithic material have also been noted on the North York Moors, often around springheads, for example, at Snilesworth Moor and Upleatham (Simmons 1996), though as these are undated it is unclear whether or not they represent a few, temporally clustered larger encampments or repeated, small-scale visits over millennia. Recent surveys have shown concentrations of small Late Mesolithic scatters in particular areas: Bransdale moor, the Farndale-Westerdale-Baysdale watershed, Glaisdale-Rosedale moors, West Bilsdale and Snilesworth moors (Waughman 2017). These may represent repeated return to particular places on a similar temporal scale to the Pennine sites.

Despite investment in cooking pits and stone-built hearths, evidence for additional structures amongst fifth millennium sites is slight. A single stakehole was noted in the very small trench at Lominot C (Spikins 2002). In the Northern Pennines, two features have been found at the two rod sites at South Haw (Chatterton 2006). The most extensive was in TP1, where an earth oven was found surrounded by an arc of stakeholes enclosing an area measuring around 2 m in diameter. A larger post-hole was located adjacent to the firepit, which was surrounded by dark sediment. The pit seems to have been reused and filled with debris from the occupation. At RA1, a shallow scoop measuring 2 by 1.4 m was found, which seemed to represent an occupation floor, though without associated posts or stakeholes.

The last hunters in the uplands

Little has thus far been said about the final site excavated by the West Yorkshire Mesolithic Project. This is March Hil Top (trench B), located just below the brow of the hill. Here, a small scatter of lithic material was recovered, surrounding a stone-built hearth that had two phases of use. Material cleared out from the hearth seems to have been dumped adjacent to it, rather than placed within a pit, as was often the custom at earlier sites. This evidence from the top of March Hill differs from that on March Hill Carr: The scatter is very small in size, most lithic material derives from only 2 m^2; it is made on translucent flint only, rather than the mix of flint and chert at trench A, and the only microliths represented are straight-backed bladelets, often known as 'rods'.

About 300 of these 'rod' sites are known in the north and are confined to the uplands of the Pennines and the North York Moors, though stray finds, probably representing composite tools, are known from the lowlands of Northern England (Jacobi 1978a; Switsur and Jacobi 1975). As Griffiths (2014) notes, the term 'rod' has been used very variably in Mesolithic studies. Jacobi used the term rod to describe any narrow-backed bladelet where the backing seemed designed to produce a straight edge; it was originally employed by Rankine to refer to a double-backed bladelet. However, others have used rod to mean any form of backed bladelet microlith, while others reserve the term to refer to steeply retouched single or double backed bladelets (the latter sometimes more akin to Jacobi's needle point; Preston 2012), which perhaps appear more characteristic of the Pennine Final Mesolithic sites. While traditionally associated with the very end of the Mesolithic, narrow straight-backed bladelets occur throughout assemblages traditionally defined as Late Mesolithic. They are present in the earliest of these, such as Filpoke Beacon, where they slightly outnumber scalenes, and in much later ones, such as the early fifth millennium BC assemblage from March Hill Carr, where scalenes are more dominant (Conneller 1999). A find of a composite tool composed only of backed bladelets from Seamer K in the Vale of Pickering has been radiocarbon dated to 7570–6805 cal BC (HAR-6498) (David 1998). Ellaby (1987) also makes a strong case that straight-backed bladelets were the dominant microlith type in Southeastern England around the same time. However, there are also a series of dated assemblages with steeply retouched straight-backed bladelets as the only microlith form present that date to the very end of the Mesolithic, at least in the Pennines, where they are associated with small sites at high altitudes and made entirely or predominantly on flint. The combination of these specifically rod-like microlith types, raw material differences, site size and upland location in the Pennines does provide greater confidence in assigning undated sites with these features to this distinct chronological phenomenon.

Several radiocarbon dates from the March Hill Top hearth indicate that it was in use between 4190 and 3970 cal BC (Griffiths 2011). Three other of these 'rod' sites have dates. From the Central Pennines are Dunford Bridge B at 4360–4000 cal BC (Q-799, 5380 ± 80 BP) and Rocher Moss South 2 at 4935–4460 (Q-1190, 5830 ± 100 BP). Both are on unidentified bulked wood so should be regarded as *termini post quos* for rod assemblages, while the date on charcoal from Rocher Moss South 2 does not come from a sealed context and thus may be particularly suspect (Jacobi 1994). Finally, in the Northern Pennines, South Haw in Nidderdale has radiocarbon dates from two separate hearths, both on birch charcoal, indicating occupation between 4230–3985 cal BC (Beta-189653, 5270 ± 40 BP) and 3945–3705 cal BC (Beta-189652, 5010 ± 40 BP) (Chatterton 2006; Griffiths 2014). These indicate rod sites in this region date to the very end of the Mesolithic, at a time when people pursuing Neolithic ways of life were already present in Britain (Griffiths 2014).

March Hill Top is microlith dominated (see Figure 1.5), though a burin and re-sharpening spalls are also present. Other rod sites show more variability (Table 6.9). At Dunford Bridge B, though microliths were most common, a relatively high frequency of scrapers and two burins were recorded. South Haw has 42 microliths but six burins, two scrapers and an awl (Chatterton 2006), while the small assemblage of Rocher Moss South 2 yielded only microliths (Stonehouse 1980). The March Hill Top scatter is small, only 9 m² in area. Rod sites in the Pennines tend to be small in size, with assemblages of less than 650 pieces; larger sites are present on the North York Moors, though these are undated (Jacobi 1975; Switsur and Jacobi 1975). Jacobi (1975) noted they tended to be found on the higher points of the Pennines, a finding recently confirmed by Preston (2012), who notes they are confined to the top 20% of the Central Pennine altitudinal range. The March Hill Top site is similar to Rocher Moss South 2, in its small area, dominance of microliths and high frequency of burnt material, which is likely in both cases to be the result of site/hearth maintenance activities. A feature of many rod sites is a focus on the production of relatively (for the Pennines) large blades. This has been noted at South Haw (Chatterton 2006), Rocher Moss South 2 (Stonehouse 1972), and in a group of rods accompanied by a group of blades measuring around 40 by 12 mm from Tintwistle site MST01 ACC, which may represent a cache (Garton 2017).

Chert is rare or absent at rod sites; instead, the dominant material is flint: Only five pieces of chert were recovered at March Hill Top (Conneller 1999); of the 42 rod microliths at South Haw RA1, only one was on chert, and all 25 from TP1 were on flint (Chatterton 2006). A translucent brown flint was used at March Hill Top and South Haw TP1, a grey opaque flint at Dunford Bridge B and a mottled grey flint at South Haw RA1. Both March Hill Top and the two rod sites at South Haw have low quantities of cortical flakes in comparison to the triangle dominated assemblages, indicating flint cores were brought in already partly reduced (Chatterton 2006; Conneller 1999). This, combined with the evidence for the production of large blades, may suggest changes in technological and transportation strategies in comparison to the triangle sites where Myers (1986) has argued that both flint and chert were brought in as unworked nodules. These changes may indicate shifts in mobility or may be the product of the emergence of new networks of exchange and obligation which guaranteed previous supplies.

There is evidence for disturbances in the local vegetation in the last centuries of the fifth millennium, suggesting that burning of the vegetation continued as a practise amongst groups using rod microliths. This can be seen at Soyland Moor, for example, where late burning is accompanied by the presence of cereal-type pollen dating to the 42nd or 41st centuries BC (Williams 1985). There is also very late Mesolithic evidence for burning at Rishworth Moor, where a hiatus in the charcoal record of around a century perhaps marks the end of the moor's use by Mesolithic groups, before the area was reoccupied during the Neolithic (Albert et al. 2021, 13).

Similar evidence is present on the North York Moors, where burning episodes dated to between the 42nd and 40th century cal BC have been recorded at Esklets, Bonfield Gill Head, North Gill and Bluewath Beck Head (Albert and Innes 2015; Innes et al. 2010). There are suggestions that small-scale disturbance episodes at Esklets were associated with the cultivation of barley, and cereal-type pollen has also been found associated with a sequence of this date at North Gill 1 A (Simmons and Innes 1996). A TPQ for oak charcoal of 4360–4250 cal BC (5449 ± 30 BP; SUERC-62297) from Esklets ECW2 is associated with a shallow cooking pit and a small knapping scatter focused on the working of small, partially worked cores and scalene microtriangles (Carter 2016). There have been suggestions that a rod microlith phase also existed on the North York Moors (Spratt 1982), though this has not been confirmed by radiocarbon dating, and inconsistency in the use of the term 'rods' and the persistent presence of backed bladelets throughout the Late Mesolithic mean this phase cannot yet be substantiated. Two sites at Esklets have been suggested to represent rod sites, site ECW6 and Hayes' Esklets site. These are both small assemblages whose only microliths are straight backed bladelets (ibid).

North Wales

Fifth millennium radiocarbon dates are relatively rare in North Wales, consisting often of determinations from isolated pits, as at Rough Close, Powys and Parc Bryn Cegin, Gwynedd. The only area that has seen more systematic investigation is Nant Hall, Prestatyn. Here, several small shell middens have been located, lying on the eastern side of what was then the estuary of the river Cwyd. To the south, the land rises steeply to the limestone of the Clwydian hills. At a time of higher sea-level, an estuary around 9 km wide was created, stretching from Abergele to Rhyl.

Excavations at Nant Hall were carried out in 1991 by CPAT in advance of development and identified three middens, with additional fieldwork carried out the following year in conjunction with University of Wales, Lampeter, during which two further middens were located (Figure 6.20). Two middens, composed primarily of cockles, were dated to the Early Neolithic, and two others (D and E), composed of mussels, were dated to the last few centuries of the Mesolithic (Bell 2007). This change in composition may reflect changing coastal morphology as a result of shifting sea-levels. Mussels are species of the rocky shore, while cockles are associated with sandy and muddy sediments.

Environmental evidence indicates that the vegetation near the mussel middens was woodland, possibly with small clearings. The middens themselves are close to the wetland edge, probably in an area of mixed deciduous woodland of oak, hazel and lime. Salt marsh lay beyond, with the spring tide highwater level around 45 m distant (ibid, 309).

The midden at site D was located on a palaeosol that itself contained charcoal and occasional worked flint, which has been dated to 4470–4050 cal BC (5470 ± 80 BP; CAR-1424). The midden was between 2 and 20 cm thick. Its full extent was not uncovered, but it measured 5 m from north to south and at least 5.5 m from east to west. It appeared to have been composed of several merging, smaller heaps of mussels and other shells (periwinkles, cockles and oyster), a few animal bones (red deer) and occasional lithics and burnt stone. Beach pebble flint was predominantly

Figure 6.20 Excavations at Nant Hall, Prestatyn (copyright Martin Bell)

used, a contrast to the reliance on chert at the earlier site of Prestatyn (Bryn Newydd) (see chapter 3). Charcoal from the midden itself dates to 4330–3950 cal BC (5270 ± 80 BP; CAR-1423).

The midden at site E was smaller, only 2 m by 3 m and 10–50 mm thick, and composed of mussels with occasional cockles, periwinkles and welks. Some animal bone was preserved, but only a single red deer antler was identifiable to species. Two dates, one on the lower part of the midden, the other on the upper part, indicate use in the second half of the fifth millennium BC, perhaps into the first part of the fourth. Two additional middens (F and G), both composed of mussels, and thus likely to be Mesolithic, were located but not excavated. Augering suggests F was less than 5 m in diameter, and G measured around 3 m by 1.5 m. The small size of the middens suggest these may have played a short-term, specialist role.

The Midlands

There are only three fifth millennium radiocarbon dates in the whole of the Midlands that might be reliably attributed to human activity, and as ever the nature of the Mesolithic in this region remains elusive. Two early fifth millennium dates on roe deer bones incorporated into the pre-barrow Neolithic midden may indicate Final Mesolithic activity at Ascott-under-Wychwood. A handful of left lateralised scalene triangles and backed bladelets might be compatible with this date: Four scalenes were found beneath the barrow, and two scalenes and two backed bladelets were recovered from the area of the Roman quarry around 10 m distant from these, which are likely to have moved down slope (Jacobi archive, British Museum). However, distinguishing the extent of Final Mesolithic activity on a site disturbed by Neolithic activity within an assemblage including Early Mesolithic types is difficult. The remaining radiocarbon date comes from a wooden stake from a palaeochannel at Manor Farm, Milton Keynes, an area where there are Late Mesolithic lithic scatters (Billington 2017).

Microlith typology may provide a few more candidates if symmetric micro-tranchets, like their asymmetric cousins, also belong to the fifth millennium, and if a late date for four-sided pieces can be confirmed. Over-Whiteacre Spring in Warwickshire, a site with extensive Honey Hill and possibly also Late Mesolithic occupation has yielded a handful of asymmetric micro-tranchets and four-sided types (Saville 1981a, Figure 6.9). Four-sided microliths are also present in the Sturge collection (BM) from Lakenheath (Jacobi 1984, Figure 4.15) indicating that this location – another noted long ago by Clark as a node of Mesolithic activity – remained a focus at the end of the period. Four-sided pieces are also present at Peacock's Farm, Shippea Hill (as are both asymmetric and symmetric micro-tranchets) (Clark et al. 1935), another place repeatedly revisited in the Mesolithic, as well as Lackford and Stow, Suffolk. Micro-tranchets are also known from several surface collections in the region. These have mainly an eastern distribution, with examples found at Risby Warren, Crosby Warren, Roxby, Salmonby, Manton Warren, West Keal and Belchford in Lincolnshire, New Fen at Lakenheath, Cavenham Heath, West Row Fen and Eriswell in Suffolk; but there are also finds in the west at Long Newnton and Syreford in Gloucestershire (Jacobi and Wessex Archaeology 2014).

The Thames and its tributaries

Fifth millennium evidence comes mainly from the west of the area, from the Colne and its tributaries and from the Kennet. Evidence for the use of the Lea is currently lacking, but there are two sites with microtranchets further north on the Essex river, the Blackwater (Jacobi and Wessex Archaeology 2014). To the south, asymmetric micro-tranchets are present at Orchard Hill, by the springs that form the head of the Wryse that flows into the Wandle, and a place repeatedly occupied in the Mesolithic. A stray antler beam mattock from Staines of fifth millennium date (Elliott 2012) could come from a Thames or Colne related context. On the Thames, evidence for continued, perhaps even intensified occupation, at Runnymede Bridge has been recorded, as a silt island formed that was less affected by flooding. Residual charcoal recovered from a ditch falls between 4835 and 4450 cal BC (5780 ± 85; OxA-3582). Three microliths, including a needle point and a scalene, were also recovered from the ditch. Five of the 25 microliths from the site are needle points. TL dates on two clusters of burnt flint probably also indicate late fifth millennium occupation (Needham 2000).

There is some evidence for continued occupation on the Colne. In 1971, around a kilometre to the west of Tolpits Lane B101 (see chapter 5), the partial remains of an aurochs were located by the Rickmansworth Historical Society in peaty deposits overlying Colne Terrace gravels. These consisted of lumbar vertebrae, part of the frontal and a left horn core, the base of which revealed cut-marks associated with skinning. This has a radiocarbon date that falls into the second half of the fifth millennium BC (4500–4260 cal BC at 1σ; 5540 ± 110 BP, BM-1676R) (Burleigh et al. 1982, 263).

The more significant fifth millennium sites lie in the upper reaches of the Colne's tributaries, following the Late Mesolithic pattern. Excavations at Misbourne Viaduct were small in scale, and undertaken in a short period prior to the building of the M25. This work yielded an important assemblage of lithics and animal bone beneath and within tufa. Microliths consisting of small scalenes and narrow-backed bladelets were associated with three radiocarbon measurements on samples from the two lowest layers, which date to the late sixth or early fifth millennium BC. An extremely varied faunal assemblage came from a small area, including aurochs, red deer, roe deer, pig, beaver, wild cat, otter and badger. Wood charcoal from the site included oak and ash (Farley 2010).

More detailed evidence is available from another small excavation, at Stratford's Yard, Chesham (Stainton 1989). At Chesham, several narrow valleys meet, and the waters of three chalk springs converge to form the river Chess. Near to the confluence of the most northerly of these, the Vale Stream, with the Chess, a dense spread of Mesolithic debris was located. Overlying floodplain alluvium are what may represent a buried soil containing the majority of the artefacts. Overlying this was around 60 cm of colluvium, containing material of a range of dates, from post-medieval to Mesolithic. Behind the site, the ground rises steeply to the east and the chalk scarp of the Chilterns. In addition to burying the site, erosion of the Upper Chalk down this slope would have provided flint nodules for the site's inhabitants.

The integrity of the possible buried soil is uncertain. Much of the later Prehistoric material (Neolithic flintwork and Iron Age pottery) present on the site derives from the colluvium, as does a substantial quantity of medieval and post-medieval pottery. However the majority of the small assemblage of highly fragmented Iron Age pottery comes from the uppermost 5 cm (context 4/X) of the potential buried soil sequence. Charred cereal grains are also found throughout the sequence. These have been suggested to be medieval in date, though would also be compatible with the Iron Age evidence. It may be that the buried soil was active until the Iron Age; however, a more likely scenario is that the context 4/X, thought to be in situ, is an older colluvial layer, burying the site. This uncertainty as to the nature of these sediments means that question marks remain over the reliability of a radiocarbon date on bulked bone from the site.

Fieldwork was undertaken by the Chess Valley Archaeological and Historical Society (CVAHS) in 1969 and 1982, who excavated two small trenches in advance of development. The 1969 trench measured 4 × 3 m; the 1982 test pit, located 2 m away from the earlier excavation, only 1 m². Service trenches for the development were also monitored and lithic material recovered (Stainton 1989). The area to the north of the site also underwent excavation in 1989, when substantial quantities of lithic material were recovered. While this is of mixed date, it includes an important Mesolithic component, including microlith types not represented in the CVAHS excavations. In all, it appears that a large and complex site is present, with occupation spanning the Middle to Final Mesolithic.

Examination of the microliths from the CVAHS excavations indicates that they fall broadly into two or perhaps three groups. The first consists of obliquely blunted points and part-backed points, curve-backed pieces, lanceolates and microliths with inverse retouch. These would be compatible with a Middle Mesolithic date and though lacking classic Honey Hill Points, are broadly comparable to assemblages from sites such as Asfordby (see chapter 3). This activity may be dated by two radiocarbon dates on burnt hazelnut shells from the lowest spits of the excavation that fall into the second quarter of the eighth millennium BC.

The larger group consists of small scalenes with three sides retouched, small crescents, symmetric microtranchets and asymmetric microtranchets (Figure 1.5). One of the latter has a lower concave truncation, which forms a tang that is covered on the inverse with invasive retouch. These highly distinctive types have been named 'Bexhill Points' (Champness et al. 2019). Microtranchets are diagnostic of the latest Mesolithic industries and, along with four sided points, were noted by Jacobi to belong to the last millennia of the Mesolithic (Jacobi 1978b, 19). A group of backed bladelets, most with a single retouched edge, may belong with them but could easily be earlier. A date of 5005–4505 cal BC (5890 ± 100; BM-2404) obtained for the site (Stainton 1989) was perhaps significant in Jacobi's suggestion of a late date for microtranchets and similar forms. However, this date may be problematic: It is on bulked bone from the lower part of the possible buried soil (context XII/V) that may have been sealed rather later than the Mesolithic. In its favour, the sample comes from a layer that has relatively little evidence for intrusive material and was made up from three bones from a single wild species (aurochs). The measurement is also compatible with new dates for similar lithic assemblages from Bexhill (Champness et al. 2019).

Though the small size of the CVAHS excavations precludes detailed understanding of the Mesolithic occupation at Stratford's Yard, it is clear that this is a large and complex site that was repeatedly reoccupied over the course of the Mesolithic. Features were also present: Four small pits or post-holes were recorded. The tools recovered indicate a variety of activities: Microlith production and re-tooling, tranchet axe use and resharpening and use of scrapers. A large assemblage was recovered, despite some material being lost. The new dating indicates processing of hazelnuts took place in the Middle Mesolithic, while processing of faunal remains – mostly aurochs, but also red deer, roe deer, pig, and possibly frog and birds – occurred, perhaps towards the end of the Mesolithic.

Continuity of occupation has also been noted on the Kennet. The large Mesolithic site of Wawcott III has amongst its wide range of Late Mesolithic types a small Final Mesolithic component of four-sided pieces and asymmetric microtranchets. A late radiocarbon date of 5345–4725 cal BC (6120 ± 134; BM-767) comes from bulked material from pit 2 (Froom 1976, 160). This measurement, though not without its uncertainties, is compatible with other dates for microtranchets and four-sided microliths. Pit 2 is a hollow that was only partially excavated as it extends into the section, though augering of the unexcavated area revealed it measured around 3.5 m × 1.5 m. Its morphology suggests it may represent a tree throw, albeit one that may have seen human use, as its base contained concentrations of burnt stone, charcoal and charred hazelnut shells.

A similar date has been obtained for Mesolithic activity, just 1200 m to the east at Wawcott XXIII (Froom 2012). This site is on the floodplain (Figure 6.21), close to a relict channel. Lithic material numbering just over 5000 pieces was recovered from the lower of two layers of organic sand-silt, sealed by a layer of marl or tufa. Particle-size analysis suggests this sand may be windblown and that occupation took place on a low

Figure 6.21 View across the floodplain at Wawcott

river dune, capping a gravel rise (Barnett et al. 2019). While a small Early or Middle Mesolithic component may be present, the majority of this assemblage is Late and Final Mesolithic. Microliths consist of scalene triangles with three sides retouched, micro-crescents and a handful of double-backed bladelets (Froom 2012, Figure 7.5). Several asymmetric micro tranchets indicate a Final Mesolithic component, and a date on charcoal from a small hearth of 5295–4730 cal BC (6079 ± 113; BM-2404) would be compatible with this element.

In addition to this hearth, spreads of charcoal and burnt stones were relatively common at the site. A single pit, 1 m in diameter, was located; this was infilled with silt containing flint, burnt stone and charcoal. Some faunal remains were present, though poorly preserved, and include aurochs, red deer and pig (all of the latter possibly from the same individual) (Carter 1975; Froom 2012). A single human tooth, a lower right incisor from an elderly individual, was also recovered (Froom 2012, 238–9). It is not known whether this was lost ante-mortem, and none of the bone from the site is dated. The lithic assemblage is dominated by microliths and microburins (Table 6.10). Scrapers are rare, with only two recovered. Burins and truncations are common, though some of the former appear to have served as bladelet cores. A large axe, possibly a roughout, was recovered, made from Dorset chert (Froom 2012).

At Wawcott I, occupation was located on a low gravel spur. A 6.5 × 5.5 m trench uncovered a sub-circular feature that may have originally been a tree throw, but subsequently underwent human modification. A pile of flint nodules from the

Table 6.10 Tools from final Mesolithic Kennet sites

Tool/tool spall	Wawcott I	Wawcott XXIII
Axe/pick	5	1
Axe flake	4	0
Burin	4	31
Burin spall	4	0
Microlith	51	58
Microburin	61	30
Micro-denticulate	1	0
Notch/denticulate	0	3
Scraper	5	2
Truncation	0	40
Retouch/utilised	55	present
Cores	72	76

underlying gravel close to the feature may suggest it was as a source of flint (gravel flint was the main source used at this site). Subsequently four post-holes were dug either side of the feature (three on the east, one on the west) and a hearth built in the depression, marked by burnt flint and charcoal. One piece of charcoal gave a radiocarbon date of 4350–3790 cal BC (5260 ± 130 BP; BM-449) (Froom 1971).

The toolkit at the site is characterised by microlith production debris and discarded microliths and utilised flakes and blades. A wide variety of other tools are also represented, albeit in small numbers (Table 6.10). Notable is the presence of seven axes, including an axe of black Portland chert recovered from initial fieldwalking of the site, and two resharpening flakes (Froom 1971). The microliths are dominated by four-sided pieces, suggesting most of the material belongs to a single occupation. If the four-sided microliths belong with this radiocarbon measurement, this would suggest a very late date for this type.

South of the rivers

Typological evidence for this period indicates continued occupation of favoured places. At Farnham, symmetric and asymmetric micro-tranchets suggest that occupation continued on a site that had been a persistent place for several millennia. Micro-tranchets are also present at both North Park Farm, Bletchingly and Puttenham Heath on the Lower Greensand, and at Roffey Holt, the well-known Horsham and Late Mesolithic site in the Ashdown forest. There are also fifth millennium dates for the Wealden rockshelters, though as these are based on bulked charcoal from sites with Neolithic evidence, they should be treated with some caution. Other sites with long histories in the region, such as Selmeston or Beedings Wood, show no visible evidence for fifth millennium activity.

The richest evidence for fifth millennium settlement comes from Combe Haven and the excavations in advance of the Bexhill relief road. Here, a large number of Final Mesolithic scatters are associated with Bexhill points and a range of other microliths (Champness et al. 2019). In common with the sites described above, Bexhill was a place that had been revisited for millennia, though the environment and geomorphology of the place changed considerably over this period. Following a period of intermittent marine incursions during the Late Mesolithic when the area was less frequently visited, in the fifth millennium the landscape became more stable. Peat began to develop in the lower reaches of the valleys in a landscape of alder carr, dissected by freshwater streams. Higher, drier ground was characterised by mixed lime/hazel/oak woodland, while ferns grew in clearings and on the woodland edge. Mesolithic occupation is concentrated on drier spurs and peninsulas extending from the valley margins into the wetlands, with the highest densities found on site 15, a spur sloping down towards a river channel (Champness et al. 2019).

Of the 210 lithic scatters located by the excavations, around 60% belong to the Late/ Final Mesolithic. Of these, dating and typochronological work indicate that the majority belong to the period 5200–4000 BC, with assemblages containing Bexhill points dating to between 5200 and 4200 BC (Champness et al. 2019). The area seems to have become more attractive as it became more stable and ceased to be subject to intermittent marine incursions, perhaps as a barrier developed, though the sea would still have been close. Most scatters are microlith dominated, though other formal tools were also found within most of them. Features associated with the scatters include hearths, stakeholes, pits and tree throws used for the deposition of lithic material. Depositionary practises seem to have focused on the debris from specific events rather than the generation of middens that accumulated over a long period of time (Champness et al. 2019). The full publication of this site will undoubtedly transform our understanding of this period and provide a nuanced history of the last Mesolithic groups and the transformations leading up to and encompassing the appearance of elements of the Neolithic package.

Beyond Bexhill, radiocarbon dates come mainly from pits. A late episode of pit-digging was located at Charlwood in Surrey, amongst what was an extensive lithic scatter, now truncated by the plough (Ellaby 2004). More than 21,000 lithics were recovered from the scatter, the densest part of which was centred on the area where the pits had been dug. Seven pits were excavated, which enclosed an area of 15 by 9 m. All were heavily truncated. Pit 1 survived best, to 32 cm depths and with a diameter of 2.24 m. All contained flint: Quantities of lithics in each feature range from 22 to 1088, with an average of 398. Given that these pits are all heavily truncated, they must have originally contained substantial quantities of material, which seem an unselective sample of on-site debris. The tools are dominated by microliths: Bexhill points (inversely retouched oblique microtranchets) and micro-scalenes. Burins and truncations are also represented; scrapers, as at the Wealden rockshelters, are rare. Microburins outnumber microliths, indicating a focus on retooling. Burnt flint is common, with up to 50% of the total flint in pit 3, and an average for all pits of 36%, though this is similar to that from the ploughsoil. Three pits contained burnt bone as well as flint. Larger pieces from pit 1 may represent roe deer. Three dates on bulked charcoal from the lowest fills of pit 1 returned inconsistent Late Mesolithic and Early Neolithic dates, which could indicate contamination or old wood effect. Given the lack of Neolithic evidence at the site, it is likely this pit belongs broadly to the fifth millennium BC.

The Southwest

There also appears continuity in the use of favoured locations in Southwest England, with several of the key seventh and sixth millennium sites discussed in the previous chapter showing evidence for fifth millennium activity. Faunal remains have been re-covered from several of these sites. Species diversity appears lessened, though the numbers involved are very small (Table 6.11). At Langley's Lane, a final Mesolithic phase, thought to date from this period, followed the cessation of tufa deposition. At this time, the tufa would have formed a low mound, into which were dug a large pit, two post-holes and six stakeholes. A layer of stones was spread across the edge of the tufa mound, where the white of the tufa and brown of adjacent sediments would have made a notable contrast. Within the layer of stones was a deposit of lithics and animal bones (Lewis et al. 2019). Radiocarbon evidence indicates occupation also continued at Blashenwell.

At Blick Mead, there may, if anything, be a greater intensity of use in the fifth millennium. In the lower lying trench 19, which was dense with animal bone and where the focus of radiocarbon dating efforts were concentrated, slightly more Final Mesolithic dates were obtained than those belonging to previous millennia (Jacques et al. 2018; see Table 6.12). There also appears evidence for Final Mesolithic activity on the dryland trench 24. Here, the lower fills of a possibly modified tree throw have two late fifth millennium dates, albeit on oak. There is also a late fifth millennium date on unidentified charcoal from a possible post-hole a few metres to the north, and a fourth date on oak charcoal from a layer described as loess within the same trench. An lithic assemblage of 808 pieces, including 20 microliths, two truncations, a notch and a piercer as well as several utilised flakes and blades, was recovered from the tree throw. The microliths are all micro-scalenes or backed bladelets, which would be compatible with these dates. A Final Mesolithic element also seems represented more generally amongst the lithic assemblage from the entire site, with the presence of both asymmetric micro-tranchets and four-sided pieces.

Less than 2 km from Blick Mead, an assemblage from a large pit known as the Coneybury Anomaly has been claimed as unique evidence for contact between Final Mesolithic and Neolithic groups. The faunal remains have been seen as the remains of a feast: The Neolithic groups providing cattle, Mesolithic groups roe deer (Gron et al. 2018). A Mesolithic input has been claimed on the basis that the lithics show Mesolithic traits, and a wild fauna component is rare in Early Neolithic assemblages;

Table 6.11 Fauna (MNE) from fifth millennium contexts in Southwest England

Site	Aurochs	Red deer
Blashenwell		P
Blick Mead (dated fifth millennium bones only)	P	P
Langley's Lane 1e (fifth millennium?)	4	

Table 6.12 Radiocarbon dates from Trench 19

Date	No of dates
Eighth millennium	1
Seventh millennium	2
Sixth millennium	3
Fifth millennium	4

yet, an assemblage focused on roe deer would also be unprecedented in local Late Mesolithic contexts. The species is rare at Blick Mead, with only eight examples out of 271 identified fragments. Further study of the lithic assemblage, which was not examined in this study but is suggested to be Mesolithic, would resolve this issue. If this assemblage derives from a Mesolithic tradition, it may reinforce hints of a fifth millennium interest in large pits and shafts in this region.

A feature more securely associated with Mesolithic activity is the Fir Tree Field Shaft, a solution pit 5 m wide. It has infilled with a chalk rubble, weathered from the sides, within which are several layers of soil, also slumped in from above, the lowest at 10 m deep (Allen and Green 1998). The soil layers frequently contained charcoal and burnt flint, a common feature of Mesolithic pit deposits (Blinkhorn et al. 2016). Two roe deer skeletons, one at 7 m deep, the other at 5.2 m, have been dated to the final centuries of the Mesolithic (Griffiths 2011). These have been seen as natural deaths of animals that fell into the shaft and were trapped; however, given the rarity of this species in Mesolithic faunal assemblages and the association of roe deer with the Coneybury anomaly, these could hint at practises of formal deposition. Further up the shaft, at the base of a weathering cone, a group of straight-backed bladelets, elements of a possible composite object, were recovered. The date of this has been modelled to 4160–3980 cal BC (Griffiths 2011, 233). In the layer above the microliths, Early Neolithic activity has been recorded. This took place 0–40 years (68% probability) after the microliths were left behind. Griffiths (2011, 296) has suggested the Fir Tree Field Shaft may also have been a place where groups with differing histories met in the years around 4000 BC. Further west in Devon at Little Dartmouth Farm, the large 1.5 m deep sixth millennium pit (see chapter 5) was recut for a final time in the early fifth millennium (Green et al. 2012).

Moving further west, the little evidence that can be associated with the fifth millennium also suggests landscape continuity. The exception may be the shell midden sites where, apart from Blashenwell, there are no fifth millennium dates, though the presence of four-sided microliths at Culverwell may suggest some late occupation. In the case of Westward Ho!, this is likely to be as a result of rapidly changing coastal geomorphology; by the fifth millennium, peat had started to grow over the midden. Elsewhere there is more continuity: In addition to the recut of the Little Dartmouth Farm Pit, there is a late fifth millennium date from Birdcombe, in Somerset.

Continuity is also seen in areas where the landscape was changing. On the Somerset Levels, an estuarine phase of mudflats and salt marshes between 5500 and 4500 cal BC was followed by a slowing of sea-level rise and the development of extensive areas of reedswamp (Bell et al. 2015). Recent work by Bell and colleagues has recovered traces of post-transgression Mesolithic occupation: A lithic scatter in the base of a peat dated to the last couple of centuries of the Mesolithic at Chedzoy and a backed bladelet associated with a landsurface post-dating the transgression but sealed by an Early Neolithic peat at Shapwick (Bell et al 2015). Plant macrofossils from late fifth millennium peat at Chedzoy are indicative of wetland fen, with lime-dominated deciduous woodland on the adjacent sandy island, while pollen from Shapwick indicates Late Mesolithic damp woodland growing in fen carr with expanses of reeds and sedge swamp. The evidence suggests similar small-scale use of the area to the Late Mesolithic, focused on fishing and fowling.

In Cornwall, probable Final Mesolithic microliths have been recovered from the Late Mesolithic site of Polowrian (Smith and Harris 1982, see chapter 5). A second site on the Lizard, Windmill Farm, has seven radiocarbon dates spanning the fifth millennium, as well as two dates showing evidence for earlier occupation at the start of the sixth millennium (Smith in press). The site located on flat ground by a stream, just before it dips into a boggy valley that leads down to the sea. Ploughing in 1982 uncovered lithic material that appeared to represent the edge of a scatter that continued to the west and north into an adjacent unploughed area. Following fieldwalking of the ploughzone, which suggested the presence of two separate scatters, a 10 × 11 m trench was excavated by the Central Excavation Unit and the Cornwall Archaeological Society in the area immediately to the north.

The excavations located a significant site with an assemblage of nearly 80,000 lithic artefacts and a rich assemblage of coarse stone tools (Smith 1984; Smith in press). A number of small, shallow hollows contained fragments of oak charcoal, charred hazelnut shells and small pebbles c.10 mm in diameter. These latter have been suggested perhaps to be gastroliths from the stomachs of seals (following Jones et al. 2019). Tasks at the site seem focused on microlith production. One thousand five hundred ninety-two microburins and 968 microliths were recovered, despite only a sample of the excavated sediments being sieved. Beyond microliths, the denticulate scrapers, characteristic of the Mesolithic of the region, are also common with 246 recovered. Other tools, such as scrapers and notches, are present in smaller numbers. Bevel-ended and other coarse stone tools, with macrowear suggesting a variety of different functions, are well-represented. Unused examples are common, suggesting they may have been collected and cached for future use at the site. Microliths are mainly focused in the southwest of the main trench, surrounding two of the hollows. Denticulate scrapers and coarse stone tools are spread more evenly throughout the site (Smith in press). Proportions of tertiary bladelets are higher in the north of the site, and microburins are also most common here, suggesting this is an area to which bladelet blanks were imported for microlith production.

South Wales

At Goldcliff, intermittent occupation continued, though environments were changing. There are fifth millennium dates for site J, a site lacking earlier radiocarbon dates, though on stratigraphic grounds occupation here probably also extended back into the sixth millennium. Site J is on the edge of Goldcliff island and the highest of the sites investigated, at 1.5 m asl (Bell 2007). It was also the most extensively investigated with 64 m² excavated. It lay in an area of hazel woodland, probably close to a spring. Charcoal indicates that oak, elm, ash, blackthorn, elder and ivy were also present nearby. The site was rich in lithics and animal bone, and five distinct clusters of material were located within the buried soil horizon. Of these, the central cluster B is the most substantial and displays a sharp fall-off in material, which may be the result of a tent wall. This structure would be about 3 m in diameter and was not associated with stakeholes or any other structural evidence. As for the Star Carr hut, larger material seems to have been pushed to the edges of the structure. Large quantities of lithics were present, including 28 cores and core fragments, a microlith and 19 other tools – scrapers, notches, denticulates and retouched pieces. Microwear suggests butchery and craftwork with scraping of siliceous plants. Very little microdebitage was present. perhaps suggesting knapping stations were located elsewhere, and scatter B represents an area of tool use and caching. Animal bone, often calcinated and mostly consisting of deer remains, is present within the putative structure as are a number of enigmatic wooden artefacts. A boar's tusk was found on the edge of scatter B, which could represent a formal deposit (Bell 2007, 79).

Other scatters are more diffuse. Microliths are associated with scatter A, to the west of the structure. Three of these are remarkably similar scalene triangles, which may represent a composite tool; one of these has traces of butchery, suggesting they may have been hafted as a knife. Scatter A is also associated with animal processing and cooking activities, indicated by faunal remains and clusters of burnt stones. The latter may have been obtained from the Usk or the Ebbw, a journey, probably by canoe, given their weight of 5–10 kg. A probable tree throw was located in area A whose fill contained flint along with bones red deer, pig and aurochs, and may have been used as a midden. The different species representation between scatters A and B may suggest separate occupation episodes, though a cluster of animal bones in the northernmost scatter (E) is similar to area A. A small cluster of fish bones was associated with knapping debris in the eastern scatter C. The evidence gives the impression of repeated small-scale occupation.

Two dates are available on wooden artefacts from site J, one on the edge of scatter B, the other from scatter C, suggesting one or more of these visits dates to between 4940–4710 cal BC, though it is likely that this is just one of several Late Mesolithic visits to the site. In the late sixth and early fifth millennium, site J would have been on the margins of the estuary, whose silts cover the lower part of this site; tidal influences appear to have reached it around 4700 cal BC. Silt input is present in the upper layers of the buried soil, and there are episodes of peat growth in the silts, indicating fluctuation between marine input and periods of stabilisation. Smaller quantities of lithics, including retouched pieces, some deer bones and a 1.16 m long piece of worked oak, which may represent a spear or a digging stick were found in the estuarine silts, indicative of continued activity during the fifth millennium in this environment for specific tasks, perhaps in the context of more substantial occupation of the adjacent dryland zone. For many centuries, this site would have been at the margins of the fluctuating waters of the estuary, and as a place of dryland in close proximity to wetland environments, may have been favoured for short stays, some of which, seasonality evidence suggests, took place in spring or early summer.

Around 4800 cal BC, estuarine sedimentation ceased at Goldcliff as the waters regressed. As surfaces stabilised, peat began to develop across the lower lying areas of the landscape, though episodes of marine inundation continued to occur within its lowest lying levels, and areas of salt marsh persisted. Initially, reeds grew on the peat surface, with areas of tall-herb fen developing, where sedges, hemp agrimony and nettles grew. Aquatics, such as pondweed, indicate pools. This wetland vegetation seems to have been regularly burnt, indicated by large quantities of charcoal. At site J on the drier ground, reedswamp was succeeded by alder and willow carr and finally at the end of the Mesolithic by mixed deciduous woodland (Figure 6.22). The marine regression and peat development saw a marked reduction in human activity. While charcoal has been found at high levels in the reed peat, there is very little associated with alder carr and subsequent developments. A handful of flints, a couple of pieces of worked wood and some charcoal fragments are known from these later levels at site J, and there is similar ephemeral evidence to the west of the island for occupation at this time. However, there is none of the debris typical of the short-term campsites that characterise sites on the flanks of the island in the

Figure 6.22 Tree stump in the peat of the upper submgered forest (copyright Martin Bell)

sixth and early fifth millennium; by the end of the Mesolithic, the role this place played seems to have changed.

Elsewhere in Wales, there is more evidence for continuity. In the uplands, at Waun Fignen Felen, the discovery of an asymmetric micro-tranchet indicates continued ephemeral use of the uplands during the Final Mesolithic, while similar examples are known from upland areas at Nant Melyn, west of Aberdare and Mynydd Blaenrhondda, just south of Craig-y-Llyn (Barton et al. 1995). On the upland plateau on the other side of the Rhondda valley and close to a stream is a remarkable carved oak post from Maerdy wind farm (Figure 6.23). Radiocarbon dating of sapwood suggests this object belongs to the last two centuries of the fifth millennium. The timber measures 1.7 m in length and 0.26 m in width, with one side lost through degradation. The post seems to be rounded at one end and possibly tapered at the other. The intact edge shows a length of chevron patterning and above this a concentric diamond, which has been interpreted as a possible eye (the other side of the post where a second eye might have been located has been lost). While natural causes for this patterning have been explored, it has been determined more likely to be the product of human action. The post may have originally stood up as a marker, or have been

(a)

(b)

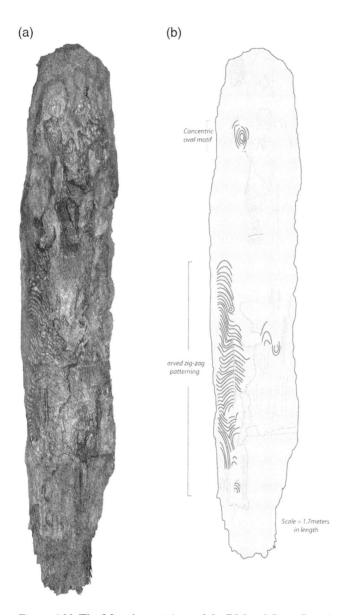

Concentric
oval motif

arved zig-zag
patterning

Scale = 1.7meters
in length

Figure 6.23 The Maerdy post (copyright Richard Scott Jones)

deposited in the bog (Scott Jones 2018). If the concentric diamond does indeed re-present an eye, this and the length of the post might suggest this represents a person. It can perhaps be compared to the Shirgir idol (Lillie et al. 2005; Zhilin et al. 2018), an Early Holocene wooden post from Russia, several metres long, with a carved head and geometric designs on the body. There may also be connections with other British Mesolithic contexts, where wooden posts may have been erected, at Stonehenge, and Bryn Celli Ddu (see chapters 4 and 5). One difference from these earlier examples is the species involved, with a move to oak from earlier use of pine. If the life histories of the trees used to form these posts was significant, this may suggest a shift in the importance of particular tree species, as indeed we see the significant of particular animal species changing across the period.

Continuity between Late and Final Mesolithic is also evinced in the areas of dense activity in Pembrokeshire (see chapter 5). There is a noticeable presence of small numbers of asymmetric micro-tranchet types on sites that also have evidence for Late Mesolithic occupation (see chapter 5). A single microtranchet has been recovered at The Nab Head, showing that this site with its long history continued to be visited (David 2007). Several examples have been found at Penpant, Solva, which lies on a south-facing slope close to springs at the head of a small valley cut by a stream that runs into St Bride's Bay (David 2020). Cwm Bach I, another site with micro-tranchets, is in a very similar environmental situation. Other examples are known from Pointzcastle, where Mesolithic material clusters around springs in a narrow valley (David 2007). There are also examples from inland locations, such as Cutty Bridge on the Western Cleddau river (David and Painter 2014) (Box 6.6).

Box 6.6   The last pig

The only dated evidence for the Final Mesolithic in Pembrokeshire comes from Lydstep. Here, the remains of a pig, associated with narrow-backed bladelets was located in intertidal peats by Leach following a storm in 1917 (Leach 1918). The peats seem to have formed in shallow lagoons behind barriers, such as storm beaches (Murphy et al. 2014), and pollen evidence suggests the area where the pig was found was alder carr with areas of reed and sedge swamp towards dryland. The pig has been directly dated to 4345–3950 cal BC (5300 ± 100; OxA-1412). The relatively small size of the pig has been the basis of a suggestion that this was a domesticated animal rustled from the earliest Neolithic groups in the region (Lewis 1992).

The pig is presumed to have escaped its hunters but died of blood loss (Jacobi 1980a). Chatterton (2005) has by contrast suggested this may represent an episode of formal deposition, with the pig laid in a small pool, weighed down with a tree trunk. This may be worth considering given the lack of representation of pig amongst footprints recently discovered at Lydstep, as well as at more distant, but more thoroughly researched intertidal wetland areas such as Goldcliff. Charcoal and burnt flints had been discovered in the same layer by Leach, only c.23 m from the pig, while in 2010 human and animal footprints were exposed and evidence of burning of the vegetation has also been noted in environmental profiles (Murphy et al. 2014). This perhaps suggests that the pig can be put in the context of a reasonable level of human activity in the wetland. This increases the possibility that its deposition is the product of human action, though whether it tells us about the nature of relations between Mesolithic and Neolithic groups remains to be seen. If this pig is the result of an act of formal deposition, this event, at the very end of the Mesolithic, is a curious echo of one right at the start: The deposition of a composite red deer at Star Carr (chapter 2). While much has changed over 5300 years, some concerns perhaps united the first and last Mesolithic people.

Neolithic epilogue

In many accounts of the transition, the Mesolithic only seems to exist as a foil for the sort of Neolithic that various archaeologists have imagined; an account in which the Mesolithic is reduced to a 'reasonable paragraph' (Achebe 1958). The paucity of radiocarbon dates and typochronologies has meant that an unchanging Mesolithic is presented, with a few key sites combined to produce a narrative of an unchanging way of life that lasted millennia.

The current narrative of the transition, funnelled through recent aDNA research (Brace et al. 2019), falls into this familiar pattern. Yet, the DNA analysis includes a single fifth millennium individual (from Oronsay). While this individual shows Western Hunter-Gatherer (WHG) ancestry only, sequencing of two 'Neolithic' individuals from Western Scotland indicated a WHG ancestor within four generations. These were individuals from Raschoille Cave, who were buried in a Mesolithic shell midden. It can be no coincidence that more complex processes are evident in the only region where there is coverage on a more appropriate temporal scale. Elsewhere in Britain, nothing is known of the genetic histories of fifth millennium individuals and when groups with particular lineages reached Britain. Brace and colleagues (2019) noted greater WHG ancestry amongst Neolithic individuals from Southeast England. This could reflect longer histories of continental connections in this region, and it may be that the genetic makeup of fourth millennium individuals sequenced reflects fifth millennium connections between Britain and the Continent (Lawrence et al. in press).

The Mesolithic was hugely diverse, but above all it had a history. The early pioneers had different concerns from the people of the hazelnut-loving Mesolithic house horizon and the southwestern groups who camped by colourful waters. Rather than continuing to pursue a lifestyle that had lasted millennia, in the fifth millennium, times were continuing to change. Some people were caught up in a Northwest European network of marine voyaging: Continental trapezes and transverse arrowheads were reimagined in an insular context; T- antler axes, a continental tool, were made in Scotland; cereals may have been grown in the Pennine uplands and in places, ostentatious versions of familiar things – middens, pits and posts – were made. Only when this geographical diversity, and historical complexity, is taken into consideration, and the fact that there were many different Final Mesolithics acknowledged, can the significance of the changes at the start of fourth millennium be adequately understood.

References

Achebe, C. 1958. *Things fall apart*. London: Heinemann.

Affleck, T., Edwards, K. and Clarke, A. 1988. Archaeological and palynological studies at the Mesolithic pitchstone and flint site of Auchareoch, Isle of Arran. *Proceedings of the Society of Antiquaries of Scotland* 118, 37–59.

Albert, B.M. and Innes, J. 2015. Multi-profile fine-resolution palynological and micro-charcoal analyses at Esklets, North York Moors, UK, with special reference to the Mesolithic-Neolithic transition. *Vegetational History and Archaeobotany* 24(3), 357–375.

Albert, B.M. and Innes, J.B. 2020. On the distinction of pollen grains ofearly varieties of Hordeum from Glyceria species: Addressing the early cereal cultivation problem in palynology. *Palynology* 44(2), 369–381.

Albert, B.M., Innes, J.B. and Blackford, J.J. 2021. Multi-profile fine-resolution palynology of Late Mesolithic to Bronze Age peat at Cat Stones, Rishworth Moor, Central Pennines, UK. *The Holocene* 31(3), 483–501

Aldhouse-Green, S. 2000. *Paviland Cave and the 'Red Lady': a definitive report*. Bristol: Western Academic & Specialist Press Ltd.

Aldhouse-Green, S.H.R. and Housley, R.A. 1993. The Uskmouth antler mattock: A radio-carbon date. *Archaeologia Cambrensis* 142, 340.

Aldhouse-Green, S., Pettitt, P. and Stringer, C. 1996. Holocene humans at Pontnewydd and Cae Gronw caves. *Antiquity* 70(268), 444–447.

Alexander, D. 1997. Excavation of a Mesolithic pit and a pit containing decorated Neolithic pottery at Spurryhillock, Newhaven. *Proceedings of the Society of Antiquaries of Scotland* 127, 17–27.

Allen, M.J. 1995. Chapter 4. Before stonehenge. In R.M.J. Cleal, K.E. Walker and R. Montague (eds.), *Stonehenge in its landscape: Twentieth century excavations*, pp. 41–42. London: English Heritage Archaeological Report 10.

Allen, M.J. and Gardiner, J. (eds.). 2000. *Our changing coast: A survey of the intertidal archaeology of Langstone Harbour, Hampshire*. London: Council for British Archaeology Research Report 124.

Allen, M.J. and Gardiner, J. 2002. A sense of time: Cultural markers in the Mesolithic of southern England. In B. David and M. Wilson (eds.), *Inscribed landscapes: Making and marking place*, pp. 139–153. Honolulu: University of Hawai'i Press.

Allen, M.J. and Green, M. 1998. The Fir Tree Field shaft: The date and archaeological and palaeo-environmental potential of a chalk swallowhole feature. *Proceedings of the Dorset Natural History and Archaeological Society* 120, 25–37.

Allen, M.J., Maxted, A. and Carter, R. 2008. A new Mesolithic for the Weald? Recent investigations at Chiddingly Wood Rocks. *Sussex Past and Present* 115, 4–5.

Alley, R.B. and Agustsdottir, A.M. 2005. The 8 k event: Cause and consequences of a major Holocene abrupt climate change. *Quaternary Science Reviews* 24(10–11), 1123–1149.

Alley, R.B., Mayewski, P.A., Sowers, T., Stuiver, M., Taylor, K.C. and Clark, P.U. 1997. Holocene climate instability: A prominent widespread event 8200 year ago. *Geology* 25, 483–486.

Andersen, S.H. 1985. Tybrind Vig: A preliminary report on a submerged Ertebølle settlement on the west coast of Fyn. *Journal of Danish Archaeology* 4(1), 52–69.

Anderson, J. 1898. Notes on the contents of a small cave or rock shelter at Druimvargie, Oban; and of three shell mounds on Oronsay. *Proceedings of the Society of Antiquaries of Scotland* 32, 298–313.

Anderson-Whymark, H. and Durden, T. 2013. The Mesolithic/Early Neolithic assemblage from area 3. In T.G. Allen, A. Barclay, A.M. Cromarty, H. Anderson-Whymark, A. Parker, M. Robinson and G. Jones (eds.), *Opening the wood, making the land: The archaeology of a Middle Thames landscape*, pp. 80–83. Oxford Archaeology: Thames Valley Landscape Monographs 38.

Anderson-Whymark, H., Garrow, D. and Sturt, F. 2015. Microliths and maritime mobility: A continental European-style Late Mesolithic flint assemblage from the Isles of Scilly. *Antiquity* 89(346), 954–971.

Andresen, J.M., Byrd, B.F., Elson, M.D., McGuire, R.H., Mendoza, R.G., Staski, E. and White, J.P. 1981. The deer hunters: Star Carr reconsidered. *World Archaeology* 13, 31–46.

Anon. 1797. *Sporting Magazine* 9, 283.

Anon. 1805. *Gentleman's Magazine* LIX, 1789.

ApSimon, A.M., Smart, P.L., Macphail, R., Scott, K. and Taylor, H. 1992. King Arthur's Cave, Whitchurch, Herefordshire: Reassessment of a Middle and Upper Palaeolithic, Mesolithic and Beaker site. *Proceedings of the University of Bristol Spelaeological Society* 19(2), 183–249.

Arkell, W.J. 1947. *The geology of the country around Weymouth, Swanage, Corfe & Lulworth*. London: HM Stationery Office.

Armstrong, A.L. 1922. Two East Yorkshire bone harpoons. *Man* 22, 130–131.

Armstrong, A.L. 1923. Further evidences of Maglemose culture in East Yorkshire. *Man* 23, 135–138.

Ashmore, P. 2004. A date list (to October 2002) for early foragers in Scotland. In A. Saville (ed.), *Mesolithic Scotland and its neighbours*, pp. 95–157. Edinburgh: Society of Antiquaries of Scotland.

Ashmore, P.J. and Hall, D. 1996. Shell midden at Braehead, Alloa. *Forth Naturalist and Historian* 20, 123–130.

Atkinson J.A. 2016. Ben Lawers: An archaeological landscape in time. Results from the Ben Lawers Historic Landscape Project, 1996–2005. *Scottish Archaeological Internet Reports* 62.

Atkinson, J., Banks, I. and Pollard, T. 1993. Risga (Ardnamurchan parish): Shell midden. *Discovery and Excavation in Scotland* 45.

Austin, P. 2009. The wood charcoal macro-remains from Mesolithic midden deposits at Sand, Applecross. *Scottish Archaeological Internet Reports* 31, 409–419. http://soas.is.ed.ac.uk/index.php/sair/article/view/2085.

Bagwell, M., Bishop, B. and Gibson, A. 2001. Mesolithic and Late Bronze Age activity at London Road, Beddington. *Surrey Archaeological Collections* 88, 289–307.

Balaam, N.D., Levitan, B. and Straker, V. (eds.). 1987. *Studies in palaeoeconomy and environment in South West England*. Oxford: British Archaeological Reports, British Series 181.

Ballin, T.B. 2009. *Archaeological pitchstone in Northern Britain. Characterization and interpretation of an important prehistoric source*. Oxford: British Archaeological Reports, British Series 476.

Ballin, T.B. 2018. The procurement of Rhum bloodstone and the Rhum bloodstone exchange network – a social territory in the Scottish Inner Hebrides? *Archäologische Informationen* 41, 241–254.

Ballin, T.B. and Barrowman, C. 2015. The chert assemblage from Garvald Burn, Scottish Borders. Archaeology Reports Online 15. https://www.archaeologyreportsonline.com/PDF/ARO15_Garvald_burn.pdf. Accessed 6/7/2018.

Ballin, T.B. and Ellis, C. 2019. An undisturbed Early Mesolithic retooling station at Donich Park, Lochgoilhead, Argyll, Scotland–right-handed and left-handed knappers. *Archäologische Informationen* 42, 195–218.

Ballin, T.B., Ellis, C. and Baillie, W. 2018. Arran pitchstone – different forms of exchange at different times? *CIfA Scottish Group Newsletter* Spring, 2018.

Ballin, T. and Faithfull, J. 2009. Gazetteer of Arran Pitchstone Sources presentation of exposed pitchstone dykes and sills across the Isle of Arran, and discussion of the archaeological relevance of these outcrops. Scottish Archaeological Internet Reports 38. http://journals.socantscot.org/index.php/sair/issue/view/63

Ballin, T.B., White, R., Richardson, P. and Neighbour, T. 2015. An early Mesolithic stone tool assemblage from Clachan Harbour, Raasay, Scottish Hebrides. *Lithics* 31, 94–104.

Banks, I. and Pollard, T. 1998. Risga (Ardmamurchan parish): Mesolithic shell midden; prehistoric occupation site. *Discovery and Excavation in Scotland* 46.

Barber, B., Halsey, C., Lewcun, M. and Philpotts, C. 2015. *The evolution and exploration of the Avon flood plain at Bath and the development of the southern suburb. Excavations at Southgate, Bath, 2006–9.* London: Museum of London Archaeology Monograph 68.

Barham, L.S., Priestly, P. and Targett, A.P. 1999. *In search of Cheddar Man*. Stroud: Tempus.

Barlow, C., and Mithen, S. 2000. The experimental use of elongated pebble tools. In S. Mithen, (ed.), *Hunter-gatherer landscape archaeology: the Southern Hebrides Mesolithic project 1988–1998*, 513–522. Cambridge: McDonald Institute Monographs.

Barnett, C. 2009. The chronology of Early Mesolithic occupation and environmental impact at Thatcham Reedbeds, Southern England. In P. Crombe, M. Van Strydonck, M. Boudin and M. Bats (eds.), *Chronology and evolution within the Mesolithic of North-West Europe*, pp. 57–76. Cambridge: Cambridge Scholars Publishing Cambridge.

Barnett, C., Bell, M. and Grant, M. 2019. Tracing their steps: Predictive mapping of upper Palaeolithic and Mesolithic archaeology. Historic England Research Report 87. https://research.historicengland.org.uk/Results.aspx?p=1&n=10&t=tracing&ns=1

Barrington, N. and Stanton, W. 1972. *Mendip: The complete caves and a view of the hills.* Cheddar: Cheddar Valley Press.

Bartley, D.D. 1975. Pollen analytical evidence for prehistoric forest clearance in the upland area west of Rishworth, W. Yorkshire. *New Phytologist* 74(2), 375–381.

Barton, N.J. 1962. *The lost rivers of London: A study of their effects upon London and Londoners, and the effects of London and Londoners upon them.* London: Phoenix House.

Barton, R.N.E. 1992. *Hengistbury Head, Dorset: The late upper palaeolithic and early mesolithic sites.* Oxford: Oxford University Committee for Archaeology.

Barton, R.N.E., Berridge, P.J., Walker, M.J. and Bevins, R.E. 1995. Persistent places in the Mesolithic landscape: An example from the Black Mountain uplands of South Wales. *Proceedings of the Prehistoric Society* 61, 81–116.

Barton, R.N.E. 1997. Fifth interim report on the survey and excavations in the Wye Valley, 1997 and new AMS Radiocarbon dating results from Madawg Rockshelter. *Proceedings of the University of Bristol Spelaeological Society* 21(1), 99–108.

Barton, R.N.E. and Roberts, A. 2004. The Mesolithic period in England: Current perspectives and new research. In A. Saville (ed.), *Mesolithic Scotland and its neighbours*, pp. 339–359. Edinburgh: Society of Antiquaries of Scotland.

Barton, R.N.E. and Roberts, A.J. 2015. Marine shell beads from three inland Later Mesolithic sites in western Britain. In N. Aston and C. Harris (eds.), *No stone unturned: Papers in honour of Roger Jacobi*, pp. 191–220. London: Lithic Studies Society Occasional Paper 9.

Bates, M.R., Nayling, N., Bates, R., Dawson, S., Huws, D. and Wickham-Jones, C. 2013. A multi-disciplinary approach to the archaeological investigation of a bedrock-dominated shallow-marine landscape: An example from the Bay of Firth, Orkney, UK. *International Journal of Nautical Archaeology* 42(1), 24–43.

Bates, M. and Stafford, E. 2013. *Thames Holocene: A geoarchaeological approach to the investigation of the river floodplain for High Speed 1, 1994–2003*. Oxford: Wessex Archaeology.

Bayliss, A., Boomer, I., Bronk Ramsey, C., Hamilton, D. and Waddington, C. 2007. Absolute dating. In C. Waddington (ed.), *Mesolithic settlement in the North Sea basin: A case study from Howick, north-east England*, pp. 75–109. Oxford: Oxbow Books.

Bayliss, A., Hedges, R., Otlet, R., Switsur, R. and Walker, J. 2012. *Radiocarbon dates: From samples funded by English heritage between 1981 and 1988*. Swindon: English Heritage.

Bayliss, A., Taylor, B., Bronk Ramsey, C., Dunbar, E., Kromer, B., Bamforth, M., Conneller, C., Elliott, B., Knight, B. and Milner, N. 2018. Dating the archaeology and environment of the Star Carr embayment. In N. Milner, C. Conneller and B. Taylor (eds.), *Star Carr volume 2. Studies in technology, subsistence and environment*, pp. 33–112. York: White Rose University Press.

Bayliss, A. and Woodman, P. 2009. A new Bayesian chronology for Mesolithic occupation at Mount Sandel, Northern Ireland. *Proceedings of the Prehistoric Society* 75, 101–123.

Bell, M. 2007. *Prehistoric coastal communities: The Mesolithic in western Britain*. York: Council for British Archaeology Research Report 149.

Bell, M., Brunning, R., Batchelor, R., Hill, T. and Wilkinson, K. 2015. The Mesolithic of the wetland/dryland edge in the Somerset Levels. Historic England Report 6624. https://research.historicengland.org.uk/Report.aspx?i=15855

Bell, M., Caseldine, A. and Neumann, H. 2000. *Prehistoric intertidal archaeology in the Welsh Severn Estuary*. York: Council for British Archaeology Research report 120.

Bello, S.M., Saladié, P., Cáceres, I., Rodríguez-Hidalgo, A. and Parfitt, S. A. 2015. Upper Palaeolithic ritualistic cannibalism at Gough's Cave (Somerset, UK): The human remains from head to toe. *Journal of Human Evolution* 82, 170–189.

Bennett, K.D. 1986. The rate of spread and population increase of forest trees during the postglacial. *Philosophical Transactions of the Royal Society of London. B, Biological Sciences* 314(1167), 523–531.

Bennett, K.D. 1988. Holocene pollen stratigraphy of central East Anglia, England, and comparison of pollen zones across the British Isles. *New Phytologist* 109(2), 237–253.

Bennett, K.D. 1989. A provisional map of forest types for the British Isles 5000 years ago. *Journal of Quaternary Science* 4, 141–144.

Bennett, K.D. 1996. Late-Quaternary vegetation dynamics of the Cairngorms. *Botanical Journal of Scotland* 48, 51–63.

Bennett, K.D., Simonson, W.D. and Peglar, S.M. 1990. Fire and man in post-glacial woodlands of eastern England. *Journal of Archaeological Science* 17(6), 635–642.

Berridge, P. 1985. Mesolithic sites in the Yarty Valley. *Proceedings of the Devon Archaeological Society* 43, 1–21.

Berridge, P. and Roberts, A. 1986. The Mesolithic period in Cornwall. *Cornish Archaeology*, 25, 7–34.

Berridge, P. and Roberts, A. 1994. The Mesolithic decorated and other pebble artefacts. In H. Quinnell and M.R. Blockley (eds.), *Excavations at Rhuddlan, Clwyd: 1969–73 mesolithic to medieval*, pp. 105–114. London: Council for British Archaeology Research Report 95.

Berridge, P. 1994. The lithics. In H. Quinnell and M.R. Blockley (eds.), *Excavations at Rhuddlan, Clwyd: 1969–73 mesolithic to medieval*, pp. 95–104. London: Council for British Archaeology Research Report 95.

Best, J. and Mulville, J. 2016. Birds from the water: Reconstructing avian resource use and contribution to diet in prehistoric Scottish island environments. *Journal of Archaeological Science: Reports* 6, 654–664.

Bicho, N., Cascalheira, J., Marreiros, J. and Pereira, T. 2011. The 2008–2010 excavations of Cabeço da Amoreira, Muge, Portugal. *Mesolithic Miscellany*, 21(2), 3–13.

Billington, L.P. 2017. *Lithic scatters and landscape occupation in the late upper palaeolithic and mesolithic: A case study from Eastern England.* Unpublished PhD Dissertation, The University of Manchester.

Binford, L.R. 1978a. *Nunamiut: Ethnoarchaeology.* New York: Academic Press.

Binford, L.R. 1978b. Dimensional analysis of behavior and site structure: Learning from an Eskimo Hunting Stand. *American Antiquity* 43, 330–361.

Binford, L.R. 1980. Willow smoke and dogs' tails: Hunter-gatherer settlement systems and archaeological site formation. *American Antiquity* 44, 1–17.

Birks, H.J. 1989. Holocene isochrone maps and patterns of tree-spreading in the British Isles. *Journal of Biogeography* 16(6), 503–540.

Bishop, J.H. 1914. An Oransay shell-mound – a Scottish pre-Neolithic site. *Proceedings of the Society of Antiquaries of Scotland* 48, 52–108.

Birks, H. J. B. 1982. Holocene (Flandrian) chronostratigraphy of the British Isles: a review. *Striae* 16, 99–105.

Bishop, B. 2002. Late prehistoric and Roman Brentford: Evolution of an agricultural landscape. *London Archaeologist* 10, 7–12.

Bishop, B. 2008. A microlithic industry from Woodbridge Road, Guildford. *Surrey Archaeological Collections* 94, 125–157.

Bishop, R.R., Church, M.J. and Nesbitt, C. 2012. Archaeological investigations at Northton, Harris, Western Isles, 2011. http://dro.dur.ac.uk/19349/1/19349.pdf.

Bishop, R., Church, M. and Rowley-Conwy, P. 2013. Seeds, fruits and nuts in the Scottish Mesolithic. *Proceedings of the Society of Antiquaries of Scotland* 143, 9–72.

Bishop, B., Cotton, J., Humphrey, R., Badreshany, K., Meddens, F.M. and Rielly, K. 2017. Mesolithic activity and early neolithic earthworks at 41-42 Kew Bridge Road, Hounslow. *Transactions of the London & Middlesex Archaeological Society* 68, 1–40.

Bjerck, H.B. 2009. Colonizing seascapes: Comparative perspectives on the development of maritime relations in Scandinavia and Patagonia. *Arctic Anthropology* 46(1–2), 118–131.

Black, S.L. and Thorns, A.V. 2014. Hunter-gatherer earth ovens in the archaeological record: Fundamental concepts. *American Antiquity* 79(2), 204–226.

Blinkhorn, E., Lawton-Matthews, E. and Warren, G. 2016. Digging and filling pits in the mesolithic of England and Ireland: Comparative perspectives on a widespread practice. In N. Achard-Corompt, E. Ghesquiere and V. Riquiere (eds.), *Creuser au Mésolithique/Digging in the Mesolithic*, pp. 12, 211–224. Paris: Séances de la Société Préhistorique Française.

Blinkhorn, E. and Little, A. 2018. Being ritual in Mesolithic Britain and Ireland: Identifying ritual behaviour within an ephemeral material record. *Journal of World Prehistory* 31(3), 403–420.

Blockley, S.M. 2005. Two hiatuses in human bone radiocarbon dates in Britain (17000 to 5000 cal BP). *Antiquity* 79(305), 505–513.

Blockley, S., Candy, I., Matthews, I., Langdon, P., Langdon, C., Palmer, A., Lincoln, P., Abrook, A., Taylor, B., Conneller, C. and Bayliss, A. 2018. The resilience of postglacial hunter-gatherers to abrupt climate change. *Nature Ecology and Evolution* 2(5), 810–821.

Bond, C.J. 2009a. A mesolithic social landscape in south-west Britain: The Somerset Levels and Mendip Hills. In S.B. McCartan, R. Shulting, G. Warren and P. Woodman (eds.), *Mesolithic horizons*, pp. 706–716. Oxford: Oxbow Books.

Bond, C.J. 2009b. The power of place and regional identity in the British southwestern Mesolithic. In S.B. McCartan, R. Shulting, G. Warren and P. Woodman (eds.), *Mesolithic horizons*, pp. 343–351. Oxford: Oxbow Books.

Bonnichsen, R. and Will, R.F. 1999. Radiocarbon chronology of Northeastern Paleoamerican sites: Discriminating natural and human burn features. In R. Bonnichsen and K.L. Turnmire (eds.), *Ice age people of North America*, pp. 395–415. Corvallis, Oregon: Oregon State University Press.

Bonsall, C. 1988. Morton and Lussa Wood, the case for early Flandrian settlement of Scotland: Comment on Myers. *Scottish Archaeological Review* 5, 30–33.

Bonsall, C. 1996. The 'Obanian' problem: Coastal adaptation in the Mesolithic of western Scotland. In T. Pollard and A. Morrison (eds.), *The early prehistory of Scotland*, pp. 183–197. Edinburgh: Edinburgh University Press.

Bonsall, C., Payton, R., Macklin, M.G. and Ritchie, G.A. 2009. A Mesolithic site at Kilmore, near Oban, Western Scotland. In N. Finlay, S. McCartan, N. Milner and C. Wickham-Jones (eds.), *From Bann Flakes to Bushmills*, pp. 70–77. Oxford: Oxbow Books.

Bonsall, C. and Smith, C. 1989. Late Palaeolithic and Mesolithic bone and antler artifacts from Britain: First reactions to accelerator dates. *Mesolithic Miscellany* 10(1), 33–38.

Bonsall, C., Sutherland, D. and Lawson, T.J. 1989. Ulva Cave and the early settlement of Northern Britain. *Cave Science* 16(3), 109–111.

Bonsall, C., Sutherland, D., Tipping, R. and Cherry, J. 1989. The Eskmeals Project: Late Mesolithic settlement and environment in north-west England. In C. Bonsall (ed.), *The Mesolithic in Europe*, pp. 175–205. Edinburgh: John Donald.

Boric, D. 2008. First households and 'house societies' in European prehistory. In A. Jones (ed.), *Prehistoric Europe: Theory and practice*, pp. 109–142. Oxford: Blackwell.

Bosinski, G., d'Errico, F. and Schiller, P. 2001. *Die gravierten Frauendarstellungen von Gönnersdorf*. Berlin: Franz Steiner Verlag.

Boismier, W.A. 1995. Excavation of a mesolithic site at Windmill Hill, Nettlebed, Oxon. *Oxoniensia* (1995), 1–19.

Boulestin, B. 1999. *Approche taphonomique des restes humaines. Le cas des Mésolithiques de la grotte des Perrats et le probleme du cannibalisme en préhistoire récente europeénne*. Oxford: British Archaeological Reports International Series 776.

Bowden, M., Soutar, S., Field, D. and Barber, M. 2015. *The Stonehenge landscape: Analysing the Stonehenge World Heritage Site*. Swindon: Historic England.

Boycott, A. and Wilson, L.J. 2010. Contemporary accounts of the discovery of Aveline's Hole, Burrington Combe, North Somerset. *Proceedings of the University of Bristol Spelaeological Society* 25(1), 11–25.

Brace, S., Diekmann, Y., Booth, T.J., van Dorp, L., Faltyskova, Z., Rohland, N., Mallick, S., Olalde, I., Ferry, M., Michel, M. and Oppenheimer, J. 2019. Ancient genomes indicate population replacement in Early Neolithic Britain. *Nature Ecology and Evolution* 3(5), 765–771.

Bradley, J. and Howard-Davies, C. 2018. From Mesolithic encampment to Medieval estate. The Archaeology of the Bay Gateway . Hastings: Lancaster Imprints 24.

Bradley, R. 1984. *The social foundations of prehistoric Britain: themes and variations in the archaeology of power*. London: Addison-Wesley Longman Limited.

Bradley, R. and Batey, C.E. 2000. *The good stones: A new investigation of the Clava Cairns*. Edinburgh: Society Antiquaries Scotland.

Bradley, S.L., Milne, G.A., Shennan, I. and Edwards, R. 2011. An improved glacial isostatic adjustment model for the British Isles. *Journal of Quaternary Science* 26(5), 541–552.

Brady, K. 2006. *The prehistoric and Roman landscape at Beechbrook Wood, Westwell, Kent*. CTRL Integrated Site Report Series, unpublished report.

Brassil, K.S., Owen, W.G., Britnell, W.J., Denne, P., Gibson, A.M., Green, H.S., Jenkins, D.A. and Wilkinson, J.L. 1991. Prehistoric and early medieval cemeteries at Tandderwen, near Denbigh, Clwyd. *Archaeological Journal* 148(1), 46–97.

Breuil, H. 1953. Statuette bisexuée dansle Mic rolithique de Nab Head, St. Brides, Pembrokeshire. Congrès Préhistorique de France: Compte rendue de la XIVe Session.

Bridgland, D.R., Innes, J., Long, A. and Mitchell, W. 2011. *Late quaternary landscape evolution of the Swale-Ure Washlands, North Yorkshire*. Oxford: Oxbow Books.

Britnell, W.J. and Savory, H.N. 1984. *Gwernvale and Penywyrlod: Two Neolithic long cairns in the Black Mountains of Brecknock*. Cardiff: Cambrian Archaeological Association.

Bronk Ramsey, C. 2009. Bayesian analysis of radiocarbon dates. *Radiocarbon* 51(1), 337–360.

Bronk Ramsey, C. and Bayliss, A. 2000. Dating stonehenge. In K. Lockyer, T.J.T. Sly and V. Mihailescu-Bîrliba (eds.), *CAA96: Computer applications and quantitative methods in archaeology*, pp. 29–39. Oxford: British Archaeological Reports 845.

Brown, T. 1997. Clearances and clearings: Deforestation in Mesolithic/Neolithic Britain. *Oxford Journal of Archaeology* 16(2), 133–146.

Brophy, K. 2018. The Brexit hypothesis and prehistory. *Antiquity* 92(366), 1650–1658.

Brown, F. in press. A mesolithic house on the isle of man. In A. Myers and P.R. Preston (eds.), *The mesolithic of North-Western England. Archaeology Northwest*. Salford: Council for British Archaeology Northwest.

Brown, F., Clark, P. Dickson, A., Gregory, R.A. and Zant, J. in press. *From an Ancient Eden to a new frontier: An archaeological journey along the Carlisle Northern development route*. Hastings: Lancaster Imprints.

Brunning, R. and Firth, H. 2012. An early Mesolithic cemetery at Greylake, Somerset, UK. *Mesolithic Miscellany* 22(1), 19–21.

Buckley, F. 1921. *A microlithic industry, Marsden, Yorkshire*. Spottiswoode: Balantyne and Co.

Buckley, F. 1924. *Microlithic industry of the Pennine Chain, related to the Tardenois of Belgium*. Privately printed.

Buckland, W. 1825. Reply to some observations in Dr Fleming's remarks on the distribution of British animals. *Edinburgh philosophical Journal* 12, 304–319.

Burke, T. 1966. Excavations at Pant Sychbant, Penderyn (Brecken.). *Bulletin of the Board of Celtic Studies* 22, 78–87.

Burkitt, M.C. 1926. *Our early ancestors: An introductory study of mesolithic, neolithic and copper age cultures in Europe and adjacent regions*. Cambridge: Cambridge University Press.

Burleigh, R. 1976. Excavations at Creffield Road, Acton in 1974 and 1975. *London Archaeologist* 2(15), 379–383.

Burleigh, R., Ambers, J. and Matthews, K. 1982. British Museum natural radiocarbon measurements XV. *Radiocarbon* 24(3), 262–290.

Burns, A. 2014. *The prehistoric footprints at Formby: Discover the footprints on the Sefton Coast and tale a glimpse into prehistoric Britain*. Liverpool: Sefton Coast Landscape Partnership Scheme.

Burns, A. 2021. The mesolithic footprints retained in one bed of the former Saltmarshes at Formby Point, Sefton Coast, North West England. In A. Pastoors and T. Lenssen-Erz Tilman (eds.), *Reading prehistoric human tracks: Methods & material*, pp. 295–315. New York: Springer.

Burrow, S. 2010. Bryn Celli Ddu passage tomb, Anglesey: Alignment, construction, date, and ritual. *Proceedings of the Prehistoric Society* 76, 249–270.

Bush, M.B. 1988. Early Mesolithic disturbance: A force on the landscape. *Journal of Archaeological Science* 15(4), 453–462.

Butler, C. 2001. A mesolithic and later prehistoric flintworking site at East and West Hills, Pyecombe, West Sussex. *Sussex Archaeological Collections* 139, 7–25.

Butler, C. 2007. A mesolithic site at Streat Lane, Streat, East Sussex. *Sussex Archaeological Collections* 145, 7–31.

Cadman, S., Knight, B., Elliott, B., Schadla-Hall, T., Robson, H.K. and Milner, N. 2018. The discovery of mesolithic red deer at Skipsea Withow. *Yorkshire Archaeological Journal* 90(1), 1–12.

Campbell, J. 1977. *The upper palaeolithic of Britain*. Oxford: Clarendon Press.

Care, V. 1979. The production and distribution of Mesolithic axes in southern England. *Proceedings of the Prehistoric Society* 45, 93–102.

Care, V. 1982. The collection and distribution of lithic materials during the Mesolithic and Neolithic periods in southern England. *Oxford Journal of Archaeology* 1(3), 269–285.

Carter, H.H. 1975. Fauna of an area of Mesolithic occupation in the Kennet Valley considered in relation to contemporary eating habits. *Berkshire Archaeological Journal* 68, 1–3.

Carter, R.J. 1997. Age estimation of the roe deer (Capreolus capreolus) mandibles from the Mesolithic site of Star Carr, Yorkshire, based on radiographs of mandibular tooth development. *Journal of Zoology* 241(3), 495–502.

Carter, R.J. 1998. Reassessment of seasonality at the Early Mesolithic site of Star Carr, Yorkshire based on radiographs of mandibular tooth development in red deer (Cervus elaphus). *Journal of Archaeological Science* 25(9), 851–856.

Carter, R.J. 2001. New evidence for seasonal human presence at the Early Mesolithic site of Thatcham, Berkshire, England. *Journal of Archaeological Science* 28(10), 1055–1060.

Carter, S.D. 2014. Unpicking the palimpsest. A late Mesolithic upland activity area in Northern England. https://timevista.co.uk/about/research/.

Carter, S.D. 2016. Monitoring of mesolithic lithic sites at Esklets, Westerdale, North York Moors, England. https://timevista.co.uk/about/research/.

Caulfield, S. 1978. Star Carr – an alternative view. *Irish Archaeological Research Forum* 5, 15–22.

Cauwe, N. 2001. Early Mesolithic collective tombs in southern Belgium. *Cambridge Archaeological Journal* 11(2), 147–163.

Chambers, F.M., Mighall, T.M. and Keen, D.H. 1996. Early Holocene pollen and molluscan records from Enfield Lock, Middlesex, UK. *Proceedings of the Geologists' Association*, 107(1), 1–14.

Champness, C., Donnelly, M., Davies, A. and Boothroyd, J. 2019. *Bexhill to Hastings Link Road. Post-excavation assessment and updated project design.* Oxford Archaeology South unpublished client report.

Champness, C., Donnelly, M., Ford, B.M. and Haggart, A. 2015. Life at the floodplain edge: Terminal Upper Palaeolithic and Mesolithic flint scatters and early prehistoric archaeology along the Beam River Valley. *Transactions of the Essex Society for Archaeology and History* 6, 5–45.

Charlton, S., Alexander, M., Collins, M., Milner, N., Mellars, P., O'Connell, T.C., Stevens, R.E. and Craig, O.E. 2016. Finding Britain's last hunter-gatherers: A new biomolecular approach to 'unidentifiable' bone fragments utilising bone collagen. *Journal of Archaeological Science* 73, 55–61.

Chatterton, R. 2005. *Transition and persistence: material culture in the Mesolithic landscape of north Yorkshire.* Unpublished PhD Dissertation, The University of Manchester.

Chatterton, R. 2006. Ritual. In C. Conneller and G. Warren (eds.), *Mesolithic Britain and Ireland: New approaches,* pp. 101–120. Oxford: Tempus.

Cherry, J. and Cherry, P.J. 1983. Prehistoric habitation sites in west Cumbria: Part 1, the St Bees area and north to the Solway. *Transactions of the Cumberland and Westmorland Antiquarian and Archaeological Society* 83, 1–14.

Cherry, J. and Cherry, P.J. 1986. Prehistoric habitation sites in West Cumbria: Part IV, the Eskmeals area. *Transactions of the Cumberland and Westmorland Antiquarian and Archaeological Society* 86, 1–18.

Cherry, J. and Cherry, P.J. 1987. *Prehistoric habitation sites on the limestone uplands of Eastern Cumbria.* Kendall: Cumberland and Westlorland Antiquarian and Archaeological Society Research Series, volume 2.

Chisham, C. 2004. *Early Mesolithic human activity and environmental change: A case study of the Kennet valley.* Doctoral dissertation, University of Reading.

Childe, V. G. 1925. *The Dawn of European Civilization.* New York: Alfred A. Knopf.

Church, M.J., Bishop, R.R., Blake, E.R.R., Nesbitt, C., Perri, A., Piper, S. and Rowley-Conwy, P.A. 2012. Tràigh na Beirigh. *Discovery and Excavation in Scotland* 13, 190.

Churchill, D.M. 1963. The stratigraphy of the Mesolithic sites III and V at Thatcham, Berkshire, England. *Proceedings of the Prehistoric Society* 28, 362–370.

Churchill, D.M. and Wymer, J.J. 1965. The kitchen midden site at Westward Ho!, Devon, England: Ecology, age, and relation to changes in land and sea level. *Proceedings of the Prehistoric Society* 31, 74–84.

Clark, J.G.D. 1932. *The mesolithic age in Britain.* Cambridge: Cambridge University Press.

Clark, J.G.D. 1933. The classification of a microlithic culture: The Tardenoisian of Horsham. *Archaeological Journal* 90(1), 52–77.

Clark, J.G.D. 1934. A late Mesolithic settlement site at Selmeston, Sussex. *The Antiquaries Journal* 14(2), 134–158.

Clark, J.G.D. 1936. *The mesolithic settlement of Northern Europe.* Cambridge: Cambridge University Press.

Clark, J.G.D. 1938. Microlithic industries from tufa deposits at Prestatyn, Flintshire and Blashenwell, Dorset. *Proceedings of the Prehistoric Society* 4(2), 330–334.

Clark, J.G.D. 1939. *Archaeology and society.* London: Methuen.

Clark, J.G.D. 1947. Whales as an economic factor in Prehistoric Europe. *Antiquity* 21(82), 84–104.

Clark, J.G.D. 1949. A preliminary report on excavations at Star Carr, Seamer, Scarborough, Yorkshire, 1949. *Proceedings of the Prehistoric Society* 15, 52–69.

Clark, J.G.D. 1950. Preliminary report on excavations at Star Carr, Seamer, Scarborough, Yorkshire (Second Season, 1950). *Proceedings of the Prehistoric Society* 16, 109–129.

Clark, J.G.D. 1952. *Prehistoric Europe: The economic basis.* Cambridge: Cambridge University Press.

Clark, J.G.D. 1954. *Excavations at Star Carr: An early mesolithic site at Seamer near Scarborough, Yorkshire.* Cambridge: Cambridge University Press.

Clark, J.G.D. 1972. *Star Carr: A case study in bioarchaeology.* Reading, Massachusetts: Addison-Wesley Modular Publications, Module 10.

Clark, J.G.D. 1974. Prehistoric Europe: The economic basis. In G.R. Willey (ed.), *Archaeological researches in retrospect,* pp. 35–57. Cambridge, Massachusetts: Winthrop.

Clark, J.G.D. 1989. *Prehistory at Cambridge and beyond.* Cambridge: Cambridge University Press.

Clark, J.G.D. and Godwin, H. 1957. A maglemosian site at Brandesburton, Holderness, Yorkshire. *Proceedings of the Prehistoric Society* 22, 6–22.

Clark, J.G.D. and Godwin, H. 1962. The neolithic in the Cambridgeshire fens. *Antiquity* 36(141), 10–23.

Clark, J.G.D., Godwin, M.E. and Clifford, M.H. 1935. Report on recent excavations at Peacock's Farm, Shippea Hill, Cambridgeshire. *The Antiquaries Journal* 15(3), 284–319.

Clark, J.G.D. and Rankine, W.F. 1939. Excavations at Farnham, Surrey (1937–38): The Horsham culture and the question of Mesolithic dwellings. *Proceedings of the Prehistoric Society* 5, 61–118.

Clarke, D. 1976. Mesolithic Europe: The economic basis. In G.de.G Sieveking, I.H. Longworth and K.E. Wilson (eds.), *Problems in Economic and Social Archaeology,* pp. 449–481. London: Duckworth.

Cloutman, E.W. 1988. Palaeoevnironments in the Vale of Pickering, part 1: Stratigraphy and palaeogeography of Seamer Carr, Star Carr and Flixton Carr. *Proceedings of the Prehistoric Society* 54, 1–19.

Clutton-Brock, J. and Noe-Nygaard, N. 1990. New osteological and C-isotope evidence on Mesolithic dogs: Companions to hunters and fishers at Star Carr, Seamer Carr and Kongemose. *Journal of Archaeological Science, 17*(6), 643–653.

Cobb, H. 2005. Midden, meaning, person, place: Interpreting the Mesolithic of Western Scotland. In H. Cobb, F. Coward, L. Grimshaw and S. Price (eds.), *Investigating prehistoric hunter-gatherer identities: Case studies from palaeolithic and mesolithic Europe,* pp. 69–78. Oxford: British Archaeological Reports, International Series 1411.

Cobb, H. and Jones, A.G. 2018. Being mesolithic in life and death. *Journal of World Prehistory* 31(3), 367–383.

Coggins, D., Laurie T.C. and Young R. 1989. The late upper palaeolithic and mesolithic of the north Pennine dales in the light of recent fieldwork. In C. Bonsall (ed.), *The mesolithic in Europe*, pp. 164–175. Edinburgh: John Donald.

Coles, B. 2006. *Beavers in Britain's past*. Oxford: Oxbow Books and WARP.

Coles, J.M. 1964. New aspects of the mesolithic settlement of SW Scotland. *Dumfriesshire and Galloway Natural History and Antiquarian Society* 41, 67.

Coles, J.M. 1983. Morton revisited. In A. O'Connor and D.Y. Clarke (eds.), *From the stone age to the forty-five*, pp. 9–18. Edinburgh: John Donald.

Coles, J.M. 1971. The early settlement of Scotland: Excavations at Morton, Fife. *Proceedings of the Prehistoric Society* 37, 284–366.

Coles, J.M. 1997. John Grahame Douglas Clark. *Proceedings of the British Academy* 94, 357–387.

Collins, D. and Lorimer, D. 1989. *Excavations at the mesolithic site on West Heath, Hampstead, 1976-1981*. Oxford: British Archaeological Reports, British Series 217.

Collins, P.E., Worsley, P., Keith-Lucas, D.M. and Fenwick, I.M. 2006. Floodplain environmental change during the Younger Dryas and Holocene in Northwest Europe: Insights from the lower Kennet Valley, south central England. *Palaeogeography, Palaeoclimatology, Palaeoecology* 233(1–2), 113–133.

Conneller, C.J. 1999. *The Lithics*. West Yorkshire Mesolithic Project. West Yorkshire Archaeological Service, unpublished report.

Conneller, C.J. 2000. *Space, time and technology: The early mesolithic of the Vale of Pickering, North Yorkshire*. Doctoral thesis, University of Cambridge.

Conneller, C. 2004. Becoming deer: Corporeal transformations at Star Carr. *Archaeological Dialogues* 11, 37–56.

Conneller, C. 2006. Death. In C. Conneller and G. Warren (eds.), *Mesolithic Britain and Ireland: New approaches*, pp. 139–164. Oxford: Tempus.

Conneller, C. 2011. *An archaeology of materials: Substantial transformations in early prehistoric Europe*. New York: Routledge.

Conneller, C., Bayliss, A., Milner, N., andTaylor, B. 2016a. The Resettlement of the British Landscape: Towards a chronology of Early Mesolithic lithic assemblage types. Internet Archaeology 42. 10.11141/ia.42.12.

Conneller, C., Bates, M., Bates, R., Schadla Hall, T., Blinkhorn, E., Cole, J., Pope, M., Scott, B., Shaw, A. and Underhill, D. 2016b. Rethinking human responses to sea-level rise: The Mesolithic occupation of the Channel Islands. *Proceedings of the Prehistoric Society* 82, 27–71.

Conneller, C. and Higham, T. 2015. The early Mesolithic colonisation of Britain: Preliminary results. In N. Ashton and C. Harris (eds), *No stone unturned. Papers in honour of Roger Jacobi*, pp. 157–166. London: Lithic Studies Society Occasional Paper 9.

Conneller, C., Little, A. and Birchenall, J. 2018a. Making space through stone. In N. Milner, C. Conneller and B. Taylor (eds.), *Star Carr. Volume 1: A persistent place in a changing world*, pp. 157–221. York: White Rose University Press.

Conneller, C., Little, A., Garcia-Diaz, V. and Croft, S. 2018b. The worked flint. In N. Milner, C. Conneller and B. Taylor (eds.), *Star Carr Volume 2: Studies in technology, subsistence and environment*, pp. 493–534. York: White Rose Press.

Conneller, C., Milner, N., Taylor, B. and Taylor, M. 2012. Substantial settlement in the European Early Mesolithic: New research at Star Carr. *Antiquity* 86(334), 1004–1020.

Conneller, C. and Overton, N.J. 2018. The British mesolithic context. In N. Milner, C. Conneller and B. Taylor (eds.), *Star Carr Volume 1: A persistent place in a changing world*, pp. 275–303. York: White Rose Press.

Conneller, C. and Schadla-Hall, T. 2003. Beyond Star Carr: The Vale of Pickering in the 10th millennium BP. *Proceedings of the Prehistoric Society* 69, 85–105.

Conneller and Griffiths. In prep. A new chronology for the Mesolithic.

Cooper, L.P. and Jarvis, W. 2017. Making and breaking microliths: A middle mesolithic site at Asfordby, Leicestershire. *Proceedings of the Prehistoric Society* 83, 43–96.

Corcoran, J., Halsey, C., Spurr, G., Burton, E. and Jamieson, D. 2011. *Mapping past landscapes in the lower Lea valley: A geoarchaeological study of the Quaternary sequence.* London: Museum of London Archaeology Monograph 55.

Corcoran, J. and Howell, I. 2002. *Sanderson site, Oxford Road, Denham, Buckinghamshire: A report on the evaluation.* London: Museum of London Archaeology Service.

Cormack, W.F. 1970. A mesolithic site at Barsalloch, Wigtownshire. *Dumfriesshire and Galloway Natural History and Antiquarian Society* 47, 63–78.

Cormack, W.F. and Coles, J.M. 1968. A mesolithic site at Low Clone, Wigtownshire. *Dumfriesshire and Galloway Natural History and Antiquarian Society* 45, 44–72.

Coupland, G. 1925. A microlithic industry, Durham. *Proceedings of the Prehistoric Society of East Anglia* 5(1), 62–64.

Coupland, G. 1948. *A mesolithic industry at 'The Beacon', SE Durham.* Gloucester: J. Bellows.

Cowell, R.W. 1992. Greasby, North Wirral, Merseyside: Interim report on the excavation of an early Mesolithic site. *Archaeology North West* 4, 7–15.

Cowell, R. 2018. An interim characterisation of two potential Later Mesolithic structures at Lunt Meadows Site 1, Sefton, Merseyside, England. In A. Myers and P.R. Preston (eds.), *The mesolithic of North-Western England. Archaeology Northwest*, pp. 71–99. Salford: Council for British Archaeology Northwest.

Cowling, E.T. and Strickland, H.J. 1947. Two mesolithic riverside sites in Yorkshire. *Yorkshire Archaeological Journal* 36, 445–462.

Cramp, K. and Leivers, M. 2010. The worked flint (section 4). In J. Lewis (ed.), *Landscape evolution in the Middle Thames Valley, Heathrow Terminal 5 Excavations Volume 2, CD section 1, unpaginated.* Oxford: Framework Archaeology Monograph/Oxbow Books.

Crombé, P., Perdaen, Y., Sergant, J. and Caspar, J.P. 2001. Wear analysis on early Mesolithic microliths from the Verrebroek site, East Flanders, Belgium. *Journal of Field Archaeology* 28(3–4), 253–269.

Damon, R. 1884. *Geology of Weymouth, Portland, and coast of Dorsetshire, from Swanage to Bridport-on-the-sea: With natural history and archæological notes.* Privately Published.

Dark, P. 2000. Revised 'absolute' dating of the early Mesolithic site of Star Carr, North Yorkshire, in the light of changes in the early Holocene tree-ring chronology. *Antiquity* 74(284), 304–307.

Dark, P. 2003. Dogs, a crane (not duck) and diet at Star Carr: A response to Schulting and Richards. *Journal of Archaeological Science* 30(10), 1353–1356.

Darvill, T. and Wainwright, G. 2014. Beyond Stonehenge: Carn Menyn Quarry and the origin and date of bluestone extraction in the Preseli Hills of south-west Wales. *Antiquity*, *88*(342), 1099–1114.

David, A. 1998. Two assemblages of later Mesolithic microliths from Seamer Carr, North Yorkshire: Fact and fancy. In N. Ashton, F. Healy and P. Pettitt (eds.), *Stone age archaeology: Essays in honour of John Wymer*, pp. 196–204. Oxford: Oxbow Monograph 102/Lithic Studies Society Occasional Paper 6.

David, A. 2007. *Palaeolithic and mesolithic settlement in Wales, with special reference to Dyfed.* British Archaeological Reports, British Series 448. Oxford: Archaeopress.

David, A. 2019a. Review of 'Blick Mead: Exploring the "First Place" in the Stonehenge landscape' by David Jacques, Tom Phillips and Tom Lyons. *Antiquaries Journal* 99, 440–441.

David, A. 2019b. Between a rock and a hard place. Flint working in west Wales. *Archaeology in Wales* 57–58, 71–89.

David, A. 2020. Six millennia and counting: A prehistoric 'persistent place' at Penpant, north Pembrokeshire. *Archaeologia Cambrensis* 169, 31–62.

David, A. and Kowlaski, R. 2019. New Mesolithic finds from the Lower Greensand near Petworth, West Sussex, and their wider affiliations. *Sussex Archaeological Collections* 57, 1–29.

David, A. and Painter, T. 2014. Hunter-gatherers in the western Cleddau valley, Pembrokeshire, West Wales. *Archaeologia Cambrensis* 163, 43–98.

David, A., Painter, T., and Wensley, P. 2015. Llangwm: a newly identified early. Mesolithic site in southwest Wales. *Archaeology in Wales* 54, 15–24.

Davies, J.A. 1921. Aveline's Hole, Burrington Combe. An Upper Palaeolithic station. *Proceedings of the University of Bristol Speleological Society* 1, 61–72.

Davies, J.A. 1922. Second report on Aveline's Hole. *Proceedings of the University of Bristol Speleological Society* 1, 113–118.

Davies, J.A. 1923. Third report on Aveline's Hole. *Proceedings of the University of Bristol Speleological Society* 2, 5–15.

Davies, J.A. 1924. Fourth report on Aveline's Hole. *Proceedings of the University of Bristol Speleological Society* 2, 104–114.

Davies, J. 1963. A mesolithic site on Blubberhouses Moor, Wharfedale, West Riding of Yorkshire. *Yorkshire Archaeological Journal* 41, 60–70.

Davies, M. 1989. Recent advances in cave archaeology in southwest Wales. In T.D. Ford (ed.), *Limestones and caves of Wales*, pp. 79–91. Cambridge: Cambridge University Press.

Davies, G. 2001. *Interim statement on the archaeological works at Staythorpe Power Station (ARCUS 438f)*. ARCUS, unpublished report.

Davies, P., Robb, J. G., and Ladbrook, D. 2005. Woodland clearance in the Mesolithic: the social aspects. *Antiquity* 79(304), 280–288.

Davis, R. 2012. *The nature of Mesolithic activity at selected spring sites in South West England.* Doctoral dissertation, University of Worcester.

Dawkins, W.B. 1864. On the caverns of Burrington Coombe. *Proceedings of the Somerset Archaeology and Natural History Society* 12, 161–176.

Dawson, A. 1994. Geomorphological effects of tsunami run-up and backwash. *Geomorphology* 10, 83–94. 10.1016/0169-555X(94)90009-4.

Dawson, A.G., Long, D. and Smith, D.E. 1988. The Storegga slides: Evidence from eastern Scotland for a possible tsunami. *Marine geology 82*(3–4), 271–276.

Dawson, A.G., Smith, D.E. and Long, D. 1990. Evidence for a tsunami from a Mesolithic site in Inverness, Scotland. *Journal of Archaeological Science* 17(5), 509–512.

De Bie, M. and Caspar, J.P. 2000. *Rekem. A Federmesser camp on the Meuse river bank*. Leuven: Leuven University Press.

Deaville, R. 2016. Cetacean Strandings Investigation Programme, Annual report 2015. http://ukstrandings.org/csip-reports/ Accessed 2/9/2019.

Deith, M.R. 1983. Molluscan calendars: The use of growth-line analysis to establish seasonality of shellfish collection at the Mesolithic site of Morton, Fife. *Journal of Archaeological Science* 10(5), 423–440.

Deith, M.R. 1986. Subsistence strategies at a Mesolithic camp site: Evidence from stable isotope analyses of shells. *Journal of Archaeological Science* 13(1), 61–78.

Descola, P. 1992. Societies of nature and the nature of societies. In A. Kuper (ed.), *Conceptualising society,* pp. 107–126. London: Routledge.

Descola, P. 1999. Constructing natures: Symbolic ecology and social practice. In P. Descola and G. Palsson (eds.), *Nature and society. Anthropological perspectives*, pp. 82–102. London: Routledge.

Deveraux, D. and Sloane, D. 1983. Inveravon. *Discovery and Excavation in Scotland* 1983, 3.

Devoy, R.J.N. 1979. Flandrian sea level changes and vegetational history of the lower Thames estuary. *Philosophical Transactions of the Royal Society of London. B, Biological Sciences* 285(1010), 355–407.

Dingwall, K., Ginnever, M., Tipping, R., van Wissel, J. and Wilson, D. 2019. *The land was forever; 15,000 years in north-east Scotland.* Oxford: Oxbow Books.

Dimbleby, G. W. 1957. Pollen analysis of terrestrial soils. *New Phytologist* 56(1), 12–28.

Dimbleby, G. W. 1959. Thatcham pollen analyses. *Berkshire Archaeological Journal* 57, 25–29.

Dimbleby, G. W. 1985. *The palynology of archaeological sites.* London: Academic Press.

Dockall, J.E. 1997. Wear traces and projectile impact: A review of the experimental and archaeological evidence. *Journal of Field Archaeology* 24, 321–331.

Donahue, R.E. and Lovis, W.A. 2006. Regional settlement systems in Mesolithic northern England: Scalar issues in mobility and territoriality. *Journal of Anthropological Archaeology*, 25(2), 248–258.

Donnelly, M. and Macgregor, G. 2005. The excavation of Mesolithic activity, Neolithic and Bronze Age burnt mounds and Romano-British ring groove houses at Gallow Hill, Girvan. *Scottish Archaeological Journal* 27(1), 31–69.

Draper, C. 1951. Stone industries from Rainbow Bar, Hants. *Archaeological Newsletter* 3(9), 147–149.

Draper, C. 1968. Mesolithic distribution in south-east Hampshire. *Proceedings of the Hampshire Field Club* 23, 110–119.

Ducrocq, T. 2013. The 'Beuronian with crescents' in Northern France: The beginnings of a palethnological approach. In B. Valentin, B. Souffi, T. Ducrocq, J.-P. Fagnart, F. Séara and C. Verjux (eds.), *Mesolithic palethnography. Research on open-air sites between Loire and Neckar*, pp. 189–206. Paris: Séances de la Société Préhistorique Française 2-2.

Ducrocq, T., Le Goff, I. and Valentin, F. 1996. La sépulture secondaire mésolithique de la Chaussée-Tirancourt (Somme). *Bulletin de la Société préhistorique française*, 211–216.

Dumont, J.V. 1988. *A microwear analysis of selected artefact types from the Mesolithic sites of Star Carr and Mount Sandel.* Oxford: British Archaeological Reports, British Series 187.

Edmonds, M., Johnston, R., La Trobe-Bateman, E., Roberts, J. and Warren, G. 2009. Ynys Enlli: Shifting horizons. In S. McCartan, R. Schulting, G. Warren and P. Woodman (eds.), *Mesolithic horizons. Seventh International Conference on the Mesolithic in Europe, Belfast 2005*, pp. 385–391. Oxford: Oxbow.

Edwards, K.J. 1990. Fire and the Scottish Mesolithic: Evidence from microscopic charcoal. In C. Bonsall (ed.), *Contributions to the mesolithic in Europe*, pp. 71–79. Edinburgh: John Donald.

Edwards, K.J. 1996. The contribution of Tom Affleck to the study of the Mesolithic of Southwest Scotland. In T. Pollard and A. Morrison (eds.), *The early prehistory of Scotland*, pp. 108–122. Edinburgh: Edinburgh University Press.

Edwards, K.J. 2000. Vegetation history of the southern Inner Hebrides during the Mesolithic period. In: S. Mithen (ed.), *Hunter-gatherer landscape archaeology: The Southern Hebrides Mesolithic Project 1988–1998*, pp. 115–127. Cambridge: McDonald Institute Monographs.

Edwards, K.J. 2004. Palaeoenvironments of the late upper Palaeolithic and Mesolithic periods in Scotland and the North Sea area: New work, new thoughts. In *Mesolithic Scotland and its neighbours*, pp. 55–72. Edinburgh: Society of Antiquaries of Scotland.

Edwards, K.J., Bennett, K.D. and Davies, A.L. 2018. Palaeoecological perspectives on Holocene environmental change in Scotland. *Earth and Environmental Science Transactions of the Royal Society of Edinburgh* 109, 1–19.

Ellaby, R. 1987. The upper palaeolithic and mesolithic in Surrey. In J. Bird and D.G. Bird (eds.), *The archaeology of Surrey to 1540*, pp. 53–70. Guildford: Surrey Archaeological Society.

Ellaby, R. 2004. Food for thought: A late Mesolithic site at Charlwood, Surrey. In J. Cotton and D. Field (eds.), *Towards a new stone age*, pp. 12–23. York: CBA Research Report 137.

Elliott, B. 2012. *Antlerworking practices in mesolithic Britain.* Doctoral dissertation, University of York.

Elliott, B. 2015. Facing the chop: Redefining British antler mattocks to consider larger-scale maritime networks in the early fifth millennium cal BC. *European Journal of Archaeology*, 18(2), 222–244.

Elliott, B. and Griffiths, S. 2018. Living Mesolithic time: Narratives, chronologies and organic material culture. *Journal of World Prehistory* 31(3), 347–365.

Elliott, B., Knight, B. and Little, A. 2018. Antler frontlets. In N. Milner, C. Conneller and B. Taylor, *Star Carr Volume 2: Studies in technology, subsistence and environment*, pp. 297–334. York: White Rose Press.

Ellis, C.J., Allen, M.J., Gardiner, J., Harding, P., Ingrem, C., Powell, A., Scaife, R.G., Gale, R. and Heathcote, J. 2003. An early Mesolithic seasonal hunting site in the Kennet Valley, Southern England. *Proceedings of the Prehistoric Society* 69, 107–135.

English, J., Ellaby, R., Taylor, C. 2018. Excavations at Orchard Hill, Carshalton, 1964–5. *Surrey Archaeological Collections* 101, 195–208.

Eriksson, G. and Zagorska, I. 2003. Do dogs eat like humans? Marine stable isotope signals in dog teeth from inland Zvejnieki. In Larsson, L. (ed.), *Mesolithic on the move: Papers presented at the Sixth International Conference on the Mesolithic in Europe, Stockholm 2000*, pp. 160–168. Oxford: Oxbow Books.

Evans, A.A. 2009. *Microwear analysis and the role of the microlith in Mesolithic Britain*. Unpublished PhD thesis, University of Bradford.

Evans, A.A. 2017. Making and breaking microliths: A middle mesolithic site at Asfordby, Leicestershire. In L.P. Cooper and W. Jarvis (eds.), *Proceedings of the Prehistoric Society* 83, 43–96.

Evans, A.A., Langer, J.L., Donahue, R.E., Wolframm, Y.B. and Lovis, W.A. 2010. Lithic raw material sourcing and the assessment of Mesolithic landscape organization and mobility strategies in northern England. *The Holocene* 20(7), 1157–1163.

Evans, A.A., Wolframm, Y.B., Donahue, R.E. and Lovis, W.A. 2007. A pilot study of 'black chert' sourcing and implications for assessing hunter-gatherer mobility strategies in northern England. *Journal of Archaeological Science* 34, 2161–2169.

Evans, J.G. 1972. *Land snails in archaeology*. London: Seminar Press.

Evans, J.G. 1975. *The environment of early man in the British Isles*. Berkley: University of California Press.

Evans, C., Pollard, J. and Knight, M. 1999. Life in the Woods: Tree-throws, 'Settlement' and Forest Cognition. *Oxford Journal of Archaeology* 18(3), 241–254.

Evans, C., Tabor, J. and van der Linden, M. 2016. *Twice-crossed river: Prehistoric and palaeoenvironmental investigations at Barleycroft Farm/Over, Cambridgeshire*. Cambridge: MacDonald Institute for Archaeological Research.

Evans, J.G. and Smith, I.F. 1983. Excavations at Cherhill, North Wiltshire, 1967. *Proceedings of the Prehistoric Society* 49, 43–117.

Fagan, B. 2018. *Grahame Clark: An intellectual biography of an archaeologist*. London: Routledge.

Farley, M. 1978. Excavations at Low Farm, Fulmer, Bucks. 1: The Mesolithic occupation. *Records of Bucks* 20, 601–616.

Farley, M. 2010. *An illustrated history of early Buckinghamshire*. Aylesbury: Buckinghamshire Archaeological Society.

Farrell, M., Bunting, M.J., Lee, D. and Thomas, A. 2014. Neolithic settlement at the woodland's edge: Palynological data and timber architecture in Orkney, Scotland. *Journal of Archaeological Science* 51, 225–236. 10.1016/j.jas.2012.05.042.

Fausto, C. 2007. Feasting on people: Eating animals and humans in Amazonia. *Current Anthropology* 48(4), 497–530.

Field, D. 1989. Tranchet axes and Thames picks: Mesolithic core-tools from the West London Thames. *Transactions of the London and Middlesex Archaeological Society* 40, 1–46.

Fienup-Riordan, A. 1987. The eye of the dance. *Artic Anthropology* 24(2), 40–55.

Finlay, N. 2000. Deer prudence. *Archaeological Review from Cambridge* 17(1), 67–79.

Finlay, N. 2003. Microliths and multiple authorship. In L. Larsson, H. Kindgren, K. Knutsson, D. Loeffler and A. Akerlund (eds.), *Mesolithic on the move*, pp. 169–176. Oxford: Oxbow Books.

Finlay, N. 2004. E-scapes and E-motion. *Before Farming* 1, 1–10.

Finlay, N., Cerón-Carrasco, R., Housley, R., Huggett, J., Jardine, W.G., Ramsay, S., Smith, C., Wright, D., Augley, J. and Wright, P.J. 2019. Calling time on Oronsay: Revising settlement models around the mesolithic–neolithic transition in Western Scotland, new evidence from Port Lobh, Colonsay. *Proceedings of the Prehistoric Society* 85, 83–114.

Finlay, N., Finlayson, B. and Mithen, S. 2000. The primary technology: Its character and inter-site variability. *Hunter-gatherer landscape archaeology. The Southern Hebrides Mesolithic Project 1988–98.* Vol. 2, pp. 547–569. Cambridge: McDonald Institute for Archaeological Resarch.

Finlayson, B. 1990. The functions of microliths: Evidence from Smittons and Starr, SW Scotland. *Mesolithic Miscellany* 11(1), 2–6.

Finlayson, B. 1996. Complexity in the mesolithic of the Western Scottish seaboard. In A. Fischer (ed.), *Man and sea in the mesolithic: Coastal settlement above and below present sea-level*, pp. 261–265. Oxford: Oxbow.

Finlayson, B. and Mithen, S. 1997. The microwear and morphology of microliths from Gleann Mor. In H. Knecht (ed.), *Projectile technology,* pp. 107–129. New York: Plenum Press.

Fischer, A. 1974. An ornamented flint core from Holmegård V, Zealand, Denmark. Notes on Mesolithic ornamentation and flintknapping. *Acta Archaeologica*, 45, 155–168.

Fitzpatrick, A.P., Powell, A.B. and Allen, M.J. 2008 Archaeological Excavations on the Route of the A27 Westhampnett Bypass, West Sussex, 1992: The late Upper Palaeolithic - Anglo-Saxon. Salisbury: Wessex Archaeology.

Florescu, G., Brown, K.J., Carter, V.A., Kuneš, P., Veski, S. and Feurdean, A. 2019. Holocene rapid climate changes and ice-rafting debris events reflected in high-resolution European charcoal records. *Quaternary Science Reviews* 222, 105877.

Framework Archaeology. 2011. Archaeology at Heathrow Terminal Five. https://framearch.co.uk/t5/2006/08/23/8500-4000-bc-deep-forest-and-a-river/.

French, C., Lewis, H., Allen, M.J., Scaife, R.G., Green, M., Gardiner, J. and Gdaniec, K. 2003. Archaeological and palaeo-environmental investigations of the upper Allen Valley, Cranborne Chase, Dorset (1998–2000): A new model of earlier Holocene landscape development. *Proceedings of the Prehistoric Society* 69, 201–234.

Froom, F.R. 1971. A mesolithic site at Wawcott. *Berkshire Archaeological Journal* 66, 23–44.

Froom, F.R. 1976. *Wawcott III: A stratified Mesolithic succession.* British Archaeological Reports 27.

Froom, R. 2012. *The mesolithic of the Kennet Valley.* Oxford: Oxbow Books.

Gabel, G. 1976. St. Catherine's Hill: A mesolithic site near Guildford. *Research Volume of the Surrey Archaeological Society* 3, 77–101.

Gaffney, V., Fitch, S., Bates, M., Ware, R.L., Kinnaird, T., Gearey, B., Hill, T., Telford, R., Batt, C., Stern, B. and Whittaker, J. 2020. Multi-proxy characterisation of the Storegga Tsunami and its impact on the early Holocene landscapes of the southern North Sea. *Geosciences* 10(7), 270. 10.3390/geosciences10070270.

Gaffney, V.L., Fitch, S., Ramsey, E., Yorston, R., Ch'ng, E., Baldwin, E., Bates, R., Gaffney, C.F., Ruggles, C., Sparrow, T. and McMillan, A. 2013. Time and a place: A luni-solar 'time-reckoner' from 8th millennium BC Scotland. *Internet Archaeology* 34. 10.11141/ia.34.1.

Gardiner, J. 1984. Lithic distributions and settlement patterns in central-southern England. In R. Bradley and J. Gardiner (eds.), *Neolithic studies: A review of some current research*, pp. 15–40. Oxford: British Archaeological Reports, British Series 133.

Gardiner, J. 1988. *The composition and distribution of Neolithic surface flint scatters in central southern England.* Doctoral thesis, University of Reading.

Gardiner, P.J. 2007. Mesolithic activity at Hawkcombe Head, Somerset: An interim report on the 2002–3 excavations. In C. Waddington and K. Pedersen (eds.), *Mesolithic studies in the North Sea Basin and Beyond*, pp. 81–95. Oxford: Oxbow.

Gardiner, P.J. 2009. South-western regional identities: Birdcombe, Totty Pot and Hawkcombe Head. In S. McCartan, R. Schulting, G. Warren and P. Woodman (eds.), *Mesolithic horizons: Papers presented at the Seventh International Conferenceon the Mesolithic in Europe, Belfast 2005*, pp. 485–493. Oxford: Oxbow Books.

Gardiner, P.J. 2016. Totty Pot, Cheddar Somerset: A history of the archaeological excavations and finds from 1960 to 1998. *Proceedings of the University of Bristol Spelaeological Society* 27(1), 39–72.

Gardiner, P., Mapplethorpe, K. and Waddington, C. 2011. *An archaeological excavation at Hawcombe Head, Exmoor National Park*. Archaeological Research Services. 10.5284/1016164. Accessed 1/8/2020.

Garland, N. and Anderson-Whymark, H. 2015. Mesolithic and late Neolithic/Bronze Age activity on the site of the American Express Community Stadium, Falmer, East Sussex. Sussex Archaeological Collection 154, 1–44.

Garrow, D. and Sturt, F. 2011. Grey waters bright with Neolithic argonauts? Maritime connections and the Mesolithic–Neolithic transition within the 'western seaways' of Britain, c. 5000–3500 BC. *Antiquity* 85(327), 59–72.

Garton, D. 2017. Prior to peat: Assessing the hiatus between Mesolithic activity and peat inception on the Southern Pennine Moors. *Archaeological Journal* 174(2), 281–334.

Ghesquière, E. 2012. Les rapports entre les deux rives de la Manche au mésolithique moyen (8000 à 6500 BC). In C. Marcigny (ed.), *Archéologie, histoire et anthropologie de la presqu'île de la Hague (Manche)*, pp. 6 ,11–21. Beaumont-Hague: Etudes ettravaux.

Ghesquière, E., Lefèvre, P., Marcigny, C. and Souffi, B. 2000. *Le Mésolithique Moyen du Nord-Cotentin Basse-Normandie, France*. Oxford: BAR (International Series) 856.

Ghilardi, B. and O'Connell, M. 2013. Early Holocene vegetation and climate dynamics with particular reference to the 8.2 ka event: Pollen and macrofossil evidencefrom a small lake in western Ireland. *Vegetation History and Archaeobotany* 22, 99–114.

Gilmour, N. and Lowe, L. 2015. A Mesolithic cremation-related deposit from Langford, Essex, England: A first for the British Mesolithic. *Mesolithic Miscellany* 23(2), 55–57.

Godwin, H. 1940a. Pollen analysis and forest history of England and Wales. *New Phytologist* 39, 370–400.

Godwin, H. 1940b. Studies of the post-glacial history of British vegetation. III. Fenland pollen diagrams. IV. Post-glacial changes of relative land- and sea-levels in the English fenland. *Philosophical Transactions of the Royal Society of London (Series B)* 230, 239–303.

Godwin, H. 1956. *History of the British Flora*. Cambridge: Cambridge University Press.

Godwin, H. 1954. Lake-stratigraphy and vegetational history. In J. G. D. Clark. (ed)., *Excavations at Star Carr*. Cambridge:Cambridge University Press.

Gooder, J. 2007. Excavation of a Mesolithic house at East Barns, East Lothian, Scotland: An interim view. In C. Waddington and K. Pedersen (eds.), *Mesolithic studies in the North Sea Basin and beyond: Proceedings of a conference held at Newcastle in 2003*, pp. 49–58. Oxford: Oxbow Books.

Gordon-Williams, J.P. 1926. The Nab Head chipping floor. *Archaeologia Cambrensis* 81, 86–111.

Gowlett, J.A.J., Hedges, R.E.M., Law, I.A. and Perry, C. 1986. Radiocarbon dates form the Oxford AMS system: Archaeometry datelist 4. *Archaeometry* 28, 206–221.

Grant, E. 2018. Exciting discoveries in the Black Isle. *History Scotland* 18(4).

Grant, M.J., Norcott, D. and Stevens, C.J. 2012. *By river, fields and factories: The making of the Lower Lea Valley – archaeological and cultural heritage investigations on the site of the London 2012 Olympic Games and Paralympic Games. Section 1: Palaeo-environmental*. Salisbury: Wessex Archaeology.

Grey, E.W. 1839. *The history and antiquities of Newbury and its environs: Including twenty-eight parishes, situate in the county of Berkshire.* Newbury: Hall and Marsh.

Grey, H. 1928. Human remains found at Greylake, Middlezoy. *Proceedings of the Somerset Archaeology and Natural History Society* 74, 156.

Greatorex, C. and Seager Thomas, M. 2000. Rock shelter stratigraphy. *Sussex Archaeological Collections* 138, 49–56.

Green, F. and Edwards, K. 2009. Palynological Studies in Northeast Skye and Raasay. *Scottish Archaeological Internet Reports* 31, 481–490. http://soas.is.ed.ac.uk/index.php/sair/article/view/2176.

Green, T., Morris, B. and Tingle, M. 2012. *Little Dartmouth Farm, Dartmouth, Devon. Results of a desk-based assessment, archaeological monitoring and excavation.* Unpublished client report. South Moulton, Devon: Southwest Archaeology.

Gregory, R.A., Murphy, E.M., Church, M.J., Edwards, K.J., Guttmann, E.B. and Simpson, D.D. 2005. Archaeological evidence for the first Mesolithic occupation of the Western Isles of Scotland. *The Holocene* 15(7), 944–950.

Griffiths, S. 2011. *Chronological modelling of the mesolithic-neolithic transition in the midlands and north of England.* Doctoral thesis, Cardiff University.

Griffiths, S. 2014. Points in time: The mesolithic–neolithic transition and the chronology of Late Rod microliths in Britain. *Oxford Journal of Archaeology* 33(3), 221–243.

Griffiths, S. and Saunders, N.J. 2020. Forged in conflict: Francis Buckley, the First World War, and British Prehistory. *International Journal of Historical Archaeology* 25, 469–485. 10.1007/s10761-020-00572-6.

Grigson, C. nd. The faunal remains. Cherhill: Wiltshire Museum.

Grigson, C. 1981. Fauna. In I.G. Simmons and M.J. Tooley (eds.), *The environment in British prehistory*, pp. 191–199. London: Duckworth.

Grigson, C. and Mellars, P. 1987. The mammalian remains from the middens. In P. Mellars (ed.), *Excavations on Oronsay: Prehistoric human ecology on a small island*, pp. 243–289. Edinburgh: Edinburgh University Press.

Grøn, O. 2003. Mesolithic dwelling places in south Scandinavia: Their definition and social interpretation. *Antiquity* 77(298), 685–708.

Gron, K.J., Rowley-Conwy, P., Fernandez-Dominguez, E., Gröcke, D.R., Montgomery, J., Nowell, G.M. and Patterson, W.P. 2018. A meeting in the forest: Hunters and farmers at the Coneybury 'anomaly', Wiltshire. *Proceedings of the Prehistoric Society* 84, 111–144.

Guéret, C. and Bénard, A. 2017. "Fontainebleau rock art" (Ile-de-France, France), an exceptional rock art group dated to the Mesolithic? Critical return on the lithic material discovered in three decorated rock shelters. *Journal of Archaeological Science: Reports* 13, 99–120.

Gupta, S., Collier, J.S., Palmer-Felgate, A. and Potter, G. 2007. Catastrophic flooding origin of shelf valley systems in the English Channel. *Nature* 448(7151), 342–346.

Hart, C. R. 1981. *The North Derbyshire Archaeological Survey.* Leeds: A. Wigley & Sons.

Haflidason, H., Sejrup, H.P., Nygård, A., Mienert, J., Bryn, P., Lien, R., Forsberg, C.F., Berg, K. and Masson, D. 2004. The Storegga Slide: Architecture, geometry and slide development. *Marine Geology* 213(1–4), 201–234.

Hallowell, A.I. 1926. Bear ceremonialism in the northern hemisphere. *American Anthropologist* 28(1), 1–75.

Halsey, C. 2006. *The Former Sanderson Site, Oxford Rd, Denham. An archaeological post-excavation assessment and updated project design.* London: Museum of London Archaeology Service.

Harbord, N.H. 1996. A North York Moors mesolithic marginal site on Highcliff Nab Guisborough. *Durham Archaeological Journal* 12, 17–26.

Harding, P. 2000. A mesolithic site at Rock Common, Washington, West Sussex. *Sussex Archaeological Collections* 138, 29–48.

Harding, A.F. and Ostoja-Zagórski, J. 1987. Excavations in Rocks Wood, Withyham. *Sussex Archaeological Collections* 125, 11–32.

Hardy, K. and Birch, S. 2009. Worked bone from Sand. *Scottish Archaeological Internet Reports* 31, 274–304. http://soas.is.ed.ac.uk/index.php/sair/article/view/2158.

Hardy, K. and Wickham-Jones, C. 2002. Scotland's first settlers: The mesolithic seascape of the Inner Sound, Skye and its contribution to the early prehistory of Scotland. *Antiquity* 76(293), 825–833.

Hardy, K. and Wickham-Jones, C. 2009. Mesolithic and later sites around the Inner Sound, Scotland the work of the Scotland's First Settlers Project 1998–2004. *Scottish Archaeological Internet Reports* 31 (January). http://soas.is.ed.ac.uk/index.php/sair/article/view/1405.

Harris, S. 2014. Sensible dress: The sight, sound, smell and touch of Late Ertebølle Mesolithic cloth types. *Cambridge Archaeological Journal* 24(1), 37–56.

Harris, S. 2019. The sensory archaeology of textiles. In R. Skeates and J. Day (eds.), *Routledge handbook of sensory archaeology*. London: Routledge.

Healey, E. 1993. The lithics. In F. Lynch (ed.), *Excavations in the Brenig Valley: A mesolithic and bronze age landscape in North Wales*. Cardiff: Cambrian Archaeological Association.

Healy, F., Bayliss, A., Whittle, A., Pryor, F., French, C., Allen, M., Evans, C., Edmonds, M., Meadows, J. and Hey, G. 2011. Eastern England. In A. Whittle, F. Healy and A. Bayliss (eds.), *Gathering time. Dating the Early Neolithic enclosures of Southern Britain and Ireland*, pp. 263–347. Oxford: Oxbow Books.

Healy, F., Heaton, M., Lobb, S.J., Allen, M.J., Fenwick, I.M., Grace, R. and Scaife, R.G. 1992. Excavations of a mesolithic site at Thatcham, Berkshire. *Proceedings of the Prehistoric Society* 58, 41–76.

Hedges, R.E.M., Housley, R.A., Law, I. A. and Bronk, C.R. 1989. RAdiocarbon dates from the Oxford AMS system: Archaeometry datelist 9. *Archaeometry* 31, 207–234.

Hellewell, E.R. 2015. *An investigation into the placement of disarticulated human remains into shell middens during prehistory*. Doctoral dissertation, University of York.

Hemingway, M.F. 1980. Preliminary explorations at the Rocks, Uckfield. *Sussex Archaeological Society Newsletter* 31, 209–210.

Henson, D. 1982. *Flint as a raw material in prehistory*. M.Phil thesis, University of Sheffield.

Hey, G. 2014. Later upper palaeolithic and mesolithic resource assessment. In G. Hey and J. Hind (eds.), *Solent-Thames research framework for the historic environment resource assessments and research agenda*. Oxford: Oxford Wessex Monographs 6.

Higgs, E. 1959. Excavations at a mesolithic site at Downton, near Salisbury, Wiltshire. *Proceedings of the Prehistoric Society* 25, 209–232.

Higham, N.J. and Cane, T. 1999. The Tatton Park Project, part 1: Prehistoric to sub-Roman settlement and land use. *Journal of the Chester Archaeological Society* 74, 1–61.

Hind, D. 1998. Chert use in the Mesolithic of Northern England. *Assemblage* 4.

Hirons, K.R. and Edwards, K.J. 1990. Pollen and related studies at Kinloch, Isle of Rhum, Scotland, with particular reference to possible early human impacts on vegetation. *New Phytologist*, 116(4), 715–727.

Hodgson, J. and Brennand, M. 2006. The prehistoric period resource assessment. In M. Brennand (ed.), *Research and archaeology in North West England. An archaeological research framework for North West England: Volume 1, resource assessment*, pp. 23–58. Bolton: Council for British Archaeology North West.

Holyoak, D.T. 1980. *Late pleistocene sediments and biostratigraphy of the Kennet Valley, England*. Doctoral dissertation, University of Reading.

Hopson, P.M. 2005. *A stratigraphical framework for the Upper Cretaceous Chalk of England and Scotland, with statements on the Chalk of Northern Ireland and the UK Offshore Sector*. Keyworth: British Geological Survey Research Report.

Howard-Davis, C., Bain, M., Bamford, H., Barnes, B., Leech, R.H. and Quartermaine, J. 1996. Seeing the sites: Survey and excavation on the Anglezarke Uplands, Lancashire. *Proceedings of the Prehistoric Society* 62, 133–166.

Huang, C.C. 2002. Holocene landscape development and human impact in the Connemara uplands, western Ireland. *Journal of Biogeography* 29, 153–165.

Hughes, M. and ApSimon, A. 1977. A mesolithic flint working site on the south coast motorway (M27) near Fort Wallington, Fareham, Hampshire, 1972. *Proceedings of the Hampshire Field Club* 34, 23–35.

Ingold, T. 1993. The temporality of the landscape. *World Archaeology* 25(2), 152–174.

Ingold, T. 2000. Totemism, animism and the depiction of animals. In *The Perception of the environment. Essays in livelihood, dwelling and skill,* pp. 111–131. London: Routledge.

Innes, J.B. and Blackford, J.J. 2003. The ecology of late Mesolithic woodland disturbances: Model testing with fungal spore assemblage data. *Journal of Archaeological Science* 30(2), 185–194.

Innes, J., Laurie, T. and Simmons, I. 2012. The age of the late mesolithic on the North York Moors, England: Radiocarbon dating a small flint tool stratified in peat from East Bilsdale Moor. *Journal of Wetland Archaeology* 12(1), 48–57.

Innes, J. and Tipping, R. 2016. Geoarchaeology and landscape reconstruction. In C. Waddington and C. Bonsall (eds.), *Archaeology and environment on the North Sea littoral: A case study from Low Hauxley,* pp. 214–252. Bakewell: Archaeological Research Services/ Northumberland Wildlife Trust.

Iversen, J. 1973. Geology of Denmark III: The Development of Denmark's Nature since the Last Glacial. *Danmarks Geologiske Undersøgelse V. Række* 7, 1–126.

Jackson, R., Bevan, B., Hurst, D. and de Rouffignac, C. 1994. Salvage recording of a Mesolithic site at Lightmarsh Farm, Kidderminster Foreign. Archaeological Service, Hereford and Worcester County Council, internal report, 199.

Jackson, R.A., Bevan, L., Hurst, J.D. and de Rouffignac, C. 1996. Archaeology on the Trimpley to Blackstone Aqueduct. *Transactions of the Worcester Archaeological Society* 15, 93–126.

Jacobi, R.M. 1975. *Aspects of the Post-Glacial Archaeology of England and Wales.* Doctoral thesis, University of Cambridge.

Jacobi, R. nd. Roger Jacobi archive, British Museum.

Jacobi, R.M. 1976. Britain inside and outside Mesolithic Europe. *Proceedings of the Prehistoric Society* 42, 67–84.

Jacobi, R.M. 1978a. Northern England in the Eighth millennium BC. In P.A. Mellars (ed.), *The Early Post-Glacial Settlement of Northern Europe,* pp. 295–332. London: Duckworth.

Jacobi, R.M. 1978b. The Mesolithic of Sussex. In A. Ellison and P.L. Drewett (eds.), *Archaeology in Sussex to AD 1500,* pp. 15–22. London: CBA Research Report 29.

Jacobi, R.M. 1979. Early Flandrian hunters in the South-West. In V.A. Haxfield (ed.), *Devon Archaeological Society: Prehistoric Dartmoor in its Context,* pp. 48–93. Devon Archaeological Society Jubilee Conference Proceedings 37. Exeter: Devon Archaeological Society.

Jacobi, R.M. 1980a. The Early Holocene settlement of Wales. In J.A. Taylor (ed.), *Culture and Environment in Prehistoric Wales,* pp. 131–206. Oxford: British Archaeological Reports, British Series 76.

Jacobi, R.M. 1980b. The Mesolithic of Essex. In D.G. Buckley, (ed.), *Archaeology in Essex to AD 1500,* pp. 14–25. Council for British Archaeology.

Jacobi, R.M. 1981. The last hunters in Hampshire. In S. Shennan and R.T. Schadla-Hall (eds.), 1981. *The Archaeology of Hampshire: From the Palaeolithic to the Industrial Revolution,* pp. 10–25. Winchester: Hampshire Field Club and Archaeological Society.

Jacobi, R.M. 1982a. When did man come to Scotland? *Mesolithic Miscellany* 3(2), 8–9.

Jacobi, R.M. 1982b. Mesolithic findspots near Horsham. *Warnham Historical Society Newsletter* 5, 1–4.

Jacobi, R.M. 1982c. Last hunters in Kent, Tasmania and the earliest Neolithic. In P.E. Leach (ed.), *Archaeology in Kent to AD 1500*, pp. 12–24. London: CBA. Research Report 48.

Jacobi, R. 1984. The Mesolithic of northern East Anglia and contemporary territories. *Aspects of East Anglian Prehistory (twenty years after Rainbird Clarke)*, pp. 43–76. Norwich: Geo Books.

Jacobi, R.M. 1987. Misanthropic miscellany: Musings on British early Flandrian archaeology and other flights of fancy. In P. Rowly-Conwy and H. Blankholm (eds.), *Mesolithic Northwest Europe: Recent trends*, pp. 163–168. Sheffield: Department of Archaeology.

Jacobi, R.M. 1994. Mesolithic radiocarbon dates: A first review of some recent dates. In N. Ashton and A. David (eds), *Stories in Stone. Proceedings of Anniversary Conference at St. Hilda's College, Oxford, April 1993*, pp. 192–198. London: Lithic Studies Society Occasional paper 4.

Jacobi, R.M. 2005. Some observations on the lithic artefacts from Aveline's Hole, Burrington Combe, North Somerset. *Proceedings of the University of Bristol Spelaeological Society* 23(3), 267–295.

Jacobi, R.M., Martingell, H.E. and Huggins, P.J. 1978. A Mesolithic industry from Hill Wood, High Beach, Epping Forest. *Essex Archaeology and His*tory 10, 206–219.

Jacobi, R.M., Tallis, J.H. and Mellars, P.A. 1976. The southern Pennine Mesolithic and the ecological record. *Journal of Archaeological Science* 3(4), 307–320.

Jacobi, R.M. and Tebbutt, C.F. 1981. A Late Mesolithic rock-shelter site at High Hurstwood, Sussex. *Sussex Archaeological Collections* 119, 1–36.

Jacobi, R. and Higham, T. 2011. The Later Upper Palaeolithic recolonisation of Britain: new results from AMS radiocarbon dating. *Developments in Quaternary Sciences* 14, 223–247.

Jacobi, R.M. and Wessex Archaeology. 2014. *Palaeolithic and Mesolithic Lithic Artefact (PaMELA) database [data-set]*. York: Archaeology Data Service [distributor]. 10.5284/102 8201.

Jacques, D., Phillips, T., Hoare, P., Bishop, B., Legge, T. and Parfitt, S. 2014. Mesolithic settlement near Stonehenge: Excavations at Blick Mead, Vespasian's Camp, Amesbury. *Wiltshire Archaeological and Natural History Magazine* 107, 7–27.

Jacques, D., Phillips, T. and Lyons, T. 2018. *Blick Mead: Exploring the 'first Place' in the Stonehenge Landscape: Archaeological Excavations at Blick Mead, Amesbury, Wiltshire 2005–2016*. Oxford: Peter Lang Limited.

Jessen, C.A., Pedersen, K.B., Christensen, C., Olsen, J., Mortensen, M.F. and Hansen, K.M. 2015. Early Maglemosian culture in the Preboreal landscape: Archaeology and vegetation from the earliest Mesolithic site in Denmark at Lundby Mose, Sjælland. *Quaternary International* 378, 73–87. 10.1016/j.quaint.2014.03.056.

Jochim, M.A. 1991. Archaeology as long-term ethnography. *American Anthropologist* 93, 309–319.

Johnson, M. and Cameron, K. 2012. An Early Bronze age unenclosed cremation cemetery and Mesolithic pit at Skilmafilly, near Maud, Aberdeenshire. *Scottish Archaeological Internet Reports 53*. 10.9750/issn.1773-3808.2012.53.

Johnson, N. and David, A. 1982. A Mesolithic site on Trevose Head and contemporary geography. *Cornish Archaeology* 21, 67–103.

Jones, S.J. 1938. The excavation of Gorsey Bigbury. *Proceedings of the University of Bristol Spelaeological Society* 5(1), 3–56.

Jones, P. 2013. *Upper Palaeolithic sites in the lower courses of the Rivers Colne and Wey: Excavations at Church Lammas and Wey Manor Farm*. Dorchester: SpoilHeap Monographs 5.

Jones, A.M. 2015. An incised Mesolithic pebble from Trevose Head, St Merryn, Cornwall. *Cornish Archaeology* 54, 219–223.

Jones, A.M. 2016. A Mesolithic pit at Penans Farm, Grampound, Cornwall. *Cornish Archaeology* 55, 241–248.

Jones, A.M., Lawson-Jones, A. and Quinnell, H. 2019. Excavations at the North Cliffs 2016: Investigating Mesolithic flint scatters in Hudder Field. *Cornish Archaeology* 58, 1–26.

Jones, A.M., Lawson-Jones, A., Quinnell, H. and Tyacke, A. 2018. The North Cliffs Project. *Mesolithic Miscellany* 26(1), 23–48.

Jones, P., Marples, N. and Bailey, R.M. 2013. *A Mesolithic 'Persistent Place' at North Park Farm, Bletchingley, Surrey,* p. 8. Dorchester: Spoil Heap Monographs.

Jordan, P. 2003. Investigating post-glacial hunter-gatherer landscape enculturation: Ethnographic analogy and interpretive methodologies. In L. Larsson, K. Kindgren, D. Loeffer and A. Akerlund (eds.), *Mesolithic on the Move*, pp. 128–138. Oxford: Oxbow.

Karsten, P. and Knarrström, B. 2003. *The Tågerup Excavations.* Trelleborg: National Heritage Board.

Keef, P.A.M., Wymer, J.J. and Dimbleby, G.W. 1965. A Mesolithic site on Iping Common, Sussex, England. *Proceedings of the Prehistoric Society* 31, 85–92.

Kelly, R.L. 1995. *The foraging spectrum: Diversity in hunter-gatherer lifeways.* Washington: Smithsonian Inst Press.

Kenney, J. 1993. *The beginnings of agriculture in Great Britain: A critical assessment.* Doctoral thesis, University of Edinburgh.

Kenney, J. 2008. *Recent Excavations at Llandygai, near Bangor, North Wales.* Gwynedd Archaeological Trust Report 764.

Kenney, J. and Hopewell, D. 2016. *Ynys Enlli Management Plan*, prepared for Cadw, Gwyedd Archaeological Trust Report 1304.

Kenworthy, J.B. 1982. The flint. In H. Murray (ed.), *Excavations in the medieval burgh of Aberdeen 1973–81*, pp. 200–215. Edinburgh: Society of Antiquaries of Scotland Monograph Series 2.

Knight, B., Milner, N., Taylor, B., Elliot, B., O'Connor, T., Milner, N., Conneller, C. and Taylor, B. 2018. Assembling animals. In N. Milner, C. Conneller, B. Taylor (eds.), *Star Carr: A persistent place in a changing world*, pp. 123–156. York: White Rose Press.

Lacaille, A.D. 1954. *The stone age in Scotland.* Oxford: Oxford University Press.

Larsson, L., Sjöström, A. and Heron, C. 2016. The Rönneholm arrow: a find of a wooden arrow-tip with microliths in the Bog Rönneholms Mosse, Central Scania, Southern Sweden. *Lund Archaeological Review* 22, 7–20.

Larson, G., Karlsson, E.K., Perri, A., Webster, M.T., Ho, S.Y.W., Peters, J., Stahl, P.W., Piper, P.J., Lingaas, F., Fredholm, M., Comstock, K.E., Modiano, J.F., Schelling, C., Agoulnik, A.I., Leegwater, P.A., Dobney, K., Vigne, J.-D., Vila, C., Andersson, L., and Lindblad-Toh, K. 2012. Rethinking dog domestication by integrating genetics, archeology, and biogeography. *Proceedings of the National Academy of Sciences* 109, 8878–8883. 10.1073/pnas.1203005109.

Lacaille, A.D. 1963. Mesolithic industries beside Colne Waters in Iver and Denham. *Records of Bucks* 17, 143–181.

Lacaille, A.D. 1966. Mesolithic facies in the transpontine fringes. *Surrey Archaeological Collection* 66, 1–43.

Lacaille, A.D. and Grimes, W.F. 1956. The prehistory of Caldey. *Archaeologia Cambrensis* 104, 85–165.

Lacaille, A.D. and Grimes, W.F. 1961. The prehistory of Caldey, Part 2. *Archaeologia Cambrensis* 110, 30–63.

Lane, P., Schadla-Hall, R.T. and Taylor, B. in press. *Hunter-gatherers in the landscape: Investigations of the Early Mesolithic in the Vale of Pickering, North Yorkshire. 1976–2000.* Cambridge: MacDonald Institute for Archaeological Research.

Larsson, L. 1990. Dogs in fraction–symbols in action. In P.M. Vermeersch and P. Van Peer (eds.), *Contributions to the Mesolithic in Europe: Papers Presented at the Fourth International Symposium, The Mesolithic in Europe, Leuven, 1990*, pp. 153–160. Leuven: Leuven University Press.

Larsson, L. 2004. The Mesolithic period in Southern Scandinavia, with special reference to burials and cemeteries. In Saville, A. (ed.), *Mesolithic Scotland and its neighbours*, pp. 371–392. Edinburgh: Society of Antiquaries for Scotland.

Lawrence, T., Donnelly, M., Kennard, E., Souday, C. and Grant, R. in press. Britain in or out of Europe during the late Mesolithic? A new perspective. In T. Perrin, B. Marquebielle, S. Philibert and N. Valdeyron (eds.), *Proceedings of the Mesolithic in Europe 2020 Conference*. Berlin: Open Archaeology.

Lawrence, T., Long, A.J., Gehrels, W.R., Jackson, L. and Smith, D.E. 2016. Relative sea-level data from southwest Scotland constrain meltwater-driven sea-level jumps prior to the 8.2kyrBP event. *Quaternary Science Reviews* 151, 292–308.

Lawson, T.J. and Bonsall. C. 1986. The Palaeolithic of Scotland: A reconsideration of evidence from Reindeer Cave, Assynt. In S.N. Colicutt (ed.), *The Palaeolithic of Britain and its nearest neighbours: Recent trends*, pp. 85–89. Sheffield: University of Sheffield, Department of Archaeology.

Layard, N.F. 1927. A Late Palaeolithic settlement in the Colne Valley, Essex. *The Antiquaries Journal* 7(4), 500–514.

Leach, A.L. 1918. Flint-working sites on the submerged land (submerged forest) bordering the Pembrokeshire coast. *Proceedings of the Geologists' Association* 29, 46–67.

Leakey, L.S.B. 1951. *Preliminary excavations of a Mesolithic site at Abinger Common, Surrey.* Surrey Archaeological Society Research Papers 3.

Leary, J. 2015. *The remembered land: Surviving sea-level rise after the last Ice Age.* London: Bloomsbury Publishing.

Legge, A. and Rowley-Conwy, P. 1988. *Star Carr Revisited.* London: Birkbeck College.

Lee, D. and Woodward, N. 2009. Links House, Stronsay. *Discovery and Excavation in Scotland* 10, 141.

Leivers, M., Barnett, C. and Harding, P. 2007. Excavation of Mesolithic and Neolithic flint scatters and accompanying environmental sequences at Tank Hill Road, Purfleet, Essex, 2002. *Essex Archaeology and History* 38, 1–44.

Lesvignes, E., Robert, E., Valentin, B., Ballinger, M., Bénard, A., Bellanger, F., Bouet, B., Bougnères, F., Cantin, A., Costa, L. and Dardignac, C. 2019. Using digital techniques to document prehistoric rock art: First approaches on the engraved panels of the Paris Basin shelters. *Digital Applications in Archaeology and Cultural Heritage* 15, p. e00122.

Lévi-Strauss, C. 1966. *The savage mind.* London: Weidenfeld and Nicolson.

Lévi-Strauss, C. 1982. *The way of the masks.* London: Jonathan Cape.

Lewis, M.P. 1992. *The prehistory of south west Wales, 7500–3600 BP: An interdisciplinary palaeoenvironmental and archaeological investigation.* Unpublished Ph.D. thesis, University of Lampeter.

Lewis, J.S. 2000. *The Archaeology of Greater London.* London: Museum of London Archaeological Service Monograph.

Lewis, J.S. and Rackham, J. 2011. *Three Ways Wharf, Uxbridge: A late glacial and early Holocene hunter-gatherer site in the Colne Valley.* London: Museum of London Archaeology Monograph.

Lewis, J., Rosen, C., Booth, R., Davies, P., Allen, M. and Law, M. 2019. Making a significant place: Excavations at the Late Mesolithic site of Langley's Lane, Midsomer Norton, Bath and North-East Somerset. *Archaeological Journal* 176(1), 1–50.

Lillie, M. 2015. *Hunters, Fishers and Foragers in Wales: Towards a social narrative of Mesolithic lifeways.* Oxford: Oxbow Books.

Lillie, M.C., Zhilin, M., Shavchenko, S. and Taylor, M. 2005. Carpentry dates back to Mesolithic. *Antiquity* 79(305). https://antiquity.ac.uk/projGall/lillie/index.html.

Little, A., Elliott, B., Conneller, C., Pomstra, D., Evans, A.A., Fitton, L.C., Holland, A., Davis, R., Kershaw, R., O'Connor, S. and O'Connor, T. 2016. Technological analysis of the world's earliest shamanic costume: A multi-scalar, experimental study of a red deer headdress from the Early Holocene site of Star Carr, North Yorkshire, UK. *PLoS One* 11(4), p. e0152136.

Little, A. and van Gijn, A. 2017. Enigmatic plant-working tools and the transition to farming in the Rhine Meuse Delta. *Excerpta Archaeologica Leidensia II, Analecta Praehistorica Leidensia* 47, 1–10.

Louwe Kooijmans, L.P. 2003. The Hardinxveld sites in the Rhine/Meuse delta, the Netherlands, 5500-4500 cal BC. In L. Larsson, F. Kindgren, K. Knutsson, D. Loeffer and A. Akerlund (eds.), *Mesolithic on the Moue: Papers presented at the sixth international conference on the Mesolithic in Europe, Stockholm 2000*, pp. 608–624. Oxford: Oxbow.

Loveday, R. 2012. The Greater Stonehenge Cursus–the Long View. *Proceedings of the Prehistoric Society* 78, 341–350.

Lucas, G. 2019. Periodisation in archaeology. Starting from the ground. In S. Souvatzi, A. Baysal and E. Baysal (eds.), *Time and history in prehistory*, pp. 77–94. London: Routledge.

Lynch, F. 1970. *Prehistoric Anglesey: The archaeology of the island to the Roman conquest.* Llangefni: Anglesey Antiquarian Society.

Lynch, F. 1993. *Excavations in the Brenig Valley: A Mesolithic and Bronze Age Landscape in North Wales.* Cardiff: Cambrian Archaeological Association.

Lynch, F. and Musson, C. 2001. A prehistoric and early medieval complex at Llandegai, near Bangor, North Wales. *Archaeologia Cambrensis* 150, 17–142.

MacGregor, G. 2009. Changing people changing landscapes: Excavations at The Carrick, Midross, Loch Lomond. *Historic Argyll* 8, 8–13.

MacGregor, G. and Donnelly, M. 2001. A Mesolithic scatter from Littlehill Bridge, Girvan, Ayrshire. *Scottish Archeological Journal* 23(1), 1–14.

MacKie, E.W. 1972. Radiocarbon dates for two Mesolithic shell heaps and a Neolithic axe factory in Scotland. *Proceedings of the Prehistoric Society* 38, 412–416.

Manby, T.G. 1966. Creswellian site at Brigham, East Yorkshire. *The Antiquaries Journal* 46(2), 211–228.

Mannino, M.A., Spiro, B.F. and Thomas, K.D. 2003. Sampling shells for seasonality: Oxygen isotope analysis on shell carbonates of the inter-tidal gastropod Monodonta lineata (da Costa) from populations across its modern range and from a Mesolithic site in southern Britain. *Journal of Archaeological Science* 30(6), 667–679.

Mannino, M.A. and Thomas, K.D. 2001. Intensive Mesolithic exploitation of coastal resources? Evidence from a shell deposit on the Isle of Portland (Southern England) for the impact of human foraging on populations of intertidal rocky shore molluscs. *Journal of Archaeological Science* 28(10), 1101–1114.

Mansrud, A. 2017. Untangling social, ritual and cosmological aspects of fishhook manufacture in the Middle Mesolithic coastal communities of NE Skagerrak. *International Journal of Nautical Archaeology* 46(1), 31–47.

Marchand, G. and Perrin, T. 2017. Why this revolution? Explaining the major technical shift in Southwestern Europe during the 7th millennium cal. BC. *Quaternary International* 428, 73–85.

Marean, C.W. and Kim, S.Y. 1998. Mousterian large-mammal remains from Kobeh Cave behavioral implications for Neanderthals and early modern humans. *Current Anthropology* 39(S1), S79–S114.

Marshall, G.D. 2000. The distribution and character of flint beach pebbles on Islay as a source for Mesolithic chipped stone artefact production. *Hunter-gatherer landscape archaeology: The Southern Hebrides Mesolithic Project Volume 1*, pp. 79–90. Cambridge: McDonald Institute Monographs.

Marsland, A. 1986. The floodplain deposits of the lower Thames. *Quarterly Journal of Engineering Geology* 19, 223–247.

Mayewski, P.A., Rohling, E.E., Stager, J.C., Karlén, W., Maasch, K.A., Meeker, L.D., Meyerson, E.A., Gasse, F., van Kreveld, S., Holmgren, K. and Lee-Thorp, J. 2004. Holocene climate variability. *Quaternary Research* 62(3), 243–255.

McBurney, C. 1959. Recent excavations in the Mendip Caves. *Proceedings of the Prehistoric Society* 25, 260–269.

McCullagh, R. 1988. Excavation at Newton, Islay. *Glasgow Archaeological Journal* 15(15), 23–51.

McFadyen, L. 2006. Landscape. In C. Conneller and G. Warren (eds.), Mesolithic Britain and Ireland: New approaches, pp. 121–138. Stroud: Tempus.

McInnes, E. 2015. *(Re) creating the World in Everyday Engagements: A material approach to elements and cosmologies during the Mesolithic-Neolithic transition.* Doctoral thesis, University of Manchester.

McKinley, J., Riddler, I. and Trevarthan, M. 2006. The Prehistoric, Roman and Anglo-Saxon Funerary Landscape at Saltwood Tunnel, Kent. *CTRL Integrated Report Series.*

Meiklejohn, C., Chamberlain, A.T. and Schulting, R.J. 2011. Radiocarbon dating of Mesolithic human remains in Great Britain. *Mesolithic Miscellany* 21(2), 20–58.

Meiklejohn, C. and Denston, B. 1987. The human skeletal material: Inventory and initial interpretation. In P.A. Mellars, *Excavations on Oronsay: Prehistoric human ecology on a small island*, pp. 290–300. Edinburgh: Edinburgh University Press.

Meiklejohn, C., Merrett, D.C., Nolan, R., Richards, M.P. and Mellars, P.A. 2005. Spatial relationships, dating and taphonomy of the human bone from the Mesolithic site of Cnoc Coig, Oronsay, Argyll, Scotland. *Proceedings of the Prehistoric Society* 71, 85–105.

Mellars, P.A. 1976a. Settlement patterns and industrial variability in the British Mesolithic. In G. de G Sieveking, I.H. Longworth and K.E. Wilson (eds.), *Problems in Economic and Social Archaeology*, pp. 357–399. London: Duckworth.

Mellars, P.A. 1976b. December. Fire ecology, animal populations and man: A study of some ecological relationships in prehistory. *Proceedings of the Prehistoric Society* 42, 15–45.

Mellars, P.A. 1987. *Excavations on Oronsay: Prehistoric human ecology on a small island.* Edinburgh: Edinburgh University Press.

Mellars, P. and Dark, P. 1998. *Star Carr in context.* Cambridge: McDonald Institute Monographs.

Mellars, P.A. and Reinhardt, S.C. 1978. Patterns of Mesolithic land-use in southern England: A geological perspective. In P. Mellars (ed.), *The early postglacial settlement of Northern Europe*, pp. 234–294. London: Duckworth.

Mellars, P.A. and Wilkinson, M.R. 1980. Fish otoliths as indicators of seasonality in prehistoric shell middens: The evidence from Oronsay (Inner Hebrides). *Proceedings of the Prehistoric Society* 46, 19–44.

Melton, N. 2009. Shells, seals and ceramics: An evaluation of a midden at West Voe, Sumburgh, Shetland, 2004–2005. In S. McCartan, P. Woodman, R. Schulting and G. Warren (eds.), *Mesolithic horizons: Papers presented at the seventh international conference on the Mesolithic in Europe, Belfast 2005*, pp. 184–189. Oxford: Oxbow.

Melton, N., Russ, H. and Johnson, D.S. 2014. *Excavation of a Mesolithic site at Kingsdale Head (SD712 799) by the Ingleborough Archaeology Group 2009-2010.* Carnforth: Ingleborough Archaeology Group.

Mercer, J. 1968. Stone tools from a washing-limit deposit of the highest postglacial transgression, Lealt Bay, Isle of Jura, *Proceedings of the Society of Antiquaries of Scotland* 100 (1967-8), 1–46.

Mercer, J. 1969. Flint tools from the present tidal zone, Lussa Bay, Isle of Jura, Argyll. *Proceedings of the Society of Antiquaries of Scotland* 102, 1–30.

Mercer, J. 1970. A regression-time stone-workers' camp, 33ft OD, Lussa River, Isle of Jura. *Proceedings of the Society of Antiquaries of Scotland* 103, 1–32.

Mercer, J. 1972. Microlithic and Bronze Age camps, 75-26 ft O.D., N. Cam, Isle of Jura', *Proceedings of the Society of Antiquaries of Scotland* 104 (1971-2), 1–22.

Mercer, J. 1974. Glenbatrick Waterhole, a microlithic site on the Isle of Jura. *Proceedings of the Society of Antiquaries of Scotland* 105, 9–32.

Mercer, J. 1978. Lussa Wood 1: The late-glacial and early post-glacial occupation of Jura. *Proceedings of the Society of Antiquaries of Scotland* 110, 1–31.

Milner, N. 2006. Subsistence. In C. Conneller and G. Warren (eds.), *Mesolithic Britain and Ireland: New approaches*, pp. 61–82. Oxford: Oxbow.

Milner, N. 2009. Mesolithic middens and marine molluscs, procurement and consumption of shellfish at the site of sand. *Scottish Archaeological Internet Reports* 31, 384–400. http://soas.is.ed.ac.uk/index.php/sair/article/view/2067. Accessed 15/3/2019.

Milner, N., Conneller, C. and Taylor, B. 2018. *Star Carr, Volume 1: A persistent place in a changing world.* York: White Rose University Press.

Mithen, S. 2000. *Hunter-gatherer landscape archaeology: The Southern Hebrides Mesolithic project 1988–1998.* Cambridge: McDonald Institute Monographs.

Mithen, S. 2019. Mesolithic fireplaces and the enculturation of Early Holocene landscapes in Britain, with a case study from western Scotland. *Proceedings of the Prehistoric Society* 85, 131–159.

Mithen, S. J. and Finlayson, B. 1991. Red Deer Hunters on Colonsay? The Implications of Staosnaig for the Interpretation of the Oronsay Middens. *Proceedings of the Prehistoric Society* 57(2), 1–8.

Mithen, S. and Finlay, N. 2000. Coulererach, Islay: Test-pit survey and trial excavation. *Hunter-Gatherer landscape Archaeology: The Southern Hebrides Mesolithic Project Volume 1*, pp. 217–229. Cambridge: Cambridge University Press.

Mithen, S.J. and Wicks, K. 2008. Inner hebrides archaeological project: Fiskary Bay. *Discovery and Excavation in Scotland* 9, 36.

Mithen, S. and Wicks, K. 2018. The interpretation of Mesolithic structures in Britain: New evidence from Criet Dubh, Isle of Mull, and alternative approaches to chronological analysis for inferring occupation tempos and settlement patterns. *Proceedings of the Prehistoric Society* 84, 77–110.

Mithen, S., Wicks, K. and Berg-Hansen, I.M. 2019. The Mesolithic coastal exploitation of western Scotland: The impacts of climate change and use of favoured locations. In A. Schülke (ed.), *Coastal landscapes of the Mesolithic*, pp. 147–178. London: Routledge.

Mithen, S.J., Wicks, K. and Hill, J. 2007. Fiskary Bay: A Mesolithic fishing camp on Coll. *Scottish Archaeology News* 55, 14–15.

Mithen, S., Wicks, K., Pirie, A., Riede, F., Lane, C., Banerjea, R., Cullen, V., Gittins, M. and Pankhurst, N. 2015. A lateglacial archaeological site in the far north-west of Europe at Rubha Port an t-Seilich, Isle of Islay, western Scotland: Ahrensburgian-style artefacts, absolute dating and geoarchaeology. *Journal of Quaternary Science* 30(5), 396–416.

Momber, G., Mason, B., Gillespie, J., Heamagi, C., Satchell, J., Ferreira, R. and Noble-Shelly, J. 2020. New evidence from Bouldnor Cliff for technological innovation in the Mesolithic, population dispersal and use of drowned landscapes. *Quaternary International* 584, 116–128.

Momber, G., Tomalin, D., Scaife, R., Satchell, J. and Gillespie, J. 2011. *Mesolithic occupation at Bouldnor Cliff and the submerged prehistoric landscapes of the Solent.* London: CBA Research Report 164.

Money, J.H. 1960. Excavations at high rocks, Tunbridge Wells, 1954–1956. *Sussex Archaeological Collections* 98, 173–221.

Moore, J.W. 1950. Mesolithic sites in the neighbourhood of Flixton, North-East Yorkshire. *Proceedings of the Prehistoric Society* 16, 101–108.

Moore, J. 2003. Beyond hazelnuts and into the forest. In L. Bevan and J. Moore (eds.), *Peopling the Mesolithic in a northern environment*, pp 53–58. Oxford: British Archaeological Reports 1157.

Morey, D. 2010. *Dogs: Domestication and the development of a social bond.* Cambridge: Cambridge University Press.

Movius, H.L. 1940. An early post-glacial archaeological site at Cushendun, County Antrim. *Proceedings of the Royal Irish Academy. Section C: Archaeology, Celtic Studies, History, Linguistics, Literature* 46, 1–84.

Mullan, G.J. and Wilson, L.J. 2004. A possible Mesolithic engraving in Aveline's Hole, Burrington Combe, north Somerset. *Proceedings of the University of Bristol Spelaeological Society* 23(2), 75–85.

Munnery, T. 2014. *Late Upper Palaeolithic/Early Mesolithic, Roman and Saxon discoveries at Fetcham near Leatherhead*. Dorchester: Spoilheap Occasional Papers 4.

Murphy, K., Caseldine, A.E., Barker, L., Fielding, S., Burrow, S. and Carlsen, S. 2014. Mesolithic human and animal footprints at Lystep Haven, Pembrokeshire, 2010: The environmental context. *Archaeologia Cambrensis* 163, 23–41.

Murray, H. and Murray, J.F. 2014. Mesolithic and early Neolithic activity along the Dee: Excavations at Garthdee Road, Aberdeen. *Proceedings of the Society of Antiquaries of Scotland* 144, 1–64.

Murray, H.K., Murray, J.C. and Fraser, S. 2009. *A tale of the unknown unknowns: A Mesolithic pit alignment and a Neolithic timber hall at Warren Field, Crathes, Aberdeenshire*. Oxford: Oxbow Books.

Myers, A.M. 1986. *The organisation and structural dimensions of lithic technology: Theoretical perspectives from ethnography and ethnoarchaeology as applied to the Mesolithic of mainland Britain with a case study from Northern England*. Doctoral thesis, University of Sheffield.

Myers, A. 1987. All shot to pieces. In A.G. Brown and M.R. Edmonds (eds.), *Lithic analysis and later British prehistory*, pp 137–153. Oxford: British Archaeological Reports, British Series 162.

Myers, A.M. 1989. Reliable and maintainable technological strategies. In R. Torrence (ed.), *Time, energy and stone tools*, pp. 78–91. Cambridge: Cambridge University Press.

Myers, A.M. 2006. An archaeological resource assessment and research agenda for the Mesolithic in the East Midlands. In N.J. Cooper (ed), *The Archaeology of the East Midlands: An Archaeological Assessment and Research Agenda*, pp. 51–68. Leicester: University of Leicester Archaeology Services.

Myers, A.M. 2020. North west regional research framework update. Prehistory resource assessment. Available at https://researchframeworks.org/nwrf/ . Accessed 21/12/2020.

Myers, A. and Gourlay, R. 1991. Muirtown, inverness: Preliminary investigation of a shell midden. *Proceedings of the Society of Antiquaries of Scotland* 121, 17–25.

Needham, A., Little, A., Conneller, C., Pomstra, D., Croft, S. and Milner, N. 2018. Beads and pendant. In N. Milner, C. Conneller and B. Taylor (eds.), *Star Carr. Volume 2: Studies in technology, subsistence and environment*, pp. 463–477. York: White Rose University Press.

Needham, S. 2000. *The passage of the Thames: Holocene environment and settlement at Runnymede* (Vol. 1). London: British Museum Publications Limited.

Newell, R. 1981. Mesolithic dwelling structures: Fact and fantasy. In B. Gramsch (ed.), *Mesolithikum in Europa*, pp. 235–284. Berlin: Veroffentlichungen des Museums fur Ur-und Fruhgeschichte Potsdam 14/15.

Nicholls, M., Corcoran, J., Eastbury, E.,Cotton, J., Scaife, R.C., Whittaker, J.E., Macphail, R., Cameron, N. and Stewart, K. 2013. A prehistoric eyot at Canning Town, Newham: A geoarchaeological investigation. Essex Archaeology and History 4, 3–26.

Nolan, R.W. 1986. *Cnoc Coig: The spatial analysis of a late Mesolithic shell midden in western Scotland*. Doctoral thesis, University of Sheffield.

Norman, C. 1975. Four Mesolithic assemblages from west Somerset. *Proceedings of the Somerset Archaeological and Natural History Society* 119, 26–37.

Norman, C. 1982. Mesolithic hunter-gatherers 9000-4000 BC. In M. Aston and I. Burrow (eds.), *The Archaeology of Somerset: A review to, 1500*, pp. 15–21. Taunton: Somerset County Council.

Norman, C. 2001. Mesolithic to Bronze Age activity at Parchey Sand Batch, Chedzoy. *Proceedings of the Somerset Archaeological and Natural History Society* 145, 9–38.

Olalde, I., Allentoft, M.E., Sánchez-Quinto, F., Santpere, G., Chiang, C.W., DeGiorgio, M., Prado-Martinez, J., Rodríguez, J.A., Rasmussen, S., Quilez, J. and Ramírez, O. 2014. Derived immune and ancestral pigmentation alleles in a 7,000-year-old Mesolithic European. *Nature* 507(7491), 225–228.

O'Malley, M. 1982. *When the Mammoth Roamed Romsey, a study of the prehistory of Romsey and district*. Romsey: Lower Test Valley Archaeology Society.

O'Malley, M. and Jacobi, R.M. 1978. The excavation of a Mesolithic occupation site at Broom Hill, Braishfield, Hampshire. *Rescue Archaeology in Hampshire* 4, 16–39.

Orschiedt, J. 2005. The head burials from Ofnet cave: An example of warlike conflict in the Mesolithic. In M. Parker Pearson and I.J.N. Thorpe (eds.), *Warfare, violence and slavery in prehistory*, pp. 67–74. Oxford: British Archaeological Reports, International Series 1374.

Overton, N.J. 2014. *Memorable meetings in the Mesolithic: Tracing the biography of human-nonhuman relationships in the Kennet and Colne Valleys with Social Zooarchaeology*. Unpublished PhD thesis, University of Manchester.

Overton, N.J. 2016. More than skin deep: Reconsidering isolated remains of 'fur-bearing species' in the British and European Mesolithic. *Cambridge Archaeological Journal* 26(4), 561–578.

Overton, N.J. and Taylor, B. 2018. Humans in the environment: Plants, animals and landscapes in Mesolithic Britain and Ireland. *Journal of World Prehistory* 31(3), 385–402.

Owen, R. 1846. *A history of British mammals and birds*. London: J. Van Voorst.

Palmer, S. 1878. On the antiquities found in the peat of Newbury. *Transactions of the Newbury Field Club* 2, 123–134.

Palmer, S. 1970. The Stone Age industries of the Isle of Portland, Dorset, and the utilization of Portland chert as artifact material in southern England. *Proceedings of the Prehistoric Society* 36, 82–115.

Palmer, S. 1972. The Mesolithic industries of Mother Siller's Channel, Christchurch, and the neighbouring areas. *Proceedings of the Hampshire Field Club and Archaeology Society* 27, 9–32.

Palmer, S. 1977. *Mesolithic cultures of Britain*. Poole: Dolphin Press.

Palmer, S. 1999. *Culverwell Mesolithic Habitation Site, Isle of Portland, Dorset. Excavation report and research studies*. Oxford: British Archaeological Reports 287.

Palmer, S. and Dimbleby, G. 1979. A Mesolithic habitation site on Winfrith Heath, Dorset. *Proceedings of the Dorset Natural History and Archaeology Society* 101, 27–56.

Pannett, A. and Baines, A. 2006. Making things, making places: The excavation of Mesolithic flint knapping sites at Oliclett, Caithness. *Scottish Archaeological Journal* 28(1), 1–26.

Parfitt, K. and Halliwell, G. 2014. Exploiting the wildwood: Evidence from a Mesolithic activity site at Finglesham, near Deal. *Archaeologia Cantiana* 134(9), 221–262.

Parker-Pearson, M. 2013. Researching stonehenge: Theories past and present. *Archaeology International* 16 (2012–2013), 72–83. 10.5334/ai.1601. Accessed 3/7/2019.

Parker-Pearson, M., Pollard, J., Richards, C., Welham, K., Casswell, C., French, C., Schlee, D., Shaw, D., Simmons, E., Stanford, A. and Bevins, R. 2019. Megalith quarries for Stonehenge's bluestones. *Antiquity* 93(367), 45–62.

Parks, R. and Barrett, J. 2009. The Zooarchaeology of sand. *Scottish Archaeological Internet Reports* 31, 331–383. http://soas.is.ed.ac.uk/index.php/sair/article/view/2053.

Parry, R. 1928. Recent excavations at the Cheddar Caves. *Nature* 122, 735–736. 10.1038/122735a0.

Peake, A.E. 1915. A cave site at Nettlebed, S. Oxon. *Proceedings of the Prehistoric Society of East Anglia* 2(1), 71–80.

Peake, A.E. 1917. A prehistoric site at Kimble, S. Bucks. *Proceedings of the Prehistoric Society of East Anglia* 2(3), 437–458.

Peake, H. and Crawford, O.G.S. 1922. A flint factory at Thatcham, Berks. *Proceedings of the Prehistoric Society of East Anglia* 3, 499–514.

Peake, H. 1934. Mesolithic Implements at Newbury. *Transactions of the Newbury District Field Club* 7, 50–51.

Pedersen, M.A. 2007. Talismans of thought: Shamanist ontologies and extended cognition in northern Mongolia. In Henare, A., Holbraad, M. and Wastell, S. (eds.), *Thinking through things: Theorising artefacts ethnographically* pp. 151–176. London: Routledge.

Peglar, S.M. 1993a. Mid- and late-Holocene vegetation history of Quidenham Mere, Norfolk, UK interpreted using recurrent groups of taxa. *Vegetation History and Archaeobotany* 2, 15–28.

Peglar, S.M. 1993b. The mid-Holocene Ulmus decline at Diss Mere, Norfolk, UK: A year-by-year pollen stratigraphy from annual laminations. *The Holocene* 3, 1–13.

Pengelly, W. 1872. The literature of the Oreston Caves near Plymouth. *Transactions of the Devonshire Association* 5, 249–361.

Perrin, T., Marchand, G., Allard, P., Binder, D., Collina, C., Puchol, O.G. and Valdeyron, N. 2009. Le second Mésolithique d'Europe occidentale: Origines et gradient chronologique. *Annales de la Fondation Fyssen* 24, 160–176.

Petch, J.A. 1924. *Early man in the district of Huddersfield*, Huddersfield: 3. Advertiser Press.

Pettitt, P. and White, M. 2012. *The British Palaeolithic: Human societies at the edge of the Pleistocene world*. London: Routledge.

Pickard C. and Bonsall C. 2004. Deep-sea fishing in the European Mesolithic: Fact or fantasy? *European Journal of Archaeology* 7, 273–290.

Pickard, C. and Bonsall, C. 2009. Some observations on the Mesolithic crustacean assemblage from Ulva Cave, Inner Hebrides, Scotland. In J.M. Burdukiewicz, K. Cyrek, P. Dyczek and K. Szymczak (eds.), *Understanding the past: Papers offered to Stefan K. Kozlowski*, pp. 305–313. Warsaw: University of Warsaw Centre for Research on the Antiquity of Southeastern Europe.

Pierpoint, S.J. and Hart, C.R. 1980. A Mesolithic surface collection from Harry Hut, Chunal Moor, Charlesworth, Derbyshire. *Derbyshire Archaeological Journal* 100, 5–11.

Piper, S.F., Bishop, R.R., Rowley-Conwy, P.A., Elliott, L. and Church, M.J. 2018. Fire in the Moor: Mesolithic carbonised remains in riverine deposits at Gleann Mor Barabhais, Lewis, Western Isles of Scotland. *Journal of the North Atlantic* 35, 1–22.

Piper, S. and Church, M.J. 2012. Small-scale sampling at Traigh an Teampuill (Temple Bay), Toe Head Peninsula, Northton, Harris, 2012; data structure report., Technical Report. http://dro.dur.ac.uk/16662/1/16662.pdf?DDD6+drk0mjc+dul4eg. Accessed 26/11/2019.

Pirie, A., Mellars, P.A. and Mithen, S.J. 2006. Cnoc Coig: A Mesolithic shell midden assemblage. *Lithics: The Journal of the Lithic Studies Society* 27, 4–11.

Pitts, M.W. nd. Lithic catalogue. Cherhill: Wiltshire Museum.

Pitts, M. 1979. Hide and Antlers: A new look at the gatherer-hunter site at Star Carr, N. Yorks, England. *World Archaeology* 11(1), 32–42.

Pitts, M.W. and Jacobi, R.M. 1979. Some aspects of change in flaked stone industries of the Mesolithic and Neolithic in southern Britain. *Journal of Archaeological Science* 6(2), 163–177.

Pollard, J. 2017. Substantial and significant pits in the Mesolithic of Britain and adjacent regions. *Hunter Gatherer Research* 3(1), 165–185.

Pollard, T. 1990. Down through the ages: A review of the Oban cave deposits. *Scottish Archaeological Review* 7, 58–74.

Pollard, T. 1996. Time and tide: coastal environments, cosmology and ritual practice in prehistoric Scotland. In T. Pollard and A. Morrison (eds.) *The Early Prehistory of Scotland*, pp. 198–212. Edinburgh: Edinburgh University Press.

Pollard, T. 2000. Risga and the Mesolithic occupation of Scottish islands. In R. Young (ed.), *Mesolithic lifeways: Current research from Britain and Ireland*, pp. 143–152. Leicester: University of Leicester.

Pollard, T., Atkinson, J. and Banks, I. 1996. It is the technical side of the work which is my stumbling block: A shell midden site on Risga reconsidered. In. Pollard, T. and Morrison, A. (eds.), *The early prehistory of Scotland*, pp. 165–182. Edinburgh: Edinburgh University Press.

Poole, S. 1986. A Late Mesolithic and Early Bronze Age site at Piethorn Brook, Milnrow. *Greater Manchester Archaeological Journal* 2, 11–30.

Poole, S. 2020. *The use and origin of Chert on Early Mesolithic sites in the Pennines and Rossendale*. M.Phil Thesis, University of Manchester.

Pope, A. 2017. *UK Shaded Relief Tiff, [Dataset]*. University of Edinburgh. 10.7488/ds/1772.

Porr M. and Bell H.R. 2012. 'Rock-art', 'Animism' and two-way thinking: Towards a complementary epistemology in the understanding of material culture and 'Rock-art' of hunting and gathering people. *Journal of Archaeological Method and Theory* 19, 161–205.

Poulton, R., Hayman, G. and Marples, N. 2017. *Foragers and farmers: 10,000 years of history at Hengrove Farm, Staines: Excavations between 1997 and 2012*. Woking: SpoilHeap Monograph 12.

Powell, A.B. 2012. *By river, fields and factories: The making of the Lower Lea Valley*. Wessex Archaeology Report 29.

Powell, A.B. and Leivers, M. 2013. Mesolithic, Neolithic and Bronze Age activity on an eyot at Addington Street, Lambeth. *London and Middlesex Archaeological Society Transactions* 63, 10–32.

Preece, R.C. 1980. The biostratigraphy and dating of the tufa deposit at the Mesolithic site at Blashenwell, Dorset, England. *Journal of Archaeological Science* 7(4), 345–362.

Preston, P.R. 2012. *Lithics to landscapes: Hunter gatherer tool use, resource exploitation and mobility during the Mesolithic of the Central Pennines, England*. Doctoral thesis, Oxford University.

Preston, P.R. and Kador, T. 2018. Approaches to interpreting Mesolithic mobility and settlement in Britain and Ireland. *Journal of World Prehistory* 31(3), 321–345.

Proctor, J. and Bishop, B. 2002. Prehistoric and environmental development on Horsleydown: Excavations at 1-2 Three Oak Lane. *Surrey Archaeological Collections* 89, 1–26.

Quinnell, H. and Blockley, M.R. 1994. *Excavations at Rhuddlan, Clwyd: 1969–73 Mesolithic to Medieval*. London: Council for British Archaeology Research Report 95.

Radley, J. 1968. A Mesolithic structure at Sheldon. *Derbyshire Archaeological Journal* 88, 26–36.

Radley, J. 1969a. A note on four Maglemosian bone points from Brandesburton, and a flint site at Brigham, Yorkshire. *The Antiquaries Journal* 49(2), 377–378.

Radley, J. 1969b. The Mesolithic period in North-East Yorkshire. *Yorkshire Archaeological Journal* 42(3), 14–327.

Radley, J. and Marshall, G. 1965. Maglemosian sites in the Pennines. *Yorkshire Archaeological Journal* 41, 394–402.

Radley, J. and Mellars, P. 1964. A Mesolithic structure at Deepcar, Yorkshire, England, and the affinities of its associated flint industries. *Proceedings of the Prehistoric Society* 30, 1–24.

Radley, J., Tallis, J.H. and Switsur, V.R. 1974. The excavation of three 'narrow blade' Mesolithic sites in the southern Pennines, England. *Proceedings of the Prehistoric Society* 40, 1–19.

Radovanovic, I. 1996. *The iron gates mesolithic*. Ann Arbor (Michigan): International Monographs in Prehistory.

Raistrick, A., Coupland, G. and Coupland, F. 1936. A Mesolithic Site on the South East Durham Coast. *Transactions of the Northern Naturalists Union* 1(4), 207–216.

Rankine, W.F. 1936. A Mesolithic site at Farnham. *Surrey Archaeological Collections* 44, 25–46.

Rankine W.F. 1949a. Pebbles of non-local rock from Mesolithic chipping floors. *Proceedings of the Prehistoric Society* 15, 188–190.

Rankine, W.F. 1949b. Mesolithic chipping floors in the wind-blown deposits of West Surrey. *Surrey Archaeological Collections* 50, 1–8.

Rankine, W.F. 1951a. A Mesolithic site on the foreshore at Cams, Fareham, Hants. *Proceedings of the Hampshire Field Club* 17, 141–142.

Rankine, W.F. 1951b. Artifacts of Portland chert in southern England. *Proceedings of the Prehistoric Society* 17(1), 93–94.

Rankine, W.F. 1953. A Mesolithic chipping floor at the Warren, Oakhanger, Selborne, Hants. *Proceedings of the Prehistoric Society* 18, 21–35.

Rankine, W.F. 1956. *The Mesolithic of southern England.* Surrey: Surrey Archaeological Society 4.

Rankine, W. F. 1961. A Mesolithic flaking floorat Oakhanger, Selbourne, Hants. Epitomised supplement to the abstract of the report published in the Proceedings of the Prehistoric Society 1960, 26, 246–262.

Rankine, W.F., Rankine, W.M. and Dimbleby, G. 1960. Further excavations at a Mesolithic site at Oakhanger, Selborne, Hants. *Proceedings of the Prehistoric Society* 26, 246–262.

Reader, F.W. 1911. A Neolithic floor in the bed of the Crouch river, and other discoveries near Rayleigh, Essex. *The Essex Naturalist* 16, 249–264.

Reid, C. 1896. An early neolithic kitchen-midden and tufaceous deposit at Blashenwell, near Corfe Castle. *Proceedings of Dorset Natural History and Antiquarian Field Club* 17, 67–75.

Reid, C. 1897. Supplementary note (February 1897) on the worked-flints from Blashenwell, near Corfe Castle. *Proceedings of Dorset Natural History and Antiquarian Field Club* 17, 67–75.

Reimer, P.J., Bard, E., Bayliss, A., Beck, J.W., Blackwell, P.G., Ramsey, C.B., Buck, C.E., Cheng, H., Edwards, R.L., Friedrich, M. and Grootes, P.M. 2013. IntCal13 and Marine13 radiocarbon age calibration curves 0–50,000 years cal BP. *Radiocarbon 55*(4), 1869–1887.

Reynier, M.J. 1997. Radiocarbon dating of Early Mesolithic technologies from Great Britain. In J.P. Fagnart and A. Thévenin (eds.), *Le Tardiglaciaire en Europe du Nord-Ouest*, pp. 529–542. Paris: Éditions du CTHS.

Reynier, M.J. 2002. Kettlebury 103: A Mesolithic 'Horsham' type stone assemblage from Hankley Common, Elstead. *Surrey Archaeological Collections* 89, 211–231.

Reynier, M.J. 2005. *Early Mesolithic Britain: Origins, development and directions.* Oxford: British Archaeological Reports, British Series 393.

Reynier, M. 2011. An Early Mesolithic stone assemblage from Marsh Benham, Berkshire UK. *Berkshire Archaeological Journal* 80, 5–21.

Richards, E. P. 1897. The gravelsand associated deposits at Newbury. *Quarterly Journal of the Geological Society* 53(1-4), 420–437.

Richards, T. 1989. Initial results of a blood residue analysis of lithic artefacts from Thorpe Common Rockshelter, South Yorkshire. In I.P. Brooks and P. Phillips (eds.), *Breaking the stony silence: Papers from the Sheffield Lithics Conference 1988*, pp. 73–90. Oxford: British Archaeological Reports, British Series 213.

Richards, M.P. and Mellars, P.A. 1998. Stable isotopes and the seasonality of the Oronsay middens. *Antiquity* 72, 178–184.

Ritchie, A. 2005. Kilellan Farm, Ardnave, Islay: Excavations of a prehistoric to Early Medieval site by Colin Burgess and others 1954-1976. Edinburgh: Society of Antiquaries of Scotland.

Ritchie, G.A. 2010. *Chronological and regional variability in Late Mesolithic narrow-blade lithic assemblages from northern Britain.* Doctoral dissertation, University of Edinburgh.

Roberts, D., Moorhead, S., Robinson, P., Payne, A., Winton, H., Hembrey, N., Bishop, B., Campbell, G., Dungworth, D., Forward, A., Middleton, A., Russell, M., Timby, J., Worley, F., Carpenter, E., Edwards, Z., Linford, N., Linford, P., Vallender, J., Henry, R., Marshall, P., Reimer, P. and Russell, N. 2017. Recent work on Urchfont Hill, Urchfont, Wiltshire. *Wiltshire Archaeological and Natural History Magazine* 110, 134–170.

Roberts, M.J., Scourse, J.D., Bennell, J.D., Huws, D.G., Jago, C.F. and Long, B.T. 2011. Late Devensian and Holocene relative sea-level change in North Wales, UK. *Journal of Quaternary Science* 26(2), 141–155.

Robertson, A., Lochrie, J., Timpany, S., Bailey, L., Mynett, A., Shillito, L.M. and Smith, C. 2013. Built to last: Mesolithic and Neolithic settlement at two sites beside the Forth estuary, Scotland. *Proceedings of the Society of Antiquaries of Scotland* 143, 73–136.

Robins, P. 1998. Mesolithic sites at two mile bottom, near Thetford, Norfolk. In N. Ashton, F. Healy and P. Pettitt (eds.), *Stone Age Archaeology: Essays in honour of John Wymer*, pp. 205–210. Oxford: Oxbow Monograph 102/Lithic Studies Society Occasional Paper 6.

Robinson, G. 2013. The excavation of a multi period rock-shelter at Garreg Hylldrem, Llanfrothen 2011-2012. *Archaeology in Wales 52*, 3–10.

Rockman, M. 2003. Knowledge and learning in the archaeology of colonization. In M. Rockman and J. Steele (eds.), *The Colonization of Unfamiliar Landscapes*, pp. 27–43. New York: Routledge.

Rogers, W. 1990. Mesolithic and Neolithic flint tool-manufacturing areas buried beneath Roman Watling Street in Southwark. *London Archaeologist* 6(9), 227–231.

Rosen, C.J. 2016. *The use of caves in the Mesolithic in South West Britain.* Unpublished PhD Thesis, University of Worcester.

Rots, V. and Plisson, H. 2014. Projectiles and the abuse of the use-wear method in a search for impact. *Journal of Archaeological Science* 48, 154–165.

Rowley-Conwy, P. 1994. Mesolithic settlement patterns: New zooarchaeological evidence from the Vale of Pickering, Yorkshire. *Archaeological Reports (University of Durham and Newcastle-upon-Tyne)* 1994, 1–7.

Rozoy, J.-G. 1984. The age of red deer or of bowmen. *Mesolithic Miscellany* 5, 14–16.

Rozoy, C. and Rozoy, J.G. 2002. *Les camps mésolithiques du Tillet: Analyses typologique, typométrique, structurelle et spatiale.* Paris: Société préhistorique française.

Russell, N.J., Bonsall, C. and Sutherland, D.G. 1995. The exploitation of marine molluscs in the Mesolithic of western Scotland: Evidence from Ulva Cave, Inner Hebrides. In Fischer, A. (ed.), *Man and sea in the Mesolithic: Coastal settlement above and below present sea level.* Oxford: Oxbow Monograph 53, 273–288.

Ryan, P.A. and Blackford, J.J. 2009. Late Mesolithic environmental change in the Upland Zone of Britain: High resolution records of woodland disturbance and fire. In Crombe, P., van Strydonk, M., Sergant, J., Boudin, M. and Bats, M. (eds.), *Chronology and evolution within the Mesolithic of north-west Europe* pp. 591–613. Cambridge: Cambridge Scholars Publishing.

Saint-Périer, R. de. 1922. Statuette de femme stéatopyge découverte à Lespugue (Haute-Garonne). *L'Anthropologie* 32, 1922.

Sainty, J.E. 1924. A flaking site on Kelling Heath, Norfolk. *Proceedings of the Prehistoric Society of East Anglia* 4(2), 165–176.

Sainty, J.E. 1925. Further notes on the Flaking Site on Kelling Heath Norfolk. *Proceedings of the Prehistoric Society of East Anglia* 5(1), 56–61.

Sainty, J.E. 1927. The Kelling Flaking Site. *Proceedings of the Prehistoric Society of East Anglia* 5(3), 283–288.

Sarkissian, C., Balanovsky, O., Brandt, G., Khartanovich, V., Buzhilova, A., Koshel, S., Zaporozhchenko, V., Gronenborn, D., Moiseyev, V., Kolpakov, E., Shumkin, V., Alt, K.W., Balanovska, E., Cooper, A., Haak, W., Genographic C. and Schurr, T.G. 2013. Ancient DNA reveals prehistoric gene-flow from Siberia in the complex human population history of North East Europe. *PLoS Genetics 9* (8), e1003296. 10.1371/journal.pgen.1003296.

Saville, A. 1981a. Mesolithic industries in Central England: An exploratory investigation using microlith typology. *Archaeological Journal* 138(1), 49–71.

Saville, A. 1981b. Honey Hill, Elkington: A Northamptonshire Mesolithic site. *Northamptonshire Archaeology* 16, 1–13.

Saville, A. 2008. The beginning of the later Mesolithic in Scotland. In Z. Sulgostowska and A.J. Tomaszewski (eds.), *Man - Millennia - Environment. Studies in honour of Romuald Schild*, pp. 207–213. Warsaw: Institute of Archaeology and Ethnology, Polish Academy of Sciences.

Saville, A., Hardy, K., Miket, R., Ballin, T., Bartosiewicz, L., Bonsall, C., Bruce, M., Carter, S., Cowie, T., Craig, O. and Hallén, Y. 2012. An Corran, Staffin, Skye: A rockshelter with Mesolithic and later occupation. *Scottish Archaeological Internet Reports* 51.

Savory, H.N. 1961. Mesolithic sites on Craig-y-Llyn, Glamorgan. *Bulletin of the Board of Celtic Studies* 19, 163–165.

Scaife, R.G. 1995. Boreal and sub-boreal chalk landscape: Pollen evidence. In R.M.J. Cleal, K.E. Walker and R. Montague (eds.), *Stonehenge in its landscape: Twentieth century excavations*, pp. 51–55. London: English Heritage Archaeological Report 10.

Schadla-Hall, R.T. 1987. Recent investigations of the early Mesolithic landscape in the Vale of Pickering, East Yorkshire. In M. Zvelebil and H. Blankholm (eds.), *Mesolithic Northwest Europe: Recent trends*, pp. 46–54. Sheffield: Department of Archaeology, University of Sheffield.

Schadla-Hall, R.T. 1989. The Vale of Pickering in the Early Mesolithic in context. In C. Bonsall (ed.), *The Mesolithic in Europe, papers presented at the third International Symposium, Edinburgh, 1985*, pp. 218–224. Edinburgh: John Donald.

Schlanger, S.H. 1992. Recognising persistent places in Anasazi settlement systems. In J. Rossignol and L. Wandsnider (eds.), *Space, time and archaeological landscapes*, pp. 91–112. New York: Plenum Press.

Schulting, R. J. 1996. Antlers, bone pins and flint blades: the Mesolithic cemeteries of Téviecand Hoëdic, Brittany. *Antiquity* 70(268), 335–350.

Schulting, R. 2009. Worm's head and Caldey Island (South Wales UK) and the question of Mesolithic territories. In S. McCartan, R.J. Schulting, G. Warren and P. Woodman (eds.), *Mesolithic horizons*, pp. 354–361. Oxford: Oxbow Books.

Schulting, R. 2013. 'Tilbury Man': A Mesolithic skeleton from the Lower Thames. *Proceedings of the Prehistoric Society* 79, 19–37.

Schulting, R., Fibiger, L., Macphail, R., McLaughlin, R., Murray, E., Price, C. and Walker, E.A. 2013. Mesolithic and Neolithic human remains from Foxhole Cave, Gower, South Wales. *The Antiquaries Journal* 93, 1–23.

Schulting, R.J., Bello, S.M., Chandler, B., and Higham, T.F.G. 2015. A cut-marked and fractured Mesolithic human bone from Kent's Cavern, Devon, UK. *International Journal of Osteoarchaeology* 25(1), 31–44.

Schulting, R.J., Booth, T., Brace, S., Diekmann, Y., Thomas, M. G., Barnes, I., Meiklejohn, C., Babb, J., Budd, C., Charlton, S., van der Plic ht, H., Mullan, G., and Wilson, L.J. 2019. Aveline's Hole: an unexpected twist in the tale. *Proceedings of the University of Bristol Spelaeological Society* 28(1), 9–63.

Schulting, R.J. and Richards, M.P. 2000. The use of stable isotopes in studies of subsistence and seasonality in the British Mesolithic. In R. Young (ed.), *Mesolithic lifeways: Current research from Britain and Ireland*, pp. 55–65. Leicester: University of Leicester, School of Archaeological Studies.

Schulting, R.J. and Richards, M.P. 2002. Finding the coastal Mesolithic in Southwest Britain: AMS dates and stable isotope results on human remains from Caldey Island, South Wales. *Antiquity* 76(294), 1011–1025.

Schulting, R.J. and Richards, M.P. 2009. Dogs, divers, deer and diet. Stable isotope results from Star Carr and a response to Dark. *Journal of Archaeological Science 36*(2), 498–503.

Schulting, R.J., Snoeck, C., Loe, L. and Gilmour, N. 2016. Strontium isotope analysis of the Mesolithic cremation from Langford, Essex, England. *Mesolithic Miscellany* 24(1), 19–21.

Schulting, R.J. and Wysocki, M. 2005. 'Pursuing a rabbit in Burrington Combe': New research on the Early Mesolithic burial cave of Aveline's Hole. *Proceedings of the University of Bristol Spelaeological Society* 23(3), 171–265.

Scott, B. and Shaw, A. nd. *Greylake Quarry 1, Middlezoy, Somerset*. Unpublished lithic report.

Scott Jones, R. 2018. Mardy Windfarm, Glamorgan (2012–3). https://hrswales.co.uk/maerdy-windfarm. Accessed 20/1/2021.

Scottish Agricultural College. 2000. Cetacean Strandings Investigation Scotland. Report to the Department of the Environment, published online at http://ukstrandings.org/csip-reports/ Accessed 2/9/2019.

Séara, F., Bridault, A., Ducrocq, T. and Souffi, B. 2009. Chasser au Mésolithique. L'apport des sites de vallées du quart nord-est de la France. *Archéopages: Archéologie et Société 28*, 26–35.

Shennan, I., Milne, G. and Bradley, S. 2012. Late Holocene vertical land motion and relative sea-level changes: Lessons from the British Isles. *Journal of Quaternary Science 27*(1), 64–70.

Sheridan, R., Sheridan, D., and Hassen, P. 1967. Rescue excavation of a Mesolithic site at Greenham Dairy Farm, Newbury, 1963.*Newbury and District Field Club, Transactions* 11(4), 66–73.

Sidell, J., Cotton, J., Rayner, L. and Wheeler, L. 2002. *The prehistory and topography of Southwark and Lambeth*. London: Museum of London Archaeology Service Monograph 14.

Sidell, J., Wilkinson, K., Scaife, R. and Cameron, N. 2000. *The Holocene evolution of the London Thames*. London: Museum of London Archaeology Service Monograph 14.

Simmonds, M. 2016. *Examining the relationship between environmental change and human activities at the dryland-wetland interface during the Late Upper Palaeolithic and Mesolithic in Southeast England*. Doctoral thesis, Reading University.

Simmons, I.G. 1975. Towards an ecology of Mesolithic man in the uplands of Great Britain. *Journal of Archaeological Science 2*, 1–15.

Simmons, I.G. 1996. *The environmental impact of later Mesolithic cultures: The creation of moorland landscape in England and Wales*. Edinburgh: Edinburgh University Press.

Simmons, I.G. and Innes, J.B. 1996. Disturbance phases in the mid-holocene vegetation at North Gill, North York Moors: Form and process. *Journal of Archaeological Science 23*(2), 183–191.

Sloane, D. 1986. Inveravon. *Discovery and Excavation in Scotland 1986*, 6.

Smith, A.G. 1970. *The influence of Mesolithic and Neolithic man on British vegetation: A discussion*. In D. Walker and R.G. West (eds.), *Studies in the vegetational history of the British Isles*, pp. 81–96. Cambridge: Cambridge University Press.

Smith, A.G. and Cloutman, E.W. 1988. Reconstruction of Holocene vegetation history in three dimensions at Waun-Fignen-Felen, an upland site in South Wales. *Philosophical Transactions of the Royal Society of London. B, Biological Sciences 322*(1209), 159–219.

Smith, A. G. and Pilcher, J. R. 1973. Radiocarbon dates and vegetational history of the British Isles. *New Phytologist 72*(4), 903–914.

Smith, A.G., Whittle, A., Cloutman, E.W. and Morgan, L.A. 1989. Mesolithic and Neolithic activity and environmental impact on the south-east fen-edge in Cambridgeshire. *Proceedings of the Prehistoric Society 55*, 207–249.

Smith, C. 2002. *Late Stone Age hunters of the British Isles*. London: Routledge.

Smith, D.E., Davies, M.H., Brooks, C.L., Mighall, T.M., Dawson, S., Rea, B.R., Jordan, J.T. and Holloway, L.K. 2010. Holocene relative sea levels and related prehistoric activity in the Forth lowland, Scotland, United Kingdom. *Quaternary Science Reviews 29*(17–18), 2382–2410.

Smith, D.E., Harrison, S. and Jordan, J.T. 2013. Sea level rise and submarine mass failures on open continental margins. *Quaternary Science Reviews 82*, 93–103.

Smith, D.E., Shi, S., Cullingford, R.A., Dawson, A.G., Dawson, S., Firth, C.R., Foster, I.D., Fretwell, P.T., Haggart, B.A., Holloway, L.K. and Long, D. 2004. The holocene storegga slide tsunami in the United Kingdom. *Quaternary Science Reviews 23*(23–24), 2291–2321.

Smith, G. 1924. Some evidences of early man within and near to the northern portion of the Vale of Clwyd. *Proceedings of the Liverpool Geological Society 14*, 117–122.

Smith, G. 1926. Prehistoric remains at Bryn Newydd, Prestatyn. *Proceeding of the Llandudno and District Field Club 13*, 62–72.

Smith, G. 1984. Excavation at Windmill Farm, Predannack Moor. *Cornish Archaeology* 23, 179.

Smith, G. 1987. The Lizard Project: Landscape survey Stevanović, 1978–1983. *Cornish Archaeology* 26, 13–68.

Smith, G. 2005. The north-west Wales lithic scatters project. *Lithics: The Journal of the Lithic Studies Society* 26, 38–56.

Smith, G. in press. A Later Mesolithic activity area at Windmill Farm, Predannack Moor, The Lizard, Cornwall. *Cornish Archaeology* 59.

Smith, G. and Harris, D. 1982. The excavation of Mesolithic, Neolithic and Bronze Age settlements at Poldowrian, St. Keverne, 1980. *Cornish Archae*ology 21, 23–62.

Smith, G. and Walker, E. 2014. Snail Cave rock shelter, North Wales: A new prehistoric site. *Archaeologia Cambrensis* 163, 99–131.

Smith, I.R., Wilkinson, D.M. and O'Regan, H.J. 2013. New Lateglacial fauna and early Mesolithic human remains from Northern England. *Journal of Quaternary Science* 28(6), 542–544.

Smith, P.J. 1994. *Grahame Clark, the Fenland research Committee and prehistory at Cambridge*. Unpublished MPhil thesis, University of Cambridge.

Smith, P.J. 1999. 'The Coup': How did the Prehistoric Society of East Anglia become the Prehistoric Society? *Proceedings of the Prehistoric Society* 65, 465–470.

Smith, O., Momber, G., Bates, R., Garwood, P., Fitch, S., Pallen, M., Gaffney, V. and Allaby, R.G. 2015. Sedimentary DNA from a submerged site reveals wheat in the British Isles 8000 years ago. *Science* 347(6225), 998–1001.

Speed, G., Rowe, P., Russ, H. and Gardiner, L. 2018. A game of two (unequal) halves: An Early Mesolithic site at Little Holtby, near Leeming, North Yorkshire. *Mesolithic Miscellany* 26(1), 49–87.

Spikins, P. 1999. Mesolithic Northern England: Environment, population and settlement. British Archaeological Reports, British Series 283.

Spikins, P. 2002. *Prehistoric people of the Pennines: Reconstructing the lifestyles of Mesolithic hunter-gatherers on Marsden Moor*. Wakefield: West Yorkshire Archaeology Service and English Heritage.

Spratt, D.A. 1982. *Prehistoric and Roman Archaeology of North-East Yorkshire*. Oxford: British Archaeological Reports, British Series 104.

Spratt, D.A., Goddard, R.E. and Brown, D.R. 1976. Mesolithic settlement sites at Upleatham, Cleveland. *Yorkshire Archaeological Journal* 48, 19–26.

Stanton, Y. 1984. The Mesolithic period: Early post-glacial hunter-gatherer communities in Glamorgan. In H.N. Savory (ed.), *Glamorgan County History volume 2, Early Glamorgan*, pp. 33–131. Cardiff: University of Wales Press.

Stainton, B. 1989. Excavation of an early prehistoric site at Stratford's Yard, Chesham. *Records of Buckinghamshire* 31: 49–74.

Stevanović, M. 1997. The Age of Clay: The social dynamics of house destruction. *Journal of Anthropological Archaeology* 16(4), 334–395.

Stewart, R.J. 2017. The Isle of Portland, Portland chert and Neolithic arrowheads: Qualities and connections. *Lithics: The Journal of the Lithic Studies Society* 38, 57–71.

Stonehouse, P.B. 1972. Rocher Moss South 2. A Late Mesolithic site in Saddleworth. *Saddleworth Historical Society Bulletin* 10 (2), 21–23.

Stonehouse, P.B. 1980. Rocher Moss South. *Saddleworth Historical Society Bulletin* 2(3), 21–24.

Stonehouse, P.B. 1986. Dean Clough 1: A Late Mesolithic site in the Central Pennines. *Greater Manchester Archaeological Journal* 2, 1–9.

Stonehouse, P.B. 1987. Mesolithic sites on the Pennine watershed. *Greater Manchester Archaeological Journal* 3, 5–17.

Stonehouse, P.B. 1992. Two Early Mesolithic sites in the central Pennines. *Yorkshire Archaeological Journal* 64, 1–15.

Stonehouse, P.B. 1997. Pule Bents: A possible kill site in the Central Pennines. *Yorkshire Archaeological Journal* 69, 1–8.

Stonehouse, P.B. 2001. *The prehistory of Saddleworth and adjacent areas*. Saddleworth: Saddleworth Archaeological Trust.

Sturt, F. 2006. Local knowledge is required: A rhythmanalytical approach to the late Mesolithic and early Neolithic of the East Anglian Fenland, UK. *Journal of Maritime Archaeology* 1(2), 119–139.

Sturt, F., Garrow, D. and Bradley, S. 2013. New models of North West European Holocene palaeogeography and inundation. *Journal of Archaeological Science* 40(11), 3963–3976.

Suddaby, I. 2007. Downsizing in the Mesolithic? The discovery of two associated post-circles at Silvercrest, Lesmurdie Road, Elgin, Scotland. In C. Waddington & K. Pedersen (eds.), *Mesolithic studies in the North Sea Basin and Beyond*, pp. 60–68. Oxford: Oxbow Books.

Summers, P.G. 1941. A Mesolithic site, near Iwerne Minster, Dorset. *Proceedings of the Prehistoric Society* 7, 145–146.

Switsur, V.R. and Jacobi, R.M. 1975. Radiocarbon dates for the Pennine Mesolithic. *Nature* 256(5512), 32–34.

Switsur, V.R. and Jacobi, R.M. 1979. A radiocarbon chronology for the early postglacial stone industries of England and Wales. In R. Berger and H.E. Suess (eds.), *Radiocarbon dating, Radiocarbon dating: Proceedings of the ninth international conference, Los Angeles and La Jolla, 1976*, pp. 41–68. Berkley: University of California Press.

Sykes, C.M. and Whittle, S.L. 1965. A Flint Chipping Site on Tog Hill, near Marshfield. *Transactions of the Bristol and Gloucestershire Archaeological Society* 84, 5–14.

Taborin, Y. 2004. *Langage sans parole. La parure aux temps préhistoriques*. Paris: La Maison des Roches.

Tallis, J. 1975. Tree remains in southern Pennine peats. *Nature* 256, 482–484.

Tallis, J.H. 1991. Forest and Moorland in the South Pennine Uplands in the Mid-Flandrian Period.: III. The Spread of Moorland--Local, Regional and National. *The Journal of Ecology*, 79(2), 401–415.

Tallis, J.H. and Switsur, V.R. 1990. Forest and Moorland in the South Pennine Uplands in the Mid-Flandrian Period.: II. The Hillslope Forests. *The Journal of Ecology* 78(4), 857–883.

Taylor, B. and Gray-Jones, A. 2009. Definitely a pit, possibly a house? Recent excavations at Flixton School House Farm in the Vale of Pickering. Mesolithic Miscellany 20(2), 21–26.

Thomson, D. 1939. The seasonal factor in human culture. *Proceedings of the Prehistoric Society* 5, 209–221.

Thomas, E.R., Wolff, E.W., Mulvaney, R., Steffensen, J.P., Johnsen, S.J., Arrowsmith, C., White, J.W., Vaughn, B. and Popp, T. 2007. The 8.2 ka event from Greenland ice cores. *Quaternary Science Reviews* 26(1–2), 70–81.

Thomas, J. and Tilley, C. 1993. The axe and the torso: symbolic structures in the Neolithic of Brittany. In C. Tilley (ed.), *Interpretative archaeology*, pp. 225–324. Oxford: Berg.

Tipping, R. 1994. The form and the fate of Scotland's woodlands. *Proceedings of the Society of Antiquaries of Scotland* 124, 1–54.

Tipping, R. 1996. Microscopic charcoal records, inferred human activity and climatic change in the Mesolithic of northernmost Scotland. In Pollard, A., Morrison, A. (eds.), *The early prehistory of Scotland*, pp. 39–61. Edinburgh: Edinburgh University Press.

Tipping, R. 1997. Vegetational history of southern Scotland. *Botanical Journal of Scotland* 49, 151–162.

Tipping, R. 2010a. *Bowmont: An environmental history of the Bowmont Valley and the northern Cheviot Hills, 10000 BC-AD 2000*. Edinburgh: Society of Antiquaries of Scotland.

Tipping, R. 2010b. The case for climatic stress forcing choice in the adoption to agriculture in the British Isles. In B. Finlayson and G. Warren (eds.), *Landscapes in transition*, pp. 66–76. Oxford: Oxbow Books.

Todd, K.C.R. nd. Lackford Heath. Unpublished Manuscript, British Museum.

Tolan-Smith, C. and Bonsall, C. 1999. Stone Age studies in the British Isles: The impact of accelerator dating. *Mémoires de la Société Préhistorique Française 26*, 249–257.

Tooley, M.J. and Huddart, D. 1972. Cumberland coastal sections. Durham: Quaternary research association handbook.

Tratman, E.K. 1975. The cave archaeology and palaeontology of Mendip. In I. Smith and D. Drew (eds.), *Limestones and caves of the Mendip Hills*, pp. 352–403. Newton Abbott: David and Charles.

Trigger, B.G. 1989. *A history of archaeological thought*. Cambridge: Cambridge University Press.

Trinkaus, E., Humphrey, L., Stringer, C., Churchill, S. and Tague, R. 2003. Gough's cave 1 (Somerset, England): An assessment of the sex and age at death. *Bulletin of the Natural History Museum. Geology Series* 58(S1), 45–50. 10.1017/S0968046203000081.

Turner, J. and Hodgson, J. 1991. Studies in the vegetational history of the Northern Pennines: IV. Variations in the composition of the late Flandrian forests and comparisons with those of the early and mid-Flandrian. *New Phytologist* 117(1), 165–174.

Turner, W. 1889. On some implements of stag's horn associated with whale skeletons found in the Carse of Stirling. *Report on the Meetings of the British Association* 59, 789–791.

Uchiyama, J. 2016. From Awashimadai to Star Carr: A Japanese Jomon perspective on the subsistence strategies and settlement patterns of Early Mesolithic hunter–gatherers in the Vale of Pickering, UK. *Quaternary International* 419, 17–26.

van Nedervelde, B.J., Davies, M. and John, B.S. 1973. Radiocarbon dating from Ogof-yr-Ychen, a new Pleistocene site in west Wales. *Nature* 245(5426), 453–455.

Vatcher, F. de M. & Vatcher, L. 1973. Excavation of three post-holes in the Stonehenge carpark. *Wiltshire Archaeology and Natural History Magazine* 68, 57–63.

Vincent, P.J., Lord, T.C., Telfer, M.W. and Wilson, P. 2010. Early Holocene loessic colluviation in northwest England: New evidence for the 8.2 ka event in the terrestrial record? *Boreas* 10.1111/j.1502-3885.2010.00172.x.

Vita-Finzi, C. and Higgs, E.S. 1970. Prehistoric economy in the Mount Carmel area of Palestine: Site catchment analysis. *Proceedings of the Prehistoric Society* 36, 1–37.

Viveiros de Castro, E. 1998. Cosmological deixis and Amerindian perspectivism. *Journal of the Royal Anthropological Institute 4(3)*, 469–488.

Waddington, C. ed. 2007. *Mesolithic settlement in the North Sea Basin: A case study from Howick, North-East England*. Oxford: Oxbow Books.

Waddington, C. 2015. Mesolithic re-colonisation of Britain following the drowning of North Sea landscapes. In N. Ashton and C. Lucas (eds.), *No stone unturned: Papers in honour of Roger Jacobi*, pp. 221–232. London: Lithic Studies Occasional Paper 9.

Waddington, C., Bailey, G., Bayliss, A. and Milner, N. 2007. Howick in its North Sea context. In C. Waddington (ed.), *Mesolithic settlement in the North Sea Basin: A case study from Howick, North-East England*, pp. 203–224. Oxford: Oxbow Books.

Waddington, C. and Bonsall, C. 2016. *Archaeology and environment on the North Sea littoral: A case study from Low Hauxley*. Bakewell: Archaeological Research Services/ Northumberland Wildlife Trust.

Waddington, C. and Wicks, K. 2017. Resilience or wipe out? Evaluating the convergent impacts of the 8.2 ka event and Storegga tsunami on the Mesolithic of northeast Britain. *Journal of Archaeological Science: Reports* 14, 692–714.

Wainwright, G.J. 1960. Three microlithic industries from south-west England and their affinities. *Proceedings of the Prehistoric Society* 26, 193–201.

Walker, J., Gaffney, V., Fitch, S., Muru, M., Fraser, A., Bates, M. and Bates, R. 2020. A great wave: The Storegga tsunami and the end of Doggerland? *Antiquity* 94(378), 1409–1425. 10.15184/aqy.2020.49.

Wanner, H., Mercolli, L., Grosjean, M. and Ritz, S.P. 2015. Holocene climate variability and change; a data-based review. *Journal of the Geological Society* 172(2), 254–263.

Ward, T. 2012. *Mesolithic chert quarry at Burnetland Farm. Biggar Archaeology Group Reports.* http://217.199.187.196/biggararchaeology.org.uk/wp-content/uploads/2017/09/BURNETL-AND_CHERTMINE_REPORT2012.pdf. Accessed 7/7/2019.

Ward, T. 2017. *Daer Valley and Clydesdale Mesolithic. Biggar Archaeology Group Reports.* http://217.199.187.196/biggararchaeology.org.uk/wp-content/uploads/2017/09/BAG_Mesolithic.pdf. Accessed 14/7/2019.

Warren, G. 2001. *Towards a social archaeology of the Mesolithic in eastern Scotland: Landscapes, contexts and experience.* Doctoral thesis, Edinburgh University.

Warren, G. 2006. Technology. In: C. Conneller and Warren G. (eds.), *Mesolithic Britain and Ireland.* Oxford: Tempus.

Warren, G. 2007. Mesolithic myths. *Proceedings of the British Academy* 144, 311–328.

Warren, G., Fraser, S., Clarke, A., Driscoll, K., Mitchell, W., Noble, G., Paterson, D., Schulting, R., Tipping, R., Verbaas, A., Wilson, C. and Wickham-Jones, C. 2018. Little house in the Mountains? A small Mesolithic structure from the Cairngorm Mountains, Scotland. *Journal of Archaeological Science: Reports* 18, 936–945.

Warren, S.H. 1912a. The classification of the prehistoric remains of Eastern Essex. *The Journal of the Royal Anthropological Institute of Great Britain and Ireland* 42, 91–127.

Warren, S.H. 1912b. On a late glacial stage in the valley of the river Lea, subsequent to the epoch of river-drift man. *Quarterly Journal of the Geological Society* 68(1–4), 213–228.

Warren, S.H., Clark, J.G.D., Godwin, H., Godwin, M.E. and Macfadyen, W.A. 1934. An early Mesolithic site at Broxbourne sealed under Boreal peat. *The Journal of the Royal Anthropological Institute of Great Britain and Ireland* 64, 101–128.

Waughman, M. 1996. Excavations of a Mesolithic site at Highcliffe Nab, Guisborough. *Durham Archaeological Journal* 12, 1–16.

Waughman, M. 2017. Hunter-gatherers in an upland landscape: The Mesolithic period in North East Yorkshire. *Yorkshire Archaeological Journal* 89(1), 1–22.

Weiß, C.L., Dannemann, M., Preufer, K. and Burbano, H.A. 2015. Contesting thepresence of wheat in the British Isles 8,000 years ago by assessingancient DNA authenticity from low-coverage data. *eLife* 4, e10005. 10.7554/eLife.10005.

Weninger, B., Schulting, R., Bradtmöller, M., Clare, L., Collard, M., Edinborough, K., Hilpert, J., Jöris, O., Niekus, M., Rohling, E.J. and Wagner, B. 2008. The catastrophic final flooding of Doggerland by the Storegga Slide tsunami. *Documenta Praehistorica* 35, 1–24.

Wessex, 2005. Wessex archaeology. Preferred area 4, Denham, Buckinghamshire. Archaeological Evaluation Report. Wessex Archaeology unpublished report 50692.08.

Weyman, J. 1984. The Mesolithic in North-East England. In C. Burgess and R. Miket (eds.), *Between and beyond the walls: Essays on the prehistory and history of north Britain in honour of George Jobey,* pp. 38–51. Edinburgh: J. Donald.

White, D.A. 1974. The excavation of three round barrows on Chaldon Down, Dorset, 1969. *Proceeding of the Dorset Natural History and Archaeological Society* 95, 34.

White, R.B. 1978. Excavations at Trwyn Du, Anglesey, 1974. *Archaeologia Cambrensis* 127, 16–39.

Wickham-Jones, C.R. 1990. *Rhum: Mesolithic and later sites at Kinloch, excavations 1984–86.* Edinburgh: Society of Antiquaries of Scotland.

Wickham-Jones, C.R. 1994. Scotland's first settlers. London: Batsford.

Wickham-Jones, C.R. 2009. Excavations at Sand, the Flaked Lithic Assemblage. *Scottish Archaeological Internet Reports* 31, 244–273. http://soas.is.ed.ac.uk/index.php/sair/article/view/2151.

Wickham-Jones, C.R., Clark, A. and Noble, G. in press. *Prehistoric Communities of the River Dee: Mesolithic and other lithic scatter sites of central Deeside, Aberdeenshire. Scottish Archaeological Internet Reports.*

Wickham-Jones, C. and Dalland, M. 1998. A small Mesolithic site at Fife Ness, Fife, Scotland. *Internet Archaeology* 5(1). 10.11141/ia.5.1.

Wickham-Jones, C. and Downes, J. 2007. Long Howe, Orkney (St Andrew's and Deerness parish), excavation. *Discovery and Excavation in Scotland* 8, 147.

Wickham-Jones, C., Hardy, K., Clarke, A., Cressey, M., Edwards, K. and Newton, A. 2004. Camas Daraich: A Mesolithic site at the Point of Sleat, Skye. *Scottish Archaeological Internet Reports* 1–7. http://journals.socantscot.org/index.php/sair/article/view/572

Wickham-Jones, C.R., Kenworthy, J.B., Gould, A., MacGregor, G. and Noble, G. 2016. Archaeological excavations at Nethermills Farm, Deeside, 1978-81. *Proceedings of the Society of Antiquaries of Scotland* 146, 7–55.

Wickham-Jones, C.R., Noble, G., Fraser, S.M., Warren, G., Tipping, R., Paterson, D., Mitchell, W., Hamilton, D. and Clarke, A. 2020. New evidence for upland occupation in the Mesolithic of Scotland. *Proceedings of the Prehistoric Society*, 1–30. 10.1017/ppr. 2020.8.

Wicks, K. and Mithen, S. 2014. The impact of the abrupt 8.2 ka cold event on the Mesolithic population of western Scotland: A Bayesian chronological analysis using 'activity events' as a population proxy. *Journal of Archaeological Science* 45, 240–269.

Wicks, K., Pirie, A. and Mithen, S.J. 2014. Settlement patterns in the late Mesolithic of western Scotland: The implications of Bayesian analysis of radiocarbon dates and inter-site technological comparisons. *Journal of Archaeological Science* 41, 406–422.

Wild, M. 2019. An evaluation of the antler headdress evidence from Hohen Viecheln. In D. Groß, J. Meadows, D. Jantzen and H. Lübke (eds.), *Working at the sharp end: From bone and antler to Early Mesolithic Life in Northern Europe*, pp. 1–14. Kiel/Hamburg: Wachholtz Verlag.

Wilkinson, T.J. and Murphy, P. 1995. *The Archaeology of the Essex Coast: The Hullbridge Survey*. East Anglian Archaeology Monograph 71.

Williams, C.T. 1985. *Mesolithic exploitation patterns in the Central Pennines: A palynological study of Soyland Moor*. Oxford: British Archaeological Reports.

Williams Thorpe, O. and Thorpe, R.S. 1984. The distribution and sources of archaeological pitchstone in Britain, *Journal of Archaeological Science* 11, 1–34.

Woodman, P.C. 1978. *The Mesolithic in Ireland*. Oxford: British Archaeological Report 58.

Woodman, P.C. 1985. *Excavations at Mount Sandel, 1973–1977, County Londonderry*. London: HM Stationery Office.

Woodman, P. 1989. A review of the Scottish Mesolithic: A plea for normality! *Proceedings of the Society of Antiquaries of Scotland* 119, 1–32.

Woodman, P. and McCarthy, M. 2003. Contemplating some awful(ly interesting) vistas: Importing cattle and red deer into prehistoric Ireland. Neolithic settlement in Ireland and western Britain In: I. Armit, E. Murphy, E. Nelis and D. Simpson (eds.), *Neolithic Settlement in Ireland and Western Britain*, pp. 31–39. Oxford: Oxbow Books.

Wordsworth, J. 1985. The excavation of a Mesolithic horizon at 13-24 Castle Street, Inverness. *Proceedings of the Society of Antiquaries of Scotland* 115, 89–103.

Woodhead, T. W. 1929. History of the vegetation of the southern Pennines. *Journal of Ecology* 17, 1–31.

Wymer, J.J. 1959. Excavations on the Mesolithic Site at Thatcham, Berks 1958. Interim Report, *Berkshire Archaeological Journal* 57, 1–24.

Wymer, J.J. 1962. Excavations at the Maglemosian sites at Thatcham, Berkshire, England. *Proceedings of the Prehistoric Society* 28, 329–361.

Wymer, J. 1996. Barrow excavations in Norfolk, 1984–88. EAA 77, Norfolk Museums Service.

Wymer, J.J. and Robins, P.A. 1995. A Mesolithic site at Great Melton. *Norfolk Archaeology* 42, 125–147.

Young, D.S., Branch, C.P., Elias, N.P., Bateson, S.A. and Batchelor, C.R. 2018. Environmental setting: Geoarchaeological investigations and environmental analysis In: Jacques D., Phillips T. and Lyons T. (eds.), *Blick Mead: Exploring the 'first Place' in the Stonehenge Landscape: Archaeological Excavations at Blick Mead*. 2005–2016, pp. 35–66. Amesbury: Wiltshire.

Young, R. 2007. 'I must go down to the sea again.' A review of early research on the 'coastal' Mesolithic of the North-East of England. In C. Waddington and K. Pedersen (eds.), *Mesolithic studies in the North Sea Basin and beyond: Proceedings of a conference held at Newcastle in 2003*, pp. 16–24. Oxford: Oxbow Books.

Yu, S.Y., Colman, S.M., Lowell, T.V., Milne, G.A., Fisher, T.G., Breckenridge, A., Boyd, M. and Teller, J.T. 2010. Freshwater outburst from Lake Superior as a trigger for the cold event 9300 years ago. *Science* 328, 1262–1266.

Zhilin, M., Savchenko, S., Hansen, S., Heussner, K. and Terberger, T. 2018. Early art in the Urals: New research on the wooden sculpture from Shigir. *Antiquity* 92(362), 334–350.

Zvelebil, M. 1994. Plant use in the Mesolithic and its role in the transition to farming. *Proceedings of the Prehistoric Society* 60, 35–74.

Index

Note: Page numbers in italics denotes figures; bold denotes tables, and those followed by b denotes boxes.